आ नो भद्राः क्रतवो यन्तु विश्वतः। [Rigveda, I-89-i]

Let noble thoughts come to us from every side (i.e., quaquaversally).

* * *

To

ANGSUMAN DUTTA
as a token of regard for
his accomplishments and in
the hope that we can
collaborate, even on so-called
"white papers" in the future...

With warm, personal, regards,

(Sridhar Ramamoorti)

October 15, 2009

Naperville, Illinois

INTERNAL AUDITING:
Assurance & Consulting Services

Kurt F. Reding, Ph.D., CIA, CPA, CMA
Paul J. Sobel, CIA, CPA
Urton L. Anderson, Ph.D., CIA, CCSA, CGAP, CFSA
Michael J. Head, CIA, CPA, CISA
Sri Ramamoorti, Ph.D., CIA, CPA, CFE, CFSA, CGAP, CGFM, CICA
Mark Salamasick, CIA, CISA, CSP

Contributing Writer
Cris Riddle, M.A.

The Institute of
Internal Auditors

RESEARCH
FOUNDATION
Understanding, Guiding, Shaping

Book design by ren morrison, www.renco.org
Illustrations by Richard Tuschman.

The IIARF publishes this document for informational and educational purposes. This document is intended to provide information, but is not a substitute for legal or accounting advice. The IIARF does not provide such advice and makes no warranty as to any legal or accounting results through its publication of this document. When legal or accounting issues arise, professional assistance should be sought and retained.

The Professional Practices Framework for Internal Auditing (PPF) comprises the full range of existing and developing practice guidance for the profession. The IIA's Professional Practices Framework provides guidance to internal auditors globally and paves the way to world-class internal auditing.

This guidance fits into the Framework under the heading Development and Practice Aids.

The mission of The IIA Research Foundation (IIARF) is to be the global leader in sponsoring, disseminating, and promoting research and knowledge resources to enhance the development and effectiveness of the internal auditing profession.

ISBN 978-0-89413-610-8

06741 06/07

First Printing

TABLE OF CONTENTS

Preface

Chapter 3   Governance and Risk Management

Chapter 4   Business Processes and Business Risks

Chapter 5   Internal Control

Chapter 6   Information Technology Risks and Controls

Chapter 7   Fraud Risks and Controls

Chapter 8   Managing the Internal Audit Function

Chapter 9   Gathering and Documenting Audit Evidence

Chapter 10   Conducting the Assurance Engagement

Chapter 11   Communicating Assurance Engagement Outcomes and Performing Follow-up Procedures

Chapter 12   The Consulting Engagement

Glossary

Appendix

Index

Preface

I asked Paul Sobel, Urton Anderson, Mike Head, Sri Ramamoorti, and Mark Salamasick to coauthor *Internal Auditing: Assurance & Consulting Services* because they have several things in common:

- Many years of distinguished experience as an internal auditor practitioner and/or educator,
- A reputation of internal audit thought leadership,
- A history of volunteer leadership service to The Institute of Internal Auditors,
- The designation of Certified Internal Auditor, and most importantly,
- An awareness of the significant need for a textbook that reflects contemporary, real-world internal auditing.

We added Cris Riddle to the team, and she not only contributed to the writing of several chapters, but also leveraged her education and experience with written text to help us ensure the disparate styles of six other authors fit together well, making this textbook a cohesive read for all who pick it up. Our shared vision was to work together as a team of internal audit educators and practitioners to write such a textbook. Our goal was to provide students with the fundamental knowledge and a sense of the skills they will need to succeed as entry-level internal audit professionals.

Our primary target audience is, accordingly, undergraduate and graduate college students enrolled in introductory internal auditing courses. We believe, however, that internal audit practitioners also will find the book useful as a training and reference tool.

— Kurt F. Reding
Textbook Project Manager

Textbook Overview

The textbook includes the following key content components:

- Extensive coverage of governance, risk management, and internal control.
- A risk-based, process and controls-focused internal audit approach.
- Integration of IT and fraud risks, control activities, and auditing.
- Alignment with The IIA's Professional Practices Framework (PPF) and Certified Internal Auditor® (CIA) examination content specifications. Readers should note that the textbook addresses the PPF as it stands today. The IIA is in the process of updating the PPF to reflect the dramatic change in the role of internal auditing in recent years with the intent of expanding the guidance currently provided, enhancing its clarity, and making it easier to use.

The first eight chapters, which we refer to collectively as Fundamental Audit Concepts chapters, cover basic audit concepts that internal auditors need to know and understand. Chapters 9 through 12, which we refer to as the Internal Audit Processes chapters, focus on how internal audit assurance and consulting engagements are planned and performed and how engagement outcomes are communicated.

Each chapter concludes with review, multiple-choice, and discussion questions and one or more application-oriented cases. Unless otherwise indicated in the individual chapters, all end-of-chapter questions are the original work of the authors or have been adapted from The Certified Internal Auditor Model Exams published by The IIA in 1998 and 2004 or from CIA exams prior to the The IIA's closure of the exam in 1997.

Textbook Supplements

The following supplemental materials are available for instructors:

- **ACL and IDEA Software.** Both ACL and IDEA, the two most widely used commercially available audit software programs, accompany this textbook on CD-ROMs. Instructors can decide individually the extent to which they want to give their students practical, hands-on experience with generalized audit software using ACL and/or IDEA.
- **Case Study Chapters.** The authors have prepared supplemental chapters intended to provide students with more in-depth, application-oriented coverage of operational, financial, and compliance auditing. These chapters will be distributed separately from the textbook to instructors interested in using them in their courses.
- **Solutions Manual.** The Solutions Manual contains answers prepared by the textbook authors for the end-of-chapter questions and cases
- **Key-Point Slides.** The authors have prepared a small set of key-point slides for each chapter. Individual instructors can use these key-point slides as is or as starting points for preparing customized sets of slides.
- **Illustrative Exams.** The illustrative exams prepared by the authors are intended to give instructors a head start on constructing exams best suited for their classes.

Acknowledgements

We would like to thank the following organizations and individuals for their contributions to the textbook:

- The Institute of Internal Auditors Research Foundation for sponsoring the writing of the textbook.

- The Institute of Internal Auditors for permission to incorporate the Professional Practices Framework and other materials, including questions from The Certified Internal Auditor Model Exams and from past CIA examinations.

- Bonnie Ulmer, Director, Educational Products, The Institute of Internal Auditors, for coordinating and directing the project and keeping us on task. We also want to thank Bonnie for "thinking outside the box" with respect to the textbook's design.

- Joanne Hodges, Vice President, Educational Materials, and her team at The Institute of Internal Auditors, for directing the final textbook production process and providing her creative input to ensure this textbook had a distinctive look to emphasize the written content.

- Jeffrey E. Perkins, CIA, CPA, CISA, CISSP, CISM, Vice President, Internal Audit, TransUnion, for reviewing the entire textbook from a practitioner's perspective and providing us with constructive feedback that significantly improved the quality of the textbook.

- The following individuals, and their students, who graciously pilot tested portions of the textbook:
    - Audrey A. Gramling, Ph.D., CIA, CPA, Associate Professor of Accounting, Kennesaw State University.
    - Alan N. Siegfried, CIA, CFSA, CCSA, CGAP, CPA, CISA, CBA, CSB, Auditor General, Inter-American Development Bank and Adjunct Professor of Internal Auditing, University of Maryland.
    - James G. Swearingen, Ph.D., CPA, Professor of Accounting, Weber State University

- The following organizations for granting us permission to copy and/or adapt proprietary information:
    - The American Institute of Certified Public Accountants
    - The University of Texas at Austin
    - Deloitte & Touche
    - PricewaterhouseCoopers
    - Protiviti, Inc.

- The following members of The Institute of Internal Auditors' Advanced Technology Committee for reviewing Chapter 6, "Information Technology Risks and Controls":
    - Lily Bi, Manager, Technology Practices, The Institute of Internal Auditors
    - Gene Kim, Chief Technology Officer, Tripwire Inc.
    - David S. Lione, Senior Manager, Grant Thornton

- ■ Heriot Prentice, MIIA, FIIA, QiCA, Director, Technology Practices, The Institute of Internal Auditors
- ■ Jay Taylor, CIA, CISA, CFE, General Director – IT Audit, General Motors Corporation
- The following individuals from TD AMERITRADE for reviewing Chapter 5, "Internal Control," and answering the Chapter 5 questions and cases:
  - ■ John Dwyer, IT Audit Director
  - ■ Russ Hancock, Audit Administration Director
  - ■ Kate Kastens, Audit Risk Manager
  - ■ Melissa Simmons, Audit Director
- Ronald Banse, General Director, Accounting, Union Pacific Railroad, for providing reference materials for Chapter 11, Communicating Outcomes and Performing Follow-up Procedures.
- The following individuals for reviewing Chapter 12, "The Consulting Engagement":
  - ■ Chris Desjardins, Audit Director, Essilor
  - ■ Steve Shepherd, Chief Auditor, City of Garland
- Margaret Christ, CIA, Ph.D. Candidate, The University of Texas at Austin, for offering comments on the text and working on end-of-chapter questions and cases.
- Julie Danahy, Senior Executive Assistant for Corporate Audit, TD AMERITRADE, for creating and revising many of the exhibits throughout the textbook.

About the Authors

Kurt F. Reding, Ph.D., CIA, CPA, CMA
Professor of Accounting
Friends University
Wichita, Kansas

Kurt currently serves on The Institute of Internal Auditors' Academic Relations Committee and The IIA Wichita Chapter's Board of Governors. He has previously served on The IIA's Board of Directors, North American Board, Board of Research and Education Advisors, and Board of Research Advisors and as an ex officio member of The IIA Kansas City Chapter's Board of Governors. Kurt received The IIA's 2003 Leon R. Radde Educator of the Year Award. He also has received both The IIA's John B. Thurston Award (2001) and the Institute of Management Accountants' Lybrand Gold Medal (2004), the highest annual writing awards bestowed by these organizations. He coauthored Introduction to Auditing: Logic, Principles, and Techniques, a textbook published by The IIA in 2002 and has published articles in Internal Auditor, Internal Auditing, Managerial Auditing Journal, Management Accounting Quarterly, and other journals. Kurt has 25 years of experience as an audit educator and practitioner and holds a Ph.D. in Accounting from The University of Tennessee. He is a member of The Institute of Internal Auditors, the American Institute of Certified Public Accountants, the Institute of Management Accountants, and the American Accounting Association.

Paul Sobel, CIA, CPA
Vice President, Internal Audit
Mirant Corporation

Prior to joining Mirant, Paul was Vice President, Risk Assessment at Aquila, Inc. His responsibilities at these two energy companies have included directing the worldwide internal audit activities, and developing and implementing risk assessment and enterprise risk management methodologies. Paul was a Senior Manager in Arthur Andersen's Business Risk Consulting practice, with focus on risk assessments and internal audit co-sourcing arrangements. His career has also included the positions of Audit Director with Harcourt General and International Audit Manager for PepsiCo. He began his career with Arthur Andersen, focusing on financial and information systems audits.

Paul is a frequent speaker on ERM and governance topics at IIA and other conferences, and achieved Distinguished Faculty honors as an instructor of IIA seminars. He has published a book titled Auditor's Risk Management Guide: Integrating Auditing and ERM. He has also authored or co-authored articles for Internal Auditor and Management Accounting Quarterly, the last of which was awarded the Institute of Management Accountants' Lybrand Gold Medal in 2004. Paul has been an active volunteer with The IIA. He has served on The IIA's Board of Directors, the North American Board, The IIA Research Foundation's Board of Trustees, and as the Midwest Region Representative and Midwest District #1 Representative. He has also served on the Board of Governors of the Atlanta, Kansas City, and Central Florida Chapters, and was President for the Kansas City Chapter.

Urton L. Anderson, Ph.D, CIA, CCSA, CGAP
Clark W. Thompson, Jr., Professor in Accounting Education
Associate Dean for Undergraduate Programs
McCombs School of Business
The University of Texas at Austin

Urton joined the Department of Accounting at the University of Texas at Austin in 1984, teaching auditing and managerial accounting. Urton received his Ph. D. from The University of Minnesota in 1985. Urton's research has addressed various issues in internal and external auditing – particularly corporate governance, compliance, enterprise risk management, and internal control. He has written several books, his most recent being Implementing the Professional Practices Framework: 2nd Edition (with Andrew Dahle), as well as papers published in a variety of scholarly and professional journals. He is also editor/author of the Handbook for Internal Auditors published by LexisNexis/MatthewBender. Urton is active in The Institute of Internal Auditors. He has been a member and Chair of The IIA's Board of Regents and served on the CCSA Steering Committee which developed the professional examination for Control Self-Assessment and the CGAP Steering Committee for the new professional examination in governmental auditing. He has also been a member and Chair of the International Internal Auditing Standards Board. In 1997 he was named Leon R. Radde Educator of the Year by The Institute of Internal Auditors. In June 2006, The Institute of Internal Auditors recognized his outstanding contributions to the field of internal auditing by awarding him The Bradford Cadmus Memorial Award. Urton also has served on the board of directors for the Health Care Compliance Association and the advisory board of the Society of Corporate Compliance and Ethics.

Michael J. Head, CIA, CPA, CMA, CBA, CISA
Managing Director of Corporate Audit
TD AMERITRADE

Michael is responsible for the coordination and delivery of risk-based and process-driven review, assurance, and advisory services specific to internal controls and risk management throughout TD AMERITRADE. During his 27-year career, he has served in various capacities, including director of internal audit, audit manager, and controller, with companies including PricewaterhouseCoopers, KPMG, The Guarantee Life Companies Inc., Bank of America (formerly NationsBank), FirsTier Financial, Inc., and Standard Havens, Inc. His experience includes the development and implementation of comprehensive, risk-based internal audit functions, and strategic, financial, operational, and compliance control consultant to the financial services industry.
Michael is a National Association of Securities Dealers Registered General Securities Representative (Series 7), General Securities Principal (Series 24), and a Financial and Operations Principal (Series 27). He is also an active member and director of The IIA, serving on the International Board's Audit Committee. In the past, Michael has served on The IIA North American Board and also as The IIA's Midwestern Region District Advisor. Mike, who earned a BSBA degree at the University of Missouri – Columbia, is also a member of the American Institute of CPAs, the Nebraska Society of CPAs, Missouri Society of CPAs, Information Systems Audit & Control Association, and Institute of Management Accountants.

Sridhar Ramamoorti, Ph.D., CIA, ACA, CPA, CFE, CFSA, CRP, CGAP, CGFM, CICA
Partner, National Corporate Governance Group
Grant Thornton LLP
Chicago, Illinois

Sri contributes to the firm's thought leadership efforts in the areas of corporate governance and accountability, consults on Sarbanes-Oxley as well as technical matters in financial reporting and auditing, and on anti-fraud programs and controls. He assists with global client pursuits across Grant Thornton's practices, helps design in-house professional development programs, and mentors younger professionals.

Previously, Sridhar was the Sarbanes-Oxley Advisor for the National Advisory Practices of Ernst & Young in North America. He was one of the Ernst & Young Fraud Investigation & Dispute Services (FIDS) faculty who conducted training on fraud awareness for over 1,000 U.S. audit partners and principals. Earlier in his career, Sridhar was a principal with Arthur Andersen's firm-wide Professional Standards Group. He was the Andersen representative on the AICPA's financial instruments task force that produced SAS 92: Auditing Derivatives, Hedging Activities, and Investments in Securities, and served as a key liaison for the multi-million dollar Andersen-MIT research collaboration.

Sridhar earned a Bachelor of Commerce (BCom) degree from Bombay University, India, and the MAcc. and Ph.D. degrees from The Ohio State University. After finishing his Ph.D., Sridhar served on the accountancy faculty of the University of Illinois at Urbana-Champaign. He has published extensively, in research and professional journals such as Management Science, European Management Journal, International Journal of Accounting, Journal of Information Systems, Research in Accounting Ethics, Journal of Government Financial Management, Internal Auditor, The White Paper, and Internal Auditing. Among his IIA-funded research monographs are: Research Opportunities in Internal Auditing (ROIA, co-edited by Bailey, Gramling & Ramamoorti, 2003), and Using Neural Networks for Risk Assessment in Internal Auditing (Ramamoorti & Traver, 1998). He is a core member of the Grant Thornton authoring team for a recently commissioned COSO project on monitoring. He has won prestigious research grants and teaching excellence awards.

Sridhar has been an active volunteer as the Chairman of the Academy for Government Accountability, a member of The IIA Research Foundation's Board of Trustees, Chairman of The IIA's Academic Relations Committee, as well as a member of the Board of Governors of the Chicago IIA Chapter. Over the last decade or so, Sridhar has made professional presentations in the USA, Brazil, France, India, Japan, Spain, and Turkey.

Mark Salamasick, CIA, CISA, CSP
Director of the Center for Internal Auditing Excellence
University of Texas at Dallas (UTD)

One of the largest internal audit programs worldwide, the Center for Internal Auditing Excellence has been in place for four years and has an emphasis on internal auditing, technology, audit software, information security, and forensic accounting. Mark was the principal researcher on a project with The IIA Research Foundation and Intel on PC Management Best Practices along with another publication Auditing Vendor Relationships, both published in 2003. Mark was previously with Bank of America for over 20 years. During the last two years at the bank, he was Senior Vice President of Internet/Intranet Services. Prior to that, he served as Senior Vice President and Director of Information Technology Audit. He worked within the Internal Audit Group of the bank for eighteen years with experience in technology, financial, and operational auditing. He had responsibility for partnering and auditing technology, information security, and business continuity during that time period. Prior to joining Bank of America, Mark was a senior consultant with Accenture (Andersen Consulting).

Mark has served on The IIA Board of Education and Research Advisors and its predecessor, the Board of Research Advisors, since 1997 and has served on a number of other IIA International Committees including the Advanced Technology Committee and Seminars Committee. He received the 1994 IIA International Audit and Technology award. In 2005 he was named Leon R. Radde Educator of the Year by The Institute of Internal Auditors. He is a frequent conference speaker on emerging technology issues and internal audit practices. He is on the Dallas Chapter IIA Board of Governors. Mark holds a BS in Business Administration and MBA from Central Michigan University, where he taught accounting and information systems as a graduate student and as a full time faculty member.

Cris Riddle, M.A.
Audit Administration Analyst
TD AMERITRADE

Cris is responsible for managing the processes, systems, and databases for the administration of the Internal Audit department. Additionally, she reviews and edits audit materials including audit reports, meeting presentations, and the Audit Manual. Cris is a member of The IIA, as well as an NASD Registered General Securities Representative (Series 7). She received both her B.A. and M.A. degrees in English/Creative Writing from Creighton University in Omaha, Nebraska, where she held a Presidential Fellowship as a graduate student. She writes and presents on numerous topics and is currently working on a novel.

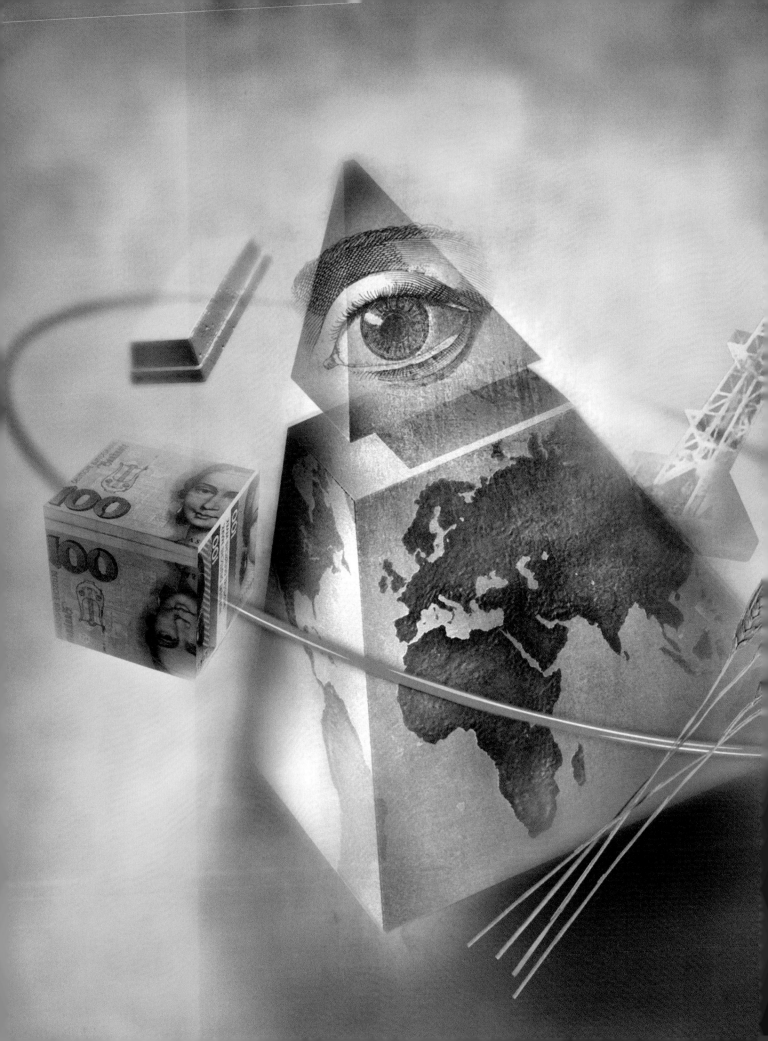

CHAPTER 1
INTRODUCTION TO
INTERNAL AUDITING

Learning Objectives

- Obtain a basic understanding of internal auditing and the internal audit process.

- Understand the relationship between auditing and accounting.

- Distinguish between financial reporting assurance services provided by internal auditors and those provided by independent outside auditors.

- Become familiar with the internal audit profession and The Institute of Internal Auditors.

- Understand the competencies needed to excel as an internal auditor.

- Be aware of the various internal audit career opportunities it is possible to pursue.

Think about the term "internal auditing" for a moment. What pops into your mind? What does the term mean to you? Now consider the following statements.

Time *names Cynthia Cooper, WorldCom Vice President of Internal Audit, one of three Persons of the Year.*[1]

"Each listed company must have an internal audit function."
— New York Stock Exchange[2]

"[Internal] auditors are rock stars now. This is their day in the sun."
— Bruce Nolop
Chief Financial Officer, Pitney Bowes Inc.[3]

"Global companies should look at processes that are material to them, not processes that really don't make that much difference. We need to focus on areas that could create a real risk to the institution. We also need greater reliance on internal audits."
– John A. Thain
Chief Executive Officer, NYSE[4]

Did your initial thoughts about internal auditing coincide with these statements? Probably not. Internal auditing has not, until recently, been widely viewed as a prestigious, high profile profession. Many

people have long held the view that auditing is merely a boring branch of accounting—only a nerd would want to sit behind a desk working with numbers day after day. To others, internal auditing conveys a negative connotation—after all, the only thing auditors do is check other peoples' work and report the mistakes they make. These are just two of the widespread misperceptions about internal auditing.

As the authors of this textbook, we hope to dispel these misperceptions. The fact is that the stature of the internal audit profession has never been higher. The demand for talented individuals at all levels of internal auditing far exceeds the supply. Chief audit executives (CAEs) of most public companies report directly to the audit committee of the board of directors and are viewed as peers among senior management executives. Membership in The Institute of Internal Auditors (IIA) currently exceeds 130,000[5] and is projected to surpass 200,000 in 2010.

We also hope to convey our shared passion for internal auditing—we really like it. We even enjoy getting together and talking about it. We want to share our collective expertise about internal auditing with you in a way that enables you to make informed decisions as to whether it is a career option you should consider.

We begin this introductory chapter by walking through the definition of internal auditing and introducing you to the internal audit process. We next clarify the relationship between auditing and accounting and distinguish the financial reporting assurance services provided by internal auditors from those provided by independent outside auditors. We then introduce you to the internal audit profession and The IIA. We wrap up the chapter by discussing the competencies needed to excel as an internal auditor and the various internal audit opportunities interested, competent individuals can pursue.

DEFINITION OF INTERNAL AUDITING

The IIA's Board of Directors adopted the current definition of internal auditing in 1999:

> *Internal auditing is an independent, objective, assurance and consulting activity designed to add value and improve an organization's operations. It helps an organization accomplish its objectives by bringing a systematic, disciplined approach to evaluate and improve effectiveness of risk management, control, and governance processes.*[6]

The key components of this definition are listed here and will be discussed in turn below:

- Helping the organization accomplish its objectives.
- Evaluating and improving the effectiveness of risk management, control, and governance processes.
- Assurance and consulting activity designed to add value and improve operations.
- Independence and objectivity.
- A systematic and disciplined approach (specifically, the engagement process).

Internal Auditing

An independent, objective, assurance and consulting activity designed to add value and improve an organization's operations.

Add Value

Value is provided by improving opportunities to achieve organizational objectives, identifying operational improvement, and/or reducing risk exposure through both assurance and consulting services.

Helping the Organization Accomplish Its Objectives

An organization's objectives define what the organization wants to achieve and its ongoing success depends on the accomplishment of its objectives. At the highest level, these objectives are reflected in the organization's mission and vision statements. The mission statement expresses, in broad terms, what the organization wants to achieve today. The vision statement conveys what the organization aspires to achieve in the future.

There is no single right way to categorize business objectives. This textbook uses the following categorization promulgated by the Committee of Sponsoring Organizations of the Treadway Commission (COSO) in 2004.

> **Strategic objectives** pertain to the value creation choices management makes on behalf of the organization's stakeholders. Note: Hereafter the term *objectives* is used when referring to what an organization wants to achieve and the term *strategy* when referring to how management plans to achieve the organization's objectives. For example, an organization may specify "increase market share" as an objective and implement a strategy of "acquire other companies" to achieve this objective.

> **Operations objectives** pertain to the effectiveness and efficiency of the organization's operations, including performance and profitability goals and safeguarding resources against loss.

> **Reporting objectives** pertain to the reliability of internal and external reporting of financial and nonfinancial information.

> **Compliance objectives** pertain to adherence to applicable laws and regulations.[7]

Understandable and measurable business objectives represent achievement targets and, accordingly, establish parameters for evaluating actual achievements over time. From an internal auditor's perspective, business objectives provide a framework for defining engagement objectives (in other words, what the auditor wants to achieve). The direct linkage between business objectives and audit engagement objectives sets the stage for internal auditors to help the organization achieve its objectives. This is an important concept that will be emphasized throughout the text. Exhibit 1-1 illustrates a set of business objectives and corresponding internal audit engagement objectives.

Evaluating and Improving the Effectiveness of Risk Management, Control, and Governance Processes

An organization cannot achieve its objectives and sustain success without effective risk management, control, and governance processes. These processes are complex and interrelated; an in-depth discussion of them at this point would be premature. They are covered extensively in later chapters.

Simple definitions are provided here to facilitate thinking about the various roles internal auditors might play in evaluating and

Internal Auditing

It helps an organization accomplish its objectives by bringing a systematic, disciplined approach to evaluate and improve effectiveness of risk managment,control, and governance processes.

COSO

A voluntary private-sector organization dedicated to improving the quality of financial reporting through business ethics, effective internal controls, and corporate governance.

Objectives

What an organization wants to achieve.

EXHIBIT 1-1

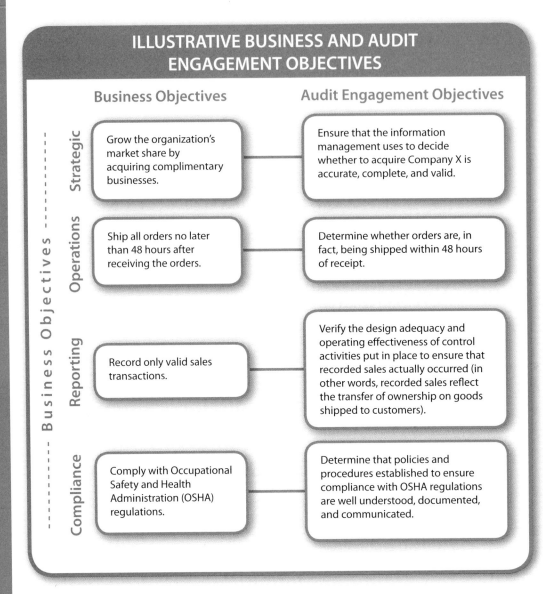

ILLUSTRATIVE BUSINESS AND AUDIT ENGAGEMENT OBJECTIVES

Business Objectives — — — — — — — — — — — — — — — —

Business Objectives	Audit Engagement Objectives
Strategic Grow the organization's market share by acquiring complimentary businesses.	Ensure that the information management uses to decide whether to acquire Company X is accurate, complete, and valid.
Operations Ship all orders no later than 48 hours after receiving the orders.	Determine whether orders are, in fact, being shipped within 48 hours of receipt.
Reporting Record only valid sales transactions.	Verify the design adequacy and operating effectiveness of control activities put in place to ensure that recorded sales actually occurred (in other words, recorded sales reflect the transfer of ownership on goods shipped to customers).
Compliance Comply with Occupational Safety and Health Administration (OSHA) regulations.	Determine that policies and procedures established to ensure compliance with OSHA regulations are well understood, documented, and communicated.

improving these processes. Governance provides a good starting point because it is generally viewed as the broadest of the three.

Governance is the process conducted by the board of directors to authorize, direct, and oversee management toward the achievement of the organization's objectives.

Risk management, which is closely interlinked with governance, is the process conducted by management to understand and deal with uncertainties (i.e., risks and opportunities) that could affect the organization's ability to achieve its objectives. Note that hereafter the term *risk* is used when referring to the possibility that an event will occur and negatively affect the achievement of objectives (e.g., employee fraud) and the term *opportunity* is used when referring to the possibility that an event will occur and positively affect the achievement of objectives (e.g., introducing a new product).

Control, which is imbedded in risk management, is the process conducted by management to reduce risks to acceptably low levels.

All three processes focus on the achievement of the organization's objectives. Whereas the board of directors is responsible for conducting the governance process, management is responsible for conducting the risk management and control processes. The term *conducting* here means guiding or leading the process as opposed to unilaterally performing or completing the steps in the process. The board and management need each other to effectively implement governance, risk management, and control. They also need the internal audit function, which plays a prominent role in evaluating and improving these processes. Note, however, that the internal audit function's responsibility stops well short of actually guiding or leading governance, risk management, and control. Chapter 3, "Governance and Risk Management," and Chapter 5, "Internal Control," discuss in detail the internal audit function's responsibilities in these areas.

Assurance and Consulting Activity Designed to Add Value and Improve Operations

The title of this textbook, *Internal Auditing: Assurance and Consulting Services,* was chosen because it clearly identifies the two types of services — assurance and consulting — that internal auditors provide to add value and improve operations. Assurance and consulting engagements differ in three respects: the primary purpose of the engagement, who determines the nature and scope of the engagements, and the parties involved.

The primary purpose of internal assurance services is to assess evidence relevant to subject matter of interest to someone and to provide conclusions regarding the subject matter. The internal audit function determines the nature and scope of assurance engagements, which generally involve three parties: The *first-party auditee* directly involved with the subject matter of interest, the *second-party auditor* making the assessment and providing the conclusion, and the *third-party user* relying on the auditor's assessment of evidence and conclusion.

The primary purpose of internal consulting services is to provide advice, generally at the specific request of engagement customers. The customer and the internal audit function mutually agree on the nature and scope of consulting engagements, which generally involve only two parties: the first-party auditee seeking and receiving the advice, and the second-party auditor offering and providing the advice.

Independence and Objectivity

Both The IIA's Code of Ethics and the The IIA's *International Standards for the Professional Practice of Internal Auditing (Standards)* emphasize the criticality of independence and objectivity to the practice of internal auditing. Independence refers to the organizational status of the internal audit function. Objectivity refers to the mental attitude of individual auditors.

For the internal audit function to be independent, the CAE must report to a level within the organization that has sufficient authority to ensure broad engagement coverage, due consideration of engagement outcomes, and appropriate responses to those outcomes. The IIA recommends that ideally the CAE report functionally to the

---

Assurance Services

An objective examination of evidence for the purpose of providing an independent assessment on risk management, control, or governance processes for the organization.

Consulting Services

Advisory and related services, the nature adn scope of which are agreed to with the customer and which are intended to improve an organization's governance, risk managment, and control processes without the internal auditor assuming management resonsibility.

organization's board of directors and administratively to the organization's chief executive officer (CEO) (Practice Advisory 1110-1, Organizational Independence).

Objectivity means that an auditor is able to make impartial, unbiased judgments. To ensure objectivity, internal auditors should not involve themselves in day-to-day operations, make management decisions, or otherwise put themselves in situations that result in actual or potential conflicts of interest. For example, if an auditor moves into the internal audit function from another area of the organization, the auditor may not provide assurance services to that area for one year (Standard 1130.A1-1). The reasoning behind this policy is that the auditor would be put in a position of auditing his or her own work. Chapter 8, "Managing the Internal Audit Function, goes into greater depth on the subjects of independence and objectivity.

A Systematic and Disciplined Approach (Specifically, the Engagement Process)

To truly add value and improve operations, internal assurance and consulting engagements must be performed in a systematic and disciplined manner. The three fundamental phases in the internal audit engagement process are planning the engagement, performing the engagement, and communicating engagement outcomes. These three phases are covered in depth in Chapter 10, "Conducting the Assurance Engagement" and Chapter 11, "Communicating Assurance Engagement Outcomes and Performing Follow-up Procedures." However, a brief overview is provided here.

Planning the engagement involves, among other activities:

- Obtaining an understanding of the auditee. An auditor cannot provide value-adding assurance or consulting services to a client that is not well understood. The auditor needs to understand the auditee's business objectives and the risks that threaten the achievement of those objectives. Other aspects of the auditee that the auditor must understand include, for example, the auditee's personnel, resources, and operations.

- Setting the engagement objectives. Because the overall purpose of internal assurance and consulting services is to help the organization achieve its objectives, the auditor will use the auditee's business objectives as a framework for defining the desired outcomes of a specific engagement.

- Determining the required evidence. The auditor must design the engagement to obtain sufficient competent evidence to achieve the engagement objectives.

- Deciding the nature, timing, and extent of the procedures that the auditor will perform to gather the required evidence.

Performing the engagement involves the application of specific audit procedures. Procedures include, for example, making inquiries, observing operations, inspecting documents, and analyzing the reasonableness of information. A second important aspect of gathering evidence is documenting the procedures performed and the results of performing the procedures.

Evaluating the evidence gathered during an assurance engagement involves reaching logical conclusions based on the evidence. For example, an internal auditor might reach the conclusion that internal controls over sales transactions are effective. Evaluating the evidence gathered during a consulting engagement involves formulating practical advice based on the evidence. For example, an internal auditor might advise the customer that specific application controls need to be built into a new computerized information system.

Communicating outcomes is a critical component of all internal assurance and consulting engagements. Regardless of the content or form of the communications, which may vary, communications of engagement outcomes should be accurate, objective, clear, concise, constructive, complete, and timely (Standard 2420, Quality of Communications).

THE RELATIONSHIP BETWEEN ACCOUNTING AND AUDITING

Students beginning their first auditing course have a tendency to assume that auditing is a subset of accounting. Although such an assumption is understandable, it is not correct. Exhibit 1-2 contains a quote from *The Philosophy of Auditing* that explains the difference between auditing and accounting.

Although the context of this quote is the audit of financial statements conducted by an independent outside auditor, the ideas expressed are just as relevant to internal assurance and consulting services. Internal assurance and consulting services are analytical and investigative; they are based on logic, which involves reasoning and drawing inferences. Auditors use logic when they reach conclusions or formulate advice based on evidence they gather and evaluate. The quality of auditors' conclusions or advice depends on their ability to gather and evaluate sufficient, competent evidence.

FINANCIAL REPORTING ASSURANCE SERVICES: EXTERNAL VERSUS INTERNAL

Publicly traded companies in the United States are required by the federal securities acts to have their annual financial statements audited by an independent outside auditor, for example, a certified public accounting (CPA) firm. A financial statement audit is a form of assurance service in which the CPA firm issues a written attestation report that expresses an opinion about whether the financial statements are fairly stated in accordance with generally accepted accounting principles (GAAP). Many privately held companies, government organizations, and not-for-profit organizations also have annual financial statement audits.

The U.S. Sarbanes-Oxley Act of 2002 requires a U.S. public company's independent outside auditor (frequently referred to as the external auditor) to also attest to the effectiveness of the company's internal control over financial reporting as of the balance sheet date. The CPA firm's opinion on internal control over financial reporting must be based on a recognized framework such as the *Internal Control—Integrated Framework* issued by COSO. The COSO Framework, as it is often called, as well as other internal control frameworks, are discussed

EXHIBIT 1-2

Relationship Between Auditing and Accounting

"The relationship of auditing to accounting is close, yet their natures are very different; they are business associates, not parent and child. Accounting includes the collection, classification, summarization, and communication of financial data; it involves the measurement and communication of business events and conditions as they affect and represent a given enterprise or other entity. The task of accounting is to reduce a tremendous mass of detailed information to manageable and understandable proportions. Auditing does none of these things. Auditing must consider business events and conditions too, but it does not have the task of measuring or communicating them. Its task is to review the measurements and communications of accounting for propriety. Auditing is analytical, not constructive; it is critical, investigative, concerned with the basis for accounting measurements and assertions. Auditing emphasizes proof, the support for financial statements and data. Thus, auditing has its principal roots, not in accounting, which it reviews, but in logic on which it leans heavily for ideas and methods."

Mautz, R. K. and Hussein A. Sharaf, The Philosophy of Auditing *(Sarasota, Fla.: American Accounting Association, 1961, p. 14).*

Independent Outside Auditor

A registered public accounting firm, hired by the organization's board or executive management, to perform a financial statement audit providing assurance for which the firm issues a written attestation report that expresses an opinion about whether the financial statements are fairly presented in accordance with applicable generally accepted accounting principles.

---

in detail in Chapter 5, "Internal Control." Both the CPA firm's financial statement audit report and the firm's report on the effectiveness of internal control over financial reporting are public documents—they are included in the company's annual report and submitted to the U.S. Securities and Exchange Commission (SEC). This requirement is not restricted to the United States. Many other countries have similar financial reporting laws with similar requirements.

CPA firms provide their financial reporting assurance services primarily for the benefit of third parties. Third parties rely on the CPA firm's independent attestations when making financial decisions about the organization. The independent attestations provide credibility to the information being used by the third-party decision makers and, accordingly, increase the users' confidence regarding the accuracy, completeness, and validity of the information upon which they base their decisions.

Internal auditors also provide financial reporting assurance services. The primary difference between internal and external financial reporting assurance services is the audience. Internal auditors provide their financial reporting assurance services primarily for the benefit of management and the board of directors. For example, the Sarbanes-Oxley Act requires the CEO and chief financial officer (CFO) of U.S. public companies to certify the company's financial statements as part of their quarterly and annual filings. It also requires management to assess and report on the effectiveness of internal control over financial reporting. Senior management relies on the financial reporting assurance services provided by the company's internal audit function to provide them with confidence regarding the truthfulness of their financial reporting assertions.

THE INTERNAL AUDIT PROFESSION

Modern Internal Auditing: A Dynamic Profession in High Demand

"The profession of auditing in general, and internal auditing in particular, is ancient." [8]

Although historians have traced the history of internal auditing to centuries B.C., many people associate the genesis of modern internal auditing with the establishment of The IIA in 1941. At its inception, The IIA was a national organization with 24 charter members. [9]

Both The IIA and the internal audit profession have evolved dramatically since then. A time line of selected IIA milestones is presented in Exhibit 1-3. Two items that stand out in the time line are the phenomenal growth of The IIA, especially during the last 30 years, and its globalization. IIA members now reside in nearly 170 countries and territories, with more than 50% of the membership residing outside North America. [10] Internal auditing is now a truly global profession and the demand for internal audit services continues to grow.

A number of interrelated circumstances and events have fueled the dramatic increase in demand for internal audit services over the past 30 years. The business world during this time has changed dramatically. Examples include globalization, increasingly complex corporate structures, and e-commerce and other technological advances. Simultaneously, the business world has experienced a rash of devastating corporate scandals, which have precipitated a groundswell of new laws and regulations and professional guidance. These forces, in combination, continue to generate an ever-widening array of risks that corporate executives must understand and address. As a result, internal auditors are increasingly being called upon to help organizations strengthen their corporate governance, risk management, and internal control processes.

The Nature and Scope of Modern Internal Audit Services

The overarching objective of the internal audit function is to help an organization achieve its business objectives. Consequently, the targets of internal audit attention may include:

- Operational effectiveness and efficiency of business processes.
- Reliability of information systems and the quality of the decision-making information produced by those systems.
- Safeguarding assets against loss, including losses resulting from management and employee fraud.
- Compliance with organization policies, contracts, laws, and regulations.

The internal audit function helps the organization achieve its business objectives by evaluating and improving the effectiveness of risk management, control, and governance processes. Evaluating and improving these processes propels the internal audit function into virtually all aspects of the organization, including, for example, production of goods and services, financial management, human resources, research and development, logistics, and information technology. The customers served by internal auditing range from the board of directors and senior management to business process managers.

Internal auditors use a wide variety of procedures to test the design adequacy and operating effectiveness of the organization's risk management, control, and governance processes. These procedures include:

EXHIBIT 1-3

Time Line of Selected IIA Milestones

1941	The Institute of Internal Auditors is established. IIA membership totals 24.
1947	The *Statement of Responsibilities of the Internal Auditor* is issued.
1948	The first chapters outside North America are formed in London and Manila.
1953	"Progress Through Sharing" is adopted as The IIA's official motto.
1957	The *Statement of Responsibilities of the Internal Auditor* is revised to include more responsibility for operational areas.
1968	The IIA Code of Ethics is approved.
1973	The first Board of Regents is appointed. The Certified Internal Auditor (CIA) program is established.
1976	The Foundation of Auditability, Research, and Education (FARE) is founded; the name is later changed to The IIA Research Foundation.
1978	The *Standards for the Professional Practice of Internal Auditing* is approved.
1979	The National Institute Agreement is approved; five national institutes are established.
1980	IIA membership totals 21,549.
1984	*The Quality Assurance Review Manual* is published. A pilot school is established at Louisiana State University. The first *Statement on Internal Auditing Standards* (SIAS) is published.
1986	The target school program is started.
1988	An IIA National Institute is established in The People's Republic of China.
1989	The United Nations grants consultative status to The IIA.
1990	The IIA elects A.J. Hans Spoel as the first chairman from outside North America.
1995	The IIA becomes an official member body of the American National Standards Institute (ANSI) and the sole U.S. representative to the International Standards Organization (ISO).
1996	*Accounting Today* names IIA President, William G. Bishop III, CIA, as one of the "top 100 most influential people in accounting." The IIA begins to aggressively promote the CIA program in Europe, Asia, the Middle East, and South America.
1998	The first all-objective CIA exam is offered with a record-breaking 5,165 candidates sitting for one or more parts.
1999	The new definition of internal auditing is introduced. The 25th anniversary of the CIA designation is celebrated.
2000	The new *International Standards for the Professional Practice of Internal Auditing* are introduced. IIA membership totals 68,985.
2002	The *Standards* become mandatory guidance for all IIA members and CIAs.
2003	The new IIA Professional Practices Framework is issued.
2006	IIA membership exceeds 120,000.
2007	To continue to use the statement "conducted in accordance with the *Standards*," internal audit functions that existed as of January 1, 2002, must have an external quality assessment completed by January 1, 2007.

Source: www.theiia.org

- Inquiring of managers and employees.
- Observing activities.
- Inspecting resources and documents.
- Reperforming control activities.
- Performing trend and ratio analysis.
- Performing data analysis using computer-assisted audit techniques.
- Gathering corroborating information from independent third parties.
- Performing direct tests of events and transactions.

The Professionals Who Perform Internal Audit Services

Internal audit service providers are employed by all types of organizations: public and private companies; local, state, and federal government agencies; and nonprofit entities. Until recently, these services were provided exclusively "in-house," in other words, by employees of the organizations employing them. This is no longer the case. Some organizations are choosing to outsource their internal audit functions, either fully or partially, to external service providers. External providers of internal audit services include public accounting firms and other third-party vendors. The most common form of outsourcing is referred to as "co-sourcing." Co-sourcing means that an organization is supplementing its in-house internal audit function to some extent via the services of third-party vendors. Common situations in which an organization will cosource its internal audit function with a third-party service provider include circumstances in which the third-party vendor has specialized audit knowledge and skills that the organization does not have in-house and circumstances in which the organization has insufficient in-house audit resources to fully complete its planned audits. Chapter 8, "Managing the Internal Audit Function," goes into more detail regarding co-sourcing.

THE INSTITUTE OF INTERNAL AUDITORS

An Overview

The IIA, headquartered in Altamonte Springs, Fla., is recognized around the world as "the internal audit profession's leader in certification, education, research, and technological guidance."[11] The IIA headquarters, with a staff of more than 150 professionals, serves the internal audit profession at the international level. In addition, The Institute has more than 250 affiliates (chapters and national institutes) that serve IIA members at the local level.[12]

The IIA's vision, mission, and motto are presented in Exhibit 1-4 on page 1-12.

The IIA Leadership Structure

The IIA headquarters' leadership team includes the president, chief operating officer, chief administrative officer, and chief advocacy officer. Hundreds of volunteers also provide IIA leadership. These leaders include the IIA Board of Directors, international committees, district representatives, and affiliate officers and board members.

The 37 member Board of Directors oversees the affairs of The IIA. The Board's Executive Committee comprises the Chairman of the Board, the Senior Vice Chairman, four Vice Chairmen, the Treasurer, the Secretary, and the two most recent former Chairmen of the Board. The board also includes the North American Board, which holds specific authority and oversight of North American activities, Affiliate Directors, Directors-at-Large, and The IIA President as an Ex-Officio Director.[13]

Numerous international committees undertake specific tasks directed at meeting the ever-changing needs of the IIA membership. Thirty-one district representatives oversee the activities of approximately 170 North

The Institute of Internal Auditors
Headquartered in Altamonte Springs, Fla., it is recognized around the world as the internal audit profession's leader in certification, education, research, and technological guidance.

EXHIBIT 1-4

The IIA's Vision, Mission, and Motto

Vision
The IIA will be the global voice of the internal audit profession: Advocating its value, promoting best practice, and providing exceptional service to its members.

Mission
The mission of The Institute of Internal Auditors is to provide dynamic leadership for the global profession of internal auditing. Activities in support of this mission will include, but not be limited to:

- Advocating and promoting the value that internal audit professionals add to their organizations.
- Providing comprehensive professional education and development opportunities; standards and other professional practice guidance; and certification programs.
- Researching, disseminating, and promoting to practitioners and stakeholders knowledge concerning internal auditing and its appropriate role in control, risk management, and governance.
- Educating practitioners and other relevant audiences on best practices in internal auditing.
- Bringing together internal auditors from all countries to share information and experiences.

Motto
Progress Through Sharing

Source: www.theiia.org

American chapters in Canada, the United States, Bermuda, and the Caribbean.[14] Each of the nearly 150 IIA affiliates (chapters and national institutes) worldwide elects its own officers and board members.

Professional Guidance

Professional guidance provided by The IIA includes the Professional Practices Framework, position papers, and other resources. The following is a brief introduction to the Professional Practices Framework. It is described in detail in Chapter 2, "The Professional Practices Framework: Ethics and Standards of Practice."

The Professional Practices Framework comprises three categories of guidance:

Category 1: The Code of Ethics and Standards. The Code of Ethics and *Standards* are mandatory guidance that is considered essential to the professional practice of internal auditing.

Category 2: Practice Advisories. The Practice Advisories are strongly recommended, not mandatory, guidance. They are intended to help interpret the *Standards* and apply them in specific internal audit environments.

Category 3: Development and Practice Aids. This guidance includes a wide range of materials developed or endorsed by The IIA such as research studies, books, seminars, conferences, and other products and services pertaining to internal auditing.

More detailed information about the Professional Practices Framework and the other guidance resources provided by The IIA can be found on The Institute's Web site (www.theiia.org).

Professional Certifications

The premier certification sponsored by The IIA is the Certified Internal Auditor® (CIA®), the only globally accepted certification for internal auditors. The CIA exam tests a candidate's expertise in four parts: The Internal Audit Activity's Role in Governance, Risk, and Control; Conducting the Internal Audit Engagement; Business Analysis and Information Technology; and Business Management Skills. In addition to passing the CIA examination, candidates must have a minimum of two years of internal audit experience or its equivalent to become a certified internal auditor.

The IIA also sponsors three specialty certification programs: Certification in Control Self-Assessment®; Certified Government Auditing Professional®; and Certified Financial Services Auditor®. Detailed information about each of the certification programs can be found on The IIA's Web site.

Note: Professional organizations other than The IIA also sponsor certification programs relevant to internal auditors. For example, ISACA sponsors the Certified Information Systems Auditor® program and the Association of Certified Fraud Examiners sponsors the Certified Fraud Examiner® program.

Research and Educational Products and Services

The IIA is known as the "profession's chief educator and global leader in professional development," which is reflected in its official motto, "Progress Through Sharing,"[15] for good reason. The wide variety of research and education products and services offered by The IIA are briefly described below. More detailed information can be found on The IIA's Web site.

The IIA Research Foundation (IIARF) was established in 1976. Its mission is "to be the integrated research and educational products arm of The IIA dedicated to facilitating the effective management of the internal audit guidance life cycle and developing global guidance resources." Its major objective is "to expand knowledge and understanding of internal auditing by providing relevant research and educational products to advance the profession globally."[16] The foundation sponsors research projects and publishes research reports. The IIARF Bookstore offers hundreds of educational products, including books and videos, covering topics of interest to internal audit professionals.

The IIA's Global Auditing Information Network Benchmarking Services and Flash Surveys enable internal audit functions to share information and learn from each other. *Internal Auditor*, The IIA's bi-monthly magazine, publishes articles of widespread interest to internal auditors around the world. Numerous newsletters published by The IIA also cover top-

Certified Internal Auditor® (CIA®)
The premier certification sponsored by The IIA; the only globally accepted certification for internal auditors.

The IIA Research Foundation
Established in 1976, its mission is "to be the integrated research and educational products arm of The IIA dedicated to facilitating the effective management of the internal audit guidance life cycle and developing global guidance resources."

ics of interest to internal auditors, including topics of specific interest to CAEs and to various internal audit industry and specialty groups such as financial services, gaming, and information technology (IT) auditing.

Professional development opportunities offered by The IIA include meetings, seminars, and conferences as well as technology-based training, books, and webcasts. The premier IIA conference is the annual International Conference, which attracts thousands of internal auditors from around the world. Other IIA opportunities include industry-specific conferences such as the Financial Services Conference and the Government Auditing Conference, specialty opportunities such as the General Audit Management Conference, which is targeted toward CAEs, and district and regional conferences.

The IIA, through its Academic Relation Committee, also promotes and supports internal audit education around the world. The Internal Auditing Education Partnership (IAEP) is designed to support universities and colleges that have made formal commitments to offer internal audit education. The level of support provided by The IIA to a particular school is directly related to the level of development of the internal audit program at that school.

COMPETENCIES NEEDED
TO EXCEL AS AN INTERNAL AUDITOR

Reflecting back on the definition and description of internal auditing presented earlier in this chapter, what must a person know to achieve success as an internal auditor? What must a person be able to do? Are there certain personal characteristics that are indicative of success? The good news is that there is no single right answer to these questions; different people with different competency profiles can achieve success as internal auditors. Moreover, the competencies needed to succeed are not unique to internal auditing.

There are, however, certain competencies that tend to be common among successful internal auditors. Some of these competencies are inherent personal qualities. Others are knowledge and skills that can be learned and developed. An understanding of these competencies will provide information with which an informed decision can be made about internal auditing as a desirable vocation for anyone considering the profession.

Inherent Personal Qualities

Different people have different inherent personal qualities or characteristics. For example, some people are by nature more introverted (shy and reserved), while others are more extroverted (outgoing and sociable). Personal qualities that are common among successful internal auditors at all levels include the following:

Integrity. Integrity is not an option for internal auditors; they must have it. People of integrity build trust, which in turn establishes the foundation for reliance on what they say and do. Users of internal audit work products rely on the auditors' professional judgments to make important business decisions. These stakeholders must have confidence that internal auditors are trustworthy.

Passion. It is virtually impossible to be very good at something you do not really like to do. Successful internal auditors have a deep interest in, and intense enthusiasm for, their work.

Work ethic. All successful professional service providers are adept at meeting their clients' quality, cost, and timing expectations. Successful internal auditors not only work hard; they also work smart. They cost-effectively accomplish what auditees want when they want it. They get the right things done the right way.

Curiosity. Successful internal auditors are naturally inquisitive. They like to know how things work and why they work the way they do.

Creativity. Successful internal auditors like to solve problems. They constantly think outside the box to generate improvement ideas for their organizations.

Initiative. Successful internal auditors are self-starters. They voluntarily seek out and pursue opportunities to add value and want to play the role of change agent within their organizations.

Flexibility. Change is the only constant in today's business world. Successful companies continuously adapt to change and change brings new risks, which must be managed. Successful internal auditors embrace change; they adapt quickly to new situations and challenges.

The characteristics described above are illustrative of the inherent personal qualities that are required to succeed as an internal auditor. Does this mean that someone lacking one or more of these traits is destined to failure as an internal auditor? Not necessarily. Integrity is imperative and it would be foolish for anyone to pursue a vocation they really do not believe in or to which they are not fully committed. The other qualities listed above can be exercised—they can be strengthened, if desired.

Knowledge, Skills, and Credentials

The IIA *Standards* require internal auditors to perform their assurance and consulting engagements with proficiency, which means they must possess the knowledge and skills needed to fulfill their responsibilities (Standard 1210). What knowledge and skills are needed to succeed as an internal auditor? The answer to this question will depend, to a certain extent, on the current stage in a person's career. Those planning to pursue a long-term career in internal auditing will need to continuously advance their knowledge and skills. For example, an internal auditor will be expected to know and do things as an in-charge auditor with four years of experience that would not be expected of someone directly out of school. Accordingly, one of the most important skills to start to develop while in school is learning how to learn—internal auditors continue to learn throughout their careers.

Nobody is an expert internal auditor when they graduate from college. Internal auditing, like any other profession, is learned primarily by doing, in other words, through on-the-job experience. It is like learning how to drive a car. It is impossible to learn how to drive merely by reading about it, listening to someone talk about it, or watching someone else drive. It must be experienced—it is necessary to get in a car and practice, preferably under the supervision of a well-qualified instructor. Such is the case with internal auditing—it is learned by doing it under the watchful eyes of experienced supervisors and mentors.

An obvious example of a very important skill for all internal auditors is the application of internal audit standards and procedures. All internal auditors must possess a working knowledge of The IIA's *Standards* and be well versed in the Practice Advisories. Because a large part of internal auditors' responsibilities involves gathering and evaluation of evidence, they must be proficient in applying the various types of audit procedures introduced earlier in this chapter—inquiry, observation, inspection, reperformance, analysis of trends, ratios and data, gathering information from independent sources, and performing direct tests of events and transactions.

All internal auditors must also become well versed in fundamental management principles so they can recognize and evaluate deviations from good business practices. They must thoroughly understand the organization and industry in which it operates. Among many other things, internal auditors need to understand the:

- Organization's business objectives, strategies, and operations.
- External and internal risks that threaten the organization's success.
- Organization's risk management, control, and governance processes.

What about accounting and IT? Must internal auditors be proficient in these areas? An auditor must be proficient in accounting if he or she works extensively in the area of financial reporting. Likewise, an auditor who works extensively in the area of computerized information systems must possess deep IT risk, control, and audit expertise. Such auditors are commonly referred to as information systems or IT auditors. In today's business world, however, it is practically impossible for any auditor to completely avoid computerized information systems. Accordingly, all internal auditors should have a sound understanding of fundamental IT risks, controls, and audit techniques. Chapter 6, "IT Risks and Controls," covers this topic in greater depth.

The internal audit function as a whole must be sufficiently competent to provide effective and efficient assurance and consulting services in any area within its scope of responsibilities, which invariably covers operating, reporting, and compliance objectives. Worthy of consideration at this point is the fact that it is virtually impossible for internal auditors to effectively reach valid conclusions or provide meaningful advice about anything they do not thoroughly understand.

Internal auditors must have good interpersonal skills and be able to communicate effectively, both orally and in writing. Why? Auditing involves gathering evidence, much of which comes from other people. Auditors need to know how to ask the right questions in the right way to get the information they need to reach well-founded conclusions.

Standard

A professional pronouncement promulgated by the International Internal Auditing Standards Board that delineates the requirements for performing a broad range of internal audit activities and for evaluating internal audit performance.

They also need to listen well to the answers they are given. Every internal audit engagement culminates in some form of communication. The communications the internal audit function produces contain information used by a wide variety of decision-makers, including senior management and the board of directors. Accordingly, engagement communications must convey information that facilitates informed decisions clearly and effectively. Communication requirements are discussed in detail in Chapter 11, "Communicating Assurance Engagement Outcomes and Performing Follow-up Procedures."

There are many things a student can do to prepare for an entry-level internal audit position. Knowledge and skills that can be developed include:

- Expertise in auditing, accounting, information systems and technology, business risks and controls, management, finance and economics, commercial law, or quantitative methods. Specialized expertise in more than one area is especially beneficial. Specialized expertise in both auditing and information systems, for example, is in very high demand.

- Hands-on working knowledge of audit-related software such as flowcharting, spreadsheet, and database, as well as generalized audit software.

- Interpersonal and communication skills.

- Ability to think analytically, assimilate new information quickly, cope with ambiguity, handle unstructured multi-dimensional tasks, and effectively manage several projects simultaneously.

The credentials students attain and report on their resumes will reflect the knowledge and skills they have obtained. The completion of a degree with a good grade point average displays mastery of a field of study. Working while in school or actively participating in extracurricular activities shows the ability to multitask successfully. Scholarships and other awards signify respect for a student's abilities. Completion of an internship demonstrates the ability to apply what has been learned. Serving as an officer in a student organization signifies motivation and the ability to lead. Completing the CIA examination before graduation signals competency in internal auditing and related subjects.

Progression from a staff auditor to an experienced in-charge auditor indicates a readiness to coach and share expertise with subordinates, make presentations and facilitate meetings, communicate persuasively with all levels of people, build rapport and lasting relationships with auditees, and proactively stimulate change. Credentials to accrue during this stage of an internal audit career may include, for example, a track record of engagement successes, testimonials from auditees (being recognized as a "go to" person), a Master of Business Administration degree, multiple professional certifications, and a volunteer leadership position in a professional organization such as a local IIA chapter.

Internal audit professionals will continue to develop their management and leadership skills if they decide to continue into internal audit management. These individuals will be expected to foster an internal

Knowledge and Skills to Be Developed
Expertise

Technology

Communication

Analytical thinking

audit environment that engenders creativity, adeptly addresses strategic management issues, and commands respect among senior executives and professional colleagues. As an individual gains a reputation as an internal audit thought leader, he or she will likely be called upon to share his or her expertise by doing such things as serving as an IIA volunteer at the international level, delivering presentations at professional meetings, and writing professional journal articles.

INTERNAL AUDIT CAREER PATHS

Pathways into Internal Auditing

Until very recently, most internal auditors began their careers in public accounting. Accounting graduates would start out as financial statement auditors in public accounting and, after gaining experience, move into internal audit positions, oftentimes with former clients. While this is still a common pathway into internal auditing, it is by no means the only one.

Hiring of internal auditors directly out of school has become much more common in recent years. Companies, government, and not-for-profit organizations, and firms that provide internal audit services to other companies and organizations are increasingly recruiting internal auditors directly out of colleges and universities. Colleges and universities that have established internal audit programs endorsed by The IIA are growing in number and popularity among recruiters. Top-tier students with degrees in accounting, information systems, and other business and nonbusiness fields from these and other schools are in high demand. Those students who have completed one or more audit-related internships are in especially high demand because of their experience and credentials.

Some organizations consider internal auditing to be an important component of their management trainee programs because it offers management candidates a unique opportunity to gain relevant risk management, control, and governance expertise across many areas of the organization. In these organizations, prospective managers from different areas of the organization are required to spend a certain amount of time in the internal audit function as a prerequisite to moving upward into management.

Pathways Out of Internal Auditing

The vast majority of people who work in internal auditing do not spend their entire careers there. As indicated above, internal auditing serves as an excellent training ground for aspiring business executives. Many internal auditors use the expertise they gain in internal auditing as a stepping stone into financial or nonfinancial management positions, either in the organization they have been working for or another organization.

Moving from internal auditing into a position with a firm that provides internal assurance and consulting services was virtually unheard of a few years ago. This is now a viable opportunity, especially for individuals with specialized, high-demand expertise in a particular industry (e.g., energy or banking) or subject matter (e.g., information systems or fraud prevention, deterrence, and detection).

Careers in Internal Auditing

Some people, however, do choose to make internal auditing their career and even they have options. One option is to progress upward through the ranks of a single organization's internal audit function into internal audit management. Another option is to stay in internal auditing but advance up the ladder toward internal audit management, moving from one organization to another. A third option is to move upward through the various levels in a firm that provides internal assurance and consulting services.

The ultimate destination of a career internal auditor in an organization is CAE. CAEs are highly respected within their organizations, often holding senior executive positions. They interact with the highest level of senior management and the board of directors. They commonly report functionally to the audit committee of the board of directors and administratively to a senior executive such as the CEO or CFO. Chapter 8, "Managing the Internal Audit Function," comprehensively addresses the roles and responsibilities of the CAE.

In a firm that provides internal audit services to many organizations, an auditor can rise to the level of a partner or comparably prestigious position. Unlike CAEs in an organization, they interact with and report to senior executives and boards of directors of several organizations.

SUMMARY

This chapter provides a basic understanding of internal auditing and introduces the internal audit process. The difference between auditing and accounting and the difference between the financial reporting assurance services internal auditors provide and those that public accountants provide is covered. An introduction to the internal audit profession and The IIA also is provided. Finally, the competencies needed to excel as an internal auditor and the various internal audit career paths that are available are outlined.

Chief Audit Executive
The top position within the organization responsible for internal audit activities.

1. Define *internal auditing*.

2. Define *objective* and *strategy*. Describe the four categories of business objectives introduced in this chapter.

3. Define *governance, risk management,* and *control*.

4. Explain the difference between internal assurance services and internal consulting services.

5. Define *independence* and *objectivity* as they pertain to internal auditors.

6. What are the three fundamental phases in the internal audit engagement process?

7. Explain the relationship between accounting and auditing.

8. Explain the primary difference between internal and external financial reporting assurance services.

9. Identify some of the factors that have fueled the dramatic increase in demand for internal audit services over the past 30 years.

10. List the types of procedures an internal auditor might use to test the design and operating effectiveness of risk management, control, and governance processes.

11. Define *cosourcing.*
    Why might an organization choose to cosource its internal audit function?

12. Describe The IIA leadership structure.

13. What are the three categories of guidance included in the Professional Practices Framework?

14. Identify the areas of expertise tested on the CIA exam.

15. What is The IIA's official motto?

16. Identify five inherent personal qualities that are common among successful internal auditors.

17. Explain why it is imperative that internal auditors have integrity.

18. Explain why internal auditors must have good interpersonal and communications skills.

19. Describe some of the things a student can do to prepare for an entry-level internal audit position.

20. Describe three ways individuals enter the internal audit profession.

21. Do most people who work in internal auditing spend their entire careers there? Explain.

22. What options does an individual have if he or she chooses to be a career internal auditor?

Select the best answer for each of the following questions.

1. AVF Company's new CFO has asked the company's CAE to meet with him to discuss the role of the internal audit function. The CAE should inform the CFO that the overall responsibility of internal auditing is to:

   a. Serve as an independent assurance and consulting activity designed to add value and improve the company's operations.

   b. Assess the company's methods for safeguarding its assets and, as appropriate, verify the existence of the assets.

   c. Review the integrity of financial and operating information and the methods used to accumulate and report information.

   d. Determine whether the company's system of internal controls provides reasonable assurance that information is effectively and efficiently communicated to management.

2. Which of the following statements is not true about business objectives?

   a. Business objectives represent targets of performance.

   b. Establishment of meaningful business objectives is a prerequisite to effective internal control.

   c. Establishing meaningful business objectives is a key component of the management process.

   d. Business objectives are management's means of employing resources and assigning responsibilities.

3. Within the context of internal auditing, assurance services are best defined as:

   a. Objective examinations of evidence for the purpose of providing independent assessments.

   b. Advisory services intended to add value and improve an organization's operations.

   c. Professional activities that measure and communicate financial and business data.

   d. Objective evaluations of compliance with policies, plans, procedures, laws, and regulations.

4. The IIA's Professional Practices Framework indicates that all internal auditors should individually:

   I. Understand human relations and be skilled in dealing with people.

   II. Be able to recognize deviations from good business practice.

   III. Be experts on subjects such as economics, taxes, commercial law, and statistics.

   IV. Be skilled in oral and written communication.

a. I and III.

b. II and IV.

c. I, II, and IV.

d. I, II, III, and IV.

5. While planning an internal audit, the auditor obtains knowledge about the client to, among other things:

   a. Develop an attitude of professional skepticism about management's assertions.

   b. Make constructive suggestions to management concerning internal control improvements.

   c. Evaluate whether misstatements in the client's performance reports should be communicated to senior management and the audit committee.

   d. Develop an understanding of the client's objectives and risks.

DISCUSSION QUESTIONS

1. Describe the relationship between objectives and strategies. What is your foremost objective as a student in this course? Explain your strategy for achieving this objective.

2. Ina Icandoit has an 8:00 AM class everyday. It is very important to Ina that she gets to class on time. What risks threaten the achievement of Ina's objective? What controls can Ina implement to mitigate these risks?

3. Prim Rose owns five flower shops in the suburbs of a large mid-western city. Each shop is managed by a different person. One of the tests Prim performs to monitor the performance of his shops is a simple trend analysis of month-to-month sales for each shop. Assume that Prim's analysis of the reported sales performance for his flower shop on Iris Street shows that monthly sales remained relatively consistent from January through June. Should Prim be pleased or concerned about the sales performance report for the shop on Iris Street over this six-month period? Explain.

4. Discuss:

   a. The inherent personal qualities common among successful internal auditors.

   b. The knowledge, skills, and credentials entry-level internal auditors are expected to possess.

   c. The knowledge, skills, and credentials in-charge internal auditors are expected to possess.

   d. The knowledge, skills, and credentials internal audit executives are expected to possess.

CASE

Visit The Institute of Internal Auditors' Web site (www. theiia.org). Locate, print, read, and prepare to discuss the following items:

a. The printer-friendly comprehensive version of "Frequently Asked Questions (FAQs) About the Internal Audit Profession."

b. "What Does it Take to be an Internal Audit Professional?"

c. The CIA exam content outlines for "Part I: The Internal Audit Activity's Role in Governance, Risk, and Control" and "Part II: Conducting the Internal Audit Engagement."

REFERENCES

[1] Lacayo, Richard and Amanda Ripley, "Persons of the Year," *Time,* Dec. 30, 2002–Jan. 6, 2003, 30.

[2] NYSE Listed Company Manual, Section 303A.07(d), http://www.nyse.com/Frameset.html?nyseref=&displayPage=/listed/1022221393251.html.

[3] Lieb, Scott, "New Terrain," *CFO Magazine,* Feb. 1, 2004, 40.

[4] "Up Front Question of the Week," *BusinessWeek,* Dec. 18, 2006, 18.

[5] www.theiia.org.

[6] Institute of Internal Auditors, The Professional Practices Framework or Internal Auditing (Altamonte Springs, Fla: The Institute of Internal Auditors, 2004), xxvii.

[7] Committee of Sponsoring Organizations of the Treadway Commission (COSO), Enterprise Risk Management – Integrated Framework (Jersey City, N.J.: AICPA, 2004), 35-36.

[8] Calloway, David, *Internal Auditing: A Guide for the New Auditor* (Altamonte Springs, Fla: The Institute of Internal Auditors, 1995), 1.

[9] www.theiia.org.

[10] www.theiia.org.

[11] www.theiia.org.

[12] www.theiia.org.

[13] www.theiia.org.

[14] www.theiia.org.

[15] www.theiia.org.

[16] www.theiia.org.

CHAPTER 2
THE PROFESSIONAL PRACTICES FRAMEWORK: ETHICS AND STANDARDS OF PRACTICE

Learning Objectives

- Understand the structure of the Professional Practices Framework and type of guidance it provides.

- Apply the professional guidance in the practice of internal auditing.

- Use the Professional Practices Framework to address issues that arise in internal audit practice.

- Understand the ethical principles and behavioral norms relevant to the profession and practice of internal auditing.

- Identify the essential characteristics of functions, organizations, and individuals for the performance of effective internal audit activities.

- Understand the nature of internal audit activities and the criteria against which performance of these activities can be measured.

What does it take to be a good internal auditor? What makes for a successful internal audit function? What should the users, the customers, of internal audit services expect of their internal auditors? What are the responsibilities of the chief audit executive (CAE)? How do the audit committee and senior management evaluate internal audit services? In other words, how does internal auditing add value?

In this chapter, you will learn how the internal audit profession addresses such questions through The Institute of Internal Auditors' Professional Practices Framework (PPF). The PPF reflects the global nature of the profession and has achieved worldwide acceptance with approved translations of the Code of Ethics and the *International Standards for the Professional Practice of Internal Auditing (Standards)* in more than 25 languages.

THE PROFESSIONAL PRACTICES FRAMEWORK

The definition of *internal auditing* presented in Chapter 1, "Introduction to Internal Auditing," describes the role and responsibilities of the profession as the delivery of professional services consisting of independent, objective assurance and consulting activities that add value and improve an organization's operations. Internal auditors provide these professional services to a diverse set of organizations ranging from publicly traded and private companies to government and not-for-profit entities. Within these organizations, they serve a number of customers, each with their own needs and demands. These customers include boards of directors (particularly the audit committee), executive management, financial and operating managers, auditees, regulators, and even, indirectly, the organization's suppliers, investors, and patrons. This chapter explores how the internal audit profession can deliver services that provide value by meeting the needs of these various customers.

Although the complete answer to how internal auditing can provide value will involve an in-depth understanding of the specifics of the organization in which the internal audit services are being performed, the fundamental elements of the answer can be found in the PPF. The PPF represents the collective knowledge of the internal audit profession as codified by The IIA and contains what is considered to be the essential elements of the effective delivery of internal audit services. These elements include the attributes of the individual internal auditor, the characteristics of the function or organization providing these services, the nature of internal audit activities, and their performance criteria. The PPF thus provides guidance to the profession and sets expectation for its customers regarding the performance of internal audit services.

Guidance for the Internal Audit Practice

The practice of internal auditing developed over a long period of time. As organizations grew in size and complexity and developed geographically dispersed operations, managers could no longer personally observe operations for which they were responsible nor have significant direct contact with people reporting to them. With the founding of The IIA in 1941, internal audit practice began the move toward becoming a profession, including agreement among practitioners about the role of internal auditing and its basic concepts and practices. The development of guidance for the emerging profession proceeded relatively slowly in the early years of The IIA. The first guidance came with the issuance of the *Statement of the Responsibilities of the Internal Auditor* in 1947. This short document set out to define the objectives and scope of internal auditing. As the profession evolved, the broadening of its scope was reflected in subsequent revisions. For instance, in the original 1947 *Statement* the scope was focused primarily on financial matters, but by 1957 it had been broadened to include numerous services to management regarding review and evaluation of operations as well.[1] Over the years, the *Statement* was periodically revised (1957, 1971, 1976, 1981, and 1990) until its replacement in 1999 by the current definition.

The Professional Practices Framework

Comprises the official definition of internal auditing, the *International Standards for the Professional Practice of Internal Auditing*, the Code of Ethics, Practice Advisories, and development and practice aids.

The IIA provided additional guidance for the profession in 1968 with the issuance of a Code of Ethics for IIA members. This code consisted of eight articles of which the basic principles are still found in the current code. The IIA also provided specifics on what knowledge and skills internal audit practitioners should possess with the publication of the *Common Body of Knowledge* in 1972 and implementation of the Certified Internal Auditor™ (CIA) certification program the subsequent year. Finally, in 1978, The IIA issued *The Standards for the Professional Practice of Internal Auditing*. These standards consisted of five general and 25 specific guidelines as to how the internal audit function should be managed and how audit engagements should be performed. These standards were widely adopted and translated into several different languages. Additionally, they were incorporated into the laws and regulations of various government entities.

The 1978 *Standards* proved relatively robust and were able to accommodate the evolving profession, remaining relatively unchanged for the next 20 years. However, there was a large amount of additional guidance provided to interpret these standards coming from a number of different sources (ranging from guidelines that accompanied the *Standards*, to a series of Professional Standards Practice Releases providing IIA staff's response to frequently asked questions in terms of implementing the *Standards*, to IIA position papers, as well as several research studies). By the end of the 1990s, the body of guidance that had developed alongside the Code of Ethics and the *Standards* had reached a point where there were no clear levels of authority among the various sources of guidance, and there were instances of conflicting guidance.

The landscape of the profession in the 1990s had also altered in terms of how internal audit services were being provided, with a significant share of the services now being delivered by external service providers. In some internal audit functions, there was a dramatic shift in the amount of time being allocated to the traditional services of audits and reviews of operations. Nontraditional audit services such as control self-assessment programs, proactive training on internal control, participation as advisors in system implementation projects, and other consulting activities consumed a growing proportion of the internal audit resources. Further, since the mid-1980s the concept of risk management as a method of allocating internal audit resources had rapidly developed within the profession. The 1978 *Standards* did not specifically address these emerging issues.

Recognizing the important role that the *Statement of Responsibilities,* the Code of Ethics, and particularly, the *Standards* had played in the development of the now global internal audit profession, The IIA established a Guidance Task Force in 1997 to consider the needs and mechanisms for providing guidance to the profession in the future. After over a year of study, the Guidance Task Force issued its report—*A Vision for the Future: Professional Practices Framework for Internal Auditing.*[2] This report proposed a new definition of internal auditing to replace the one found in the *Statement of Responsibilities* and a new structure for providing relevant and timely guidance to the profession. The proposed definition and structure was approved in 1999. Implementation began with the revision of the Code of Ethics in 2000 and

The International Standards for the Professional Practice of Internal Auditing consists of five general and four broad attribute standards and seven broad performance standards, most containing more specific sandards and implementation standards.

the completion of the new *International Standards for the Professional Practice of Internal Auditing* in 2003.

The Structure of the Professional Practices Framework

The goal of the PPF is to elaborate on and support The IIA's definition of internal auditing. Recall that this definition identified the role and responsibilities of the internal audit profession as adding value and improving an organization's operation through independent, objective assurance and consulting activities and established the profession's scope of expertise (specifically, governance, risk management, and control processes). The PPF provides the means for internal auditing to fulfill its role and effectively meet its responsibilities.

The components of the PPF are the Code of Ethics, the *Standards*, the Practice Advisories, and other guidance (Exhibit 2-1). The Code of Ethics and the *Standards* provide mandatory guidance in the sense that these guidelines must be followed for the effective delivery of internal audit services. The Practice Advisories give endorsed, but nonmandatory, guidance. They provide interpretations of the *Standards* and the

EXHIBIT 2-1

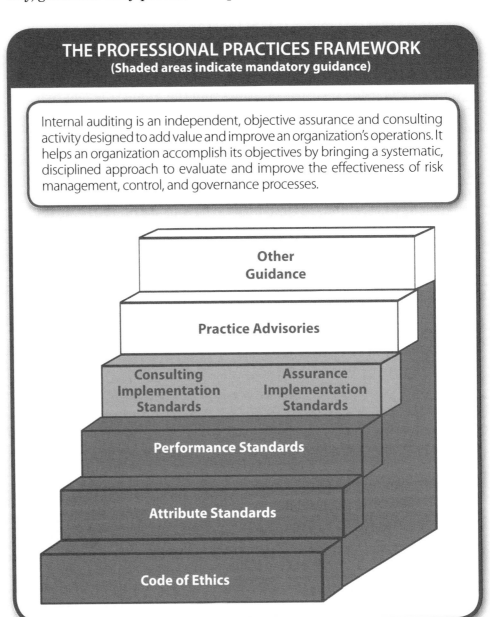

THE PROFESSIONAL PRACTICES FRAMEWORK
(Shaded areas indicate mandatory guidance)

Internal auditing is an independent, objective assurance and consulting activity designed to add value and improve an organization's operations. It helps an organization accomplish its objectives by bringing a systematic, disciplined approach to evaluate and improve the effectiveness of risk management, control, and governance processes.

Other Guidance

Practice Advisories

Consulting Implementation Standards

Assurance Implementation Standards

Performance Standards

Attribute Standards

Code of Ethics

means by which the *Standards* may be implemented. Other guidance consists of development and practice aids that include a variety of materials endorsed or developed by The IIA. These include practice tools such as textbooks, research studies, position papers, seminars, conference presentations, and other resources related to the practice of internal auditing.

The Code of Ethics consists of two components: the Principles and the Rules of Conduct. These two components go beyond the definition of internal auditing by expanding on the necessary attributes and behaviors of the individuals providing internal audit services. The Principles set out the four ideals internal audit professionals should aspire to maintain in conducting their work. The Rules describe 12 behavioral norms that the internal auditor should follow to put the Principles into practice. The Code applies to both individuals and to entities that provide internal audit services.

The *Standards* consist of three classifications of standards: Attribute Standards, Performance Standards, and Implementation Standards. The Attribute Standards describe the defining characteristics of organizations (traditional internal audit functions and/or external service providers), as well as the individuals performing internal audit services. The Performance Standards describe the nature of internal audit services and provide quality criteria against which the performance of these services can be measured. The Attribute and Performance Standards apply to the performance of all types of internal audit services (including, among other things, compliance audits, fraud investigations, and control self-assessment projects). The Implementation Standards, in contrast, apply to specific types of internal audit services. They augment the Attribute and Performance Standards by providing more explicit detail about how these would apply in the delivery of a given type of service. The PPF envisions potentially numerous sets of Implementation Standards, such as standards for specialized types of engagements like fraud investigation or control self-assessment, or industry-specific standards in areas such as insurance, government, or health care. However, there are currently only Assurance and Consulting Implementation Standards.

The *Standards* use a numbering system to identify each specific type of standard. Attribute Standards make up the 1000 series and Performance Standards, the 2000 series. For example, the Attribute Standard titled "Proficiency and Due Professional Care" is 1200, with more specific discussion of this topic in 1210 (Proficiency), 1220 (Due Professional Care), and 1230 (Continuing Professional Development). The Implementation Standards are covered under the related Attribute and Performance Standards and are indicated by a letter. Thus, the Implementation Standards for assurance services are nnnn.A1, nnnn.A2 etc., and for consulting activities, nnnn.C1, etc. An example of how this system applies to an assurance implementation standard is 1210.A3 as shown in Exhibit 2-2.

The *Standards* also include a glossary that provides definitions of terms that have been given a specific meaning as they are used in the *Standards*. For example, the term *board* is defined as:

Attribute Standards describe the defining characteristics of organizations, as well as the individuals performing internal audit services.

Performance Standards describe the nature of internal audit services and provide quality criteria against which the performance of these services can be measured.

Implementation Standards apply to specific types of internal audit services.

An organization's governing body, such as a board of directors, supervisory board, head of an agency or legislative body, board of governors or trustees of a nonprofit organization, or any other designated body of the organization, including the audit committee, to whom the chief audit executive may functionally report.

While in U.S. public companies the term *board* would be read to mean "the audit committee," in other situations, such as in the case of a government agency, it would be read to mean "agency head" if there were no additional governing group. The glossary is an important part of the *Standards* and is necessary for their correct interpretation.

The Practice Advisories provide guidance as to how specific standards might be implemented or add clarity as to how a standard should be interpreted in a specific context. Unlike the Code of Ethics and the *Standards*, it is not mandatory that the Practice Advisories be followed, although it is strongly encouraged by The IIA. The Practice Advisories are organized by the number of the specific standard to which the given advisory relates.

EXHIBIT 2-2

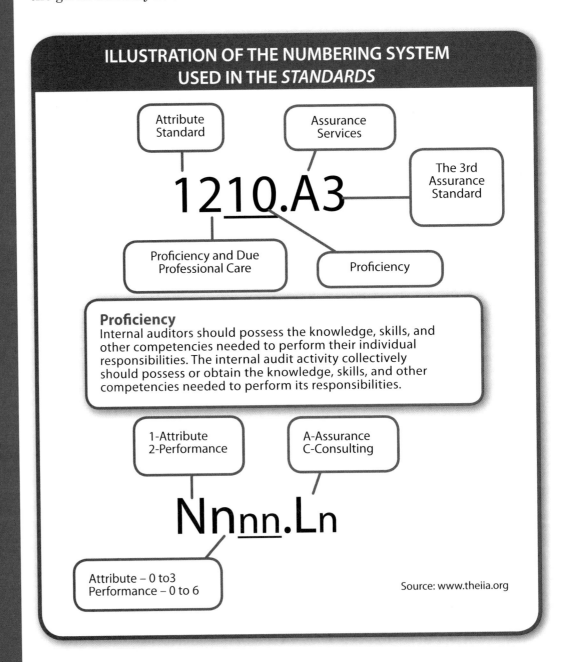

ILLUSTRATION OF THE NUMBERING SYSTEM USED IN THE *STANDARDS*

Attribute Standard

Assurance Services

The 3rd Assurance Standard

1210.A3

Proficiency and Due Professional Care

Proficiency

Proficiency
Internal auditors should possess the knowledge, skills, and other competencies needed to perform their individual responsibilities. The internal audit activity collectively should possess or obtain the knowledge, skills, and other competencies needed to perform its responsibilities.

1-Attribute
2-Performance

A-Assurance
C-Consulting

Nnnn.Ln

Attribute – 0 to 3
Performance – 0 to 6

Source: www.theiia.org

Other Guidance, also called Development and Practice Aids, refers to the multitude of other sources of information pertaining to the practice of internal auditing. This includes textbooks such as this one, articles in professional journals such as *Internal Auditor,* IIA webcasts, research reports, information presented at seminars and conferences, and other practice aids such as sample documents and model engagement programs. For development and practice aids available from The IIA, The IIA's Web site contains a page under "Guidance" linking the specific standards to either the relevant practice aid itself or instructions for how to obtain the relevant practice aid.

THE CODE OF ETHICS

The stated purpose of the Code of Ethics is to promote an ethical culture in the internal audit profession. The code does this by setting out four basic principles that contain the four core values that must be upheld for the customers of internal auditors to put their trust in the services provided. While some might have differing views about how specific engagements are carried out or whether internal audit services are better provided by external providers or an internal function, it is hard to imagine there is anyone who would not want the internal audit professional to follow these four principles:

- Integrity
- Objectivity
- Confidentiality
- Competency

By *integrity*, the code means that internal auditors will do their work with diligence and truthfulness and in accordance with the law and ethical values of their organization. It is easy to understand that a report issued by internal auditors that lied about what they found would not be of much value to anyone. What trust could the user put in such a report? The code specifically gives four rules of conduct that guide how the concept of integrity would be put into internal audit practice. They are outlined in Exhibit 2-3. It is the internal auditor's integrity that engenders trust and thus forms the basis for reliance on the internal auditor's judgments.

Objectivity is mentioned as a fundamental attribute of internal auditing in the definition of internal auditing. It is indeed one of the essential ingredients necessary for internal audit services to add value. In conducting their work, it is imperative that internal auditors exercise the highest level of objectivity in gathering, evaluating, and communicating information about the activity or process being examined. They should make a balanced assessment of all the relevant circumstances and not be unduly influenced by their own interests or by others when forming judgments. This means that in performing their work, internal auditors need to be aware of potential threats to their objectivity such as personal relationships or conflicts of interest. These could be such things as accepting gifts from auditees, auditing an operation in which their spouse works, or agreeing with the divisional manager to transfer to the division at the end of the audit. The specific rules are spelled out in the code as outlined in Exhibit 2-3. Note that the rules

The Code of Ethics **contains principles relevant to the profession and practice of internal auditing and Rules of Conduct that describe behavior expected of internal auditors.**

EXHIBIT 2-3

THE CODE OF ETHICS
Rules of Conduct

1. Integrity

Internal auditors:

1.1   Shall perform their work with honesty, diligence, and responsibility.

1.2   Shall observe the law and make disclosures expected by the law and the profession.

1.3   Shall not knowingly be a party to any illegal activity, or engage in acts that are discreditable to the profession of internal auditing or to the organization.

1.4   Shall respect and contribute to the legitimate and ethical objectives of the organization.

2. Objectivity

Internal auditors:

2.1   Shall not participate in any activity or relationship that may impair or be presumed to impair their unbiased assessment. This participation includes those activities or relationships that may be in conflict with the interests of the organization.

2.2   Shall not accept anything that may impair or be presumed to impair their professional judgment.

2.3   Shall disclose all material facts known to them that, if not disclosed, may distort the reporting of activities under review.

3. Confidentiality

Internal auditors:

3.1   Shall be prudent in the use and protection of information acquired in the course of their duties.

3.2   Shall not use information for any personal gain or in any manner that would be contrary to the law or detrimental to the legitimate and ethical objectives of the organization.

4. Competency

Internal auditors:

4.1   Shall engage only in those services for which they have the necessary knowledge, skills, and experience.

4.2   Shall perform internal auditing services in accordance with the *International Standards for the Professional Practice of Internal Auditing*.

4.3   Shall continually improve their proficiency and the effectiveness and quality of their services.

Source: www.theiia.org

do not specify that the auditor's judgment actually be biased, only that it could be presumed to be biased. In addition, rule 2.3 prohibits the potential biasing of the communication of the message in the report of the auditor's work by not disclosing all information critical for the user to correctly understand the report. For example, stating that inventory controls were at the same level of effectiveness as in the last audit, but neglecting to point out that in the previous audit, control activities were found to be unsatisfactory.

In providing internal audit services, the internal auditor will need unrestricted access to all relevant data in the organization. For the organization and auditees to grant such access, they need confidence that the internal auditor will not inappropriately disclose or make use of the data. The principle of confidentiality requires internal auditors to respect the value and ownership of information they receive and to not disclose information without appropriate authority unless there is a legal or professional obligation to do so. The code stipulates two rules regarding *confidentiality* (see Exhibit 2-3). The first requires prudence in the use and protection of data obtained in the course of providing internal audit services, and the second prohibits the use of this information for personal gain or in other ways that would be contrary to the law. For instance, this principle would require internal auditors to use passwords and other security measures if they were carrying personally identifiable information of employees or client customers in files on their laptop. This principle would also prohibit the internal auditor from making trades in the stock of a company they learned was going to be acquired by their employer (in other words, insider trading).

Finally, the code requires that the internal auditor must have and apply the *competency* necessary to deliver the required internal audit services. One could obtain internal audit services from people who had integrity, were objective, and maintained confidentiality, but those services would be of little value if those persons did not have the necessary knowledge and skills to perform the work. This is required in rule 4.1 (see Exhibit 2-3). In addition, the code also specifically requires that the work be performed in accordance with the *Standards* and that internal auditors continually work to improve the effectiveness and quality of their services.

Unlike the prior IIA Code of Ethics, the code issued in 2000 expands the applicability of the code to all individuals and organizations that provide internal audit services, not just those who are IIA members or hold IIA certifications. However, The IIA is only able to exercise enforcement over IIA members and recipients of, or candidates for, IIA professional certifications. Breaches of the code for those in the purview of The IIA are subject to censure, suspension of membership and/or certifications, and expulsion and/or revocation of certification as determined by The IIA's Ethics Committee. It should also be noted that conduct need not be explicitly mentioned in the Rules of Conduct for it to be considered unacceptable or discreditable and thus subject to disciplinary action.

These four principles and the 12 Rules of Conduct thus set expectations for what the customer of internal audit services can expect in terms of behavior from an internal audit professional. Each of the four principles is equally critical. Violation of any of the four will preclude the delivery of value added and, thus, effective internal audit services. Further, although enforcement of the code by The IIA is relatively limited, in the United States at least, regulators and the courts have looked to the code as well as the *Standards* in determining cases involving adequacy of the performance of internal audit services.

THE INTERNATIONAL STANDARDS FOR THE PROFESSIONAL PRACTICE OF INTERNAL AUDITING

The *Standards* serve as the foundation for the internal audit profession and the core of the PPF. The objectives of the *Standards* are to:

- Delineate basic principles that represent the practice of internal

auditing as it should be.

- Provide a framework for performing and promoting a broad range of value-added internal audit activities.
- Establish the basis for the evaluation of internal audit performance.
- Foster improved organizational processes and operations.

The *Standards* lay out the fundamental concepts on which the internal audit profession is built and establish the benchmarks for measuring the performance of internal audit services. The *Standards* allow the customers of internal audit services to have clear expectations about the nature and quality of the services they are acquiring.

As discussed earlier in this chapter, there are three types of standards:

- **Attribute Standards.** The critical characteristics that individuals, teams, and organizations must have to provide effective internal audit services.
- **Performance Standards.** The description of the nature of internal audit services and the quality criteria against which the performance of these services can be evaluated.
- **Implementation Standards.** More specific guidance as to how the Attribute and Performance Standards apply to each major type of internal audit activity.

The *Standards* can be found in Appendix B of this textbook. The Attribute Standards will be covered first, followed by coverage of the Performance Standards. Discussion of the Implementation Standards will be integrated into the respective discussion of the Attribute and Performance Standards. However, prior to this discussion, the major types of audit services will be reviewed in terms of how the nature of these services influences their respective Implementation Standards.

The Nature of Audit Services and the Standards

In Chapter 1, "Introduction to Internal Auditing," the two types of basic internal audit services were described—assurance and consulting. Specifically, the glossary to the *Standards* defines them as:

Assurance Services. An objective examination of evidence for the purpose of providing an independent assessment on risk management, control, or governance processes for the organization.

Consulting Services. Advisory and related client service activities, the nature and scope of which are agreed with the client and which are intended to add value and improve an organization's governance, risk management, and control processes without the internal auditor assuming management responsibility.

To understand how the Attribute and Performance Standards apply, one must keep in mind the key phrase in the definition of Consulting Services "the nature and scope of which are agreed to with the client." This phrase reflects a fundamental difference in the structure and relationships involved in the delivery of the two types of services (see Exhibit 2-4). Consulting services generally involve two parties: (1) the

Auditee

The subsidiary, business unit, department, group, or other established subdivision of an organization that is the subject of an assurance engagement.

person or group offering the advice—the internal audit function, and (2) the person or group seeking and receiving the advice—the client. In assurance services there are typically three parties involved: (1) the person or group directly involved with the process, system, or other subject matter—the auditee, (2) the person or group making the assessment—the internal audit function, and (3) the person or group using the assessment—the user.

This structural difference is critical to the need for standards in the delivery of the respective services. In consulting, the service provider typically has direct contact with an identifiable customer. Thus, the two parties are able to work together to assess and tailor the work to the customer's needs. However, in assurance services the relationships are more complex. Often the parties using the internal audit function's assessment are remote from any direct involvement with the engagement, and in some cases, may not even be specifically known. The interests of these parties must be protected if the service is to effectively meet their needs, as the auditee's interests may have actual or potential conflicts with the interests of the users. It is up to the provider of assurance services, whose interests need to be aligned with those of the third-party users, to watch over the users' interests by taking responsibility for determining the nature and scope of the engagement and the reporting of the results. Many of the attributes and practices required by the *Standards* and Code of Conduct are particularly concerned with keeping the interests of assurance service providers and of the third-party users aligned. Because of this issue, we find considerably more stringent requirements and a higher number of implementation standards for the delivery of assurance as compared to consulting services.

Customer

Business unit, department, group, indivdual, or other established subdivision of an organization that is the subject of a consulting engagement.

ASSURANCE AND CONSULTING SERVICES

Assurance Services

User

Internal Auditor ⟷ Auditee

Consulting Services

Internal Auditor ⟷ Customer

EXHIBIT 2-4

The Attribute Standards

The Attribute Standards address four critical groups of characteristics that the internal audit function or its individuals must possess to perform effective internal audit services. These groups are:

- Purpose, authority, and responsibility.
- Independence and objectivity.
- Proficiency and due professional care.
- Commitment to quality assurance and improvement.

Purpose, Authority, and Responsibility. The 1000 series of the Attribute Standards applies to those providing the internal audit services, whether a traditional function embedded within an organization or an external service provider who either provides the services or supplements the competencies or work done by the internal audit function. For the traditional internal audit function, the *Standards* state that the function should have a charter that states the function's purpose, authority, and responsibilities and specifies the types of assurance and consulting activities provided. It is particularly important to specify in the charter the types and extent of consulting services provided so that the audit committee and board have a clear understanding of how the two are balanced. The charter needs to be consistent with the *Standards* and typically includes a statement that the function follows the *Standards*. Standard 1000.A.1 also requires that the charter define the nature of any assurance being provided to parties outside the organization from the internal audit function's work because it is important that the audit committee and upper management be aware of any such specific use being made of the internal audit function's work. This does not encompass the general assurance that people outside the organization might gain simply by knowing that the organization has an effective internal audit function, but rather relates to specific reports being used to provide assurance to outside parties (for example, for information systems interchange or joint ventures). When services are being provided by a third-party provider, the charter may be the service contract. This contract would naturally list the types of services being provided, but it also should state that the provider follows The IIA's *Standards* in the delivery of those services. More information about the charter and the means for fulfilling this group of standards are found in Chapter 8, "Managing the Internal Audit Function."

Independence and Objectivity. The 1100 series of the Attribute Standards addresses organization independence, individual objectivity, and what to do in cases where there might be impairments to either. It is important to note that, in the *Standards*, independence and objectivity refer to two distinct, yet related, concepts that are fundamental to the value of audit services. The PPF uses the terms in a very precise manner that has evolved over time as the internal audit profession has developed. A research study sponsored by The IIA Research Foundation, *Independence and Objectivity: A Framework for Internal Auditors*, provided the profession with much needed clarity regarding these concepts.[3] However, this precise usage is not always similar to the use of the terms in everyday language or even to that used in much of the audit literature.

Standard 1100 makes it clear that *the internal audit activity should be independent*, while *internal auditors should be objective.* This is a subtle, yet extremely important, distinction. Independence is viewed as an attribute of the internal audit function, whereas objectivity is an attribute of the individual auditor. The glossary defines the terms as:

- **Independence.** The freedom from conditions that threaten objectivity or the appearance of objectivity. Such threats to objectivity must be managed at the individual auditor, engagement, functional, and organizational levels.

- **Objectivity.** An unbiased mental attitude that allows internal auditors to perform engagements in such a manner that they have an honest belief in their work product and that no significant quality compromises are made. Objectivity requires internal auditors not to subordinate their judgment on audit matters to that of others.

Further, these definitions imply that it is the objectivity of the individual internal auditor's judgment (one of the three foundations of effective internal audit services, as shown in Exhibit 2-5) that is the goal and that independence is viewed as the effective management of threats to that objectivity. Objectivity is a state of mind and is defined as freedom from bias. It is the expression of a professional opinion involving the use of facts without distortions by personal feelings or prejudices.[4] In an applied sense, it would mean that two people with the same level of expertise and facing the same facts and circumstances will come to similar conclusions.

An internal auditor's objectivity can be undermined or threatened by many things, which can be grouped in three basic categories:

- Incentives.
- Personal relationships.
- Task-related threats.

Incentives refer to the presence of economic interests that could influence an auditor's judgment when the auditor has an economic stake in the directional outcome of his or her work. This could be an economic interest in the outcome of the internal auditor's evaluation of the performance of the auditee. For instance, auditors would be vulnerable if the managers of the area under audit made a promise that they would give the internal auditor a job in their operations or a promotion if the audit goes well and no problems are found. Or, in the other direction, a compensation structure that awards a bonus based on the number of observations the internal auditor puts in the report could also represent an incentive. Moreover, if the auditee has given a gift to, or done a favor for, the internal auditor, the gesture could create an expectation that this be reciprocated. Social pressure also can be viewed as an incentive threat. Such would be the case when an internal auditor is pressured, or perceives there is pressure, from a group with which the internal auditor identifies, to come to a particular outcome.

Personal relationships present a threat when the internal auditor

Independence

The freedom from conditions that threaten objectivity or the appearance of objectivity. Such threats to objectivity must be managed at the indivdual auditor, engagement, functional, and organizational levels (also see *Organizational Independence*).

Individual Objectivity

An impartial, unbiased mental attitude and avoidance of conflicts of interest, allowing internal auditors to perform engagements in such a manner that they have an honest belief in their work product and that no significant quality compromises are made. Objectivity requires internal auditors not to subordinate their judgment on audit matters to that of others.

performs an engagement involving an area where the managers or employees are relatives or close friends. In such situations, the internal auditor may be tempted to overlook problems or soften negative conclusions.

Finally, task-related threats come from the nature of the work itself. For example, it would be a problem if an individual who recently joined the audit department were asked to audit the area for which he or she was previously responsible. This may be perceived as auditing his or her own work. The threat to objectivity exists because there is always a tendency to save face and not acknowledge weakness in one's own work. Human beings exhibit an unconscious "self-serving bias" that is a cognitive weakness. For example, research has shown that people are not as good at identifying weaknesses in systems they design as they are in seeing the weaknesses in systems designed by others.[5]

There are a number of other potential cognitive biases as well, such as hindsight bias, anchoring on an initial judgment and then making insufficient adjustments for additional information, and the tendency to favor confirming evidence. Cultural, gender, and racial biases can also be a threat, as can over-familiarity where judgment is formed on repeated past experience and not current evidence. For example, suppose an internal auditor has audited a manager five times in the past six years and each time found serious control weaknesses, in some cases the same weakness identified the year before. Discussions with the manager in the past give the impression that he doesn't think control activities are important. If the internal auditor is assigned, yet again, to audit an area under this manager's control, will he or she really be objective in these circumstances?

A review of these various potential threats indicates how difficult it

EXHIBIT 2-5

THE THREE FOUNDATIONS OF EFFECTIVE INTERNAL AUDIT SERVICES

Effective Internal Audit Services

OBJECTIVITY   COMPETENCE   DUE CARE

can be to remain objective; indeed, for an auditor to maintain a state of pure, absolute objectivity is probably impossible. Pragmatically, independence is not the complete absence of any threat; rather it is a state where threats to objectivity are managed to the extent that the risks of ineffectual internal audit services are acceptably controlled. Standard 1110 provides for one of the basic mechanisms for removing incentive threats: having the CAE report to relatively high levels of the organization. This better aligns the internal audit function's interest with the organization as a whole and allows objective internal audit services to be provided to a wider range of the activities of the organization. In contrast, reporting to an assistant controller where many of the organization's most significant activities take place would create a conflict for the function by making it potentially in the function's interest to deliver favorable assessments. Further, reporting to high levels also provides more certainty that the reports of the internal audit function's work get to the appropriate levels and are not suppressed at lower levels of the organizational hierarchy. Chapter 8, "Managing the Internal Audit Function," covers this topic in greater detail.

Standard 1130 recognizes that there may be times when real or perceived individual objectivity and organizational independence problems occur. For example, there may be times when, due to his or her professional expertise, a member of the internal audit staff might be asked to temporarily take on an operating role, such as accounts payable manager or treasurer, until a specific problem is resolved or a replacement can be found. Internal auditors also may be asked to develop operating policy and procedures in areas where control activities are weak and the organization does not have other staff available with the necessary skills. Often it also happens that a person from operations is moved into internal auditing or that the internal audit director may have come from a position where he or she had significant operating responsibilities. While this is not particularly problematic for consulting services (Standard 1130.C1), it is for assurance services. Standard 1130.A1 specifically states that, for a period of at least one year, internal auditors should refrain from assessing specific operations for which they were previously responsible. In smaller organizations, or in the case of the audit director, this is not always possible. When such impairments occur, the *Standards* provide guidance for how to deal with the situation. Disclosure is the primary mechanism. This prevents the users of the service from unknowingly placing unwarranted confidence in the work product and allows them to determine for themselves the extent to which they want to rely on the work.

There are also cases where the CAE has responsibilities for functions in addition to internal auditing. This might be responsibility for enterprise risk management or serving as the organization's compliance officer. In such cases, assurance engagements for these areas should be conducted by someone outside of the internal audit function.

Proficiency and Due Professional Care. The 1200 series of standards addresses the other two parts of the foundation for effective internal audit services (refer back to Exhibit 2-5). As with objectivity, assurance and consulting services provided by individuals or teams lacking the knowledge and skills to perform the work or by those who do not make sufficient effort or apply appropriate care will not be of value. Thus the *Standards* require that internal auditors have the knowledge, skills, and competencies needed to carry out their responsibilities and that they apply due professional care.

In terms of proficiency, the *Standards* do not mandate a specific set of skills and competencies. Additional guidance on specific knowledge and skills is found in Practice Advisory 1210-1 and specifically in the syllabus for the Certified Internal Auditor™ (CIA™) examination.[6] The Practice Advisory calls for proficiency in applying internal audit standards, procedures, and techniques as well as an understanding of management principles. Written and oral communication skills, as well as skills in dealing with people, are also important. The internal auditor should have an understanding sufficient to the recognition of potential issues in subjects such as accounting, economics, commercial law, and taxation. Because of increased importance of information technology to the functioning of most organizations and operating processes, the *Standards* explicitly require internal auditors to have knowledge of the key risks and controls related to information technology as well as the available computer-based audit tools and techniques (Standard 1210.A3). Refer to Chapter 6, "Information Technology Risks and Controls," for an overview of what internal auditors should know about this area. The *Standards* also require every internal auditor to have sufficient knowledge to recognize indicators of fraud (1210.A2). Chapter 7, "Fraud Risks and Controls," covers this topic in greater detail. However, in the case of knowledge of either information technology or fraud, individuals are not expected to have the level of knowledge of persons specializing in those respective areas.

Proficiency applies to the internal audit function as a whole as well as to the individual. It is the responsibility of the CAE to obtain the knowledge and skills for the function to fulfill its responsibilities. In cases where the function lacks the skills needed to perform the assurance engagements necessary to address significant risks to the organization, steps such as investing in staff training or contracting with outside service providers may be required. This type of cosourcing is addressed in more detail in Chapter 8, "Managing the Internal Audit Function." When a request for consulting services that require knowledge the internal audit function lacks is received, it can be addressed by declining such engagements (Standard 1210.C1).

Standard 1220 defines due professional care as "apply[ing] the care and skill expected of a reasonably prudent and competent internal auditor." This does not mean that auditors will not make mistakes or errors in judgment, but that they will work with the same diligence and competence as other professional internal auditors in similar situations and circumstances. Nor does it mean that they will look at each transaction, visit every location, or talk to every person working in the area. It does, however, mean that they will put forth the same effort as other internal audit professionals in similar situations. In determining the appropriate level of care, the *Standards* prescribe what needs to be considered for assurance and consulting engagements. Exhibit 2-6 presents the factors the *Standards* require the internal auditor to consider for assurance engagements and consulting engagements, respec-

Due Professional Care

Applying the care and skill expected of a reasonably prudent and competent internal auditor.

EXHIBIT 2-6

DUE PROFESSIONAL CARE CONSIDERATIONS IN ASSURANCE AND CONSULTING SERVICES

Assurance

- Extent of work needed to achieve the engagement's objectives.
- Relative complexity, materiality, or significance of matters to which assurance procedures are applied.
- Adequacy and effectiveness of risk management, control, and governance processes.
- Probability of significant errors, irregularities, or noncompliance.
- Cost of assurance in relation to potential benefits (Standard 1220.A1).
- Alertness to the significant risks that might affect objectives, operations, or resources (Standard 1220.A3).
- The use of computer-assisted audit tools and other data analysis techniques (Standard 1220.A2).

Consulting

- Needs and expectations of clients, including the nature, timing, and communication of engagement results.
- Relative complexity and extent of work needed to achieve the engagement's objectives.
- Cost of the consulting engagement in relation to potential benefits (Standard 1220.C1).

tively. As Exhibit 2-6 indicates, due care in assurance engagements is more demanding than in consulting engagements in that the internal auditor needs to consider the possibility that significant irregularities, noncompliance, or operating risks exist.

Finally, proficiency and due care imply that internal audit professionals will continue to enhance their "knowledge, skills, and competency through continuing professional development" (Standard 1230). Internal auditors who have not yet achieved the relevant certifications such as the CIA, the CISA (Certified Information Systems Auditor), CCSA (Certified in Control Self-assessment), CFSA (Certified Financial Services Auditor), CGAP (Certified Governmental Audit Professional) should pursue an educational program that supports efforts to obtain the respective certifications. Those with professional certifications need to obtain sufficient continuing professional education to meet the requirements of the certifications held. This standard is complementary to rule 4.3 of the Code of Ethics, which requires internal auditors to continually improve their proficiency and the effectiveness and quality of their services.

Quality Assurance and Improvement Programs. The basic concept of quality assurance is the same for internal audit services as it is in the manufacturing of products or the delivery of any other service. It is a process that assures the product or service has the essential features and characteristics that it was designed to have. For example, manufacturers thinking about quality assurance in terms of the production of a ¼ inch metal bolt, they would be looking to see that it was of a particular length, that it fit a particular size nut, that it was of a particular strength, etc.—in essence, that the bolt fit the engineering specifications. Quality assurance for internal audit services has a similar purpose: to provide reasonable assurance that the internal audit function carries out its responsibilities to management, the audit committee, and the organization as a whole. In the bolt example, the criteria were the engineering specifications. In internal auditing, the criteria are The IIA's *Standards*, the Code of Ethics, and the organization's internal audit charter, which, combined, set out the function's specific responsibilities.

The CAE has the responsibility for designing and maintaining the quality assurance program. It is important to note that the program should cover all aspects of the internal audit function (it does not just apply to assurance services, but to the full range of services provided by the function). Both continuous monitoring activities and periodic reviews need to be part of the program's design. Standard 1310 requires two types of assessments: internal and external. Internal assessments include ongoing reviews of the internal audit function's work, which is a significant part of the engagement's supervisory process, and periodic reviews conducted by the internal audit function's staff or other members of the organization who have knowledge of internal audit practice and the *Standards* (Standard 1311). External reviews of the function as a whole are required at least once every five years. These external reviews need to be conducted by persons independent of the organization and knowledgeable of internal audit practices and the *Standards* (Standard 1312).

Exhibit 2-7 provides a framework for designing the quality assurance program. There is a principle of substitutability underlying the framework. Quality assurance elements can be substituted for those higher up in the hierarchy. The limit of this substitution is determined by independence. For example, internal review can be substituted for external review to the extent that the internal reviewers are independent (in other words, outside the line of authority/responsibility of the aspect of the work they are reviewing). Thus, in large organizations with several decentralized audit units (for example an Asian office, a North and South American office, and a European office) internal review can be used to cover much of the internal audit function's work—leaving the external review to focus on the internal quality assurance process—the internal audit function's organizational independence, risk assessment process, and relations with and expectations of the audit committee and senior management. On the other hand, in the case of a small, centralized internal audit function, the external review would require a much greater focus on the individual engagement.

In addition to assurance regarding compliance with the *Standards* and Code of Ethics, the *Standards* require that the program evaluate the extent to which the internal audit function adds value and improves organizational effectiveness. This implies that the internal audit function needs to implement a system of performance measurement that tracks the accomplishment of its objectives and the value it adds. Standard 1320 also requires that the result of the external review be communicated to the audit committee.

Quality Assurance

Providing reasonable assurance that the internal audit function carries out its responsibilities to management, the audit committee, and the organization as a whole.

Assurance Services

An objective examination of evidence for the purpose of providing an independent assessment on risk management, control, or governance processes for the organization.

2-18

Standard 1330 discusses the issue of claiming that an audit function follows the *Standards* and what such a claim implies. Specifically, it states that internal audit functions should make such a claim "only if assessments of the quality improvement program demonstrate that the internal audit activity is in compliance with the *Standards*." In the case of noncompliance, Standard 1340 requires that if the non-compliance impacts the overall operations of the internal audit function, the issue be communicated to senior management as well as the audit committee (or board). Such a case might be the result of a lack of organizational independence, competency gaps because of excessive staff turnover, or instances where the internal audit function has had to take on significant operating responsibility. It would not be a situation that applied to only one engagement, for example in the case of an auditor assigned to audit an area that he or she had previously managed. This latter situation would only require disclosure in the specific engagement report.

Chapter 8, "Managing the Internal Audit Function," will provide more details regarding the implementation of quality assurance programs. Specific procedures for carrying out internal and external reviews can be found in The IIA's *Quality Assessment Manual*.

The Performance Standards

As discussed previously, the Performance Standards describe the nature of internal audit services and the criteria against which the performance of these services can be assessed. The Performance Standards are composed of seven series of standards: one addressing the management of the internal audit function, one the nature of internal auditing, four dealing with the stages involved in the performance of

Consulting Services
Advisory and related client service activities, the nature and scope of which are agreed to/with the client and which are intended to add value and improve an organization's governance, risk management, and control processes without the internal auditor assuming management responsibility.

FRAMEWORK FOR QUALITY ASSURANCE PROGRAM DESIGN
Hierarchy of Quality Assurance Elements

Control Element	Control Objective	Source	Assurance Level
Professionalism (Due Care)	Individual Auditor's Work	Individual	Individual Auditor
Supervisory Review	Engagement	Supervisor *Within* Line of Responsibility	Audit Function Management
Internal Review	Aggregate of Engagements or Divisional Offices or Autonomous Audit Units	Supervisor/Peer *Outside* Line of Responsibility	Chief Audit Executive
External Review	Audit Function as a Whole	Qualified Persons From Outside the Organization	Audit Committee and Senior Management

EXHIBIT 2-7

engagements, and a final standard regarding the issue of the organization's acceptance of risk. The specific structure is:

- 2000 – Managing the Internal Auditing Activity.
- 2100 – Nature of Work.
- 2200 – Engagement Planning.
- 2300 – Performing the Engagement.
- 2400 – Communicating Results.
- 2500 – Monitoring Progress.
- 2600 – Management's Acceptance of Risks.

Managing the Internal Audit Activity

The 2000 series of the *Standards* sets out the responsibility of the CAE. In the traditional internal audit function, the CAE is typically the internal audit director (may also be called the general auditor, inspector general, etc.). This is the top person within the organization with responsibility for the internal audit activities. Even when the internal audit activities are outsourced to a third party provider, there needs to be a CAE within the organization. In such cases, the CAE is the person responsible for overseeing the service contract and the overall quality assurance of these activities, reporting to senior management and the board regarding internal audit activities, and following up on engagement results and observations. Although the performance of engagements can be conducted by persons outside the organization, basic responsibilities of the CAE remain within the organization. These responsibilities are to:

- Effectively manage the internal audit function to add value to the organization.
- Establish a risk-based plan to accomplish the objectives of the internal audit function consistent with the organization's goals.
- Communicate the internal audit function's plans and resource requirements to senior management and the board for review and approval.
- Ensure that internal audit resources are appropriate, sufficient, and effectively deployed.
- Coordinate with other internal and external providers of audit and consulting services to ensure proper coverage and minimize duplication.
- Report periodically to the board and senior management on the internal audit function's purpose, authority, responsibility, and performance relative to its plan.
- Monitor whether appropriate management actions have been taken on significant reported risks or that senior management has accepted the risk of not taking action.

These responsibilities are covered in Standards 2010 to 2060 and will be discussed in more detail in Chapter 8, "Managing the Internal Audit Function."

Performance Standards

describe the nature of internal audit services and the criteria against which the performance of these services can be assessed.

Nature of Work. The definition of *internal auditing* sets the scope of internal audit work as assisting an organization in accomplishing its objectives by evaluating and improving the effectiveness of governance, risk management, and control processes. It does this by bringing a disciplined and systematic approach to the evaluation and improvement of each of these three groups of processes. The internal audit function helps the organization improve the governance process (as discussed in Standard 2130) by assisting in:

- Promoting appropriate ethics and values within the organization.

- Ensuring effective organizational performance management and accountability.

- Effectively communicating risk and control information to appropriate areas of the organization.

- Effectively coordinating the activities of and communicating information among the board, external and internal auditors, and management.

The internal audit function helps the organization manage risk (as discussed in Standard 2110) by:

- Identifying and evaluating significant exposure to risk.

- Contributing to the improvement of risk management and control systems.

- Monitoring and assessing enterprise risk management activities.

Finally, the internal audit function helps the organization maintain effective controls (as discussed in Standard 2120) by:

- Assessing the effectiveness and efficiency of controls.

- Promoting continuous improvement in the control environment.

Chapter 1, "Introduction to Internal Auditing," introduced the notion of governance, risk management, and control processes. In Chapter 3, "Governance and Risk Management," a detailed examination of the governance and risk management processes is given. Control processes are discussed in Chapter 5, "Internal Control."

The Engagement Process. The performance of engagements, whether assurance or consulting, can be broken into four stages. Standards 2200 to 2500 cover what needs to be done in each phase of the engagement, with specifics for each type of engagement in the corresponding implementation standards. Exhibit 2-8 shows the phases and the corresponding standards.

Each engagement requires the internal auditor to develop and record a plan. In assurance engagements this plan must always be documented, whereas in consulting engagements, this would be required only if it were a significant engagement. For example, consulting engagements—such as conducting a one hour training session on general internal control concepts for the accounts payable staff using materials already developed for training of the purchasing staff—would not need a documented plan. Planning the engagement starts with understanding the objectives of the area or process on which the engagement is focused. With this understanding and considerations of the area's or process's systems of risk management and control, the engagement objectives, scope, and resource allocation are then set. Standard 2220.A2 makes a subtle point regarding the scope. It essentially prohibits blending assurance and consulting engagements, stating that if significant consulting opportunities arise during an assurance engagement they should be developed as a separate engagement. The point of this distinction is to ensure that all work associated with an assurance engagement must meet the more stringent requirements of the Assurance Standards so that users place appropriate reliance on engagement results. Chapter 10, "Conducting the Assurance Engagement," further describes the assurance engagement planning process.

The standards that cover engagement performance are general in nature to accommodate the varying objectives of the engagement. The guidance regarding methods of identifying information and its subsequent analysis and evaluation is provided primarily through development, practice aids, and other nonmandatory guidance and is discussed in Chapter 9, "Gathering and Documenting Audit Evidence," and in Chapter 10, "Conducting the Assurance Engagement." The *Standards* do, however, require that conclusions and engagement results be supported by relevant information and that a record of this information be kept for an appropriate amount of time (Standard 2330). Appropriate supervision is also required: first, to make sure that the engagement objectives are indeed met; second, to guarantee that the work is done consistently with the internal audit function's quality assurance standards, and finally, to develop the internal audit staff.

For internal audit engagements to have value, their outcomes must be communicated to the appropriate users. It is not enough, however, for the user just to receive the report. The communication must be in a form that minimizes the risk of misinterpretation. Specifically, the appropriate conclusions and recommendations must be communicated, as well as the engagement's objectives and scope, so that the user does not place undue reliance on the work or otherwise misunderstand the results. The *Standards* do not require a specific mode of communication. Assurance engagements typically result in a formal, written report. The outcomes of other engagements may be communicated in an oral presentation. Regardless of the method, "communications should be accurate, objective, clear, concise, constructive, complete, and timely" (Standard 2420). The *Standards* also provide guidance on what should be done in the case of errors in the final report or if the engagement work did not comply with the *Standards*. The *Standards* charge the CAE with responsibility to make sure the appropriate users get the results (Standard 2440). Chapter 11, "Communicating Assurance Engagement Outcomes and Performing Follow-up Procedures," provides information about how to structure effective engagement communications.

The final phase of the engagement process is monitoring progress. This requires the CAE to establish a follow-up system to track the disposition of engagement results. For assurance engagements, this means that the CAE must be certain that necessary management ac-

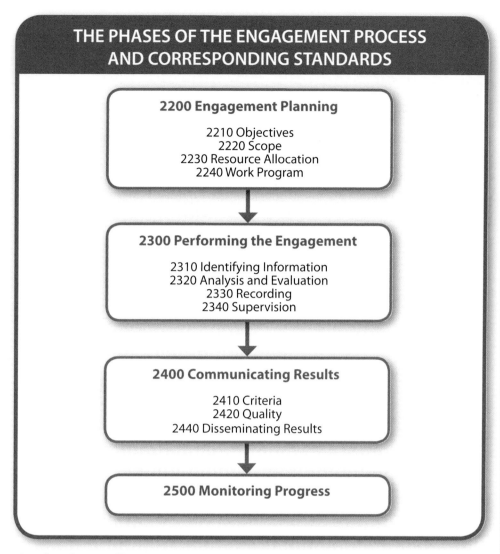

EXHIBIT 2-8

THE PHASES OF THE ENGAGEMENT PROCESS AND CORRESPONDING STANDARDS

2200 Engagement Planning

2210 Objectives
2220 Scope
2230 Resource Allocation
2240 Work Program

2300 Performing the Engagement

2310 Identifying Information
2320 Analysis and Evaluation
2330 Recording
2340 Supervision

2400 Communicating Results

2410 Criteria
2420 Quality
2440 Disseminating Results

2500 Monitoring Progress

tion has been effectively implemented or that senior management has accepted the risk of not taking the action (Standard 2500.A1). In the case of consulting engagements, the extent of follow-up is agreed upon with the customer.

Resolution of Management's Acceptance of Risks. The final Performance Standard addresses the issue of significant residual risk. The glossary defines *residual risk* as the risk remaining after management takes action to reduce the impact and likelihood of an adverse event, including control activities in responding to a risk. When the CAE believes that residual risk exists that may be unacceptable to the organization, the *Standards* require the CAE to discuss it with senior management and if it is not resolved, to communicate it to the audit committee. While this potentially puts the CAE in direct conflict with senior management, the audit committee must be made aware of the CAE's views as it is the audit committee (or other appropriate governing body) that has ultimate responsibility for the organization's risk tolerance. The audit committee may accept the risk, but it must be made aware of it first.

THE PRACTICE ADVISORIES

It should be apparent at this point that the guidance provided in the *Standards* is quite general. The *Standards* are designed to apply to all

Residual Risk

The portion of inherent risk that remains after management executes its risk responses (sometimes referred to as net risk).

EXHIBIT 2-9

EXAMPLE OF PRACTICE ADVISORY

Practice Advisory 1130.A1-1:
Assessing Operations for Which Internal Auditors Were Previously Responsible

Interpretation of Standard 1130.A1 from the *International Standards for the Professional Practice of Internal Auditing*

Related Standard
1130.A1 – Internal auditors should refrain from assessing specific operations for which they were previously responsible. Objectivity is presumed to be impaired if an auditor provides assurance services for an activity for which the auditor had responsibility within the previous year.

Nature of this Practice Advisory: Internal auditors should consider the following suggestions when faced with a situation where the auditor has been assigned to assess an operation for which they were previously responsible. This guidance is not intended to represent all the considerations that may be necessary during such an evaluation, but simply a recommended set of items that should be addressed. **Compliance with the Practice Advisory is optional.**

1. Internal auditors should not assume operating responsibilities. If senior management directs internal auditors to perform non-audit work, it should be understood that they are not functioning as internal auditors. Moreover, objectivity is presumed to be impaired when internal auditors perform an assurance review of any activity for which they had authority or responsibility within the past year. This impairment should be considered when communicating audit engagement results.

   - If internal auditors are directed to perform non-audit duties that may impair objectivity, such as preparation of bank reconciliations, the chief audit executive should inform senior management and the board that this activity is not an assurance audit activity; and, therefore, audit-related conclusions should not be drawn.

   - In addition, when operating responsibilities are assigned to the internal audit activity, special attention must be given to ensure objectivity when a subsequent assurance engagement in the related operating area is undertaken. Objectivity is presumed to be impaired when internal auditors audit any activity for which they had authority or responsibility within the past year. These facts should be clearly stated when communicating the results of an audit engagement relating to an area where an auditor had operating responsibilities.

2. At any point that assigned activities involve the assumption of operating authority, audit objectivity would be presumed to be impaired with respect to that activity.

3. Persons transferred to or temporarily engaged by the internal audit activity should not be assigned to audit those activities they previously performed until a reasonable period of time (at least one year) has elapsed. Such assignments are presumed to impair objectivity, and additional consideration should be exercised when supervising the engagement work and communicating engagement results.

4. The internal auditor's objectivity is not adversely affected when the auditor recommends standards of control for systems or reviews procedures before they are implemented. The auditor's objectivity is considered to be impaired if the auditor designs, installs, drafts procedures for, or operates such systems.

5. The occasional performance of non-audit work by the internal auditor, with full disclosure in the reporting process, would not necessarily impair independence. However, it would require careful consideration by management and the internal auditor to avoid adversely affecting the internal auditor's objectivity.

Origination date: Jan. 5, 2001

internal audit activities. However, internal audit activities are performed in a number of very different types of organizations, by persons functioning inside the organization and by outside third parties, centrally and decentrally, and in diverse cultures and legal environments. The Practice Advisories provide more specific guidance, but that guidance is not mandatory.

The Practice Advisories are issued by The IIA's Professional Issues Committee. To date, more than 80 advisories have been issued, but as multiple advisories are issued each year, that number has probably already increased. An up-to-date listing, as well as the text of all issued advisories, is available at The IIA's Web site. You must, however, be a current IIA member to access them. They are also available in the published edition of the PPF, which is usually updated each year. The IIA's Web site has listings of the Practice Advisories by date issued and by topics, as well as by standard number, which are useful reference tools.

Exhibit 2-9 presents an example of a practice advisory. This practice advisory provides an interpretation of Standard 1130.A1 regarding the impairment of objectivity if an internal auditor performs assurance work in an area in which he or she had previous operating responsibility. The advisory provides the text of the related standard and then a standard paragraph reminding the reader of the nature of practice advisories, specifically, that compliance is not mandatory. As paragraph 1 illustrates, very specific guidance is given about what the CAE should do. The complete text of all of the Practice Advisories can be found on The IIA's Web site or in the printed version of the PPF.

OTHER STANDARDS

Organizations other than The IIA provide professional guidance that may have relevance for certain specialized aspects of internal audit practice or that apply to particular industries. These include:

- The U.S. Government Accountability Office (GAO).
- International Organization of Supreme Audit Institutions (INTOSAI).
- The Information Systems Audit and Control Association (ISACA).
- The International Auditing and Assurance Standards Board (part of the International Federation of Accountants – IFAC).
- The International Standards Organization (ISO).
- Standards Australia.
- The Health Care Compliance Association (HCCA).

The IIA's Framework recognizes that there may be other guidance that applies to internal audit practice and allows for the possibility that some Implementation Standards may be standards issued by other standard setting bodies and adopted by The IIA. These might include standards such as the GAO's Governmental Auditing Standards or standards issued by the International Standards Organization (ISO). While to date The IIA's International Internal Auditing Standards Board has not incorporated any standards from other organizations into the *Standards*, many internal audit functions have done

The International Standards Organization (ISO)

An international standard-setting body composed of representatives from various national standards bodies.

so. For instance, the internal audit functions in many state and local government agencies have incorporated both The IIA's *Standards* and the *Government Auditing Standards (Yellow Book)* issued by the U.S. Government Accountability Office in their charters. In addition, other standards have been incorporated into The IIA's PPF. For example, in 2005, seven guidelines from the Guidelines of the Information Systems Audit and Control Association (ISACA) were incorporated into the Practice Advisories (Practice Advisories 1220-2, and 2100-9 through 2100-14).

Standards for Internal Auditing in Government. The U.S. Government Accountability Office (GAO) has issued standards for governmental audits that are known as Generally Accepted Governmental Auditing Standards or GAGAS. These standards are commonly referred to as the Yellow Book standards because of the yellow cover used when publishing the standards. The Yellow Book standards apply to federal financial audits, performance (or operational) audits, and other audit-related activities. U. S. Federal legislation requires that both federal and nonfederal auditors comply with the Yellow Book standards for audits of federal organizations, programs, and functions. The standards are generally relevant to, and are recommended for use by, state and local government auditors and public accountants in most state and local government audits. The Yellow Book explicitly recognizes The IIA's *Standards* as relevant for internal audit work in governmental entities; however, it does require that in cases of conflict, or where the Yellow Book standards are more restrictive, that the Yellow Book be followed. An example of this is the requirement for external quality assurance review: The IIA's *Standards* require review every five years, but the Yellow Book requires it every three years.

As in the United States, most countries have established some system of standards for audit of governmental entities and contracts. Many have modeled their standards after the principles established by the International Organization of Supreme Audit Institutions (INTOSAI). Like the *Yellow Book*, these standards tend to focus on financial statement and performance audits for external users.

Standards for Information Technology Audits. Auditing of computerized information systems is a significant part of the coverage of most internal audit functions. Although The IIA's *Standards* provide a sufficient framework for conducting assurance engagements of computerized systems, additional specialized guidance is provided by the Information Systems Audit and Control Association (ISACA). ISACA issues "standards," "guidelines," and "procedures" for conducting information systems audits. The ISACA standards are mandatory and very similar to The IIA *Standards,* except that they are directed to a much more specific practice. There is not, at present, any incompatibility between the two. ISACA guidelines provide more specific information about how to apply the standards and require justification for departure from them when appropriate. "Procedures" provide examples of what an information systems auditor might do in performing an audit engagement but they are not requirements. Internal audit functions whose work involves a significant portion of information systems audits should be aware of the ISACA guidance and consider adopting the

Generally Accepted Governmental Auditing Standards (GAGAS)

Standards for financial audits issued by the Comptroller General of the United States through the U.S. Government Accountability Office.

standards for their systems work.

Standards for Financial Audits. Until recently, standards for audits of financial statements were set by each country, for example, by the American Institute of Certified Public Accountants in the United States. However, as with accounting standards, there is an attempt to unify the audit standards as well. The International Auditing and Assurance Standards Board, which is a part of International Federation of Accountants (IFAC), has issued international audit standards that are being adopted by a number of countries. Although these standards are for the external audit of the financial statements, they can have a bearing on internal audit work, particularly those standards dealing with internal/external audit coordination.

Other Standards. In conducting internal audit engagements, there may be occasions where other standards are relevant. The International Standards Organization (ISO) sets standards for quality and environmental audits. Standards Australia has issued standards for risk management and governance processes. The Health Care Compliance Association (HCCA) provides ethical practice and compliance standards for ethics and compliance professionals in the health-care industry. Internal auditors practicing in industries that may have specialized standards need to be aware of those standards as well as The IIA's PPF. For instance, in the case of banking and financial institutions operating internationally, standards established by the Basel Committee on Banking Supervision (referred to as Basel I and Basel II) have some specific requirements for internal auditing of the organization's risk management and rating systems.

THE EVOLUTION OF THE PROFESSIONAL PRACTICES FRAMEWORK

The IIA's PPF is not intended to be a static body of guidance, but to evolve along with the internal audit professional as the profession responds to a continually changing environment. The charge of maintaining the relevance of the PPF is distributed over three international committees:

The Ethics Committee. A five-member committee charged with developing and promoting ethical values and standards for the profession. Any changes in the Code of Ethics, such as incorporating additional rules, would be initiated by this committee. Adoption of new rules would require an exposure period allowing for public comment and final approval by The IIA's Board of Directors. This committee also evaluates conduct of members and candidates for, or recipients of, IIA professional certification, when necessary.

International Internal Auditing Standards Board. This board's mission is to develop, monitor, and promote the *International Standards for the Professional Practice of Internal Auditing.* New standards or modifications are initiated with this committee and require an exposure period for public comment. Exposure includes translation into Spanish and French, and often into other major member languages (Chinese, Italian, German,

Japanese, and potentially others). After considering the responses, a majority vote of the committee is required for the final issuance.

Professional Issues Committee. The mission of this committee is to provide timely guidance to the members of the profession on concepts, methodologies, and techniques included in the PPF and to comment on, or develop positions on, other matters that directly or indirectly impact the profession of internal auditing. The Practice Advisories are initiated and developed by this committee. Exposure drafts of potential practice advisories are circulated as appropriate, but this circulation is not mandatory. A practice advisory is issued with the vote of a majority of the Professional Issues Committee.

The Standards Board and the Professional Issues Committee work closely with one another. The Standards Board usually reviews any practice advisory before it is issued for consistency with the *Standards*. The Standards Board and the Professional Issues Committee also work on the development of new standards with the notion that there should be a bottom-up approach to setting standards, with practices moving from optional to mandatory as practice evolves.

With the rise in status and growth of the internal audit profession, the PPF and particularly the *Standards* are being increasingly acknowledged as the global criteria for the practice of internal auditing. They have been specifically recognized as such in legislation in a number of jurisdictions and regulations. Such an example of this recognition is found in the PCAOB's Auditing Standard No. 2 regarding implementation of Section 404 of the U.S. Sarbanes-Oxley Act of 2002:

> 121. Internal auditors normally are expected to have greater competence with regard to internal control over financial reporting and objectivity than other company personnel. Therefore, the auditor may be able to use his or her work to a greater extent than the work of other company personnel. This is particularly true in the case of internal auditors who follow the *International Standards for the Professional Practice of Internal Auditing* issued by The Institute of Internal Auditors. If internal auditors have performed an extensive amount of relevant work and the auditor determines they possess a high degree of competence and objectivity, the auditor could use their work to the greatest extent an auditor could use the work of others.[7]

Another example is the adoption of the PPF by the government of Canada and its departments for their internal audit work.[8]

SUMMARY

This chapter has presented the role of professional guidance and how it is provided to the profession. The different types of guidance that make up the PPF and how to use it to address issues that might arise in practice were discussed in detail. The ethical principles and behavioral norms relevant to the profession, as delineated in the Code of Ethics, were outlined. The Attribute Standards provided an understanding of the essential characteristics of internal audit functions and internal audit practitioners necessary for the delivery of effective internal audit services. An introduction to the nature of internal audit work and what is required of the CAE to effectively administer the internal audit function as required by the *Standards* was provided. Finally, the critical elements of the internal audit engagement were presented.

1. What are the four components of the Professional Practices Framework? Briefly describe each.

2. Name the four principles of The Code of Ethics. Why would the users of internal audit services want the internal audit professional to strive to attain these principles?

3. What is the purpose of the Code of Ethics?

4. Explain the difference between Attribute and Performance standards.

5. What is the difference between assurance and consulting services? Why does each service have its own Implementation Standards?

6. What is the difference between standards and practice advisories?

7. Which standards and practice advisories would you look to for guidance if you were developing a document outlining the purpose, authority, and responsibilities for a new internal audit function? For a complete list of the Practice Advisories, consult The IIA's Web site, www.theiia.org.

8. You are part of a three-person internal audit function. If your internal audit function was asked by your chief executive officer to conduct an audit of internal controls over the company's commodities trading and hedging activities but no one in the internal audit function has any training in trading and hedging, which standards and practice advisories would you consult for guidance?

9. If you were conducting an audit of business-to-customer e-commerce, where should you look besides the *Standards* and Practice Advisories for guidance?

10. Which committee of The Institute of Internal Auditors is responsible for developing the Practice Advisories?

Select the best answer for each of the following questions.

1. A major purpose of the *International Standards for the Professional Practice of Internal Auditing* is to:

    a. Promote coordination of internal and external audit efforts.

    b. Establish a basis for the evaluation (measurement) of internal audit performance.

    c. Develop consistency in internal audit practices.

    d. Provide a codification of existing practices.

2. In The IIA's Professional Practice Framework, which of the following is "mandatory guidance"?

    I.   Practice Advisories.

    II. The Code of Ethics.

    III. The definition of internal auditing.

    IV. The *International Standards for the Professional Practice of Internal Auditing*.

    a. I, II, and IV only.

b. II and IV only.

c. II, III, and IV only.

d. I, II, III, and IV.

3. An internal auditor engages in the preparation of income tax forms during tax season. For which of the following activities would the auditor most likely be considered in violation of The IIA's Code of Ethics?

a. Preparing the personal tax return, for a fee, for one of the company's divisional managers.

b. Appearing on a radio show on the local public broadcasting station to discuss retirement planning and tax issues.

c. Teaching an evening tax class, for a fee, at the local junior college.

d. On the weekends, working on an hourly basis for a friend who has a small CPA firm.

4. Assume that an internal auditor is auditing a division in which the division's chief financial officer is a close personal friend. The auditor learns that the friend is to be replaced after a series of critical contract negotiations with the U.S. Department of Defense. The auditor relays this information to the friend. Which principle of The IIA's Code of Ethics has been violated?

a. Integrity.

b. Objectivity.

c. Confidentiality.

d. Privacy.

5. In conducting an assurance engagement, the *Standards* require that the internal auditor exercise due professional care. Which of the following is not something an internal auditor is required to consider in determining what is needed for the exercising of due care in an assurance engagement of treasury operations?

a. The audit committee has requested assurance on the treasury function's compliance with a new policy on use of financial instruments.

b. Treasury management has not instituted any risk-management policies.

c. The independent outside auditors have requested to see the report and workpapers from the engagement.

d. The treasury function just completed implementation of a new real-time investment tracking system.

6. In which of the following situations does the internal auditor potentially lack objectivity?

a. A payroll accounting employee assists an internal auditor in verifying the physical inventory of small motors.

b. An internal auditor discusses a significant issue with the vice president to whom the auditee reports prior to drafting the audit report.

c. An internal auditor recommends standards of control and performamance measures for a contract with a service organization for the processing of payroll and employee benefits.

d. A former purchasing assistant performs a review of internal controls over purchasing four months after being transferred to the internal audit department.

1. The Professional Practices Framework divides the *International Standards for the Professional Practice of Internal Auditing* into two types: (1) Attribute Standards and (2) Performance Standards. Explain the difference between these two types of standards.

2. What is the role of the Practice Advisories in the Professional Practices Framework?

3. Why do non-IIA members working as internal auditors still need to follow The IIA's Professional Practices Framework?

4. How does The IIA's Code of Ethics differ from the *International Standards for the Professional Practice of Internal Auditing* in governing the behavior and activities of internal auditors?

5. The chief audit executive for Sargon Products reports administratively to the chief executive officer and functionally to the audit committee. The scope of the internal audit function's assurance services includes financial, operational, and compliance engagements.

   Required:
   Indicate whether the internal auditors' objectivity regarding accounting related matters has been impaired in each of the situations described below. Briefly explain your answer.

   a. The internal auditors are frequently asked to make accounting entries for complex transactions that the company's accountants do not have the expertise to handle.

   b. A staff accountant reconciles the company's monthly bank statements. An internal auditor reviews the bank reconciliations to make sure they are completed properly.

6. Does including the chief audit executive in a company's stock option program violate The IIA's Code of Ethics or the *Standards*?

CASES

CASE 1
Several years ago, *The Wall Street Journal* (April 7, 1999, page c1) described a now-settled U.S. Securities Exchange Commission (SEC) case against W. R. Grace & Co., claiming that the company engaged in "profit management" in its National Medical Care unit.[9]

> In the early 1990s, executives at W.R. Grace & Co. became troubled about the performance of the company's National Medical Care Inc. unit. The Problem: Earnings were growing too fast. Profit was increasing more than 30% a year, exceeding the unit's growth target. While most companies would be ecstatic, Grace executives worried that the unit couldn't keep it up. So they quietly stashed the excess profit in an all-purpose reserve, which they later would tap in a way that masked real problems—including slowing earnings.

> The profit stockpile soon was discovered by _____* auditors, who repeatedly told Grace that this was wrong, internal _____* memos show. But instead of standing firm, the accountants gave the financial statements a clean bill of health ...

> Internal company and audit-firm memos, as well as deposition excerpts, show a breakdown in controls at Grace and far larger distortions to earnings than previously disclosed. At least six _____* auditors and Norman Eatough, Grace's former in-house audit chief, questioned the propriety of Grace's accounting maneuvers ...

> Some business people insist the SEC's initiative is much ado about very little, noting that companies have leeway to use accounting techniques to deliver consistent earnings, as long as any adjustments aren't "material." That's the fuzzy disclosure standard under securities laws, often defined by accountants as events that have more than a 5% or 10% impact on earnings.

> "Any CFO anywhere has managed earnings in a way the SEC is now jumping up and down and calling fraud," maintains Wallace Timmeny, a lawyer ...

> Mr. Eatough, Grace's in-house audit chief, meanwhile, was growing concerned (in a report to the CFO he laid out what he called "deliberate deferral of reported income.") But, fearing his job was in jeopardy, he stopped short of calling it fraud ...

What would you advise Mr. Eatough to do in this situation? Justify your advice with the guidance provided in The IIA's Professional Practices Framework, referencing specific sections of the Standards and the Code of Ethics as well as any other practical considerations.

Mark Hobson is an internal auditor employed by Comstock Industries. He is nearing completion of an audit of the Avil Division conducted during the first five weeks of the year. The Avil Division is one of three manufacturing divisions in Comstock and manufactures inventories to supply about 50% of Comstock's sales. In addition to the manufacturing divisions, Comstock has two marketing divisions (domestic and international) and a technical service division that offers worldwide technical support. Each customer is assigned to the most suitable manufacturing division, which functions as the supplier for that customer. The manufacturing division then approves the customer's credit, ships against orders obtained by the sales representatives, and collects the customer receivables when due. This allows order-to-order monitoring of customer credit limits against customer orders received.

Two Potential Observations

Two items concern Mark. First, there was a material dollar amount of inventory of part number A2 still carried on the Avil books at year-end, despite the fact that the Fast-tac machining component in which part A2 was used is now considered first generation and is no longer manufactured. Company policy requires an immediate write-off of all obsolete inventory items. Second, some accounts receivable still carried as collectible at year-end were more than 180 days old. All receivables are due in 30 days, which is standard for the industry. Mark believes many of these old accounts are uncollectible.

The division manager's administrative assistant, Brenda Wilson, performed the aging of accounts receivable rather than the division accountant, as is standard practice. The division accountant refused to discuss the circumstances of Brenda's actions.

The Auditee's Comments

Mark scheduled a meeting with Brenda to discuss his concerns.

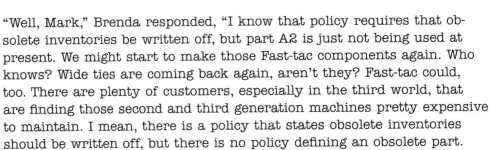

"Well, Mark," Brenda responded, "I know that policy requires that obsolete inventories be written off, but part A2 is just not being used at present. We might start to make those Fast-tac components again. Who knows? Wide ties are coming back again, aren't they? Fast-tac could, too. There are plenty of customers, especially in the third world, that are finding those second and third generation machines pretty expensive to maintain. I mean, there is a policy that states obsolete inventories should be written off, but there is no policy defining an obsolete part.

"And as for those receivables," Brenda continued, "that is certainly a judgment call, too. Who knows if those accounts will be collected? We're in a slight recession now. When things pick up, we'll probably collect a few. There isn't even a policy in this division on writing off receivables. I checked. Nothing says I have to write them off. So who are you to say I have to?"

"Brenda, be straight. You know those parts will never be used. And you know those receivables are bad."

"Look, Mark," Brenda finally bargained, "it's only two weeks from the close of the year. Let's let these items ride until after the close so that everyone gets their bonuses. Then, I promise I'll take a fresh look at both inventories and receivables. I'll write them down after year-end, after the financial reports are issued. No one will know. And, after all, who's to be hurt?"

The Division Manager

Mark continued his audit, drafted his report containing observations related to the inventory and receivables, and reviewed the report with the division manager, Hal Wright. Hal was visibly disturbed.

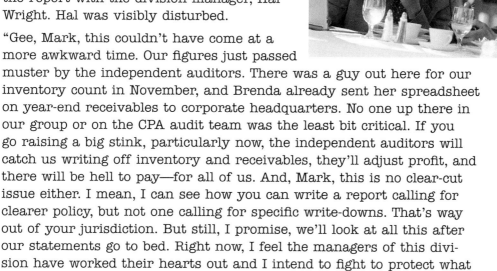

"Gee, Mark, this couldn't have come at a more awkward time. Our figures just passed muster by the independent auditors. There was a guy out here for our inventory count in November, and Brenda already sent her spreadsheet on year-end receivables to corporate headquarters. No one up there in our group or on the CPA audit team was the least bit critical. If you go raising a big stink, particularly now, the independent auditors will catch us writing off inventory and receivables, they'll adjust profit, and there will be hell to pay—for all of us. And, Mark, this is no clear-cut issue either. I mean, I can see how you can write a report calling for clearer policy, but not one calling for specific write-downs. That's way out of your jurisdiction. But still, I promise, we'll look at all this after our statements go to bed. Right now, I feel the managers of this division have worked their hearts out and I intend to fight to protect what little bonuses they have coming. If we write down as you suggest, those bonuses will go and the stockholders will lose, too. Earnings per share (EPS) will drop like a rock. They might even close this division. Now you don't want that, do you?"

"Well, Hal, I could word my observations as they are in the draft but include your response." Hal was suddenly angry. "What? And let the audit committee decide the issue? They have nothing to do with this. They accepted the CPA's report. If you want to make the audit committee happy, you'll accept it, too, and leave this adjustment stuff alone."

The Internal Audit Director

Concerned, Mark delayed finalizing his report and discussed the draft with Gail Wu, Director of Internal Audit. Gail is not trained as an auditor and was promoted to Director of Internal Audit from Corporate Finance so that she might develop a better understanding of operating relationships. Still, Gail is very smart and Mark has always respected her opinion. The discussion was by telephone, with Mark still at the Avil Division headquarters and Gail at the corporate office.

"Mark, Hal is right. If you, in essence, blow the whistle on management bonuses this year, we can kiss all the goodwill I've been struggling to build for this department good-bye. It will all go out the window."

"I know you've been trying to put us on a better footing, Gail, but Hal is intractable. As far as he is concerned, the only observation he will accept in the report is that of deficient policy, with nothing mentioned about the inventory or receivables needing adjustment."

"Well, do what you have to," Gail ended the discussion. "But I insist that you submit a report that Hal agrees to and has signed. I don't want to stir up hornets and then have to try to explain my loose cannon to the board when everyone is howling about the bonus problem."

Answer the following questions.

1. Refer to The IIA's Code of Ethics. Identify three specific Rules of Conduct relevant to this case. Using the Rules of Conduct you identify as the context, discuss the ethical issues raised in the case.

2. Discuss how the ethical dilemma Mark faces might have been avoided. In other words, discuss specific things Comstock's management and/or the internal audit function might have done to reduce the risk of such a situation arising.

3. Clearly indicate what you would do if you found yourself in Mark's position. Briefly explain why.

REFERENCES

[1] Ramamoorti, Sridhar, "Internal Auditing: History, Evolution, and Pros pects," in Bailey et al. Research Opportunities in Internal Auditing, (Al tamonte Springs, FL, 2003), p. 5.

[2] The Institute of Internal Auditors, A Vision for the Future: Professional Practices Framework for Internal Auditing, (Altamonte Springs, FL: The Institute of Internal Auditors, 1999).

[3] The research study was conducted by a task force of leading auditing researchers from around the globe under the auspices of the Auditing Section of the American Accounting Association and published by The IIA Research Foundation in 2001.

[4] Independence and Objectivity: A Framework for Internal Auditors (Al tamonte Springs, FL: The Institute of Internal Auditors, 2001, p.15).

[5] Plumlee, R. David, "The Standard of Objectivity for Internal Auditors: Memory and Bias Effects," Journal of Accounting Research (Autumn, 1985), p. 683-699.

[6] The Syllabus for the CIA examination is available from the IIA's Web site under "Certification".

[7] Public Company Accounting Oversight Board. Auditing Related Profes sional Practice Standards: Auditing Standard No. 2—An Audit of Internal Control Over Financial Reporting Performed in Conjunction With An Audit of Financial Statements. September 8, 2004, paragraph 121.

[8] The Treasury Board of Canada Secretariat, Internal Auditing Standards for the Government of Canada, (Ottawa, ON: The Treasury Board of Canada Secretariat, October 21, 2005).

[9] Davis, A. "SEC Case Claims Profit Management by Grace," Wall Street Jour nal, April 7, 1997, C1.

[10] Adapted from Case 37, "Comstock Industries," by G. Thomas Friedlob and E. Lewis Bryan, included in Case Studies in Internal Auditing: Volume 2, compiled by M. Dittenhofer and R. A. Roy, and issued by The Institute of Internal Auditors' Academic Relations Committee, March 1994.

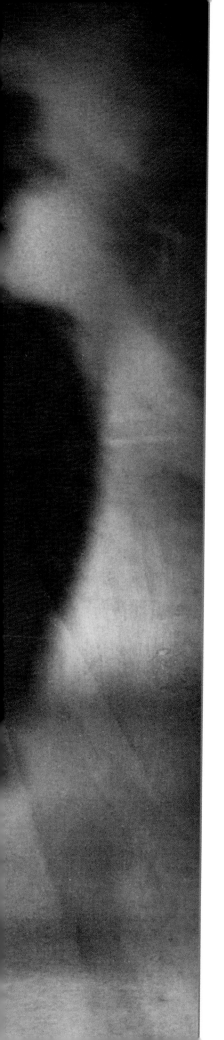

CHAPTER 3
GOVERNANCE AND
RISK MANAGEMENT

Learning Objectives

- Define governance and contrast the different roles and responsibilities within governance.

- Articulate the different enterprisewide governance principles.

- Describe the changes in regulations and how governance has evolved into its present state.

- Describe the role of the internal audit function in the governance process.

- Define risk and enterprise risk management.

- Discuss the different dimensions of the Committee of Sponsoring Organizations of the Treadway Commission's *Enterprise Risk Management– Integrated Framework*.

- Articulate the relationship between governance and enterprise risk management.

- Describe the different roles the internal audit function can play in enterprise risk management.

- Evaluate the impact of enterprise risk management on internal audit assurance activities.

Life is full of uncertainty. If you stop to think about it, there are many day-to-day activities about which you simply don't know what the outcome will be in advance. How you deal with those uncertainties determines what kind of success you'll have in life.

Operating a business is no different. Organizations face uncertainties in all aspects of conducting business, and their success is dependent on how well they manage those uncertainties. Internal auditing can be a key enabler to that success. Before you can fully understand how an internal audit function can serve such a role, it's important first to understand how organizations are structured and operate to achieve success. Although the actual organizational structure will vary from one organization to the next, each must establish an overall governance structure to ensure key stakeholder needs are met. This governance structure provides direction to those executing the day-

EXHIBIT 3-1

2110 – Risk Management

2130 – Governance

Practice Advisory 2010-2: Linking the Audit Plan to Risk and Exposures

Practice Advisory 2100-3: Internal Auditing's Role in the
Risk Management Process

Practice Advisory 2100-4: Internal Auditing's Role in Organizations
Without a Risk Management Process

Practice Advisory 2110-1: Assessing the Adequacy of
Risk Management Processes

Practice Advisory 2210.A1-1: Risk Assessment in Engagement Planning

Practice Advisory 2600-1: Management's Acceptance of Risks

to-day activities of managing the risks inherent in an organization's business model. Finally, these day-to-day activities represent internal control activities. These elements are depicted in Exhibit 3-2.

This figure shows that governance surrounds all activities in an organization. The governance structure may be established to comply with laws and regulations in the jurisdictions in which an organization operates. These laws and regulations are typically promulgated to protect the public's interest. Additionally, the board and management of an organization may establish governance structures to ensure the needs of key stakeholders are met and that the organization operates within the boundaries and values established by the board and senior management.

Risk management is the next layer in the governance structure. Risk management is intended to identify and manage the risks that may adversely affect the organization's success. Management develops strategies regarding how to best manage the key risks. Risk management activities should operate within the overall direction of the governance structure.

Internal control activities are shown in the center as they represent a subset, but integral part of, the broader risk management activities. Internal control activities are designed to execute the risk management strategies.

Finally, there are arrows that represent the flow of information throughout the governance structure. The board provides direction to senior management to guide them in carrying out the risk management activities. Senior management in turn provides direction to lower levels of management who are responsible for the internal control activities. However, lower level managers are accountable to senior management with regard to the success of those internal control activities. And senior management is accountable to provide the board assurances regarding the effectiveness of risk management activities. The arrows in the figure depict that flow of direction and accountability from one layer to the next.

This chapter will describe governance and risk management in detail, discussing the key elements and principles of each, as well as the respective roles and responsibilities. Other illustrations will be provided to depict, in greater detail, how one might envision the key elements of governance and risk management.

Finally, as indicated, the internal audit function can play a key, and integral, role in both governance and risk management. The role of the internal audit function will be discussed, as will the impact governance and risk management may have on the annual audit plan.

GOVERNANCE CONCEPTS

To perform effective internal assurance and consulting services, it is imperative to have an understanding of an organization's business. As part of gaining that understanding, it is necessary to determine how an organization operates from a top-down perspective. The overall means by which organizations operate is commonly referred to as corporate governance (referred to more generally as "governance" throughout this chapter).

Definition of Governance

As discussed in Chapter 1, "Introduction to Internal Auditing," governance is the process conducted by the board of directors to authorize, direct, and oversee management toward the achievement of the

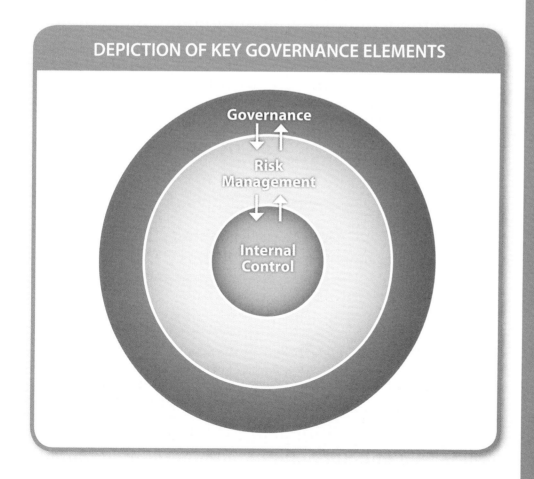

DEPICTION OF KEY GOVERNANCE ELEMENTS

Governance

Risk Management

Internal Control

EXHIBIT 3-2

organization's objectives. An often-used definition of governance comes from the Paris-based forum of democratic markets, the Organisation for Economic Co-operation and Development (OECD):

> Corporate governance involves a set of relationships between a company's management, its board, its shareholders, and other stakeholders. Corporate governance also provides the structure through which the objectives of the company are set, and the means of attaining those objectives and monitoring performance are determined.[1]

Although there are many other definitions of governance, there are certain common elements present in most of them. These elements describe governance as the policies, processes, and structures used by an organization to direct and control its activities, to achieve its objectives, and to protect the interests of its diverse stakeholder groups in a manner consistent with appropriate ethical standards.[2]

In addition to the elements described by the OECD, the discussion of governance that follows will include the element of organizations determining their objectives and values, and establishing boundaries for conduct. Taking into consideration the different governance definitions and associated elements, governance can be depicted in a diagram as shown in Exhibit 3-3.

The first broad area of governance is depicted in the exhibit as strategic direction. The board is responsible for providing strategic direction and guidance relative to the establishment of key business objectives, consistent with the organization's business model. Directors bring varied and diverse business experience to the board and, thus, are in a position to provide the strategic direction and guidance that will help ensure the organization is successful. The board can also influence the organization's risk-taking philosophy and establish broad boundaries of conduct based on the organization's overall risk appetite and cultural values. Monitoring progress toward meeting the goals and objectives of the organization is another key reason for the board's existence.

Governance

The process conducted by the board of directors to authorize, direct, and oversee management toward the achievement of the organization's objectives.

EXHIBIT 3-3

OVERVIEW OF GOVERNANCE

Governance Umbrella
Board of Directors

Strategic Direction

Governance Oversight

KEY COMPONENTS OF GOVERNANCE OVERSIGHT

Stakeholders

Governance Umbrella
Board of Directors

Risk Management
Senior Management

Risk Owners

Assurance

Internal ⟷ *External*

EXHIBIT 3-4

The second broad area of governance is depicted in the exhibit as governance oversight. Expanding on the view in Exhibit 3-3, the key components of governance oversight are shown in Exhibit 3-4. Because this oversight responsibility is where the risk management and internal audit activities are most relevant, governance oversight is discussed in much greater detail following this exhibit.

The key points that should be taken from this definition are:

- Governance begins with the board of directors and its committees. The board serves as the "umbrella" of governance oversight for the entire organization. It provides direction to management, empowers them with the authority to take actions, and oversees the overall results of operations.

- The board must understand and focus on the needs of key stakeholders. Ultimately, stakeholders are the ones to whom the board has a fiduciary responsibility.

- Day-to-day, governance is executed by management of the organization. Both senior executives and line managers have important, although somewhat different, roles in governance. These roles are carried out through risk management activities.

- Internal and external auditors provide management and the board with assurances regarding the effectiveness of governance activities.

Roles and Responsibilities Within Governance

The Board and its Committees

Frequently through its various committees governance is ultimately the responsibility of the board. The first of the board's responsibilities is to identify the key stakeholders of an organization. A stakeholder is any party with a direct or indirect interest in an organization's activities and outcomes. Stakeholders can be divided into the following groupings:

- **Direct Stakeholders.** Those stakeholders who are directly involved in the operation of the organization's business.

- **Indirect Stakeholders.** Those stakeholders who are not directly involved in the organization's business, but who are affected by the success or other outcomes of the business.

- **Influencing Stakeholders.** Those stakeholders who are not involved in or affected by the organization's business, but who may themselves influence aspects of the organization's business and, as a result, the organization's success.

Common stakeholders in each of these groupings are:

Employees. All of the individuals working for an organization, whether management or line employees, are **direct stakeholders** as they are integrally involved in the conduct of the organization's business. Employees have a vested interest in the organization's ongoing viability and success. If the organization ceases to exist, or has to downsize due to the lack of success in a market, employees may lose their source of livelihood. Therefore, a board must ensure an organization is operating in a manner that serves the best interest of its employees.

Customers. Customers are typically the lifeblood of an organization's success, and, as such, are **direct stakeholders** in an organization. In exchange for some form of payment, customers rely on an organization to build safe and reliable products, deliver agreed-upon services, and comply with other aspects of sales contracts and arrangements. Because the organization has obligations to customers, the board has a responsibility to ensure these obligations are met.

Vendors. Vendors provide the goods and services needed for an organization to conduct its business and, therefore, are **direct stakeholders**. Similar to customers, an organization has certain obligations to vendors, the most obvious of which is the obligation to pay for the goods and services received from those vendors. Therefore, a board has oversight responsibilities to ensure that the organization meets its obligations under vendor contracts and arrangements.

Shareholders/Investors. Shareholders are **indirect stakeholders** as they have an investment in the company, either through shares of stock, ownership units, or some other legal instrument that vests them in the future success of the company. Shareholders may be individual investors, institutions, or funds that invest on behalf of a group of investors. Typically, shareholders have the right to elect individuals to serve as directors on the board who they believe will best serve and

Board

An organization's governing body, such as a board of directors, supervisory board, head of an agency or legislative body, etc., to whom the chief audit executive may functionally report.

Stakeholder

Any party with a direct or indirect interest in an organization's activities and outcomes.

protect their interests. Therefore, shareholders are frequently considered the most important and powerful stakeholders from the board's perspective.

Regulatory Agencies. These governmental agencies may be either **indirect stakeholders** or **influencing stakeholders**. The rules and regulations promulgated by these agencies may dictate certain operational and reporting requirements of an organization, or influence the decisions made by management of the organization. For example, the U.S. Securities and Exchange Commission (SEC) influences all publicly held companies in the United States. Examples of regulatory agencies affecting most U.S. companies include the Department of Labor, the Environmental Protection Agency (EPA), and the Occupational Safety and Health Administration (OSHA). Additionally, some industries are subject to specific regulators such as banking [the Federal Deposit Insurance Corporation (FDIC) and others] and utilities [for example, the Federal Energy Resources Commission and state regulatory commissions that are responsible for approving the rates that can be charged to customers]. Virtually every country or legal jurisdiction will have agencies or similar bodies that promulgate regulations. A board must understand the requirements of these agencies to exercise their oversight responsibilities.

Financial Institutions. Organizations typically have some form of capital structure composed of debt and/or equity. The equity component was covered under the discussion of shareholders above. Debt stakeholders are typically financial institutions, such as banks or other institutions that provide financing to an organization. Financial institutions are willing to provide financing in exchange for a return, most commonly in the form of an interest rate on the outstanding balance. However, such institutions frequently have other stipulations, or covenants, with which an organization must comply. These covenants typically relate to the overall financial health and liquidity of an organization, and provide ongoing assurances to the financial institutions regarding the organization's ability to repay its obligations. Therefore, a board must provide oversight to ensure management is mindful of and complying with all relevant covenants of financing arrangements with these **influencing stakeholders**.

Other Influencing Stakeholders. Although the above are the most common types of stakeholders, there may be other parties who are **influencing stakeholders**. Examples include rating agencies, industry associations, and competitors of the organization. The key point is that a board must make the effort and spend the time to ensure it has identified all of the key stakeholders in an organization.

Once the key stakeholders are identified, the next step the board must undertake is to understand the needs and expectations of these stakeholders. Some of those needs and expectations are self-evident. For example, customers expect that products are generally free of defects and vendors expect obligations to be paid on time. However, other expectations, such as shareholders' desire for dividends versus share price growth, may require some research and analysis to fully understand. Boards may be able to determine these expectations through internal discussions, but they also may need to discuss expectations directly with key stakeholders.

Finally, the board should identify the potential outcomes that would be unacceptable to key stakeholders. For example, certain investors may be disappointed if the company misses its earnings estimate by 1 cent per share in a given quarter, but may not find that unacceptable, as some components of earnings are more volatile than others. However, if the company misses its earnings estimates for several consecutive quarters, investors may find that unacceptable and question whether the board should consider a change in senior management.

Because the various stakeholders will likely have different expectations, the outcomes each type of stakeholder deems unacceptable will vary as well. The board may need to consider the following types of outcomes:

- **Financial.** For example, earnings per share, cash liquidity, credit rating, return on investments, capital availability, tax exposures, material weaknesses, and disclosure transparency.

- **Compliance.** For example, litigation, code of conduct violations, EPA/OSHA violations, restraining orders, governmental investigations, indictments, and arrests.

- **Operations.** For example, achievement of objectives, efficient use of assets, protection of assets (insurance coverage, asset impairments, asset destruction), protection of people (health and safety, work stoppages), protection of information (data integrity, data confidentiality), and protection of community (environmental spills, plant shutdowns).

- **Strategic.** For example, reputation, corporate sustainability, employee morale, and customer satisfaction.

Once the board determines the outcomes key stakeholders deem unacceptable, it can establish tolerance levels based on those outcomes. The tolerance levels, which are consistent with the organization's overall risk appetite, can be communicated to management as boundaries within which the board would like the organization to operate. The concepts of risk appetite and tolerance levels will be discussed further in the ERM section later in this chapter.

The board can best execute its governance responsibilities by:

- Establishing a Governance Committee.
  - This committee could be a new committee or an expansion of responsibilities for an existing committee (for example, many companies have expanded the responsibilities of the Nominating Committee to become a Nominating and Governance Committee).
  - It should be made up of independent directors.
  - The committee should have the responsibilities outlined above.
- Articulating requirements for reporting to the board.
  - The board should delegate to management the authority

Risk Appetite

The amount of risk, on a broad level, an organization is willing to accept in pursuit of its business objectives.

3-8

to operate the business within the board's tolerable limits relative to unacceptable outcomes. Management must have the authority to make day-to-day business decisions, but must also have a clear understanding of the board's tolerance limits within which to manage the business.

- As part of its oversight role, the board must also establish reporting thresholds for management—that is, which outcomes must be approved by the board, reported directly to the board, or summarized for the board as part of quarterly meetings.

● Re-evaluating governance expectations on a periodic basis (probably annually).

- Key stakeholder expectations may evolve and change. Therefore, the board must identify those changes and re-evaluate its governance direction.

- As a result of those changes, the board's tolerance levels should also be re-evaluated.

In summary, the board of directors plays a very key and comprehensive role in corporate governance. Without that umbrella of authority, direction, and oversight, governance will not be sufficient over the long term.

Senior Management

Although the board provides the umbrella of governance oversight, management executes the day-to-day activities that help ensure effective governance is achieved. Once the board determines its tolerance levels relative to the boundaries of operations, it must next delegate authority to senior management so they can manage the operations within those tolerance levels. Senior management then has the responsibility to execute the board's direction in a manner that achieves corporate objectives, but within the tolerance limits outlined by the board.

To execute its governance responsibilities, senior management is responsible for:

● Ensuring that the full scope of direction and authority delegated is understood appropriately. Senior management must understand the board's governance expectations, the amount of authority the board has delegated to management, its tolerance levels relative to unacceptable outcomes, and requirements for reporting to the board.

● Identifying the processes and activities within the organization that are integral to executing the governance direction provided by the board. That is, senior management must determine:

- Where in the organization to manage the specific risks that could result in unacceptable outcomes.

- Who will be responsible for managing those risks (that is, risk owners).

- How those risks will be managed.

● Evaluating what other business considerations or factors might create a justification for delegating a lower tolerance level to risk owners than that delegated by the board. For example, the board may specify that management must maintain controls to ensure there are no adjustments or control weaknesses beyond a certain level of severity. However, senior management, desiring to avoid the situation where multiple significant control deficiencies aggregate to an unacceptable level, may specify to risk owners that control activities be maintained to ensure there are no control deficiencies exceeding a lower level of severity.

● Ensuring that sufficient information is gathered from the risk owners to support its reporting requirements to the board.

Senior management can best execute its governance responsibilities by:

● Establishing a Risk Committee.

■ This committee is typically led by a senior executive; a chief risk officer (CRO), if one exists; or some other executive who has broad risk oversight responsibility.

■ It is responsible for determining that all key risks are identified, linked to risk management activities, and assigned to risk owners. As part of this responsibility, the committee must ensure that it comprehensively considers all possible outcomes for key risks, not just the financial outcomes.

■ It evaluates the organization's ongoing risk appetite and ensures that tolerance levels delegated to the risk owners are consistent with this risk appetite.

● Articulating reporting requirements.

■ Risk owners must understand the nature, format, and timing of communications regarding the effectiveness of the risk management activities. These communications typically should be consistent with the tolerance levels delegated to the risk owners.

■ This reporting may occur through regularly scheduled Risk Committee meetings or as part of the process of compiling information for reporting to the board.

● Re-evaluating governance expectations on a periodic basis (probably annually).

■ As an organization evolves and changes, senior management must re-evaluate its governance direction and the corresponding tolerance levels that have been delegated to risk owners. These changes may come from the board or from other external and internal factors. Such changes may result in the need for new risk management activities or modifications to existing risk management activities.

■ As a result of those changes, senior management's tolerance levels should also be re-evaluated.

■ This also gives senior management the opportunity to evaluate the overall effectiveness of the company's risk management program.

Senior management plays an integral role in enterprise risk management, which is a key component of governance.

Risk Owners

Individuals who have day-to-day responsibility for ensuring risk management activities effectively manage risks within the organization's risk appetite are called risk owners. Risk owners work with senior management to carry out the risk management activities of an organization. The responsibilities of risk owners include:

- Evaluating whether the risk management activities are designed adequately to manage the related risks within the tolerance levels specified by senior management. Although senior management may provide direction relative to the risk management activities, the risk owners typically will determine the specific tasks that are necessary to carry out those activities.

- Assessing the ongoing capabilities of the organization to execute the risk management activities as they are designed. This assessment should evaluate the maturity of the procedures in place, the competence and experience of the people performing those procedures, the sufficiency of any enabling technologies (for example, computer systems), and the availability of external and internal information to support decision-making.

- Determining whether the risk management activities are currently operating as designed—that is, whether the people and systems are executing the processes consistently with the desired objectives.

- Establishing monitoring activities to identify, in a timely manner, whether anomalies or divergences from expected outcomes have occurred.

- Ensuring that the information needed by senior management and the board is accurate and readily available, and is provided to senior management on a timely basis.

Risk owners can best execute their governance responsibilities by:

- Presenting governance proposals to the Risk Committee.
  - If an individual becomes a new risk owner, or is responsible for a risk that was not previously subject to formal risk management and reporting, the risk owner should prepare a proposal for the Risk Committee. This proposal should cover the inherent nature and source of the risk, its potential impact, proposed tolerance levels, and expected risk management activities. This information is presented to, discussed with, and agreed upon by the Risk Committee.

- Re-evaluating risk management activities on a periodic basis (at least annually, but potentially more frequently).
  - The design of risk management activities should continue to align with companywide risk strategies and ensure the risks are managed within the delegated tolerance levels.
  - The risk management capabilities should be reassessed in light of turnover, systems changes, and other events

Risk Management
The process conducted by management to understand and deal with uncertainties (that is, risks and opportunities)— that could affect the organization's ability to achieve its objectives.

that could impact the maturity and effectiveness of those capabilities.

- Risk management monitoring activities should provide the risk owners with timely information on the effectiveness of the risk management activities.

- The reporting of risk management results up to senior management should be assessed periodically with management to ensure it is meeting its needs.

Risk owners are on the front lines of managing risks and, as such, are key contributors to good governance. Their role in executing and monitoring risk management activities, along with reporting on the effectiveness of those activities, will greatly influence the success an organization will have in avoiding or mitigating unacceptable outcomes.

Assurance Activities

The final component of governance is represented by the assurance activities, which help provide the board with an objective assessment regarding the effectiveness of the risk management activities. These assurance activities can be performed by a variety of parties, either internal or external to the organization. The most common internal group to provide such assurances is the internal audit function.

The extent of assurance activities performed by the internal audit function will depend on (a) the internal audit charter, which specifies the internal audit function's role in governance assurance, and (b) specific direction from the board regarding current or ongoing expectations to perform such activities. Depending on these two factors, the internal audit function's governance responsibilities may include any or all of the following:

- Evaluating whether the various risk management activities are designed adequately to manage the risks associated with unacceptable outcomes.

- Testing and evaluating whether the various risk management activities are operating as designed.

- Determining whether the assertions made by the risk owners to senior management regarding the effectiveness of the risk management activities accurately reflect the current state of risk management effectiveness.

- Determining whether the assertions made by senior management to the board regarding the effectiveness of the risk management activities provide the board with the information it desires about the current state of risk management effectiveness.

- Evaluating whether risk tolerance information is communicated timely and effectively from the board to senior management, and from senior management to the risk owners.

- Assessing whether there are any other risk areas that are currently not included in the governance process, but should be (for example, a risk for which risk tolerance and reporting expectations have not been delegated to a specific risk owner).

The internal audit function can be an effective part of the governance

Assurance Services

An objective examination of evidence for the purpose of providing an independent assessment on risk management, control, or governance processes for the organization.

process by:

- Ensuring it fully understands the board's governance direction and expectations.
  - The internal audit function should understand the direction provided to senior management, including the tolerance levels and reporting expectations.
  - Additionally, it is important to understand the board's expectations of the role the internal audit function should play with regard to governance assurance.
- Supporting management's risk management program.
  - The internal audit function can help bring structure and discipline to the risk management program which may be managed in a manner similar to managing internal audit activities.
  - The internal audit function can help educate management and other employees on risk and control topics.
  - Organizational and divisional risk assessments can be facilitated or monitored by the internal audit function.
  - Ongoing oversight and input can be provided formally (for example, sitting on a risk steering committee) or informally (for example, periodic discussions with management).
- Developing an internal audit plan that appropriately encompasses the governance assurance activities and allows for periodic communications to senior management and the board on the effectiveness of risk management activities.

Some organizations have other groups that may provide governance assurances (for example, environmental and safety departments, quality assurance groups, etc.). These groups may provide assurances directly to the board, or they may communicate to members of management who provide the assurances to the board.

Assurances from external parties are less common but still can be important to the board. For example, although the attestation opinions provided by outside independent auditors are primarily for the purpose of meeting regulatory or contractual requirements, unqualified opinions may indirectly provide the board and management with some assurances regarding the effectiveness of activities designed to mitigate financial reporting risks. Similarly, third-party consultants may be hired to provide management or the board with assurances regarding specific risk management activities.

The assurance activities performed by internal auditors as well as other parties provide valuable information to senior management and the board so that they can monitor the ongoing effectiveness of governance and risk management activities.

THE EVOLUTION OF GOVERNANCE

Despite the publicity that corporate governance has received in recent years, effective governance is not a new concept. An underlying premise of the public equity markets is that investors will provide capital to organizations in exchange for a potential return on that investment. To instill confidence in the capital markets, investors need sufficient information to evaluate the potential risks and rewards of their investments. They also need assurances that it's a level playing field—that is, all investors will be able to transact in a consistent and fair manner. Various regulations and standards have been written to achieve the transparency objective. Frequently, new regulations and standards have been promulgated in response to events in the business world. These regulations and standards were designed to eliminate or minimize the undesirable outcomes of those events. Exhibit 3-5 summarizes some of those key business events in the United States and the legislation that resulted. Appendix 3-A, Summary of Key U.S. Regulations, at the end of this chapter presents a summary of key U.S. regulations and a description of each piece of legislation shown in Exhibit 3-5.

Regulations in Other Parts of the World

Similar business events have occurred in other countries around the world, resulting in the promulgation of legislation by their legislative bodies. Each piece of legislation was designed to improve overall governance, as well as the control activities surrounding the preparation of financial statements, and enhance the fairness and transparency of financial reporting.

EXHIBIT 3-5

KEY U.S. BUSINESS EVENTS AND RESULTING LEGISLATION

Key Business Events	Legislation/Guidance
The U.S. stock market crash in 1929, combined with the subsequent failures of several major corporations because of fraud, precipitated the need for investor faith to be restored. The intent of the resulting regulations was to provide a level playing field for investors through consistent, timely, complete, and relevant public reporting of financial information.	Securities Act of 1933 Securities Exchange Act of 1934
In the aftermath of the Watergate investigation at the beginning of the 1970s, more than 450 American companies were reported to have paid bribes or made questionable payments to foreign government officials or political parties.	Foreign Corrupt Practices Act (FCPA) of 1977
In the 1980s, there were multiple incidents of financial reporting that were inaccurate, incomplete, or misleading.	Report of the National Commission on Fraudulent Financial Reporting (Treadway Commission Report) 1987
In the 1980s, several savings and loan institutions required bailout by the federal government, bringing into question, among other things, the strength of their system of internal controls.	Federal Deposit Insurance Corporation Improvement Act (FDICIA) of 1991
After the turn of the new century, several U.S. corporations were beset by fraud and bankruptcy (for example, Enron Corp. and WorldCom).	Sarbanes-Oxley Act of 2002, which amends the 1933 and 1934 Securities Acts U.S. Stock Exchange Listing Standards (NYSE, AMEX, NASDAQ)

A description of key guidance/regulations from other countries can be found in Appendix 3-B, Summary of Governance Codes From Other Countries. Additionally, Appendix 3-C, Other Governance Reference Sources, provides links to other governance reference sources.

Commonly Identified Governance Principles

As is probably evident from the previous discussions, governance is a broad concept. However, as described in an IIA white paper on governance, principles often included in defining effective governance processes are:[2]

1. Ensure a properly organized and functioning board that has the correct number of members; an appropriate board committee structure; established meeting protocols; sound, independent judgment about affairs of the organization; and periodically reaffirmed membership.

2. Ensure board members possess appropriate qualifications and experience, with a clear understanding of their role in the governance activities, a sound knowledge of the organization's operations, and an independent/objective mindset.

3. Ensure that the board has sufficient authority, funding, and resources to conduct independent inquiries.

4. Maintain an understanding by executive management and the board of the organization's operating structure, including structures that impede transparency.

5. Articulate an organizational strategy against which the success of the overall enterprise and the contributions of individuals are measured.

6. Create an organizational structure that supports the enterprise in achieving its strategy.

7. Establish a governing policy for the operation of key activities of the organization.

8. Set and enforce clear lines of responsibility and accountability throughout the organization.

9. Ensure effective interaction among the board, management, external and internal auditors, and any other assurance providers.

10. Secure appropriate oversight by management, including establishment and maintenance of a strong set of internal controls.

11. Make sure that compensation policies and practices—especially related to senior management—are consistent with the organization's ethical values, objectives, strategy, and control environment, and encourage appropriate behavior.

12. Communicate and reinforce throughout the organization an ethical culture, organizational values, and appropriate tone at the top, which includes an environment that allows employees to raise concerns without fear of retaliation, as well as monitors and investigates potential conflicts of interest.

13. Effectively use internal auditors, ensuring the adequacy of their independence, resources, scope of activities, and effectiveness of operations.

14. Clearly define and implement risk management policies, processes, and accountabilities at the board level and throughout the organization.

15. Effectively use external auditors, ensuring their independence, adequate resources, and scope of activities.

16. Provide appropriate disclosure of key information, in a transparent manner, to stakeholders.

17. Provide disclosure of the organization's governance processes, comparing those processes with recognized national codes or best practices.

18. Ensure appropriate oversight of related party transactions and conflict of interest situations.

Although there may be additional principles cited in other resources, this list comprehensively supports the discussion of governance provided earlier in this chapter.

OVERVIEW OF RISK MANAGEMENT

A Brief History of Risk

The concept of risk is not a recent phenomenon or new way of approaching the management of a business. Peter L. Bernstein provides an extensive history of risk in *Against the Gods: The Remarkable Story of Risk*.[3] His book outlines the evolving acceptance and understanding of risk over the centuries. For example:

- Gambling has been documented back several centuries to early Greek and Egyptian civilizations as well as in the Bible (for example, Pontius Pilate's soldiers cast lots for Christ's robe as he suffered on the cross). While games of chance have been common throughout history, the theory of probability was not discovered until the Renaissance period in the mid-17th century. After that discovery, probability theory advanced from the mathematical exercise of explaining outcomes in games of chance to a key tool used in the business world to support decision making.

- Chinese and Babylonian traders displayed risk transfer and distribution practices as early as the 3rd and 2nd century BC, respectively. The Greeks and Romans introduced early forms of health and life insurance around 600 AD. Toward the end of the 17th century, the growing importance of London as a center for trade led to rising demand for marine insurance. In the late 1680s, Edward Lloyd opened a coffee house that became a popular haunt of ship owners, merchants, and ships' captains, and thereby a reliable source of the latest shipping news. It became the meeting place for parties wishing to insure cargoes and ships, and those willing to underwrite such ventures. Today, Lloyd's of London remains one of the leading specialty insurance companies in the world.

- Similar to insurance businesses, banks and other financial institutions have been dealing with risks in all aspects of their

business throughout the years. The first banks were probably the religious temples of the ancient world. There are records of loans from the 18th Century BC in Babylon that were made by temple priests to merchants. And the Greek and Roman empires helped evolve banking practices surrounding loans, deposits, and currency exchange. Banks use concepts of risk to determine the rates they can charge for loans based on their own cost of funds and the probabilities of default. Financial institutions have also developed financial instruments, such as options, swaps, and derivative instruments that create value based on the probabilities of uncertain future events.

Definitions of Risk

The English language word *risk* comes from an Italian word *risicare*, which means "to dare: a choice under uncertain conditions (rather than fate)." The key to that definition is the notion of uncertainty. Expanding on that definition, The Committee of Sponsoring Organizations of the Treadway Commision (COSO) defines risk as the possibility that an event will occur and adversely affect the achievement of an objective.[5]

Embedded in COSO's definition of risk are certain key, fundamental points that must be understood before proceeding to the concepts of risk management:

- Risk begins with strategy formulation and objective setting. An organization is in business to achieve particular strategies and objectives, and risks represent the barriers to successfully achieving those objectives. Therefore, because each organization has somewhat different strategies and objectives, they will also face different types of risks.

- Risk does not represent a single point estimate (for example, the most likely outcome). Rather it represents a range of possible outcomes. Because many different outcomes are possible, the concept of a range is what creates uncertainty when understanding and evaluating risks.

- Risks may relate to preventing bad things from happening, or failing to ensure good things happen. Most people focus on preventing bad outcomes—for example, a hazard that needs to be mitigated or eliminated. While many risks do, in fact, present a threat to an organization, failure to achieve positive outcomes may also create a barrier to achievement of an objective and is also a risk.

- Risks are inherent in all aspects of life—that is, wherever uncertainty exists, one or more risks exist. The examples provided in the previous section on the history of risk illustrate how the understanding of risk has evolved. Those risks specifically associated with organizations conducting a form of business are commonly referred to as business risks. This can be thought of in quite simple terms: uncertainties related to the achievement of business objectives are considered business risks.

Using this definition of risk, the extensive number of risks that organizations face as they try to execute their strategies and achieve their objectives becomes apparent. This extensiveness can be somewhat overwhelming, which brings greater appreciation for the need to have a process to effectively understand and manage risks across an organization. This need can be addressed through ERM.

COSO ERM Framework

In the United States, COSO published its *ERM—Integrated Framework* (COSO ERM) in 2004. COSO identified a need for a robust framework to help companies effectively identify, assess, and manage risk. The resulting framework expanded on the previously issued *Internal Control–Integrated Framework*, incorporating all key aspects of that framework in the broader ERM framework.

COSO defines ERM as:

> A process, effected by an entity's board of directors, management and other personnel, applied in strategy setting and across the enterprise, designed to identify potential events that may affect the entity, and manage risk to be within its risk appetite, to provide reasonable assurance regarding the achievement of entity objectives.

COSO explains that this definition reflects certain fundamental concepts. ERM is:

- A process, ongoing and flowing through an entity.
- Effected by people at every level of an organization.
- Applied in a strategy setting.
- Applied across the enterprise, at every level and unit, and includes taking an entity-level portfolio view of risk.
- Designed to identify potential events that, if they occur, will affect the entity and to manage risks within its risk appetite.
- Able to provide reasonable assurance to an entity's management and board of directors.
- Geared to achievement of objectives in one or more separate but overlapping categories.

The ERM framework was graphically depicted as a three-dimensional matrix, in the form of a cube, recreated in Exhibit 3-6. This depiction shows the interrelationship between the objectives categories (vertical columns across the top of the cube), the components of ERM (horizontal rows), and an entity's business structure (side of the cube). It portrays the ability to focus on the entirety of an entity's ERM, or by objectives category, component, entity unit, or any subset thereof.

Categories of Objectives

Within the context of an entity's established mission or vision, management establishes strategic objectives, selects strategy, and sets aligned objectives cascading through the enterprise. This ERM framework is geared to achieving an entity's objectives in the following four categories:

Opportunity
The possibility that an event will occur and *positively* affect the achievement of objectives.

- **Strategic.** High-level goals, aligned with and supporting its mission.
- **Operations.** Effective and efficient use of its resources.
- **Reporting.** Reliability of reporting (both external and internal).
- **Compliance.** Compliance with applicable laws and regulations.

This categorization of entity objectives allows a focus on separate aspects of ERM. These distinct but overlapping categories—a particular objective can fall into more than one category—address different entity needs and may be the direct responsibility of different executives.

Because objectives relating to reliability of reporting and compliance with laws and regulations are within the entity's control, ERM can be expected to provide reasonable assurance of achieving those objectives. Achievement of strategic and operations objectives, however, may be subject to external events not always within the entity's control. Accordingly, for these objectives, ERM can provide reasonable assurance that management, and the board in its oversight role, are made aware, in a timely manner, of the extent to which the entity is moving toward achievement of the objectives.

Components of ERM

ERM consists of eight interrelated components. These are derived from the way management runs an enterprise and are integrated with the management process. These components are:

- **Internal Environment.** Management sets a philosophy regarding risk and establishes a risk appetite. The internal environment encompasses the tone of an organization, and sets the basis for how risk and control are viewed and addressed by an entity's people. The core of any business is its people—their individual attributes, including integrity, ethical values, and competence—and the environment in which they operate.

  The internal environment is the basis for all other components of ERM, providing discipline and structure. It influences how strategies and objectives are established, business activities are structured, and risks are identified, assessed, and acted upon. It also influences the design and functioning of control activities, information and communication systems, and monitoring activities.

  The internal environment is influenced by an entity's history and culture. It comprises many elements, including:

  - **Risk management philosophy.** The set of shared beliefs and attitudes characterizing how the entity considers risk in everything it does.
  - **Risk appetite.** The amount of risk, on a broad level, an entity is willing to accept.
  - **Board of directors.** The structure, experience, independence, and oversight role played by the entity's primary governing body.

Objectives
What an entity desires to achieve. When referring to what an organization wants to achieve, these are called business objectives, and may be classified as strategic, operational, reporting, and compliance.

EXHIBIT 3-6

Copyright 2004 by The Committee of Sponsoring Organizations of the Treadway Commission. Reproduced with permission from the American Institute of Certified Public Accountants acting as authorized copyright administrator for COSO.

Enterprise Risk Management

A process, effected by an entity's board of directors, management, and other personnel, applied in strategy setting and across the enterprise, designed to identify potential events that may affect the entity, and manage risk to be within its risk appetite, to provide reasonable assurance regarding the achievement of entity objectives.

- **Integrity and ethical values.** Preferences, standards of behavior, and style.
- **Commitment to competence.** Knowledge and skills needed to perform assigned tasks.
- **Organizational structure.** A framework to plan, execute, control, and monitor activities.
- **Assignment of authority and responsibility.** The degree to which individuals and teams are authorized and encouraged to use initiative to address issues and solve problems, as well as limits to their authority.
- **Human resource standards.** Practices pertaining to hiring, orientating, training, evaluating, counseling, promoting, compensating, and taking remedial actions.
- **Objective Setting.** Objectives are set at the strategic level, establishing a basis for operations, reporting, and compliance objectives. Every entity faces a variety of risks from external and internal sources, and a precondition to effective event identification, risk assessment, and risk response is establishment of objectives.

  Objectives are aligned with the entity's risk appetite, which drives risk tolerance levels for the entity. Risk tolerances are the acceptable levels of size and variation relative to the achievement of objectives, and must align with the risk appetite.

- **Event Identification.** Management identifies potential events that, if they occur, will affect the entity, and determines whether these events represent opportunities or whether they might adversely affect the entity's ability to successfully implement strategy and achieve objectives. Events with negative impact represent risks, which require management's assessment and response. Events with positive impact represent opportunities, which management channels back into the strategy and objective-setting processes. When identifying events, management considers a variety of internal and external factors that may give rise to risks and opportunities, in the context of the full risk scope of the organization.

  External factors, along with examples of related events, include:

  - **Economic.** Price movements, capital availability, or lower barriers to competitive entry.
  - **Natural environment.** Flood, fire, earthquake, or weather-related events.
  - **Political**. Election of government officials with new political agendas, or enactment of new laws and regulations.
  - **Social**. Changing demographics, social mores, family structures, or work/life priorities.
  - **Technological**. New means of electronic commerce, storage, or processing.

  Internal factors, along with examples of related events, include:

  - **Infrastructure**. Increasing capital allocation to preventive maintenance or call center support.
  - **Personnel**. Workplace accidents, fraudulent activities, or labor agreement expiration.
  - **Process**. Process modifications, process execution errors, or outsourcing decisions.
  - **Technology**. Increasing resources to handle volume volatility, security breaches, or systems downtime.

- **Risk Assessment.** Risk assessment allows an entity to consider the extent to which potential events have an impact on achievement of objectives. Management assesses events from two perspectives—likelihood and impact—and normally uses a combination of qualitative and quantitative methods. The impact of potential events should be examined, individually or by category, across the entity. Risks are assessed on both an inherent and residual basis.

  In simplest terms, inherent risk represents the "gross" risk while residual risk is the "net" risk. Inherent risk is the risk to an entity in the absence of any actions management might take to alter either the risk's likelihood or impact. These risks may be inherent in the entity's business model or relate to decisions management

Strategic Objectives
What an entity desires to achieve through the value creation choices management makes on behalf of the organization's stakeholders.

has made regarding how to operate and execute that business model. Residual risk is the risk that remains after management's response to the risk (for example, to reduce or transfer the risk). Risk assessment should be applied first to inherent risks. Once the risk responses have been developed, management then considers residual risk (relative to the organization's risk appetite).

There are many different ways to assess the impact and likelihood of risks, ranging from obtaining the overall judgments and perspectives of individuals, to benchmarking against other companies, to running sophisticated probabilistic models. Regardless of which option, or combination of options, is used, it is important that the assessment also consider the relationships between risks. That is, the realistic worst-case impact and likelihood of risk events may be dependent on how combinations of risks interrelate; assessing each risk on its own may overlook realistic worst-case scenarios that the entity needs to consider.

- **Risk Response.** Having assessed relevant risks, management determines how it will respond. Responses fall within four categories: risk avoidance, reduction, sharing, and acceptance.

  - **Avoidance.** Exiting or divesting of the activities giving rise to the risk. Risk avoidance may involve exiting a product line, declining expansion to a new geographical market, or selling a division.

  - **Reduction.** Action is taken to reduce risk likelihood or impact, or both. This typically involves any of a myriad of everyday business decisions, such as implementing controls.

  - **Sharing.** Reducing risk likelihood or impact by transferring or otherwise sharing a portion of the risk. Common techniques include purchasing insurance products, engaging in hedging transactions, or outsourcing an activity.

  - **Acceptance.** No action is taken to affect risk likelihood or impact. In effect, the entity is willing to accept the risk at the current level rather than spend valuable resources deploying one of the other risk response options.

In considering its response, management assesses the effect on risk likelihood and impact, as well as costs and benefits, selecting a response that brings residual risk within desired risk tolerances. Management identifies any opportunities that might be available, and takes an entitywide, or portfolio, view of risk, determining whether overall residual risk is within the entity's risk appetite.

It is important to consider the portfolio effect of risk responses. In some cases, a certain risk response may not appear to be the best or most cost-effective response for a given risk. However, if that risk response helps manage other risks, the benefit to the organization may justify the selection of that particular option. By looking at risks from a portfolio perspective, management can best ensure that risks are optimally managed within the entity's established risk appetite.

- **Control Activities.** Control activities are the policies and procedures that help ensure that management's risk responses are carried out. While control activities are most commonly associated with risk reduction strategies, certain control activities may also be necessary when executing one of the other risk responses as well. Control activities occur throughout the organization, at all levels and in all functions. They are classified in a variety of ways and include a range of activities that may be preventive or detective, manual or automated, and at the process level or the management level. Examples of commonly used control activities include:

  - **Top-level reviews.** Controls executed at the entity level, such as performance against budget reviews, updated forecasts, monitoring of competitor actions, or cost containment initiatives.

  - **Direct functional or activity management.** Controls executed by managers running specific functions or activities, such as reviewing performance reports for the area or overseeing the execution of detailed level controls (for example, reconciliations).

  - **Information processing.** Controls designed to check the accuracy, completeness, and authorization of transactions. Additionally, this area includes general infrastructure controls, such as physical and logical security; controls over systems implementation, upgrades, or modifications; disaster recovery; and systems operations controls.

  - **Physical controls.** These include physical counts of cash, securities, inventories, equipment, or other fixed assets, and comparing those counts with amounts recorded in the books and records.

  - **Performance indicators.** Analyzing and following up on deviations from expected or targeted performance norms.

  - **Segregation of duties.** Separating the duties of different people to reduce the risk of error or fraud. For example, different people would perform the establishment of a new vendor in the system, authorization of a transaction to pay that vendor, and physical processing of the check that disburses funds to the vendor.

- **Information and Communication.** Pertinent information is identified, captured, and communicated in a form and time frame that enable people to carry out their responsibilities. Information must be in sufficient depth consistent with an entity's need to identify, assess, and respond to risk, and remain within its risk tolerance. Information systems use internally generated data and information from external sources, providing information for managing risks and making informed decisions relative to objectives. Finally, information must be of sufficient quality to support decision-making. The quality of information relates to the following:

  - Content is appropriate and at the right level of detail.

Risk Response

An action or set of actions taken by management to achieve a desired risk management strategy. Risk responses can be categorized as risk avoidance, reduction, sharing, or acceptance.

- Information is timely and available when needed.

- Information is current, reflecting the most recent financial or operational information.

- Information is accurate and reliable.

- Information is accessible to those who need it.

Effective communication also occurs, flowing down, across, and up the organization. All personnel receive a clear message from top management that ERM responsibilities must be taken seriously. They understand their own role in ERM, as well as how individual activities relate to the work of others. They must have a means of communicating significant information upstream. There is also effective communication with external parties, such as customers, suppliers, regulators, and shareholders.

Communications may take different forms, such as policy manuals, memoranda, e-mails, bulletin board notices, and video messages. When messages are transmitted orally, tone of voice and body language may influence how messages are interpreted.

- **Monitoring**. ERM is monitored—assessing the presence and functioning of its components over time. This type of back-end control activity is accomplished through ongoing monitoring activities, separate evaluations, or a combination of the two. Ongoing monitoring occurs in the normal course of management activities. The scope and frequency of separate evaluations will depend primarily on an assessment of risks and the effectiveness of ongoing monitoring procedures. ERM deficiencies are reported upstream, with serious matters reported to top management and the board.

  In addition to management's ongoing monitoring activities, other individuals may be involved in the monitoring process. For example, individuals responsible for the performance of key activities may perform self-assessments to evaluate the effectiveness of their risk management activities. Internal auditors typically are part of the overall monitoring system, whereby the results of individual audits help assess the effectiveness of the related risk management activities. In certain circumstances, the work performed by the outside independent auditors may also influence management's assessment of ongoing risk management effectiveness.

In essence, the components of ERM provide an outline for answering some common, everyday questions that summarize risk management thinking:

1. What are we trying to accomplish (that is, what are our objectives)?

2. What could stop us from accomplishing it (that is, what are the risks, how bad could they be, and how likely are they to occur)?

3. What can we do to make sure those things don't happen (that is, what are the risk management options or strategies)?

4. Do we have the ability to execute those things (that is, have we

---

Control Activities

Any action taken by management, the board, and other parties to manage risk and increase the likelihood that established objectives will be achieved. Management plans, organizes, and directs the performance of sufficient actions to provide reasonable assurance that objectives will be achieved.

designed control activities, and can we execute those activities to carry out the risk strategies)?

5. How will we know that we have accomplished what we wanted to accomplish (that is, does the information exist to evidence success, and can we monitor performance to verify that success)?

These five questions apply to more than just risk management in the business world. They can apply to almost any objective or decision in life. Answering these questions instills a risk management-based type of thinking and discipline that aligns with COSO ERM and other risk management frameworks.

Roles and Responsibilities in ERM

The board of directors, management, risk officers, financial officers, internal auditors, and indeed, every individual within an entity contribute to effective ERM. The roles and responsibilities of each of these groups align with those discussed in the governance section earlier in this chapter.

- **The board of directors.** The board provides oversight and direction to an entity's management. The board can play a role in strategy setting, formulating high-level objectives, broad-based resource allocation, and shaping the ethical environment. The board provides oversight with regards to ERM by:

    - Knowing the extent to which management has established effective ERM in an organization.

    - Being aware of and concurring with the entity's risk appetite.

    - Reviewing the entity's portfolio view of risk and considering it against the entity's risk appetite.

    - Being apprised of the most significant risks and whether management is responding appropriately.

    The board is also part of the internal environment component of ERM and must have the requisite composition and focus for ERM to be effective. Typically, the board will exercise its responsibilities through its various committees, such as an audit committee and a nominating and governance committee.

- **Management.** Management is responsible for all activities of an entity, including ERM. However, these responsibilities will vary, depending on the level in the organization and the entity's characteristics.

    The chief executive officer (CEO) has ultimate ownership responsibility of ERM. One of the most important aspects of this responsibility is ensuring the presence of a positive internal environment. The CEO sets the tone at the top, influences the composition and conduct of the board, provides leadership and direction to senior managers, and monitors the entity's overall risk activities in relation to its risk appetite. Where evolving circumstances, emerging risks, strategy implementation, or anticipated actions indicate potential misalignment with risk appetite, the CEO will take the necessary action to reestablish alignment.

Monitoring
A process that assesses the presence and functioning of governance, risk management, and control components over time.

Senior managers in charge of organizational units have responsibility for managing risks related to their units' objectives. They convert strategy into operations, identify events and assess risks, and effect risk responses. Managers guide application of ERM components within their spheres of responsibility, ensuring application consistent with risk tolerances. They usually assign responsibility for specific ERM procedures to managers in specific processes, functions, or departments. Accordingly, these managers usually play a more hands-on role in devising and executing particular risk procedures that address unit objectives, such as techniques for event identification and risk assessment, and in determining responses, for example, developing protocols for purchasing goods or accepting new customers.

Staff functions, such as human resources, compliance, or legal, also have important supporting roles in designing or shaping effective ERM components. These functions may design and implement programs that help manage certain key risks across the entire organization.

- **Risk Officer.** Some organizations have established a centralized coordinating point to facilitate ERM. A risk officer—referred to in some organizations as a CRO or risk manager—typically operates in a staff function, working with other managers in establishing ERM in their areas of responsibility. The risk officer has the resources to help effect ERM across subsidiaries, businesses, departments, functions, and activities. This individual may have responsibility for monitoring risk management progress and for assisting other managers in reporting relevant risk information up, down, and across the entity. Specific responsibilities of a risk officer may include:

  - Establishing ERM policies, defining roles and responsibilities, and setting goals for implementation.

  - Framing authority and accountability for ERM in business units.

  - Promoting an ERM competence throughout the entity.

  - Guiding integration of ERM with other business planning and management activities.

  - Establishing a common risk management language that includes measures around likelihood and impact, and risk categories.

  - Facilitating managers' development of reporting protocols, including quantitative and qualitative thresholds, and monitoring the reporting process.

  - Reporting to the CEO on progress and outliers and recommending action as needed.

- **Financial Executives.** Finance and controllership executives and their staffs are responsible for activities that cut across the organization. These executives often are involved in developing entitywide budgets and plans, and tracking and analyzing performance, from an operations, compliance, and reporting perspective. They play an important role in preventing and detecting fraudulent reporting, and influence the design, implementation, and monitoring of the organization's reporting system.

- **Internal Auditors.** The internal audit function plays a key role in evaluating the effectiveness of—and recommending improvements to—ERM. Standards established by The IIA specify that the scope of the internal audit function should encompass risk management and control systems. This includes evaluating the reliability of reporting, effectiveness and efficiency of operations, and compliance with laws and regulations. In carrying out these responsibilities, the internal audit function assists management and the board by examining, evaluating, reporting on, and recommending improvements to the adequacy and effectiveness of the entity's ERM.

- **Other Entity Personnel.** ERM is, to some degree, the responsibility of everyone in an entity and therefore should be an explicit or implicit part of everyone's job description. This is true because:

  - Virtually all personnel play some role in effecting ERM, ranging from producing information used in identifying or assessing risks, to taking actions needed to manage those risks.

  - All personnel are responsible for supporting information and communication flows inherent in ERM.

  Although some of the executives mentioned above may be considered owners of certain risks, typically an organization's risk owners are individuals with management responsibilities from throughout the organization.

- **External Auditors.** Outside independent auditors can provide management and the board of directors a unique, independent, and objective view that can contribute to an entity's achievement of its external financial reporting objectives, as well as other objectives. External audit findings relating to risk management deficiencies, analytical information, and other recommendations for improvement can all provide management with valuable information to enhance its risk management program.

- **Legislators and Regulators.** Legislators and regulators can affect the ERM of many entities, either through requirements to establish risk management mechanisms or systems of internal controls (for example, the U.S. Sarbanes-Oxley Act of 2002) or through examinations of particular entities (for example, by federal and state bank examiners). Legislators and regulators may establish rules that provide the impetus for management to ensure that risk management and control systems meet minimum statutory and regulatory requirements. Also, pursuant to a regulatory examination, they provide information useful to the entity in applying ERM, and recommendations or directives to management regarding needed improvements.

- **Other External Parties.** Finally, others may impact an entity's ERM activities:

- Customers, vendors, business partners, and others who conduct business with an entity are an important source of information used in ERM.

- Creditors can provide oversight or direction influencing how organizations achieve their objectives. For example, debt covenants may require companies to monitor and report information differently than they otherwise might.

- Financial analysts, rating agencies, news media, and other external parties can influence risk management activities. Their investigative and monitoring activities can provide insights on how others perceive the entity's performance, industry and economic risks, innovative operating or financing strategies, and industry trends. Management must consider the insights and observations of these parties and, if necessary, adjust the corresponding risk management activities.

- Outsource service providers are becoming a more prevalent way for companies to delegate their day-to-day management of certain non-core functions. Although the external parties discussed above may directly influence an organization's ERM activities, using outside service providers may result in a different set of risks and responses than if the organization did not outsource any functions. These external parties may execute activities on behalf of the entity; however, management cannot abdicate its responsibility to manage the associated risks and, thus, should establish a program to monitor outsourced activities. Refer to Chapter 4, "Business Processes and Business Risks," where business process outsourcing is discussed in greater detail.

Formal ERM is not yet embedded in the business practices of most organizations, but there is a growing trend to either implement ERM or at least practice many of its key principles. COSO ERM lists potential value drivers from ERM:

- Aligning risk appetite and strategic planning.

- Enhancing risk response decisions.

- Reducing operational surprises and losses.

- Identifying and managing cross-enterprise risks.

- Providing integrated responses to multiple risks.

- Improving deployment of capital.

Other Frameworks

Although COSO ERM is widely recognized within the United States, other countries have developed their own frameworks. As indicated in Appendix 3-B, "Summary of Governance Codes from Other Countries," business conditions and regulatory initiatives have resulted in a variety of codes and regulations to meet the needs of the local capital markets and businesses. While all of these frameworks are fundamentally similar to COSO ERM, each of them has unique characteristics that readers are encouraged to study. Certain frameworks will prove to be more intuitive to some individuals than others.

Independent Outside Auditor

A registered public accounting firm, hired by the organization's board or executive management, to perform a financial statement audit providing assurance for which the firm issues a written attestation report that expresses an opinion about whether the financial statements are fairly presented in accordance with applicable generally accepted accounting principles.

THE ROLE OF THE INTERNAL AUDIT FUNCTION IN ERM

Internal auditors typically possess skill sets and have broad experience levels that lend themselves to playing a valuable role in ERM. In fact, considering the broad purview of most internal audit functions, as well as their role in the overall monitoring process, failure to involve the internal audit function in some manner would likely result in the ERM initiative falling short of expectations. The following discussion focuses on the role that the internal audit function can play in ERM, depending on whether or not the organization is formally implementing ERM.

Organizations With ERM

The IIA published a position paper in September 2004, "The Role of Internal Audit in Enterprise-wide Risk Management," which outlines several opportunities for the internal audit function to be involved. In its summary, the paper states, "Internal auditing's core role with regard to ERM is to provide objective assurance to the board on the effectiveness of an organization's ERM activities to help ensure key business risks are being managed appropriately and that the system of internal control is operating effectively."

The position paper depicts the various roles that the internal audit function could or should not undertake in a fan- or dial-shaped diagram, as shown in Exhibit 3-7. The following types of roles are discussed in the paper.[7]

Core Internal Audit Roles. These roles, which are on the left of the dial in Exhibit 3-7, represent assurance activities. They are part of the wider objective of giving assurance on risk management.

- Giving assurance on risk management processes.
- Giving assurance that risks are correctly evaluated.
- Evaluating risk management processes.
- Evaluating the reporting of key risks.
- Reviewing the management of key risks.

Legitimate Internal Audit Roles With Safeguards. These roles represent consulting services that may improve the organization's governance, risk management, and control processes. The extent of such services will depend on the other resources available to the board and on the risk maturity of the organization. The consulting roles are shown in the middle of the dial in Exhibit 3-7. In general, the further to the right of the dial that the internal audit function ventures, the greater the safeguards that are required to ensure that its independence and objectivity are maintained.

- Facilitating identification and evaluation of risks.
- Coaching management in responding to risks.
- Coordinating ERM activities.
- Consolidating the reporting on risks.
- Maintaining and developing the ERM framework.

- Championing establishment of ERM.
- Developing risk management strategy for board approval.

Roles Internal Auditing Should Not Undertake. These roles, which are depicted on the right of the dial in Exhibit 3-7, should not be undertaken by the internal audit function as the roles represent management responsibilities that would impair the internal auditors' independence and objectivity.

- Setting the risk appetite.
- Imposing risk management processes.
- Being the sole source for management's assurance that risks are effectively managed (this would be considered the same as the internal audit function performing a management function).
- Taking decisions on risk responses.
- Implementing risk responses on management's behalf.
- Accountability for risk management.

When determining the role the internal audit function plays in ERM, the chief audit executive (CAE) must evaluate whether each activity raises any threats to the internal audit function's independence or objectivity. It is important that the organization fully understands that management remains responsible for risk management. As the internal audit function extends its roles further to the right of the dial, the following safeguards should be put in place:

- It should be clear that management remains responsible for risk management.
- The nature of the internal audit function's responsibilities should be documented in the audit charter and approved by the audit committee.
- The internal audit function cannot manage any of the risks on behalf of management.
- The internal audit function should provide advice, challenge, and support to management's decision making, as opposed to making risk management decisions itself.
- The internal audit function cannot give objective assurance on any part of the ERM framework for which it is responsible. Such assurance should be provided by other suitably qualified parties, whether internal or external to the organization.
- Any work beyond the assurance activities should be recognized as a consulting engagement, and the implementation standards related to such engagements should be followed.

Organizations With Internal Audit-driven ERM

Practice Advisory 2100-4, Internal Auditing's Role in Organizations Without a Risk Management Process, relates to Standard 2100 which

---

Reasonable Assurance

A level of assurance that is supported by generally accepted audit procedures and judgments. Reasonable assurance can apply to judgments surrounding the effectiveness of internal controls, the mitigation of risks, achievement of objectives, or other engagement-related conclusions.

EXHIBIT 3-7

INTERNAL AUDIT'S ROLE IN ENTERPRISE RISK MANAGEMENT

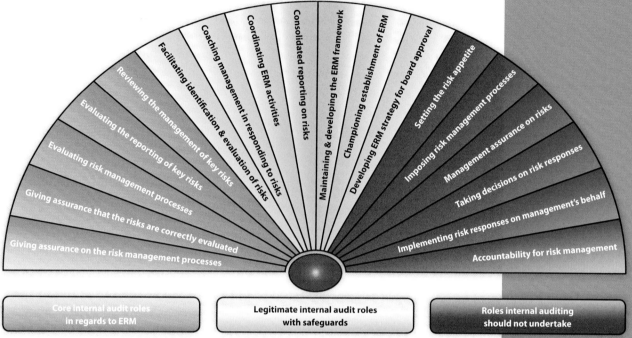

Core internal audit roles in regards to ERM

Legitimate internal audit roles with safeguards

Roles internal auditing should not undertake

This diagram is taken from "Position Statement: The Role of Internal Auditing in Enterprise-wide Risk Management," reproduced with the permission of the Institute of Internal Auditors – United Kingdom and Ireland. For the full statement visit, www.iia.org.uk. © The Institute of Internal Auditors – UK and Ireland Ltd., July 2004

states, "The internal audit activity should evaluate and contribute to the improvement of risk management, control, and governance processes using a systematic and disciplined approach." The following practice advisory provides the following broad guidance for internal auditors:

> Internal auditors should assist both management and the audit committee by examining, evaluating, reporting, and recommending improvements on the adequacy and effectiveness of management's risk processes. Management and the board are responsible for their organization's risk management and control processes. However, internal auditors acting in a consulting role can assist the organization in identifying, evaluating, and implementing risk management methodologies and controls to address those risks."

When an organization has not established a risk management process, the practice advisory offers the following guidance:

● The internal auditor should bring the lack of a risk management process to management's attention along with suggestions for establishing such a process. The internal auditor should seek direction from management and the board as to the audit activity's role in risk management. The charters for the audit activity and audit committee should document the role of each in the risk management process.

- If requested, internal auditors can play a proactive role in assisting with the initial establishment of a risk management process for the organization. A more proactive role supplements traditional assurance activities with a consultative approach to improving fundamental processes. If such assistance exceeds normal assurance and consulting activities conducted by internal auditors, independence could be impaired. In these situations, internal auditors should comply with the disclosure requirements of the *International Standards for the Professional Practice of Internal Auditing*.

THE IMPACT OF ERM ON INTERNAL AUDIT ASSURANCE

Standard 2010 on planning states, "The chief audit executive should establish risk-based plans to determine the priorities of the audit activity, consistent with the organization's goals." Supporting this standard, Practice Advisory 2010-2, Linking the Audit Plan to Risk and Exposures, notes that "The organization's risk strategy should be reflected in the design of the internal audit activity's plan. A coordinated approach should be applied to leverage synergies between the organization's risk management and internal audit processes."

This practice advisory offers the following relative to linking the audit plan to risk and exposures:

- The audit plan should be designed based on an assessment of risk and exposures that may affect the organization. Ultimately, key audit objectives are to provide management with information to mitigate the negative consequences associated with accomplishing the organization's objectives, as well as an assessment of the effectiveness of management's risk management activities.

- The audit universe can include components from the organization's strategic plan. By incorporating components of the organization's strategic plan, the audit universe will consider and reflect the overall business objectives. Strategic plans also likely reflect the organization's attitude toward risk and the degree of difficulty to achieving planned objectives. The audit universe will normally be influenced by the results of the risk management process. The organization's strategic plan should have been created considering the environment in which the organization operates. These same environmental factors will likely impact the audit universe and assessment of relative risk.

- Changes in management direction, objectives, emphasis, and focus should be reflected in updates to the audit universe and related audit plan. It is advisable to assess the audit universe on at least an annual basis to reflect the most current strategies and direction of the organization. In some situations, audit plans may need to be updated frequently (for example, quarterly) in response to changes in the organization's environment or management activities.

- Audit work schedules should be based on, among other factors, an assessment of risk priority and exposure. Prioritizing is needed to make decisions for applying relative resources based on the significance of risk and exposure. A variety of risk models exist to assist the CAE in prioritizing potential audit subject areas. Most risk models use risk factors to establish the priority of engagements such as: financial impact, asset liquidity, management competence, quality of internal controls, degree of change or stability, time of last audit engagement, complexity, and employee and government relations. In conducting audit engagements, methods and techniques for testing and validating exposures should reflect the risk severity and likelihood of occurrence.

- Management reporting and communication should convey risk management conclusions and recommendations to reduce exposures. For management to fully understand the degree of exposure, it is critical that audit reporting identify the criticality and consequence of the risk exposure to achieving objectives.

The points above, which apply at the level of establishing an annual audit plan, are also relevant at the audit engagement level. For example, the scope and approach to an individual project will be influenced by:

- How risks at the process level relate to the strategic plans and objectives of the organization. Process-level risks are discussed in greater detail in Chapter 10, "Conducting the Assurance Engagement."

- Changes in the process (for example, objectives, procedures, personnel, and performance measures) that have occurred over the last year or since the last audit of the process.

- Relevant risk model factors, (for example, financial impact and asset liquidity).

- The severity and likelihood of the process-level risks.

In summary, management's approach to risk management, regardless of whether or not an organization has implemented ERM, will have a significant influence on both the internal audit charter and annual audit plan.

EXHIBIT 3-8

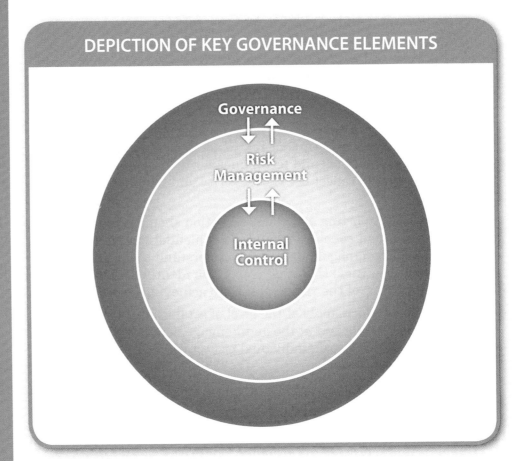

DEPICTION OF KEY GOVERNANCE ELEMENTS

Governance

Risk Management

Internal Control

SUMMARY

Organizations must take great care to implement effective governance structures and risk management approaches. The governance structure provides direction to those executing the day-to-day activities of managing the risks inherent in an organization's business model. These activities must be monitored to ensure consistent operation. The three elements of governance can be depicted as shown in Exhibit 3-8.

Governance involves a set of relationships between an organization's management, its board, and its stakeholders. The board typically provides the "umbrella" of governance direction, authority, and oversight. The board must understand and strive to meet the needs and expectations of the organization's various stakeholders. Thus, the board must articulate its direction, advise on the creation of business objectives, establish boundaries of business conduct, and empower management to carry out its direction. Management executes its risk management activities to fulfill the direction of the board. These activities may be carried out by lower-level risk owners in the organization, but senior management is ultimately accountable for the effectiveness of risk management activities. Finally, internal and external auditors carry out activities that can provide levels of assurance to management and the board regarding the effectiveness of risk management activities.

ERM is a process, affected by the board, management, and other personnel, applied in a strategy setting and across the enterprise, designed to identify potential events that may affect an organization's ability to achieve its objectives and manage risks to be within its risk appetite.

An organization's objectives may be strategic, operational, reporting, or compliance oriented. ERM can be assessed across several components: internal environment, objective setting, event identification, risk assessment, risk response, control activities, information and communication, and monitoring.

Internal auditors typically possess skill sets and have broad experience levels that lend themselves to playing a valuable role in ERM. The internal audit function may take on a variety of roles relative to ERM, some of which are consistent with the assurance activities as outlined in its charter, and some of which may be consulting services provided to assist the organization in improving its governance, risk management, and control processes. However, an internal audit function must establish appropriate safeguards to ensure that it does not take on roles that could be equivalent to management's responsibilities, thus impairing independence and objectivity of internal auditors.

An organization's strategic plan and inherent risks will have a direct and profound impact on both the charter of an internal audit function as well as its annual audit plans. Changes in management direction, objectives, emphasis, and focus may also impact the annual internal audit plan. The CAE must consider risks when prioritizing and scheduling the upcoming internal audit engagements.

1. Why are there arrows flowing in both directions between the different elements of governance depicted in Exhibit 3-2?

2. What is the difference between the two areas of governance depicted in Exhibit 3-3?

3. What are the three different types of stakeholders that the board must understand? Give examples of each type.

4. What are the key responsibilities of senior management in governance?

5. What role does the internal audit function play in governance?

6. What is the definition of risk used by the Committee of Sponsoring Organizations of the Treadway Commission (COSO)?

7. According to COSO, what are the fundamental concepts in its definition of enterprise risk management (ERM)?

8. What are the eight components of the COSO *Enterprise Risk Management– Integrated Framework* (COSO ERM)?

9. What are typical responsibilities of a chief risk officer?

10. What roles in ERM should the internal audit function not undertake?

11. According to IIA Practice Advisory 2010-2, Linking the Audit Plan to Risk and Exposures, how should the internal audit function's audit plan be determined?

Select the best answer for each of the following questions.

1. Which of the following is not an appropriate governance role for an organization's board of directors?

    a. Evaluating and approving strategic objectives.

    b. Influencing the risk-taking philosophy.

    c. Providing assurances directly to third parties that the organization's governance processes are effective.

    d. Establishing broad boundaries of conduct, outside of which the organization should not operate.

2. Which of the following are typically governance responsibilities of senior management?

    I.   Delegating risk tolerance levels to risk managers.

    II. Establishing monitoring activities to determine whether expected outcomes have occurred.

    III. Establishing a governance committee of the board.

    IV. Ensuring that sufficient information is gathered to support reporting to the board.

a. I and IV.

b. II and III.

c. I, II, and IV.

d. II, III, and IV.

e. I, II, III, and IV.

3. According to COSO ERM, all of the following are elements of an entity's internal environment except for:

   a. Setting organizational objectives.

   b. Establishing risk appetite.

   c. Developing human resource standards.

   d. Assigning authority and responsibility.

   e. Having predominantly independent directors on the board.

4. Which of the following is not an example of a risk-sharing strategy?

   a. Outsourcing a non-core, high-risk area.

   b. Selling a non-strategic business unit.

   c. Hedging against interest rate fluctuations.

   d. Buying an insurance policy to protect against adverse weather.

5. Who is responsible for implementing ERM?

   a. The chief financial officer.

   b. The chief internal auditor.

   c. The chief compliance officer.

   d. The external auditor.

   e. Management throughout the organization.

6. Which of the following is not a potential value driver for implementing ERM?

   a. Financial results will improve in the short run.

   b. There will be fewer surprises from year-to-year.

   c. There will be better information available to make risk decisions.

   d. An organization's risk appetite can be aligned with strategic planning.

   e. Critical assets can be deployed more effectively.

7. Which of the following is the best reason for the chief audit executive (CAE) to consider the organization's strategic plan in developing the annual audit plan?

   a. To emphasize the importance of the internal audit function to the organization.

b. To ensure that the internal audit plan will be approved by senior management.

c. To make recommendations to improve the strategic plan.

d. To ensure that the internal audit plan supports the overall business objectives.

e. To provide assurance that the strategic plan is consistent with the organization's values.

8. When senior management accepts a level of residual risk that the CAE believes is unacceptable to the organization, the CAE should:

a. Report the unacceptable risk level immediately to the chair of the audit committee and the external audit partner.

b. Resign his or her position in the organization.

c. Discuss the matter with knowledgeable members of senior management and, if not resolved, take it to the audit committee.

d. Notify the appropriate regulatory agency (for example, securities commission).

e. Accept senior management's position because it establishes the risk appetite for the organization.

9. The CAE is asked to conduct the enterprise risk assessment as part of an organization's implementation of ERM. Which of the following would be least effective in protecting the internal audit function's independence and the objectivity of its internal auditors from perceived impairment?

a. A cross section of management is involved in assessing the impact and likelihood of each risk.

b. Risk owners are assigned responsibility for each key risk.

c. The internal audit function defers to management when decisions are made regarding how to best manage each key risk.

d. A member of senior management presents the results of the risk assessment to the board and communicates that it represents the organization's risk profile.

e. The internal audit function obtains assistance from an outside consultant in the conduct of the formal risk assessment session.

10. An internal audit engagement was included in the approved audit plan. This is considered a moderately high risk audit based on the internal audit function's risk model. It is currently on a two year audit cycle. Which of the following will likely have the greatest impact on the scope and approach of the audit engagement?

a. The area being audited involves the processing of a high volume of transactions.

b. The process affects multiple account balances.

c. Certain components of the process are outsourced.

d. A new system was implemented during the year, which changed how the transactions are processed.

e. The total dollars processed in this area are material.

1. Describe ways in which an organization's business model may affect its approach to governance oversight.

2. Describe the difference between risk management philosophy, risk appetite, and risk tolerance. Give examples of each.

3. COSO ERM recognizes four categories of objectives (strategic, operations, reporting, and compliance). If an organization were unable to effectively manage the risks around the objectives in one of those categories, for which category would the impact on the organization *be* the greatest?

4. Define inherent risk and residual risk. Which of the two types of risk would have a greater impact on the annual internal audit plan?

5. For an organization that has not implemented ERM, describe some of the steps the internal audit function can take without impairing its independence and/or objectivity.

CASES

CASE 1

Recall the five "everyday questions" outlined earlier in this chapter that can be used to apply risk management thinking:

a. What are we trying to accomplish (that is, what are our objectives)?

b. What could stop us from accomplishing it (that is, what are the risks, how bad could they be, and how likely are they to occur)?

c. What can we do to make sure those things don't happen (that is, what are the risk management options or strategies)?

d. Do we have the ability to execute those things (that is, have we designed control activities, and can we execute those activities to carry out the risk strategies)?

e. How will we know that we have accomplished what we wanted to accomplish (that is, does the information exist to evidence success, and can we monitor performance to verify that success)?

Think about the reasons you decided to take this course and answer each of those questions with a focus on achieving your desired level of success.

CASE 2

Your organization has implemented a robust ERM program similar to the one outlined in this chapter. The audit committee has asked you to assess the design and operation of the program. Because members are familiar with COSO ERM, they would like you to assess the veracity of the ERM program relative to the eight components of ERM. Based on this request, develop a list of steps you would follow to test each of the ERM components that includes at least two work steps for each component.

REFERENCES

[1] Organization for Economic Co-operation and Development, Principles of Corporate Governance, Revised May 2004.

[2] Institute of Internal Auditors, *Enterprise-Wide Governance for Internal Auditors*, (Altamonte Springs, FL: The Institute of Internal Auditors, May 2006).

[3] Bernstein, Peter L., *Against the Gods: The Remarkable Story of Risk*, (Indianapolis, IN: John Wiley & Sons, 1996).

[4] Bernstein, Peter L., *Against the Gods: The Remarkable Story of Risk*, (Indianapolis, IN: John Wiley & Sons, 1996).

[5] The Committee of Sponsoring Organizations of the Treadway Commission, *Enterprise Risk Management–Integrated Framework*, (Jersey City, NJ: American Institute of Certified Public Accountants, September 2004).

[6] The Committee of Sponsoring Organizations of the Treadway Commission, *Enterprise Risk Management–Integrated Framework*, (Jersey City, NJ: AICPA, September 2004).

[7] Institute of Internal Auditors, The Role of Internal Audit in Enterprise-wide Risk Management, September 2004.

[8] U.S. Foreign Corrupt Practices Act, Section 78m.(b) (2)(a). Available at http://www.usdoj.gov/criminal/fraud/fcpa/fcpastat.htm.

[9] Institute of Internal Auditors Research Foundation, *Factors Affecting Corporate Governance and Audit Committees in Selected Countries*, (Altamonte Springs, FL: Institute of Internal Auditors, 2005).

[10] Bromilow, Catherine, L., Barbara L. Berlin, and Richard J. Anderson, "Stepping Up," *Internal Auditor*, December 2005.

APPENDICES

Appendix 3-A
Summary of Key U.S. Regulations

Securities Act of 1933

This U.S. piece of federal legislation was enacted after the market crash of 1929 and the ensuing Great Depression. The market crash raised some serious questions about the effectiveness of governance over the sale of securities. It was signed into law by President Franklin D. Roosevelt as part of his "New Deal" with America to bring back stability and investor confidence in the securities markets. The legislation had two main goals: (1) to ensure greater transparency in financial statements so investors can make informed decisions about securities being offered for public sale, and (2) to establish laws against deceit, misrepresentation, and other fraudulent activities in the sale of securities in the public markets.

Securities Exchange Act of 1934

The Securities Exchange Act of 1934 was created to provide governance of securities transactions on the secondary market (after issue) and regulate the different exchanges and broker-dealers to protect the investing public. From this act, the Securities and Exchange Commission (SEC) was created. The SEC's responsibility is to enforce securities laws. Primary requirements include registration of any securities listed on U.S. stock exchanges, disclosure, proxy solicitations, and margin and audit requirements. Contrasted with the Securities Act of 1933, which regulates these original issues, the Securities Exchange Act of 1934 regulates the secondary trading of those securities between persons often unrelated to the issuer. Trillions of dollars are made and lost through trading in the secondary market.

Foreign Corrupt Practices Act

Due to questionable corporate political campaign finance practices and foreign corrupt practices in the mid-1970s, the SEC and the U.S. Congress enacted campaign finance law reforms and the 1977 Foreign Corrupt Practices Act (FCPA), which criminalizes transnational bribery and requires companies to implement internal control programs. Specifically, the FCPA requires publicly traded companies to "make and keep books, records, and accounts, which, in reasonable detail, accurately and fairly reflect the transactions and dispositions of the assets of the issuer …"[8] The act, in effect, broadens the focus on internal controls to provide reasonable assurance that transactions are appropriately authorized and accurately recorded, assets are physically safeguarded, and there is periodic substantiation of recorded assets.

Report of the National Commission on Fraudulent Financial Reporting (Treadway Commission Report)

A private-sector initiative, called the National Commission on Fraudulent Financial Reporting (commonly known as the Treadway Commission) was formed in October 1985. Its mission was to identify causal factors that could lead to fraudulent financial reporting and steps to reduce the incidence of those factors. The Commission studied cases that had been brought before the SEC during the years leading up to its initial report in 1987. This report recommended that the organizations sponsoring the Commission work together to develop integrated guidance on internal control. Additionally, it had recommendations for public companies, independent public accounting firms, the SEC and others with regulatory power, and educators.

As a result of this report, the Committee of Sponsoring Organizations of the Treadway Commission (COSO) was created. COSO was composed of the American Institute of Certified Public Accountants (AICPA), American Accounting Association (AAA), Financial Executives International (FEI), The IIA, and the Institute of Management Accountants (IMA). COSO commissioned the creation of an internal control framework, which was issued in 1992, titled *Internal Control–Integrated Framework*. This framework became the only widely accepted internal control framework in the United States.

FDICIA

The U.S. Federal Deposit Insurance Corporation Improvement Act of 1991 requires FDIC insured depository institutions with assets in excess of U.S. $500 million to certify that their system of internal controls is functioning effectively. It also requires the institution's outside independent auditors to attest to management's assertions regarding the effectiveness of its system of internal controls. Many aspects of this act were later included in the U.S. Sarbanes-Oxley Act of 2002.

Sarbanes-Oxley Act of 2002

After a series of significant bankruptcies and incidents of fraudulent financial reporting at major U.S. corporations (for example, Enron Corp., Tyco, WorldCom), legislation was passed in the United States with the overall objectives of creating more accountability over the integrity of financial reporting by chief executive and chief financial officers, and restoring investor confidence in the capital markets. This legislation, the Sarbanes-Oxley Act, contained numerous sections promulgating rules and regulations on many aspects of governance for public companies. The two sections that received the most public awareness and scrutiny were Sections 302 and 404.

- Section 302 requires the chief executive and chief financial officers of public companies to certify each quarter, in connection with the company's quarterly filing of its financial results on Form 10-Q, as to the effectiveness of the disclosure controls and procedures that were in place in connection with preparing that filing.

- Section 404 requires the company to provide assertions, in connection with the annual filing of its financial results on Form 10-K, as to the effectiveness of internal controls over financial reporting. This section, in particular, requires most companies to improve the documentation and testing surrounding those internal controls to support the required assertions.

APPENDICES

U.S. Stock Exchange Listing Standards

The major stock exchanges in the United States (New York Stock Exchange (NYSE), American Stock Exchange (AMEX), and NASDAQ have promulgated certain standards that must be met by any public company that desires to be listed on those exchanges. These listing standards cover such items as: the organization and responsibilities of the board and audit committee, code of business conduct, personal loans to executives, the need for an internal audit function, and stock options.

Appendix 3-B
Summary of Governance Codes
From Other Countries

Corporate Governance Codes in General [9] [10]

Many nations have promulgated regulations or issued codes pertaining to governance principles. Following is a summary of those from certain countries.

Australia – The Corporate Governance Council of the Australian Stock Exchange (ASX) issued Principles of Good Corporate Governance and Best Practice Recommendations in 2003. This document outlines 10 essential corporate governance principles and includes recommendations regarding the composition and role of the audit committee. The ASX recommends that audit committees be composed of nonexecutive directors, a majority of whom are independent, and that the audit committee's role include, among other things, assessing the performance and objectivity of the internal audit function, reviewing results of risk management and internal compliance and control systems, and assessing whether external reporting is consistent with audit committee members' information and knowledge and is adequate for shareholder needs.

Canada – Canadian Securities Administrators issued rules to improve investor confidence in early 2004. The rules mandate an independent audit committee, require written committee charters, authorize audit committees to communicate directly with internal audit functions, and cover a variety of other issues.

China – The China Securities Regulatory Commission, Code of Corporate Governance for Listed Companies in China (2001), requires at least one-third of board members to be independent directors, and its rules provide for the optional appointment of an audit committee. If an audit committee is established, a majority of its members must be independent, and at least one independent director must be an accounting expert. The committee's principal responsibilities should include supervision of the internal audit function.

France – L'Autorite des Marches Financiers (AMF) established new obligations in 2003 with respect to the information to be given at shareholders' meetings, including work methods of the board of directors and the internal control procedures for the company. The internal audit function is required to present to shareholders' meetings a report relative to the established procedures where they concern accounting and financial information. Listed companies should publish relevant information. In 2007, the AMF issued a reference framework for internal control, which includes an application guide.

Germany – A government commission appointed by the Ministry of Justice adopted the German Corporate Governance Code (Kodex) in February 2002. In July 2002, the Transparency and Disclosure Act was passed, requiring companies to publish an annual statement of compliance or noncompliance with the code's recommendations. The code, which has been amended since it was originally published, recommends the establishment of audit committees to deal with issues of accounting, auditing, and risk management.

Hong Kong – The Rules Governing the Listing of Securities on the Stock Exchange of Hong Kong Limited and The Rules Governing the Listing of Securities on the Growth Enterprise Market of the Stock Exchange of Hong Kong Limited require listed companies to establish an audit committee composed of nonexecutive directors, a majority of whom are independent. The audit committee should have clear terms of reference, including oversight of the financial reporting system and internal controls procedures. For issuers with an internal audit function, the audit committee should review and monitor its effectiveness and ensure it has adequate resources and appropriate standing. The rules also require directors to report to shareholders annually on whether they have conducted a review of the effectiveness of the system of internal controls and, if not, the reasons why.

Italy – The Corporate Governance Code issued by Borsa Italiana in 2006 significantly changed the 2002 version of the code. In particular, it requires the establishment of an internal control committee made up of nonexecutive directors (the majority of whom need to meet additional independence requirements), and the appointment of an executive director position (one of the managing directors) specifically responsible for internal controls. The internal controls committee is a distinct committee from the Board of Auditors, which oversees the auditing of financial statements. An internal audit function is also required.

Japan – The Standards and Implementation Standards for Evaluation and Auditing of Internal Control Over Financial Reporting were issued in early 2007. These standards, which support the Japanese Financial Instruments and Exchange Law, require all listed companies to submit internal control reports on a consolidated basis. Management must evaluate and report on the sufficiency of internal control over financial reporting.

Mexico – The Securities Market Law, Ley del Mercado de Valores, was last updated in 2004. It requires listed companies to establish an audit committee with a majority of independent directors. The Mexican Securities and Banking Commission recommends that all public companies adopt its Code of Best

APPENDICES

Practices, which recommends the size, role, and responsibilities of the audit committee. Among those responsibilities are assisting the board in reviewing financial information for external reporting and helping to oversee internal control systems and to evaluate their effectiveness.

The Netherlands – The Dutch Corporate Governance Code, issued in 2003, recommends practices for the supervisory board and the audit committee. The supervisory board should supervise the operation of the internal risk management and control systems. To give the code more corporate governance structure, the committee proposes that listed companies that fail to adhere to certain aspects of the code must state the reasons for this noncompliance in their annual report (the "comply or explain" principle).

Russia – A Corporate Behavior Code was developed through the efforts of regulators, the business community, and professional advisers and recommended by the government in November 2001. The Federal Commission for Financial Markets in April 2002 recommended the code for adoption by all regulated exchanges and listed companies. Compliance is voluntary. The code recommends the establishment of an audit committee for purposes of implementing and monitoring controls over an organization's financial and business activities. The code also recommends that the audit committee consist solely of independent directors.

South Africa – The King Report on Corporate Governance (King II Report), issued in 2002, focuses on board and audit committee practices and their conduct to improve governance. The role, function, and reporting requirements of internal auditing are specifically covered. Audit committees are required to concur in the appointment and dismissal of the chief audit executive (CAE). The report also recommends that internal audit plans be based on risk assessment as well as on issues highlighted by the audit committee and senior management.

United Kingdom – The Combined Code on Corporate Governance, issued in 2003, has appended guidance on internal control from the Turnbull Committee, guidance on audit committees from the Smith Group, and suggestions for good practice from the report authored by Sir Derek Higgs. Regarding internal auditing, audit committees are advised to monitor and review the effectiveness of the internal audit function—including reviewing internal auditing's remit, appointing or terminating the CAE, and meeting privately with the CAE at least annually. The Turnbull guidance recommends that directors acknowledge, in annual reports, their responsibility for the company's system of internal controls and for reviewing its effectiveness. It also recommends that boards disclose whether there is an ongoing process for identifying, evaluating, and managing significant risks faced by the company.

Appendix 3-C
Other Governance Reference Sources

Many different reference sources are available on the Internet with relevant information regarding governance and ERM principles. The authors have found the following sample to be of interest in terms of their comprehensiveness and relevance relative to the topics in this textbook.

- Links to various countries' governance codes or guidelines as assembled by the European Corporate Governance Institute.
  http://www.ecgi.org/codes/all_codes.php.

- The Basel Committee on Banking Supervision is an institution created by the central bank governors of the Group of Ten Nations. The Basel Committee formulates broad supervisory standards and guidelines and recommends statements of best practice in banking supervision. The purpose of the committee is to encourage convergence toward common approaches and standards.
  http://www.bis.org.

- The Open Compliance and Ethics Group focuses on compliance matters.
  http://www.oceg.org

- National Association of Corporate Directors.
  http://www.nacdonline.org.

- COSO.
  http://www.coso.org.

- The Business Roundtable.
  http://www.businessroundtable.org/.

- The Institute of Internal Auditors governance Web page.
  http://www.theiia.org/guidance/standards-and-practices/additional-resources/corporate-governance

- Institutional Shareholder Services Inc.
  http://www.issproxy.com.

- The International Corporate Governance Network.
  http://www.icgn.org.

CHAPTER 4
BUSINESS PROCESSES
AND BUSINESS RISKS

LEARNING OBJECTIVES

- Understand how organizations structure their activities to achieve their objectives.

- Identify key business processes in an organization.

- Obtain an understanding of a given business process and be able to document it.

- Understand basic types of business risks organizations face.

- Identify and assess the key risks to the organization's objectives and how they are linked to business processes.

- Develop an audit universe for an entity and develop an annual audit plan based on business risk to allocate internal audit resources across the organization.

- Understand how to use risk assessment techniques within assurance engagements.

- Obtain an awareness of additional risk when an organization outsources some of its key processes.

All of us have goals and objectives. You want to earn your degree by next May. You want to get a job as an internal auditor when you graduate. You want to get your Master of Business Administration degree before you are 30.

Let's take a simple goal. You want to get to tomorrow's 8:00 a.m. class on time. What do you do?

You might do the following:

- Put the notes, assignments, and books you will need for tomorrow in your backpack along with your cell phone and laptop.
- Set your alarm clock for 6:00 a.m., and then go to sleep.
- Get up when your alarm clock rings.
- Get dressed and eat breakfast.
- At 7:00 a.m., get in your car and drive to campus.
- Find a parking space.
- Walk to the building.
- Get coffee.
- Walk to the classroom and find a seat.

EXHIBIT 4-1

PROFESSIONAL STANDARDS AND PRACTICE ADVISORIES RELEVANT TO CHAPTER 4

2010—Planning

2110—Risk Management

2200—Engagement Planning

2201—Planning Considerations

2210—Engagement Objectives

Practice Advisory 2010-2: Linking the Audit Plan to Risk and Exposures

Practice Advisory 2100-3: Internal Auditing's Role in the Risk Management Process

Practice Advisory 2210-1: Engagement Objectives

Practice Advisory 2210.A1-1: Risk Assessment in Engagement Planning

This is the list of activities you need to achieve your objective of being to class on time. To achieve this objective, you made specific choices from any number of other choices that could have been made. For instance, you could have packed your backpack in the morning instead of doing it the night before, or you could have decided to take the bus to campus instead of driving your car. So, why did you make these choices?

In some cases, it may have just been personal preference. For example, if you pack your backpack the night before, you can sleep five minutes longer the next morning. In other cases, your choice may have a direct impact on your ability to achieve your objective. For instance, you decided to drive rather than take the bus because the bus is often late or is frequently full and you might have to wait for the next one. In this case, you are exercising the same type of risk management thinking described in Chapter 3, "Governance and Risk Management."

In this chapter, you will learn organizations go through the same type of thought process to plan steps to achieve their objectives, including identifying the potential risks to the objectives managing those risks to acceptable levels. You will also learn how risk assessment techniques and methodology are used by internal auditors to carry out their responsibilities.

BUSINESS PROCESSES

Chapter 3, "Governance and Risk Management," discussed the importance of the governance process when setting objectives for the organization and the boundaries within which it will operate. This chapter examines how organizations actually structure their activities to

Business Process

The set of connected activities linked with each other for the purpose of achieving an objective or goal.

implement their strategies and achieve their business (organizational) objectives. Organizations structure activities into either (1) business processes or (2) projects. Although there are some common processes across organizations, the exact mix and structure will be unique for each organization. Even within an organization, there may be considerable variability in processes across divisions.

What is a business process? It is simply the set of connected activities linked with each other for the purpose of achieving an objective or

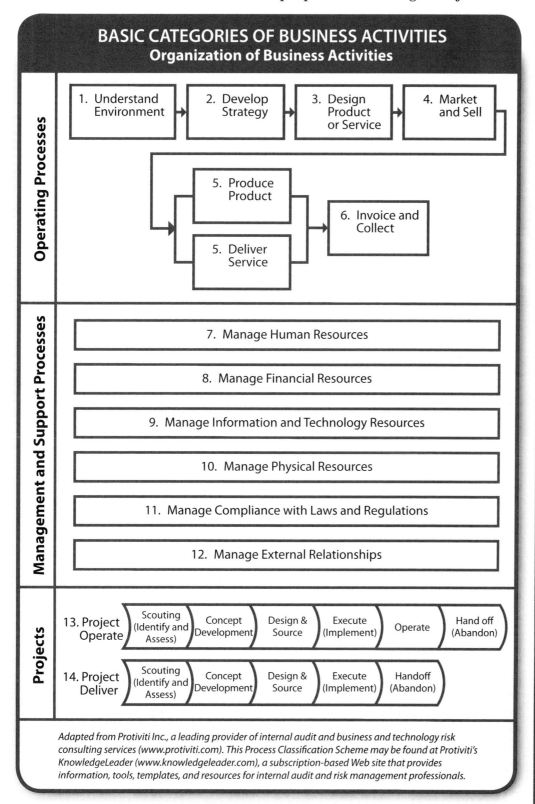

EXHIBIT 4-2

BASIC CATEGORIES OF BUSINESS ACTIVITIES
Organization of Business Activities

Operating Processes

1. Understand Environment → 2. Develop Strategy → 3. Design Product or Service → 4. Market and Sell

5. Produce Product
5. Deliver Service
6. Invoice and Collect

Management and Support Processes

7. Manage Human Resources

8. Manage Financial Resources

9. Manage Information and Technology Resources

10. Manage Physical Resources

11. Manage Compliance with Laws and Regulations

12. Manage External Relationships

Projects

13. Project Operate — Scouting (Identify and Assess) | Concept Development | Design & Source | Execute (Implement) | Operate | Hand off (Abandon)

14. Project Deliver — Scouting (Identify and Assess) | Concept Development | Design & Source | Execute (Implement) | Handoff (Abandon)

Adapted from Protiviti Inc., a leading provider of internal audit and business and technology risk consulting services (www.protiviti.com). This Process Classification Scheme may be found at Protiviti's KnowledgeLeader (www.knowledgeleader.com), a subscription-based Web site that provides information, tools, templates, and resources for internal audit and risk management professionals.

goal. Exhibit 4-2 outlines a basic classification of business activities. There are three types of business processes: operating processes, management and support processes, and projects.

Operating processes for most organizations include the core processes through which the organization achieves its primary objectives. For a manufacturing company, this would be the processes through which it makes and sells products. For service providers such as a consulting firm or financial institution, it would be the process by which they market and deliver their services. Government entities such as a city fire department or not-for-profit organizations (for example, the Boy Scouts) also have operating processes through which they deliver services. Once the product or service is designed (processes 1 to 3 in Exhibit 4-2), these processes (processes 4 to 6) are viewed as essentially continuous, being repeated many times in a business cycle. It is through these processes that organizations create value and deliver it directly to their customers.

For some organizations, a different method is used to organize value-creating activities. This structure, called *projects,* is used when activities happen over an extended period of time, require a complex sequencing, and are relatively unique in that a specific activity is not done on a continuing basis. Examples of organizations that often set up their core activities in this manner are engineering and construction firms; mining, oil, and gas companies; and defense contractors. Processes 13 and 14 of Exhibit 4-2 show the two different types of projects. Process 13 applies when the organization designs and constructs the asset and operates it, as well. For example, a petroleum company drills an oil well. Process 14 applies when the organization designs and constructs the asset, then hands it off to another organization to actually operate (for example, construction of a factory or building by an engineering firm where the facility is passed to another company for operation). Projects are also frequently used in most organizations to structure nonroutine activities to create assets for the organization's use. For example, a project structure would be used for selection and implementation of a new accounting system, initial implementation of the U.S. Sarbanes-Oxley Act of 2002 or other countries' financial reporting requirements, or construction of a new production facility.

Management and support processes are the activities that oversee and support the organization's core value-creation processes. These include the activities involved in organizational governance that set the strategic direction of the organization and provide oversight of the organization as was discussed in Chapter 3, "Governance and Risk Management." Examples of governance processes include strategic planning, the organization's compliance and ethics program, activities of the board and board committees, the enterprise risk management system, and various monitoring and assurance activities. Management and support processes also include the processes used to administer the organization's human, financial, information and technology, and physical resources (processes 7 to 10). Such support processes include recruitment, accounting, cash management, payroll, purchasing, etc. Finally, this category also includes processes the organization uses to manage its external relationships such as those with suppliers, customers, governmental entities, and regulators, as well as relations with capital markets and venture and alliance partners.

Exhibit 4-2 looks at business processes from a highly aggregated perspective. Each of these 14 categories can be further divided into more specific sets of activities. For example, if we consider the case of a retail organization, we could look at the activities of making a sale in general (customer selects goods, pays for goods with cash or promise to pay, accepts possession of goods); or more specifically, at the activities involved in a sale in a store setting compared to the process used for a sale over the Internet. This is illustrated in Exhibit 4-3. The level of aggregation used to conceptualize the processes will vary depending on whether you are trying to get an overview of the organization, in which case you would look at a high level of aggregation, or are considering the detailed steps in a specific process. Further, some of the processes are made of subprocesses. For example, in Exhibit 4-3,

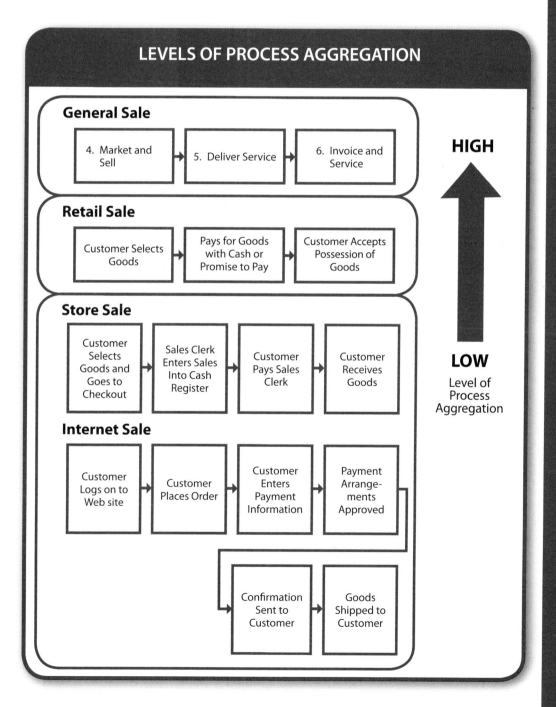

EXHIBIT 4-3

Business Model

The objectives of the organization and how the organization's business processes are structured to achieve these objectives.

Objectives

What an entity desires to achieve. When referring to what an organization wants to achieve, these are called business objectives, and may be classified as strategic, operational, reporting, and compliance.

Top-down Approach

To begin at the entity level, with the organization's objectives, and then identify the key processes critical to the success of each of the organization's objectives.

the "store sale" process of entering information into the cash register could involve a number of subprocesses such as updating inventory numbers, recording sales revenue, and opening the cash drawer.

Understanding Business Processes

For internal auditors to add value and improve an organization's operation, they must first understand the organization's business model. The business model includes the objectives of the organization and how the organization's business processes are structured to achieve these objectives. The model also includes the organization's vision, mission, and values, as well as sets of boundaries for the organization—what products or services it will deliver, what customers or markets it will target, and what supply and delivery channels it will use. While the model includes the high-level strategies and tactical direction for how the organization will implement the model, it also includes the annual goals that set the specific steps the organization intends to undertake in the next year and the measures for their expected accomplishment.

Although all members of the organization, including internal auditors, should have a basic understanding of the organization's objectives, there are many sources with more detailed information about the organization's strategy. These include:

- Vision and mission statements.
- Organizational objectives (strategic, operations, reporting, compliance).
- Value statements.
- Annual goals for the organization.
- Annual goals for key executives.
- Strategic planning presentations and related documents.

For publicly traded companies, additional sources are required such as regulatory filings (for example, for companies publicly traded in the United States, the 10-K filing with the U.S. Securities and Exchange Commission [SEC]) and analysts' reports, which contain an external perspective on the company's strategies. While an organization's vision, mission, values, and objectives are relatively stable from year to year, the internal audit function should still periodically update their understanding of the organization's strategy. Usually, this would be done on an annual basis when reviewing the annual goals for the organization and executive management.

There are two approaches that can be taken to understand business processes and their role in the business model: a top-down approach and a bottom-up approach. In the top-down approach, one begins at the entity level, with the organization's objectives, and then identifies the key processes critical to the success of each of the organization's objectives. A process is considered *key* relative to a specific objective if failure of the process to function effectively would directly result in the organization not achieving the objective. For example, if a specific objective was to increase shareholder value by consistently delivering growth in operating earnings (historically, 12% per year), then—referring to the high-level entity processes in Exhibit 4-2—processes in categories 3, 4, and 5 would be key, whereas some of the support processes—[such as the monthly accounting closing process (process category 8)] would not be. While processes may not be *key* to one specific objective, they may be a key process for another. Thus, in the example above, while the monthly accounting closing process might not be a key process to the earnings growth objective, it would be a key process for an organizational objective such as "provide reliable and timely accounting information." Once the key processes are identified, they are analyzed in more detail, breaking the process into levels of subprocesses, and eventually reaching the activity level. This approach is effective because it yields a manageable set of critical processes. However, there is the potential to overlook processes that are critical but are omitted. This approach is usually undertaken by a team of individuals with a broad perspective of the organization, but not with detailed knowledge of each area.

The bottom-up approach begins by looking at all processes directly at the activity level. Such an approach would require each area of the organization to identify and document the business processes in which they are involved. This should be done by the people in the area who are involved in the actual activities. The identified processes are then aggregated across the organization. While this approach works well for smaller organizations with a relatively limited number of processes, it becomes less effective in large and complex organizations as it becomes cumbersome to prioritize the significance of each process relative to the others.

Bottom-up Approach
To begin by looking at all processes directly at the activity level, and then aggregating the identified processes across the organization.

Once a process is identified, the next step in either the top-down or bottom-up approach is to determine the key objectives of the process. Essentially, determining the key objectives involves getting the answers to the following questions:

- Why does the process exist?
- How does the process support the organization's strategy and contribute to its success?
- How are people expected to act?
- What else does the process do that is important to management?

For an internal auditor, or someone not directly involved in the process, the first source of information is the process owner and the existing policy and procedures documentation for the process. Ideally, the process owner has established formal process objectives that provide the answers to the four questions above. If not, the auditor will need to work with key people involved with the process to get information.

Once the process objectives have been identified, the next step is to look at the process inputs and specific activities needed to achieve the objectives (the process outputs). To understand how inputs and activities combine to generate the output, start with a review of existing documents. This should include:

- Process procedural manuals.

Key Performance Indicator

A metric or other form of measuring whether a process or individual tasks are operating within prescribed tolerances.

- Policies related to the process.
- Job descriptions of people involved in the process.
- Any process maps that describing the process flow.

Although documents are a start, it is usually necessary to discuss aspects of the process with the people performing significant activities in the process. Exhibit 4-4 presents the type of questions typically asked during this step.

In addition to identifying the key objectives, understanding the process necessitates an understanding of how management and the process owner know the process is performing as intended. The process owner should have established key performance indicators (KPIs) that are used to monitor the performance of the process. These indicators should be observable (they can be measured objectively), be relevant to the objective (not just used because they can be quantified), available on a timely basis, and communicated to people involved in the process.

DOCUMENTING BUSINESS PROCESSES

Documentation of the business process is required. It should be done by the process owner and people involved in the process. However, there are instances when that is not the case because of the daily demands of their jobs or because they do not see the value of formal documentation. While not completing the process documentation may have little immediate consequence, as time passes and those involved in the process move on to other positions or leave the organization, the objective of the process may be lost or distorted. Process documentation can be very effective in (1) orienting new personnel, (2) defining areas of responsibility, (3) evaluating the efficiency of systems, (4) determining areas of primary concern, and (5) identifying key risks and controls. Internal auditors also must document their understanding to

EXHIBIT 4-4

UNDERSTANDING A BUSINESS PROCESS
Useful Questions to Ask a
Process Owner and Key Personnel

1. Why does the process exist?
2. Which of the organization's strategic objectives can the process affect and how?
3. What initiatives should the process undertake to help the organization achieve its strategic objectives?
4. What does the process provide the organization, without which the organization would have a difficult time being successful?
5. In the end, what gives employees involved in the process a sense of accomplishment with their jobs?
6. What accomplishments tend to get employees involved in the process recognized by management or by internal customers?
7. How are people involved with the process expected to act and what happens if they don't meet this expectation?
8. Do KPIs exist to help measure and monitor performance?

Sobel, Paul., Auditor's Risk Management Guide, 2005 ed., Chicago (CCH), pp. 7.05-7.06, 7.16.

support their overall assessment of risk and control in the organization and in any specific assurance engagements they would conduct on the process.

There are two commonly used methods for documenting processes: process maps and process write-ups. Process maps may be high-level or at the detailed-activity level and involve pictorial representations of inputs, steps, workflows, and outputs. Process maps also include some accompanying narrative.

High-level process maps attempt to depict the broad inputs, activities, workflows, and interactions with other processes and outputs. They provide an overall framework to understand the detailed activity and subprocesses. The goal in the high-level flowchart is to keep it simple and focus on the forest rather than the trees. Exhibit 4-5 provides an example of a high-level process map of getting to tomorrow's 8:00 a.m. class on time.

There are no absolute standards regarding the format and symbols for process mapping, although some internal audit functions and outsource firms try for consistency. Exhibit 4-6 presents the basic symbols with typical meanings. The process maps are usually structured so the sequence of activities runs from left to right, as in Exhibit 4-5, or from top to bottom.

Exhibit 4-7 presents a detailed-level process map for getting to tomorrow's 8:00 a.m. class on time. Here, the high-level process in Exhibit 4-5 is broken down to the specific activity or subprocess. Narrative is often included along with the process map to explain activities in more detail. Exhibit 4-7 illustrates how narrative supports the process map. In this case, the narrative provides more detail about the activity, but could also include descriptions of control activities

Exhibits 4-5 and 4-7 are sometimes referred to as process or procedures flowcharts. Other types of flowcharts and maps are also used. Internal auditors frequently use document flowcharts, which depict the flow of documents through specific processing steps. Deployment flowcharts are used to depict the flow of a document or materials through different departments within an organization.

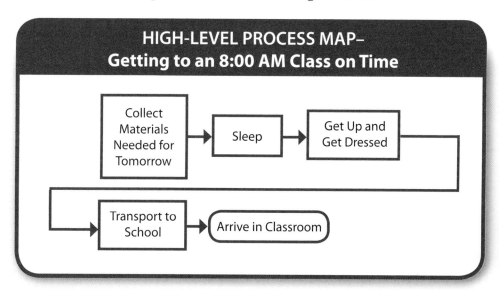

HIGH-LEVEL PROCESS MAP–
Getting to an 8:00 AM Class on Time

Collect Materials Needed for Tomorrow → Sleep → Get Up and Get Dressed → Transport to School → Arrive in Classroom

EXHIBIT 4-5

BUSINESS RISKS

Once the internal auditor obtains an understanding of the organization's objectives and the key processes used to achieve them, he or she should evaluate the business risks that could impede the accomplishment of the objectives. The ability of the chief audit executive (CAE) and internal audit management to get a thorough understanding of the organization's business risks will determine the extent to which the internal audit function will be able to fulfill its mission and add value to the organization. The first step in developing the understanding of the organization's business risks is to develop an overall risk profile of the organization that identifies the critical risk to each strategic objective. Historically, development of the profile has been left to the internal audit function. However, with the implementation of enterprise risk management (ERM) in an increasing number of organizations, the internal audit function frequently can begin building from an established base.

There are a number of different tools and methodologies to assist in developing the profile. This chapter will look only at a small set of those. Note also that despite the array of tools available, the assessment of organizational risk remains a very subjective process that requires experience and sound judgment.

EXHIBIT 4-6

COMMON FLOWCHARTING SYMBOLS	
□	**Process or operation** – A process, sub-process, or activity.
◇	**Decision** – Indicates alternative choices (for example, yes/no or accept/reject), each of which results in different flows of activities and/or documents.
⬗	**Document** – A hard copy input source document or output report.
→	**Flow line** – The direction of activities, workflow, information flow, documents, and hand offs.
⬢	**Computer system or application** – Information technology that is used to store data, run an application, or perform other computer-based functions.
○	**On-page connector** – Used to connect different parts of a flowchart on the same page without the use of flow lines.
⬠	**Off-page connector** – Used to connect parts of a flowchart documented on different pages.
⬭	**Terminator** – The start or end of a flow.
⊣	**Annotation** – An explanatory note attached to a specific point in a flowchart.

DETAILED LEVEL PROCESS MAP
Getting to an 8:00 AM Class on Time

EXHIBIT 4-7

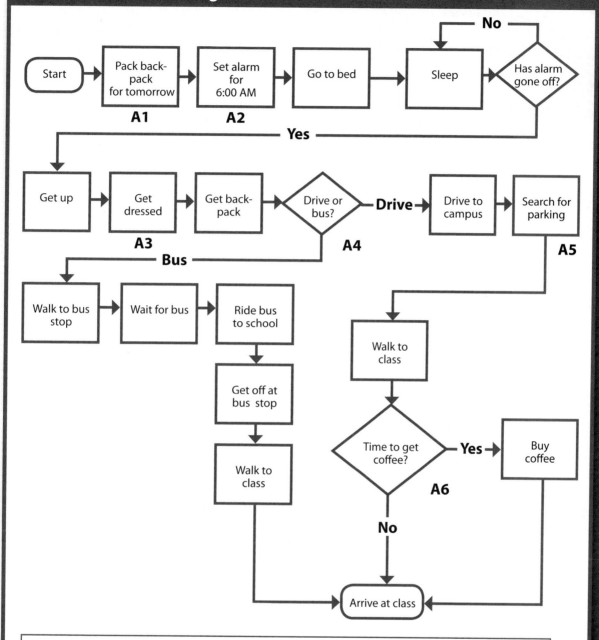

A1	Determine what books and papers will be needed for class and study for tomorrow. Put cell phone and laptop in backpack.
A2	Set alarm for 6:00 AM—5:45 AM if want to make breakfast.
A3	Includes showering, brushing teeth, fixing hair, ironing shirt, if necessary.
A4	Evaluate the chance of finding parking and the chance of the bus being late.
A5	Start at lot C1: if no parking space, go to lot C3: if none there, go to remote lot D3.
A6	If still 15 minutes before class when walking past coffee shop, stop and get coffee. If not, go directly to class.

Returning to the example of getting to class on time, assume the mission this semester is to gain the necessary knowledge and skills to be successful in an entry-level internal audit position. Several specific strategic objectives could be developed to accomplish this mission:

1. Attend all classes.

2. Be on time for each class.

3. Do assigned reading before the class in which it will be discussed.

4. Complete all assignments on time.

5. Obtain a B+ or better on all exams.

The process depicted in Exhibits 4-5 and 4-7 that outlines getting to an 8:00 a.m. class contributes to objective 2 and, to an extent, objective 1. Other processes such as study processes would be critical to objectives 3, 4, and 5. Chapter 3, "Governance and Risk Management," defines risk as "the possibility that an event will occur and adversely affect the achievement of an objective." Keeping the definition in mind, a number of risks can be identified that could impede the achievement of the five objectives. For instance, becoming sick would impact the achievement of objectives 1, 2, and 4. Exhibit 4-8 presents seven critical risks and their potential to impede these five strategic objectives.

The type of analysis done to gain the necessary knowledge and skills to be successful in an entry-level internal audit position and the requisite objectives can be done for organizations as well. Exhibit 4-9 presents an analysis for an online financial services firm. As mentioned in our discussion of business processes earlier in the chapter, the objectives can usually be found in the 10-K filing for publicly traded companies in the United States or in other organizational planning documents.

The critical risks are more difficult to derive, however. A typical approach might be to begin with a brainstorming session with senior managers or with just the internal audit staff. The group might start with a generic risk model that lays out the categories and types of risks an organization might encounter. Such a risk model is presented in Exhibit 4-10. In this model, the potential risks are broken down into four categories and 10 subcategories. The various risks are then assessed in terms of impact and likelihood.

Impact is usually assessed in terms of categories. Typically, three (high, medium, low) or five categories are used. A five-category model is presented in Exhibit 4-11. Establishing boundaries for each category is useful for gathering input from multiple people. In this model, the boundaries are set in terms of dollar values. However, some organizations set boundaries in other measures as well. For instance, some organizations establish impact in terms of reputation, health and safety, legal, or damage to assets. For heath and safety, the categories might be: slight injury, minor injury, major injury, fatality, multiple fatalities, with the scale going from negligible to extreme (the impact scale shown in Exhibit 4-11) respectively.

Risk

The possibility that an event will occur and adversely affect the achievement of objectives.

EXHIBIT 4-8

OBJECTIVES AND CRITICAL RISK MATRIX

	CRITICAL RISKS						
Mission: Gain the necessary knowledge and skills to be successful in an entry-level auditing position.	CR1 Illness.	CR2 Forget deadline.	CR3 Delays or oversleeps.	CR4 Does not have needed course materials.	CR5 Inadequate time to do all the work.	CR6 Unable to understand material.	CR7 Social or other distractions.
1. Attend all classes.	X		X				
2. Be on time for each class.	X		X				X
3. Do assigned reading prior to the class in which it will be discussed.				X	X		
4. Complete all assignments on time.	X	X		X	X	X	X
5. Obtain a B+ or better on all exams.		X			X	X	X

(Left margin label: OBJECTIVES)

Likelihood can be evaluated by directly assessing the probability in terms of odds or probabilities. However, given the subjective nature of these assessments, most managers and internal auditors are more comfortable in expressing the likelihood in less precise categories. Again, a three-category scale (high, medium, low) or a five-category scale (Exhibit 4-11) is often used. As with impact, it does help to specify the category boundaries. This is usually done in terms of specific or a range of probabilities (as in the scale in Exhibit 4-11).

Using the risk assessment model in Exhibit 4-11, the various risks from the basic business risk model (Exhibit 4-10) can be placed on the matrix. Frequently, this is done in a group session of senior managers or, if they are not available, the management and more experienced staff of the internal audit function. Using senior management and operations managers is preferable because they have the best understanding of the risks in their areas of responsibility. In this meeting, risks are discussed and consensus is obtained regarding impact, likelihood, and position of the respective risk on the matrix. The combination of impact and likelihood determines the importance of the risks. Exhibit 4-11 shows the matrix broken into 25 boxes. In this model, boxes 20 to 25 represent critical risks, and boxes 16 to 19, high risks. These risks present the most serious challenge to meeting the organizational objectives. Boxes 7 to 15 are moderate risks and boxes 1 to 6, low risks.

Exhibit 4-12 presents a mapping of the risk model to the risk assessment matrix for the online financial services company previously discussed. Four risks identified as critical from Exhibit 4-9 appear in

EXHIBIT 4-9

OBJECTIVES AND CRITICAL RISK MATRIX
Online Financial Services Firm

Mission: To continue projected growth of the delivery of online financial services in North America and capitalize on our low-cost infrastructure to grow market share and profitability. To enhance the client experience while increasing shareholder value.	CRITICAL RISKS				
	CR1 Economic — Changes in market dynamics.	**CR2** Product Stagnation — Inability to deliver product innovation.	**CR3** Availability — Systems or service outages.	**CR4** Business Continuity — Incomplete business continuity planning.	**CR5** Privacy — Compromise of client privacy.
OBJECTIVES 1. Focus on investor services. Plan to focus on attracting independent and active investors to our services.	X	X	X	X	X
2. Leverage infrastructure to add incremental revenue. Capitalize on our superior proprietary technology, which allows exceptional online experience for investors.		X	X	X	X
3. Continue to aggressively pursue growth through acquisitions.	X	X			
4. Leverage our strong brand.	X	X			
5. Continue to offer innovative technologies and service enhancements to our customers.	X	X	X	X	X
6. Continue to be the low-cost provider of quality services.		X	X	X	

EXHIBIT 4-10

BASIC BUSINESS RISK MODEL

Strategic Risks

External	Internal
Change in laws and regulations Competition Change in market dynamics Industry Technology	Reputation Strategic focus Customer satisfaction Governance

Compliance Risks

External	Internal
Contractual Regulatory Litigation Permits	Ethics Policies Fraud and illegal acts

Reporting Risks

External	Internal
Accounting and financial reporting Taxation	Budgeting Performance measures Internal control and regulatory reporting

Information Resources

Access
Availability
Data integrity
Infrastructure
Privacy

Operations Risks

Process	People	Financial
Supply chain Capacity Process execution Health and human safety Business continuity Cycle time Catastrophic events Lack of product innovation	Manpower supply Leadership/key employees Performance incentives Empowerment Change readiness Communication	Interest rates Foreign currency exchange Capacity Default Concentration Capital availability Cash management Commodity pricing Duration

boxes 21 and 22. Product stagnation was also included as one of the five critical risks in Exhibit 4-9, even though it appears in box 19 because of its pervasive potential effect on all five business objectives.

Mapping Risks to the Business Processes

From the ERM perspective discussed in Chapter 3, "Governance and Risk Management," the next step would be to develop appropriate responses to each risk. There are four responses the organization can take to a risk:

- **Avoidance.** Exiting or divesting of the activities giving rise to the risk. Risk avoidance may involve exiting a product line, declining expansion to a new geographical market, or selling a division.

- **Reduction.** Action is taken to reduce risk likelihood or impact, or both. This involves any of the myriad everyday business decisions, such as implementing controls.

- **Sharing.** Reducing risk likelihood or impact by transferring or otherwise sharing a portion of the risk. Common techniques include purchasing insurance products, engaging in hedging

Four Responses to a Risk:
- **Avoid**
- **Reduce**
- **Share**
- **Accept**

EXHIBIT 4-11

RISK ASSESSMENT MODEL

IMPACT		Remote (0-10%)	Unlikely (10-25%)	Possible (25-50%)	Probable (50-90%)	Certain (90-100%)
	Extreme	15	19	22	24	25
	High	10	14	18	21	23
	Medium	6	9	13	17	20
	Low	3	5	8	12	16
	Negligible	1	2	4	7	11

LIKELIHOOD

Impact

Extreme: >$80m — Threatens ongoing existence.
High: $15-$80m — Difficult to achieve business objectives.
Medium: $2-$15m — Makes achieving some business objectives challenging.
Low: $.5-$2m — Some undesirable outcomes.
Negligible: <$.5m — No noticeable impact on objectives.

- Critical Risks
- High Risks
- Moderate Risks
- Low Risks

transactions, or outsourcing an activity.

- **Acceptance.** No action is taken to affect risk likelihood or impact. The entity is willing to accept the risk at the current level rather than spend valuable resources deploying one of the other risk response options.

To effectively select appropriate response strategies, an understanding of how the risk relates to the organization's business processes is necessary. Internal auditors also must establish the link between risk and business process to whether or not the risk is being managed to an appropriate level within management's response strategy and to identify where in the organization the critical risk resides. Recall that Standard 2010 explicitly requires the CAE to "establish risk-based plans to determine the priorities of the internal audit activity, consistent with the organization's goals."

One method used to establish the linkage is a risk by process ma-

EXHIBIT 4-12

IDENTIFICATION OF CRITICAL RISKS

	Remote (0-10%)	Unlikely (10-25%)	Possible (25-50%)	Probable (50-90%)	Certain (90-100%)
Extreme	Catastrophic events Governance	Product stagnation	Availability Economics Business continuity		
High	Changes in laws and regulations Industry Strategic focus	Reputation Technology Competition Customer satisfaction Acct and fin reporting Access Infrastructure Cash management	Litigation Fraud and illegal acts Budgeting Data integrity	Privacy	
Medium	Concentration	Contractual Regulatory IC & reg. reporting Duration Capital availability Leadership/key employees Manpower supply			
Low	Health and safety Permits	Taxation Commodity Pricing	Foreign currency Supply chain		
Negligible					

trix (the linkage approach). Risks are listed along the top of the matrix, and processes are listed down the side. Exhibit 4-13 illustrates this matrix. The risks would be those identified in the business risk model (Exhibit 4-10). Typically, these will be from 30 to 70 risks. The risk evaluation process used above (Exhibit 4-12) can also be used to shorten the list of risks. For instance, it might be desirable to limit the risks to which processes are linked to only those risks in cells 7 to 25 (see Exhibit 4-11.)

The next step is to analyze each process or functional groups of processes to determine if there is any association between the process and the risk. Returning to the initial process example of getting to an 8:00 a.m. class on time, linkages between that process (Exhibit 4-7) and the seven critical risks listed in Exhibit 4-8 can be assessed. There is clearly a strong direct association between this process and Critical Risk 3, Delay or Oversleep. There would also be an association with Critical Risk 4, Not Having the Needed Course Materials, because part of getting to the 8:00 a.m. class on time involves gathering needed

EXHIBIT 4-13

materials for classes and studying the rest of the day. Critical Risk 5, Inadequate Time to do All Work, and Critical Risk 6, Unable to Understand Material, are clearly not related to this process. They would be related to other processes such as time management, scheduling, and study processes. After identifying with which risks a particular process is associated, the associations should be evaluated as to whether the linkages are a key linkage or a secondary linkage. Key linkages are those in which the process plays a direct and key role in managing the risk. Secondary linkages are ones in which the process helps to manage the risk in an indirect manner. In the example above, Critical Risk 3 would be judged as a key linkage, while Critical Risk 4 may only be considered a secondary linkage. When the linkages are viewed across a particular risk, there should be one or two processes (at most three) identified as having key linkages and any number of additional processes identified as having secondary linkages.

Once the risk/process matrix is complete, it can be used by the internal audit function to develop the function's annual plan for what engagements it will undertake. A first step could be to tally the number of key and secondary linkages of each process. A cycle for auditing each process could then be established for those with a key linkage to the critical risks or to several significant and moderate risks on a one-or two-year cycle and those with only secondary linkages to critical and significant risks on a three-, four-, or five-year cycle. Some considerations should also be given to past audit results. For instance, even a process on a three-or four-year cycle should be audited before its cycle ends if the prior audit identifies significant problems.

Key Linkages
Those in which the process plays a direct and key role in managing the risk.

Secondary Linkages
Those in which the process helps to manage the risk in an indirect manner.

PROCESS/RISK MATRIX

K — Key linkage S — Secondary Linkage	Risk 1	Risk 2	Risk 3	Risk 4	Risk 5	Risk 6	Risk 7	...	Risk m
Process 1		S							
Process 2				S					
Process 3			S						
Process 4	K						S		
Process 5				S					
Process 6									
Process 7				S	S	S	K		
Process 8		K							
Process 9	S				K	K			
Process 10		K							
Process 11	S		K		S				
...									
Process n									

Another, more indirect, approach of linking business processes and risks is through the development of basic risk factors used to evaluate risks across processes (risk factor approach). Typically, the risk factor models identify seven to 15 factors that can be used to assess each process. These factors are not identical to risks in the earlier basic business risk model (Exhibit 4-10). They are a higher level of abstraction, one that can be applied to each process. Most models are composed of two basic types of factors—external risk factors and internal risk factors. The external risk factors pertain to factors built into the environment and the nature of the process itself. They can be characteristics such as relative level of activity, amount and liquidity of assets involved in the process, complexity of the process in terms of number of steps and inputs, level of legal and regulatory constraints, and so forth. Internal risk factors relate to extent of control activities designed into the process to assure the process achieves its objectives, performance of the people involved in the activities and in managing the process, and the degree of changes in the process and environment in which it operates. Some models include several additional factors, most commonly—time since the last audit, prior audit results, and specific management concerns.

After the factors have been identified, three other decisions must be made before implementing the model. First, the scale used to assess each factor must be set. Typically, a three-, five-, or seven-point scale is used. For example, in a three-point scale, 1 is low, 2 is medium, and 3 is high. The boundaries on the three categories can also be set for each factor. For example, if one factor is "amount of assets involved," then low (a score of 1) might be $500,000 or less, medium (a score of 2) $500,000 to $10 million, and high (a score of 3) more than $10 million. The important thing to note is regardless of which scale is selected (a three-, five-, seven-, or n-point scale), the same scale should be used for the assessment of all factors. Exhibit 4-14 shows an example of a 10-factor model using a three-point scale.

The next decision is about the relative importance (or weight) of one factor to another. If each of the risk factors is considered to be of equal importance, they would be given the same numeric weighting. Usually, weighting is done by assigning numbers between 0 and 100, so the sum of weights equals 100. Thus, if we had five risk factors and each of the factors was considered to be of the same importance as the others, each factor would be assigned a weight of 20. In the risk factor model shown in Exhibit 4-15, the Internal Control Stability factor is given a weight of 5, which means it is considered only half as important as the Assets at Risk factor and only one-third as important as the Significant Changes factor.

The final decision is how the risk factors are combined. Most risk factor approaches use a weighted-additive model—each factor score is multiplied by factor weight and summed across factors to give an overall risk score (Exhibit 4-15). Overall scores can a range from 100 to 300 and can be interpreted as low (scores below 150), medium (scores 150 to 239), and high (scores above 240) risk. The category cutoff scores should be adjusted once distribution of scores over all processes is determined. The categories can then be used to assign the process an audit cycle of one, two, three, or four years. Thus, if a process is assigned to a two-

External Risk Factors

Factors built into the environment and the nature of the process itself.

Internal Risk Factors

Factors related to the extent of control activities designed into the process to assure that the process achieves its objectives.

EXHIBIT 4-14

RISK FACTOR APPROACH
Factor Descriptions and Scales

Risk Factor Description		
External Risk Factors	**Factor Score**	**Explanation**
1. Assets at risk.	1	Less than $500,000.
	2	Greater than $500,000, less than $5 million.
	3	Greater than $5 million.
2. Visibility.	1	Operating unit/direct customer.
	2	Divisional/limited set of customers.
	3	Organization/national press.
3. Complexity.	1	Simple, unskilled assignments make up process.
	2	Requires several steps and interaction of multiple people.
	3	Multiple steps, requiring coordination of multiple individuals both within process and with other processes.
4. Size of process/ operation.	1	Process affects less than 3% of organization's activities.
	2	Process affects 3% to 15% of the organization's activities.
	3	Process affects more than 15% of organization's activities.
5. Legal/regulatory/ external requirements.	1	Few requirements, unregulated.
	2	Some regulatory requirements.
	3	Significant number and complexity of requirements.
Internal Risk Factors	**Factor Score**	**Explanation**
6. Internal control (IC) stability.	1	Mature risk and control system.
	2	Stable control and compliance system.
	3	Ad hoc approach to control and compliance.
7. Internal control effectiveness.	1	No IC or compliance issues in past two years.
	2	Multiple instances of fraud, IC weakness, or compliance failures, but not of major significance in the past two years.
	3	Significant fraud, IC weaknesses, or compliance failures in past two years.
8. Significant changes in business operations, processes, personnel, or technology.	1	No significant change in last 12 months.
	2	Some changes in process or key personnel in last 12 months.
	3	Major change in business and process or new IT system in last 12 months.
Other Factors	**Factor Score**	**Explanation**
9. Management condition or concern.	1	No concern.
	2	Some concern expressed by senior management.
	3	Senior management or board expressed notable concern.
10. Prior audit results.	1	No control or compliance issues in last audit.
	2	Minor control or compliance issues in last audit.
	3	Significant IC weaknesses in last audit.

RISK FACTOR APPROACH WEIGHTING AND SCORING

Risk Factor

External Risk Factors	Score	X Weight	Weighted Score
1. Assets at Risk	___	10	___
2. Visibility	___	10	___
3. Complexity	___	10	___
4. Size of Process/Operation	___	10	___
5. Legal/Regulatory/External Requirements	___	10	___

Total External Risk Score

Internal Risk Factors	Score	X Weight	Weighted Score
6. Internal Control Stability	___	5	___
7. Internal Control Effectiveness	___	10	___
8. Significant Changes in Business Operations, Processes, Personnel, or Technology	___	15	___

Total Internal Risk Score

Other Factors	Score	X Weight	Weighted Score
9. Management Condition or Concern	___	10	___
10. Prior Audit Results	___	10	___

Total Other Risk Score

Overall Risk Score

EXHIBIT 4-15

EXHIBIT 4-16

RISK FACTOR APPROACH
Risk Analysis by Business Process

	External	Internal	Other
Process 1			
Process 2			
Process 3			
Process 4			
Process 5			
Process 6			
Process 7			
Process 8			
Process 9			
Process 10			
Process 11			
...			
Process n			

Risk Level	External	Internal	Other
Potential Range of Scores	50 to 150	30 to 90	20 to 60
Low	<90	<50	<35
Medium	90-124	50-74	35-49
High	>125	>75	>50

Process Priority Map

A diagram which visually shows the relationship between inherent risk and process significance.

year cycle it would be scheduled for audit every two years.

As an alternative to assigning each process to a cycle, the prioritizing of processes to audit can be done by sorting the processes by their risk scores and selecting the one with the highest score to audit (then the next, and so forth) until available audit hours for the planning period have been exhausted. If such an approach is used, it is important to note when the process was last audited. One technique for doing this is to add *time since last audit* as one of the risk factors. In the model presented in Exhibit 4-14, this factor would be added as a factor under *Other Factors* and could be scored 1—*process audited in past 12 months,* 2—*process audited in past 12 to 36 months,* and 3—*process has not been audited in past 36 months.*

Some internal audit functions prefer not to make judgments using total scores, but look at the scores by factor (External, Internal, Other). This can be done by assigning a low, medium, or high rating to each factor. Note the range of scores varies in terms of number of individual factors in each category (5, 3, and 2 in the current example) and difference in weightings. Thus, in the model presented in Exhibit 4-15, the total External Risk Score can range from 50 to 150, the total Internal Risk Scores from 30 to 90, and total Other Factors Score, from 20 to 60. Thus we might set *Low* for External Risk as 50 to 90 and *High* as more than 125. With Other Factors Scores, *Low* might be scores between 20 and 35 and *High* for scores more than 50. Exhibit 4-16 illustrates visually how this might be displayed to assist in determining the audit cycle. As before, the process can be placed on a cycle of one, two, three, or four years.

Business Process and Business Risk in the Assurance Engagement

Once a process or area of the organization has been selected for an audit, a second risk evaluation and process analysis is done. If the audit function structures its engagements by area rather than specific processes, the various processes in the area must be identified and prioritized in terms of importance to overall business objectives and inherent risk to these objectives. One could list processes in order of their significance and evaluate them as high, medium, or low risk. However, one technique that is often used is to place the process on a Process Priority Map that visually shows the relationship between inherent risk and process importance. An example of such a map is presented in Exhibit 14-17.

Let us return to the example presented earlier in this chapter (Exhibit

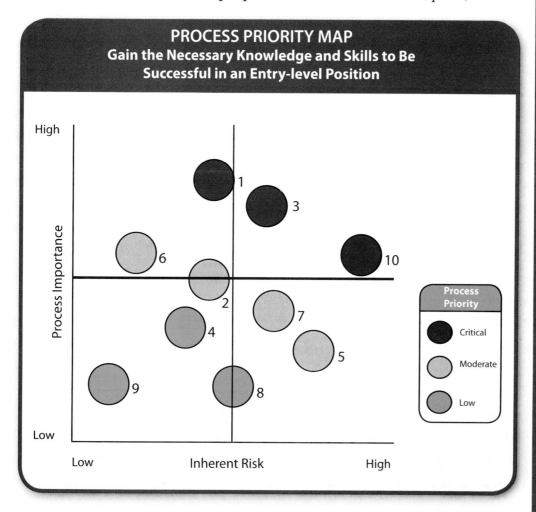

PROCESS PRIORITY MAP
Gain the Necessary Knowledge and Skills to Be Successful in an Entry-level Position

EXHIBIT 4-17

4-8)—the mission of gaining the necessary knowledge and skills to be a successful internal auditor and the five objectives established to accomplish this mission. Suppose a student's parents wanted some assurance the objectives and mission would be accomplished and asked an older sibling, recently graduated and working as an internal auditor, to visit the student and perform an audit. The audit begins with the student and the sibling sitting down and listing a number of activities and processes the student carries out to achieve this mission:

1. Studying to prepare for an exam.
2. Reading the assigned materials.
3. Completing class assignments and projects.
4. Eating meals.
5. Paying tuition and other bills.

EXHIBIT 4-18

RISK/CONTROL MATRIX
Partially Completed for Process 10

KEY PROCESS — PROCESS 10 Getting to an 8:00 AM Class on Time				
Activity Sub-process Within Key Process	**Risk Statement**	**Potential Impact**	**Impact Rating**	**Likelihood Rating**
Pack Backpack.	1. Forget to pack homework assignments.	Loss of points for late work.	Medium	Medium
	2. Forget to pack cell phone.	Unable to receive or make calls.	Low	High
	3. Forget to shutdown and pack laptop.	Late because of delay with shutdown.	Low	Medium
Set Alarm.	4. Forget to turn on alarm.	Oversleep and miss class.	High	High
	5. Power goes out during the night.	Oversleep and miss class.	High	Low
Go to Bed.	6. Not be able to get to sleep.	Tired next day.	Medium	Low
	7. Go to bed too late to get sufficient sleep.	Tired next day.	Medium	Medium
Sleep/Wake up.	8. Turn off alarm and go back to sleep.	Miss class	High	Medium
	9. Push snooze repeatedly.	Miss or be late to class.	High	Low
Get Dressed.	10. Cannot decide which clothes to wear.	Late to class.	Medium	Medium
	11. No clean clothes.	Late to class.	Medium	High
Get Backpack.	12. Leave without backpack.	Late because of delay to go back for backpack.	Medium	Low
Drive to Campus.	13. Traffic.	Late to class.	Medium	High
Search for Parking	14. No parking space.	Late to class	Medium	High

6. Listening and taking notes in class.

7. Selecting and registering for the appropriate classes.

8. Exercising.

9. Cleaning the apartment.

10. Getting to the first class of the day on time.

Exhibit 4-17 shows the priority of how these processes and activities might relate to the risk of not achieving the mission. The map indicates Processes 1, 3, and 10 are the most critical. While Processes 1 and 3 are considered the most significant to success, Process 10, though less significant, has a high level of inherent risk. The next step will be to look at the three key processes in more detail.

Beginning with Process 10, the auditor/sibling proceeds to ask the student a series of questions about how preparations for the next day are conducted and about getting up in the morning and going to class. The student explains although class is only on Monday, Wednesday, and Friday this semester, the first class begins at 8:00 AM. After answering all the questions asked, the auditor/sibling creates a flowchart and asks if it represents the information provided. The student suggests a few changes and the auditor/sibling makes them, producing the process map shown in Exhibit 4-7.

The next step is to identify and evaluate specific risks in each activity or subprocess within the key process. The auditor/sibling does this by placing each activity on a matrix and listing a description of each risk down the side of the page as shown in Exhibit 4-18. Each risk statement describes an event which has an effect on the activity or subprocess achieving its goal or working as intended. Potential impact of the event is then identified and evaluated by its seriousness. Finally, likelihood of the event is assessed. Exhibit 4-18 is a partially completed risk/control matrix for the first several activities in Process 10.

Risk evaluation can also be displayed using a risk map to prioritize risk within the key process. Those in the upper right quadrant of the risk map would be the most critical, while those in the lower left quadrant would be of relatively low concern. A risk map for the risks identified in Exhibit 4-18 is shown in Exhibit 4-19. On the risk map, impact and likelihood are combined to determine if the risk is critical, moderate, or low.

Once specific risks have been identified, the next step is to determine how they are managed and if the response is effective in reducing the risk to an acceptable level. As mentioned earlier, there are four general responses: avoid, reduce, share, and accept. Within processes, most often the response to a specific risk is either to accept the risk or attempt to reduce the risk through control activities. The topic of control activities is addressed in more detail in Chapter 5, "Internal Control," and subsequent chapters. However, to complete the discussion of the risks in our process example, Exhibit 4-20 adds two additional columns to the risk matrix. The first is a column to indicate the response strategy and the second specifies how one might get assurance the response strategy (in particular, the control activity) was effective at managing the risks.

Risk Assessment

A process whereby the potential impact and likelihood of one or more risks are estimated.

Risk Control Map

A diagram that plots risk significance against control effectiveness.

EXHIBIT 4-19

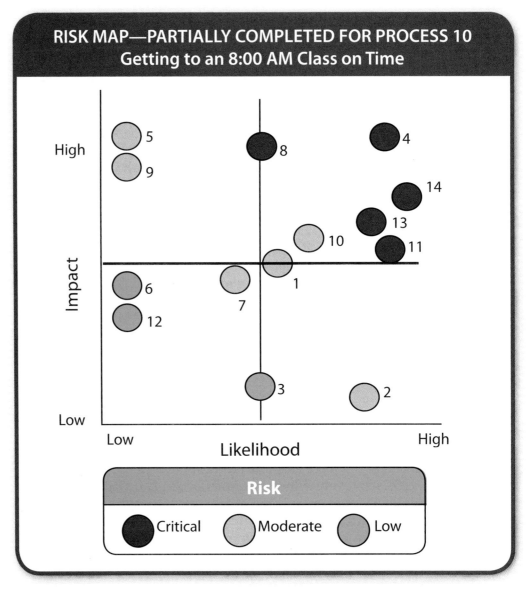

RISK MAP—PARTIALLY COMPLETED FOR PROCESS 10
Getting to an 8:00 AM Class on Time

After the response strategies have been determined, and both before and after the strategies have been tested for effectiveness, an overview of the risk response strategy can be obtained by creating a Risk Control Map, which plots risk significance (the combination of impact and likelihood; in our example: low, moderate, and critical) against control effectiveness. This is illustrated by the example (using the specific risks in Exhibit 4-18 for Process 10 (Getting to an 8:00 AM Class on Time) in Exhibit 4-21. The risk control map shows where there is an appropriate balance between risk and the control activity; that is, more effective control activities on critical risks (high-impact and likelihood) than on low risks (low-impact and low chance of occurrence). Risks falling between the two dotted parallel lines (Risks 4, 8, 11, 10, 1, 3, 6, and 12) are shown to be appropriately balanced. In the left upper quadrant of the map (Risks 14, 13, and 7), the control/risk relationship is not appropriately balanced; the response strategy does not appropriately mitigate the risks. On the other hand, in the lower right quadrant are a number of risks that may be over-controlled (9, 5, and 2). They represent situations where efficiencies might be gained by loosening control activities.

EXHIBIT 4-20

RISK/CONTROL MATRIX FOR PROCESS 10
Getting to an 8:00 AM Class on Time

KEY PROCESS — PROCESS 10

Getting to an 8:00 AM Class on Time

Activity Sub-process within Key Process	Risk Statement	Potential Impact	Impact Rating	Likelihood Rating	Risk Response	Technique for Assessing Effectiveness
Pack Backpack	1. Forget to pack homework assignments.	Loss of points for late work.	Medium	Medium	Accept	—
	2. Forget to pack cell phone.	Unable to receive or make calls.	Low	High	Always keep cell phone in backpack.	Call phone to test location.
	3. Forget to shutdown and pack laptop.	Late because of delay with shutdown.	Low	Medium	Accept	—
Set Alarm	4. Forget to turn on alarm.	Oversleep and miss class.	High	High	Turn on alarm in morning when getting up.	Inquire to find out if this is being done.
	5. Power goes out during the night.	Oversleep and miss class.	High	Low	Second battery-powered alarm clock.	Observation
Go to Bed	6. Not be able to get to sleep.	Tired next day.	Medium	Low	Accept	—
	7. Go to bed too late to get sufficient sleep.	Tired next day.	Medium	Medium	Accept	—
Sleep/Wake up	8. Turn off alarm and go back to sleep.	Miss class.	High	Medium	Put alarm across room.	Investigate to see if there is an alarm across room.
	9. Push snooze repeatedly.	Miss or be late to class.	High	Low	Second alarm.	Observation

EXHIBIT 4-21

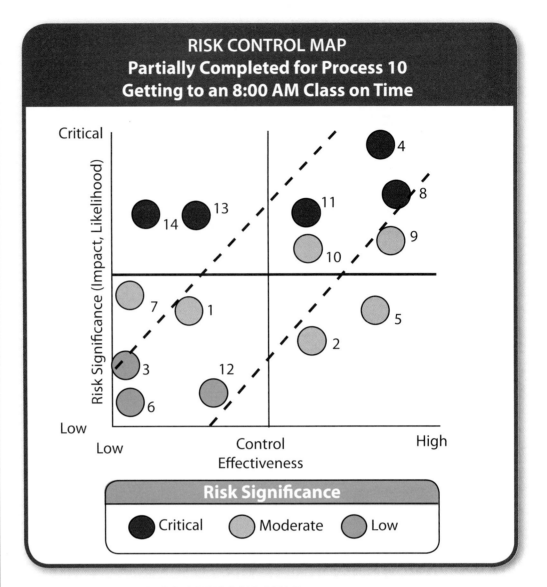

RISK CONTROL MAP
Partially Completed for Process 10
Getting to an 8:00 AM Class on Time

Business Process Outsourcing

The act of transferring some of an organization's business processes to an outside provider to achieve cost reductions, operating effectiveness, or operating efficiency while improving service quality.

BUSINESS PROCESS OUTSOURCING

In an effort to streamline operations and reduce costs, organizations are increasing the degree to which they are outsourcing specific business processes. In developing the audit universe, these outsourced processes should also be considered and included in the risk analysis.

Business Process Outsourcing (BPO) is the act of transferring some of an organization's business processes to an outside provider to achieve cost reductions while improving service quality and efficiency. Because the processes are repeated and a long-term contract is used, outsourcing goes far beyond the use of consultants. Historically, payroll and information technology (IT) functions were the first critical business processes outsourced. However, the trend has grown to include human resources, engineering, customer service, finance and accounting, and logistics as companies seek to reduce costs through the leverage and economies of scale gained by those in the outsourcing business.

Even though functions may be outsourced, it is critical that management and the internal audit function ensure an adequate system of

EXHIBIT 4-22

BEST PRACTICES IN BUSINESS PROCESSING OUTSOURCING

- Involve internal audit throughout entire process.
- Verify other corporate support departments such as legal, information security, and human resources are involved.
- Gain an understanding of how and why decisions to outsource were made.
- Verify that alternatives were considered.
- Create a document that guides the conversion process.
- Flowchart the key processes.
- Verify a strategic analysis was done to ensure alignment with goals.
- Verify a cost benefit analysis was done.
- Conduct thorough risk assessment.
- Verify how processes will be overseen and by which management personnel.
- Verify a documented vendor selection process exists.
- Gain an understanding of the vendor selection process.
- Assess risk of vendor before selection, including any country-specific risks.
- Create unique and robust contract.
- Monitor vendor and contract for compliance.
- Monitor outsourcing process to ensure it meets management's objectives.
- Procure SAS 70 reports or outside audit reports when available.
- If no outside report is available, determine if audit is required and document controls of vendor.

Adapted from Salamasick, Mark and Linsteadt, Chris. Auditing Vendor Relationships. *Altamonte Springs, Fla. The Institute of Internal Auditors. 2003..*

internal controls exists with the outsource vendor. In many cases, the system of internal controls and efficiency of the vendor may be better than if the processes were kept internally. However, there are new risks, particularly those encountered in the transition phase of either outsourcing business functions or bringing them back to be managed internally. Exhibit 4-22 presents some of the recommend practices that organizations should follow for effective risk management and control of outsourced business processes.

SUMMARY

Risk Management as an Everyday Management Tool

The risk management concepts and tools that have been discussed in this chapter are not limited to the use of internal auditors. They should be a part of the fundamental tools of every manager. Nor are they only for large organizations. This was illustrated throughout the chapter through the application of the tools in a personal setting via the example of the student with the mission of becoming an internal auditor. The following example, which will close this chapter, presents techniques that are applicable to the management of activities and events in student organizations. This particular methodology was developed by the Office of the Dean of Students at The University of Texas at Austin, but draws from similar risk management practices used at several other universities, corporations, and government entities.

The methodology involves a six-step process that the officers or committees of student organizations are encouraged to go through when planning events (i.e., a concert or dance) or activities (i.e., a field trip to visit organizations or a softball tournament). The steps are to:

1. List all aspects of your event on the management risk worksheet (Exhibit 4-23).

2. Identify risks associated with each activity, thinking broadly about potential risks.

3. Use the matrix (Exhibit 4-24) to determine the level of risk associated with each activity before applying any risk management strategies.

4. Brainstorm methods to manage risks. Find strategies you can apply to reduce the severity of the risk and probability that something can go wrong.

5. Use the matrix (Exhibit 4-24) to reassess the activities now that risk management strategies have been applied.

6. Determine if an acceptable level of risk has been reached by applying risk management strategies. Consider modifying or eliminating activities with unreasonable risks. Remember to consider how the activity relates to the mission and purpose of the organization.

Exhibit 4-24 shows the link between impact and likelihood. It uses slightly different scales and definitions but is conceptually identical with other models discussed in this chapter.

Whether it is a student organization or a multinational corporation, achievement of an organization's mission will involve taking necessary risks. In today's competitive environment, those who manage risk the best and focus on improved business processes will outperform the competition. Internal auditors are in a unique position to see the entire enterprise and make recommendations that can have impact across organizational boundaries. In addition to providing assurance of business processes, the internal audit function can have an even bigger impact when providing consulting on major changes to business processes. In today's volatile business environment, it is even more important to look to the future and assess how the business processes can be changed to prepare organizations for the challenges ahead. It is imperative internal auditors take a leadership role and be agents of change. The internal audit function can be of great assistance in evaluating of the degree of business risk the organization can take to achieve the goals established by management.

EXHIBIT 4-23

MANAGING RISK WORKSHEET

Be sure to list all aspects of your event, both risky and less risky ones.	Think through all the things that could go wrong, including worst-case scenarios.	Consider what your organization could do to manage the risk and bring it to a reasonable level.
Examples: driving, sports/recreation, collecting money, concerts, outdoor events, etc.		

The University of Texas at Austin, Office of the Dean of Students.

RISK MODEL FOR STUDENT ORGANIZATION AND ACTIVITIES

Probability That Something Will Go Wrong

Category	Unlikely — Unlikely to occur.	Seldom — Not likely to occur but possible.	Occasional — May occur at times.	Likely — Quite likely to occur in time.	Frequent — Likely to occur immediately or in a short period of time.
CATASTROPHIC May result in death.	M	H	H	E	E
CRITICAL May cause severe injury, major property damage, significant financial loss, and/or result in negative publicity for the organization and/or institution.	L	M	H	H	E
MARGINAL May cause minor injury, illness, property damage, financial loss, and/or result in negative publicity of organization or institution.	L	L	M	M	M
NEGLIGIBLE Hazard presents a minimal threat to safety, health, and well-being of participants.	L	L	L	L	M

Severity of Risk

E	Extremely High Risk	Activities in this category contain unacceptable levels of risk, including catastrophic and critical injury that are likely to occur. Organizations should consider whether they should eliminate or modify activities that still have an "E" rating after applying all reasonable risk management strategies.
H	High Risk	Activities in this category contain potentially serious risks that are likely to occur. Applications of proactive risk management strategies to reduce risk is advised. Organizations should consider ways to modify or eliminate unacceptable risks.
M	Moderate Risk	Activities in this category contain some level of risk that is unlikely to occur. Organizations should consider what can be done to manage the risk to prevent negative outcomes.
L	Low Risk	Activities in this category contain minimal risk that is unlikely to occur. Organizations can proceed with these activities as planned.

1. What is a business process?

2. Describe the standard business processes common to most organizations.

3. What is included in a company's business model?

4. How do you determine the key objectives of a business process?

5. What are the two commonly used methods for documenting processes? Describe each.

6. What are "critical risks?"

7. Describe the four responses an organization can take toward a risk?

8. What is the difference between a key linkage and a secondary linkage?

9. Explain how the risk factor approach can be used to identify areas of high-risk in an organization.

10. What is the difference between inherent risk factors and control risk factors?

11. How does outsourcing business processes change the risks?

1. In assessing organizational risk in a manufacturing firm, which of the following would have the most long-range impact on the organization?

   a. Advertising budget

   b. Production scheduling

   c. Inventory policy

   d. Product quality

2. Internal auditors often flowchart a control system and reference the flowchart to narrative descriptions of certain activities. This is an appropriate procedure to:

   a. Determine the ability of the activities to produce reliable information.

   b. Obtain the understanding necessary to test the effectiveness of the system.

   c. Document that the system meets international auditing standards.

   d. Determine if the system meets established management objectives.

Use the chart to answer questions 3 and 4.

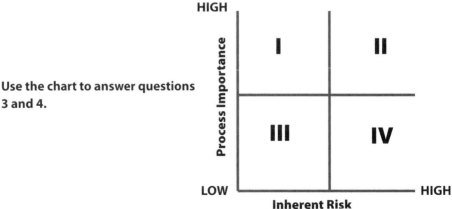

3. If a process appears in quadrant II of the above process priority map, it means that:

   a. The process should be audited by the independent outside auditor rather than the internal auditor.

   b. The process will need to be analyzed further to evaluate the effectiveness of management's risk response.

   c. The process has an imbalance between risk and control.

   d. The process should be classified as having a significant weakness

4. In the case of an effective system of internal controls, in which quadrant would you expect to find the lowest investment in control activities?

   a. I   b. II   c. III   d. IV

5. Which of the following are business processes?

   I.   Compliance with environmental regulations
   II. Review and write-off of delinquent loans
   III. Safeguarding of assets
   IV. Remittance of payroll taxes to the respective local and federal tax authorities.

        a. II only

        b. I and III only

        c. II and IV only

        d. I, II, III, and IV

6. Which of the following is true regarding business process outsourcing?

   a. Outsourcing a core, high-risk business process reduces the overall operational risks.

   b. Outsourced processes should not be included in the audit universe.

   c. The independent outside auditor is required to review all significant outsourced business processes.

   d. The internal audit function should review the contract to make sure it will meet management's objectives before being signed.

1. How would an oil exploration and production company differ from a company like Wal-Mart in terms of how it organizes business processes?

2. What are five of the most important business processes and business risks for a large auto manufacturer like Toyota?

3. The objectives of Sargon's purchasing process are to obtain the right goods, at the right price, at the right time. What are the significant risks to achievement of those objectives?

4. For an event your internal audit student organization (or other organization) is planning, apply the risk assessment methodology for student activities presented in the summary of this chapter (Exhibits 4-23 and 4-24).

CASES

Pizza Inc.
Applying the Risk Solutions Approach

Pizza Inc., a pizza take-out and delivery chain, is experiencing decreasing revenues and is steadily losing market share despite favorable market testing of its products/recipes. The company strategy has traditionally been defined as gaining increased market share through customer satisfaction. Management has asked your internal audit function to help them understand the reasons for declining sales at the Uptown location and how the decline might be related to internal operations. Your prior audit experience and direct observation of work performed at the troubled location identified the following information.

In 2003, Pizza Inc.'s corporate office screened this site location prior to construction to ensure that neighborhood demographics supported the ideal business environment. This resulted in locating the chain near a suburb where typical residents were in the mid- to upper-middle class income range and who owned homes with 3 to 4 bedrooms. Despite the favorable location, the site you are reviewing continues to have gross and operating margins lower than their local competitors.

On-the-job training is the primary method used by managers to communicate corporate policy and procedures. However, documented Pizza Inc. policies and detailed procedures do exist for each key process and are available by request from the shift manager. Employees are typically male (comprising 65% of total staff), 17 to 23 years old, with no prior work experience at the time of hire. Unscheduled absenteeism is high and part-time shift assignments are rotated frequently to reward those individuals who regularly work as scheduled. The internal audit team noted in last year's review that management has documented an average annual turnover rate of 18%.

The shift manager is responsible for ensuring that all pizza orders are completed within established deadlines, a long held competitive advantage. Drivers are required to record the time of their arrival at the location of delivery on a delivery ticket. This time is compared with the time recorded on the order ticket to calculate total elapsed minutes. Review of the last six month's delivery tickets indicates that the corporate benchmark delivery cycle time of 25 minutes from "placing the order to when we're on the doorbell" has slipped to an average 43.8 minutes. For months there have been persistent rumors about bets placed on one driver's notorious reputation for beating the delivery deadline every time.

Delivery promptness is also dependent on the volume of completed pizzas at any given time and the neighborhood traffic pattern. Drivers are initially screened at hire for outstanding traffic violations or DWI infractions. The original site manager posted a large map on the wall so drivers can identify their routes. Mileage is reimbursed as part of the compensation for using their own vehicles so each driver turns in a mileage log at the end of the shift to indicate both start and ending mileage. The manager checks the recorded beginning or ending mileage with the car's odometer on a random basis.

Pizza Inc.'s corporate policy requires that each location restricts itself to a 5 mile service area, however, if an order comes in, the work is never refused. Phone orders occur in predictable patterns, but walk-in orders are more random and less frequent. Scheduling staff requirements to match the need is done one week in advance. The average workload during peak hours is 29 orders taken per hour. Orders are manually written on pre-numbered pads. When mistakes are made, the original order ticket is tossed out and a new order form is created to avoid confusion. Information captured includes: date, time of call (or walk in), name, address, phone number, type of crust, and toppings requested. Hand calculators are available to assist with pricing quotes that are told to the customer and recorded on the delivery ticket. Shift managers check every order to ensure that information is complete prior to processing the order.

Employees who make the pizza are instructed in the proper quantity of ingredients for various standard topping combinations. Frequently, special request orders are received that add items to the standard recipe. Measuring cups are available but your internal audit team noted on prior visits that when activity reaches peak load employees generally "know" how much pepperoni to use. The manager monitors the supply cabinets and refrigerators at the end of the shift to ensure adequate inventory is on hand. Several months ago, the evening shift manager determined that inventory deliveries should be increased to four per week, up from the usual three. Oven temperatures are monitored closely to ensure that pizzas are properly cooked. Employees who bake the pizza rely on a centrally located wall clock to time the various combinations. There are cooking guidelines posted for each standard topping combination with instructions on what to do if a pizza is overcooked. Generally these are available to employees for snacking.

All employees are responsible for ensuring the baked pizzas are cut, boxed, hand-labeled for delivery, and assigned to the next available driver. (Drivers work in a first-in first-out method.)

Your internal audit team determined, after reviewing information received from various external sources and reading Pizza Inc.'s internal communications on strategy, mission, and vision, that using the business risk to business process framework will assist Pizza Inc.'s chief executive officer, chief financial officer, and chief operations officer with identifying the critical business processes and key success factors for each process.

As leader of the internal audit team, you have agreed to:

1. Identify and list the key processes used by Pizza Inc.

2. Determine and prioritize each of these key processes based on the level of inherent risk. (Complete a Process Priority Map – see Exhibit 4-17.)

3. Select the key process (the one you consider most critical to the success of Pizza Inc.) and map the sub-activities within the key process. (Create a detailed level process map of the process deemed most critical for success.)

4. Identify the specific risks associated with the sub-activities of the key process (that is, the process you selected for process mapping). (Complete the risk portion of a risk/control matrix – Exhibit 4-18.)

5. Map the identified risks related to their level of inherent risk and probability of occurrence. (complete Risk Map – Exhibit 4-19.)

6. Identify control activities (actions management currently takes) to mitigate the identified risk and put them on the risk/control matrix. (Exhibit 4-20.)

7. Determine the best method for assessing the effectiveness of the existing control activities.

8. Map the risks related to their importance and potential risk response effectiveness. (Complete Risk/Control Map – Exhibit 4-21.)

9. Based on your observations and opinion of the potential effectiveness of the current risk response activities to address risks in the critical process you selected, provide additional recommendations to mitigate existing risk and improve performance.

CASE 2

Select a company with a recent IPO and obtain the prospectus (these are usually available on the company's Web site, EDGAR, or other information services).

1. What is the business strategy and business model?

2. Identify the strategic objectives.

3. Identify the critical risks.

4. Construct a matrix with the strategic objectives on the Y axis and the critical risks on the X axis. For each objective, indicate which critical risk applies.

5. Discuss which risk you think the internal audit function should set as the highest priority.

REFERENCES

[1] Sobel, Paul. *Auditor's Risk Management Guide*. 2005 edition. (Chicago CCH, 2005, pp. 7.04-7.05).

CHAPTER 5
INTERNAL CONTROL

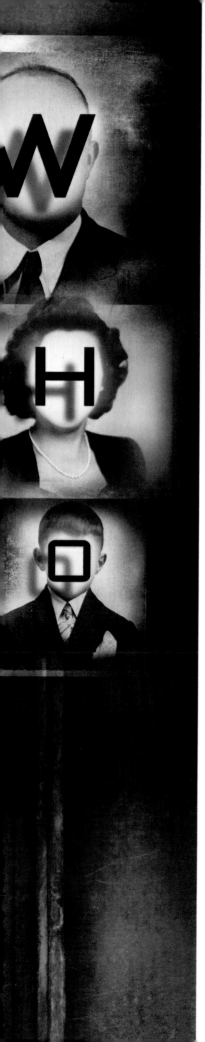

> **Learning Objectives**
>
> - Understand what is meant by internal control in a variety of frameworks.
> - Identify the components of an effective internal control framework.
> - Know the roles and responsibilities each group in an organization has regarding internal control.
> - Identify the different types of internal control and the appropriate application for each of them.
> - Understand the process of evaluating the system of internal controls.
> - Become familiar with an internal control maturity model.

"We can think of few activities within an organization that are more important to its success than maintaining internal control. Internal auditing provides management with genuine assurance that adequate controls are in place, that they are being performed as intended, and that any failures are investigated and remedied on a timely basis."[1]

Every organization has business objectives that it intends to achieve, and every organization has risks that threaten the achievement of those objectives. In this chapter, we will discuss the various components of the system of internal controls that organizations develop to mitigate and manage those risks. You will come away from this chapter with an understanding of what is meant by internal control and be able to identify a variety of frameworks that consider internal control. Additionally, you will be able to identify the components that must be present for an adequately designed and effectively operating system of internal controls. Everybody within an organization has responsibility for control activities, and this chapter will outline the specific roles and responsibilities each group of people in the organization has in that respect, including management's process for evaluating the organization's system of internal controls. Most importantly for the purpose of this chapter, we will delineate the specific role the internal audit function has relative to monitoring the system of internal controls within the organization. There are several different types of control activities employed to mitigate the many varieties of risks facing

EXHIBIT 5-1

PROFESSIONAL STANDARDS AND PRACTICE ADVISORIES RELEVANT TO CHAPTER 5

2100—Nature of Work
2120—Control

Practice Advisory 1000.C1-2: Additional Considerations for Formal
    Consulting Engagements
Practice Advisory 2100-1: Nature of Work
Practice Advisory 2100-2: Information Security
Practice Advisory 2100-5: Legal Considerations in Evaluating Regulatory
    Compliance Programs
Practice Advisory 2120.A1-1: Assessing and Reporting on Control Processes
Practice Advisory 2120.A1-2: Using Control Self-assessment for Assessing the
    Adequacy of Control Processes
Practice Advisory 2120.A1-3: Internal Auditing's Role in Quarterly Financial
    Reporting, Disclosures, and
    Management's Certifications
Practice Advisory 2120.A4-1: Control Criteria

an organization. By the end of this chapter, you will be able to identify the different types of control activities available, as well as the appropriate application of each one. Finally, we will wrap up the chapter by presenting an example of an internal control maturity model and explaining how it adds value to an organization.

FRAMEWORKS

A framework is a body of guiding principles that form a template against which organizations can evaluate a multitude of business practices. These principles are comprised of various concepts, values, assumptions, and practices intended to provide a yard stick against which an organization can assess or evaluate a particular structure, process, or environment or a group of practices or procedures. Specific to the practice of internal auditing, various frameworks are used to assess the design and operating effectiveness of internal controls.

The *International Standards for the Professional Practice of Internal Auditing (Standards)* provides the following guidance relative to the use of frameworks: "In general, a framework provides a structural blueprint of how a body of knowledge and guidance fit together. As a coherent system, it facilitates consistent development, interpretation, and application of concepts, methodologies, and techniques useful to a discipline or profession."

It is important to begin by making a few distinctions so that confusion doesn't arise regarding the different frameworks discussed in this chapter—specifically, enterprise risk management (ERM) frameworks and frameworks more specifically designed to address internal control. Both deal with risk mitigation and aspects of internal control; however, those frameworks that focus on internal control alone are more narrowly defined and tend to be less strategic in nature. While this chapter deals specifically with the subject of internal control and will focus on internal control frameworks, it would be incomplete without identifying

Framework

A body of guiding principles that form a template against which organizations can evaluate a multitude of business practices.

EXHIBIT 5-2

GLOBALLY RECOGNIZED FRAMEWORKS

Internal Control Frameworks

Internal Control—Integrated Framework (COSO), Committee of Sponsoring Organizations of the Treadway Commission, United States, 1992

Guidance on Control (CoCo), The Canadian Institute of Chartered Accountants, Canada, 1995

Internal Control Guidance for Directors on the Combined Code (Turnbull), The Institute of Chartered Accountants, England and Wales, 1999

COBIT 4.0, IT Governance Institute, United States, 2005

Enterprise Risk Management Frameworks

Australian/New Zealand Standard Risk Management (Australian Standard 4360), Joint Technical Committee OB/7—Risk Management, Australia/New Zealand, 1995

Enterprise Risk Management—Integrated Framework (COSO), Committee of Sponsoring Organizations of the Treadway Commission, United States, 2004

Governance Frameworks

Report of the Committee on the Financial Aspects of Corporate Governance (Cadbury), England, 1992

King Committee on Corporate Governance, Institute of Directors, South Africa, 2002

Other Globally Recognized Risk Mitigation Frameworks

International Convergence of Capital Measurement and Capital Standards (Basel Accord), Basel Committee on Banking Supervision, 1988

International Convergence of Capital Measurement and Capital Standards: A Revised Framework (Basel II or The New Accord), Basel Committee on Banking Supervision, 2005

ERM frameworks and other globally recognized frameworks dealing with governance, risk management, and internal control that have also been developed or have evolved over time. Chapter 3, "Governance and Risk Management," addresses the Committee of Sponsoring Organizations of the Treadway Commission (COSO) ERM framework in more detail. Exhibit 5-2 is a presentation of these frameworks.

Internal Control Frameworks

Although the frameworks discussed above contain elements of internal control, there are currently only three internal control frameworks recognized globally by management, independent outside accountants/auditors, and internal audit professionals: *Internal Control–Integrated Framework,* issued by COSO in 1992; *Guidance on Control* (often referred to as the CoCo Framework), published in 1995 by the Canadian Institute of Chartered Accountants (CICA), and *Internal Control Guidance for Directors on the Combined Code* (referred to as the Turnbull Report), published by the Institute of Chartered Accountants in England & Wales, which came out in 1999. COBIT, the information technology (IT) internal control framework referenced in Exhibit 5-2,

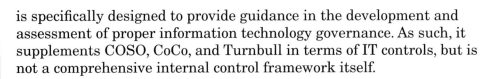

is specifically designed to provide guidance in the development and assessment of proper information technology governance. As such, it supplements COSO, CoCo, and Turnbull in terms of IT controls, but is not a comprehensive internal control framework itself.

There are no substantive differences among COSO, CoCo, and Turnbull. All of the frameworks include definitions of internal control that describe a process that provides reasonable assurance for achieving the objectives of an organization in three specific categories: effectiveness and efficiency of operations, reliability of financial reporting, and compliance with applicable laws and regulations. The three frameworks also agree regarding responsibility for internal control, specifically putting responsibility not only on the board of directors, senior management, and internal auditors, but also on each associate within the organization. Although called by different titles among the frameworks, the components of each internal control framework are basically the same and can be examined using the COSO titles for each component. They are: Control Environment, Risk Assessment, Control Activities, Information and Communication, and Monitoring. For a comparison of the three internal control frameworks using the language specific to each one, see Exhibit 5-3.

EXHIBIT 5-3

COMPARISON OF ACCEPTED INTERNAL CONTROL FRAMEWORKS			
	COSO	**CoCo**	**Turnbull**
Definition of Internal Control	A process effected by an entity's board of directors, management, and other personnel, designed to provide reasonable assurance regarding the achievement of objectives in the following categories: effectiveness and efficiency of operations, reliability of financial reporting, and compliance with laws and regulations.	Those elements of an organization that support people and offer reasonable assurance in the achievement of the organization's objectives in the following categories: effectiveness and efficiency of operations, reliability of internal and external reporting, compliance with laws and regulations, and internal policies.	Encompasses the policies, processes, tasks, behaviors, and other aspects of a company that offer reasonable assurance in facilitating its effective and efficient operation, enabling it to respond appropriately to significant business, operational, financial, compliance, and other risks to achieving the company's objectives relative to safeguarding assets, identifying and managing liabilities, the quality of reporting, compliance with laws & regulations.
Components of Internal Control	Control Environment, Risk Assessment, Control Activities, Information & Communication, and Monitoring	Purpose, Commitment, Capability, Monitoring, and Learning	Control Activities, Information & Communication Processes, Monitoring, Embeddedness in Operations of Company, Response to Risk and Changes, and Reporting

In the United States, the Sarbanes-Oxley Act of 2002 legislation put responsibility for the design, maintenance, and effective operation of internal control squarely on the shoulders of senior management, specifically, the chief executive officer (CEO) and chief financial officer (CFO). To comply with this legislation, the U.S. Securities and Exchange Commission (SEC) requires the CEO and CFO of publicly traded companies to opine on the adequate design and effective operation of internal control over financial reporting (ICFR) as part of the annual filing of financial statements with the SEC, as well as report any substantial changes in ICFR on a quarterly basis, if any. Specifically, the SEC requires evidence of compliance, ruling that "…management must base its evaluation [or, opinion] of the effectiveness of the company's internal control over financial reporting on a suitable, recognized control framework that is established by a body or group that has followed due-process procedures, including the broad distribution of the framework for public comment." [2] For details regarding the SEC's evaluation of appropriate internal control frameworks, see Exhibit 5-4.

The SEC further ruled, "The COSO Framework satisfies our criteria and may be used as an evaluation framework for purposes of management's annual internal control evaluation and disclosure requirements. However, the final rules do not mandate use of a particular framework, such as the COSO Framework, in recognition of the fact that other evaluation standards exist outside the United States. …'
The SEC, in footnote 67 of the final ruling, specifically identified the Guidance on Assessing Control, published by the Canadian Institute of Chartered Accountants (CoCo) and the Turnbull Report, published by the Institute of Chartered Accountants in England & Wales as examples of other suitable frameworks. In addition to the three frameworks specifically referred to, the SEC recognizes "…that frameworks other than COSO may be developed within the United States in the future, that satisfy the intent of the statute without diminishing the benefits to investors. The use of standard measures that are publicly available will enhance the quality of the internal control report and will promote comparability of the internal control reports of different companies. The final rules require management's report to identify the evaluation framework used by management to assess the effectiveness of the company's internal control over financial reporting. Specifi-

COSO

A voluntary private-sector organization dedicated to improving the quality of financial reporting through business ethics, effective internal controls, and corporate governance.

U.S. SARBANES-OXLEY ACT OF 2002 COMPLIANCE

The Securities and Exchange Commission (SEC) in the United States specifically refers to the COSO framework as an example of a framework suitable for organizations to compare their system of internal controls against to be compliant with Section 404 of the Sarbanes-Oxley Act, which governs all entities, foreign or domestic, wishing to access the U.S. capital market. The SEC also recognizes the CoCo framework of Canada and the Turnbull Report of England and Wales as suitable frameworks. Outside England and Wales and Canada, however, COSO represents the primary framework used to assess an organization's system of internal controls.

EXHIBIT 5-4

cally, a suitable framework must: be free from bias; permit reasonably consistent qualitative and quantitative measurements of a company's internal control; be sufficiently complete so that those relevant factors that would alter a conclusion [or opinion] about the effectiveness of a company's internal controls are not omitted; and be relevant to an evaluation of internal control over financial reporting [ICFR]" (SEC final ruling 33-8238).

Many organizations were able to successfully apply these frameworks in their efforts to comply with Section 404 of Sarbanes-Oxley, despite encountering significant unanticipated costs. Smaller publicly held companies (as defined in Exhibit 5-5), on the other hand, struggled to comply due to the prohibitive costs as well as several other challenges unique to smaller organizations, including "... sufficient resources to achieve adequate segregation of duties, management's ability to dominate activities [management override of control] ..., recruiting individuals with requisite financial reporting and other expertise to serve effectively on the board of directors and audit committee, recruiting and retaining personnel with sufficient experience and skill in accounting and financial reporting, ... [and] maintaining appropriate control over computer information systems. ..." In response to this, COSO issued *Internal Control Over Financial Reporting—Guidance for Smaller Public Companies* (The Guidance) in July 2006 as a supplement to the original COSO framework. Primarily designed to provide guidance to smaller public companies to assist them with a cost effective means to comply with Section 404 of Sarbanes-Oxley, The Guidance had the added benefit of supplying direction to all organizations, regardless of size, in the application of the original COSO framework when evaluating the effectiveness of ICFR by providing "a set of twenty basic principles representing the fundamental concepts associated with, and drawn directly from, the five components of the [COSO] Framework." These 20 basic principles are outlined in Exhibit 5-6.

As a result of the increased public scrutiny over ICFR, the subject of internal control has been elevated to the prominence formerly reserved for topics such as sales, marketing, profits (EPS), and capital

EXHIBIT 5-6

BASIC PRINCIPLES FROM THE COSO FRAMEWORK

Control Environment

Integrity and Ethical Values—Sound integrity and ethical values, particularly of top management, are developed and understood and set the standard of conduct for financial reporting.

Board of Directors—The board of directors understands and exercises oversight responsibility related to financial reporting and related internal control.

Management's Philosophy and Operating Style—Management's philosophy and operating style support achieving effective internal control over financial reporting.

Organizational Structure—The company's organizational structure supports effective internal control over financial reporting.

Financial Reporting Competencies—The company retains individuals competent in financial reporting and oversight roles.

Authority and Responsibility—Management and employees are assigned appropriate levels of authority and responsibility to facilitate effective internal control over financial reporting.

Human Resources—Human resource policies and practices are designed and implemented to facilitate effective internal control over financial reporting.

Risk Assessment

Financial Reporting Objectives—Management specifies financial reporting objectives with sufficient clarity and criteria to enable the identification of risks to reliable financial reporting.

Financial Reporting Risks—The company identifies and analyzes risks to the achievement of financial reporting objectives as a basis for determining how the risks should be managed.

Fraud Risk—The potential for material misstatement due to fraud is explicitly considered in assessing risks to the achievement of financial reporting objectives.

Control Activities

Integration With Risk Assessment—Actions are taken to address risks to the achievement of financial reporting objectives.

Selection and Development of Control Activities—Control activities are selected and developed considering their cost and their potential effectiveness in mitigating risks to the achievement of financial reporting objectives.

Policies and Procedures—Policies related to reliable financial reporting are established and communicated throughout the company, with corresponding procedures resulting in management directives being carried out.

Information Technology—Information technology controls, where applicable, are designed and implemented to support the achievement of financial reporting objectives.

Information and Communication

Financial Reporting Information—Pertinent information is identified, captured, used at all levels of the company, and distributed in a form and time frame that supports the achievement of financial reporting objectives.

Internal Control Information—Information used to execute other control components is identified, captured, and distributed in a form and time frame that enables personnel to carry out their internal control responsibilities.

Internal Communication—Communications enable and support understanding and execution of internal control objectives, processes, and individual responsibilities at all levels of the organization.

External Communication—Matters affecting the achievement of financial reporting objectives are communicated with outside parties.

Monitoring

Ongoing and Separate Evaluations—Ongoing and/or separate evaluations enable management to determine whether internal control over financial reporting is present and functioning.

Reporting Deficiencies—Internal control deficiencies are identified and communicated in a timely manner to those parties responsible for taking corrective action, and to management and the board as appropriate.

adequacy in many organizations. In addition to using COSO, CoCo, and Turnbull as vehicles to assess ICFR, many organizations are also using these frameworks to more broadly evaluate the entire system of internal controls.

> Control had long been a component of the "unique" franchise of internal auditing. The emergence of broad management control frameworks such as Internal Control-Integrated Framework from the Committee of Sponsoring Organizations of the Treadway Commission (COSO) and Criteria of Control from the Canadian Institute of Chartered Accountants (CoCo) has elevated the internal auditor's focus from financial and compliance-oriented controls to management controls and governance processes that address broad organizational risks. The COSO and CoCo focus widens the spectrum of controls addressed by internal auditors and more closely aligns their control activities with an organization's objectives and core value-creating processes.[3]

As previously indicated, these three frameworks include similar definitions of internal control that describe a process that provides reasonable assurance for achieving the business objectives of an organization in three specific categories: effectiveness and efficiency of operations, reliability of financial reporting, and compliance with applicable laws and regulations. Again, they are called by different titles among the frameworks, but the components of each internal control framework are basically the same. Therefore, going forward, the COSO Framework will be used to study the various components of the system of internal controls in more depth.

DEFINITION OF INTERNAL CONTROL

COSO broadly defines internal control as:

> … a process, effected by an entity's board of directors, management, and other personnel, designed to provide reasonable assurance regarding the achievement of objectives in the following categories:

- Effectiveness and efficiency of operations.

- Reliability of financial reporting.

- Compliance with applicable laws and regulations.

This definition reflects certain fundamental concepts:

- Internal control is a process. It's a means to an end, not an end in itself.

- Internal control is effected by people. It's not merely policy manuals and forms, but people at every level of an organization.

- Internal control can be expected to provide only reasonable assurance, not absolute assurance, to an entity's management and board.

Internal Control (COSO definition)

A process, effected by an entity's board of directors, management, and other personnel, designed to provide reasonable assurance regarding the achievement of objectives in the following categories:

• Effectiveness and efficiency of operations.

• Reliability of financial reporting.

• Compliance with applicable laws and regulations.

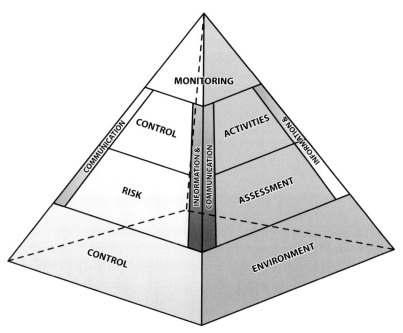

EXHIBIT 5-7

The *control environment* provides an atmosphere in which people conduct their activities and carry out their control responsibilities. It serves as the foundation for the other components. Within this environment, management *assesses risks* to the achievement of specified objectives. *Control activities* are implemented to help ensure that management directives to address the risks are carried out. Meanwhile, relevant *information* is captured and *communicated* throughout the organization. The entire process is *monitored* and modified as conditions warrant.

Copyright 1992 by the Committee of Sponsoring Organizations of the Treadway Commission. Reproduced with permission from the AICPA acting as authorized administrator for COSO.

- Internal control is geared to the achievement of objectives in one or more separate but overlapping categories.[4]

Although this definition may seem very general, broadly defining internal control accommodates the exploration of its categories individually or taken as a whole. When internal control categories are looked at as a whole, they are collectively referred to as the system of internal controls. COSO indicates, "Those who want to can focus separately, for example, on controls over financial reporting or controls related to compliance with laws and regulations. Similarly, a directed focus on controls in particular units or activities of an entity can be accommodated." Likewise, an organization can choose to focus on its overall system of internal controls.

Note that while COSO defines achievement of compliance objectives strictly as "adherence to laws and regulations to which the entity is subject," The IIA's Professional Practices Framework defines it more broadly as "conformity and adherence to policies, plans, procedures, laws, regulations, contracts, or other requirements." COSO considers compliance with those additional governance related requirements a part of the achievement of operations objectives instead of compliance objectives. The classification is much less important than the actual achievement of the objectives no matter how an organization chooses to classify them. This distinction is, however, an important consideration when the internal audit function is planning and determining the scope of an assurance engagement. For a detailed review of assurance engagement planning, scope setting, and communications, refer to Chapter 9, "Gathering and Documenting Audit Evidence," Chapter 10, "Conducting the Assurance Engagement," and Chapter 11, "Communicating Assurance Engagement Outcomes and Performing Follow-up Procedures."

THE COMPONENTS OF INTERNAL CONTROL

Control Environment

The control environment sets the tone of an organization, influencing the control consciousness of its people. It is the foundation for all other components of internal control, providing discipline and structure. Control environment factors include the integrity, ethical values, and competence of the entity's people; management's philosophy and operating style; the way management assigns authority and responsibility, and organizes and develops its people; and the attention and direction provided by the board of directors.

The control environment has a pervasive influence on the way business activities are structured, objectives established, and risks assessed. It also influences control activities, information and communication systems, and monitoring activities. This is true not only of their design but also the way they work day to day. The control environment is influenced by the entity's history and culture. It influences the control consciousness of its people. Effectively controlled entities strive to have competent people, instill an enterprisewide attitude of integrity and control consciousness, and set a positive "tone at the top." They establish appropriate policies and procedures, often including a written code of conduct, which foster shared values and team work in pursuit of the entity's objectives.[5]

The control environment, then, is the sphere in which entitywide (entity level) controls are created. Entitywide controls will be addressed in more detail later in this chapter.

Risk Assessment

Every entity faces a variety of risks from external and internal sources that must be assessed. A precondition to risk assessment is establishment of objectives, linked at different levels and internally consistent. Risk assessment is the identification and analysis of relevant risks to achievement of the objectives, forming a basis for determining how the risks should be managed. Because economic, industry, regulatory, and operating conditions will continue to change, mechanisms are needed to identify and deal with the special risks associated with change. [6]

Objective setting is the precondition to effective event identification, risk assessment, and risk response. There must first be objectives, established in a strategy-setting environment, before manage-

Compliance

Conformity and adherence to applicable laws and regulations (COSO definition). May also include conformity and adherence to policies, plans, procedures, contracts, or other requirements.

Risk Assessment

The identification and analysis of relevant risks to achievement of the objectives, forming a basis for determining how the risks should be managed.

EXHIBIT 5-8

Internal Control and the Management Process

Management Activities	Internal Control
Entity-level [entitywide] objective setting—mission, value statements	
Strategic planning	
Establishing control environment factors	✓
Activity-level [process-level] objective setting	
Risk identification and analysis	✓
Risk management	
Conducting control activities	✓
Information identification, capture, and communication	✓
Monitoring	✓
Corrective actions	

ment can identify risks (event identification) that might impede the achievement of the objectives and take necessary actions to manage those risks (risk response). Objective setting, event identification, risk assessment, and risk response, then, are key elements of the risk management process. While objective setting is not an internal control component, it is a prerequisite to and enabler of internal control. COSO describes the objective setting process and its importance to an organization's system of internal controls as follows:

> Objective setting can be a highly structured or informal process. Objectives may be explicitly stated, or be implicit, such as to continue a past level of performance. At the entity level, objectives often are represented by the entity's mission and value statements. Along with assessments of the entity's strengths and weaknesses, and of opportunities and threats, they lead to an overall strategy. Generally, the strategic plan is broadly stated, dealing with high-level resource allocations and priorities.

> More specific objectives flow from the entity's broad strategy. Entity-level objectives are linked and integrated with more-specific objectives established for various "activities," such as sales, production, and engineering, making sure they are consistent. These sub-objectives, or activity-level objectives, include establishing goals and may deal with product line, market, financing, and profit objectives.

By setting objectives at the entity and activity [process] levels, an entity can identify critical success factors. These are key things that must go right if goals are to be attained. Critical success factors exist

for the entity, a business unit, a function, a department, or an individual. Objective setting enables management to identify measurement criteria for performance, with focus on critical factors.

Despite the diversity of objectives, certain broad categories can be established:

- **Operations Objectives.** These pertain to effectiveness and efficiency of the entity's operations, including performance and profitability goals and safeguarding resources against loss. They vary based on management's choices about structure and performance.

- **Financial Reporting Objectives.** These pertain to the preparation of reliable published financial statements, including prevention of fraudulent public financial reporting. They are driven primarily by external requirements.

- **Compliance Objectives.** These objectives pertain to adherence to laws and regulations to which the entity is subject. They are dependent on external factors, such as environmental regulations, and tend to be similar across all entities in some cases and across an industry in others.[7]

Control Activities

Control activities are the policies and procedures that help ensure management directives are carried out. They help ensure that necessary actions are taken to address risks to achievement of the entity's objectives. Control activities occur throughout the organization, at all levels and in all functions. They include a range of activities as diverse as approvals, authorizations, verifications, reconciliations, reviews of operating performance, security of assets, and segregation of duties.

Control activities can be divided into three categories based on the nature of the entity's objectives to which they relate: operations, financial reporting, or compliance.

Although some controls relate solely to one area, there is often overlap. Depending on circumstances, a particular control activity could help satisfy entity objectives in more than one of the three categories. Thus, operations controls also can help ensure reliable financial reporting, financial reporting controls can serve to effect compliance, and so on.

Although these categories are helpful in discussing internal control, the particular category in which a control happens to be placed is not as important as the role it plays in achieving a particular activity's objectives.

Many different descriptions of types of control activities have been put forth, including preventive controls, detective controls, manual controls, computer controls, and management controls.[8]

Various types of controls and their definitions will be addressed in more detail later in this chapter.

Every organization has its own set of business objectives and implementation strategies for such. Because each organization is managed by different people who use individual judgments in unique operating environments with varying complexity, no two organizations have the same set of control activities, even though they might have very similar business strategies. Control activities, therefore, serve a vital role in the management process of an organization by ensuring that its uniquely identified risks are mitigated, allowing the organization to achieve its business objectives.

Information and Communication

Pertinent information must be identified, captured, and communicated in a form and time frame that enable people to carry out their responsibilities. Information systems produce reports, containing operational, financial, and compliance-related information, that make it possible to run and control the business. They deal not only with internally generated data, but also with information about external events, activities, and conditions necessary to informed business decision-making and external reporting. Effective communication also must occur in a broader sense, flowing down, across, and up the organization. All personnel must receive a clear message from top management that control responsibilities must be taken seriously. They must understand their own role in the internal control system, as well as how individual activities relate to the work of others. They must have a means of communicating significant information upstream. There also needs to be effective communication with external parties, such as customers, suppliers, regulators, and shareholders.

Information is needed at all levels of an organization to run the business and move toward achievement of the entity's objectives in all categories—operations, financial reporting, and compliance.

Keeping information consistent with [business] needs becomes particularly important when an entity operates in the face of fundamental industry changes, highly innovative and quick-moving competitors, or significant customer demand shifts.[9]

Information is only useful when communicated appropriately. This interdependency is why COSO combines information and communication in this component. Accurate and timely information must be available to those management representatives that need it at all levels of an organization to run the business effectively. Not only must information be provided "to appropriate personnel so they can carry out their operating, financial reporting, and compliance responsibilities," but "communication also must take place in a broader sense, dealing with expectations, responsibilities of individuals and groups, and other important matters."[10] Communications with external parties are also important and can provide critical information on the functioning of control activities. These parties include, but are not limited to, customers, suppliers, service providers, regulators, external auditors, and shareholders.

Communication takes such forms as policy manuals, memoranda, bulletin board notices, and videotaped messages. Where messages are transmitted orally—in large groups, smaller meetings, or one-on-one sessions—tone of voice and body language serve to emphasize what is being said.

Another powerful communications medium is the action taken by management in dealing with subordinates. Managers should remind themselves, "Actions speak louder than words." Their actions are, in turn, influenced by the history and culture of the entity, drawing on past observations of how their superiors dealt with similar situations.

An entity with a long and rich history of operating with integrity, and whose culture is well understood by people throughout the organization, will likely find little difficulty in communicating its message. An entity without such a tradition will likely need to put more effort into the way messages are communicated.[11]

Monitoring

Monitoring

A process that assesses the presence and functioning of governance, risk management, and control components over time.

Internal control systems need to be monitored—a process that assesses the quality of the system's performance over time. This is accomplished through ongoing monitoring activities, separate [periodic] evaluations, or a combination of the two. Ongoing monitoring occurs in the course of operations. It includes regular management and supervisory activities, and other actions personnel take in performing their duties. The scope and frequency of separate evaluations will depend primarily on an assessment of risks and the effectiveness of ongoing monitoring procedures. Internal control deficiencies should be reported upstream, with serious matters reported to top management and the board [of directors].

Monitoring ensures that internal control continues to operate effectively. This process involves assessment by appropriate personnel of the design and operation of controls on a suitably timely basis, and the taking of necessary actions. It applies to all activities within an organization, and sometimes to outside contractors as well.

Monitoring can be done in two ways: through ongoing activities or separate evaluations. Internal control systems usually will be structured to monitor themselves on an ongoing basis to some degree. The greater the degree and effectiveness of ongoing monitoring, the less need for separate evaluations. The frequency of separate evaluations necessary for management to have reasonable assurance about the effectiveness of the internal control system is a matter of management's judgment. In making that determination, consideration should be given to the following: the nature and degree of changes occurring and their associated risks, the competence and experience of the people implementing the controls, as well as the results of the ongoing monitoring. Usually, some combination of ongoing monitoring and separate evaluations will ensure that the internal control system maintains its effectiveness over time.

It should be recognized that ongoing monitoring procedures are built into the normal, recurring operating activities of an entity. Because they are performed on a real-time basis, reacting dynamically to changing conditions, and are ingrained in the entity, they are more effective than procedures performed in connection with separate evaluations. Since separate evaluations take place after the fact, problems will often be identified more quickly by the ongoing monitoring routines.

Activities that serve to monitor the effectiveness of internal control in the ordinary course of operations are manifold. They include regular management and supervisory activities, comparisons, reconciliations, and other routine actions.

Exhibit 5-9 provides examples of different types of monitoring.

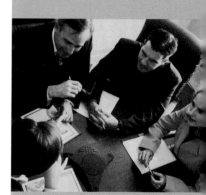

While ongoing monitoring procedures usually provide important feedback on the effectiveness of other control components, [separate evaluations provide] a fresh look from time to time, focusing directly on the system's effectiveness. This also provides an opportunity to consider the continued effectiveness of the ongoing monitoring procedures.

Often [separate] evaluations take the form of self-assessments, where persons responsible for a particular unit or function will determine the effectiveness of controls for their activities. Internal auditors normally perform internal control evaluations as part of their regular duties, or upon special request of the board of directors, senior management, or subsidiary or divisional executives. Similarly, management may use the work of external auditors in considering the effectiveness of internal control. A combination of efforts by both parties may be used in conducting whatever [separate] evaluative procedures management deems necessary.[12]

During the performance of ongoing monitoring and separate evaluations, deficiencies in an organization's system of internal controls may be identified. COSO broadly defines a deficiency as "a condition within an internal control system worthy of attention." COSO elaborates that "a deficiency, therefore, may represent a perceived, potential, or real shortcoming, or opportunity to strengthen the internal control system to provide a greater likelihood that the entity's objectives will be achieved."[13] Deficiencies (also referred to as audit observations) identified as a result of ongoing monitoring and separate evaluations must be reported in a timely manner to the appropriate parties within the organization. Depending on the impact a specific deficiency has on the potential effectiveness of the system of internal controls, it should be reported to business unit management, senior management, and/or board of directors. Reported deficiencies are important considerations

More than any other individual, the *chief executive* sets the "tone at the top" that affects integrity and ethics and other factors of a positive control environment.

EXHIBIT 5-9

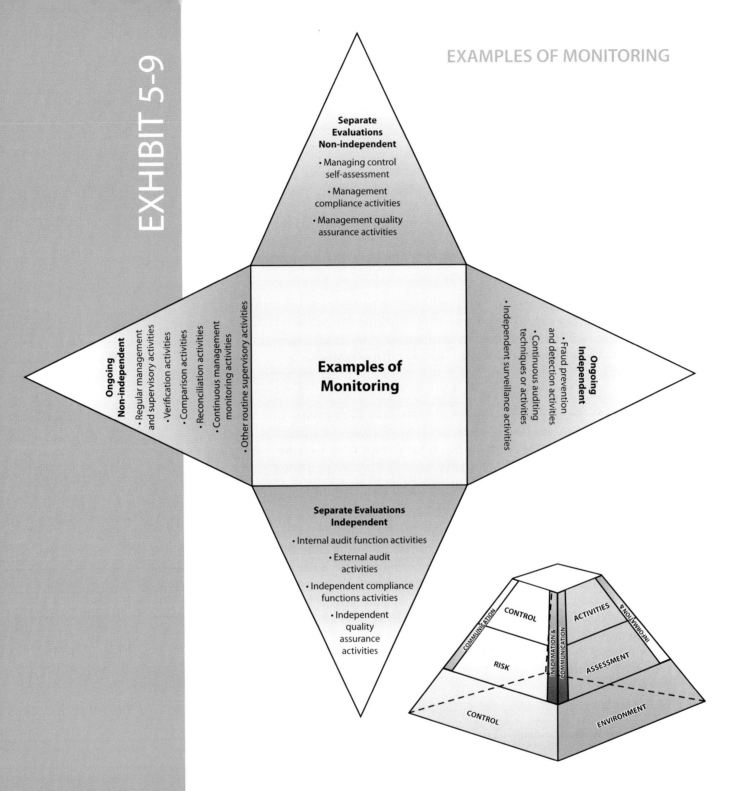

Separate Evaluations Non-independent

• Managing control self-assessment

• Management compliance activities

• Management quality assurance activities

Ongoing Non-independent

• Regular management and supervisory activities
• Verification activities
• Comparison activities
• Reconciliation activities
• Continuous management monitoring activities
• Other routine supervisory activities

Examples of Monitoring

Ongoing Independent

• Fraud prevention and detection activities
• Continuous auditing techniques or activities
• Independent surveillance activities

Separate Evaluations Independent

• Internal audit function activities

• External audit activities

• Independent compliance functions activities

• Independent quality assurance activities

in the evaluation of the system of internal controls. Evaluating the system of internal controls will be explored in more detail later in this chapter. Formal communications relative to assurance engagements completed by the internal audit function are addressed in detail in Chapter 11, "Communicating Assurance Engagement Outcomes and Performing Follow-up Procedures."

INTERNAL CONTROL ROLES AND RESPONSIBILITIES

Everyone in an organization has responsibility for internal control:

Management

The chief executive officer is ultimately responsible and should assume "ownership" of the system. More than any other individual, the chief executive sets the "tone at the top" that affects integrity and ethics and other factors of a positive control environment. In a large company, the chief executive fulfills this duty by providing leadership and direction to senior managers and reviewing the way they're controlling the business. Senior managers, in turn, assign responsibility for establishment of more specific internal control policies and procedures to personnel responsible for the unit's functions. In a smaller entity, the influence of the chief executive, often an owner-manager, is usually more direct. In any event, in a cascading responsibility, a manager is effectively a chief executive of his or her sphere of responsibility. Of particular significance are financial officers and their staffs, whose control activities cut across, as well as up and down, the operating and other units of an enterprise.

Board of Directors

Management is accountable to the board of directors, which provides governance, guidance, and oversight. Effective board members are objective, capable, and inquisitive. They also have knowledge of the entity's activities and environment, and commit the time necessary to fulfill their board responsibilities. Management may be in a position to override controls and ignore or stifle communications from subordinates, enabling a dishonest management that intentionally misrepresents results to cover its tracks. A strong, active board, particularly when coupled with effective upward communications channels and capable financial, legal, and internal audit functions, is often best able to identify and correct such a problem.[14]

The board of directors' roles and responsibilities as described by COSO eventually evolved into what is today known as an "effective" governance structure for an organization. For a visual depiction of this process, see Exhibit 3-3 in Chapter 3, "Governance and Risk Management." Chapter 3 describes governance as the process conducted by the board of directors to authorize, direct, and oversee management toward the achievement of the organization's business objectives.

Internal Auditors

While management, in the form of the chief executive officer, has ultimate responsibility for the adequate design and effective operation of the system of internal controls, internal auditors play a significant role in the verification that management has met its responsibility. Initially, management performs the primary assessment, testing, and certification of the system of internal controls, and then the internal audit function independently validates management's results. The internal audit function provides reasonable assurance that the system of internal controls is properly designed and operating effectively, increasing the likelihood the organization's business objectives and goals will be met efficiently and economically. The COSO framework

Internal Control Function

A process, effected by an entity's board of directors, management, and other personnel, designed to provide reasonable assurance regarding the achievement of objectives in the following categories:

- Effectiveness and efficiency of operations.

- Reliability of financial reporting.

- Compliance with applicable laws and regulations.

defines the role of the internal auditor similarly, although in more general terms: "Internal auditors play an important role in evaluating the effectiveness of control systems, and contribute to ongoing effectiveness. Because of organizational position and authority in an entity, an internal audit function often plays a significant monitoring role." [15] The relationship between management and the internal audit function relative to evaluating the system of internal controls and reporting on such is further explored later in this chapter and in Chapter 8, "Managing the Internal Audit Function."

Other Personnel

Internal control is, to some degree, the responsibility of everyone in an organization and therefore should be an explicit or implicit part of everyone's job description. Virtually all employees produce information used in the internal control system or take other actions needed to effect control. Also, all personnel should be responsible for communicating upward problems in operations, noncompliance with the code of conduct, or other policy violations or illegal actions.

A number of external parties often contribute to achievement of an entity's objectives. External auditors, bringing an independent and objective view, contribute directly through the financial statement audit and indirectly by providing information useful to management and the board in carrying out their responsibilities. Others providing information to the entity useful in effecting internal control are legislators and regulators, customers and others transacting business with the enterprise, financial analysts, bond raters, and the news media. External parties, however, are not responsible for, nor are they a part of, the entity's internal control system. [16]

In many cases, outside vendors are used to perform elements of the internal control system. However, in those cases, ownership or accountability for those outsourced elements remains with internal management, who has the ultimate responsibility for testing and certifying outsourced key controls. Examples would include data processing, payroll, or even the internal audit function itself. Since internal management representatives are ultimately responsible for any outsourced control activities, these vendors are not considered responsible for, nor are they a part of, the entity's internal control system, per se.

LIMITATIONS OF INTERNAL CONTROLS

Internal control, no matter how well designed and operated, can provide only reasonable assurance to management and the board of directors regarding achievement of an entity's objectives. The likelihood of achievement is affected by limitations inherent in all internal control systems. These include the realities that human judgment in decision-making can be faulty, and that breakdowns can occur because of such human failures as simple error or mistake. Additionally, controls can be circumvented by the collusion of two or more people, and management has the ability to override the internal control system. Another limiting factor is

Inherent Limitations of Internal Control

The confines that relate to the limits of human judgment, resource constraints and the need to consider the cost of controls in relation to expected benefits, the reality that breakdowns can occur, and the possibility of collusion or management override.

the need to consider controls' relative costs and benefits.

Internal control has been viewed by some observers as ensuring an entity will not fail—that is, the entity will always achieve its operations, financial reporting, and compliance objectives. In this sense, internal control sometimes is looked upon as a cure-all for all real and potential business ills. This view is misguided. Internal control is not a panacea.

In considering limitations of internal control, two different concepts must be recognized: First, internal control—even effective internal control—operates at different levels with respect to different objectives. For objectives related to the effectiveness and efficiency of an entity's operations—achievement of its basic mission, profitability goals and the like—internal control can help to ensure that management is aware of the entity's progress, or lack of it. But it cannot provide even reasonable assurance that the objectives themselves will be achieved. Second, internal control cannot provide absolute assurance with respect to any of the three objectives categories.[17]

Inherent Limitations and Reasonable Assurance

COSO concludes that inherent limitations are "the limitations [that] relate to the limits of human judgment; resource constraints and the need to consider the cost of controls in relation to expected benefits; the reality that breakdowns can occur; and the possibility of management override and collusion."[18] All internal control systems have inherent limitations.

Because all internal control systems have inherent limitations, there is no guarantee (absolute assurance) that an organization's business objectives in any of the three objectives categories will be met. This concept is what COSO refers to as reasonable assurance.

Establishing business objectives is a prerequisite to designing an effective system of internal controls. Business objectives provide the measurable targets for which an organization conducts its operations. A key to understanding the concepts of inherent limitations and reasonable assurance lies in also understanding the linkage and interdependency of the business objectives and the risks that directly or indirectly affect an organization's ability to achieve their business objectives. Only then can an organization properly design and implement an effective system of internal controls. As COSO indicates, "The process of identifying and analyzing risk is an ongoing iterative process and is a critical component of an effective internal control system. Management must focus carefully on risks at all levels of the entity and take necessary actions to manage them." [19]

Risk Analysis—Inherent Risk, Risk Appetite, Controllable Risk, and Residual Risk

An organization's ability to achieve established business objectives is affected by both internal and external risk factors. The combination of internal and external risk factors in their pure, uncontrolled state is referred to as inherent risk. Said another way, inherent risk is the

Inherent Risk
The combination of internal and external risk factors in their pure, uncontrolled state, or, the gross risk that exists assuming there are no internal control activities in place.

gross risk that exists assuming there are no internal control activities in place. The acknowledgement of the existence of inherent risk and that certain events or conditions are simply outside of management's control (external risk factors) is the basis for inherent limitations.

Identifying external and internal factors that contribute to risk at an entity and activity (process and transaction) level is critical to effective risk assessment. As discussed in Chapter 4, "Business Processes and Business Risks," once the major contributing risk factors have been identified, management can then consider their importance and, where possible, link risk factors to business objectives and related business operations.

> After the entity has identified entitywide and activity risks, a risk analysis needs to be performed. The methodology for analyzing risks can vary, largely because many risks are difficult to quantify. Nonetheless, the process—which may be more or less formal—usually includes:
>
> - Estimating the significance of a risk [severity or impact].
>
> - Assessing the likelihood (or frequency) of the risk occurring [probability].
>
> - Considering how the risk should be managed—that is, an assessment of what actions need to be taken [control activities].
>
> A risk that does not have a significant effect on the entity and that has a low likelihood of occurrence generally does not warrant serious concern. A significant risk with a high likelihood of occurrence, on the other hand, usually demands considerable attention. Circumstances in between these extremes usually require difficult judgments. It is important that the analysis be rational and careful.
>
> Once the significance and likelihood of risk have been assessed, management needs to consider how the risk should be managed. This involves judgment based on assumptions about the risk, and reasonable analysis of costs associated with reducing the level of risk [to an acceptable level]. Actions that can be taken to reduce significance or likelihood of the risk occurring include a myriad of decisions management may make every day.[20]

The specific action management chooses to take to reduce the significance or likelihood of a risk depends largely on the risk appetite established by an organization's management and board of directors. COSO's *Enterprise Risk Management—Integrated Framework* defines risk appetite as "the broad-based amount of risk a company or other entity is willing to accept in pursuit of its mission or vision."[21] Additionally, risk appetite takes into consideration the amount of risk that management consciously accepts after balancing the cost and benefits of implementing control activities. It is important to recognize that there is a direct relationship between the amount of risk mitigated and the cost associated with implementing control activities designed to achieve that level of mitigation. Consequently, an organization must ensure it

EXHIBIT 5-10

BALANCING RISKS AND CONTROLS

Consequences of Accepting Excessive Risk:	Consequences of Implementing Excessive Controls:
• Potential loss of assets	• Increased bureaucracy
• Poor or ineffective business decision making	• Excess cost of production
• Potential noncompliance with laws and regulations	• Unnecessary complexity of controls
• Potential for fraud to occur	• Increased cycle time
	• Non-value add activities

has neither excessive risk nor excessive control. Exhibit 5-10 lists some of the possible consequences of accepting excessive risk or implementing excessive control. The balance that management is able to achieve results in an organization accepting a higher or lower level of risk and depends on the nature of the risk, the regulatory environment in which the organization operates, and management's philosophy.

With that said, there are many factors management must consider when determining the specific actions (control activities) management should take to manage inherent risk within the risk appetite established by an organization. To begin with, management must consider controllable risk.

Controllable risk is that portion of inherent risk specifically related to risk factors internal to an organization. Said another way, controllable risk is the risk that management can directly influence and that can be reduced or managed through day-to-day business operations.

Once management has implemented cost-effective control activities to address controllable risk, then and only then can they determine if the organization is operating within the risk appetite established by executive management and the board of directors. The portion of inherent risk that remains after mitigating controllable risk is defined as residual risk. If the remaining uncontrolled risk (residual risk) is less than the established risk appetite, then the system of internal controls is operating at an acceptable level and within an organization's defined risk appetite.

If, however, residual risk exceeds the organization's established risk appetite, it is necessary to re-evaluate the system of internal controls to determine if additional cost effective control activities can be implemented to further reduce residual risk to a level within management's risk appetite. If not, management must consider other options such as sharing or transferring a portion of the uncontrolled risk to a willing independent third party through insurance or outsourcing. If the uncontrolled risk cannot be effectively transferred or shared, management can either accept the higher level of risk (and adjust their risk appetite accordingly), or the organization must decide if it wants to remain engaged in the activity causing the risk. Refer to Chapter 3, "Governance and Risk Management," for an in-depth review of risk

Residual Risk

The portion of inherent risk that remains after management executes its risk responses (sometimes referred to as net risk).

management and related mitigation techniques.

A properly designed and effectively operating system of internal controls, by definition, is designed to manage risk within the organization's established risk appetite. It should mitigate inherent risk related to the three COSO categories of objectives (effective and efficient operations, reliable financial reporting, and compliance with applicable laws and regulations) within management's risk appetite.

VIEWING INTERNAL CONTROL FROM DIFFERENT PERSPECTIVES

Because everyone in an organization has some responsibility for internal control, there naturally will be different perspectives from which individuals in the organization approach internal control. "Different perspectives on internal control are not undesirable," according to COSO. "Internal control is concerned with entity objectives, and different groups are interested in different objectives for different reasons."[22]

Management

Management views internal control from the broad perspective of the entire organization. Its responsibility is to develop the entity's objectives and strategies, and to direct its human and material resources to achieve the objectives.

For management, internal control covers a wide spectrum, including policies, procedures, and actions to help ensure that an entity achieves its objectives. It includes all personally carried out and delegated activities that enable management to: direct and monitor operations, be aware of relevant internal and external events, and identify and deal with risks.

Internal control enables management to take timely action when conditions change. Information is provided, for example, on production, sales, inventory levels, and other areas that bear on effective decision-making. Broader-based events—such as technology changes, industry innovations, actions of competitors, customers and suppliers, and legislative initiatives—also are addressed. This allows management to lessen adverse impacts or take advantage of emerging opportunities. Internal control also helps management ensure that it complies with environmental, social, and legal responsibilities. These include fiduciary rules for employee benefit plans, worker safety regulations, and rules for proper disposal of hazardous waste. Ensuring compliance protects the reputation of the enterprise.[23]

Internal Auditors

The IIA defines internal control as "any action taken by management to enhance the likelihood that established objectives and goals will be achieved," and elaborates on the nature of these actions by noting that control is the result of proper planning, organizing, and directing by management.

Internal Control (IIA definition)

Any action taken by management to enhance the likelihood that established objectives and goals will be achieved.

This broad view of internal control is consistent with The IIA's view of internal auditing's role in an entity: that "internal auditing examines and evaluates the planning, organizing, and directing processes to determine whether reasonable assurance exists that goals and objectives will be achieved." All of an entity's systems, processes, operations, functions, and activities are included within the purview of internal control. In practice, the scope of internal auditing organizations will vary, depending on their charter in the entity.[24]

Independent Auditors

Independent certified public accountants, because of their role as auditors of financial statements, have focused their perspective of internal control primarily on those aspects that support or affect the entity's external financial reporting.

Although for audit-planning purposes, independent auditors gain knowledge of an entity's business and industry—including its business objectives, strategies, and competitive position—they do not need to address the totality of internal control to audit the enterprise's financial statements. This narrowing of focus is the same process that many others must perform to carry out their duties.[25]

Other External Parties

Legislators and regulatory agencies have developed various definitions of internal control to conform to their responsibilities. These definitions generally relate to the types of activities monitored, and may encompass achievement of the entity's goals and objectives, reporting requirements, use of resources in compliance with laws and regulations, and safeguarding resources against waste, loss, and misuse.

Investors and creditors need information, primarily financial, that generally is consistent with the type addressed by independent auditors. Other external parties need a variety of information about an entity. However, these constituencies have limited ability to require specific entities to provide information and usually are not in a position to impose their perspectives on internal control.[26]

TYPES OF CONTROL ACTIVITIES

There are many types of control activities that are used by an organization to increase the likelihood that objectives will be met. It is important to note that specific controls can be referred to by different organizations (and even different individuals within an organization) by different names. More significant than the name used to describe a particular control is the type of control it is. This can create confusion because many controls fit into more than one category simultaneously. This will be addressed in more detail later in the chapter.

One critical concept common to all control activities, however, is the concept that COSO defines as *segregation of duties*. Segregation of du-

Control Activities
Any action taken by management, the board, and other parties to manage risk and increase the likelihood that established objectives and goals will be achieved. Management plans, organizes, and directs the performance of sufficient actions to provide reasonable assurance that objectives and goals will be achieved.

ties is the concept of dividing, or segregating, control activities related to the authorization of transactions from the processing of those transactions from physical access to the assets related to those underlying transactions. The primary purpose of segregating duties (dividing control activities) among different people is to reduce the risk of error or inappropriate actions taken by any single individual.

In addition to segregation of duties, there are many commonly recognized control activities that are present in a well-designed system of internal controls, including:

● Performance reviews and follow-up.

● Authorization (approvals).

● IT access control activities.

● Documentation (rigorous and comprehensive).

● Physical access control activities.

● IT application (input, processing, output) control activities.

● Independent verifications and reconciliations.

Depending on the specific application of these control activities, they can be classified any number of ways and may take on multiple classifications simultaneously. The following sections outline the various types of control activities and their individual purposes that these and other control activities will assume.

Entitywide and Process-level Control Activities

All control activities are designed to mitigate risk either at the enterprise level or at the operational level within an organization. The original COSO framework uses the terms "entity level" and "activity level" respectively to describe these controls, although it is not uncommon for organizations within the internal audit profession to use different terminology such as "company wide" to refer to entity-level controls and "process," "transaction," or "application" to refer to activity-level controls. More recently, however, COSO published the guide *Internal Control over Financial Reporting—Guidance for Smaller Public Companies*, in which the terminology for these concepts has been changed to "entitywide" and "process level" respectively. Exhibit 5-11 goes into more detail on the specific control activities comprising the more general category of process level control activities, however, in the interest of simplicity and consistency, this chapter uses the most recently adopted COSO terms "entitywide" and "process level," going forward. More important than the specific terms used when discussing these types of controls, however, is the purpose of the control and its operating effectiveness.

Entitywide control activities are very broadly focused and often deal with the organizational environment or atmosphere. They are designed to mitigate risks that exist at the organizationwide level including those that arise internally as well as externally. These control activities "have a pervasive effect on the achievement of many overall objectives

Entitywide Control

A control that operates across an entire entity and, as such, is not bound by, or associated with, individual processes.

EXHIBIT 5-11

CONTROL ACTIVITIES COMPRISING PROCESS-LEVEL CONTROL ACTIVITIES

COSO recognizes entitywide and process-level as the two levels of control activities. Other professional organizations within the internal auditing profession, however, often recognize subsets of what COSO refers to as process level control activities. These subsets are defined as follows:

Transaction level: Transaction-level control activities are very specifically focused on reducing risk related to individual operational tasks or processing of individual transactions. They are designed to ensure individual activities (tasks or transactions) are accurately processed in a timely manner.

Application level: Application-level control activities are implemented to ensure that systems operate as intended.

of the control criteria."[27] The U.S. Public Company Accounting Oversight Board (PCAOB) lists the following examples of entitywide control activities in its Auditing Standard No. 2: "controls within the control environment, including tone at the top, the assignment of authority and responsibility, consistent policies and procedures, and company-wide programs, such as codes of conduct and fraud prevention, that apply to all locations and business units; management's risk assessment process; centralized processing and controls, including shared service environments; controls to monitor results of operations; controls to monitor other controls, including activities of the internal audit function, the audit committee, and self-assessment programs; the period-end financial reporting process; and board-approved policies that address significant business control and risk management practices."[28]

Process-level control activities are more detailed in their focus than entitywide control activities and reduce risk relative to a group or variety of operational level activities (tasks) or transactions within an organization. They are designed to ensure individual operational activities, tasks, or transactions, as well as related groups of operational activities (tasks) or transactions, are accurately processed in a timely manner. Examples of process-level control activities include such tasks as transaction approval, transaction verification, transaction re-calculation, transaction confirmation, and various system integrity and validation checks.

Adequately designed and effectively operating entitywide and process-level control activities work in unison and serve as an organization's defense against the risks that threaten the achievement of business objectives.

Key Control Activities and Secondary Control Activities

Control activities can also be categorized in terms of their importance. As such, a control activity can be categorized either as a key control activity or as a secondary control activity.

A key control activity (often referred to as the "primary" control activity) is a control activity designed to reduce risk associated with a critical business objective. Failure to implement adequately designed and effectively operating key controls can result in the failure of the orga-

Key Control Activity

A control activity designed to reduce risk associated with a critical business objective.

Secondary Control Activity

A control activity designed to either reduce risk associated with business objectives that are not critical to the organization's survival or success, or serve as a back up to a key control.

Compensating Control Activity

An activity designed to supplement key control activities that may be either ineffective or do not fully mitigate a risk or group of risks by themselves to an acceptable level.

nization not only to achieve critical business objectives but to survive.

A secondary control activity is one that is designed to either reduce risk associated with business objectives that are not critical to the organization's survival or success, or serve as a backup to a key control. When a secondary control activity serves as the second line of defense for key control activities, they come into play only when, and if, the key control activity fails. They reinforce (back up) key control activities but are not adequate to mitigate a particular risk to an acceptable level, were there not a key control activity or other secondary controls already in place. Secondary control activities are typically a subset of compensating or complementary control activities.

Compensating Control Activities

Compensating control activities are essentially redundant controls designed to supplement key controls that are either ineffective or cannot fully mitigate a risk or group of risks by themselves to an acceptable level within the risk appetite established by management and the board.

A compensating control activity also serves as a backup or a redundancy to multiple key control activities at the same time. In contrast, a secondary control activity typically serves as a backup to a single key control activity only.

As previously mentioned, secondary control activities and compensating control activities are necessary when an effective key control activity cannot be created or designed to adequately mitigate a risk or group of risks within management's established risk appetite. This may be a result of economic restraints or operational complexity or both. No matter the reason, secondary and compensating controls are required for which no effective key control activity is realized. Often, compensating controls work concurrently with related or overlapping key control activities, while serving as a secondary control activity for a specific key control activity.

Complementary Control Activities

A complementary control activity is not directly related to the risk it mitigates, and is not enough to fully mitigate the risk by itself but when taken together with other control activities that are in place, does contribute to the overall effective mitigation of risk. Frequently, complementary control activities operate across multiple processes and risks. They are not designed to be key control activities in and of themselves, but they can assist other control activities address risks more effectively.

Detective, Preventive, Directive, and Corrective Control Activities

Often, the many different control activities that exist are referred to by labels that describe what they are intended to do in an attempt to differentiate between them. Included here is a short list of these types of control activities and their definitions.

A *detective control* is one that is designed to discover undesirable

Complementary Control Activity

A control activity that is not directly related to the risk it mitigates, and is not enough to fully mitigate the risk by itself, but when taken together with other control activities that are in place, does contribute to the overall effective mitigation of risk.

Detective Control

A control activity designed to discover undesirable events that have already occurred.

Preventive Control

A control activity designed to deter unintended events from occurring.

Directive Control

A control activity that gives explicit direction regarding what actions need to take place to cause or encourage a desirable event to occur.

Corrective Control

A control activity in which detected omissions and errors are corrected.

events that have already occurred. A detective control must occur on a timely basis (before the undesirable event has had a negative impact on the organization) to be considered effective.

Conversely, a *preventive control* is a control designed to deter unintended events from occurring in the first place. Because of the dynamic nature and complexity of day-to-day business operations, it is much more difficult and costly to design a preventive control activity that is both economical and efficient. As a result, most organizations use a combination of preventive control activities and detective control activities when designing both an effective and efficient system of internal controls.

A *directive control,* as its name suggests, is a control that gives explicit direction regarding what actions need to take place to cause or encourage a desirable event to occur.

A *corrective control* is one in which detected omissions and errors are corrected.

Information Systems Control Activities

Due to the prevalent dependence on information systems that exists today, control activities must be implemented to mitigate the risks associated with automated systems necessary to run the core business of an organization.

> Two broad groupings of information systems control activities can be used. The first is general [computing] controls—which apply to many if not all application systems and help ensure their continued, proper operation. The second category is application controls, which include computerized steps within the application software and related manual procedures to control the processing of various types of transactions. Together, these controls serve to ensure completeness, accuracy, and validity of the financial and other information in the system.[29]

General computing control activities specific to information systems are considered entitywide controls. Application control activities have characteristics of both entitywide and process-level control activities. They are considered entitywide control activities in instances when they are relied upon throughout the organization and support other entitywide control activities. Applications such as the general ledger and payroll, for example, are used and relied upon by business units throughout the organization, and in these cases the application control activities could be considered entity-wide. However, application control activities also take on many of the characteristics of process-level control activities in cases such as authorization and accuracy of individual transactions for a specific process or business unit. While some ambiguity may exist regarding whether to classify a specific application control activity as entitywide or process level, it is far more important that the control activity itself is adequately designed and operating effectively within an adequately designed, effectively operating system of internal controls.

General Information Technology Control Activities

Control activities that operate across all IT systems and are in place to ensure the integrity, reliability, and accuracy of the application systems. Also represents a specific example of an entitywide control.

Simultaneous Categorization of Control Activities

As alluded to earlier in the chapter, specific control activities can fit into several categories at the same time. For example, a control activity can be an entitywide control at the same time that it is a key control. That same control activity can also be a directive control. It could not, however, be a secondary control or a transaction-level control at the same time that it is a key control and an entitywide control. While these nuances can be confusing in the beginning, time spent working with control activities will lead to a better understanding of how the various categories of control activities can exist in a single control.

EVALUATING THE SYSTEM OF INTERNAL CONTROLS

As previously mentioned, management, in the form of the chief executive officer, has ultimate responsibility for the adequate design and effective operation of the system of internal controls. As such, management is responsible for putting in place adequately designed and effectively operating entitywide and process-level control activities to manage risks associated with the achievement of business objectives in each of the three COSO-defined categories: effective and efficient operations, reliable financial reporting, and compliance with laws and regulations.

Internal auditors play a significant role in the verification that management has met its responsibility. Initially, management performs the primary assessment, testing, and certification of internal controls, and then the internal audit function independently validates management's results. Additionally, a report is typically submitted to the audit committee by either senior management or the chief audit executive (CAE) outlining the results of management's self assessment regarding the proper design and efficacy of the organization's internal controls.

As indicated in The IIA's *Standards*, the internal audit function is responsible for assessing and reporting on an organization's control activities (either elements of, or the entirety of, the system of internal controls) as outlined in Practice Advisory 2120.A1-1, Assessing and Reporting on Control Processes:

> Three key considerations in reaching an evaluation of [conclusion on] the overall effectiveness of the organization's risk management and control processes are:
>
> ● Were significant discrepancies or weaknesses [deficiencies] discovered from the audit work performed and other assessment information gathered?
>
> ● If so, were corrections or improvements made after the discoveries?
>
> ● Do the discoveries and their consequences lead to the conclusion that a pervasive condition exists resulting in an unacceptable level of business risk [or operating effectiveness]?

System of Internal Controls

Comprises the five components of internal control: the control environment, risk assessment, control activities, information and communication, and monitoring that are in place to manage risks related to the financial reporting, compliance, and operational objectives of an organization. See also Internal Control.

Sarbanes-Oxley additionally requires management of organizations registered to participate in the U.S. capital markets to publicly report on the reliability of ICFR. As previously indicated, in the United States, Sarbanes-Oxley put responsibility for the design, maintenance, and effective operation of ICFR squarely on the shoulders of senior management, specifically, the CEO and CFO. To comply with this legislation, the SEC requires the CEO and CFO of publicly traded companies to opine on the reliability of financial reporting (that is, the adequate design and effective operation of ICFR) as part of the annual filing of financial statements with the SEC, as well as report any substantial changes, if any, in ICFR on a quarterly basis.

Reliable financial reporting, "… in the context of published financial statements, … is defined [by COSO] as the preparation of financial statements fairly presented in conformity with generally accepted accounting principles and regulatory requirements for external purposes, within the context of materiality. Supporting fair presentation are five basic financial statement assertions: existence or occurrence, completeness, rights and obligations, valuation or allocation, and presentation and disclosure."[30] Entitywide and process-level control activities specifically designed for the achievement of these external reporting objectives (assertions) possess certain common elements. To be properly designed and operating effectively, these control activities should address the concepts of initiation, authorization, recording, processing, and reporting. As mentioned earlier in the chapter, these control activities are commonly referred to as internal controls over financial reporting.

The PCAOB was created to establish guidelines that independent outside auditors and, indirectly, management must adhere to in order to comply with these reporting requirements. In response, on March 9, 2004, the PCAOB issued Auditing Standard No. 2, An Audit of Internal Control Over Financial Reporting Performed in Conjunction With an Audit of Financial Statements. For additional specific guidelines, refer to Auditing Standard No. 2 itself.

CONTROL MATURITY MODEL

A control maturity model is a tool that an organization uses to assess the sophistication of its system of internal controls. Control activities for various areas of an organization are evaluated against a spectrum of maturity. It is a way for organizations to have a snapshot of where their various control activities stand at a particular point in time relative to a well defined and widely accepted standard rating scale. Since an organization's system of internal controls is dynamic in nature, a control maturity model also helps an organization assess progress (or lack thereof) in enhancing or maintaining their system of internal controls over time as compared to a single point in time. Many organizations believe the use of a control maturity model enhances management's ability to monitor the effectiveness of the system of internal controls and provides a measure of sustainability of controls over time. Exhibit 5-12 is an example of an internal control maturity model.

Control Maturity Model

A tool that an organization may use to assess the sophistication and sustainability of its system of internal controls.

EXHIBIT 5-12

CONTROLS MATURITY MODEL

Model Levels	Capability Attributes
World Class	Controls are considered "world class," based on benchmarking and continuous improvement; the control infrastructure is highly automated and self-updating, thus creating a competitive advantage; extensive use of real-time monitoring and executive dashboards.
Mature	KPIs and monitoring techniques are employed to measure success; greater reliance on prevention versus detection controls; strong self-assessment of operating effectiveness by process owners; chain of accountability exists and is well understood.
Defined	Controls are well defined and documented, thus there is consistency even in times of change; overall control awareness exists; control gaps are detected and remediated timely; performance monitoring is informal, placing great reliance on the diligence of people and independent audits.
Repeatable	Controls are established with some policy structure; formal process documentation still lacking; some clarity on roles, responsibilities, and authorities, but not accountability; increased discipline and guidelines support repeatability; high reliance on existing personnel creates exposure to change.
Immature	Controls are fragmented and ad hoc; generally managed in silos and reactive; lack of formal policies and procedures; dependent on the "heroics" of individuals to get things done; higher potential for errors; higher costs due to inefficiencies; not sustainable.

Maturity Evolution

SUMMARY

This chapter discussed the control activities that organizations develop to mitigate and manage the risks that could potentially threaten the achievement of business objectives. Beginning with a definition of internal control, the chapter moved on to explain what a framework is and how concepts like internal control and enterprise risk management are more effectively put into practice when they are implemented using well-developed and generally accepted frameworks. Additionally, the variety of frameworks that consider internal control should now be easily identifiable. From there, the components that must be present for an adequately designed and effectively operating system of internal controls were identified and defined. Everybody within an organization has some responsibility for control activities and this chapter outlined the specific roles and responsibilities each group of people in the organization has in that respect, including management's process for evaluating the organization's overall system of internal controls. The specific role the internal audit function has relative to monitoring the system of internal controls within the organization was discussed in detail. The different types of control activities employed to mitigate the many varieties of risks facing an organization were addressed and should now be easily identifiable. The appropriate application of each one should also be well understood. The chapter concluded with a definition of a control maturity model and an example was provided.

1. What does the term *internal control* mean? Draw from multiple frameworks in your answer.

2. What are the five components of an effective internal control framework?

3. Who has responsibility for internal control within an organization?

4. Briefly describe the responsibilities each of the following groups of people has regarding internal control: management, the board of directors, internal auditors, others in the organization.

5. How is the system of internal controls evaluated?

6. What is an internal control maturity model? What is its purpose?

1. Which of the following best describes an internal auditor's purpose in reviewing the organization's existing risk management, control, and governance processes?

   a. To help determine the nature, timing, and extent of tests necessary to achieve engagement objectives.

   b. To ensure that weaknesses in the internal control system are corrected.

   c. To provide reasonable assurance that the processes will enable the organization's objectives and goals to be met efficiently and economically.

   d. To determine whether the processes ensure that the accounting records are correct and that financial statements are fairly stated.

2. What is residual risk?

   a. Impact of risk.

   b. Risk that is under control.

   c. Risk that is not managed.

   d. Underlying risk in the environment.

3. The requirement that purchases be made from suppliers on an approved vendor list is an example of a:

   a. Preventive control.

   b. Detective control.

   c. Corrective control.

   d. Monitoring control.

4. An adequate system of internal control is most likely to detect an irregularity perpetrated by a:

a. Group of employees in collusion.

b. Single employee.

c. Group of managers in collusion.

d. Single manager.

5. Audit engagement programs testing internal control activities should:

   a. Be tailored for the audit of each business area within the organization.

   b. Be generalized to fit all situations without regard to departmental lines.

   c. Be generalized so as to be usable at various international locations of an organization.

   d. Reduce costly duplication of effort by ensuring that every aspect of an operation is examined.

6. The control that would most likely ensure that payroll checks are written only for authorized amounts is to:

   a. Conduct periodic floor verification of employees on the payroll.

   b. Require the return of undelivered checks to the cashier.

   c. Require supervisory approval of employee time cards.

   d. Periodically witness the distribution of payroll checks.

7. An internal auditor plans to conduct an audit of the adequacy of controls over investments in new financial instruments. Which of the following would NOT be required as part of such an engagement?

   a. Determine if policies exist that describe the risks the treasurer may take and the types of instruments in which the treasurer may make investments.

   b. Determine the extent of management oversight over investments in sophisticated instruments.

   c. Determine whether the treasurer is getting higher or lower rates of return on investments than are treasurers in comparable organizations.

   d. Determine the nature of controls established by the treasurer to monitor the risks in the investments.

8. Appropriate internal control for a multinational corporation's branch office that has a department responsible for the transfer of money requires that:

   a. The individual who initiates wire transfers does not reconcile the bank statement.

   b. The branch manager receives all wire transfers.

   c. Foreign currency rates be computed separately by two different employees.

   d. Corporate management approves the hiring of monetary transfer unit employees.

1. An audit report contains the following observations:

   a) A service department's location is not well suited to allow adequate service to other units,

   b) Employees hired for sensitive positions are not subjected to background checks,

   c) Managers do not have access to reports that profile overall performance in relation to other benchmarked organizations, and

   d) Management has not taken corrective action to resolve past engagement observations related to inventory controls.

   Which two of these observations are *most likely* to indicate the existence of control weaknesses over safeguarding of assets? Why?

2. To meet waste discharge standards, a factory implements a control system designed to prevent the release of waste water that does not meet those standards. One of the control activities in that control system is performing chemical analysis of the water, prior to discharge, for components specified in the permit. Is this an appropriate control activity? Why or why not?

3. An organization wants to prevent the ordering of quantities in excess of its needs. One individual in the organization wants to design a control activity that requires a review of all purchase requisitions by a supervisor in the user department prior to submitting them to the purchasing department. Another individual wants to institute a policy requiring agreement of the receiving report and packing slip before storage of new receipts. Is one control activity more appropriate than the other or are they equally appropriate? Explain your answer.

CASE: [31]

Control activities mitigate risks that threaten objectives and thus provide assurance that objectives will be achieved. Risks encompass both threats of bad things happening and threats of good things not happening. Some controls are visible and therefore can be photographed.

Required:

A. Choose one or two classmates you want to work with on this assignment. Each team will need a camera.

B. As a team, photograph five different control activities you observe around campus and/or the surrounding community. Use your imagination and ingenuity. Each team must work independently to produce a unique set of pictures. At least two of the control activities photographed must be control activities designed to mitigate risks of something good not happening (i.e., that is controls designed to help something good happen).

C. For each control photographed:

1. Clearly indicate whether the control activity is designed to mitigate the threat of bad things happening or the threat of good things not happening.

2. Then briefly and separately describe:

   a. An objective the control activity is designed to help achieve.

   b. A risk the control activity is designed to mitigate. (Note: The risk you describe must be something other than merely the inverse of the objective.)

   c. How the control is meant to operate (that is, how the control works).

   d. How you would test the control to determine whether it is operating effectively.

To be submitted:

1. The set of 5 pictures.

2. The descriptions of the 5 controls the pictures represent, as called for in requirement C.

REFERENCES

[1] The Institute of Internal Auditors. *A Vision for the Future: Professional Practices Framework for Internal Auditing*. (Altamonte Springs, FL: The Institute of Internal Auditors, 1999, p. 54).

[2] U.S. Securities and Exchange Commission. Final Rules 2003 (Rule 33-823). Available at http://www.sec.gov.

[3] The Institute of Internal Auditors. *A Vision for the Future: Professional Practices Framework for Internal Auditing*. (Altamonte Springs, FL: The Institute of Internal Auditors, 1999, p. 9).

[4] Committee of Sponsoring Organizations of the Treadway Commission. *Internal Control—Integrated Framework*. (Jersey City, NJ: The Committee of Sponsoring Organizations of the Treadway Commission, 1994, p. 13).

[5] Committee of Sponsoring Organizations of the Treadway Commission. *Internal Control—Integrated Framework*. (Jersey City, NJ: The Committee of Sponsoring Organizations of the Treadway Commission, 1994, p. 23).

[6] Committee of Sponsoring Organizations of the Treadway Commission. *Internal Control—Integrated Framework*. (Jersey City, NJ: The Committee of Sponsoring Organizations of the Treadway Commission, 1994, p. 33).

[7] Committee of Sponsoring Organizations of the Treadway Commission. *Internal Control—Integrated Framework*. (Jersey City, NJ: The Committee of Sponsoring Organizations of the Treadway Commission, 1994, pp. 33-34).

[8] Committee of Sponsoring Organizations of the Treadway Commission. *Internal Control—Integrated Framework*. (Jersey City, NJ: The Committee of Sponsoring Organizations of the Treadway Commission, 1994, p. 49).

[9] Committee of Sponsoring Organizations of the Treadway Commission. *Internal Control—Integrated Framework*. (Jersey City, NJ: The Committee of Sponsoring Organizations of the Treadway Commission, 1994, p. 59).

[10] Committee of Sponsoring Organizations of the Treadway Commission. *Internal Control—Integrated Framework*. (Jersey City, NJ: The Committee of Sponsoring Organizations of the Treadway Commission, 1994, p. 63).

[11] Committee of Sponsoring Organizations of the Treadway Commission. *Internal Control—Integrated Framework*. (Jersey City, NJ: The Committee of Sponsoring Organizations of the Treadway Commission, 1994, pp. 65-66).

[12] Committee of Sponsoring Organizations of the Treadway Commission. *Internal Control—Integrated Framework*. (Jersey City, NJ: The Committee of Sponsoring Organizations of the Treadway Commission, 1994, pp. 69-72).

[13] Committee of Sponsoring Organizations of the Treadway Commission. *Internal Control—Integrated Framework*. (Jersey City, NJ: The Committee of Sponsoring Organizations of the Treadway Commission, 1994, p. 74).

[14] Committee of Sponsoring Organizations of the Treadway Commission. *Internal Control—Integrated Framework.* (Jersey City, NJ: The Committee of Sponsoring Organizations of the Treadway Commission, 1994, pp. 6-7).

[15] Committee of Sponsoring Organizations of the Treadway Commission. *Internal Control—Integrated Framework.* (Jersey City, NJ: The Committee of Sponsoring Organizations of the Treadway Commission, 1994, p. 7).

[16] Committee of Sponsoring Organizations of the Treadway Commission. *Internal Control—Integrated Framework.* (Jersey City, NJ: The Committee of Sponsoring Organizations of the Treadway Commission, 1994, p. 7).

[17] Committee of Sponsoring Organizations of the Treadway Commission. *Internal Control—Integrated Framework.* (Jersey City, NJ: The Committee of Sponsoring Organizations of the Treadway Commission, 1994, p. 79).

[18] Committee of Sponsoring Organizations of the Treadway Commission. *Internal Control—Integrated Framework.* (Jersey City, NJ: The Committee of Sponsoring Organizations of the Treadway Commission, 1994, p. 120).

[19] Committee of Sponsoring Organizations of the Treadway Commission. *Internal Control—Integrated Framework.* (Jersey City, NJ: The Committee of Sponsoring Organizations of the Treadway Commission, 1994, p. 39).

[20] Committee of Sponsoring Organizations of the Treadway Commission. *Internal Control—Integrated Framework.* (Jersey City, NJ: The Committee of Sponsoring Organizations of the Treadway Commission, 1994, p. 42).

[21] Committee of Sponsoring Organizations of the Treadway Commission. *Enterprise Risk Management—Integrated Framework.* (Jersey City, NJ: The Committee of Sponsoring Organizations of the Treadway Commission, 2004, p. 124).

[22] Committee of Sponsoring Organizations of the Treadway Commission. *Internal Control—Integrated Framework.* (Jersey City, NJ: The Committee of Sponsoring Organizations of the Treadway Commission, 1994, p. 107).

[23] Committee of Sponsoring Organizations of the Treadway Commission. *Internal Control—Integrated Framework.* (Jersey City, NJ: The Committee of Sponsoring Organizations of the Treadway Commission, 1994, p. 106}.

[24] Committee of Sponsoring Organizations of the Treadway Commission. *Internal Control—Integrated Framework.* (Jersey City, NJ: The Committee of Sponsoring Organizations of the Treadway Commission, 1994, p. 106).

[25] Committee of Sponsoring Organizations of the Treadway Commission. *Internal Control—Integrated Framework.* (Jersey City, NJ: The Committee of Sponsoring Organizations of the Treadway Commission, 1994, pp. 106-107).

[26] Committee of Sponsoring Organizations of the Treadway Commission. *Internal Control—Integrated Framework*. (Jersey City, NJ: The Committee of Sponsoring Organizations of the Treadway Commission, 1994, p. 107).

[27] Public Company Accounting Oversight Board. Auditing and Related Professional Practice Standards: *Auditing Standard No. 2—An Audit of Internal Control Over Financial Reporting Performed in Conjunction with An Audit of Financial Statements.* September 8, 2004, paragraph 50.

[28] Public Company Accounting Oversight Board. Auditing and Related Professional Practice Standards: *Auditing Standard No. 2—An Audit of Internal Control Over Financial Reporting Performed in Conjunction with An Audit of Financial Statements.* September 8, 2004, paragraph 53.

[29] Committee of Sponsoring Organizations of the Treadway Commission. *Internal Control—Integrated Framework*. (Jersey City, NJ: The Committee of Sponsoring Organizations of the Treadway Commission, 1994, p. 52).

[30] Committee of Sponsoring Organizations of the Treadway Commission. *Internal Control—Integrated Framework*. Jersey City, NJ: The Committee of Sponsoring Organizations of the Treadway Commission, 1994, p. 122).

[31] Adapted from his Snap A Control created by Dr. Glenn Sumners.

CHAPTER 6
INFORMATION TECHNOLOGY RISKS AND CONTROLS

> ## Learning Objectives
>
> - Understand the key components of modern information technology.
> - Identify the top-10 information technology risks.
> - Describe the linkage between information technology control activities and the COSO internal control framework.
> - Understand the different classifications of information technology control activities.
> - Articulate how information technology control activities should be designed and developed.
> - Understand the implications of information technology outsourcing and emerging IT issues.
> - Describe the three most critical types of general information technology control activities: information and physical security, change management, and business continuity and disaster recovery.
> - Understand how information technology affects internal auditing.

Hacked computer sites, natural disasters, and breaches of data privacy are examples of risks that threaten information technology (IT). If an organization you work for makes the news related to any of these incidents, you can bet it's not good news. On the other hand, if control activities had been put in place for a rapid recovery during a hurricane such as Katrina in 2005, your organization would be recognized in the press for its quick response to the event.

> The methods that will most effectively minimize the ability of intruders to compromise information security are comprehensive user training and education. Enacting policies and procedures simply won't suffice. Even with oversight, the policies and procedures may not be effective: My access to Motorola, Nokia, AT&T, and Sun depended upon the willingness of people to bypass policies and procedures that were in place for years before I compromised them successfully. — *Kevin Mitnick*[1]

EXHIBIT 6-1

PROFESSIONAL STANDARDS AND PRACTICE ADVISORIES RELEVANT TO CHAPTER 6

1200 – Proficiency and Due Professional Care
1210 – Proficiency
1220 – Due Professional Care
2100 – Nature of Work
2300 – Performing the Engagement

Practice Advisory 1220-2:	CAATS
Practice Advisory 2100-2:	Information Security
Practice Advisory 2100-6:	Control and Audit Implications of E-commerce Activities
Practice Advisory 2100-8:	The Internal Auditor's Role in Evaluating an Organization's Privacy Framework
Practice Advisory 2100-9:	Applications Systems Review
Practice Advisory 2100-11:	Effect of Pervasive IS Controls
Practice Advisory 2100-12:	Outsourcing of IS Activities
Practice Advisory 2100-13:	Effect of Third Parties on an Organization's IT Controls
Practice Advisory 2100-14:	Audit Evidence Requirement
Practice Advisory 2110-2:	The Internal Auditor's Role in the Business Continuity Process
Practice Advisory 2300-1:	The Internal Auditor's Use of Personal Information in Conducting Audits

During the 9/11 crisis, if it weren't for the foresight to have computer and work areas established in New Jersey prior to the disaster, we would not have been able to transfer millions in funds that afternoon. Not only were we able to complete our wire transfers but those for a number of other financial services organizations.

— *Mark Salamasick,*
Former Senior Vice President, Bank of America[2]

The internal audit function can play a major role in addressing IT risks. Historically, assessing technology risk and evaluating control activities have been the responsibility of IT audit specialists. Technology has now advanced, however, to a point where it is integral to everything we do. Although many internal audit functions employ internal auditors who specialize in IT, this chapter is intended to provide the basic knowledge required for any internal auditor to perform basic technology risk assessments and assist in the implementation of adequately designed and effectively operating IT control activities.

KEY COMPONENTS OF MODERN INFORMATION TECHNOLOGY

Exhibit 6-2 illustrates many of the key components of modern IT. These key components are briefly described below:

Computer Hardware. The physical devices such as disk drives, monitors, keyboards, printers, computer chips, and memory. Physical control activities over computers are the most critical to mitigating risks related to computer hardware. Exhibit 6-2 shows different types of servers including a front-end security router, Web servers, and database and content servers. All of

Operating Systems
Software programs that run the computer and perform basic tasks, such as recognizing input from the keyboard, sending output to the printer, keeping track of files and directories on the hard drive, and controlling various computer peripheral devices.

these are components required to support an Internet-based application and should be kept in a secured location.

Operating Systems. The software programs that run the computer and perform basic tasks, such as recognizing input from the keyboard, sending output to the printer, keeping track of files and directories on the hard drive, and controlling various peripheral devices.

Every computer, no matter what size, requires an operating system to work properly. This is one of the highest risk areas related to technology because it deals with the lowest-level machine language. Exhibit 6-2 shows a Windows Server configuration that would include the operating system that runs the various servers that support the Internet applications.

Application Systems. Sets of programs that are designed for end users such as payroll, accounts payable, and in some cases, large applications such as enterprise resource planning (ERP) systems that provide many business functions. Many organizations now install large ERP systems that require the internal audit function to have specialized training to enable them to efficiently audit those systems. The servers that are to the far right on Exhibit 6-2 would execute specific business applications.

Information Technology Operations. The area that performs the function of running the computer and various devices. In a personal computer (PC) environment, the end user is performing those functions. For large enterprise systems, individuals are responsible for handling the running of computers, networks, and the various peripheral devices. IT operations would be responsible for the ongoing support, maintenance, and operations.

Database Systems. Provide a system of programs that enable the storage, modification, and extraction of data. The Structured

COMMON TECHNOLOGY COMPONENTS

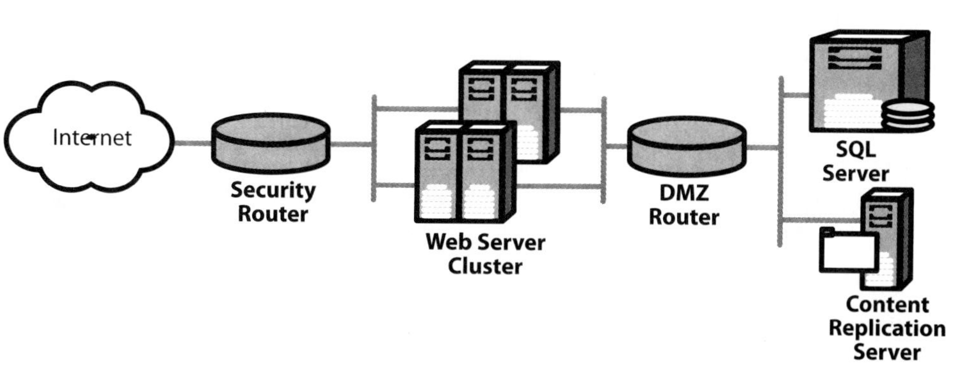

Internet — Security Router — Web Server Cluster — DMZ Router — SQL Server — Content Replication Server

EXHIBIT 6-2

Query Language (SQL) server in Exhibit 6-2 is a relational database management system produced by Microsoft.

Networks. Enable computers and devices to communicate and are linked together to provide transfer of data and operations among the various computers and devices in an organization. The network consists of all the components, including the Internet connection to the outside world. The firewall provides security and filtering of the corporate network's access, providing protection to the intranet from the Internet.

Technology has long existed for the purpose of assisting businesses in operating more effectively and efficiently. With the advent of the Internet and Web technology, information systems have become even more critical to business operations. All internal auditors need to have a baseline of technology knowledge and must integrate technology into their internal audit work.

The IIA maintains a Web site (www.theiia.org/itaudit) that provides internal auditors with current information on the changes occurring in IT as it pertains to the practice of internal auditing. It is considered the premier IT resource for internal auditors and is designed to enhance internal auditors' knowledge of IT.

THE TOP 10 INFORMATION TECHNOLOGY RISKS

Many of the issues related to technology risk have remained constant with the passing of time. As new technology is introduced, however, so are new risks. The Advanced Technology Committee of The IIA, which is a volunteer group of IIA members with a focus on technology, annually summarizes the top 10 IT risks. The committee's most recent top 10 list is presented in Exhibit 6-3. Readers should note that many of the items listed involve information security issues: threat/vulnerability management, privacy, wireless security, enterprise security metrics, and identity management.

LINKING IT CONTROLS WITH THE COSO INTERNAL CONTROL FRAMEWORK

As technology advances, the need to place additional control activities as part of the technology infrastructure also increases. Organizations have struggled over the years to find a suitable IT control framework to use. In the past, most IT functions have decided either not to use a standard framework or to customize an approach that best fits the organization. With additional regulatory requirements, along with pressures to reduce costs and streamline operations of technology, a shift to a standard IT framework makes sense. Adoption of a standard IT control framework will allow IT management to better measure how they are doing.

Because U.S. organizations are using the Committee of Sponsoring Organizations of the Treadway Commission's (COSO's) *Internal Control–Integrated Framework* as their model for complying with the U.S. Sarbanes-Oxley Act of 2002, and it is widely accepted by most organizations, using it as a starting point for IT control activities makes the

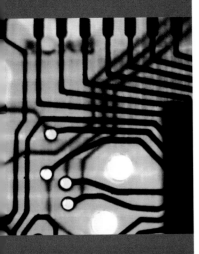

Networks

A configuration that enables computers and devices to communicate and be linked together to provide transfer of data and operations.

EXHIBIT 6-3

TOP 10 TECHNOLOGY RISK ISSUES AS IDENTIFIED BY THE IIA ADVANCED TECHNOLOGY COMMITTEE

1. Legislation and Regulatory Compliance
2. Threat / Vulnerability Management (Application exploits, DDOS, IM, SPAM, Viruses, Trojans, worms …)
3. Privacy (including identity protection)
4. Continuous Monitoring / Auditing / Assurance
5. Wireless Security
6. Intrusion Protection (including firewalls, monitoring, analysis, reaction …)
7. IT Outsourcing (including offshore)
8. Enterprise Security Metrics (dashboards, scorecards, analytics …)
9. Identity Management
10. Acquisitions & Divestitures – impacts on systems management

The Institute of Internal Auditors, Advanced Technology Committee Meeting, Dec. 2005.

most sense.[3] This framework, as well as other accepted internal control frameworks, is discussed in more detail in Chapter 5, "Internal Control."

Exhibit 6-4 illustrates how key IT control activities can be mapped to the COSO model. This mapping, which can easily be adapted to any organization, links IT control activities to the five COSO components of internal control. Organizations can use this tool to measure progress in improving control over IT risks.

CLASSIFYING IT CONTROL ACTIVITIES

There are a number of methods used for classifying IT control activities. Commonly, they are classified as either general or application control activities, but they also can be classified as governance, management, or technical control activities as well. The most common methods of classifying IT control activities are described in turn below.

General Control Activities Versus Application Control Activities

General IT control activities span all IT systems and are put in place to ensure the integrity, reliability, and accuracy of the application systems. Typical general control activities include:

- Systems development standards.
- Information security policies and procedures.
- Backup and recovery standards.
- Service level agreements with vendors.
- Network monitoring procedures and practices.
- Program coding standards.
- Computer hardware architecture and product standards.
- Hardware and software installation, configuration, and testing standards.

EXHIBIT 6-4

COSO MODEL FOR TECHNOLOGY CONTROLS

Monitoring

- Monthly metrics from technology performance.
- Technology cost and control performance analysis.
- Periodic technology management assessments.
- Internal audit of technology enterprise.
- Internal audit of high risk areas.

Control Activities

- Review board for change management.
- Comparison of technology initiatives to plan and return on investment.
- Documentation and approval of IT plans and systems architecture.
- Compliance with information and physical security standards.
- Adherence to business continuity risk assessment.
- Technology standards compliance enforcement.

Information and Communication

- Periodic corporate communications (Intranet, e-mail, meetings, mailings).
- Ongoing technology awareness of best practices.
- IT performance survey.
- IT and security training.
- Help desk ongoing issue resolution.

Risk Assessment

- IT risks included in overall corporate risk assessment.
- IT integrated into business risk assessments.
- Differentiate IT controls for high risk business areas/functions.
- IT internal audit assessment.
- IT insurance assessment.

Control Environment

- Tone at the top—IT and security controls considered important.
- Overall technology policy and information security policy.
- Corporate Technology Governance Committee.
- Technology Architecture and Standards Committee.
- Full representation of all business units.

The Institute of Internal Auditors, Global Technology Audit Guide—Information Technology Controls, *(Altamonte Springs, Fla.: The Institute of Internal Auditors, 2006)*

An organization should strive to position as many of the control activities as possible at the higher-level general control activities rather than in each application. An example of this is the use of user IDs and passwords that authenticate user sign-on at the point of logging into the system instead of at the individual application level. By working to place as many of the overall, pervasive control activities into the general control activities category, a more consistent, reliable, and controlled approach can be put in place for the information systems throughout the organization. The three most critical general control activities areas are:

- Information and physical security.
- Change management.
- Business continuity/disaster recovery.

These three types of general control activities are described in-depth in a subsequent section of this chapter.

The IIA developed the Guide to the Assessment of Information Technology General Controls Scope Based on Risk (GAIT) "to help organizations identify key IT general controls where failure might indirectly result in a material error in a financial statement. More specifically, GAIT enables management and auditors to identify key IT general controls as part of, and as a continuation of, the company's top-down, risk-based scoping efforts for Section 404 compliance." Since GAIT is principles-based, it can be applied to any organization, regardless of size and industry. The four GAIT principles are presented in Exhibit 6-5.

Application Control Activities pertain to individual application systems. The primary mission of any information systems function is to run applications for the benefit of systems users. Application system integrity is critical to operational success. A set of control activities needs to be in place to ensure that the system processes and logic perform according to specifications each time the system is run. The level of resources spent on integrity control activities needs to be evaluated in light of the risk associated with the application and data. To ensure overall system integrity, a combination of input, processing, and output control activities is necessary. The better the combination of these control activities, the higher the reliability of the overall system of internal controls.

Application design is often referred to as functional specifications since those user requirements are critical to the functionality of the application itself. The functional specifications are translated into detailed specifications by system analysts, and then used to write the programs that comprise the application system. The various modules and programs described in specifications must work in concert to form a fully functional application system. If the specifications are not good, system functionality will be in jeopardy. Other actions required to produce a fully functional system include user control activities, auditability, error procedures, documentation, training plans, and backup and contingency plans.

Sound applications have very specific procedures for input, processing, output, and storage to protect the valuable application assets. Normal-

General Information Technology (IT) Control Activities

Control activities that operate across all IT systems and are in place to ensure the integrity, reliability, and accuracy of the application systems. Also represents a specific example of an "entitywide control."

Guide to the Assessment of IT General Controls Scope Based on Risk (GAIT)

A set of principles and related methodology developed by The IIA that facilitates the cost-scoping of IT general control assessment.

EXHIBIT 6-5

THE FOUR GAIT PRINCIPLES

1. The only IT infrastructure elements (e.g., databases, operating systems, networks) relevant to information technology general controls (ITGC) assessment are those that support financially significant applications and data.
2. The IT processes primarily relevant to ITGC assessment are those that directly impact the integrity of financially significant applications and data, such as:
    *   Change management and systems development.
    *   Operations management.
    *   Security management.
3. Implications to the reliability of financially significant applications and data, including controls, are based upon the achievement or failure of IT process objectives, not the design and operating effectiveness of the individual controls with those processes.
4. The basis for identifying key controls in the three IT processes is based on:
    *   Inherent risk of not achieving the IT process objectives.
    *   IT process risk objectives.

The Institute of Internal Auditors-Advanced Technology Committee, Guide to the Assessment of IT General Controls Scope Based on Risk (GAIT), August, 2006, www.theiia.org/technology.

Application Control Activities

Programmed and manual procedures designed to ensure the validity, completeness, and accuracy of information processing for individual application systems.

ly, protection is provided by a combination of application and general control activities that are designed to provide completeness and accuracy of input, appropriate update of the right version of the data files during processing, distribution of output and reports, and supervised storage of data files and programs, whether on-line or off-line.

Input control activities ensure that all transactions are entered for processing completely and accurately. They should also cover control activities over rejected data. Procedures should cover resubmissions and identify who has the authority to make system overrides. Control activities pertaining to updates include general control activities over data files, their use and protection, as well as those over changes to programs and computer operations to prevent unauthorized changes or processing runs. There is also a need to ensure that data on file remains complete, current, and accurate, and that the transactions processed are valid and authorized.

Processing control activities ensure that transactions are accurately recorded and calculations are properly made. These control activities can also pro-actively monitor transactions or situations that may adversely affect business operations.

Output control activities cover who gets which reports, the timing of receiving reports, the level of information required by various users, and exception report handling.

Storage control activities are required at both an application and a general control activities level to cover application programs, data files, input forms, and output blanks, including blank checks or requisition forms. The methods of storage depend on what is being stored, its format, and its nature. For large centralized information systems environments, much of the storage control activities reside in the librarian function.

Global Technology Audit Guide

A series of IIA publications providing guidance on information technology management, control, and security.

Governance, Management, and Technical Control Activities

Exhibit 6-6, from the *Global Technology Audit Guide—Information Technology Controls* (GTAG-1), depicts three classifications of control activities—governance, management, and technical. These classifications correspond with the organizational groups responsible for ensuring they are properly implemented and maintained.[4]

- **Governance control activities.** "The primary responsibility for internal control resides with the board of directors in its role as keeper of the governance framework. IT control at the governance level involves ensuring that effective information management and security principles, policies, and processes are in place and performance and compliance metrics demonstrate

INFORMATION TECHNOLOGY CONTROL FRAMEWORK–GTAG

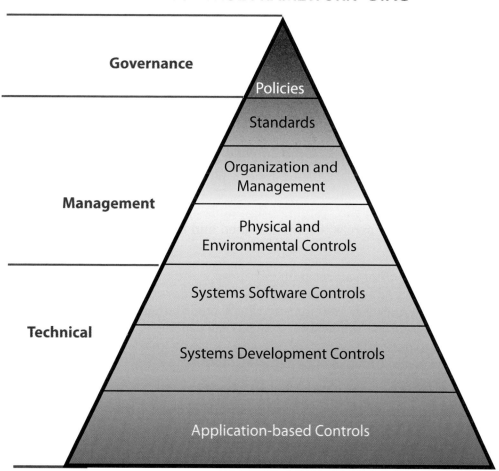

Governance

Policies

Standards

Management

Organization and Management

Physical and Environmental Controls

Systems Software Controls

Technical

Systems Development Controls

Application-based Controls

The Institute of Internal Auditors, Global Technology Audit Guide—Information Technology Controls, *(Altamonte Springs, Fla.: The Institute of Internal Auditors, 2006, p. 5.*

EXHIBIT 6-6

ongoing support for that framework." "The board's responsibility involves oversight rather than actually performing control activities."

- **Management control activities.** "Management responsibility for internal controls typically involves reaching into all areas of the organization with special attention to critical assets, sensitive information, and operational functions." "Management must make sure that IT controls needed to achieve the organization's established objectives are applied and ensure reliable and continuous processing."

- **Technical control activities.** "Technical controls form the foundation that ensures the reliability of virtually every other control in the organization. For example, by protecting against unauthorized access and intrusion, they provide the basis for reliance on the integrity of information—including evidence of all changes and their authenticity. These controls are specific to the technologies in use within the organization's IT infrastructure."

Exhibit 6-6 provides a framework for layering technology control activities with the overriding policies and management control activities setting the direction for the technical control activities. If the overall governance and management control activities are not in place, a lack of direction and inconsistent technical control activities result. The overriding components of how the business operates, along with general control activities, should first be established so the application and manual control activities can rely on the overall framework of control activities.

DESIGNING AND DEVELOPING IT CONTROL ACTIVITIES

Adequate attention must be given to the integration of control activities during the design of an application to ensure that the system will have integrity once it is installed. The proper design and implementation of control activities as an application is developed is crucial to staying within budget. It is often too expensive to add control activities that were left out of the system's original design. A poorly-controlled system may allow errors to go undetected and be prone to misuse or fraud.

The internal auditor can recommend appropriate control points and types of control activities that might be used. Internal auditors should review the application systems and the IT environment as a whole and identify appropriate application and general control activities. Application reviews are a major part of the work of many auditors, both internal and external (independent outside auditors).

When possible, it is beneficial for internal auditors to be involved in the development of an information system application as reviewers of the development process. They should evaluate the methodology, check to make sure it is being followed, and determine whether participants are properly performing their assigned roles. When the methodology is sound and is being followed, there is more assurance that the application systems themselves will be better controlled and more auditable.

Then, internal auditors should review the system itself, just before or after implementation, or as part of the normal audit process later on when it is in use.

Testing is critical to successful implementation and use of an application. Test results should be reviewed and approved by the development process participants, including users. Positive test results are important to internal control because they substantiate that reliance on the application is warranted.

Global Technology Audit Guide—Applications Control (GTAG-8) was issued by The IIA during the summer of 2007. Interested readers should refer to GTAG-8 for detailed information on application controls and best practices in reviewing application controls.

INFORMATION TECHNOLOGY OUTSOURCING

As technology has evolved, more organizations are moving toward the outsourcing of technology functions. This includes people, processes, hardware, and software. The global nature of telecommunications and the Internet have allowed organizations to leverage major technological advances without the commitment of internal corporate resources. Given the timeline to deploy newer technologies and maintain focus of personnel and financial resources on major corporate projects, outsourcing is a viable solution.

Although the technology risks and control activities may shift to the outsource provider, this does not negate senior management's responsibility to understand and periodically review the outsourced technology environment. One approach that provides a high level of coverage and comfort of the control activities that have been outsourced is documented in Statement on Auditing Standards (SAS) 70 published by the American Institute of Certified Public Accountants. The guidance provided in SAS 70 is specifically intended for public accountants (independent outside auditors) who attest to the adequate design and effective operation of outsourced control activities.

In addition to reviewing the independent outside auditor's SAS 70 report, internal auditors may rely on other reports from the outside service provider's internal audit group, or perform independent testing of the outsourced control activities themselves. A key understanding of which technology risks and control activities are addressed internally and which are addressed externally is the first step in deciding the degree of reliance that can be placed on outside testing. In cases where high risk areas are outsourced, some internal audit testing of the outsourced internal control activities should be performed.

EMERGING TECHNOLOGY

As technology continues to change at a rapid pace and the introduction of new business models continue to emerge with the rapid expansion of e-business, new technology risks will surface. Organizations continue to become more dependent on networks as interconnection between organizations and individuals increases. Many of the more advanced information systems audit areas deal with auditing networks and require a higher degree of technical expertise.

Statement on Auditing Standards (SAS) 70

A standard published by the American Institute of Certified Public Accountants that provides guidance on the factors an independent outside auditor should consider when auditing the financial statements of an organization that has outsourced the processing of certain transactions.

The advent of the Internet and e-business, and the explosion of wireless connectivity have generated new career opportunities for internal auditors to pursue. Internal audit expertise is needed in areas such as firewalls, encryption, Web applications, voice over the Internet, and extranets. These are areas in which information systems auditors can best utilize their time and talents as new technologies are deployed throughout organizations.

Sources such as The IIA's ITAudit site, www.theiia.org/itaudit, provide valuable resources for new and emerging IT audit issues. The front page of this Web site contains links to recent articles that provide emerging issue updates.

THREE CRITICAL CATEGORIES OF GENERAL IT CONTROL ACTIVITIES

Three critical categories of general IT control activities (that warrant further discussion) were introduced in a previous section of this chapter—information and physical security, change management, and business continuity and disaster recovery.

Information and Physical Security

IT control activities are key to the protection and security of data. These control activities address the risks of unauthorized access to information. For example, logon control activities of user IDs and passwords to limit access to a system provide security over unauthorized access to data and are a control technique. The risk is unauthorized access to data and is controlled by the system control activities of user IDs and passwords.

It is important for information security and control issues to be addressed with the deployment of new technologies. Not only is new technology being deployed to help improve productivity but also to improve control and security. Areas such as identity theft are a growing concern to individuals and new solutions for identity management are being explored and deployed continuously. Additional security hardware and software solutions are being developed to meet the current information security demands.

Information security (logical security) mitigates risk by preventing unauthorized users from accessing the programs and data in a system. It is also used to create an appropriate segregation of duties by preventing users from accessing programs and data that are not required as part of their job functions. Appropriate user access management should be based on job and control requirements.

There are many places in a system where logical security can be implemented. In a large mainframe environment, there are many aspects of the system software that allow control activities to be put in place. For example, the telecommunications software contains information identifying which individuals who support the systems are allowed to modify system parameters, while the applications themselves can restrict who is allowed to enter transactions. In smaller systems, there may be a more limited number of places where logical control activities can be used, but the opportunity usually exists somewhere in the system.

To provide an added layer of access control, most systems now use special access control software, the only function of which is to make sure that only authorized users access the system and only those portions of the system they are authorized to access. This access software is a general control activity that can be utilized by all applications.

The effective implementation of logical security control activities is one of the more important areas in the control of modern information systems, and is therefore critical to the system of internal controls. Without such control activities, a system is considered to be wide open and vulnerable to the potential for abuse.

An interesting recent development is the use of physical devices to control logical access to a system. Among these are things like smart cards, which contain security profiles about the user, and biometric systems that work by analyzing an individual's voice, fingerprint, or retina before allowing access. In this way, physical devices are helping provide logical access with decreased risk.

Physical security is of obvious importance to an effective system of internal controls. The protection of assets applies to the hardware, software, and data used by a system. The physical control activities are the first layer of control over access to computers. Typically, computer centers have a high degree of physical security through the use of access badges and barriers, along with other environmental control activities. Since data is maintained on many different computer systems including PCs and smaller hand-held devices, physical security over those devices must also be considered. Now, with important corporate data kept on portable devices, physical security over these devices becomes critical. In all cases, a layered approach of physical and logical security becomes even more critical, so that only those who should have access to data and other IT resources have the appropriate access.

Internal auditors should point out the serious consequences that can result from inadequately designed or ineffectively operating logical security control activities. For example, when an access control security package is in place, there is a tendency on the part of some information systems personnel to feel that everything is taken care of, when in reality, the way in which that package is set up on the system has great latitude and can be critical to its function, creating the opportunity for the existence of risk.

Internal auditors often simulate attacks on their organizations' systems with management concurrence to test the security systems for potential exposures and threats from hackers. This allows the information security area, along with management, to take appropriate actions to protect the organization from the vulnerabilities identified.

There is a lot of documentation on the Internet posted from various hacker groups and professional associations dedicated to providing improved security. One of those professional organizations that specifically addresses security is the Information Systems Security Association (ISSA). Interested readers can learn more about the ISSA by visiting its Web site at www.issa.org/index.htm.

Information Security (Logical Security)
Security measures that mitigate risk by preventing unauthorized users from accessing the programs and data in a system.

Biometric Systems
Logical security control activities that analyze an individual's voice, fingerprint, or retina before allowing access.

Physical Security
The physical protection of hardware, software, data, and other information system resources.

Change Management

Change management involves all processes of the organization, not just technology. However, technology plays an important role in moving the organization toward positive change. When developing new systems and processes, change management is an integral part of successful implementation. As a system is used, there will be changes. These can be enhancements, upgrades, additions, or responses to problems. Ongoing maintenance is needed in all systems. It is important to ensure that only authorized changes are made, that they are appropriately tested before implementation, and that when emergency changes are required, they are adequately tested and authorized after the fact.

Modified programs should be subject to the same kinds of control activities as newly developed application systems. There should be a formal process and documentation of requests for change. Probably the most important among these is the requirement that there be thorough testing of the modified system. In addition, accurate records should be maintained describing the change, the reasons for making the change, the person or people authorizing the change, and those responsible for making the change.

Communication to all parties impacted by a change is one thing that often gets overlooked during the change process. It can be difficult to ensure that not only the impact of the change is communicated to all parties but also the specific timing of the change. Despite the difficulty, however, it is important that all changes are communicated to all affected parties in a timely manner.

For PCs and other small systems, similar implementation control activities should be in place to suit the end-user environment (including the use of individual applications, such as spreadsheets and databases). Control activities should ensure that only authorized programs are installed and that there is no illegal copying that could lead to software copyright violations or virus-infected programs. These important aspects should be reinforced through user training and awareness programs.

As a system is developed, or redeveloped, the control activities over that effort must include procedures for handling all versions of the application programs. The programs are developed in the programmer's library, the individual modules are tested there, and then the entire application is tested in a test library. When it has been accepted, it is moved into the production library for operational processing. In today's systems, these libraries are normally available on-line within a set of logical libraries that are found in different partitions or logical areas of the system. The logical and physical control activities over the libraries require standards and procedures for segregating the development or programming and test libraries from the production library.

Global Technology Audit Guide—Change and Patch Management Controls: Critical for Organizational Success (GTAG-2)[5] focuses on change management and patch management. As noted in GTAG-2, the top five risk indicators of poor change management are:

- Unauthorized changes.
- Unplanned outages.
- Low change success rate.
- High number of emergency changes.
- Delayed project implementations.

The challenge for management and internal auditors is to develop improved change management policies and procedures that effectively address these issues, all of which involve the human element of change management.

Business Continuity and Disaster Recovery

Business continuity involves planning for business interruptions. Disaster recovery is the process of recovering from interruptions that impact information systems. Businesses typically plan first for the systems components, and then plan for the rest of the business when time allows. In the case of critical systems, like wire transfers in the banking industry, millions of dollars can be lost and many customers impacted in a matter of minutes.

Before an adequate contingency plan can be developed, there must be a clear understanding of the specific needs to be addressed. The disaster recovery plan covers those systems that are critical to the organization's survival. Therefore, the first step is often a risk analysis of system sensitivity, and criticality to the organization. This preliminary review helps prioritize the systems to be restored in case of a disaster.

Management must plan for a possible disaster by establishing backup and recovery procedures regarding personnel and systems following organizational standards, policies, and procedures. In addition to information systems, it is necessary to evaluate the impact on the organization, plus any other risk factors and conditions, to develop a plan to meet those needs. Information systems must be technically and organizationally ready to meet operational needs in a crisis.

As a starting point, information systems personnel, along with end users, should identify critical systems and data to ensure that they are backed up on appropriate media at appropriate intervals and rotated to an off-site location. In more advanced systems, files and transactions can be transmitted to another location for processing in case of a disaster affecting the primary site.

Recommendations regarding backup sites and processing possibilities should be reviewed by appropriate users and systems analysts to ensure that the best solution is selected. They should ensure that the critical applications are identified and dealt with appropriately, and that valuable resources are not wasted in preparing to restore nonessential systems.

The disaster recovery plan must be consistent with organizational goals, taking into consideration the systems in place, resources available, costs of alternative processing methods and locations, the capacity of the existing system, and requirements for backup. The plan should describe in detail what steps will be taken, who will be involved

Business Continuity Planning
Developing a plan to ensure that the organization will continue to function if an event causes an unscheduled interruption in normal business operations.

and what their responsibilities will be. The plan should also consider the location of the backup system; where the program and data backups reside; transaction volume; how the backup system will work, including any telecommunications requirements; the computer system configuration; methods of input and output; requirements for data authentication and other validation routines; and distribution of output.

Whenever possible, the contingency plan should be tested. This can be accomplished by walkthroughs and visits to the alternate sites to make sure that they are ready to absorb the processing requirements. The best approach, however, is actual tests where systems are brought up in a contingency environment and restore actual data in a simulation mode.

Among the considerations that should be tested are how current the information is, whether there is enough detail for people to really know what to do, whether responsible user and data processing management are available to respond during a crisis to provide required authorizations, whether the plan has been reviewed and approved by appropriate parties, and whether the arrangements with alternate processing sites are still current and viable. The goal is to ensure that during an emergency, the plan will really work.

A contingency and disaster recovery plan must be current if it is to have any real value to an organization. If it is not up-to-date, the chances are good that it will not work when it is required. In today's information system environments, things change very quickly, and the need to perform adequate maintenance on the plan is critical. Changes in capacity and versions of software are major factors. Deployment of new technologies and other changes require continuous updates for the contingency plan to be successful in meeting organizational goals.

Without adequate review and maintenance of the plan, the organization may find that it is unable to implement it in an emergency. It can be extremely expensive to acquire equipment and services quickly. When an organization has not planned well in advance, expensive stop-gap measures may be needed. Internal auditors should know what kind of plan maintenance is done, whether the plan fits into the overall corporate plan, and who is responsible for monitoring its effectiveness.

There must be business departmental plans within the overall plan to handle the application systems at the user end. Some of the contingency planning possibilities include falling back on manual processing or making use of local computers for some applications. Those areas need to be ready to take on such responsibilities if and when necessary.

Adequate planning includes creating those business plans and ensuring that they are consistent with the organizational plan. There must be a strong link between the various plans because they must all work together effectively. Backup systems should be somewhat flexible and adaptable to absorb the additional processing.

The integration of contingency plans into a total business continuation plan is important to the system of internal controls because it determines how effectively the entire information system will work after a crisis. Effective contingency planning must be a part of the overall organizational strategy in support of business objectives. Internal auditors are concerned with corporate guidelines, what kind of business planning is done, how it fits into the overall corporate plan, and who is responsible for monitoring its effectiveness.

The Association for Contingency Planners is an international association that was extremely active during the Y2K event. Interested readers can visit the organization's Web site at www.acp-international.com. As with information security, many information systems auditors have made career changes into contingency planning.

The best way to plan for a potential disaster is to complete a business impact analysis (BIA). In a BIA, organizational units are identified and any vulnerabilities are defined. The next steps are to identify strategies for minimizing risk. The result of the analysis is a BIA report, which describes the potential risks specific to the organization. One of the basic assumptions behind BIA is that every component of the organization is reliant upon the continued functioning of every other component and that some components are more crucial than others and require a greater allocation of funds in the wake of a disaster. For example, a business may be able to continue more or less normally if the cafeteria were to close but would come to a complete halt if the information system crashes.

HOW IT AFFECTS INTERNAL AUDITING

IT affects internal auditing in three ways:

- Auditing IT control activities is an integral component of auditing the business processes in which the IT control activities reside. It is imperative that internal auditors address technology issues as they are integrated into the business process.

- All internal auditors must have at least a baseline knowledge of IT risks and controls. Effectively auditing more sophisticated IT control activities may require the expertise of internal auditors trained to be IT audit specialists.

- Internal auditors use IT in conducting assurance and consulting engagements. Examples include the use of electronic workpapers and other software tools to enhance the engagement process. Audit software can be used to perform data mining techniques to identify anomalies.

Historically, the lack of a basic understanding of IT control activities has resulted in many internal audit functions either relying on IT audit specialists or performing inadequate "checklist" IT audits without the requisite knowledge and skills to properly assess IT risks, evaluate IT control activities, and formulate cost-effective recommendations for improvement.

Technology has now advanced, however, to a point where IT is integral to everything organizations do. Although many internal audit functions still employ IT audit specialists, chief audit executives are increasingly expecting internal auditors without specialized IT back-

Business Impact Analysis
An analysis of organizational units and their vulnerabilities, including strategies for minimizing risk. The result of the analysis is a business impact analysis report, which describes the potential risks specific to the organization.

grounds to perform basic technology risk assessments and assist in the implementation of adequately designed and effectively operating IT control activities.

Exhibit 6-7, The Structure of IT Auditing, is taken directly from GTAG-1. As depicted in Exhibit 6-7, "the internal auditor's role in IT controls begins with a sound conceptual understanding and culminates in providing the results of risk and controls assessments."[6]

Information systems are audited most effectively during audits of the business processes they support. This allows for auditing through the information system rather than auditing around the computer application and its supporting technology.

IT Audit Specialists

There is still a significant demand, however, for auditors with specialized IT knowledge and skills (for example, the knowledge and skills required to perform technical reviews of IT components such as firewalls, operating systems, security system software, or vulnerabilities). Whereas every internal auditor should be knowledgeable about fundamental IT risks and control activities, highly technical areas require deeper levels of expertise.

EXHIBIT 6-7

THE STRUCTURE OF IT AUDITING

ASSESSING IT CONTROLS

Understanding IT Controls	Governance, Management, Technical General/Application Preventive, Detective, Corrective Information Security
Importance of IT Controls	Reliability and Effectiveness Competitive Advantage Legislation and Regulation
Roles and Responsibilities	Governance Management Audit
Based on Risk	Risk Analysis Risk Response Baseline Controls
Monitoring and Techniques	Control Framework Frequency
Assessment	Methodologies Audit Committee Interface

The Institute of Internal Auditors, Global Technology Audit Guide—Information Technology Controls, *(Altamonte Springs, FL: The Institute of Internal Auditors, 2005, p. 18.*

Larger internal audit functions generally have the financial where-withal to support in-house IT audit specialists. Smaller internal audit functions sometimes acquire the needed knowledge and skills from cosourcing service providers. As described in Chapter 8, "Managing the Internal Audit Function," cosourcing can provide temporary internal audit personnel with highly complex and technical skills that limited resources preclude the internal audit function from retaining full time. This does not, however, discharge the CAE from the responsibility of understanding the issues being outsourced, or from providing overall management of internal audit work that may be outsourced.

Continuous Auditing

A very effective way of getting more audit coverage is to use software that runs on an ongoing basis, looking for exceptions that are outside normal boundaries. The internal audit function has been very success-ful at looking at transaction patterns that would indicate fraud. Those situations are then codified in internal audit software that can be reviewed frequently and timely for follow-up and action by the inter-nal audit function. Systems of this type have been more successful in industries with large volumes of transactions, such as the financial services and retail industries. Continuous auditing allows the internal audit function to focus in on exceptions and get much greater cover-age of high-risk areas. In addition, fraud can be detected on a timelier basis, resulting in reduced financial loss to the organization.

There are a number of recent research projects and publications from The IIA regarding this topic. *Global Technology Audit Guide—Con-tinuous Auditing: Implications for Assurance Monitoring and Risk Assessment* (GTAG-3), which was completed in 2005, is available for downloading at www.theiia.org/technology.[7] Building comprehen-sive systems of this nature requires thorough business, systems, and analytical techniques. Although most organizations want to develop systems of this type, doing so requires the right skill set along with a long-term commitment to implement the program for long-term suc-cess. Smaller internal audit functions have to rely on systems from the IT group or resources outside of the internal audit function and are not typically successful at implementing continuous auditing without the use of those resources. Additional continuous auditing resources provided by The IIA are listed in Exhibit 6-8.

Continuous Auditing

Using computerized techniques to perpetually audit the processing of business transaction

CONTINUOUS AUDITING RESOURCES FROM THE IIA

- Continuous Auditing Potential for Internal Auditors (2003)
- Proactively Detecting Occupational Fraud Using Computer Audit Reports (2004).
- Continuous Auditing: An Operational Model for Auditors (2005)
- Global Technology Audit Guide—Continuous Auditing: Implications for Assurance Monitoring and Risk Assessment (2005)

EXHIBIT 6-8

EXHIBIT 6-9

CERTIFICATIONS AVAILABLE FOR INDIVIDUALS INTERESTED IN SPECIALIZING IN INFORMATION TECHNOLOGY

Certification	Organization Sponsoring Certification	Web site	Primarily Directed Toward
CISA (Certified Information Systems Auditor)	ISACA (Information Systems Audit and Control Association)	www.isaca.org	Information Systems Auditors
CISSP (Certified Information Systems Security Professional)	ISSA (Information Systems Security Association)	www.issa.org	Information Security Professionals
CBCP (Certified Business Continuity Planner)	DRII (Disaster Recovery Institute International)	www.drii.org	Business Continuity Planners

Computer-assisted Audit Techniques (CAATs)

Automated audit techniques, such as generalized audit software, utility software, test data, application software tracing and mapping, and audit expert systems, that help the internal auditor directly test control activities built into computerized information systems and data contained in computer files.

Available Certifications for IT Auditors and Technology Risk Professionals

Professionals interested in specializing in technology risk and control activities can earn a number of specific certifications. The certifications outlined in Exhibit 6-9 are those that are most widely recognized. There are numerous other certifications, but they tend to be less recognized and more narrowly focused. Internal auditors wishing to specialize in information systems auditing or pursue careers in technology risk management should consider these certifications.

Using the Computer as an Audit Tool

Using the computer as an internal audit tool has been around since the advent of computers. Effective use of computer assisted audit techniques (CAATs) generally lags behind advancements in technology. This is usually due to a number of factors, including funding, penetration of the particular technology in the company, and the learning curve for the newer technology. Many of the specialized internal audit tools today provide for interfacing and downloading to a PC or server.

The degree of specialized tools that are available to internal auditors can be found on The IIA's Web site at: www3.theiia.org/ecm/guide-ia.cfm?doc_id=838#model. Some of these software tools are generalized software, while others are designed to handle specific problems encountered by internal auditors. CAATs and generalized audit software are discussed in more detail in Chapter 9, "Gathering and Documenting Audit Evidence."

SUMMARY

The predominance of the Internet and information systems in the achievement of business objectives necessitates an internal audit function that has a basic understanding of IT and the skills with which to assess the related risks and evaluate the related control activities. This chapter provides that baseline of knowledge and outlines the responsibility of the internal audit function to obtain the necessary knowledge and skills it doesn't already possess when the need arises. Additional IT resources on which the internal audit function can draw upon when necessary are also provided.

1. Briefly describe the key components of modern information technology.

2. Identify five information technology risks.

3. Identify two IT control activities specific to each of the five COSO components of internal control.

4. Explain the difference between general control activities and application control activities.

5. Why is it important to integrate control activities into an application as it is being developed?

6. Briefly explain how IT outsourcing and emerging technology affect the internal audit function.

7. Explain the difference between information (logical) security and physical security.

8. Identify the top five risk indicators of poor change management.

9. List five important elements of a disaster recovery plan.

10. Briefly describe three ways in which IT affects internal auditing.

11. Why is there still a need for IT audit specialists?

12. What does the term *continuous auditing* mean?

13. How might an internal auditor use the computer as an audit tool?

1. The difference between physical access control activities and logical access control activities is that:

    a. Passwords are always required for physical access.

    b. Passwords are always a requirement of logical access systems.

    c. Although logical access controls allow a person into a computer facility, physical access controls authorize a person into the computer software.

    d. Although physical access controls allow a person into a computer facility, logical access controls authorize a person into the computer software.

2. Which of the following best describes the Internet from a network security perspective?

    a. The Internet is a network with a high degree of security.

    b. The Internet is a network that is used by many and provides limited security.

    c. The Internet is a network that provides connectivity only for nonbusiness use.

    d. The Internet is a network to which it is difficult to gain access.

3. Which of the following is not a general control activity?

    a. Information security.

b. Business continuity/disaster recovery planning.

c. Change management.

d. Input/output controls.

4. Which of the following is an advantage of outsourcing technology?

a. An increased ability to modify products and services.

b. A minimum level of investment accompanied by the ability to expedite the introduction of new technology.

c. Greater security and confidentiality.

d. Priorities are easier to control.

5. Which of the following components of IT contingency planning is most important?

a. Verification of systems routines.

b. Security over the contingency site.

c. Documentation of the plan.

d. Integration of the business plans with the system plans.

6. Which of the following would not be considered an emerging technology?

a. Web technologies.

b. Firewalls.

c. Computer centers.

d. Wireless technologies.

7. Program change control activities should include all of the following except:

a. Security over the production and test libraries.

b. A formal process and documentation of requests for change.

c. Execution of only authorized programs from the production program environment.

d. Development of programs in the production environment.

1. Research the Internet and identify five information systems auditing topics of current significance.

2. Identify 10 Web sites that provide valuable information about information systems auditing.

3. Identify five areas of information system controls that commonly require improvement.

CASE

This case involves the systems development and change management processes of Dynamite Shoes, a large shoe manufacturer.

Dynamite Shoes' sales have been declining at the same time that high demand products have been unavailable in stores. The chief executive officer (CEO) couldn't understand why friends had been telling him they couldn't find the company's new Mighty shoe anywhere.

The company determined that an enterprise resouce planning (ERP) system such as SAP, together with expanding Web sales, might alleviate the problem. Web sales increased, but the problem of not having shoes in stock continued. The company decided to invest more than $300 million to implement a large enterprise-wide ERP solution to expedite the delivery of shoes, despite the fact that net income had decreased to less than $100 million the past year.

The CEO instructed the chief information officer to hire a consultant and a large enterprise ERP vendor to solve the problem, which had originated internally. The problem encompassed not just the sales process, but the production and distribution processes as well. It was determined that all of these processes needed to be automated.

The internal audit function was made aware of the project after it was started. The CEO told the CAE, "Make sure this project doesn't fail; the company's survival depends on its success. We want adequate monitoring in place to quickly identify any major problems." He also made it clear that he expected to see a significant increase in both in-store and Web-based sales.

Describe the key issues, including technology issues, that should have been resolved prior to undertaking this project. What are the technology risks associated with the project?

What steps would you take as part of the internal audit team assigned to this project? How would you ensure that adequate monitoring occurs throughout the project? At what points in the process would status updates to the CEO be appropriate? What types of update information would you provide the CEO?

REFERENCES

[1]Mitnik, Kevin, Committee on Governmental Affairs, The United States Senate, 1997, http://www.senate.gov/%7Egov_affairs/030200_mitnick.htm.

[2]Salamasick, Mark, Dallas IIA Chapter Meeting, Jan., 17, 2002.

[3]Committee of Sponsoring Organizations of the Treadway Commission *Internal Control—Integrated Framework.* (Jersey City, NJ: The Committee of Sponsoring Organizations of the Treadway Commission, 1994, p 23).

[4]The Institute of Internal Auditors, *Global Technology Audit Guide—Information Technology Controls* (Altamonte Springs, Fla.: The Institute of Internal Auditors, 2005).

[5]The Institute of Internal Auditors, *Global Technology Audit Guide—Change and Patch Management Controls: Critical for Organizational Success* (Altamonte Springs, Fla.: The Institute of Internal Auditors, 2006, p. 1).

[6]The Institute of Internal Auditors, *Global Technology Audit Guide—Information Technology Controls* (Altamonte Springs, Fla.: The Institute of Internal Auditors, 2005).

[7]The Institute of Internal Auditors, *Global Technology Audit Guide—Continuous Auditing: Implications for Assurance Monitoring and Risk Assessment* (Altamonte Springs, Fla.: The Institute of Internal Auditors, 2006).

CHAPTER 7
FRAUD RISKS AND CONTROLS

Learning Objectives

- Obtain a basic understanding of fraud risk and controls.

- Learn how fraud risks impact internal auditing.

- Define the types of fraud and fraud risk factors.

- Define governance, risk management, and internal control in the context of fraud.

- Describe fraud prevention, deterrence, and detection programs.

- Understand professional skepticism, professional judgment, and the use of computer forensics and forensic technology.

- Describe internal auditors' fraud-related responsibilities.

- Understand evolving responsibilities of the internal audit function, including the involvement of forensic accountants and fraud examination specialists.

The very mention of the word "fraud" immediately suggests a betrayal of trust and the discovery of wrongdoing. Consider your own experience of having heard the term "fraud" used to express moral outrage in general contexts, for example, "She's a fraud!" or "But, wait—isn't that fraud?" Indeed, fraud arouses much righteous indignation and emotion because it points to the basic unfairness of scheming, dishonest people knowingly deceiving honest others. In fact, the U.S. audit profession, in a civil and professional fashion, continued to refer to fraud as "accounting irregularities" until just before the 21st century. By then, financial statement fraud had increased dramatically in incidence and impact, and it became necessary to dispense with euphemisms and call it what it was.

One of the most significant risks faced by contemporary organizations is the risk of fraud. When fraud surfaces—whether it is internal fraud, third-party fraud, or collusive fraud—the afflicted organization will likely incur significant financial impact as well as serious reputational damage. In many cases, the occurrence of fraud quickly leads to precipitous declines in stock prices and market capitalization and is an early indicator of financial distress, eventually leading to bankruptcy or demise of the company. Indeed, fraud and financial distress seem to relate to each other in a "chicken-and-egg" sort of way: Fraud can

EXHIBIT 7-1

IIA STANDARDS AND PRACTICE ADVISORIES RELEVANT TO CHAPTER 7

1210.A2 — Proficiency
2130 — Governance
2210.A2 — Engagement Objectives

Practice Advisory 2130-1: Role of the Internal Audit Activity and Internal Auditor in the Ethical Culture of an Organization

Practice Advisory 2440-3: Communicating Sensitive Information Within and Outside the Chain of Command

lead to financial distress, but financial distress frequently fuels fraud. Given the serious economic consequences of fraud, senior management of many organizations is under pressure to address rising expectations associated with key business, regulatory compliance, and marketplace drivers in developing antifraud programs and control activities. This renewed global focus on corporate governance comes from a realization that fraudulent financial reporting could easily sound the death-knell for any organization.

Since 2002, the emphasis on improved corporate governance has become an increasingly global trend, with several countries such as the United Kingdom, France, and Germany (and Europe in general), Canada, Indonesia, South Africa, Australia, India, and Japan adopting new rules and regulations. Clearly, the driving factor behind such regulatory interest is to preserve market confidence by directly addressing and mitigating the risk of fraudulent financial reporting. As

EXHIBIT 7-2

U.S. AND 21ST CENTURY FRAUD

As noted in previous chapters, in the early years of the 21st century, mammoth accounting and corporate scandals involving Enron and WorldCom led to a dire situation where billions of U.S. dollars in market capitalization evaporated; investors became skittish, lost confidence, and hastily exited the capital markets. To restore public trust and confidence in the financial markets, the U.S. Congress passed sweeping corporate governance reform legislation, specifically, the Sarbanes-Oxley Act of 2002. However, fraud is certainly not the monopoly of the United States. It is a global trend, and hence, measures are being taken all over the world to mitigate fraud risk. Some statistics from the United States: During the quarter century from 1978-2002, U.S. federal regulators initiated 585 enforcement actions for public company financial misrepresentation, citing 2,310 individuals and 657 firms as being potentially liable (*Wall Street Journal*, 2005). The continuing increase in U.S. Securities & Exchange Commission (SEC) investigations and the number of financial statement restatements since 2002 suggest that corporate America is still dogged by serious governance failures. Nevertheless, there is no question that Sarbanes-Oxley, and, especially the American Institute of Certified Public Accountants' SAS 99: *Consideration of Fraud in a Financial Statement Audit,* as well as the U.S. Public Company Accounting Oversight Board's Auditing Standard No. 5, *An Audit of Internal Control Over Financial Reporting That Is Integrated With an Audit of Financial Statements*, have dramatically influenced the internal audit function's mandate and role, including its responsibilities related to fraud prevention, deterrence, and detection.

a result, the gatekeepers of financial integrity, among them internal auditors, have achieved significant prominence and are increasingly being asked to play a key role in preventing, deterring, and detecting fraud in for-profit, governmental, and nonprofit organizations globally. Examples of the kinds of fraud that led to this emphasis on improved corporate governance are presented in Exhibit 7-3.

EXHIBIT 7-3

INTERNATIONAL EXAMPLES OF FRAUD

In May 2006, Japan's Financial Services Agency took the unprecedented step of ordering one of Japan's largest accountancy firms, Chuo Aoyama Audit Corporation (CAAC was affiliated with PricewaterhouseCoopers), to suspend auditing operations for two months beginning in July as punishment for its role in the massive fraud at Kanebo Ltd., a giant cosmetics and textiles company. The fraud, involving the bloating of earnings by over 200 billion yen from 1999–2004, was exposed when Kanebo, burdened by massive debts, went into restructuring under the government's Industrial Revitalization Corporation of Japan (IRCJ). Three CPAs at Chuo Aoyama have since pleaded guilty to falsifying the cosmetics and textile manufacturer's financial statements. This is significant because Chuo Aoyama is an auditing behemoth with about 3,500 employees, including 1,700 CPAs, and audits about 5,300 companies, of which 2,300 are legally required to have their books audited. Premier clients of the firm include Toyota Motor Corp., Sony Corp., Nippon Steel Corp., Toray Industries Inc., Nippon Life Insurance Co., and Millea Holdings Inc. To control reputational damage, Chuo Aoyama changed its name to Mizusu as of September 2006. However, a new revelation that Chuo Aoyama had signed off on the 2005 financials of Nikko Cordial, Japan's 3rd largest broker that was hit with a huge regulatory fine for window dressing, further damaged Mizusu's fledgling reputation. Subsequently, the decision announced on Tuesday, Feb. 20, 2007 by Misuzu, Japan's fourth-largest accountancy firm and one of two partner firms of PricewaterhouseCoopers, to wind down its business highlights a sea of change in the country's accountancy profession. Commentators have drawn parallels between the regulatory action against Chuo Aoyama and the Andersen scenario following the Enron scandal. Interestingly, the role of internal auditors at Kanebo and Nikko Cordial, if indeed there was such a control function, has not been discussed at all.

Other noteworthy examples of massive financial frauds outside the United States include the wholesale fraud at the Bank of Credit and Commerce International, based in the United Kingdom; the multi-billion dollar fraud at Parmalat, the Italian dairy giant; the financial statement restatements at Nortel Networks, one of Canada's largest companies; and the relatively recent corruption and bribery charges levied against the Chairman of Hyundai, the Korean automobile company.

Internationally, the pertinent standard furnishing guidance for auditors is International Standard on Auditing (ISA) No. 240: The Auditor's Responsibility to Consider Fraud and Error in an Audit of Financial Statements, issued by the International Federation of Accountants (IFAC). Although this standard applies primarily to independent outside auditors, internal auditors, too, would greatly benefit from a review of its contents and guidance. Fraud, waste, and abuse are also a big concern in government, and the recently revised and updated Generally Accepted Government Auditing Standards (GAGAS) in the United States—also known as the Yellow Book—devotes several sections to government internal auditors' responsibilities in this area. In

addition, individuals and organizations that are charged with overseeing senior management (for example, audit committees) and those with responsibility for financial reporting and disclosure monitoring have high expectations of internal auditors with respect to preventing and mitigating fraud. Recent studies in comparative corporate governance find that governance reform is unmistakably a global trend, and internal auditors all over the world are facing increased expectations in combating fraud.

DEFINITIONS OF FRAUD

Organizations representing specialized professionals such as independent outside auditors and internal auditors, as well as fraud examiners, have attempted to define fraud and delineate the roles and

responsibilities of their respective member constituency. In addition to the Certified Internal Auditor (CIA) designation, practicing internal auditors frequently hold other designations such as the Certified Public Accountant (CPA), or Chartered Accountant in certain non-U.S. jurisdictions), and the Certified Fraud Examiner (CFE). Accordingly, the definitions of fraud offered by the international Institute of Internal Auditors (IIA), the American Institute of Certified Public Accountants (AICPA), and the global Association of Certified Fraud Examiners (ACFE), are discussed below.

The Institute of Internal Auditors' Definition

The IIA offers the following definition of fraud in the glossary accompanying its Professional Practices Framework:

> **Fraud.** Any illegal acts characterized by deceit, concealment or violation of trust. These acts are not dependent upon the application of threat of violence or of physical force. Frauds are perpetrated by parties and organizations to obtain money, property, or services; to avoid payment or loss of services; or to secure personal or business advantage.[1]

Specifically, the role of the internal audit function has been emphasized in recent legislation, regulatory mandates, as well as in gover-

Fraud

Any illegal acts characterized by deceit, concealment, or violation of trust.

nance-focused organizations around the world. Internal auditors, as the "eyes and ears, and arms and legs of the audit committee," are encouraged to consider the following questions:

- What fraud risks are being monitored by the internal audit function on a periodic or regular basis? How does the internal audit function address the continuous auditing of these critical risks? (An important consequence of fraud allegation is the significant reputational damage to the victim organization, its brand, products, and people.)

- What specific procedures does the internal audit function perform to address management override of internal control activities?

- Has anything occurred that would lead the internal audit function to change its assessment of the risk of management override of internal control activities?

- What competencies and skills do internal auditors need to address the risk of fraud within organizations? When do they need to bring in specialists to deal with particularly complex issues?

- How should the internal audit function devote its attention to the preventive, deterrent, detective, and investigative aspects of fraud?

- In addition to establishing direct lines of reporting to the audit committee, how can the independent organizational status of the internal audit function be strengthened? How can they come to be relied upon as competent and objective professionals in addressing the fraud risk and controls issues for organizations?

American Institute of Certified Public Accountants' Definition

Given the public accounting profession's primary focus on the financial statement audit, now expanded in the United States to include an audit of internal control over financial reporting under Section 404 of the Sarbanes-Oxley Act of 2002, it is not surprising that the AICPA discusses the concept of fraud by evaluating its relation to, and effect on, the organization's financial statements. Thus, the AICPA definition— taken from Statement on Auditing Standard (SAS) 99 that became effective for financial statement audits after Dec. 15, 2002—describes two types of fraud: misstatements arising from fraudulent financial reporting (distortion of an organization's financial statements resulting from "cooking the books") and misstatements arising from misappropriation of assets (theft or misuse of an organization's assets).

Fraudulent financial reporting involves intentional misstatements or omissions of amounts or disclosures in financial statements designed to deceive financial statement users. The nature of these misstatements or omissions is the failure of the financial statements to be presented, in all material respects, in conformity with generally accepted accounting principles (GAAP). Fraudulent financial reporting can be accomplished by the following:

- Manipulation, falsification, or alteration of accounting records or

Fraudulent Financial Reporting

Acts that involve falsification of an organization's financial statements, (for example, overstating revenues, understating liabilities and expenses).

supporting documents from which the financial statements are prepared.

- Misrepresentation in, or intentional omission from, the financial statements of events, transactions, or other significant information.
- Intentional misapplication of accounting principles relating to amounts, classification, manner of presentation, or disclosure.

Misstatements arising from misappropriation of assets (sometimes referred to as pilferage, embezzlement, or defalcation) involve the theft of an entity's assets in which the effect of the theft causes the financial statements not to be presented, in all material respects, in conformity with GAAP. Misappropriation of assets can be perpetrated in various ways, including embezzling receipts, stealing assets, or causing an entity to pay for goods or services that have not been received. Misappropriation of assets may be accompanied by false or misleading records or documents, or suppressing evidence, possibly created by circumventing internal control activities. Frequently, collusion with other employees or third parties may also be involved. For more detail regarding SAS 99, see Exhibit 7-5.

Association of Certified Fraud Examiners' Definition

The Association of Certified Fraud Examiners (ACFE), in its 2006 *Report to the Nation on Occupational Fraud* and Abuse defines *occupational fraud* as:

> The use of one's occupation for personal enrichment through the deliberate misuse or misapplication of the employing organization's resources or assets.[2]

Occupational fraud encompasses a wide range of misconduct by employees, managers, and executives. Occupational fraud schemes can be as simple as petty cash theft or as complex as fraudulent financial reporting. Four elements seem to characterize the incidence of occupational fraud. Such an act:

Asset Misappropriation

Acts involving the theft or misuse of an organization's assets (for example, skimming revenues, stealing inventory, payroll fraud).

Occupational Fraud

The use of one's occupation for personal enrichment through the deliberate misuse or misapplication of the employing organization's resources or assets.

EXHIBIT 7-5

MORE ON AICPA'S FRAUD STANDARD, SAS 99

Among the AICPA's professional standards, SAS 99: *Consideration of Fraud in a Financial Statement Audit* states that [independant outside] auditors are responsible for planning and performing an audit to obtain reasonable assurance about whether the financial statements are free of material misstatements whether caused by error of fraud. Specifically, SAS 99 contains the following:

- Increased emphasis on fraud awareness and professional skepticism.
- Audit engagement team discussion ("brainstorming session").
- Gathering information needed to identify the risk of material misstatement due to fraud.
- Summarizing identified fraud and the auditor's planned response.
- Mandatory audit procedures to address the risk of management override of internal control activities.
- Evaluating audit results.
- Communications about fraud with management, the audit committee, and others.

- Is clandestine (that is, secretive and suspicious).
- Violates the perpetrator's fiduciary duties to the victim organization.
- Is committed for the purpose of direct or indirect financial benefit to the perpetrator.
- Costs the employing organization assets, revenues, or reserves.

The ACFE's Uniform Occupational Fraud Classification System (Fraud Tree), describes three main types of fraud: *asset misappropriation*, which involves the theft or misuse of an organization's assets (for example, skimming revenues, stealing inventory, payroll fraud); *corruption*, in which fraudsters wrongfully use their influence in a business transaction in order to procure some benefit for themselves or another person, contrary to their duty to their employer or the rights of another (for example, kickbacks, self-dealing, conflicts of interest); and *fraudulent statements,* which generally involve falsification of an organization's financial statements (for example, overstating revenues, understating liabilities and expenses).

CFEs conduct forensic accounting investigations (usually after the fact, when predication exists) to resolve allegations or suspicions of fraud, reporting either to an appropriate level of management or to the audit committee or board of directors, depending upon the nature of the issue and the level of personnel involved. They may also assist the audit committee and the board of directors with aspects of the oversight process, either directly or as part of a team of internal auditors or independent outside auditors, in evaluating the fraud risk assessment and fraud prevention measures implemented by senior management. They can provide more objective input into management's evaluation of the risk of fraud (especially fraud involving senior management, such as financial statement fraud) and the development of appropriate antifraud control activities that are less vulnerable to management override. In recent years, several internal audit professionals have obtained the CFE designation and, having acquired this specialized expertise, are better equipped to discharge their responsibilities in this area.

Since 1996, the ACFE has released its Report to the Nation, which sheds light on the immense, and largely undefined, costs that occupational fraud imposes on organizations. The stated goals of the report are to:

- Summarize the opinions of experts on the percentage and amount of organizational revenue lost to all forms of occupational fraud and abuse.
- Examine the characteristics of the employees who commit occupational fraud and abuse.
- Determine what kinds of organizations are victims of occupational fraud and abuse.
- Categorize the ways in which serious fraud and abuse occurs.[3]

Exhibit 7-6 provides more detail on the 2006 Report to the Nation.

Conflict of Interest
Any relationship that is, or appears to be, not in the best interest of the organization.

Certified Fraud Examiners
conduct forensic accounting investigations (usually after the fact, when predication exists) to resolve allegations or suspicions of fraud.

EXHIBIT 7-6

ASSOCIATION OF CERTIFIED FRAUD EXAMINERS' 2006 REPORT TO THE NATION

The 2006 ACFE *Report to the Nation* is based on data compiled from 1,134 cases of occupational fraud from a wide range of industries that were investigated between January 2004 and January 2006. Information from each case was reported by a certified fraud examiner, who investigated the case.

- Occupational fraud and abuse imposes enormous costs on organizations. Study participants estimated that U.S. organizations lose 5% of their annual revenues to fraud. Applied to the estimated U.S. gross domestic product (GDP) this 5% figure would translate to approximately US$652 billion in fraud losses.

- Occupational fraud schemes can be very difficult to detect. The median length of the schemes in the 2006 study was 18 months from the time the fraud began until the time it was detected.

- Occupational frauds are more likely to be detected by a tip than by other means such as internal audits, independent outside audits, or internal control activities.

- Certain antifraud control activities can have a measurable impact on an organization's exposure to fraud. For instance, having an anonymous fraud hotline in place, or an internal audit function that regularly performs surprise audits, and conducts antifraud training for employees and managers, can significantly deter fraud and reduce losses from fraud.

- Small businesses continue to suffer disproportionate fraud losses from activities such as employees fraudulently writing company checks, skimming revenues, and processing fraudulent invoices. Small businesses do a poor job of proactively detecting fraud (for example, they may not have an internal audit function), and most of the frauds in this sector were detected by accident.

- The size of the loss caused by occupational fraud is strongly related to the position of the perpetrator and most occupational fraud schemes involved either the accounting department or upper management.

- Although a majority of organizations in the study routinely conducted background checks (nearly 67%), less than 8% of the perpetrators had convictions prior to commiting their frauds. In other words, the predominate majority of fraud perpetrators were first-time offenders, suggesting that internal audit activities and the existence of anonymous reporting mechanisms can significantly help with fraud deterence efforts.

GOVERNANCE, RISK MANAGEMENT, AND CONTROL ACTIVITIES IN THE CONTEXT OF FRAUD

In general, capital market regulators around the world are introducing rules designed to increase management's accountability for the financial reporting process and to strengthen corporate governance. Several of these legislative mandates and regulatory requirements, either directly or indirectly, will help create and sustain a stronger control environment thus enhancing the likelihood of preventing, deterring, and detecting financial statement or other fraud. Further, any enterprisewide risk management framework implementation—for example, the Committee of Sponsoring Organizations of the Treadway Commission (COSO) *Enterprise Risk Management (ERM)—Integrated Framework*—would require that considerable emphasis be placed on evaluating and assessing the risk of fraud adversely affecting the organization's achievement of strategic goals and objectives. The ERM framework and governance are discussed in detail in Chapter 3, "Governance and Risk Management."

With respect to management's responsibility for establishing and maintaining effective systems of internal control to prevent, deter, and detect fraud, IIA Practice Advisory 1210.A2-2, Responsibility for Fraud Detection, states that "management has a responsibility to establish and maintain an effective control system at a reasonable cost."

Specific provisions gleaned from a review of evolving rules and regulations, as well as professional standards, are summarized below, along with an indication of how the internal audit function may be involved in these efforts:

- Support audit committee (or others charged with governance) oversight in ensuring that management has implemented an effective system of internal controls, including control activities to help prevent, deter, and detect fraud. Audit committees are also required to establish procedures for receiving and following up on anonymous tips and complaints from employees regarding control activities, as well as questionable accounting and auditing matters. Obviously, the internal audit function has a significant role to play in supporting the audit committee in discharging its oversight responsibilities, including implementing any whistleblower provisions, effectively. Best practice in this area recommends that ethics hotlines be expanded to cover not only employees but also those outside the organization such as vendors, customers, and other third parties.

- Validate management's assessment of, and report on, the effectiveness of the company's system of internal controls and procedures for financial reporting, including fraud risk mitigation controls, where appropriate. Internal auditors can independently review and provide a certain degree of assurance about the success of these efforts prior to the independent outside auditors' formal attestation report on the same.

- Provide assurances on management [chief executive officer (CEO) and chief financial officer (CFO)] certification of financial statements in each quarterly and annual report filed, for example, with the U.S. Securities and Exchange Commission (SEC). Such a requirement underscores the primary responsibility of management in designing and implementing effective internal control activities throughout the organization, and setting the proper tone at the top. Internal auditors can usefully provide assurance to management about the underlying effectiveness of internal controls over financial reporting, as well as operational controls, and compliance with laws and regulations. They can also get a sense of the ethical climate within the organization through periodic testing of anti-fraud programs and control activities.

- Monitor the annual disclosure of whether the company has adopted a code of ethics that covers its CEO and senior financial officers. Note that the SEC defines the term *code of ethics* as written standards that reasonably deter wrongdoing and to promote:

- Honest and ethical conduct.
- Full, fair, accurate, timely, and understandable disclosure in SEC reports and public communications.
- Compliance with applicable governmental laws, rules, and regulations.
- Prompt internal reporting of violation of the code.
- Accountability for adherence to the code.

Internal auditors can consult on the design of such organizational codes of conduct/ethics as well as control activities to mitigate integrity risks. They can also test the ethical climate as well as the perception of the prevailing *tone at the top*. In addition, the internal audit function can also carry out post hoc ethics audits to determine whether an organizationwide adopted code of conduct is being implemented well and being adhered to appropriately.

Roles of Internal Auditors

Internal auditors are an integral part of organizational governance, and must support ERM activities as delineated in the COSO ERM framework. One of the most important risks affecting an organization is its vulnerability to fraud. Indeed, without mitigating fraud risk to a sufficiently low level, "effective governance" is not a meaningful phrase. In other words, the occurrence of material fraud first and foremost suggests a failure of corporate governance (including an improper assessment of the organization's risk appetite and self-insured risk acceptance). Hence it is the responsibility of every internal audit function to raise fraud awareness within an organization, including encouraging the audit committee and senior management to set the proper tone at the top, create control consciousness, and help develop a credible response to the potential risk of fraud. It should also emphasize the existence of, and adherence to, organizational values and the corporate code of conduct as well as report any activities that raise suspicions that these could be illegal, unethical, or immoral through the whistleblower hotline or other means. The audit committee and the board expect no less from a competent and value-adding internal audit function.

Moreover, Standard 2130 states that "the internal audit activity should assess and make appropriate recommendations for improving the governance process in its accomplishment of the following objectives:

- Promoting appropriate ethics and values within the organization.
- Ensuring effective organizational performance management and accountability.
- Effectively communicating risk and control information to appropriate areas of the organization.
- Effectively coordinating the activities of and communicating information among the board, external and internal auditors, and management."

Given the importance of the internal audit function in strengthening governance processes, fraud risk assessment and mitigation is an important area of audit focus. Internal auditors frequently possess the competence to identify the indicators of fraud (sometimes called "red flags"). They can usefully provide independent and objective assurance on the effectiveness of processes put in place by management to manage the risk of fraud. They are responsible for the review of specific antifraud programs and fraud prevention, deterrence and detection control activities established by management, and for making recommendations to improve the efficiency and effectiveness of such programs and control activities.

Independent Outside Auditors' Reliance on the Work of Internal Auditing

In the context of a financial statement audit, the independent outside auditor can, by reviewing the work performed by the internal audit function as well as making inquiries of internal audit personnel, enhance their understanding of the adequacy and effectiveness of internal controls over financial reporting. Such information may be beneficial to the independent outside auditor in that it is then only necessary to perform the critical audit procedures necessary to clarify or resolve significant financial reporting (disclosure) control issues. Some examples of the inquiries that may be made of the internal auditor are reliability and integrity of financial and operational effectiveness; adequacy and effectiveness of financial information, safeguarding of assets, compliance with laws, regulations, and contracts; and last but not least, indicators of fraud. Of course, it should be emphasized that the independent outside auditor continues to have overall responsibility for the opinion expressed on the organization's financial statements, whether or not it is based in part on reliance of the work performed by the internal audit function.

Understanding Fraud, Fraudsters, and Fraud Risk Factors

Behavioral science has thus far been unable to identify a unitary psychological characteristic or a set of characteristics that can serve as a reliable marker of the propensity of an individual to commit fraud. At the same time, to say that "greed and dishonesty"—a commonly heard refrain—can account for all that went on during the "irrational exuberance" of the 1990s would be overly simplistic. After all, there are many professionals in the business world who are extremely ambitious, competitive, and wealthy, but nevertheless fully abide by the law. They do not necessarily resort to fraud to achieve their stretch goals. One experienced forensic accountant and fraud examiner, Thomas Golden of PricewaterhouseCoopers, believes that financial reporting fraud perpetrators fit one of two profiles: "greater good oriented" or "scheming, self-centered" types. Those who fit the greater good oriented profile are "otherwise honest individuals who misrepresent the numbers by rationalizing that what they are doing is best for the company." The scheming, self-centered types are "individuals who exhibit a rampant disregard for the truth, are well aware of what they are doing, and who are attempting to attain goals dishonestly."[4]

From a criminology perspective, fraud, like other crime, can best be explained by three factors: a supply of motivated offenders, the availability of suitable targets, and the absence of capable guardians—controls systems or someone "to mind the store" so to speak.[5] This is similar to the conceptual framework provided by the Fraud Triangle that is discussed in the following section.

The Fraud Triangle

An important conceptual framework in understanding fraud is Cressey's Fraud Triangle, loosely based on what policemen and detectives have referred to as "means, motives, and opportunity." First conceived by sociologist Donald Cressey, and widely disseminated by the Association of Certified Fraud Examiners, the fraud triangle has three vertices or components: perceived incentives/pressures, perceived opportunities, and rationalization of fraudulent behavior.

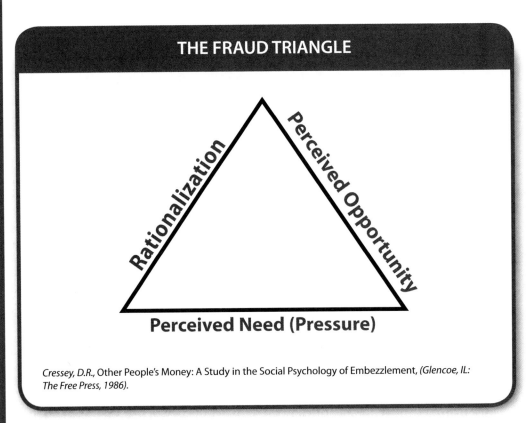

THE FRAUD TRIANGLE

Cressey, D.R., Other People's Money: A Study in the Social Psychology of Embezzlement, (Glencoe, IL: The Free Press, 1986).

Exhibit 7-7 is a visual representation of these three components.

The fraud triangle highlights the three elements that may be called the "root causes of fraud" that are always present, no matter the type of fraud. Fraud perpetrators want to relieve real or perceived pressure to show performance (for example, generating the attitude that when you can't "make" the numbers, you just "make up" the numbers), they need to see ample opportunity so that they can carry out the fraud with ease (for example, nobody's watching the store, the employee is trusted completely), and most importantly, they need to rationalize their action as acceptable. Rationalization allows fraud perpetrators to believe that they have done nothing wrong, and are "normal people." Specifically, fraud perpetrators must be able to justify their actions to themselves as a psychological coping mechanism to deal with the inevitable "cognitive dissonance" (that is, a lack of congruence between their own perception of being honest and the deceptive nature of their action or behavior). They need excuses. A typical list includes:

- Everyone's doing it, so I am no different.
- Taking money from the cash till was just a temporary "borrowing." The money will be returned when the gambling/betting winnings materialize.
- The employer is underpaying me, so I deserve these "perks" as reasonable compensation, and the company can certainly afford it.
- I am not hurting anyone—in fact, it's for a good cause!
- It is not really a serious matter.

Consider a couple of examples: A furniture store employee stealing inventory may be taking advantage of weak internal control activities (perceived opportunity), the need to furnish his new apartment for "free" (perceived pressure from spouse), and using the rationalization that other store employees are probably stealing, too (whether or not this is a fact). In the case of management fraud, the perceived pressure may be to meet earnings targets so that bonuses can be lavish, the opportunity may be weak financial reporting control activities or an inactive audit committee, and the rationalization may be that "this is in the organization's best interest and therefore an appropriate use of 'cookie jar reserves' created earlier to get over a temporary hump." Although the fraud triangle is a powerful conceptual tool, there are other factors such as basic greed and acquisitiveness, a "revenge fraud" orientation to make the organization pay for perceived inequities, or a "catch me if you can" attitude that some fraud perpetrators exhibit, and these personality characteristics do not easily fit within the fraud triangle framework. Similarly, the fraud perpetrator's assessment of the organization's attitude toward fraud even if the perpetrator is identified (for example, organizational inertia and reluctance to take any action, turning a blind eye, being content with a slap on the wrist, poor track record in vigorously prosecuting fraud) gets factored into the "opportunity space" but is not obvious as a category.

Recent research has tried to look at the relative effectiveness of certain fraud risk indicators (red flags) so that more weight can be attached to these indicators by internal auditors. On an overall basis, the average effectiveness of fraud indicators falling under the category attitude/rationalization were the most effective, followed by opportunity, and then by incentive/pressure. In general, internal auditors should be suspicious when management tries to control and reduce the scope of an audit examination—it may be an attempt to conceal fraudulent activity.

More specifically, the authors of the study furnished specific ratings on a scale from 1 to 5 (increasing effectiveness) to fraud risk factors falling under each of the three vertices of the fraud triangle. The highlights (with the assigned ranking in parenthesis) are provided here:

Opportunity

- Formal or informal restrictions on the auditors who

inappropriately limit their access to people or information, or who limit their ability to communicate effectively with the board or audit committee (4.97).

- Significant related-party transactions not in the ordinary course of business or with related entities that are not audited or are audited by another firm (4.74).

- Domination of management by a single person or a small group in a nonowner managed business without compensating control activities (4.72).

- Ineffective accounting and information systems, including situations involving significant deficiencies or material weaknesses in internal controls over financial reporting (4.47).

- Inadequate monitoring of significant internal control activities (4.43).

- Ineffective board or audit committee oversight over the financial reporting process and internal control system (4.27).

- High turnover rates or employment of ineffective accounting, internal audit, or information technology staff (4.25).

Attitude/Rationalization

- Significant, unique, or highly complex transactions, especially occurring close to year-end, that pose difficult "substance over form" questions (4.95).

- Domineering management behavior in dealing with the internal auditor, especially involving attempts to influence the scope of the internal auditor's work (4.92).

- Known history of violations of securities law, or claims against the entity, its senior management, or board members alleging fraud or violations of securities laws (4.82).

- Ineffective communication, implementation, support, or enforcement of the entity's values or ethical standards by management, or the communication of inappropriate values or ethical standards (4.52).

- Frequent disputes with the current or previous internal auditor on accounting, audit, or reporting matters (4.35).

- An interest by management in using inappropriate means to minimize reported earnings for tax-motivated reasons (4.30).

- Recurring attempts by management to justify marginal or inappropriate accounting on the basis of materiality (4.22).

- Management failure to connect known significant deficiencies or material weaknesses in internal controls over financial reporting in a timely manner[6](4.17).

Exhibit 7-8 provides an analysis of these factors as articulated by ACFE-founder Joseph Wells in *The Journal of Accountancy*.

EXHIBIT 7-8

CONTROLS VERSUS THE PERCEPTION OF BEING CAUGHT

ACFE founder Joseph Wells provides a penetrating analysis of how fraudsters think. Echoing 18th century economist Jeremy Bentham, he observes that the likelihood of committing a (white-collar) crime is a function of the perpetrator's perception of the risks and rewards, that is, those who assess the probability of getting caught as being high are naturally less inclined to commit fraud. It is well known that, on the effectiveness dimension, fraud risk control activities pale in comparison to the increase in the perception of being apprehended, and the observed follow-up consequences from the organization's track record in the handling of past incidents and allegations. Hence, from a behavioral standpoint, this raises the possibility of creating an "anticipation effect" (that is, the anticipation of being audited), including unannounced surprise checks, as part of the fraud prevention and deterrence control activities. Continuing this line of reasoning, both independent outside and internal auditors, through creative and imaginative approaches to their work using technology (for example, continuous control monitoring) or advances in statistics (for example, discovery sampling approaches, Benford's Law) or even "active brainstorming about the ways fraud could be perpetrated" can put up strong deterrents and defenses to fraud, all the while improving fraud detection capabilities. Management must act decisively and swiftly against fraud perpetrators when they are identified as a result of a fraud investigation. Such swift and decisive action can go a long way in cementing fraud deterrence efforts.

Source: www.theiia.org

Professional Skepticism, Professional Judgment, and Forensic Technology

As noted in earlier chapters, the exercise of sound professional judgment lies at the heart of the internal audit function's assurance and consulting activities. When fraud risk assessments are involved, the internal auditor must necessarily exhibit a high degree of professional skepticism, that is, an ability to critically evaluate the evidence and information available at hand. This is particularly so because fraud perpetrators typically "cover their tracks" and significant persistence may be required to unravel a well-concealed fraud scheme. (For example, the dogged perseverance by 2004 *Time Magazine* Person of the Year Cynthia Cooper and her team was essential in unearthing the massive fraud at WorldCom.)

Not all internal auditors exercise the same degree of professional skepticism—some are more skeptical, others less so—some accept explanations at face value, others want to probe further and dig deeper. The latter types, who would seem to have natural "sleuthing tendencies," also display higher levels of professional skepticism, in general. While being "paranoid" may frequently result in over-auditing, whenever facts and circumstances suggest a higher likelihood of fraud, exhibiting a heightened degree of professional skepticism may be expected, warranted, and justified.

Any complex risk assessment task involves a review of disparate pieces of evidence, with diverse characteristics and degrees of reliability. In such contexts, an experienced internal auditor has better ability to "connect the dots" and reconstruct the whole picture from incomplete information and evidence. This is why most fraud investi-

Professional Skepticism

The state of mind in which internal auditors take nothing for granted; they continuously question what they hear and see and critically assess audit evidence.

Benford's Law Analysis

Analysis of patterns in large data sets of numbers to detect anomalies that may indicate fraud.

gation groups are staffed with individuals who have significant experience with control activities. Indeed, research on the applications of artificial intelligence (including neural network technology) has shown that solving the "jigsaw puzzle," that is, aggregation of dispersed evidence, is actually a pattern recognition problem. In other words, all the available evidence cannot be considered sequentially; instead, a holistic approach that considers all the available evidence simultaneously may be required. In such circumstances, it may be important for the technology-savvy internal auditor to leverage decision aids, expert systems, and artificial intelligence to increase both effectiveness and efficiency [for example, Benford's Law or digital analysis, advanced computer-assisted audit techniques (CAATs), predictive analytics including regression models and neural networks].

With the ubiquitous use of e-mail communications, forensic investigations and fraud examination in the future will depend heavily on computer forensics, computer data imaging, electronic evidence discovery, and the analysis of structured and unstructured data. In other words, the use of technology will not be limited to data analysis (after structured data has been collected); instead, the very extraction and preservation of electronic evidence—usually in the form of textual, unstructured data requiring keyword searches, for instance—will be technology intensive. In such a context, it will be crucial for fraud examiners to have a sound understanding of, and mastery over, "digital forensics"—the latest and emerging forensic technology tools and techniques.

Internal Control Breakdown Versus Management Override of Controls

An internal control system could have flaws that can be traced to its design (for example, where certain kinds of errors or fraud were not modeled or contemplated), or to its operating effectiveness (for example, implementation challenges, including human misunderstandings), or both. When this happens, it is an *internal control breakdown*. However, when an otherwise well-designed and well-functioning internal control system is simply suspended, ignored, circumvented, or summarily dismissed by senior management—the people who implemented the control activities in the first place—it is a classic case of "management override of internal controls" (for example, a traffic cop racing through a red light because he was supposedly chasing a suspect).

Management Override

Management's intentional disregard of established policies for illegitimate purposes.

COSO states, "An internal control system, no matter how well-conceived and operated, can provide only reasonable—not absolute—assurance to management and the board regarding the achievement of the entity's objectives. The likelihood of achievement is affected by limitations inherent in all internal control systems. These include the reality that judgments in decision-making can be faulty, and that breakdowns can occur because of simple error or mistake. Additionally, control activities can be circumvented by collusion of two or more people, and management has the ability to override the system."[7]

Management override of internal control activities is extraordinarily difficult to detect especially because most internal auditors are trained to accept that "absence of evidence is evidence of absence." And when there is a motivated fraud perpetrator who is a member of senior management, the perpetrator will normally go to great lengths to conceal the evidence. Nevertheless, the internal audit function can be vigilant and take numerous steps to combat this disturbing possibility by:

- Insisting on background checks for all employees before hiring but especially so at senior executive ranks.
- Maintaining an appropriate level of professional skepticism.
- Nurturing operational risk management and compliance cultures, and gathering intelligence about potential fraud risks from separately functioning risk and compliance operations.
- Leveraging the corporate code of conduct to assess the ethical temperature of the organization.
- Working to educate the audit committee and building fraud awareness throughout the organization.
- Reporting periodically to the audit committee regarding the design of fraud control activities and their operational effectiveness.
- Ensuring that the organization actively promotes and supports a whistleblower program, including a "no retaliation expectation."
- Developing a broad information and communication feedback network.[8]

Fraud Prevention, Deterrence, and Detection Programs

Any credible approach to fraud prevention, deterrence, and detection needs to be consistent with an accepted framework, such as COSO's *Internal Control—Integrated Framework*. Exhibit 7-9 depicts the COSO cube. For more information regarding COSO's *Internal Control—Integrated Framework*, refer to Chapter 5, "Internal Control." Specifically, it is important to consider the following COSO components in looking at anti-fraud programs and controls: (1) control environment, (2) risk assessment, (3) control activities, (4) information and communication, and (5) monitoring.

A COSO-based Approach

At the very foundation, it is necessary to consider the creation of a control environment through setting the proper tone at the top and organizational culture, having an organizational code of conduct/ethics (preferably read and signed by every employee), providing fraud awareness training, and maintaining a whistleblower hotline. It is also important to develop a formal policy and methodology to investigate potential occurrences of fraud, as well as be seen as responding to fraud incidents quickly, fairly, and decisively. These latter activities help create the perception that the organization takes fraud very seriously. It also helps the organization develop a track record in terms of management's commitment in responding to fraud incidents vigorously and decisively. Next, it is critical that periodic fraud risk assessments are performed to assess the ethical climate within the organization and to follow up on specific instances arousing suspicions. This process, carried out on a regular basis, includes involving

professionals with fraud and forensic expertise, identifying fraud risk factors, brainstorming about potential fraud risks, and evaluating the feasibility of fraud schemes being perpetrated but going unnoticed or being concealed despite the existence of control activities. Following this step, there is a need to link identified fraud risks to specific control activities. This is part of the design and implementation of antifraud programs and fraud risk controls. Once this step has been carried out, it is critical that there be organizationwide communication and knowledge sharing (it may even be argued that such communication may be desirable even outside an organization with vendors and customers, so third-party fraud and collusion may be deterred and suspicious activities can be reported on the whistleblower hotline). Finally, those charged with governance (that is, typically the audit committee or equivalent) need to monitor the effectiveness of anti-fraud programs and control activities, perhaps by including testing of these control activities by the internal audit function periodically. A feedback loop is important to continue this process into the following year, and in terms of audit testing strategies, a two- or three-year cycle to achieve appropriate audit coverage may be reasonable depending on the circumstances. Ideally, using technology to drive continuous monitoring and detection activities would represent the culmination of the monitoring and oversight process. The IIA suggests that internal auditors consider fraud within the context of COSO's five components of internal control as described below:

- **Control environment.** Assess aspects of the control environment, conduct proactive fraud audits and investigations, communicate results of fraud audits, and provide support for remediation efforts. In some cases, internal auditors may also own the whistleblower hotline.

- **Risk assessment.** Evaluate management's fraud risk assessment, in particular, their processes for identifying, assessing, and testing potential fraud and misconduct schemes and scenarios, including those that could involve suppliers, contractors, and other parties.

- **Control activities.** Assess the design and operating effectiveness of fraud-related control activities, ensure that audit plans and programs address residual risk and incorporate fraud audits, evaluate the design of facilities from a fraud or theft perspective, and review proposed changes to laws, regulations or systems, and their impacts on control activities.

- **Information and communication.** Assess the operating effectiveness of information and communication systems and practices, as well as provide support to fraud-related training initiatives.

- **Monitoring.** Assess monitoring activities and related computer software, conduct investigations, support the audit committee's oversight related to control and fraud matters, support the development of fraud indicators, and hire and train employees so they can have the appropriate fraud audit or investigative experience.

EXHIBIT 7-9

THE COSO CUBE: A COSO-BASED APPROACH TO FRAUD PREVENTION, DETERRENCE, AND DETECTION

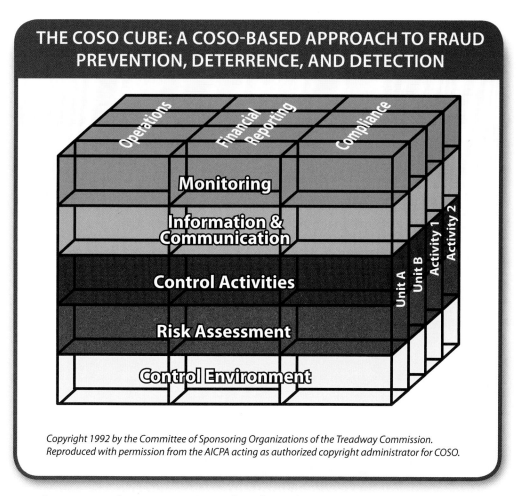

Assurance Support to Board and Senior Management

A competent and effective internal audit function can reliably support the board and senior management in performing aspects of the oversight and monitoring function with respect to antifraud programs and measures. Clearly, the internal auditors' knowledge and deep familiarity with the organization and the control activities that have been put in place enables them to identify fraud risk indicators and report these to the board and senior management. In this regard, note that IIA Standard 1210.A2 only requires that: "The internal auditor should have sufficient knowledge to identify the indicators of fraud but is not expected to have the expertise of a person whose primary responsibility is detecting and investigating fraud." Internal auditors also have the opportunity to evaluate fraud risks and control activities and to recommend action to mitigate risks and improve control activities.

Evaluating the Organizational Culture and Tone at the Top

Internal auditors should have an independent reporting line directly to the audit committee, to enable them to express any concerns about management's commitment to appropriate internal controls or to report suspicions or allegations of fraud involving senior management. They should periodically assess the ethical climate in the context of organizational culture and the tone at the top.

Internal audits can be both a deterrent as well as a detection measure. Internal auditors can assist in the deterrence of fraud by examining and evaluating the adequacy and the effectiveness of the system of in-

ternal control, commensurate with the extent of the potential exposure or risk in the various segments of the organization's operations. In carrying out this responsibility, internal auditors should, for example, determine whether:

- The organizational environment fosters control consciousness.
- Realistic organizational goals and objectives are set.
- Written policies (for example, a code of conduct) exist that describe prohibited activities and the action required whenever violations are discovered.
- Appropriate authorization policies for transactions are established and maintained.
- Policies, practices, procedures, reports, and other mechanisms are developed to monitor activities and safeguard assets, particularly in high-risk areas.
- Communication channels provide management with adequate and reliable information.
- Recommendations need to be made for the establishment or enhancement of cost-effective control activities to help deter fraud.

Internal auditors may conduct proactive auditing to search for corruption, misappropriation of assets, and financial statement fraud. This may include the use of CAATs to detect particular types of fraud. Internal auditors can also employ analytical and other procedures to isolate anomalies and perform detailed reviews of high risk accounts and transactions to identify potential financial statement fraud.

Assessing Fraud Risk

Among the most important activities in establishing a basis to design and implement anti-fraud programs and control activities is the fraud risk assessment process. As such, it is crucial to consider how to make fraud risk assessments more effective. To be effective, a fraud risk assessment:

- Is performed on a systematic and recurring basis.
- Considers possible fraud schemes and scenarios, including consideration of internal and external factors.
- Assesses risk at a companywide, significant business unit, and significant account levels.
- Evaluates likelihood, significance, and pervasiveness of each risk.
- Assesses exposure arising from each category of fraud risk by identifying mitigating control activities and considering the effectiveness of those control activities.
- Is performed with the involvement of appropriate personnel.
- Considers management override of controls (for example, nonroutine transactions and journal entries, temporary suspension of controls).

- Is updated when special circumstances arise (for example, mergers and acquisitions and new systems).

Illustrative Application Domains: Financial Statement Fraud and Procurement Fraud

In terms of implementation, a couple of practical examples are now provided to understand typical fraud schemes, detection methods, as well as possible preventative methods.

With respect to detection and prevention of financial statement fraud, some typical schemes that result in material misstatements/distortions in the financial statements are:

- Fictitious revenues.
- Concealed liabilities and expenses.
- Improper asset valuations.
- Improper disclosures.
- Timing differences (including recording amounts in the wrong period).

Some methods to detect such accounting improprieties, irregularities, and possible violation of GAAP include:

- Vertical and horizontal analyses (that is, comparatives within, between, and across periods and components).
- Ratio analyses, including cut-off testing and other analytical review procedures.
- Review of compliance with debt covenants and lender agreements.
- Review of tax returns and any notices received from the tax authorities.
- Inquiry of management about specific, unexplained variations.
- Cash flow analyses, as well as selected bank, customer, and vendor confirmations.
- In regulated industries, review of regulatory actions in the company's industry or specifically against the company.

Some preventative methods include:

- Having an independent, objective, and strong internal audit function (that does routine brainstorming about potential fraud risks).
- Ethical tone of management promoting employee integrity.
- Active oversight of management by those charged with governance.
- Reducing opportunities (for example, internal control activities) and pressures (for example, stock options tied to stock prices, not performance) related to financial statement fraud.
- Limiting rationalizations through frequent fraud awareness training.

Similarly, consider the following schemes in connection with the procurement cycle: collusion between buyer and vendor, kickback agreement, bribery, illegal gratuity, product substitution, bid rigging, conflicts of interest, side agreements, etc.

Detection methods in the procurement area include: analysis of unusual stock/inventory levels, contracts made just below approval thresholds, review of competitive sourcing policies, related party transactions, complaints from vendors, product failures and substandard performance, and matching employee and vendor databases.

Preventative methods include: proper segregation of duties, management sign-off on all procurement requests, insisting on open competition (sourcing policy), rotating procurement staff and responsibilities, monitoring performance, and regular inspections and audits.

It is clear that there is a need for much more empirically-driven research on fraud, waste, abuse, and corruption to assess the extent of fraud risk and develop ways of combating it. Accordingly, the ACFE and the AICPA have created the Institute for Fraud Prevention (IFP) to remedy the critical lack of research and data on fraud and corruption and to make public what is known about how best to prevent these financial crimes. The IFP is a partnership among ACFE, AICPA, Grant Thornton and D-Quest, numerous government and nonprofit anti-fraud agencies, and an international consortium of universities.[9] IFP's Web site is: http://www.theifp.org.

Internal Auditors' Fraud Investigation Related Responsibilities

As discussed earlier in this chapter, the internal audit function can be involved all the way from fraud awareness training and the design of antifraud programs and control activities, to testing the operating effectiveness of such control activities, to investigating improprieties and whistleblower complaints, and to conducting a full-fledged investigation at the behest of the audit committee.

Investigation of Fraud

Fraud allegations can arise from whistleblower complaints or sometimes even through sheer accident (for example, an employee substituting for another on vacation may discover some unusual arrangements or entries). Indeed, the ACFE has long maintained that anonymous tips and complaints continue to be the best source for unearthing fraud. Accordingly, they recommend ethics hotlines for every organization, and encourage employees as well as outside parties, such as customers and vendors, to call in with any suspicions of wrongdoing, unethical, or illegal acts. Of course, fraud can also be detected by the independent outside or internal auditors as a result of their recognizing fraud risk factors (red flags). Typically in such cases, the audit committee would be involved, and if the matter involves regulatory noncompliance or any potential illegal acts, then very likely, the general counsel, too.

The first question for the internal auditor to ask in such circumstances is whether litigation has already commenced or is anticipated. If such is the case, it is extremely important for the internal auditor to secure the appropriate attorney-client privilege by recommending the appointment of an outside law firm to conduct the investigation. Otherwise, the internal auditor's working papers can easily be the subject of a subpoena, and could well become the plaintiff's papers. However, when a tip or a suspicion is in the early stages of being confirmed or refuted with very little likelihood of a lawsuit, the internal auditor should be willing to take directions from the audit committee and the general counsel in exploring a particular (sensitive) issue in greater detail.

The internal audit function should plan to do a thorough job of any fraud investigation it undertakes. It should determine whether the competence, the independence, and the objectivity exist to carry out such an investigation successfully. Where the internal audit function finds the matter to be complex and beyond the scope of its expertise, it should recommend that a knowledgeable, suitably qualified and specialist forensic accountant or fraud examiner be engaged for this purpose.

When the internal audit function has been assigned an investigator's role, according to The IIA, an investigation plan must be developed for each investigation, following the organization's investigation procedures or protocols. Any possibility that there might be a potential conflict of interest with those being investigated, or with any of the organization's employees, must be cleared. According to Practice Advisory 1210.A2-2, Responsibility for Fraud Detection, the investigation plan should consider methods to:

- Gather evidence, such as surveillance, interviews, or written statements.
- Document the evidence, considering legal rules of evidence and the business uses of the evidence.
- Determine the extent of the fraud.
- Determine the scheme (techniques used to perpetrate fraud).
- Evaluate the cause.
- Identify the perpetrators.

At any point in this process, the investigator may conclude that the complaint or suspicion was unfounded and follow a process to close the case. Activities should be coordinated with management, legal counsel, and other specialists (see more on this in Use of Fraud Specialists), such as human resources and insurance risk management, as appropriate throughout the course of the investigation. Investigators must be knowledgeable and cognizant of the rights of persons within the scope of the investigation and the reputation of the organization itself. The level and extent of complicity in the fraud throughout the organization should be assessed. This assessment can be critical to ensuring that crucial evidence is not destroyed or tainted, and to avoid obtaining misleading information from persons who may be involved.

Use of Fraud Specialists

The primary qualification for fraud specialists is the CFE designation. However, when investigations involve looking into fraudulent financial reporting, possessing the CPA/CA and/or CIA credential can be very helpful. While each of the largest Standard Industry Classification

Certified Fraud Examiner (CFE)
The primary qualification for fraud specialists.

code companies typically has an internal audit function, only some of them have an additional special investigative unit (SIU) or other arrangements through which allegations and suspicions get resolved.

Organizations appear to use different structures to engage and deploy fraud specialists, including:

- Creating a separate, stand-alone SIU within the organization that has responsibility for everything to do with fraud and wrongdoing (that is, intentional and purposeful behavior designed to deceive others).

  - Occasionally, the SIU may be housed within the internal audit function and report to the CAE, the chief compliance officer, or even the general counsel.

  - Otherwise, an SIU may also be part of the global security team that has responsibility for physical (for example, warehouse guards) as well as electronic infrastructure (for example, IT authentication of passwords, access level control.).

- For smaller organizations, it is more typical that the internal audit function is supplemented by outside forensic accountants and fraud specialists as and when the situation demands it. This cosourcing approach avoids the fixed costs of maintaining an in-house SIU, and treats it purely as a variable cost of purchasing forensic and fraud examination expertise on demand.

For smaller companies, there are numerous advantages to using outside fraud specialists, in addition to the independence they bring to the job. They have intimate knowledge of similar fraud schemes that they may have worked on in the past, and can benchmark against the "usual suspects," key actors and the players, as well as the methods of investigation. Having worked with independent counsel, general counsel, state attorneys, regulators, law enforcement personnel, other accountants and auditors, and prosecutors, they have a good understanding of issues such as:

- The best approach to investigation for a specific type of fraud scheme.
- Assessing the quality and quantity of evidence needed.
- Evaluating the admissibility of evidence in consultation with outside lawyers.
- Preserving evidence and the chain of custody.
- The need for, as well as potential to act as, a fact witness or as an expert witness.

Communicating Fraud Audit Outcomes

Internal auditors should seek to identify the criteria, condition(s), cause, and effect to summarize their findings from a fraud investigation. They should try to write their communication in a systematic and organized fashion to enhance clarity and comprehension. In terms of organization, it may be useful to commence with a brief, clear state-

Fraud Reporting

Various oral or written, interim or final communications to senior management and/or the board of directors regarding the status and results of fraud investigations.

ment of the issue(s), followed by a citation of the relevant policies, rules, standards, laws, and regulations that may be applicable to the case at hand. Next, they should provide the analysis of the evidence gathered to form a professional opinion. This should be followed by the conclusions; that is, the findings and recommendations. Hopefully, the general counsel or the outside attorney conducting the investigation will find the internal auditors' communication useful and valuable so it can be made part of their own communication. At all times, the communications issued by internal auditors should contain facts only, and every effort must be made to eschew personal opinions or any kind of bias or speculation that could potentially enter the analysis. In any case, they should never seek to fix culpability on any particular employee(s), but should merely state that the evidence gathered appears to support the conclusion that fraud may have been perpetrated. The determination of culpability and the affixing of blame is a function of the court (the judge and the jury), and is typically outside the scope of the internal auditor.

According to The IIA, "fraud reporting consists of various oral or written, interim or final communications to senior management and/or the board of directors regarding the status and results of fraud investigations." As such, with respect to engagement communications, the following interpretive guidance by Practice Advisory 1210.A2-2, Auditors Responsibilities Relating to Fraud Investigation, Reporting, Resolution, and Communication, is provided:

- A draft of the proposed final communications on fraud should be submitted to legal counsel for review. In cases where the organization is able to invoke client privilege, and has chosen to do so, the report must be addressed to legal counsel.

- When the incidents of significant fraud, or erosion of trust, have been established to a reasonable certainty, senior management and the board of directors should be notified immediately.

- The results of a fraud investigation may indicate that fraud may have had a previously undiscovered adverse effect on the organization's financial position and its operational results for one or more years for which financial statements have already been issued. Senior management and the board of directors should be informed of such a discovery.

- A written report or other formal communication should be issued at the conclusion of the investigation phase. It should include the basis for beginning an investigation, time frames, observations, conclusions, resolutions, and corrective actions taken (or recommendations) to improve control activities. Depending on how the investigation was resolved, the report may need to be written in a manner that provides confidentiality to some of the people involved. The content of this report is sensitive, and it must meet the needs of the board of directors and management, while complying with legal requirements and restrictions and company policies and procedures.

SUMMARY

Fraud is a major concern among all types of organizations, encompassing the private and public sectors in today's global economy. Rising fraud awareness around the world has compelled local regulators to address management's responsibilities for fraud prevention, deterrence, and detection. For instance, in the United States, the Sarbanes-Oxley Act, especially Section 404 on internal controls over financial reporting, has underscored the significance of the internal audit function in mitigating the risk of fraud. Audit committees are increasingly looking to the internal audit function for help with the design and operating effectiveness of anti-fraud programs and control activities. The internal audit function is a key function for promoting and supporting effective governance, and has an important role to play in helping with the organization's fraud prevention, deterrence, and detection efforts. This role includes diverse activities such as: building fraud awareness among the organization's personnel, being on the alert for red flags (fraud risk factors), assessing enterprise risk, especially fraud risk, measuring the impact of such risk on the organization, recommending anti-fraud programs and control activities for management's consideration, and subsequently providing assurance about their design and operating effectiveness. Although there is professional guidance available from The IIA in terms of its *Standards* and Practice Advisories, the involvement of the internal auditor in fraud detection and investigation is an evolving area, and the internal auditor must proceed cautiously on such matters. Specifically, they are not presumed to be forensic accounting and fraud examination experts, and as such, should not undertake engagements that they may not be competent to perform. Nevertheless, internal auditors must have a good understanding of factors that pre-dispose fraud, fraud risk indicators, and how to respond when suspicious transactions or activities are observed. The best organizations have designed and adopted a communications protocol that emphasizes consultation with appropriate individuals when fraud allegations arise.

1. What is fraud? How is fraud relevant to the internal auditor? What are the internal audit function's roles and responsibilities with respect to fraud risks and control activities?

2. Why can't internal control activities eliminate all fraud? How should internal auditors provide reasonable assurance that the organization is not a victim of serious and material fraud?

3. What are some ways in which internal auditors can work with independent outside auditors (as well as in-house general counsel) in addressing fraud risk? Consider the anti-fraud responsibilities of internal audit for U.S public companies under Sarbanes-Oxley Act Sections 301.4 (whistleblowing provisions), 302 (annual certification of the financials by the CEO and the CFO), and 404 (auditor attestation about management's assessment of the effectiveness of internal control over financial reporting). (For non-U.S. jurisdictions, as well as non-public companies, consider local laws and regulations, as well as The IIA's professional standards that should be complied with internationally.)

4. Describe the role of setting the proper tone at the top, requiring all employees to sign a corporate code of conduct, any whistleblower mechanisms and follow up, and fraud awareness training as well as ethics audits by internal auditors.

5. Describe the Fraud Triangle and using illustrations involving financial reporting fraud and occupational fraud and abuse, highlight how it could be used as a conceptual framework to discuss the antecedents of fraud as well as responsive approaches to addressing fraud risk within organizations.

6. What are the fraud risk indicators that internal auditors should be aware of in general? How are these "red flags" (fraud risk factors) influenced by industry and geography? Why does it seem that certain areas and assets are more vulnerable to fraud? (That is, what "relative risk" considerations need to be factored in?) Expand these considerations to materiality and the competency and sufficiency of evidence.

7. How can the internal audit function assist the audit committee by alerting them to instances of management override of internal control activities on a timely basis?

8. How should internal auditors help, if at all, with forensic accounting investigations? What professional standards would apply in such circumstances?

1. Predication is a technical term that refers to:

    a. The ability of internal auditors to predict fraud successfully.

    b. The ability of the fraud examiner to commence an investigation given the establishment of the predicate that fraud exists and may still be occurring.

    c. The activities of fraud perpetrators in concealing their tracks so that fraud is covered up and may not be discovered.

    d. Management's analysis of fraud risks so they can put in place effective anti-fraud programs and controls.

2. The internal audit function's responsibilities with respect to fraud are limited to:

    a. The organization's operational and compliance activities only, because financial reporting matters are the responsibility of the independent outside auditor.

    b. Monitoring any calls received through the organization's whistleblower hotline but not necessarily conducting a follow-up investigation.

    c. Being aware of fraud indicators, including those relating to financial reporting fraud but not necessarily possessing the expertise of a fraud investigation specialist.

    d. Conducting fraud awareness training for organizational personnel at the behest of the audit committee and/or senior executive management.

3. Financial statement misstatements are most frequently caused by:

    a. Intentional misstatements (fraud).

    b. Unintentional misstatements (error).

    c. The CFO acting alone or in concert with the CEO.

    d. Independent outside and internal auditors not thoroughly examining the financial statements.

4. Internal auditors who hold the CIA, CPA/CA, and CFE designations must:

    a. Comply with all applicable professional standards at the level of the lowest common denominator with respect to fraud.

    b. Treat errors differently from instances of fraud, as the latter have to do with intentional misstatements.

    c. Focus on the financial statements only because fraud doesn't really occur in the operational and compliance areas.

    d. Be held to a higher standard of professional excellence in preventing, deterring, and detecting fraud as they are highly qualified.

5. Internal auditors who are asked by the audit committee to pursue a fraud investigation involving litigation by the should request:

a. Additional technical and specialist resources, particularly if they lack the fraud investigation IT and other expertise in the circumstances.

b. Attorney-client privilege for the work done so that they may insulate themselves against personal/professional risk, including the possibility of having to turn over working papers to the plaintiff's lawyers.

c. Support from the general counsel and the independent outside auditors to the extent they may be knowledgeable about the circumstances surrounding the fraud.

d. That the broadest possible "sphere of influence" be considered because fraud is rarely an isolated occurrence and is more likely to be pervasive in its impact.

6. From an organization's standpoint, because internal auditors are seen to be "internal control experts," they also are:

a. Fraud risk management process owners, and hence, the first and most important line of defense against fraudulent financial reporting or asset misappropriation.

b. The best resource for audit committees, management, and others to consult in-house when setting up anti-fraud programs and controls, even if they may not have any fraud investigation experience.

c. The key organizational unit to inquire with, should fraud ever be alleged or suspected.

d. The ideal function to design, develop, and deliver fraud awareness training within an organization.

1. Discuss why the internal audit function's organizational status, competence, and objectivity are particularly important when considering management fraud. Why might a CAE reporting line to the CFO, CEO, general counsel, or controller be problematic? Why does a direct reporting line to the audit committee (or equivalent) seem to be the best practice in this regard?

2. The OCEG recently released a guide for internal auditors to assist them in performing ethics and compliance audits. How will tone at the top, a control consciousness orientation, and a culture of integrity and ethics within organizations assist, if at all, in preventing, deterring, and detecting fraud? Is it sufficient that organizations effectively deter activities that are illegal, unethical, or immoral, and if these are observed, ensure that the whistleblower hotline will be used to report such wrongful conduct that might well be a precursor to fraud? See www.oceg.org.

3. Discuss the mix of professionals needed within an internal audit function as well as the sourcing arrangements that may be necessary to achieve optimal coverage of the audit universe particularly with respect to fraud risk assessment and response (for example, need for specialists holding CFE, CFD, CA, IFA designations). Also discuss the coordination and communication (with respect to fraud risks) among the parties that The IIA has referred to as the four pillars of corporate governance—specifically, audit committee, senior executive management, independent

outside auditors, and internal auditors. How can a breakdown in such communication and coordination become a breeding ground for fraud?

4. Fraud appears to come in different colors, stripes, shapes, and sizes. This explains why so many "cognate terms" exist to describe fraud. Consider the popular expression "unethical, illegal, or immoral." Carefully evaluate each of the following terms and explain what they mean to distinguish them:

    (1) bribery and kickbacks, (2) conflict of interest, (3) cooking the books, (4) self-dealing and corruption, (5) defalcation/embezzlement, (6) fictitious revenues or expenses, (7) identity theft, (8) industrial espionage, (9) intentionally violating GAAP, (10) kiting, (11) lapping, (12) larceny, (13) breach of fiduciary duty, (14) misrepresentation of material facts, (15) money-laundering, (16) conspiracy, (17) sham entities, (18) round-tripping, (19) forgery, (20) false or manipulated travel and entertainment reimbursement claims, (21) theft of trade secrets, (22) topside journal entries, (23) bid-rigging, (24) price fixing, (25) undisclosed side agreements, (26) ghost employees, (27) back-dating stock options, spring loading, and bullet dodging (28) illegitimate off-balance sheet transactions, (29) false claims, (30) window dressing, (31) channel stuffing, and (32) insider trading.

REFERENCES

[1] Institute of Internal Auditors, The Professional Practices Framework, (Altamonte Springs, FL: The Institute of Internal Auditors, 2004).

[2] ACFE Report to the Nation, definition of fraud, find source.

[3] ACFE Report to the Nation, find source.

[4] Ballou, B., D.L. Heitger, and C.L. Landes, "The Future of Corporate Sustainability Reporting," Journal of Accountancy, (December 2006).

[5] Cohen, I. and M. Felsen, "Social Change and Crime Rate Trends: A Routine Activity Approach," American Sociological Review, Vol. 44, (1979), pp. 588-608.

[6] Moyes, G.D., P. Lin, and R. M. Landry, Jr., "Raise the Red Flag," Internal Auditor, (October 2005).

[7] Committee of Sponsoring Organizations of the Treadway Commission, Internal Control-Integrated Framework, (New York, NY: AICPA, 1992).

[8] Watson, Mark, Moody's Special Comment Report Number 99909. (New York, NY: Moody's Investor Services, Inc., p. 3).

[9] Black, William, IFP Executive Director, University of Missouri-Kansas City, Personal interview. February, 2007.

CASE 1

Fannie Mae Ex-Officials May Face Legal Action Over Accounting, (Wall Street Journal, May 24, 2006, see pages A1 and A11).

Recently, Mr. James B. Lockhart, acting director of the Office of Federal Housing Enterprise Oversight (OFHEO), Fannie Mae's main regulator, denounced what he called an "arrogant and unethical culture" at the second largest borrower in the U.S. after the federal government. Specifically, the OFHEO's 340-page report blamed both the board and management for a corporate culture that allowed managers to disregard accounting standards when they got in the way of achieving earnings targets. The company then rewarded executives with huge bonuses for hitting those targets, the OFHEO report said.

With reference to internal auditing, the OFHEO report quotes a speech from Mr. Sam Rogers,* a former head of Fannie Mae's auditing office, as telling internal auditors they had a "moral obligation" to strive to meet a goal set by then Fannie Mae CEO, Mr. Frank Raines, in 1999 to double earnings per share to $6.46 by 2003. "By now, every one of you must have $6.46 branded in your brains," the OFHEO report quotes Mr. Rogers as saying. "You must have a raging fire in your belly that burns away all doubts, you must live, breath (sic) and dream $6.46 ... After all, thanks to Frank Raines, we all have a lot of money riding on it" in terms of bonuses. Given Mr. Rogers's responsibility for monitoring compliance with accounting rules, those remarks were "inappropriate," OFHEO said.

What's wrong with this picture? Did Mr. Rogers potentially violate The IIA's Code of Ethics and professional standards by making these remarks? Comment on his organizational status, independence, and objectivity as then Fannie Mae head of internal audit, and discuss whether there may be a conflict when internal auditors receive stock options and bonuses that are tied to financial performance.

(* Sam Rogers is a fictitious name)

CASE 2

Currently, a number of large cases of fraud are coming to trial and the post mortems are being completed. You have learned a lot related to identifying fraud risk, mitigating control activities, as well as promoting organizational ethics and compliance. You now should understand that fraud incidence is more common than previously thought, and that there are many techniques, methods, and motivations to fraud. You also should understand that fraud that is uncovered may just be a symptom of other issues and problems (for example, when management lacks integrity, a restatement of the financial statements may mean that the independent outside and/or internal auditor was successful in foiling attempted fraud). We now have a much more regulation—a classic response to similar periods in history. Previously, for instance, in the United States, it was the Samuel Insull case post the Great Depression era that lead to the Securities and Exchange Acts of 1933 and 1934.

Your group project is strategic in nature and relates to how internal auditors can deal with fraud and the impact of some of the current regulations such as the Sarbanes Oxley Act of 2002 in the U.S. The first part of this case study is to select up to five recent fraud cases, but not less than three such cases. These do not need to be Enron, WorldCom, or Tyco; you should choose only one of these high profile fraud cases. Your task is to research the root cause of each fraud and to identify techniques that may have prevented the fraud from occurring, or at least detected it in a timely manner.

As a group, prepare a PowerPoint presentation. The presentation should include two or three slides for each fraud case that summarize the fraud, the approximate loss incurred, the parties involved in the fraud, the root cause of the fraud, and the corrective actions that have been taken since the fraud occurred.. Also indicate whether Sarbanes-Oxley (or comparable local legislation and regulation) is robust enough to preclude such a fraud from occurring in the future. Additionally, describe the corrective actions your group would recommend to prevent, or detect on a timely basis, this type of fraud. On a separate slide, compare the root causes of the three to five fraud cases you study. On a final slide, convey what your group learned as a result of completing this case study.

CHAPTER 8
MANAGING THE INTERNAL AUDIT FUNCTION

Learning Objectives

- Identify the benefits of various organizational structures for an internal audit function.

- Identify the roles and responsibilities of the key positions in an internal audit function.

- Understand the policies and procedures of internal auditing and how they guide the internal audit function.

- Understand various risk management models and reflect on what role the internal audit function should have in the organization's risk management processes.

- Understand quality assurance, how it operates, and why it is important to the internal audit function.

- Understand how technology is used in the management of the internal audit function.

By now, you should recognize the depth and complexity of an internal audit function and be aware of the critical role it plays in the success of the entire organization. In this chapter, we will discuss what is involved in managing the internal audit function. When applicable, the spectrum of methods employed by different internal audit functions will be presented and the benefits of each discussed. We will begin with a discussion of the various options regarding organizational structures for an internal audit function, including where it is positioned within an organization. Then, we will identify the key positions within the internal audit function, including the chief audit executive (CAE), and outline the roles and responsibilities for each. From there, we will move on to the policies and procedures with an overview of how they provide necessary guidance and structure to the internal audit function. Next, we will examine various risk management models and look at what role the internal audit function can and should play in the organization's risk management processes. After that, we will explain quality assurance and the importance it plays with the internal audit function. Finally, we will end the chapter by touching on various technology and tools available to an internal audit function and how they are used in the management of the internal audit function.

EXHIBIT 8-1

PROFESSIONAL STANDARDS AND PRACTICE ADVISORIES RELEVANT TO CHAPTER 8

1000—Purpose, Authority, and Responsibility
1000.A1—Purpose, Authority, and Responsibility
1000.C1—Purpose, Authority, and Responsibility
1100—Independence and Objectivity
1110—Organizational Independence
1110.A1—Organizational Independence
1120—Individual Objectivity
1130—Impairments to Independence or Objectivity
1130.A1—Impairments to Independence or Objectivity
1130.A2—Impairments to Independence or Objectivity
1130.C1—Impairments to Independence or Objectivity
1130.C2—Impairments to Independence or Objectivity
1200—Proficiency and Due Professional Care
1210—Proficiency
1210.A1—Proficiency
1210.A2—Proficiency
1210.C1—Proficiency
1220—Due Professional Care
1220.A1—Due Professional Care
1220.A2—Due Professional Care
1220.C1—Due Professional Care
1230—Continuing Professional Development
1300—Quality Assurance and Improvement program
1310—Quality Program Assessments
1311—Internal Assessments

Practice Advisory 1000-1
Practice Advisory 1000.C1-1
Practice Advisory 1000.C1-2
Practice Advisory 1100-1
Practice Advisory 1110-1
Practice Advisory 1110.A1-1
Practice Advisory 1120-1
Practice Advisory 1130-1
Practice Advisory 1310-1
Practice Advisory 1130.A1-1
Practice Advisory 1130.A1-2
Practice Advisory 1200-1
Practice Advisory 1210-1
Practice Advisory 1210.A1-1
Practice Advisory 1210.A2-1
Practice Advisory 1210.A2-2
Practice Advisory 1220-1
Practice Advisory 1230-1
Practice Advisory 1311-1
Practice Advisory 1311-2

1312—External Assessments
Practice Advisory 1312-1: External Assessments

2010—Planning
2010.A1—Planning (Assurance Services)
2010.C1—Planning (Consulting Services)
Practice Advisory 2010-1: Planning
Practice Advisory 2010-2: Linking the Audit Plan to Risk and Exposures

2020—Communication and Approval
Practice Advisory 2020-1: Communication and Approval

2030—Resource Management
Practice Advisory 2030-1: Resource Management

2040—Policies and Procedures
Practice Advisory 2040-1: Policies and Procedures

2050—Coordination
Practice Advisory 2050-1: Coordination

POSITIONING THE INTERNAL AUDIT FUNCTION IN THE ORGANIZATION

There is a broad spectrum of opinions regarding where internal audit functions should and can be positioned in an organization to conform to The IIA's *International Standards for the Professional Practice of Internal Auditing* (*Standards*). On one end of the spectrum, internal audit functions are placed on an executive and/or senior management level, giving the function the visibility, authority, and responsibility to independently evaluate management's assessment of the organization's systems of internal control and the organization's ability to achieve business objectives effectively and manage, monitor, and mitigate risks associated with the achievement of those objectives. In addition to assurance services, these internal audit functions are commonly asked by management to provide consulting services in the form of initiatives or projects that allow management to use the professional expertise that the internal audit function possesses. (Consulting services are covered more extensively in Chapter 12, "The Consulting Engagement.") On the other end of the spectrum are those organizations who either do not have internal audit function, or place their internal audit functions much lower in the organizational hierarchy, typically assigning them non-audit activities to perform on a day-to-day basis, such as quality assurance, compliance, operational, and/or other transaction processing activities.

In response to The IIA's definition of internal auditing quoted in Chapter 1, "Introduction to Internal Auditing," as "an independent, objective, assurance, and consulting activity designed to add value and improve an organization's operations" that "helps an organization accomplish its objectives by bringing a systematic, disciplined approach to evaluate and improve effectiveness of risk management, control, and governance processes," many organizations have positioned their internal audit function as an activity of the board and senior or executive management. Organizations that continue to position the internal audit function to perform primarily operational and other non-audit activities, as previously mentioned, essentially render the function unable to provide management with an evaluation of the design and effectiveness of operational controls (risk management, control, and governance processes) because they lack the objectivity to independently evaluate the organization's operations and offer impartial suggestions for improvement.

Organizations that recognize the importance of placing the internal audit function in a position that maximizes its effectiveness and ability to evaluate the efficacy of the risk management, control, and governance processes that are in place often do so through a senior management position described in the *Standards* as a CAE. Standard 2000, states that "the chief audit executive should effectively manage the internal audit activity to ensure it adds value to the organization." Recognizing that the CAE is pivotal to a successful internal audit function, Practice Advisory 2000-1 outlines the role and responsibilities of the CAE:

> The chief audit executive is responsible for properly managing the internal audit activity so that:

Internal Audit Function

Various oral or written, interim or final communications to senior management and/or the board of directors regarding the status and results of fraud investigations.

- Audit work fulfills the general purposes and responsibilities described in the charter, approved by senior management, and accepted by the board.
- Resources of the internal audit activity are efficiently and effectively employed.
- Audit work conforms to the *International Standards for the Professional Practice of Internal Auditing.*

The CAE fulfills the responsibilities outlined above by creating a charter in which "the purpose, authority, and responsibility of the internal audit activity [is] formally defined ... consistent with the *Standards,* and approved by the board" (Standard 1000). In addition to specifying the purpose, authority, and responsibility of the internal audit function, the charter should take into consideration assurance and consulting services. It is important to recognize that the internal audit function and the audit committee have separate charters delineating the specific and separate obligations to the organization of each, while considering and reflecting the inherent interdependencies of the two. The internal audit function's charter is subordinate to the audit committee's charter and must support, not contradict, it. Internal audit functions often supplement the charter with formal vision and/or mission statements, as well as a detailed long-term strategy for the internal audit function. Frequently this supplemental information, along with operating budgets and resource plans, are included in an annual audit plan presented, reviewed, and approved by the audit committee. These various separate documents, along with the operating policies

EXHIBIT 8-2

REQUIREMENTS FOR ESTABLISHING AN INTERNAL AUDIT CHARTER

Practice Advisory 1000-1: Internal Audit Charter
Paragraphs 1-3

The purpose, authority, and responsibility of the internal audit activity should be defined in a charter. The chief audit executive should seek approval of the charter by senior management as well as acceptance by the board, audit committee, or appropriate governing authority. The charter should (a) establish the internal audit activity's position within the organization; (b) authorize access to records, personnel, and physical properties relevant to the performance of engagements; and (c) define the scope of internal audit activities.

The internal audit activity's charter should be in writing. A written statement provides formal communication for review and approval by management and for acceptance by the board. It also facilitates a periodic assessment of the adequacy of the internal audit activity's purpose, authority, and responsibility. Providing a formal, written document containing the charter of the internal audit activity is critical in managing the audit function within the organization. The purpose, authority, and responsibility should be defined and communicated to establish the role of the internal audit activity and to provide a basis for management and the board to use in evaluating the operations of the function. If a question should arise, the charter also provides a formal, written agreement with management and the board about the role and responsibilities of the internal audit activity within the organization.

The chief audit executive should periodically assess whether the purpose, authority, and responsibility, as defined in the charter, continue to be adequate to enable the internal audit activity to accomplish its objectives. The result of this periodic assessment should be communicated to senior management and the board.

and procedures of the internal audit function, are commonly combined into a set of guiding principles (generally referred to as an "audit manual") that, along with other procedural information, drives the internal audit function. Exhibit 8-2 outlines The IIA's recommendations regarding internal audit charters.

In addition to establishing a charter, mission and/or vision, and audit plan, the CAE is responsible for establishing and maintaining independence, objectivity, proficiency, and due professional care within the internal audit function. As stated earlier, the positioning of the internal audit function affects the degree to which it can remain objective. Being positioned on a level with senior and/or executive management with direct access to the audit committee gives the internal audit function greater independence and consequently greater objectivity. Audit committee participation in the selection, evaluation, and dismissal of the CAE further enhances the CAE's ability to maintain organizational independence and minimizes the possibility of senior and/or executive management exerting undue influence on a CAE that would impact his or her ability to act without bias (individual objectivity). Ideally, the function will be positioned high enough within the organization with direct access to the audit committee to allow conformity with the IIA requirements and recommendations as detailed below.

Independence and Objectivity

Organizational Independence. The chief audit executive should report to a level within the organization that allows the internal audit activity to fulfill its responsibilities (Standard 1110).

Relative to assurance services, Standard 1110.A1 specifies that "the internal audit activity should be free from interference in determining the scope of internal auditing, performing work, and communicating results."

More specifically, Practice Advisory 1110-1, Organizational Independence, details these particular requirements:

Internal auditors should have the support of senior management and of the board so that they can gain the cooperation of engagement clients and perform their work free from interference.

The chief audit executive should be responsible to an individual in the organization with sufficient authority to promote independence and to ensure broad audit coverage, adequate consideration of engagement communications, and appropriate action on engagement recommendations.

Ideally, the chief audit executive should report functionally to the audit committee, board of directors, or other appropriate governing authority, and administratively to the chief executive officer of the organization.

The chief audit executive should have direct communication with the board, audit committee, or other appropriate governing authority. Regular communication with the board helps assure independence and provides a means for the board and the chief

Internal Audit Charter
A formal written document that defines the internal audit function's purpose, authority, and responsibility. The charter should (a) establish the internal audit function's position within the organization, (b) authorize access to records, personnel, and physical properties relevant to the performance of engagements, and (c) define the scope of the internal audit function.

Independence
The freedom from conditions that threaten objectivity or the appearance of objectivity. Such threats to objectivity must be managed at the individual auditor, engagement, functional, and organizational levels.

audit executive to keep each other informed on matters of mutual interest.

Direct communication occurs when the chief audit executive regularly attends and participates in meetings of the board, audit committee, or other appropriate governing authority which relate to its oversight responsibilities for auditing, financial reporting, organizational governance, and control. The chief audit executive's attendance and participation at these meetings provide an opportunity to exchange information concerning the plans and activities of the internal audit activity. The chief audit executive should meet privately with the board, audit committee, or other appropriate governing authority at least annually.

Independence is enhanced when the board concurs in the appointment or removal of the chief audit executive.

Individual Objectivity: Internal auditors should have an impartial, unbiased attitude and avoid conflicts of interest. (Standard 1120)

The IIA further outlines these requirements in Practice Advisory 1120-1, Individual Objectivity:

Objectivity is an independent mental attitude that internal auditors should maintain in performing engagements. Internal auditors are not to subordinate their judgment on audit matters to that of others.

Objectivity requires internal auditors to perform engagements in such a manner that they have an honest belief in their work product and that no significant quality compromises are made. Internal auditors are not to be placed in situations in which they feel unable to make objective professional judgments.

Staff assignments should be made so that potential and actual conflicts of interest and bias are avoided. The chief audit executive should periodically obtain from the internal audit staff information concerning potential conflicts of interest and bias. Staff assignments of internal auditors should be rotated periodically whenever it is practicable to do so.

The results of internal audit work should be reviewed before the related engagement communications are released to provide reasonable assurance that the work was performed objectively.

It is unethical for an internal auditor to accept a fee or gift from an employee, client, customer, supplier, or business associate. Accepting a fee or gift may create an appearance that the auditor's objectivity has been impaired. The appearance that objectivity has been impaired may apply to current and future engagements conducted by the auditor. The status of engagements should not be considered as justification for receiving fees or gifts. The receipt of promotional items (such as pens, calendars, or samples) which are available to the general public and have minimal value should not hinder internal auditors' professional judgments. Internal auditors should report the offer of all material fees or gifts immediately to their supervisors.

If independence or objectivity is impaired in fact or appearance, the details of the impairment should be disclosed to appropriate parties. The nature of the disclosure will depend upon the impairment. (Standard 1130, Impairments to Independence or Objectivity)

Regarding impairments to independence or objectivity, The IIA recommends the following:

Internal auditors should report to the chief audit executive any situations in which a conflict of interest or bias is present or may reasonably be inferred. The chief audit executive should then reassign such audits.

A scope limitation is a restriction placed upon the internal audit activity that precludes the audit activity from accomplishing its objectives and plans. Among other things, a scope limitation may restrict the:

a. Scope defined in the charter.

b. Internal audit activity's access to records, personnel, and physical properties relevant to the performance of engagements.

c. Approved engagement work schedule.

d. Performance of necessary engagement procedures.

e. Approved staffing plan and financial budget.

A scope limitation along with its potential effect should be communicated, preferably in writing, to the board, audit committee, or other appropriate governing authority.

The CAE should consider whether it is appropriate to inform the board, audit committee, or other appropriate governing authority regarding scope limitations that were previously communicated to and accepted by the board, audit committee, or other appropriate governing authority. This may be necessary particularly when there have been organization, board, senior management, or other changes (Practice Advisory 1130-1).

Additional IIA recommendations regarding impairments to independence or objectivity can be found in Exhibit 8-3.

Often the internal audit function will work with and coordinate efforts with other departments in the organization that have similar risk mitigation objectives and responsibilities, such as compliance and risk management. As long as the internal audit function is not asked to perform operating activities or design processes and procedures they will later need to evaluate as part of their audit function, there is no impairment to independence or objectivity. This type of coordination can add significant value to the organization and promote efficient

Impairment to Independence or Objectivity

The introduction of threats that may result in a substantial limitation, or the appearance of a substantial limitation, to the internal auditor's ability to perform an engagement without bias or interference.

EXHIBIT 8-3

IIA REQUIREMENTS REGARDING IMPAIRMENTS TO INDEPENDENCE AND OBJECTIVITY

Standard 1130.A1

Internal auditors should refrain from assessing specific operations for which they were previously responsible. Objectivity is presumed to be impaired if an auditor provides assurance service for an activity for which the auditor had responsibility within the previous year.

Standard 1130.A2

Assurance engagements for functions over which the chief audit executive has responsibility should be overseen by a party outside the internal audit activity.

Standard 1130.C1

Internal auditors may provide consulting services relating to operations for which they had previous responsibilities.

Standard 1130.C2

If internal auditors have potential impairments to independence or objectivity relating to proposed consulting services, disclosure should be made to the engagement client prior to accepting the engagement.

resource utilization in the risk mitigation efforts of the organization.

Proficiency and Due Professional Care

Standard 1200 states simply that "engagements should be performed with proficiency and due professional care."

Standard 1210, Proficiency, goes into more detail, stating that "internal auditors should possess the knowledge, skills, and other competencies needed to perform their individual responsibilities. The internal audit activity collectively should possess or obtain the knowledge, skills, and other competencies needed to perform its responsibilities."

Regarding due professional care, Standard 1220 states that "internal auditors should apply the care and skill expected of a reasonably prudent and competent internal auditor. Due professional care does not imply infallibility."

PLANNING

As previously mentioned, one of the CAE's primary responsibilities is the creation of an operating budget and resource allocation plan designed to accomplish the annual audit plan. The annual audit plan is developed by the internal audit function through a process that identifies and prioritizes possible audit entities (business units or processes, referred to as the "audit universe") responsible for the mitigating efforts designed to reduce essential strategic, operations, reporting, and compliance risk to a level acceptable to the board of directors and executive management of the organization. Essential risks are those risks confronting the organization, as identified by senior and executive management through various self-assessment activities, that have been independently confirmed and collaborated by the internal audit function, and that must be controlled and monitored for an organization to successfully accomplish its defined business objectives. These self-assessment activities often include strategic planning

or risk management procedures, but may also include other informal business planning and risk assessment activities performed by senior and executive management throughout an organization. After the essential risks have been identified and agreed upon, the CAE determines which specific business units and processes are responsible for the mitigation efforts of these risks. The resulting information is then subject to a process that prioritizes and ranks the risks and associated business units or processes. The CAE takes all of this information and determines the cost in human and financial resources necessary to provide appropriate audit coverage of the prioritized audit universe. The result is a comprehensive audit plan that includes both the assurance services and consulting services necessary to monitor and control the risks to the organization's business objectives. The audit plan can then be implemented by assigning specific personnel to individual engagements in the plan over the following fiscal year. Internal audit functions will implement and assign resources to execute the audit plan throughout the fiscal year and many will update and recast the audit plan more frequently than annually (for example, quarterly or monthly).

There are multiple theories for the structuring of an audit plan. Many internal audit functions have moved toward a comprehensive process whereby executive management and the internal audit function collaborate to complete a formal risk assessment on an enterprisewide basis to establish a prioritized list of essential risk scenarios facing the organization that must be appropriately controlled and managed by the organization to achieve key business objectives. It is much more common, however, for the process to be informal and much less collaborative in nature. Whichever process is used, maximum effectiveness is achieved when the risk assessment process is completed annually at the beginning of or prior to an organization's fiscal year. This allows the CAE to align audit resources for the upcoming year with the conclusions drawn by management during the risk assessment process. Providing the CAE with a definitive list of audit entities related to the prioritized risks allows for the creation of an audit plan using a top-down, risk-based approach. However, many organizations and their internal audit functions still do not use a top-down, risk-based approach. Instead, they continue to create audit plans that cyclically audit each and every area of the organization with highly prioritized business units or processes cycled in for audit coverage more frequently and lower prioritized business units or processes cycled in less frequently.

The IIA specifically defines the relationship between risk mitigation and the audit plan in Practice Advisory 2010-2, Linking the Audit Plan to Risk and Exposures, which is provided in Exhibit 8-4.

The IIA addresses the differences between assurance services and consulting services relative to Standard 2010 with Standards 2010.A1 and 2010.C1:

> **Assurance Services.** The internal audit activity's plan of engagements should be based on a risk assessment, undertaken at least annually. The input of senior management and the board should be considered in this process. (Standard 2010.A1)

Audit Universe

A compilation of the subsidiaries, business units, departments, groups, processes, or other established subdivisions of an organization that exist to manage one or more business risks.

EXHIBIT 8-4

THE RELATIONSHIP BETWEEN THE AUDIT PLAN AND RISK AS DESCRIBED BY THE IIA

Practice Advisory 2010-2:
Linking the Audit Plan to Risk and Exposures
Paragraphs 1-7

The internal audit activity's audit plan should be designed based on an assessment of risk and exposures that may affect the organization. Ultimately, the audit objective is to provide management with information to mitigate the negative consequences associated with accomplishing the organization's objectives. The degree or materiality of exposure can be viewed as risk mitigated by establishing control activities.

The audit universe can include components from the organization's strategic plan. By incorporating components of the organization's strategic plan, the audit universe will consider and reflect the overall business plan objectives. Strategic plans are also likely to reflect the organization's attitude toward risk and the degree of difficulty to achieving planned objectives. It is advisable to assess the audit universe on at least an annual basis to reflect the most current strategies and direction of the organization. The audit universe can be influenced by the results of the risk management process. When developing audit plans the outcomes of the risk management process should be considered.

Audit work schedules should be based on, among other factors, an assessment of risk priority and exposure. Prioritizing is needed to make decisions for applying relative resources based on the significance of risk and exposure. A variety of risk models exist to assist the chief audit executive in prioritizing potential audit subject areas. Most risk models utilize risk factors to establish the priority of engagements such as: dollar materiality; asset liquidity; management competence; quality of internal controls; degree of change or stability; time of last audit engagement; complexity; employee and government relations; etc.

Changes in management direction, objectives, emphasis, and focus should be reflected in updates to the audit universe and related audit plan.

In conducting audit engagements, methods and techniques for testing and validating exposures should be reflective of the risk materiality and likelihood of occurrence.

Management reporting and communication should convey risk management conclusions and recommendations to reduce exposures. For management to fully understand the degree of exposure, it is critical that audit reporting identify the criticality and consequences of the risk activity to achieving objectives.

The chief audit executive should, at least annually, prepare a statement of the adequacy of internal controls to mitigate risks. This statement should also comment on the significance of unmitigated risk and management's acceptance of such risk.

Consulting Services. The chief audit executive should consider accepting proposed consulting engagements based on the engagement's potential to improve management of risks, add value, and improve the organization's operations. Those engagements that have been accepted should be included in the plan. (Standard 2010.C1)

The key elements necessary for effective planning as outlined in IIA Practice Advisory 2010-1 include the following:

Planning for the internal audit activity should be consistent with its charter and with the goals of the organization. The planning process involves establishing:

- Goals.
- Engagement work schedules.
- Staffing plans and financial budgets.
- Activity reports.

The goals of the internal audit activity should be capable of being accomplished within specified operating plans and budgets and, to the extent possible, should be measurable. They should be accompanied by measurement criteria and targeted dates of accomplishment.

Engagement work schedules should include: what activities are to be performed; when they will be performed; and the estimated time required, taking into account the scope of the engagement work planned and the nature and extent of related work performed by others.

Matters to be considered in establishing engagement work schedule priorities should include:

- The dates and results of the last engagement.
- Updated assessments of risks and effectiveness of risk management and control processes.
- Requests by senior management, the audit committee, and the governing body.
- Current issues relating to organizational governance.
- Major changes in enterprise's business, operations, programs, systems, and controls.
- Opportunities to achieve operating benefits.
- Changes to and capabilities of the audit staff. The work schedule should be sufficiently flexible to cover unanticipated demands on the internal audit activity.

COMMUNICATION AND APPROVAL

After the audit plan has been established, it is incumbent upon the CAE to present it to senior management and the board (typically the audit committee) to be approved. Resource requirements, significant interim changes, and the potential implications of resource limitations should all be included in the communication to senior management and the board (Standard 2020).

Specific recommendations for meeting this requirement are spelled out in Practice Advisory 2020-1, Communication and Approval:

The chief audit executive should submit annually to senior management for approval, and to the board for its information, a summary of the internal audit activity's work schedule, staffing plan, and financial budget. The chief audit executive should also submit all significant interim changes for approval and information. Engagement work schedules, staffing plans, and financial budgets should inform senior management and the board of the scope of internal audit work and of any limitations placed on that scope.

The approved engagement work schedule, staffing plan, and financial budget, along with all significant interim changes, should contain sufficient information to enable the board to ascertain whether the internal audit activity's objectives and plans support those of the organization and the board.

RESOURCE MANAGEMENT

A significant consideration in implementing an internal audit function's plan is how to allocate resources. It is the CAE's responsibility to "ensure that internal audit resources are appropriate, sufficient, and effectively deployed to achieve the approved plan" (Standard 2030). This is achieved by carefully orchestrating a number of factors as disclosed below.

Staffing Plans/Human Resources

The essential components of a staffing plan and the effective use of human resources is outlined in detail in Practice Advisory 2030-1, Resource Management, as follows:

Staffing plans and financial budgets, including the number of auditors and the knowledge, skills, and other competencies required to perform their work, should be determined from engagement work schedules, administrative activities, education and training requirements, and audit research and development efforts.

The chief audit executive should establish a program for selecting and developing the human resources of the internal audit activity. The program should provide for:

- Developing written job descriptions for each level of the audit staff.
- Selecting qualified and competent individuals.
- Training and providing continuing educational opportunities for each internal auditor.
- Appraising each internal auditor's performance at least annually.
- Providing counsel to internal auditors on their performance and professional development.

Organizational Structure and Staffing Strategy

Internal audit functions should be structured in a way that is consistent with the needs and culture of the organization. The CAE may choose to employ a flat organizational structure in which most of the internal auditors have more or less the same level of skills, experience, and seniority. Typically, this type of organization creates an internal audit function that is stable, highly knowledgeable, and very collaborative. Little supervision is necessary and the work performed is consistent and reliable. However, a flat organizational structure tends to result in a higher cost base due to the higher salaries necessary to retain auditors who all have a high degree of knowledge and experience. Other internal audit functions are much more hierarchical with field auditors reporting to and learning from senior auditors who in turn report to and learn from managers and directors who mentor those in positions subordinate to theirs while supporting the CAE above them.

Internal audit functions that are structured hierarchically tend to be more dynamic due to the fact that positions are often rotating. As the people in the positions near the top of the organizational structure move up and sometimes out of the function, the people in the subordinate positions promote up into the recently vacated positions. This allows for growth within the function and leads to the cultivation of diverse skills and fresh perspectives with a lower cost base. Both types of internal audit organization, however, rely on staff members who continue to receive training and broaden their skill base.

Hiring Practices

The CAE is responsible for hiring associates to fill the organizational structure of the internal audit function in a way that maximizes efficiency, effectively provides the necessary skill base, and makes good use of the financial budget. To do this, the CAE typically tries to hire individuals with training and expertise in a variety of areas including financial accounting and reporting, information technology, business operations, applicable laws and regulations, and various industry-specific knowledge.

Training and Mentoring

Staff development is of particular significance for an internal audit function due to the requirements placed on it regarding proficiency and due professional care as discussed earlier in the chapter. While Standard 1220 specifically points out that infallibility is not required, it is incumbent on the staff to remain current in their knowledge of the industry and audit skills. This is done primarily through ongoing training and mentoring, as well as continued professional education. Individual internal audit functions establish minimum training and professional development, which typically include professional certifications (certified public accountant [CPA], certified internal auditor [CIA], certified information systems auditor [CISA], and certified fraud examiner [CFE]) and the related minimum continued professional education required to maintain them.

Career Planning and Professional Development

In addition to the training and mentoring required to meet proficiency and due professional care standards, a good internal audit function will have a process in place for career development. This allows each associate to develop and implement an overall plan to reach long term career goals while remaining a contributing member of the internal audit function.

Strategic Sourcing

Strategic sourcing, also referred to as co-sourcing or outsourcing, is a resource that allows the CAE to optimize both the skill base and the financial considerations related to staffing. The CAE, with the use of strategic sourcing, is able to maintain a cost effective internal audit

Certified Internal Auditor® (CIA®)

The premier certification sponsored by The IIA; the only globally accepted certification for internal auditors.

function by hiring permanent associates who have a broad, more generalized base of skills while maintaining the flexibility of bringing in technical experts that are necessary for specific projects or audits but who would be cost prohibitive to keep permanently on staff. Strategic sourcing is also used in scheduling when the projected hours necessary to accomplish the audit plan exceeds the number of hours available from the permanent staff, but when hiring another staff member would be inefficient, cost prohibitive, or impractical under existing market conditions.

Scheduling

Once the right mix of permanent associates and strategic sourcing is in place and appropriately organized within the internal audit function, the CAE can begin scheduling or assigning specific audits and projects to the personnel best suited to perform them. This is where the benefits of good hiring practices and right sizing become apparent. The CAE maximizes the financial budget by creating teams that, based on their skills and placement in the organizational structure, will most efficiently and effectively accomplish the objectives of a specific engagement.

Right Sizing

Right sizing is an important concept in the hiring and scheduling of an internal audit function. It is important to achieve and maintain a balance of knowledgeable and skilled staff to complete the audit plan without putting undue stress on the staff by creating oppressive work loads while simultaneously maintaining a reasonable financial budget. This is true whether the internal audit structure is flat or hierarchically organized and in fact is often a factor when determining what type of organization structure is appropriate for an organization. The CAE relies on various sources to help validate right sizing decisions, including networking, benchmarking, and other consultative venues.

Financial Budget

As mentioned previously in the chapter, the financial budget is driven primarily by the audit plan, organizational structure, and staffing strategy. The CAE must carefully evaluate the financial resources necessary to accomplish the objectives set forth. It should be apparent at this point that the financial budget both impacts and is impacted by each of the tasks undertaken by the CAE as described above.

POLICIES AND PROCEDURES

The standard regarding the implementation of policies and procedures simply states that "the chief audit executive should establish policies and procedures to guide the internal audit activity" (Standard 2040). The relevant Practice Advisory, 2040-1, Policies and Procedures, recommends keeping the policies and procedures consistent with the size of the internal audit function:

> The form and content of written polices and procedures should be appropriate to the size and structure of the internal audit activity and the complexity of its work. Formal administrative and techni-

cal audit manuals may not be needed by all internal audit entities. A small internal audit activity may be managed informally. Its audit staff may be directed and controlled through daily, close supervision and written memoranda. In a large internal audit activity, more formal and comprehensive policies and procedures are essential to guide the audit staff in the consistent compliance with the internal audit activity's standards of performance.

COORDINATION WITH EXTERNAL AUDITORS

According to Practice Advisory 2050-1, Coordination, "Coordination of audit efforts involves periodic meetings to discuss matters of mutual interest" including:

Audit Coverage. Planned audit activities of internal and external auditors should be discussed to assure that audit coverage is coordinated and duplicate efforts are minimized. Sufficient meetings should be scheduled during the audit process to assure coordination of audit work and efficient and timely completion of audit activities, and to determine whether observations and recommendations from work performed to date require that the scope of planned work be adjusted.

Access to Each Others' Audit Programs and Workpapers. Access to the external auditors' programs and working papers may be important in order for internal auditors to be satisfied as to the propriety for internal audit purposes of relying on the external auditors' work. Such access carries with it the responsibility for internal auditors to respect the confidentiality of those programs and working papers. Similarly, access to the internal auditors' programs and working papers should be given to the external auditors in order for external auditors to be satisfied as to the propriety, for external audit purposes, of relying on the internal auditors' work.

Exchange of Audit Reports and Management Letters. Internal audit final communications, management's responses to those communications, and subsequent internal audit activity follow-up reviews should be made available to external auditors. These communications assist external auditors' management letters. Matters discussed in management letters assist internal auditors in planning the areas to emphasize in future internal audit work. After review of management letters and initiation of any needed corrective action by appropriate members of management and the board, the chief audit executive should ensure that appropriate follow-up and corrective action have been taken.

Common Understanding of Audit Techniques, Methods, and Terminology. First, the chief audit executive should understand the scope of work planned by external auditors and should be satisfied that the external auditors' planned work, in conjunction with the internal auditors' planned work, satisfies the requirements of Section 2100 of the *Standards*. Such satisfaction requires an understanding of the level of materiality used by external auditors for planning and the nature and extent of the

Independent Outside Auditor

A registered public accounting firm, hired by the organization's board or executive management, to perform a financial statement audit providing assurance for which the firm issues a written attestation report that expresses an opinion about whether the financial statements are fairly presented in accordance with applicable generally accepted accounting principles.

external auditors' planned procedures.

Second, the CAE should ensure that the external auditors' techniques, methods, and terminology are sufficiently understood by internal auditors to enable the CAE to (1) coordinate internal and external audit work; (2) evaluate, for purposes of reliance, the external auditors' work; and (3) ensure that internal auditors who are to perform work to fulfill the external auditors' objectives can communicate effectively with external auditors.

Finally, the CAE should provide sufficient information to enable external auditors to understand the internal auditors' techniques, methods, and terminology to facilitate reliance by external auditors on work performed using such techniques, methods, and terminology. It may be more efficient for internal and external auditors to use similar techniques, methods, and terminology to effectively coordinate their work and to rely on the work of one another.

REPORTING TO THE BOARD AND SENIOR MANAGEMENT

The CAE has the responsibility to "report periodically to the board and senior management on the internal audit activity's purpose, authority, responsibility, and performance relative to its plan. Reporting should also include significant risk exposures and control issues, corporate governance issues, and other matters needed or requested by the board and senior management" (Standard 2060). The CAE evidences the completion of these professional responsibilities by periodically reporting the results of ongoing internal audit activities to senior management and the audit committee during routinely scheduled meetings throughout the year. Additionally, management and the CAE coordinate efforts to routinely report on various risk and control activities performed by either, in accordance with roles and responsibilities set by the board and the audit committee. This typically includes reports covering the following:

- Business unit monitoring and risk monitoring reports.
- External auditor activity reports.
- Key financial activity reports.
- Risk management activity reports.
- Legal and compliance monitoring reports.

In addition to this information, a report is typically submitted to the audit committee by either senior management or the CAE outlining the results of management's self-assessment regarding the proper design and efficacy of the organization's internal controls. At minimum, the internal audit function should independently assess the process that management underwent to come to their conclusions. In many internal audit functions, however, the CAE takes on the added role of opining on the organization's system of internal controls related to financial reporting, operations, and compliance along with senior management, and reaching an independent opinion that is delivered to the audit committee concurrently with management's opinion. They see this as a natural extension of completing the annual audit plan in which the internal audit function has already independently evalu-

Board

An organization's governing body, such as a board of directors, supervisory board, head of an agency or legislative body, board of governors or trustees of a nonprofit organization, or any other designated body of the organization, including the audit committee, to whom the chief audit executive may functionally report.

ated the organization's system of internal controls as outlined in the audit plan. Other CAEs disagree with this approach and argue that it creates a direct conflict with their responsibility to be independent and objective evaluators of management's self assessment of the system of internal controls. The approach taken by an organization is largely a result of that organization's culture.

Practice Advisory 2060-1, Reporting to Board and Senior Management, makes the following clarifications regarding reporting to the board and senior management:

> The chief audit executive should submit activity reports to senior management and to the board at least annually. Activity reports should highlight significant engagement observations and recommendations and should inform senior management and the board of any significant deviations from approved engagement work schedules, staffing plans, and financial budgets, and the reasons for them.

> Significant engagement observations are those conditions that, in the judgment of the chief audit executive, could adversely affect the organization. Significant engagement observations may include conditions dealing with irregularities, illegal acts, errors, inefficiency, waste, ineffectiveness, conflicts of interest, and control weaknesses. After reviewing such conditions with senior management, the chief audit executive should communicate significant engagement observations and recommendations to the board, whether or not they have been satisfactorily resolved.

> Management's responsibility is to make decisions on the appropriate action to be taken regarding significant engagement observations and recommendations. Senior management may decide to assume the risk of not correcting the reported condition because of cost or other considerations. The board should be informed of senior management's decisions on all significant observations and recommendations.

> The chief audit executive should consider whether it is appropriate to inform the board regarding previously reported, significant observations and recommendations in those instances when senior management and the board assumed the risk of not correcting the reported condition. This may be particularly necessary when there have been organization, board, senior management, or other changes.

> In addition to subjects covered above, activity reports should also compare (a) actual performance with the internal audit activity's goals and audit work schedules, and (b) expenditures with financial budgets. Reports should explain the reason for major variances and indicate any action taken or needed.

However, because the CAE is responsible for maintaining relationships with entities that have potentially conflicting expectations, including the audit committee, senior management, line management, and various interested outside third parties (regulators and the external audi-

Observation
A finding, determination, or judgment derived from the internal auditor's test results from an assurance or consulting engagement.

tors, in particular), this is not always as straightforward as it appears. If an audit report contains no observations and the internal controls are found to be adequately designed and operating effectively, there typically is no misalignment between parties. However, if the internal audit function finds that the internal controls are inadequately designed and/or are ineffectively operating resulting in misalignment between management and one or more of the parties, the situation becomes much more complicated. It is not enough for the CAE to simply report such a misalignment to the board and senior management as stated in Practice Advisory 2060-1. In addition to reporting the observation and the misalignment, the CAE is expected to coordinate a resolution to the observation and report to the board and senior management not only what the exception consists of but how it is being rectified as well. Only in very rare cases when the CAE and management fail to come to agreement regarding the observation and/or its resolution would the CAE report an observation that was not accompanied by its resolution. Communication obligations are covered in detail in Chapter 11, "Communicating Assurance Engagement Outcomes and Performing Follow-up Procedures" and in Chapter 12, "The Consulting Engagement."

RISK MANAGEMENT

Risk mitigation is most effectively accomplished when it is decentralized to the areas affected most by the specific risks. In contrast, risk management is typically more effective when it is a centralized function. Generally defined, risk management is a participatory process designed to identify, document, evaluate, communicate, and monitor the most significant risk events facing an organization requiring risk mitigation to successfully achieve business objectives. Risk management is most effective when senior management is actively engaged in the process in a way in which contributors step back from their specific area/department (silo) and consider the risks confronting the organization as a whole. Unfortunately, many organizations make the mistake of letting risk management get dispersed throughout the organization along with risk mitigation. Consequently, the various silos responsible for mitigating risks also become responsible for the risk management activities described above. This results in a situation where different areas of the organization are unaware of what is happening in each other's areas to mitigate similar risk events, culminating in inconsistent risk responses due to the application of differing risk appetites and mitigation approaches by the individual areas.

Historically, risk management has been designed to focus efforts on avoiding potential danger and preventing harmful actions from negatively impacting an organization. Organizations have been moving away from that risk management model and are finding that it is more effective and rewarding to focus their risk management efforts on identifying risk events that have the potential to either negatively or positively affect the organization and facilitate management of those events within a pre-defined risk appetite set by the board and senior management. Properly executed risk management assists the board and senior management in implementing appropriate risk responses (avoiding, reducing, accepting, and/or sharing of risk) by increasing the likelihood of achieving the desired result (mitigating a negative

Risk
The possibility that an event will occur and adversely affect the achievement of objectives.

risk event or taking advantage of a positive risk event). Effective risk management also provides reasonable (not absolute) assurance that the business objectives of an organization will be achieved.

As discussed earlier in the chapter, the results of a well-executed risk management process can also be an essential source for identifying an organization's risk drivers and provide invaluable input for the development of the internal audit function's audit universe and audit plan. Consequently, risk management is an area in which the internal audit function can and does have a critical role to play. Just how much involvement the internal audit function should have in the organization's risk management process, however, is the subject of much discussion. Although many organizations now have formal risk management functions that are responsible for monitoring and facilitating risk mitigation efforts throughout an organization, the role of the internal audit function varies widely and is predicated on the division of risk management responsibilities and the culture of the organization. At minimum, the internal audit function should evaluate the adequacy and effectiveness of the organization's risk management processes by providing input and feedback through a periodic review (audit). It is also appropriate for the internal audit function to facilitate the identification and evaluation of risks, coach management on appropriate ways to respond to risk events, and help an organization coordinate enterprisewide risk management activities. However, the internal audit function should avoid setting the organization's risk appetite, avoid making decisions on appropriate risk responses, and should not own (be accountable for) the risk management process; only management should take on these roles.

According to IIA Standard 2110, "the internal audit activity should assist the organization by identifying and evaluating significant exposures to risk and contributing to the improvement of risk management and control systems."

Practice Advisory 2110-1 goes into more depth on the subject:

> Risk management is a key responsibility of management. To achieve its business objectives, management should ensure that sound risk management processes are in place and functioning. Boards and audit committees have an oversight role to determine that appropriate risk management processes are adequate and effective. Internal auditors should assist both management and the audit committee by examining, evaluating, reporting, and recommending improvements on the adequacy and effectiveness of management's risk processes. Management and the board are responsible for their organization's risk management and control processes. However, internal auditors acting in a consulting role can assist the organization in identifying, evaluating, and implementing risk management methodologies and controls to address those risks.

> Developing assessments and reports on the organization's risk management processes is normally a high audit priority. Evaluating management's risk processes is different than the requirement that auditors use risk analysis to plan audits. However,

Risk Management
The process conducted by management to understand and deal with uncertainties (that is, risks and opportunities) that could affect the organization's ability to achieve its objectives.

information from a comprehensive risk management process, including the identification of management and board concerns, can assist the internal auditor in planning audit activities.

Each organization may choose a particular methodology to implement its risk management process. The internal auditor should determine the methodology is understood by key groups or individuals involved in corporate governance, including the board and audit committee. Internal auditors must satisfy themselves that the organization's risk management processes address five key objectives to formulate an opinion on the overall adequacy of the risk management processes. The five objectives of a risk management process are:

- Risks arising from business strategies and activities are identified and prioritized.
- Management and the board have determined the level of risks acceptable to the organization, including the acceptance of risks designed to accomplish the organization's strategic plans.
- Risk mitigation activities are designed and implemented to reduce, or otherwise manage risk at levels that were determined to be acceptable to management and the board.
- Ongoing monitoring activities are conducted to periodically reassess risk and the effectiveness of controls to manage risk.
- The board and management receive periodic reports of the results of the risk management processes. The corporate governance processes of the organization should provide periodic communication of risks, risk strategies, and controls to stakeholders.

Internal auditors should recognize that there could be significant variations in the techniques used by various organizations for their risk management practices. Risk management processes should be designed for the nature of an organization's activities. Depending on the size and complexity of the organization's business activities, risk management processes [The IIA is using "risk management processes" here to allude to both risk mitigation and risk management] can be:

- Formal or informal.
- Quantitative or subjective.
- Embedded in the business units or centralized at a corporate level.

The specific process used by an organization must fit that organization's culture, management style, and business objectives. For example, the use of derivatives or other sophisticated capital markets products by the organization would require the use of quantitative risk management tools. Smaller, less complex organizations may use an informal risk committee to discuss the organization's risk profile and to initiate periodic actions. The

What an entity desires to achieve through the value creation choices management makes on behalf of the organization's stakeholders.

auditor should determine that the methodology chosen is both comprehensive and appropriate for the nature of the organization's activities.

Internal auditors should obtain sufficient evidence to satisfy themselves that the five key objectives of the risk management processes are being met in order to form an opinion on the adequacy of risk management processes. In gathering such evidence, the internal auditor should consider the following types of audit procedures:

- Research and review reference materials and background information on risk management methodologies as a basis to assess whether or not the process used by the organization is appropriate and represents best practices for the industry.

- Research and review current developments, trends, industry information related to the business conducted by the organization, and other appropriate sources of information to determine risks and exposures that may affect the organization and related control procedures used to address, monitor, and reassess those risks.

- Review corporate policies, board, and audit committee minutes to determine the organization's business strategies, risk management philosophy and methodology, appetite for risk, and acceptance of risks.

- Review previous risk evaluation reports by management, internal auditors, external auditors, and any other sources that may have issued such reports.

- Conduct interviews with line and executive management to determine business unit objectives, related risks, and management's risk mitigation and control monitoring activities.

- Assimilate information to independently evaluate the effectiveness of risk mitigation, monitoring, and communication of risks and associated control activities.

- Assess the appropriateness of reporting lines for risk monitoring activities.

- Review the completeness of management's risk analysis and actions taken to remedy issues raised by risk management processes, and suggest improvements.

- Determine the effectiveness of management's self-assessment processes through observations, direct tests of control and monitoring procedures, testing the accuracy of information used in monitoring activities, and other appropriate techniques.

- Review risk-related issues that may indicate weakness in risk management practices and, as appropriate, discuss with management, the audit committee, and the board of directors. If the auditor believes that management has accepted a level of risk that is inconsistent with the organization's risk management strategy and policies, or that is deemed

EXHIBIT 8-5

INTERNAL AUDIT'S ROLE IN ENTERPRISE RISK MANAGEMENT

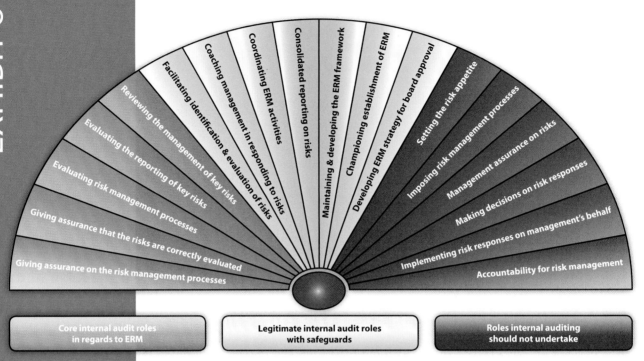

Reviewing the management of key risks

Facilitating identification & evaluation of risks

Coaching management in responding to risks

Coordinating ERM activities

Consolidated reporting on risks

Evaluating the reporting of key risks

Evaluating risk management processes

Maintaining & developing the ERM framework

Championing establishment of ERM

Developing ERM strategy for board approval

Giving assurance that the risks are correctly evaluated

Setting the risk appetite

Imposing risk management processes

Management assurance on risks

Giving assurance on the risk management processes

Making decisions on risk responses

Implementing risk responses on management's behalf

Accountability for risk management

Core internal audit roles in regards to ERM	Legitimate internal audit roles with safeguards	Roles internal auditing should not undertake

This diagram is taken from "Position Statement: The Role of Internal Auditing in Enterprise-wide Risk Management," reproduced with the permission of the Institute of Internal Auditors – United Kingdom and Ireland. For the full statement visit, www.iia.org.uk. © The Institute of Internal Auditors – UK and Ireland Ltd., July 2004

unacceptable to the organization, the auditor should refer to Standard 2600: Management's Acceptance of Risks, and any related guidance for additional direction.

In practical terms, the internal audit function should enhance risk management and mitigation, providing another level of protection. Exhibit 8-5 shows a range of activities that an internal audit function might be asked to perform, detailing which activities are appropriate and which should be avoided.

CONTROL

Standard 2120, Control, states that "the internal audit activity should assist the organization in maintaining effective controls by evaluating their effectiveness and efficiency and by promoting continuous improvement."

There are several assurance standards that address the issue of control:

Based on the results of the risk assessment, the internal audit activity should evaluate the adequacy and effectiveness of controls encompassing the organization's governance, operations, and information systems. This should include:

- Reliability and integrity of financial and operational information.
- Effectiveness and efficiency of operations.
- Safeguarding of assets.

- Compliance with laws, regulations, and contracts. (Standard 2120.A1)

Internal auditors should ascertain the extent to which operating and program goals and objectives have been established and conform to those of the organization. (Standard 2120.A2)

Internal auditors should review operations and programs to ascertain the extent to which results are consistent with established goals and objectives to determine whether operations and programs are being implemented or performed as intended. (Standard 2120.A3)

Adequate criteria are needed to evaluate controls. Internal auditors should ascertain the extent to which management has established adequate criteria to determine whether objectives and goals have been accomplished. If adequate, internal auditors should use such criteria in their evaluation. If inadequate, internal auditors should work with management to develop appropriate evaluation criteria. (Standard 2120.A4)

There are two consulting standards regarding control:

During consulting engagements, internal auditors should address controls consistent with the engagement's objectives and should be alert to the existence of any significant control weaknesses. (Standard 2120.C1)

Internal auditors should incorporate knowledge of controls gained from consulting engagements into the process of identifying and evaluating significant risk exposures of the organization. (Standard 2120.C2)

Control is addressed in detail in Chapter 5, "Internal Control."

GOVERNANCE

Standard 2130, Governance, requires the internal audit function to "contribute to the organization's governance process by evaluating and improving the process through which (1) values and goals are established and communicated, (2) the accomplishment of goals is monitored, (3) accountability is ensured, and (4) values are preserved."

The related practice advisory details the "importance of organizational culture in establishing the ethical climate of an enterprise and suggests the role that internal auditors could play in improving that ethical climate":

Governance & Organizational Culture

An organization uses various legal forms, structures, strategies, and procedures to ensure that it:

a. Complies with society's legal and regulatory rules.

b. Satisfies the generally accepted business norms, ethical precepts, and social expectations of society.

c. Provides overall benefit to society and enhances the interests

Governance
The process conducted by the board of directors to authorize, direct, and oversee management toward the achievement of the organization's objectives.

of the specific stakeholders in both the long and shortterm.

d. Reports fully and truthfully to its owners, regulators, other stakeholders, and general public to ensure accountability for its decisions, actions, conduct, and performance.

The way in which an organization chooses to conduct its affairs to meet those four responsibilities is commonly referred to as its governance process. The organization's governing body (such as a board of directors or trustees or a managing board) and its senior management are accountable for the effectiveness of the governance process.

An organization's governance practices reflect a unique and ever-changing culture that affects roles, specifies behavior, sets goals and strategies, measures performance, and defines the terms of accountability. That culture impacts the values, roles, and behavior that will be articulated and tolerated by the organization and determines how sensitive—thoughtful or indifferent—the enterprise is in meeting its responsibilities to society. Thus, how effective the overall governance process is in performing its expected function largely depends on the organization's culture.

Shared Responsibility for the Organization's Ethical Culture

All people associated with the organization share some responsibility for the state of its ethical culture. Because of the complexity and dispersion of decision-making processes in most enterprises, each individual should be encouraged to be an ethics advocate whether the role is delegated officially or merely conveyed informally. Codes of conduct and statements of vision and policy are important declarations of the organization's values and goals, the behavior expected of its people, and the strategies for maintaining a culture that aligns with its legal, ethical, and societal responsibilities. A growing number of organizations have designated a chief ethics officer as counselor of executives, managers, and others and as champion within the organization for "doing the right thing."

Internal Audit Activity as Ethics Advocate

Internal auditors and the internal audit activity should take an active role in support of the organization's ethical culture. They possess a high level of trust and integrity within the organization and the skills to be effective advocates of ethical conduct. They have the competence and capacity to appeal to the enterprise's leaders, managers, and other employees to comply with the legal, ethical, and societal responsibilities of the organization.

The internal audit activity may assume one of several different roles as an ethics advocate. Those roles include chief ethics officer (ombudsman, compliance officer, management ethics counselor, or ethics expert), member of an internal ethics council, or assessor of the organization's ethical climate. In some circumstances, the role of chief ethics officer may conflict with the independence attribute of the internal audit activity.

Chief Ethics Officer

Counselor of executives, manager, and others and champion within the organization for "doing the right thing."

Assessment of the Organization's Ethical Climate

At a minimum, the internal audit activity should periodically assess the state of the ethical climate of the organization and the effectiveness of its strategies, tactics, communications, and other processes in achieving the desired level of legal and ethical compliance. Internal auditors should evaluate the effectiveness of the following features of an enhanced, highly effective ethical culture:

- Formal code of conduct, which is clear and understandable, and related statements, policies (including procedures covering fraud and corruption), and other expressions of aspiration.

- Frequent communications and demonstrations of expected ethical attitudes and behavior by the influential leaders of the organization.

- Explicit strategies to support and enhance the ethical culture with regular programs to update and renew the organization's commitment to an ethical culture.

- Several, easily accessible ways for people to confidentially report alleged violations of the code, policies, and other acts of misconduct.

- Regular declarations by employees, suppliers, and customers that they are aware of the requirements for ethical behavior in transacting the organization's affairs.

- Clear delegation of responsibilities to ensure that ethical consequences are evaluated, confidential counseling is provided, allegations of misconduct are investigated, and case findings are properly reported.

- Easy access to learning opportunities to enable all employees to be ethics advocates.

- Positive personnel practices that encourage every employee to contribute to the ethical climate of the organization.

- Regular surveys of employees, suppliers, and customers to determine the state of the ethical climate in the organization.

- Regular reviews of the formal and informal processes within the organization that could potentially create pressures and biases that would undermine the ethical culture.

- Regular reference and background checks as part of hiring procedures, including integrity tests, drug screening, and similar measures. (Practice Advisory 2130-1, Role of the Internal Audit Activity and Internal Auditor in the Ethical Culture of an Organization)

Governance is covered in detail in Chapter 3, "Governance and Risk Management."

QUALITY ASSURANCE (QUALITY PROGRAM ASSESSMENTS)

In the current corporate governance climate, it has become imperative that internal audit functions have the appropriate tools with which to

---

Control Environment

The attitude and actions of the board and management regarding the significance of control within the organization. The control environment provides the discipline and structure for the achievement of the primary objectives of the system of internal control. The control environment includes the following elements:

- Integrity and ethical values.
- Management's philosophy and operating style.
- Organizational structure.
- Assignment of authority and responsibility.
- Human resource policies and practices.
- Competence of personnel.

self-regulate and monitor adherence to established professional standards. In the interest of maintaining consistent standards to which internal audit functions would be held relative to self-regulation, The IIA established formal quality assurance standards that must be followed for internal audit functions to be considered in compliance with the professional standards established by The IIA.

Quality assurance is the process of assuring that an internal audit function operates according to a set of standards defining the specific elements that must be present to ensure that the findings of the internal audit function are legitimate. Specifically, Standard 1300 states:

> The chief audit executive should develop and maintain a quality assurance and improvement program that covers all aspects of the internal audit activity and continuously monitors its effectiveness. The program should be designed to help the internal auditing activity add value and improve the organization's operations and to provide assurance that the internal audit activity is in conformity with the *Standards* and the Code of Ethics.

IIA Standards 1311 and 1312 detail the specific requirements for *Standard* 1300 by specifying that internal audit functions must establish both internal assessment and external assessment procedures. In practical terms, internal assessment procedures are the day-to-day quality assurance steps typically outlined in an internal audit function's operating procedures (audit manual) that ensure that the Standards are followed; and external assessment procedures are the quality assurance steps that an internal audit function has performed and/or has verified by a qualified, independent party. This process is commonly referred to as an independent peer review. Internal audit functions are required to successfully complete an external assessment on a periodic basis (at least once every five years) to confirm that the internal audit function is compliant with the *Standards*. Both internal assessment and external assessment procedures must be established and followed for an internal audit function to be able to state that its internal assurance and consulting services are "conducted in accordance with the *International Standards for the Professional Practice of Internal Auditing*" (Standard 1330). Exhibit 8-6 and Exhibit 8-7 present internal audit function quality assurance procedures and peer review quality assurance procedures suggested in the Practice Advisories.

While Standards 1300, 1311, and 1312 may seem unambiguous, particularly when clarified by the requisite Practice Advisories, questions as to how these standards should be implemented have sparked debate within the internal audit community. Standard 1312 can be very onerous, especially for "small" internal audit functions. While the latter part of Practice Advisory 1312-1 has attempted to address this concern by providing for a self-assessment option with independent validation, and agreement can generally be reached on a philosophical level, problems arise when practitioners try to define what constitutes a "small" internal audit function and the term becomes relative depending on the size of the function defining it. Exhibit 8-8 presents the suggested alternative approach for "small" internal audit functions

EXHIBIT 8-6

THE INTERNAL AUDIT FUNCTION'S QUALITY ASSURANCE PROCEDURES AS OUTLINED BY THE IIA

Practice Advisory 1311-1: Internal Assessments
Paragraphs 1-7

Ongoing Reviews: Ongoing reviews may be conducted through:

- Engagement supervision as described in Standard 2340, Engagement Supervision, and Practice Advisory 2340-1, Engagement Supervision.

- Checklists and other means to provide assurance that processes adopted by the internal audit activity (e.g., in an audit and procedures manual) are being followed.

- Feedback from audit customers and other stakeholders.

- Analysis of performance metrics, such as project budgets, timekeeping systems, audit plan completion, cost recoveries, and so forth.

Conclusions should be developed as to the quality of ongoing performance and follow-up action should be taken to assure appropriate improvements are implemented.

Periodic Reviews: Periodic assessments should be designed to assess compliance with the activity's charter, the *International Standards for the Professional Practice of Internal Auditing,* the Code of Ethics, and the efficiency and effectiveness of the activity in meeting the needs of its various stakeholders. The IIA's Quality Assessment Manual includes guidance and tools for internal reviews. Periodic assessments may:

- Include more in-depth interviews and surveys of stakeholder groups.

- Be performed by members of the internal audit activity (self-assessment).

- Be performed by CIAs, or other competent audit professionals, currently assigned elsewhere in the organization.

- Encompass a combination of self-assessment and preparation of materials subsequently reviewed by the CIAs, or other competent audit professionals, from elsewhere in the organization.

- Include benchmarking of the internal audit activity's practices and performance metrics against relevant best practices of the internal audit profession.

Conclusions should be developed as to the quality of performance and appropriate action initiated to achieve improvements and conformity to the *Standards*, as necessary.

The CAE should establish a structure for reporting results of periodic reviews that maintains appropriate credibility and objectivity. Generally, those assigned responsibility for conducting ongoing and periodic reviews should report to the CAE while performing the reviews and should communicate their results directly to the CAE.

Communicating Results: The CAE should share the results of internal assessments and necessary action plans with appropriate persons outside the activity, such as senior management, the board, and the external auditors.

finding the External Assessment Quality Assurance procedures to be too onerous.

Because neither the *Standards* nor the Practice Advisories make any distinction between functions that are primarily sourced internally to an organization and those that are primarily sourced from outside the organization (strategic outsourcing arrangements), much discussion about the applicability of, and how best to comply with, the *Standards* when the function is primarily outsourced continues to take place.

EXHIBIT 8-7

PEER REVIEW QUALITY ASSURANCE PROCEDURES AS OUTLINED BY THE IIA

Practice Advisory 1312-1: External Assessments
Paragraphs 1-12

General Considerations: External assessments of an internal audit activity should appraise and express an opinion as to the internal audit activity's compliance with the *International Standards for the Professional Practice of Internal Auditing* and, as appropriate, should include recommendations for improvement. These reviews can have considerable value to the CAE and other members of the internal audit activity. Only qualified persons (paragraph 4 below) should perform such reviews.

An external assessment is required within five years of Jan. 1, 2002. Earlier adoption of the new Standard requiring an external assessment is highly recommended. Organizations that have had external reviews are encouraged to have their next external review within five years of their last review.

On completion of the review, a formal communication should be provided to the board (as defined in the glossary to the *Standards*) and to senior management.

Qualifications for External Reviewers: External reviewers, including those who validate self-assessments (paragraph 13 below [see Exhibit 8-8]), should be independent of the organization and of the internal audit activity. The review team should consist of individuals who are competent in the professional practice of internal auditing and the external assessment process. To be considered as external assessment candidates, qualified individuals could include IIA Quality Assurance reviewers, regulatory examiners, consultants, external auditors, other professional service providers, and internal auditors from the organization.

Independence: The organization that is performing the external assessment, the members of the review team, and any other individuals who participate on the assessment should be free from any obligation to, or interest in, the organization that is the subject of the review or its personnel. Individuals who are in another department of that organization, although organizationally separate from the internal audit activity, are not considered independent for purposes of conducting an external assessment.

Reciprocal peer review arrangements between three or more organizations can be structured in a manner that alleviates independence concerns. Reciprocal peer reviews between two organizations generally should not be performed.

External assessments should be performed by qualified individuals who are independent of the organization and who do not have either a real or apparent conflict of interest. "Independent of the organization" means not a part of, or under the control of, the organization to which the internal audit activity belongs. In the selection of an external reviewer, consideration should be given to a possible real or apparent conflict of interest that the reviewer may have due to present or past relationships with the organization or its internal audit activity.

Integrity and Objectivity: Integrity requires the review team to be honest and candid within the constraints of confidentiality. Service and the public trust should not be subordinated to personal gain and advantage. Objectivity is a state of mind and a quality that lends value to a review team's services. The principle of objectivity imposes the obligation to be impartial, intellectually honest, and free of conflicts of interest.

Competence: Performing and communicating the results of an external assessment requires the exercise of professional judgment. Accordingly, an individual serving as a reviewer should:

- Be a competent, certified audit professional, for example, CIA, CPA, CA, or CISA, who possesses current knowledge of the *Standards*.

- Be well versed in the best practices of the profession.

- Have at least three years of recent experience in the practice of internal auditing at a management level.

The review team should include members with information technology expertise and relevant industry experience. Individuals with expertise in other specialized areas may assist the external review team. For example, statistical sampling specialists or experts in control self-assessment may participate in certain segments of the review.

(continued, next page)

(Exhibit 8-7, continued)

Approval by Management and the Board: The CAE should involve senior management and the board in the selection process for an external reviewer and obtain their approval.

Scope of External Assessments: The external assessment should consist of a broad scope of coverage that includes the following elements of the internal audit activity:

- Compliance with the *Standards*, the IIA's Code of Ethics, and the internal audit activity's charter, plans, policies, procedures, practices, and applicable legislative and regulatory requirements.

- The expectations of the internal audit activity expressed by the board, executive management, and operational managers.

- The integration of the internal audit activity into the organization's governance process, including the attendant relationships between and among the key groups involved in that process.

- The tools and techniques employed by the internal audit activity.

- The mix of knowledge, experience, and disciplines within the staff, including staff focus on process improvement.

- The determination whether the audit activity adds value and improves the organization's operations.

The key elements of a properly designed quality assurance program include the following:

Implementing Quality Programs

The chief audit executive (CAE) should be accountable for implementing a quality program designed to provide reasonable assurance to the various stakeholders of the internal audit activity that it:

- Performs in accordance with its charter, which should be consistent with the *Standards* and the Code of Ethics.
- Operates in an effective and efficient manner.
- Is perceived by those stakeholders as adding value and improving the organization's operations.

These processes should include appropriate supervision, periodic internal assessment and ongoing monitoring of quality assurance, and periodic external assessments.

Monitoring Quality Programs

Monitoring should include ongoing measurements and analyses of performance metrics, e.g., cycle time and recommendations accepted.

Assessing Quality Programs

Assessments should evaluate and conclude on the quality of the internal audit activity and lead to recommendations for appropriate improvements. Assessments of quality programs should include evaluation of:

- Compliance with the *Standards* and Code of Ethics.
- Adequacy of the internal audit activity's charter, goals, objectives, policies, and procedures.

EXHIBIT 8-8

INTERNAL AUDIT FUNCTION SELF-ASSESSMENT QUALITY ASSURANCE PROCEDURES FOR "SMALL" FUNCTIONS AS OUTLINED BY THE IIA

Practice Advisory 1312-1: External Assessments
Paragraphs 13-19

Self-assessment With Independent Validation: An alternative process is for the CAE to undertake a self-assessment with independent external validation with the following features:

- A comprehensive and fully documented self-assessment process.

- An independent on-site validation by a qualified reviewer (paragraph 4 [see Exhibit 8-7])

- Economical time and resource requirements.

A team under the direction of the CAE should perform the self-assessment process. The IIA's Quality Assessment Manual contains an example of the process, including guidance and tools for the self-assessment. A qualified, independent reviewer should perform limited tests of the self-assessment to validate the results and express an opinion about the indicated level of the activity's conformity to the *Standards*.

Communicating the results of the self-assessment should follow the process outlined below (paragraph 17).

While a full external review achieves maximum benefit for the activity and should be included in the activity's quality program, the self-assessment with independent validation provides an alternative means of complying with Standard 1312.

Communicating Results: The preliminary results of the review should be discussed with the CAE during and at the conclusion of the assessment process. Final results should be communicated to the CAE or other official who authorized the review for the organization.

The communication should include the following:

- An opinion on the internal audit activity's compliance with the *Standards* based on a structured rating process. The term "compliance" means that the practices of the internal audit activity, taken as a whole, satisfy the requirements of the *Standards*. Similarly, "noncompliance" means that the impact and severity of the deficiency in the practices of the internal audit activity are so significant that it impairs the internal audit activity's ability to discharge its responsibilities. The expression of an opinion on the results of the external assessment requires the application of sound business judgment, integrity, and due professional care.

- An assessment and evaluation of the use of best practice, both those observed during the assessment and others potentially applicable to the activity.

- Recommendations for improvement, where appropriate.

- Responses from the CAE that include an action plan and implementation dates.

The CAE should communicate the results of the review and necessary action plan to senior management, as appropriate, and to the board.

- Contribution to the organization's risk management, governance, and control processes.

- Compliance with applicable laws, regulations, and government or industry standards

- Effectiveness of continuous improvement activities and adoption of best practices.

- Whether the audit activity adds value and improves the organization's operations.

Continuous Improvement

All quality improvement efforts should include a communication process designed to facilitate appropriate modification of resources, technology, processes and procedures as indicated by monitoring and assessment activities.

Communicating Results

To provide accountability, the CAE should share the results of external and, as appropriate, internal quality program assessments with the various stakeholders of the activity, such as senior management, the board, and external auditors. (Practice Advisory 1310-1, Quality Program Assessments).

Disclosure of Noncompliance

In the event that an internal audit function is found to be significantly deficient as to "impact the overall scope or operation of the internal audit activity," Standard 1340 states that "disclosure should be made to senior management and the board." At that time, a determination will typically be made regarding whether said noncompliance is intentional or inadvertent, as well as what, if any, corrective action will be taken. Should senior management and the board make the decision not to take corrective action and the internal audit function remains noncompliant, the internal audit function will no longer be able to state that its internal assurance and consulting services are "conducted in accordance with the *International Standards for the Professional Practice of Internal Auditing.*" The consequences of continuing to offer internal assurance and consulting services that are not conducted in accordance with the *Standards* are far reaching and can significantly inhibit the internal audit function's relationship with interested third parties such as regulators and other interested outside parties (for example, the U.S. Securities and Exchange Commission [SEC] or the organization's registered public accounting firm).

PERFORMANCE MEASURES FOR THE INTERNAL AUDIT FUNCTION

Performance measures are integral to the internal assessment requirement outlined in Standard 1311 discussed earlier. In addition to providing the criteria against which the internal audit function judges its performance in key areas, they gauge how well the internal audit function is accomplishing its mission/goals. The CAE should consider many factors when creating performance measures, such as the size of the internal audit function, the specific services offered, industry-specific regulations, the operating environment, and the organization's culture. Performance measures should be aligned with the internal audit function charter, and all significant services addressed in the charter should be considered when establishing performance measures. The customized measurement process that results should outline activities that contribute to the achievement of the goals identified in the charter.

Practice Advisory 1311-2, Establishing Measures (Quantitative Metrics and Qualitative Assessments) to Support Reviews of Internal Audit Activity Performance, begins by outlining what a properly designed

EXHIBIT 8-9

FIGURE 1 FROM PRACTICE ADVISORY 1311-2: POSSIBLE PERFORMANCE CATEGORIES

performance measurement process includes, stating that:

> To establish effective performance measures, the CAE should establish a process that:
>
> - Identifies critical performance categories (e.g., internal stakeholder satisfaction). This advisory suggests the use of the following categories:
>   - Stakeholder satisfaction.
>   - Internal audit processes.
>   - Innovation and capability.
> - Identifies performance categories and measurements. Strategies should be pursued in a manner that complies with IIA *Standards*, other appropriate professional standards, and applicable laws and regulations, as well as ensuring stakeholder satisfaction. The use of performance measures can be an element of the internal audit activity's internal assessment process to comply with The IIA *Standards*.
> - Provides a process for performance measures to be routinely monitored, analyzed and reported.
>
> The CAE should ensure that the measures used are appropriate for their activity's size and their applicable industry, country, national laws and regulations, and operating environment. Performance measures should be specific to the organization and the CAE is cautioned against relying on general measures that

are not meaningful to the specific audit activity.

Exhibit 8-9 is taken from Practice Advisory 1311-2 and provides examples of appropriate performance categories.

USE OF TECHNOLOGY TO MANAGE THE INTERNAL AUDIT FUNCTION

Technology has an increasingly larger role in the internal audit function. There are more and more tools available that allow for increased productivity and efficiency, allowing for less time spent on administrative responsibilities and more on assurance and consulting services provided to clients. In the current environment of technological advancement, it can be difficult not to be distracted by the endless improvements, but it is important to keep in mind that technology should enhance an internal audit function's productivity, not divert attention away from the task of auditing.

In addition to decreasing the amount of time spent on administrative responsibilities, technological tools should also increase productivity inside of audit engagements, allowing for less time spent documenting, retaining, and accessing supporting documentation.

Control Self-Assessment

It should be clear at this point that internal audit functions assist an organization in assessing and mitigating risk in several ways. One way many internal audit functions do this is by establishing control self-assessment (CSA) teams and procedures. Typically, CSA teams partner with management to perform initial research and interviews to pinpoint potential risk events or scenarios facing an organization. They will assemble senior management representatives to discuss and prioritize these potential risks and assist management in identifying, documenting, evaluating, communicating, and mitigating the potential impact of the risks associated with significant risk events identified. Through the use of electronic means (database repository and tracking tool), the CSA teams can assign the various scenarios to the individuals best equipped to manage and mitigate the specific risks causing concern for management. The repository can then be used to document and track action planning and risk mitigation efforts agreed upon with management. Without the use of modern technology, CSA efforts are cumbersome, inefficient, and very difficult to manage. Control self-assessment can be used on a stand-alone basis to assist in evaluating risk in various areas or processes within an organization or as an effective tool in support of an organization's enterprisewide risk assessment efforts.

Risk Assessment

On an administrative level, automated risk assessment tools can provide the internal audit function with a repository that allows for the identification, documentation, and prioritization of risks, what areas of the organization own these risks, and key control activities designed to manage or mitigate these risks. These tools also document the audit universe, gather information about the different areas in that universe, and are used to evaluate the risks specific to those areas. Ad-

Control Self-assessment

A facilitated process where control owners provide a self-assessment of the operating effectiveness of controls for which they are responsible.

ditionally, these tools help prioritize the amount of risk that a specific area brings to the organization, which drives how often it is audited. Consequently, the resulting prioritization of the audit universe drives the budget, scheduling, audit plan, and resource requirements as described earlier in the chapter.

Data Interrogation

Often there are large amounts of data that must be reviewed by the internal auditor. This can be very difficult and time consuming without the assistance of technology. Likewise, sampling might not be effective, practical, or preferred. Sampling can also, at times, limit the internal auditor's ability to draw definitive conclusions. In these cases, data interrogation tools can be invaluable because they allow for 100% testing, resulting in definitive results and conclusions. In addition, these tools can also be used as a feeder source for continuous monitoring and/or fraud detection and prevention efforts. For a more extensive discussion of computer assisted audit techniques and sampling, refer to Chapter 9, "Gathering and Documenting Audit Evidence."

Automated Monitoring Tools

Automated monitoring tools, similar to data interrogation tools, allow the internal audit function to more efficiently perform continuous auditing by allowing the internal audit function to monitor and evaluate large amounts of data (information) that otherwise might not be possible or practical. Continuous auditing, in contrast to periodic audit efforts, "is any method used by [the internal audit function] to perform audit-related activities on a more continuous or continual basis." Continuous auditing activities often support or supplement the internal audit function's periodic audit, control assessment, and risk assessment processes. Automated monitoring tools can also enhance the internal audit function's ongoing management communication efforts by providing for "near" real-time information about the effectiveness of management's continuous monitoring activities. The availability of timely information about the adequacy and effectiveness of controls can be helpful to an internal audit function in reassessing priorities for planned assurance and consulting services, thus maximizing the audit coverage obtained of the audit universe. Automated monitoring tools can better equip an internal audit function to provide value added services, while managing its human and financial resources in the most efficient manner possible.

Automated Working Papers

The use of automated working papers by an internal audit function enhances productivity by providing a more efficient medium to document, review, store, and access information supporting audit work performed (assurance and consulting services). Productivity enhancements allow more time to be spent doing audit work rather than documenting, storing, and retrieving information. Automated working papers also serve as a repository for evidencing compliance with professional standards and due professional care.

Department Administration and Management

Most of the activities required when managing an internal audit function, including staff evaluations, tracking of time and expenses, and scheduling of audit engagements, can now be done electronically. In fact, many, if not all of these activities, can be done within the same tools that support the automated working papers and risk assessment procedures. This allows for much more efficient management of the internal audit function. Generally, the more activities that can be done with one tool, the more efficient and cost effective it is to implement the tool. When it isn't possible to choose a tool that does all of these activities, it is a good idea to choose tools that can easily interact (communicate). Many of the tools available today are cost effective enough to be viable for organizations of all sizes, large and small.

The Internet

In addition to the audit-specific tools mentioned above, the Internet can be an effective tool if used properly. It is an efficient way to do research, speeding up access to information that previously had to be retrieved through hard copy format. An increasing number of internal audit functions use Internet links to enhance the planning and delivery of services and gain access to work programs, working papers, policies, procedures, and other audit tools and resources, which results in increased efficiency and productivity.

Chapter 6, "Information Technology Risks and Controls," discusses technology as it relates to the internal audit function in some depth.

SUMMARY

This chapter presented the different philosophies regarding placement of the internal audit function within an organization and the drawbacks and benefits of each. The roles and responsibilities of the key positions within the internal audit function were identified. The policies and procedures of internal auditing were presented and how those policies and procedures guide the internal audit function was discussed. Various risk management models were explored along with what role the internal audit function should take in the organization's risk management processes. The quality assurance requirements, as stated by The IIA, were discussed and the importance of those requirements to the internal audit function was explained. The benefits of using technology, particularly as it relates to the management of the internal audit function, were discussed in detail.

1. According to The IIA, the CAE has three specific responsibilities. What are they?

2. Describe the differences between organizational independence and individual objectivity.

3. What key elements are taken into consideration when determining how to manage resources in an internal audit function?

4. According to The IIA, what "matters of mutual interest" are discussed during coordination efforts with independent outside (external) auditors?

5. What are the CAE's responsibilities when reporting to the audit committee?

6. Describe the difference between risk mitigation and risk management.

7. According to The IIA, what are the five objectives of a risk management process?

8. The IIA states that the internal audit function can play an important role in improving the ethical climate" of its organizational culture. Name the ways the internal audit function does this.

9. What are the five key elements of a properly designed quality assurance program?

10. What are the seven areas discussed in this chapter that can be enhanced by the use of technology when managing an internal audit function?

Select the best answer for each of the following questions.

1. Which of the following does not represent a key element of The IIA's quality assurance program?

   a. Implementing quality programs.

   b. Continuous improvement.

   c. Communicating results.

   d. Monitoring risk mitigation.

2. Executive management has requested that the internal audit function perform an operational review of the telephone marketing operations of a major division and to recommend procedures and policies for improving management control over the operation. The internal audit function should:

   a. Accept the audit engagement because independence would not be impaired.

   b. Accept the engagement, but indicate to management that recommending controls would impair audit independence so that management knows that future audits of the area would be impaired.

   c. Not accept the engagement because internal audit functions are presumed to have expertise on accounting controls, not marketing controls.

   d. Not accept the engagement because recommending controls would impair future objectivity of the department regarding this auditee.

3. Who is ultimately responsible for determining that the objectlves for an internal audit engagement have been met?

a. The individual internal audit staff member.

b. The chief audit executive.

c. The audit committee.

d. The internal audit engagement supervisor for the engagement.

4. Which of the following is the best reason for the CAE to consider the organization's strategic plan in developing the annual audit plan?

a. To emphasize the importance of the internal audit function to the organization.

b. To make recommendations to improve the strategic plan.

c. To ensure that the internal audit plan supports the overall business objectives.

d. To provide assurance that the strategic plan is consistent with the organization's values.

5. The *International Standards for the Professional Practice of Internal Auditing* requires policies and procedures to guide the audit staff. Which of the following statements is false with respect to this requirement?

a. A small internal audit function may be managed informally through close supervision and written memos.

b. Formal administrative and technical audit manuals may not be needed by all internal audit functions.

c. The chief audit executive should establish the function's policies and procedures.

d. All internal audit functions should have a detailed policies and procedures manual.

6. When conducting a consulting engagement to improve the efficiency and quality of a production process, the audit team is faced with a scope limitation because several months of the production data has been lost or is incomplete. Faced with this scope limitation, the CAE should:

a. Resign from the consulting engagement and conduct an audit to determine why the data was not available.

b. Discuss the problem with the client and together evaluate whether the engagement should be continued.

c. Increase the frequency of auditing the activity in question.

d. Communicate the potential effects of the scope limitation to the audit committee.

7. Which of the following is not a responsibility of the CAE?

a. To communicate the internal audit function's plans and resource requirements to senior management and the board for review and approval.

b. To oversee the establishment, administration, and assessment of the organization's system of internal controls and risk management processes.

c. To follow up on whether appropriate management actions have been taken on significant reported risks.

d. To establish a risk-based plan to accomplish the objectives of the internal auditing activity consistent with the organization's goals.

8. The *International Standards for the Professional Practice of Internal Auditing* require the chief audit executive to share information and coordinate activities with other internal and external providers of assurance services. With regard to the external auditor which of the following would not be an appropriate way for the chief audit executive to meet this requirement?

    a. Holding a meeting between the chief audit executive and the external audit firm's partner to discuss the upcoming audit of the financial statements.

    b. Providing the external auditor with access to the work papers for an audit of third party contractors.

    c. Requiring the external auditor to have the chief audit executive's approval of their annual audit plan for conducting the financial statement audit.

    d. Requesting that the internal audit function receive a copy of the external auditor's management letter.

1. How do The IIA's quality assurance professional standards (Section 1300) apply to a fully outsourced internal audit function? Specifically discuss the applicability of and compliance requirements with the external assessment procedures (Section 1312).

2. Discuss the various options for properly positioning an internal audit function within an organization and the related pros and cons for each identified option. What are the primary factors an organization should consider when establishing an effective internal audit function? Where should an effective internal audit function be positioned within an organization?

3. Should the CAE opine on the adequate design and/or effective operations of the systems of internal over financial reporting, effective and efficient operations, and compliance with applicable laws and regulations? Why or why not?

CASE

Pat Goodly accepted the CAE position with a large, global organization with a well established internal audit function. The organization is admired as an industry leader and as having very strong corporate governance practices. The organization's board is predominantly made up of outside, independent directors. The audit committee is comprised of outside, independent directors, all of whom are qualified. The chair of the audit committee is designated as the audit committee's "financial expert."

The organization's fiscal year-end is just around the corner; only a little over a month away. After a brief two months in the new position, Pat is preparing for the upcoming audit committee meeting. This typically is the meeting where next year's audit plan and budget would be presented for approval by the audit committee, as well as any necessary fiscal year-end reporting.

Recently, Pat received a "welcome" call from the audit committee chair, indicating "full" support for Pat and the internal audit function. The audit committee chair expressed an interest in meeting Pat and gaining an understanding of the vision and direction Pat has for the internal audit function going forward. The audit committee chair indicated that periodic communications between them were important and would allow for open and candid dialog in the future.

Pat was hired by and currently reports to the chief financial officer (CFO). Historically, the audit committee meeting agenda and related topic selections for such have been performed by the CFO. The CFO also has presided over the meetings in the past.

Senior management, including the chief executive officer (CEO) and the CFO, expressed support for the internal audit function and Pat's vision for the function both during the recruiting process and subsequent to Pat's joining the organization. However, the CFO firmly stated in a recent staff meeting, "I know everyone is very busy and things are going to get even more hectic with year-end upon us. I think it is in everyone's best interest not to make any 'radical' changes in our reporting processes until we get through the fiscal year-end reporting cycle. If we keep our heads down and work hard, we should be able to get through this year-end ok."

In preparation for the upcoming audit committee meeting, Pat contemplated the CFO's comments and reflected on The IIA's professional standards as they relate to the CAE's reporting responsibilities to management and the board. Put yourself in Pat's position as the newly hired CAE and consider the following:

1. How should Pat proceed with the audit committee chair? What obligations does Pat have, if any to the audit committee chair? As the CAE, what is Pat's role and responsibilities with respect to the audit committee and the audit committee chair?

2. What are Pat's reporting responsibilities to the audit committee chair? How about the audit committee? Does Pat have any? Why or why not?

3. Discuss the key issues that must be understood and addressed (and with whom) to properly discharge any reporting responsibilities noted.

REFERENCES

[1] The Institute of Internal Auditors (IIA), Global Technology Audit Guide: Continuous Auditing: Implications for Assurance, Monitoring, and Risk Assessment. (Altamonte Springs, FL: The Institute of Internal Auditors, 2005).

CHAPTER 9
GATHERING AND DOCUMENTING AUDIT EVIDENCE

Learning Objectives

- Understand the key activities involved in planning and performing an assurance engagement and reporting the engagement outcomes.

- Understand what it means to gather and properly evaluate sufficient competent evidence.

- Know the manual procedures used by internal auditors to gather audit evidence.

- Be familiar with selected computer-assisted audit techniques, including generalized audit software.

- Understand the importance of well-prepared audit working papers.

- Know how to apply statistical and nonstatistical audit sampling in tests of control activities.

- Be aware of alternative statistical sampling approaches used in tests of monetary values.

The first eight chapters of this textbook, which we refer to collectively as Fundamental Audit Concepts, cover just that—fundamental audit concepts that internal auditors need to know and understand. A firm grasp of these concepts is necessary, but not sufficient, for you to understand internal auditing. You also need to understand the internal audit process (that is, how internal audit assurance and consulting engagements are planned and performed and how engagement outcomes are communicated).

This chapter is the first of four chapters we refer to as the Internal Audit Processes chapters. In this chapter, we focus on gathering and documenting audit evidence—two very significant components of all internal audit engagements. In Chapter 10, "Conducting the Assurance Engagement," we discuss how to conduct the assurance engagement process in detail, while in Chapter 11, "Communicating Assurance Engagement Outcomes and Performing Follow-up Procedures," we cover the communication of assurance engagement outcomes. We

EXHIBIT 9-1

PROFESSIONAL STANDARDS AND PRACTICE ADVISORIES RELEVANT TO CHAPTER 9

2000 – Managing the Internal Audit Activity
2200 – Engagement Planning
2201 – Planning Considerations
2210 – Engagement Objectives
2220 – Engagement Scope
2230 – Engagement Resource Allocation
2240 – Engagement Work Program
2300 – Performing the Engagement
2310 – Identifying Information
2320 – Analysis and Evaluation
2330 – Recording Information
2340 – Engagement Supervision
2400 – Communicating Results
2410 – Criteria for Communicating
2420 – Quality of Communications
2421 – Errors and Omissions
2430 – Engagement Disclosure and Noncompliance with the *Standards*
2440 – Disseminating Results
2500 – Monitoring Progress
2600 – Resolution of Management's Acceptance of Risks

Practice Advisory 2000-1: Managing the Internal Audit Activity
Practice Advisory 2200-1: Engagement Planning
Practice Advisory 2210-1: Engagement Objectives
Practice Advisory 2210.A1-1: Risk Assessment in Engagement Planning
Practice Advisory 2230-1: Engagement Resource Allocation
Practice Advisory 2240-1: Engagement Work Program
Practice Advisory 2240.A1-1: Approval of Work Programs
Practice Advisory 2300-1: The Internal Auditor's Use of Personal Information in Conducting Audits
Practice Advisory 2310-1: Identifying Information
Practice Advisory 2320-1: Analysis and Evaluation
Practice Advisory 2330-1: Recording Information
Practice Advisory 2330.A1-1: Control of Engagement Records
Practice Advisory 2330.A1-2: Legal Considerations in Granting Access to Engagement Records
Practice Advisory 2330.A2-1: Retention of Records
Practice Advisory 2340-1: Engagement Supervision
Practice Advisory 2400-1: Legal Considerations in Communicating Results
Practice Advisory 2410-1: Communication Criteria
Practice Advisory 2420-1: Quality of Communications
Practice Advisory 2440-1: Recipients of Engagement Results
Practice Advisory 2440-2: Communications Outside the Organization
Practice Advisory 2440-3: Communicating Sensitive Information Within and Outside of the Chain of Command
Practice Advisory 2500-1: Monitoring Progress
Practice Advisory 2500.A1-1: Follow-up Process
Practice Advisory 2600-1: Management's Acceptance of Risks

shift our attention to the consulting engagement process in Chapter 12, "Performing the Consulting Engagement."

This chapter is divided into four main sections:

1. **Overview of the Assurance Engagement Process.** A brief overview of assurance engagement process activities is used to establish a context for discussing the various types of audit evidence the internal audit function gathers and the techniques used to gather and document audit evidence.

2. **Audit Evidence and Procedures.** The quality of internal auditors' conclusions and advice depends on their ability to gather and properly evaluate sufficient competent evidence. Audit procedures are performed throughout the audit process to gather the evidence needed to achieve the prescribed engagement objectives.

3. **Working Papers.** Audit working papers are used to document the engagement process. This documentation is the principal record of the procedures completed, evidence obtained, conclusions reached, and recommendations formulated by the internal audit team during the engagement. It also serves as the primary support for the internal audit team's communications to the auditee, senior management, the board of directors, and other stakeholders.

4. **Introduction to Audit Sampling.** Economic and time constraints generally preclude internal auditors from testing 100% of everything they would like to test. Audit sampling is the application of an audit procedure to less than 100% of the items in a population of audit interest for the purpose of drawing an inference about the entire population.

It is important to point out that throughout this chapter and those that follow, there are multiple references to the "internal audit function," "internal auditor," and the "internal audit team." While there might be subtle differences in the terms, depending on the circumstances described or the context in which the terms are used, generally all of these references are intended to communicate activities performed by the internal audit function under the supervision of the chief audit executive and the direction and oversight of the audit committee. As discussed in detail in Chapter 8, "Managing the Internal Audit Function," Standard 2000 states that "the chief audit executive (CAE) should effectively manage the internal audit activity to ensure it adds value to the organization." Recognizing that the CAE is pivotal to a successful internal audit function, Practice Advisory 2000-1, Managing the Internal Audit Activity, outlines the role and responsibilities of the CAE by stating,

> The chief audit executive is responsible for properly managing the internal audit activity so that:

- Audit work fulfills the general purposes and responsibilities described in the charter, approved by senior management, and accepted by the board.
- Resources of the internal audit activity are efficiently and effectively employed.
- Audit work conforms to the *International Standards for the Professional Practice of Internal Auditing (Standards)*.

OVERVIEW OF THE ASSURANCE ENGAGEMENT PROCESS

Exhibit 9-2 depicts the assurance engagement process, which comprises three fundamental phases—planning, performing, and communicating. Although this exhibit portrays the three phases of the engagement as discrete and sequential steps, actual audit engagements do not

Engagement
An internal audit assignment, task, or review activity, such as an internal audit assurance service, consulting service, control self-assessment review, fraud examination, or compliance examination.

EXHIBIT 9-2

THE ASSURANCE ENGAGEMENT PROCESS

Plan

- Determine engagement objectives and scope.
- Understand the auditee, including auditee objectives.
- Identify and assess risks.
- Identify key control activities.
- Evaluate adequacy of control design.
- Create a test plan.
- Develop a work program.
- Allocate resources to the engagement.

Perform

- Conduct tests to gather evidence.
- Evaluate evidence gathered and reach conclusions.
- Develop observations and formulate recommendations.

Communicate

- Perform observation evaluation and escalation process.
- Conduct interim and preliminary engagement communications.
- Develop final engagement communications.
- Distribute formal and informal final communications.
- Perform monitoring and follow-up procedures.

really work this way. There are no hard lines between planning, performing, and communicating. Where engagement planning ends and performance begins is debatable. In fact, planning typically continues throughout the engagement because adjustments need to be made as new evidence is uncovered. Performing the engagement begins during planning as the internal audit team applies procedures to gather information needed to plan the audit. Communicating takes place throughout the engagement process as the team communicates important matters to the auditee on an interim basis and not just at the end of the process in the final engagement communication.

Exhibit 9-2 is useful, despite its limitations, because it provides a framework for discussing the various activities included in the engagement process. As previously mentioned, it is important to be aware that although various members of the internal audit function will perform the specific activities necessary to plan, perform, and communicate during an assurance engagement, the CAE retains ultimate responsibility for the work performed. Each of the activities listed in the exhibit under Plan, Perform, and Communicate is briefly described below. The first two phases of the assurance engagement process are covered thoroughly in Chapter 10, "Conducting the Assurance Engagement," and the third phase, in Chapter 11, "Communicating Assurance Engagement Outcomes and Performing Follow-up Procedures."

Assurance Engagement Planning Activities

Effective planning is key to the successful completion of any type of project. There is an expression, sometimes referred to as the six Ps, that illustrates this principle: "Proper Prior Planning Prevents Poor Performance." Although it may be tempting to jump right in and start testing, following a structured and disciplined planning approach helps ensure that the engagement is performed effectively and efficiently. Conversely, failure to invest an appropriate amount of time and effort in planning increases the likelihood that the engagement will fail to achieve the desired objectives or that it will achieve the objectives in an inefficient manner. Studying this chapter and the next should deepen readers' appreciation of another expression, "Failing to plan means planning to fail." The following paragraphs discuss planning an engagement.

Determine engagement objectives and scope. An important first step in engagement planning is to determine the engagement objectives (what the engagement is intended to achieve) and scope (what the engagement will and will not cover). One important consideration is the business objective category or categories (strategic, operations, reporting, and/or compliance) of audit interest. For example, will the engagement focus on the operational effectiveness and efficiency of the auditee, the financial reporting aspects of the auditee, or both? Another important consideration is the deliverables the internal audit team are expected to produce. For example, the team might be expected to limit its focus to communicating individual control observations that were identified during the engagement to the appropriate levels of management, or the team might be expected to express an overall conclusion on the effectiveness of the system of internal controls for the specific area or process in question. A third important consideration is the "boundaries" of the engagement. For example, if the auditee is a business process or subprocess, where does the process or subprocess begin and where does it end? If the auditee is a specified family of geographically separated business units, such as service branches or production facilities, which specific location(s) will the internal audit team visit and what portion(s) of each business unit will the engagement cover?

Understand the auditee (including auditee objectives). It is virtually impossible to audit something effectively that is not sufficiently understood. The success of any engagement ultimately depends largely on how well the internal audit team understands the auditee. The first thing the internal auditors must understand is the auditee's business objectives (what the auditee is striving to achieve). From the auditee's perspective, clear and measurable objectives serve as meaningful targets of performance. From an internal auditor's perspective, the auditee's objectives provide a framework for defining the engagement objectives (what the internal auditor wants to achieve). Ultimately, the direct linkage between business objectives and audit engagement objectives sets the stage for internal auditors to help the auditee achieve its objectives, which in turn helps the organization as a whole achieve its objectives.

Assume, for illustrative purposes, that the auditee is a business process. Other aspects of the process that the internal audit team must understand include:

- How management deploys resources and assigns responsibilities to achieve the objectives of the process.
- The business risks threatening the process.
- The key control activities designed and placed in operation to

mitigate those risks.

- The relationships between the process and adjoining processes.

- The nature of the outputs (for example, goods and/or services) produced by the process.

- The process activities involved in producing the outputs.

- The process personnel, the responsibilities they are assigned, the authority delegated to them, and the manner in which they are held accountable.

- The tangible and intangible resources used in the process.

- Any recent changes, changes underway, and/or expected changes affecting the process. Note that significant changes affect process risks and, therefore, the design adequacy and operating effectiveness of its control activities.

Identify and assess risks. The internal audit team must identify and assess the business risks that threaten the achievement of the auditee's objectives, and ultimately, the organization's objectives. The internal audit team focuses its attention at this stage of the engagement on *inherent risk,* in other words, the risk to the auditee in the absence of any actions management might take to reduce or otherwise manage identified risks. Risk assessment involves gauging both the impact of the risk (if it should occur) and the likelihood of the risk occurring. Expressing risks in terms of causes and effects helps the internal auditor assess how big the potential problem is—how likely it is to occur. Take for example the following risk:

> Inefficient processing of vendor invoices for payment (the cause) may result in lost discounts, delays in payment, and vendor dissatisfaction (the effects).

Analyzing the potential effects (in this case, lost discounts, delays in payment, and vendor dissatisfaction) helps the internal auditor judge the size of the potential problem and whether further attention to the risk is warranted. Analyzing the potential cause (for example, inefficiencies), together with the underlying reasons for the potential inefficiencies, helps the internal auditor judge the likelihood of the risk becoming a reality.

The internal audit team also must weigh the assessed risk levels against management's risk tolerance thresholds and decide whether risks are being managed appropriately. Risks assessed at levels within management's risk tolerance thresholds may be *accepted* at their assessed levels. Risks that exceed management's tolerance thresholds must be mitigated to an acceptably low level. Mitigation options include *avoiding* risks by disbanding the activities that give rise to them, *sharing* risks by transferring a portion of them to third parties (for example, an insurance company), or *reducing* risks by implementing control activities designed to lower their impact, likelihood, or both.

Identify key control activities. The focus here is on reducing risks via control activities. The internal auditor's task is to identify those control activities that are most critical to reducing business risks to

Inherent Risk

The combination of internal and external risk factors in their pure, uncontrolled state, or, the gross risk that exists assuming there are no internal control activities in place.

acceptably low levels and thus providing assurance that established objectives are achieved. Control activities are covered extensively in Chapter 5, "Internal Control." They are discussed again in Chapter 10, "Conducting the Assurance Engagement," in the context of conducting an assurance engagement.

Evaluate adequacy of control design. The internal audit team must then decide whether the identified key control activities are designed adequately to reduce risks, both individually and collectively, to acceptably low levels, assuming that the control activities have in fact been placed in operation and are operating as intended. Internal auditors need to recognize at this point that the relationship between risks and control activities is not one-to-one—one control activity may help mitigate several risks, and multiple control activities may be needed to mitigate one risk effectively.

Key Control Activity

An activity designed to reduce risk associated with a critical business objective.

Create a test plan. The internal audit team must design the engagement to obtain sufficient competent evidence to achieve the engagement objectives. Creating a test plan involves determining the nature, timing, and extent of the procedures needed to gather the required evidence. Test plans may include tests of control activities, direct tests of performance measurements, or both. Chapter 10, "Conducting the Assurance Engagement," focuses on testing control activities. A plan for testing control activities already placed in operation should be designed to gather sufficient competent evidence to determine whether control activities that the auditee has already determined are adequately designed are also operating effectively.

Develop a work program. The work program is an extremely important planning device. It specifically outlines the audit procedures required to accomplish the engagement objectives. Over the course of the engagement, internal auditors sign off on the procedures to indicate that the work has been completed. This, in turn, enables engagement team supervisors to review the work that has been finished and monitor the work that remains to be done. At the end of the engagement, the completed program serves as a record of the work completed and documents who completed the work and when it was completed.

Allocate resources to the engagement. The last step in planning the engagement is to allocate the resources that are needed to successfully (in other words, effectively and efficiently) complete the engagement. This involves determining the audit expertise needed, estimating the time it will take to complete the engagement, assigning appropriate internal auditors to the engagement, and scheduling the work so that it is completed on a timely basis.

Assurance Engagement Performance Activities

Conduct tests to gather evidence. Performing the engagement involves the application of specific audit procedures to gather evidence. Procedures include, for example, making inquiries, observing operations, inspecting documents, and analyzing the reasonableness of information. Audit procedures are discussed in the Audit Evidence and Procedures section of this chapter. A second important aspect of gathering evidence is documenting the procedures performed and the results of performing the procedures. Documenting audit evidence is discussed in the Working Papers section of this chapter. Chapter 10, "Conducting the Assurance Engagement," focuses specifically on conducting and documenting tests to determine whether control activities are designed adequately and operating as designed.

Evaluate evidence gathered and reach conclusions. Evaluating the evidence gathered to determine, for example, whether control activities are adequately designed and operating effectively, requires a significant degree of professional judgment. The internal audit team must ultimately reach logical conclusions (in other words, make informed decisions) based on the evidence gathered. Chapter 10, "Conducting the Assurance Engagement," illustrates how an internal auditor documents conclusions that are reached based on the results of testing. Chapter 11, "Communicating Assurance Engagement Outcomes and Performing Follow-up Procedures," illustrates how an internal auditor formulates and documents conclusions on the engagement as a whole.

Develop observations and formulate recommendations. Observations (also referred to as *findings),* are defined in Practice Advisory 2410-1, Communication Criteria, as "pertinent statements of fact" that "emerge by a process of comparing what should be with what is." Well-written audit observations contain the following elements (sometimes referred to as the 4 Cs):

- **Condition.** The factual evidence the internal auditor found; the "what is."

- **Criteria.** The standards or expectations used in making an evaluation; the "what should be."

- **Consequences.** The real or potential adverse effects of the gap between the existing condition and the criteria. The *Standards* calls this element the "effect."

- **Causes.** The underlying reasons for the gap between the expected and actual condition, which lead to the adverse consequences.

Note that when the "what is" condition matches the "what should be" criteria, there is no "gap" and, therefore, no consequences or causes to deal with.

"Recommendations are based on the internal auditor's observations and conclusions" (Practice Advisory 2410-1). Audit recommendations (also referred to as *proposed corrective action),* may be documented as part of the audit observation or separately (some internal auditors refer to *corrective action* as the fifth C). Recommendations are aimed at closing the gap between the observation criteria and condition. Meaningful recommendations for corrective action address the causes of the gap between the criteria and condition, provide long-term solutions, rather than short-term fixes, and are economically feasible. Recommendations that address symptoms of problems rather than root causes tend to be of very little value.

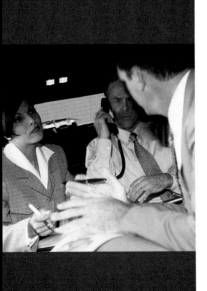

Audit Observation

Any identified and validated gap between the current and desired state arising from an assurance engagement.

EXHIBIT 9-3

ONE COMPANY'S OBSERVATION LEVELS AND DISPOSITION APPROACHES

Levels	Disposition Approaches
Not an observation: Further investigation reveals that the information upon which the observation is based is not correct.	Update the record of work done and the observation to reflect the new information and to support the appropriate conclusion.
Observation: The observation is not reportable due to mitigating controls and/or the observation is a suggested enhancement to a process and does not have a significant financial, operational, or compliance impact.	Document in the record of work done. Explain in the working papers why the observation is not reportable.
Reportable observation: The observation relates to a significant risk, and the existing control activities do not reduce the risk to an acceptable level.	Update the working papers to include the agreed upon management action plan. Track the performance of the agreed upon action plan. Include the observation in the body of the engagement communication only.
Significant observation: The observation is deemed important enough to be communicated to the audit committee.	Update the working papers to include the agreed upon management action plan. Track the performance of the agreed upon action plan. Include the observation in the executive summary of the engagement communication.

Assurance Engagement Communication Activities

Communicating outcomes is a critical component of all internal audit engagements. Regardless of the content or form of the communication, which may vary, communications of engagement outcomes should be accurate, objective, clear, concise, constructive, complete, and timely (Practice Advisory 2420-01, *Quality of Communications*).

Perform observation and evaluation process. Once one or more observations are identified, the internal audit team must assess each observation using an evaluation and escalation process and determine the implication those observations have on the resulting communications for the area (process) under review. Exhibit 9-3 illustrates one organization's approach to handling observations of varying levels of significance. Chapter 11, "Communicating Assurance Engagement Outcomes and Performing Follow-up Procedures," includes a detailed description of the observation evaluation and escalation process.

Conduct interim and preliminary engagement communications. As indicated, internal audit communications occur through-out the engagement, not just at the end. Matters often arise during internal audit engagements that warrant management's immediate or short-term attention. Timely communication of such issues allows management to address and resolve these issues sooner, sometimes before the engagement is completed. Other information that may be conveyed to the auditee on an interim basis during the engagement includes, for example, changes in engagement scope and engagement progress.

It is important for the internal audit team to give management a chance to clarify issues and express their thoughts about the internal audit team's conclusions and recommendations. Moreover, words stated in writing are sometimes interpreted differently than words spoken, and both are subject to misinterpretation. Reviewing draft versions of the report with management provides assurance that they concur with both what the internal auditors have said and what they have written in their report.

Develop final engagement communications. At this point, the internal audit team is ready to consolidate and synthesize all the evidence gathered during the engagement. There is no single prescribed way for expressing overall engagement results. Options include:

- Listing and prioritizing findings regarding control activity observations but stopping short of reaching an overall conclusion or expressing any level of assurance regarding the effectiveness of the auditee's system of internal controls.

- Reaching a conclusion known as negative assurance (also referred to as limited assurance). Internal auditors express negative assurance when they conclude that nothing has come to their attention that indicates that the auditee's system of internal controls is inadequately designed or is operating ineffectively.

- Reaching a conclusion known as positive assurance (also referred to as reasonable assurance). Internal auditors express positive assurance when they conclude that, in their opinion, the auditee's control activities are designed adequately and operating effectively.

Distribute formal and informal final communications. Several IIA standards directly pertain to preparing and issuing the final engagement report, including:

Standard 2410 – Communications should include the engagement's objectives and scope as well as applicable conclusions, recommendations, and action plans.

Standard 2410.A1 – The final communication of results should, where appropriate, contain the internal auditor's overall opinion or conclusions.

Standard 2440 – The chief audit executive should communicate results to the appropriate parties.

Standard 2440.A1 – The chief audit executive is responsible for communicating the final results to parties who can ensure that the results are given due consideration.

Also, Practice Advisory 2410-1, Communication Criteria, states that all final engagement communications "should contain, at a minimum, the purpose, scope, and results of the engagement." The purpose is the engagement objectives, in other words, why the engagement was conducted and what it was expected to achieve. The scope defines the activities included in the engagement, the nature and extent of work performed, and the time period covered. The scope may also identify related activities not included in the engagement, if necessary, to delineate the boundaries of the engagement. Results include observations, conclusions, opinions, recommendations, and action plans. The final engagement communications may also contain the auditee's responses to the internal audit team's conclusions, opinions, and recommendations.

The observations that should be included in the formal, final engagement communication are those that must be reported to support or prevent misunderstanding of the internal audit team's conclusions and recommendations. Less significant observations may be communicated informally. Conclusions and opinions express the internal audit team's evaluations of the observations. Recommendations, which are based on the observations and conclusions, are proposed actions to correct existing conditions or improve operations. Action plans are those things management has agreed to do to address the internal audit team's observations, conclusions, and recommendations.

The CAE, or another high-ranking internal auditor designated by the CAE, should review and approve the final report before it is issued to the auditee's management.

The CAE, or appointed designee, must determine to whom, other than management of the area or process audited, the final engagement report will be distributed. Appropriate recipients are those members of the organization who can ensure that the engagement results will be given due consideration. Such individuals are those who are in a position to take corrective action or ensure that corrective action is taken. Summary reports, which highlight engagement results significant to the organization as a whole, may be more appropriate for senior management, the audit committee, and the board of directors.

Briefly discussed here are two reporting situations that warrant special care on the part of internal auditing:

- Internal auditing is asked to distribute a report to a party outside the organization, possibly as an outcome of work that was performed for the benefit of the third party. Standard 2440.A2 specifically addresses this issue:

    If not mandated by legal, statutory, or regulatory requirements, prior to releasing results to parties outside the organization, the CAE should:

    - Assess the potential risk to the organization.
    - Consult with senior management and/or legal counsel as appropriate.
    - Control dissemination by restricting the use of the results.

    Practice Advisory 2440-2, Communications Outside the Organization, states that internal auditors should review guidance contained in the engagement agreement or organizational polices and procedures related to reporting information outside the organization. The internal audit charter and audit committee charter should also contain guidance regarding this situation.

- Internal auditing has uncovered highly sensitive information that could cause great harm to the organization if it ends up in the wrong hands. Practice Advisory 2440-3, Communicating Sensitive Information Within and Outside the Chain of Command, discusses this topic and provides worthwhile food for thought regarding appropriate courses of action internal auditors should consider.

Perform monitoring and follow-up procedures. As is apparent in Exhibit 9-2, the assurance engagement process does not end with reporting. Standard 2500 states that "the chief audit executive should establish and maintain a system to *monitor* [italics added] the disposition of results communicated to management." Standard 2500.A1 goes on to say that "the chief audit executive should establish a *follow-up* [italics added] process to monitor and ensure that management actions have been effectively implemented or that senior management has accepted the risk of not taking action."

It is very important for the internal audit function to determine that corrective actions on engagement observations and recommendations were, in fact, taken by management and that the actions taken remedy the underlying conditions in a timely manner. The internal audit charter should define the internal audit function's responsibility for follow-up, and the CAE should determine the nature, timing, and extent of follow-up procedures appropriate for a particular engagement. The internal audit function's monitoring and follow-up responsibilities are further discussed in Practice Advisories 2500-1, Monitoring Progress, and 2500.A1-1, Follow-up Process.

AUDIT EVIDENCE AND PROCEDURES

Recall from Chapter 1, "Introduction to Internal Auditing," that internal auditing is based on logic, which involves reasoning and drawing inferences. Internal auditors rely extensively on seasoned, professional judgment when they formulate conclusions and advice based on evidence they gather and evaluate. The quality of internal auditors' conclusions and advice depends on their ability to gather and properly evaluate sufficient competent evidence upon which their conclusions and advice are based.

Gathering sufficient competent evidence requires extensive interaction and communication with auditee personnel throughout the engagement. Such interactions and communications are critical to conducting the engagement effectively and efficiently. It is important, therefore, for internal auditors to be open, communicative, and collaborative. The internal auditor must always be mindful, however, that the managers and employees from whom evidence is gathered may not adequately understand the purpose, objectives, and scope of the engagement, or the manner in which the engagement is conducted. Moreover, some managers or employees may see the engagement as a threat to them—in other words, think that the internal auditors are specifically looking for things they have done wrong. Unfortunately, the threat of management and/or employee errors and fraud always exists.

Professional Skepticism and Reasonable Assurance

The internal auditor must always remember to apply a healthy level of professional skepticism when evaluating audit evidence. *Professional skepticism* means that internal auditors take nothing for granted; they continuously question what they hear and see and critically assess audit evidence. They do not assume by default that auditee personnel are either honest or dishonest. Applying professional skepticism throughout the engagement helps internal auditors remain unbiased and maintain an open mind to form judgments based on the preponderance of evidence gained during an engagement, and not just individual pieces of information. Professional skepticism is discussed in the context of fraud in Chapter 7, "Fraud Risks and Control."

Internal auditors are rarely, if ever, in a position to provide absolute assurance regarding the truthfulness of management's assertions regarding the system of internal controls and performance. Even experienced internal auditors are rarely convinced beyond all doubt. This is due to the nature and extent of evidence they gather and the types of decisions they make. Frequently, internal auditors must rely on evidence that is persuasive rather than absolutely convincing, and audit decisions are rarely black and white. Moreover, internal auditors' conclusions and advice must be formed at a reasonable cost within a reasonable length of time to add economic value. Accordingly, internal auditors strive to obtain sufficient competent evidence to provide a reasonable basis for formulating their conclusions and advice. This concept is referred to by internal auditors as *reasonable assurance*.

Persuasiveness of Audit Evidence

Audit evidence is *persuasive* if it enables the internal auditor to formulate well-founded conclusions and advice confidently. To be persuasive, evidence must be:

- **Relevant.** Is the evidence pertinent to the audit objective? Does it logically support the internal auditor's conclusion or advice?

- **Reliable.** Did the evidence come from a credible source? Did the internal auditor directly obtain the evidence?

- **Sufficient.** Has the internal auditor obtained enough evidence? Do different, but related, pieces of evidence corroborate each other?

Why audit evidence must be relevant to be persuasive is clear: Relying on evidence that has little or no pertinence to a specific audit objective greatly increases *audit risk*—the risk of reaching invalid conclusions and providing faulty advice.

> Example: Assume that an internal auditor wants to determine whether a particular vehicle included in the company's fixed asset ledger exists and is owned by the company. The internal auditor locates the vehicle in the company's parking lot. Can the internal auditor reasonably conclude that the vehicle exists just by seeing it? Yes. Can the internal auditor reasonably conclude that the company owns the vehicle just by seeing it? No. The internal auditor would need to inspect pertinent documentary evidence, such as a title of ownership.

Although there are no hard and fast rules regarding reliability and sufficiency of evidence, there are useful guidelines internal auditors

EXHIBIT 9-4

RELIABILITY OF DOCUMENTARY EVIDENCE		
Levels of Reliability	**Descriptions**	**Example Documents**
High	Documents prepared by the internal auditor	Inventory test counts Process maps Risk and control matrices
	Documents sent directly from a third party to the internal auditor	Confirmations Cutoff bank statements Letter from outside attorney
Medium	Documents created by a third party, sent to the organization, and requested from the organization by the internal auditor	Vendor invoices Customer purchase orders Bank statements
	Documents created by the organization, sent to a third party, returned to the organization, and requested from the organization by the internal auditor	Remittance advices Canceled checks Deposit slips
Low	Documents created by the organization and requested from the organization by the internal auditor	Written policy statements Receiving reports Time cards

can follow if they remember that guidelines are generally characterized by exceptions. Such guidelines include:

- Evidence obtained from independent third parties is *more reliable* than evidence obtained from auditee personnel.

- Evidence produced by a process or system with effective control activities is *more reliable* than evidence produced by a process or system with ineffective control activities.

- Evidence obtained directly by the internal auditor is *more reliable* than evidence obtained indirectly.

- Documented evidence is *more reliable* than undocumented evidence.

- Timely evidence is *more reliable* than untimely evidence.

- Corroborated evidence is *more sufficient* than uncorroborated or contradictory evidence.

- Larger sample sizes produce *more sufficient* evidence than smaller samples.

Documentary evidence is a significant portion of the evidence gathered during most internal audit engagements. The reliability of documentary evidence depends, to a large extent, on its origin and the route it follows before being examined by the internal auditor. Exhibit 9-4 illustrates this point.

AUDIT PROCEDURES

Audit procedures are specific tasks performed by the internal auditor to gather the evidence required to achieve the prescribed audit objectives. They are applied during the audit process to:

- Obtain a thorough understanding of the auditee, including the auditee's objectives, risks, and control activities.
- Test the design adequacy and operating effectiveness of the targeted area's system of internal controls.
- Analyze plausible relationships among different elements of data.
- Directly test recorded financial and nonfinancial information for errors and fraud.

Obtaining sufficient competent evidence to achieve the prescribed audit objectives involves determining the nature, extent, and timing of audit procedures to perform.

Nature of audit procedures. The nature of audit procedures relates to the types of tests the internal auditor performs to achieve his or her objectives. One-to-one relationships between audit objectives and audit procedures are rare. Individual audit procedures often provide evidence that is pertinent to more than one audit objective, and more than one audit procedure often is required to meet a particular audit objective. Different types of tests provide varying levels of assurance, take different amounts of time to conduct, and are more or less expensive. The internal auditor must weigh the relative benefits and costs of conducting different types of procedures. Depending on the nature of the engagement, an internal auditor may use manual audit procedures, computer-assisted audit techniques (CAATs), or a combination of the two to gather sufficient competent evidence. Manual audit procedures and CAATs are discussed in the following text.

Extent of audit procedures. The extent of audit procedures concerns how much audit evidence the internal auditor must obtain to achieve his or her objectives. An internal auditor must, for example, determine the appropriate combination of procedures to apply. The degree to which individual tests are to be conducted must also be determined. The internal auditor might decide, for example, that some types of transactions should be tested 100%, whereas others may be tested on a sample basis. Audit sampling is discussed in detail in the "Introduction to Audit Sampling" section of this chapter. Ultimately, the internal auditor must gather and evaluate enough evidence to support well-founded conclusions and advice.

Timing of audit procedures. The timing of audit procedures involves when the tests are conducted and the period of time covered by the tests. For example:

- An internal auditor testing the operating effectiveness of a manual control activity over a period of time on a sample basis must take appropriate steps to gain assurance that the sample selected is representative of the entire period.
- An internal auditor testing whether transactions are recorded in the proper fiscal year will focus his or her tests on transactions immediately before and after year-end.
- An internal auditor will test the operation of a computerized

Nature of Audit Procedures

The types of tests the internal auditor performs to achieve his or her objectives.

Extent of Audit Procedures

The quantity of audit evidence the internal auditor must obtain to achieve his or her objectives.

Timing of Audit Procedures

When audit tests are conducted and the period of time covered by the tests.

EXHIBIT 9-5

ILLUSTRATIVE APPLICATIONS OF MANUAL AUDIT PROCEDURES

Procedures	Illustrative Applications
Inquiry	• Circulate a questionnaire among senior executives asking them to identify the "top 10" risks threatening the organization. • Ask the organization's outside legal counsel to provide information about any litigation, claims, and/or assessments against the organization. • Interview managers and employees involved in the cash disbursements process to identify key process control activities.
Observation	• Tour the auditee's facility to gain a general understanding of day-to-day operations. • Observe the care with which employees count the year-end physical inventory. • Watch employees involved in executing and recording cash disbursements transactions to determine whether they are performing their assigned responsibilities and only their assigned responsibilities.
Inspection	• Review the minutes of board of director's meetings looking for authorization of significant events, for example, the acquisition of another company. • Inspect selected inventory items to determine their condition and salability. • Read the cash disbursements policies and procedures to obtain an understanding of key elements of the process, for example, assigned roles and responsibilities.
Vouching	• Vouch a sample of inventory items from the accounting records to the warehouse to see that the inventory items exist. • Vouch a sample of sales invoices to corresponding shipping documents to verify that the shipments occurred. • Vouch a sample of check copies to supporting voucher packages to test the validity of the checks.
Tracing	• Trace internal auditor test counts of inventory to the auditee's inventory compilation records to verify that the counts are properly included in the compilation. • Trace receiving reports for goods received to the corresponding voucher and then to the voucher register to verify that the receipts of goods are properly recorded as liabilities. • Trace checks dated within a period of several days before and after year-end to the accounting records to ensure the checks were recorded in the proper year.
Reperformance	• Recalculate accumulated depreciation and depreciation expense to verify that they were calculated correctly. • Independently estimate the allowance for doubtful accounts to test the reasonableness of the accounting department's estimate. • Reperform auditee-prepared bank reconciliations to test whether they were completed correctly.
Analytical procedures	• Prepare common-size financial statements for the current year and preceding two years; look specifically for variance or unexpected trends. • Compare the organization's common-size financial statements with published industry common-size information looking for unexpected inconsistencies. • Calculate accounts payable turnover for the current year and preceding two years as evidence of vendor payment periods.
Confirmation	• Confirm a sample of accounts receivable subsidiary ledger balances with customers. • Confirm the principal balance of a notes payable and interest rate with the lender. • Confirm cash account bank balances with banks.

application control at a given point in time to determine whether the control activity is operating effectively at that point in time. The internal auditor will then rely on different tests, such as tests over access and modification of application programs during a period of time, to gain assurance that the control activity operated consistently over that period of time.

Manual Audit Procedures

Commonly performed manual audit procedures include inquiry, observation, inspection, vouching, tracing, reperformance, analytical procedures, and confirmation. Each of these procedures is defined and discussed below. Example applications of each procedure are presented in Exhibit 9-5.

Inquiry. Asking questions of auditee personnel or third parties and obtaining their oral or written responses. Inquiry produces indirect evidence, which by itself is rarely persuasive. This is especially true when inquiries are directed to auditee personnel from whom the internal auditor cannot count on receiving unbiased responses. More formal types of inquiry include interviews and circulating surveys and questionnaires. Key components of effective interviewing are outlined in Exhibit 9-6.

Observation. Watching people, procedures, or processes. Observation is generally considered more persuasive than inquiry in the sense that the internal auditor is obtaining direct evidence. For example, the internal auditor's direct personal observation of an employee applying a control activity generally provides more assurance than simply inquiring of that employee about the application of the control activity. A significant limitation of observation is that it provides evidence at a point in time. The internal auditor cannot conclude that what is observed is representative of what happened throughout the year, especially given the propensity of people to behave differently when they know they are being watched.

Inspection. Studying documents and records and physically examining tangible resources. Inspection of documents and records provides direct evidence of their contents. Likewise, physical examination of tangible resources (for example, a building or piece of equipment) provides the internal auditor with direct personal knowledge of the resources' existence and physical condition. Internal auditors must, however, acknowledge and take into account their level of expertise (in other words, their capacity to comprehend what they read and see). For example, formulating valid conclusions about the value of precious gems based on inspection may be outside the scope of the internal auditor's expertise. The internal auditor might, in this case, need to rely on the assistance of a precious gems expert to help validate the gems' value.

Vouching. Tracking information *backward* from one document or record to a previously prepared document or record, or to a tangible resource. Vouching is performed specifically to test the *validity* of documented or recorded information. For example, a sale of goods typically should not be recorded unless the goods have been shipped. Vouch-

EXHIBIT 9-6

KEY COMPONENTS OF EFFECTIVE INTERVIEWING

Interviewing objectives:
- Gather information (that is, audit evidence) relevant to the engagement.
- Establish a rapport that fosters a positive working relationship throughout the engagement.

The interviewing process:

Prepare for the interview.
- Define the purpose.
- Identify the appropriate interviewee.
- Gather background information about the audit area and interviewee.
- Create the right set of questions (what, why, how, where, when, who).
- Establish expectations with the interviewee and identify information needs.
- Arrange logistics (date, time, location, length).
- Prepare an outline.

Conduct the interview.
- Establish rapport and create an atmosphere that encourages openness.
- Review the purpose of the interview, the topics to be covered, and the estimated time needed.
- Ask straightforward questions and meaningful follow-up questions.
- Avoid technical jargon.
- Use periods of silence effectively.
- Listen.
- Summarize and confirm key points.
- Discuss next steps.
- Arrange follow-up contact.
- Thank the interviewee.

Document the interview outcomes (as soon as possible after the interview).
- Reflect on the interview and review notes.
- Record the results of the interview in good form.

Characteristics of effective interviewers:
- Professionalism (for example, being prepared, respectful, courteous, and on time).
- Outstanding interpersonal and oral communication skills, including listening skills.
- The capacity to display confidence and command respect without being arrogant.
- An innate curiosity.
- Objectivity (that is, remaining impartial and refraining from interjecting personal opinions).

Common barriers to effective interviews:
- Auditee impediments such as competing demands on time, preconceived notions about internal auditors, and fear of reprisal.
- Flaws in the interview process.
- Lack of requisite competencies on the part of the internal auditor.

Critical success factors:
- Be prepared.
- Know and respect the interviewee.
- Establish credibility and trust.
- Speak the interviewee's language.
- Expect the unexpected.

ing a sales invoice to a shipping document provides evidence that the shipment upon which the invoice is based actually occurred. Likewise, vouching the recording of a vehicle in the fixed asset ledger to the actual vehicle provides evidence that the vehicle really exists. Within the context of financial audits, vouching is used to test for *overstatements* in recorded amounts.

Tracing. Tracking information *forward* from one document, record, or tangible resource, to a subsequently prepared document or record. Tracing is performed specifically to test the *completeness* of documented or recorded information. For example, purchases of goods typically should be recorded when the goods are received. Tracing a receiving report for goods received near the end of the year to the accounting records provides evidence that both the asset and liability were recorded in the same year the goods were received. Within the context of financial audits, tracing is used to test for *understatements* in recorded amounts.

Reperformance. Redoing control activities or other procedures. Reperforming a control activity provides direct audit evidence regarding its operating effectiveness. Reperforming calculations provides direct evidence as to whether the auditee's calculations are correct. Independently formulating an accounting estimate, such as the allowance for bad debts, and comparing it with the auditee's estimate provides direct evidence regarding the reasonableness of the auditee's estimate.

Analytical procedures. Practice Advisory 2320-1, Analysis and Evaluation, refers to analytical audit procedures as an effective and efficient means of assessing information that involves comparisons of the information with expectations identified or developed by the internal auditor. A basic premise underlying the use of analytical procedures in internal auditing is that the internal auditor may reasonably expect certain relationships among different pieces of information to continue in the absence of known conditions to the contrary. It is important for internal auditors to develop expectations independently based on knowledge of the auditee, industry, and economy before accumulating and analyzing information to ensure that the ensuing comparisons are unbiased.

Internal auditors use analytical procedures while planning and performing an engagement to identify anomalies in information such as unexpected fluctuations, differences, and correlations as well as the absence of expected fluctuations, differences, and correlations. Such anomalies may be indicative of unusual or nonrecurring transactions or events, errors, or fraudulent activities that warrant further attention and the gathering of corroborative evidence. Common analytical procedures performed by internal auditors include:

- **Analysis of common-size financial statements.** The internal auditor expresses financial statement line items as percentages of relevant totals (for example, income statement items are expressed as percentages of sales, and balance sheet items are expressed as percentages of total assets).

EXHIBIT 9-7

ILLUSTRATIVE PROCESS PERFORMANCE RATIOS

Sales, Accounts Receivable, and Cash Receipts:

Net Sales ÷ Average or Year-end Net Accounts Receivable (Accounts Receivable Turnover)

365 ÷ Accounts Receivable Turnover (Average Days to Collect)

Net Sales ÷ Square Footage of Sales Space

On-Time Deliveries to Customers ÷ Total Deliveries to Customers

Bad Debt Expense ÷ Net Sales

Year-end Allowance for Bad Debts ÷ Year-end Accounts Receivable

Purchases, Accounts Payable, and Cash Disbursements:

Raw Materials Purchased ÷ Cost of Finished Goods Produced

On-Time Deliveries from Suppliers ÷ Total Deliveries from Supplies

Purchase Returns ÷ Total Purchases or Cost of Goods Sold

Cost of Goods Sold or Net Purchases ÷ Average or Year-end Accounts Payable (Accounts Payable Turnover)

Inventory and Cost of Goods Sold:

Cost of Goods Sold ÷ Average or Year-end Inventory (Inventory Turnover)

365 ÷ Inventory Turnover (Average Days to Sell)

Number of Defective Units Produced ÷ Total Units Produced

Cost of Scrap/Waste/Spoilage ÷ Net Sales or Cost of Goods Sold

Gross Profit ÷ Net Sales (Gross Profit Percentage)

Human Resources and Payroll:

Number of Employees Leaving Voluntarily and/or Involuntarily During the Year ÷ Average or Year-end Number of Employees (Employee Turnover)

Man Days Lost to Absenteeism ÷ Total Man Days

Number of Overtime Hours Worked ÷ Total Hours Worked

Payroll Expense ÷ Average or Year-end Number of Employees

- **Ratio analysis.** The internal auditor calculates pertinent financial ratios (for example, current ratio, gross profit percentage, inventory turnover, cost of raw materials purchased divided by cost of finished goods produced) and ratios involving nonfinancial values (for example, sales divided by square footage of sales space, payroll expense divided by average number of employees, percentage of defective units produced). Illustrative process performance ratios are presented in Exhibit 9-7. It is important, however, to realize that the only true constraints on working with ratios are the availability of the necessary information to calculate the ratios and the internal auditor's creativity

- **Trend analysis.** The internal auditor compares performance information (for example, individual amounts, common-size percentages, and/or ratios) for the current fiscal period with like information for one or more prior periods.

- **Analysis of future-oriented information.** The internal auditor compares current fiscal period information with budgets or forecasts.

- **External benchmarking.** The internal auditor compares performance information for the organization with like information of other individual organizations or the industry in which the organization operates. Published industry data for specific industries is available for comparison purposes from sources such as Dun & Bradstreet and Standard & Poor's.

- **Internal benchmarking.** The internal auditor compares performance information of one organizational unit with like information for other organizational units.

Confirmation. Obtaining direct written verification of the accuracy of information from independent third parties. Evidence obtained via confirmation generally is considered very reliable because it comes to the internal auditor directly from independent sources. There are two common types of confirmation requests: *positive confirmations* ask recipients to respond regardless of whether or not they believe the information provided to them is correct, and *negative confirmations* ask recipients to respond only when they believe the information provided to them is incorrect. A positive confirmation may ask the recipient to provide the information of interest (referred to as a blank confirmation) or include the information of interest and ask the recipient to indicate agreement or disagreement with the information.

Computer-assisted Audit Techniques

"In exercising due professional care the internal auditor should consider the use of computer-assisted audit tools and other data analysis techniques." (Standard 1220.A2)

Practice Advisory 1220-2 was adopted from the Information Systems Audit and Control Association (ISACA) Guideline —Use of Computer-assisted Audit Techniques (CAATs), Document G3. The IIA and ISACA define *computer-assisted audit techniques* as "any automated audit techniques, such as generalized audit software, utility software, test data, application software tracing and mapping, and audit expert systems."[1] Both professional organizations define the specific techniques referred to in this definition as follows:

Generalized audit software. A computer program or series of programs designed to perform certain automated functions. These functions include reading computer files, selecting data, manipulating data, sorting data, summarizing data, performing calculations, selecting samples, and printing reports or letters in a format specified by the internal auditor. This technique includes software acquired or written for audit purposes and software imbedded in production systems.

Utility software. Computer programs provided by a computer hardware manufacturer or software vendor and used in running the system. This technique can be used to examine processing activity; test programs, system activities, and operational pro-

Computer-assisted Audit Techniques (CAATs)

Automated audit techniques, such as generalized audit software, utility software, test data, application software tracing and mapping, and audit expert systems, that help the internal auditor directly test control activities built into computerized information systems and data contained in computer files.

cedures; evaluate data file activity; and analyze job accounting data.

Test data. Simulated transactions that can be used to test processing logic, computations, and controls actually programmed in computer applications. Individual programs or an entire system can be tested. This technique includes integrated test facilities (ITFs) and base case system evaluations (BCSEs).

Application software tracing and mapping. Specialized tools that can be used to analyze the flow of data through the processing logic of the application software and document the logic, paths, control conditions, and processing sequences. Both the command language or job control statements and programming language can be analyzed. This technique includes program/system mapping, tracing, snapshots, parallel simulations, and code comparisons.

Audit expert systems. Expert or decision support systems that can be used to assist internal auditors in the decision-making process by automating the knowledge of experts in the field. This technique includes automated risk analysis, system software, and control objectives software packages.

These definitions indicate that internal auditors can use CAATs to directly test (1) controls built into computerized information systems and (2) data contained in computer files. It should be noted that, by directly testing data contained in computer files, internal auditors obtain indirect evidence about the effectiveness of the controls in the application that processed the data.

> Example: An internal auditor uses generalized audit software to directly test whether any duplicate payments of invoices exist in the company's cash disbursements transaction file. The internal auditor uncovers several duplicate payments made throughout the year. The internal auditor may properly infer that control activities to prevent and/or detect such payments on a timely basis did not exist, were inadequately designed, or did not operate effectively.

An in-depth discussion of each type of CAAT defined above is beyond the scope of this textbook. However, generalized audit software (GAS) and the types of data analyses internal auditors can perform with GAS warrant a bit more attention.

Some internal auditors continue to harbor the belief that GAS is a tool to be used only by IT audit specialists. This is no longer true because GAS has advanced to the stage where it is relatively easy to use, even by internal auditors with little audit-related IT training. It combines a user-friendly interface with powerful audit functionality and allows internal auditors to extract electronically stored auditee data and perform various operations on the data. Such operations include:

- Examining files and records for validity, completeness, and accuracy.

- Recalculating recorded values and calculating other values of audit interest.
- Selecting and printing samples and calculating sample results.
- Comparing information in separate files.
- Summarizing, resequencing, and reformatting data.
- Creating pivot tables for multi-dimensional analysis.
- Searching for potential fraud using Benford's Law analysis.
- Preparing and printing reports.
- Automatically generating a historical log of data analyses performed.

Benefits of using GAS. There are many benefits of using GAS, including:

- It allows internal auditors to conduct audit procedures in a wide variety of hardware and software environments with minimal customization.
- It enables internal auditors to perform tests on data independently of the company's IT personnel.
- Using GAS enables the internal auditor to deftly analyze very large quantities of data.
- Some applications of GAS facilitate 100% examination of data populations almost instantaneously as opposed to testing a sample of data items manually.
- Using GAS to perform necessary but routine audit tasks frees up time for the internal auditor to think analytically.

Obstacles to implementing GAS successfully. There are also legitimate obstacles that an internal auditor must overcome to implement GAS successfully:

- Obtaining access privileges to relevant and reliable data.
- Gaining physical access to the data.
- Understanding how the data is stored and formatted in the system.
- Extracting the data and downloading it to the internal auditor's personal computer (PC).
- Importing the data in a usable format into the software.

Overcoming these obstacles might, in some cases, require the assistance of an IT audit expert. However, the only "show-stopper" limitations of adding value by using GAS are the availability of relevant data in electronic format and the internal auditor's ingenuity.

ACL and IDEA software. The two most widely used, commercially available software programs, ACL (Audit Command Language) and IDEA (originally an acronym for Interactive Data Extraction and Analysis), accompany this textbook. Both ACL and IDEA are Windows-based and can be operated easily on the internal auditor's PC.

ACL Software. The ACL software that accompanies the textbook is a product of ACL Services Ltd. Interested readers can learn more about ACL Services by visiting the company's Web site at www.acl.com. The ACL CD-ROM that accompanies this text contains the following materials in addition to the software itself:

- The *Getting Started* manual.
- The *ACL in Practice* manual.
- The *Data Access Guide.*
- Help for ACL Version 9.

The *ACL in Practice* manual contains an extensive tutorial involving a hypothetical company and real-world data, which provides a good introduction to ACL's analysis and reporting capabilities.

IDEA – Data Analysis Software (IDEA). The IDEA software that accompanies the textbook is a product of CaseWare IDEA Inc., a privately held software development and marketing company. Audimation Services Inc., which is referred to on the front of the IDEA CD-ROM, is the U.S. business partner with CaseWare IDEA Inc. Interested readers can learn more about these companies and IDEA by visiting their Web sites: www.CaseWare-IDEA.com and www.audimation.com. The IDEA CD-ROM that accompanies this textbook contains the following materials in addition to the software itself:

- *IDEA Version Seven Installation Guide.*
- *IDEA Version Seven User Guide.*
- *Report Reader for IDEA Version Seven User Guide.*
- Help for IDEA Version Seven.

The Getting Started Tutorial in Section Four of the *IDEA Version Seven User Guide,* which can be completed by using the sample data files contained on the CD-ROM, provides a good introduction to IDEA's functionality. The CD-ROM also contains additional sample data files that can be used for supplemental practice with the software.

WORKING PAPERS

Standard 2330 requires internal auditors to record the evidence they accumulate as support for engagement outcomes. Practice Advisory 2330-1 provides guidance regarding working papers and their preparation.

Purposes and Content of Working Papers

Because of the many purposes working papers serve, it is difficult to overstate their importance. For example, working papers:

- Aid in planning and performing the engagement.
- Facilitate supervision of the engagement and review of the work completed.
- Indicate whether engagement objectives were achieved.
- Provide the principal support for the internal auditors' communications to the auditee, senior management, the board of

---

ACL and IDEA

The two commercially available audit software programs used most widely by internal auditors.

directors, and appropriate third parties.

- Serve as a basis for evaluating internal audit's quality assurance program.
- Contribute to the professional development of the internal audit staff.
- Demonstrate the internal audit function's compliance with The IIA's *Standards.*

The content of internal audit engagement working papers will depend on the nature of the engagement. They should always, however, provide complete, accurate, and concise documentation of the engagement process.

Types of Working Papers

A wide variety of working papers are prepared during an internal audit engagement. The following list is intended to be illustrative rather than all-inclusive:

- Work programs used to document the nature, extent, and timing of the specific audit procedures. (Work programs were briefly described above in the "Overview of the Assurance Engagement Process" section of this chapter).
- Engagement time budgets and resource allocation worksheets.
- Questionnaires used to obtain information about the auditee, including its objectives, risks, control activities, operating activities, etc.
- Process maps (flowcharts) used to document process activities, risks, and control activities. (Common flowcharting symbols and illustrative process maps are presented in Chapter 4, "Business Processes and Business Risks," and in Chapter 10, "Conducting the Assurance Engagement").
- Charts, graphs, and diagrams, such as a risk map used to plot the impact and likelihood of business risks (an illustrative risk map is presented in Chapter 10, "Conducting the Assurance Engagement").
- Agendas for internal audit team meetings and meetings with the auditee.
- Narrative memoranda used to document the results of interviews and other meetings with auditees.
- Pertinent auditee organizational information, such as organization charts, job descriptions, and operating and financial policies and procedures.
- Copies of source documents, such as purchase requisitions, purchase orders, receiving reports, vendor invoices, vouchers, and checks.
- Copies of other important documents, such as minutes of meetings and contracts.
- IT-related documents, such as program listings and exception reports.

- Accounting records, such as trial balances and excerpts from journals and ledgers.

- Evidence obtained from third parties, such as confirmation responses from customers and representations from outside legal council.

- Worksheets prepared by the auditor, such as a risk and control matrix used to document process-level risks, key control activity descriptions, the internal auditor's evaluation of control design adequacy, the tests of control activities performed, and the test results. (An illustrative risk and control matrix is presented in Chapter 10, "Conducting the Assurance Engagement").

- Other types of working papers prepared by the internal auditor that reflect work performed (for example, analytical procedures, computerized data analysis, and direct tests of transactions, events, account balances, and performance measurements).

- Evidence compiled by the auditee and tested by the internal auditor.

- Control activities performed by the auditee and reperformed by the internal auditor (for example, bank reconciliations).

- Written correspondence and documentation of oral correspondence with the auditee during the engagement.

- The internal audit team's write-ups of observations, recommendations, and conclusions. (Audit observations, recommendations, and conclusions are briefly described above in the "Overview of the Assurance Engagement Process" section of this chapter. Illustrative write-ups are discussed in Chapter 10, "Conducting the Assurance Engagement.")

- Final engagement communications and management's responses. (Illustrative audit communications are presented in Chapter 11, "Communicating Assurance Engagement Outcomes and Performing Follow-up Procedures.")

Guidelines for Working Paper Preparation

The CAE is responsible for establishing working paper policies and procedures. Well-written policies and procedures promote effective and efficient work and facilitate consistent adherence to quality assurance standards. Working papers may be prepared in paper form, electronic form, or both. Special care must be taken to maintain version control over electronic working papers and to ensure that they are properly backed up.

Standardized working paper formats help to streamline the audit process and facilitate consistent, high-quality work across engagements. Care should be taken, however, not to standardize working papers so rigidly that they inhibit internal auditor ingenuity and creativity. Appropriate working paper standardization may include:

- A uniform cross-referencing system for all engagements.
- Consistent working paper layouts.
- Standardized "tick marks" (in other words, symbols used on working papers to represent specific audit procedures).

- A prescription for the types of information to store in permanent or carry-forward files (in other words, files containing pertinent information of continuing importance for a particular auditee).

Working paper files should be complete and well-organized. At the end of an engagement, the files should be cleared out so they contain only the final versions of the working papers completed during the engagement. Each individual working paper should stand on its own merits. This means, for example, that each working paper should:

- Contain an appropriate index or reference number.
- Identify the engagement and describe the purpose or contents of the working paper.
- Be signed (or initialed) and dated by both the internal auditor who performed the work and the internal auditor(s) who reviewed the work. (Note that such a signature may be electronic.)
- Clearly identify the sources of auditee data included on the working paper.
- Include clear explanations of the tick marks used (in other words, the specific procedures performed).
- Be clearly written and easy to understand by internal auditors unfamiliar with the work performed (for example, an internal auditor who refers to the working paper at a later date).

The bottom line is that the working paper should contain sufficient information for an internal auditor other than the one who performed the work to be able to reperform it. On the other hand, working papers should not contain more information than is necessary; they should be as concise as possible.

Moreover, because time is a precious audit resource, internal auditors must always strive to prepare working papers the right way the first time. There is no time allocated for rewriting them. The vital need for working papers to be prepared correctly, clearly, concisely, and quickly is one important reason why internal auditor proficiency in written communications is not an option—it is imperative.

INTRODUCTION TO AUDIT SAMPLING

Definition of Audit Sampling

Audit sampling is the application of an audit procedure to less than 100% of the items in a population for the purpose of drawing an inference about the entire population. An audit population might be, for example, all the receiving reports prepared during the year or all the customer account balances in an accounts receivable subsidiary ledger. Sampling generally is used in performing audit procedures such as vouching and tracing, which involve the inspection of some form of manually prepared documentary audit trail. It is not applicable to the performance of audit procedures such as inquiry, observation, and analytical procedures. Walking a small set of transactions through a particular process to gain a better understanding of how the process works also is not sampling because the purpose is not to reach a conclusion about an entire population of items.

Two General Approaches to Audit Sampling

There are two general approaches to sampling: *statistical* and *nonstatistical*. Both approaches require the use of professional judgment in designing the sampling plan, executing the plan, and evaluating sample results. The internal auditor's choice between the two methods is independent of the specific audit procedures he or she intends to perform, his or her evaluation of the relevance and competence of the evidence obtained, and the actions he or she will take based on the outcomes of the sampling application. Both approaches can provide sufficient competent evidence if applied properly. (Note: Some people refer to nonstatistical sampling as "judgmental" sampling. The authors have chosen not to use this term to avoid potential confusion—both statistical sampling and nonstatistical sampling require expert audit judgment.)

The internal auditor's choice between the two methods really boils down to a cost-benefit decision. Statistical sampling is a tool, that can help the internal auditor measure the sufficiency of evidence obtained and quantitatively evaluate the sampling results. Most importantly, statistical sampling allows the internal auditor to quantify, measure, and control sampling risk. For these reasons, statistical sampling is normally thought to provide more persuasive evidence than nonstatistical sampling. However, statistical sampling also is generally thought to be more costly. It involves incremental training costs and higher costs associated with designing samples, selecting items to be examined, and evaluating sample results. Statistical sampling and nonstatistical sampling are further differentiated in subsequent sections of this chapter.

Audit Risk and Sampling Risk

As defined earlier in the chapter, audit risk is the risk of reaching a wrong audit conclusion. Within the context of sampling, audit risk comprises two types of risk: sampling risk and nonsampling risk.

Sampling risk. Sampling risk is the risk that the internal auditor's conclusion based on sample testing may be different than the conclusion reached if the audit procedure was applied to all items in the population. It is a function of testing less than 100% of the items in the population because even a properly selected sample may not be representative of the population. Sampling risk varies inversely with sample size. If the internal auditor tests 100% of a population, and therefore is not sampling, there is no sampling risk.

In performing tests of control activities, the internal auditor is concerned with two aspects of sampling risk:

The risk of assessing control risk too low (Type II risk, beta risk). Also known as the risk of over-reliance, this is the risk that the assessed level of control risk based on the sample results is lower than the internal auditor would have found it to be if the population had been tested 100%. In other words, it is the risk that the internal auditor will incorrectly conclude that a specified control activity is more effective than it really is. Stated another

Audit Sampling

The application of an audit procedure to less than 100% of the items in a population for the purpose of drawing an inference about the entire population.

way, it is the risk that the internal auditor will overstate the reliance that management can place on the control activity to reduce residual risk to an acceptably low level.

The risk of assessing control risk too high (Type I risk, alpha risk). Also known as the risk of under-reliance, this is the risk that the assessed level of control risk based on the sample results is higher than the internal auditor would have found if the population had been tested 100%. In other words, it is the risk that the internal auditor will incorrectly conclude that a specified control activity is less effective than it really is. Stated another way, it is the risk that the internal auditor will understate the reliance that management can place on the control activity to reduce residual risk to an acceptably low level.

Control risk, which is referred to for the first time in the preceding two paragraphs, is the risk that control activities fail to reduce controllable risk to an acceptable level. Remember from Chapter 5, "Internal Control," that *controllable risk* is that portion of inherent risk that management can reduce through day-to-day operations. Control activities are implemented specifically to reduce controllable risk, with the goal being to reduce it to management's level of risk tolerance (that is, the level of risk acceptable to management). *Residual risk* is the risk remaining after control activities have been implemented. If residual risk exceeds management's risk tolerance, then internal control activities are ineffective, either because they are inadequately designed or because they are not operating effectively. If the risk is managed to a level below management's risk tolerance, then internal control activities are presumed to be designed adequately and operating effectively. However, there is also the possibility that the internal control activities are excessive and utilizing more resources than may be required.

Nonsampling risk. Unlike sampling risk, nonsampling risk is not associated with testing less than 100% of the items in a population. Instead, nonsampling risk occurs when an internal auditor fails to perform his or her work properly. For example, performing inappropriate auditing procedures, misapplying an appropriate procedure (such as failure on the part of the internal auditor to recognize a control deviation or a dollar error), or misinterpreting sampling results may cause a nonsampling error. Nonsampling risk refers to the possibility of making such errors. Nonsampling risk is controlled (reduced to an acceptably low level) through proper audit planning, supervision of individual audit engagements, and the overall application of appropriate quality assurance procedures.

STATISTICAL AUDIT SAMPLING IN TESTS OF CONTROL ACTIVITIES

Attribute Sampling Approaches

Attribute sampling. A statistical sampling approach, based on the binomial distribution theory, that reaches a conclusion about a population in terms of a rate of occurrence. The binomial distribution is a distribution of all possible samples where each item in the population has one of two possible states (for example, control deviation or no con-

Sampling Risk

The risk that the internal auditor's conclusion based on sample testing may be different than the conclusion reached if the audit procedure were applied to all items in the population.

Residual Risk

The portion of inherent risk that remains after management executes its risk responses (sometimes referred to as net risk).

Control Risk

The potential that control activities will fail to reduce controllable risk to an acceptable level.

Controllable Risk

The portion of inherent risk that management can reduce through day-to-day operations and management activities.

Nonsampling Risk

The risk associated with performing inappropriate audit procedures, misapplying an appropriate procedure, or misinterpreting sampling results.

trol deviation). The most common use of attribute sampling in auditing is to evaluate the effectiveness of a particular control activity. The internal auditor tests the rate of deviation from a prescribed control activity to determine whether the occurrence rate is "acceptable" and, accordingly, whether reliance on that control activity is appropriate. Typically, the internal auditor selects a single sample of a mathematically computed size.

Stratified attribute sampling. A variation of attribute sampling from a population that can be subdivided. For example, a population of purchase transactions may be divided into those of a relatively small amount, which local managers are free to authorize, those of moderately large amounts that regional managers approve, and those of large amounts requiring central management approval. When different control activities are applied to different levels of like transactions, the different levels of transactions should be considered separately as different populations. The reason for this is simple: the levels of control effectiveness may vary when different control activities are applied.

Stop-or-go sampling. Another variation of attribute sampling. Its use is most appropriate when very low deviation rates are expected. Stop-or-go sampling is valuable in these situations, because it minimizes the required sample size for a specified level of sampling risk. An initial, relatively small, sample is drawn and analyzed. The internal auditor then decides, based on the results of this initial sample, whether the sample size should be increased. If a sufficiently low number of deviations are found in the initial sample, the internal auditor stops sampling and formulates his or her conclusion. If more than a sufficiently low number of deviations are found, more sample items are drawn and analyzed before a conclusion is reached.

Attribute Sampling

A statistical sampling approach that reaches a conclusion about a population in terms of a rate of occurrence.

Discovery sampling. A third variation of attribute sampling. The sample is designed to be large enough to detect at least one deviation if the rate of deviations in the population is at or above a specified rate. A statistical sample is drawn in a manner that enables the internal auditor to test the likelihood of finding at least one deviation. This sampling approach is used most commonly to test for fraud. Its use is appropriate when the expected deviation rate is very low and the internal auditor wants to design a sample based on a specified probability of finding one occurrence. Due to the context in which it is applied and the nature of the potential deviations being investigated, discovery sampling sample sizes are generally much larger than those used in regular attribute sampling applications.

Designing an Attribute Sampling Plan, Executing the Plan, and Evaluating the Sample Results

Attribute sampling involves the following nine steps:

1. Identify a specific internal control objective and the prescribed control activity(ies) aimed at achieving that objective.
2. Define what is meant by a control deviation.
3. Define the population and sampling unit.

4. Determine the appropriate values of the parameters affecting sample size.

5. Determine the appropriate sample size.

6. Randomly select the sample.

7. Audit the sample items selected and count the number of deviations from the prescribed control activity.

8. Determine the achieved upper deviation limit.

9. Evaluate the sample results.

Each of these steps is described here with the following hypothetical situation used as the context for illustrating each step:

An internal auditor has been instructed to use statistical sampling in her tests of control activities over materials acquisitions. The specific audit objective of interest is to determine whether all purchases of materials have been properly authorized.

Step 1: Identify a specific internal control objective and the prescribed control activity(ies) aimed at achieving that objective.

The specified audit objective is the key factor in determining what is to be sampled. The audit objective expressed in our illustrative situation above is to determine whether all purchases of materials have been properly authorized. This audit objective pertains to the business objective of validity. Management wants to be confident that all purchases are valid—in other words, that no unauthorized purchases have been made. The internal control objective pertaining to this objective is to provide reasonable assurance that management's objective is achieved—specifically, that all purchases are, in fact, properly authorized. Carefully defining the control objective and the control activity aimed at achieving that objective is very important. If the internal auditor does not do this, there is a risk of performing inappropriate audit procedures and, consequently, drawing inappropriate conclusions. This is an example of nonsampling risk.

For the illustrative example, assume that the company's materials acquisition policies specify that purchases of materials are initiated by authorized warehouse personnel preparing formal written requests (purchase requisitions) for the materials needed. Approved purchase requisitions are forwarded to the purchasing department, where they serve as authorization to order the materials requested. The purchasing department prepares prenumbered purchase orders, which become part of the trail of documentary evidence supporting purchase transactions. The internal auditor decides to test on a sample basis whether purchase orders prepared during the past 12 months, are in fact, supported by properly approved purchase requisitions.

Step 2: Define what is meant by a control deviation.

Carefully defining what is meant by a deviation from a prescribed control activity (in other words, the control attribute of interest) is just as important as carefully defining the control objective and control procedure. If the internal auditor fails to do this, there is a risk of not recognizing a deviation, which is another example of nonsampling risk.

In the illustrative example, the internal auditor wants to make sure that purchase orders are supported by properly approved purchase requisitions. A deviation from the prescribed control would include any one of the following: a missing purchase requisition, no evidence of a purchase requisition approval, approval by an unauthorized person, or a difference between the item purchased per the purchase order and the item requested per the purchase requisition.

Step 3: Define the population and sampling unit.

As stated in Step 1, the audit objective in this case is to test the validity of purchase orders. Vouching tests the validity of recorded information. It is applied by testing backward to determine whether information in a document is supported by information in previously prepared documents.

The population of interest to the internal auditor in this case is the population of prenumbered purchase orders prepared during the past 12 months. The sampling unit is each purchase order that is tested to determine whether it is supported by a properly approved purchase requisition. To test whether each purchase order is supported by a properly approved purchase requisition, the internal auditor will vouch each purchase order to the corresponding purchase requisition.

Why would it be inappropriate in this case for the internal auditor to trace purchase orders forward to determine whether a corresponding purchase order was prepared? Remember the audit objective—to determine whether purchase orders are supported by properly approved purchase requisitions. If the internal auditor selects a sample of purchase requisitions and traces them forward to subsequently prepared purchase orders, there is absolutely no chance of uncovering a situation in which a purchase requisition was not prepared for an existing purchase order.

Step 4: Determine the appropriate values of the parameters affecting sample size.

In attribute sampling, the internal auditor must specify, using audit judgment, the appropriate values for three factors affecting sample size:

- The acceptable risk of assessing control risk too low.
- The tolerable deviation rate.
- The expected population deviation rate.

Note that the size of the population has little effect on attribute sample size unless the population is very small. Statistically calculated sample sizes will increase nominally for populations ranging from 500 to 5,000 items and not increase at all for populations exceeding 5,000. The statistically derived sample size tables used below are based on large population sizes. It is, therefore, conservative to use these tables for populations less than 5,000. It may be appropriate, however, for an internal auditor to consider population size for audit efficiency purposes if a control activity is applied infrequently (for example, no more than once per day).

Assume for the example above that the population contains 2,500 individual purchase orders.

The acceptable risk of assessing control risk too low. Recall that the risk of assessing control risk too low is the risk that the internal auditor will incorrectly conclude that a specified control activity is more effective than it really is. The risk of assessing control risk too low is inversely related to sample size; in other words, the lower the acceptable level of risk, the larger the sample size.

The internal auditor's judgment about the acceptable level of assessing control risk too low is based on how confident the internal auditor wants to be in drawing a correct inference about the operating effectiveness of the control procedure being tested. In fact, the risk of assessing control risk too low is the complement of confidence (for example, if the internal auditor chooses to specify a 5% risk of assessing control risk to low, the internal auditor is indicating that 95% confidence in drawing a correct conclusion is desired). The two most commonly used levels of acceptable risk of assessing control risk too low are 5% and 10%. For our case, assume the internal auditor decides to set the acceptable level of control risk at 10%. (Note: The risk of assessing control risk too high is not explicitly controlled in determining the appropriate sample size for an attribute sampling application.)

The tolerable deviation rate. This rate is the maximum rate of deviations the internal auditor is willing to accept and still conclude that the control activity is acceptably effective (in other words, that the control activity can be relied upon to reduce residual risk to an acceptably low level). The tolerable deviation rate is inversely related to sample size.

The internal auditor's judgment about the tolerable deviation rate is based on the relative importance of the control activity being tested. If, for example, the internal auditor deems the control activity to be critical, a low tolerable deviation rate will be set. Assume for the example that the tolerable deviation rate is set at 5%.

The expected population deviation rate. This is the internal auditor's best estimate of the actual deviation rate in the population of items being examined. The expected population deviation rate has a direct effect on sample size. However, this rate will be less than the tolerable rate, or the internal auditor will not conduct the attribute sampling application being considered. Internal auditors refer to the difference between the tolerable deviation rate and the expected population deviation rate as the *planned allowance for sampling risk* or *planned precision*.

If the internal auditor has previously used attribute sampling to test the effectiveness of a particular control activity, an appropriate expected population deviation rate would be the one used in the prior audit, adjusted for any known changes in the application of the control activity. Otherwise, the internal auditor might select and audit a small pre-sample to determine the expected population deviation rate. As-

Risk of Assessing Control Risk Too Low

The risk that the internal auditor will incorrectly conclude that a specified control activity is more effective than it really is.

EXHIBIT 9-8

Tolerable Deviation Rate

The maximum rate of deviations the internal auditor is willing to accept and still conclude that the control activity is acceptably effective.

sume for the example that the internal auditor estimates the population deviation rate to be 1%.

Step 5: Determine the appropriate sample size.

Once the internal auditor has assigned the values of the factors affecting sample size, the easiest way to determine the appropriate sample size is to refer to readily available sample-size tables such as those presented in Exhibit 9-8.

The internal auditor in the example has set the risk of assessing control risk too low at 10%, the tolerable deviation rate at 5%, and the estimated population deviation rate at 1%. Exhibit 9-8 shows that the appropriate sample size is 77. The internal auditor might round the sample size up to 80 for reasons discussed in the following text.

Note that this calculation of sample size illustrates a key benefit of statistical sampling. If the internal auditor wanted to be 100% confident

ATTRIBUTE SAMPLING SAMPLE SIZE TABLES

5% Risk of Assessing Control Risk Too Low

Expected Population Deviation Rate (%)	Tolerable Deviation Rate (Number of Expected Errors)								
	2%	3%	4%	5%	6%	7%	8%	9%	10%
0.00	149(0)	99(0)	74(0)	59(0)	49(0)	42(0)	36(0)	32(0)	29(0)
0.50	——	157(1)	117(1)	93(1)	78(1)	66(1)	58(1)	51(1)	46(1)
1.00	——	——	156(2)	93(1)	78(1)	66(1)	58(1)	51(1)	46(1)
1.50	——	——	192(3)	124(4)	103(1)	66(1)	58(1)	51(1)	46(1)
2.00	——	——	——	181(4)	127(3)	88(2)	77(2)	68(2)	46(1)
2.50	——	——	——	——	150(4)	109(0)	36(0)	32(0)	29(0)
3.00	——	——	——	——	195(6)	129(4)	95(3)	84(3)	61(2)
4.00	——	——	——	——	——	——	146(6)	100(4)	89(4)
5.00	——	——	——	——	——	——	——	158(8)	116(6)
6.00	——	——	——	——	——	——	——	——	179(11)

10% Risk of Assessing Control Risk Too Low

Expected Population Deviation Rate (%)	Tolerable Deviation Rate (Number of Expected Errors)								
	2%	3%	4%	5%	6%	7%	8%	9%	10%
0.00	114(0)	76(0)	57(0)	45(0)	38(0)	32(0)	28(0)	25(0)	22(0)
0.50	194(0)	129(1)	96(1)	77(1)	64(1)	55(1)	48(1)	42(1)	38(1)
1.00	——	176(2)	96(1)	77(1)	64(1)	55(1)	48(1)	42(1)	38(1)
1.50	——	——	132(2)	105(2)	64(0)	55(1)	48(1)	42(1)	38(1)
2.00	——	——	198(4)	132(3)	88(2)	75(2)	48(1)	42(1)	38(1)
2.50	——	——	——	158(4)	110(3)	75(2)	65(2)	58(2)	38(1)
3.00	——	——	——	——	132(4)	94(3)	65(2)	58(2)	52(2)
4.00	——	——	——	——	——	149(6)	98(4)	73(3)	65(3)
5.00	——	——	——	——	——	——	160(8)	115(6)	78(4)
6.00	——	——	——	——	——	——	——	182(11)	116(7)

—— Sample size is too large to be cost-effective for most audit applications.

Note: These tables assume a large population.

Copyright 1992 by the AICPA, reproduced with permission.

in the conclusion reached about the validity of purchase orders, 100% of them would have to be vouched; however, conclusion with 90% confidence (the complement of 10% risk of assessing control risk too low) can be reached based on the sample results of vouching 80 purchase orders.

Step 6: Randomly select the sample.

When applying sampling in tests of controls, it is important that items from the entire period under audit have a chance of being selected. When applying statistical sampling, it is also very important that the internal auditor use a random-based selection technique (in other words, each item in the defined population must have an equal opportunity of being selected). The two most common approaches used to select random attribute samples are simple random sampling and systematic sampling with one or more random starts.

Simple random sampling. Simple random sampling generally is the easiest approach when sampling prenumbered documents. Using a random number table is one way for the internal auditor to achieve randomness. Another way is to use a computerized random number generator program.

Systematic sampling with one or more random starts. In this approach, the internal auditor randomly identifies a starting point and then selects every n^{th} item after that. Systematic sampling is appropriate when there is no reason to believe that the equal intervals will systematically bias the sample. To reduce the likelihood of selecting a biased sample, internal auditors will sometimes select multiple random starting points. Internal auditors most commonly use systematic selection when individual items of the population are not prenumbered.

In the example used in this chapter, the purchase orders are prenumbered, so the internal auditor decides to use a computerized random number generator program to select a random sample of purchase orders prepared during the past 12 months. The 12-month period covers the last three months of the preceding fiscal year and the first nine months of the current fiscal year. Note that it is not always feasible, in terms of timing, for an internal auditor to draw a sample covering one entire fiscal year. The internal auditor needs to take this into consideration when evaluating sample results.

Step 7: Audit the sample items selected and count the number of deviations from the prescribed control activity.

In the example, the internal auditor vouches each purchase order in the sample to the corresponding purchase requisition. Each purchase requisition is inspected for evidence of approval by an authorized person and correspondence of the item purchased per the purchase order with the item requested per the purchase requisition. Assume two possible outcomes: (1) the internal auditor finds one deviation, and (2) the internal auditor finds two deviations (in other words, two cases where no purchase requisition was found for the purchase order in the sample).

Expected Population Deviation Rate

The internal auditor's best estimate of the actual deviation rate in the population of items being examined.

Random Sample Selection

Ensuring that each item in the defined population has an equal opportunity of being selected.

Step 8: Determine the achieved upper deviation limit.

Internal auditors use attribute sampling evaluation tables such as those presented in Exhibit 9-9 to determine the achieved upper deviation limit for an attribute sampling application.

The upper deviation limits for the two possible outcomes indicated would be:

Number of Sample Deviations	Upper Deviation Limit
1	4.8%
2	6.6%

The reason why it was indicated above in Step 5 that the internal auditor might round the determined sample size of 77 up to 80 is now apparent—the tables presented in Exhibit 9-9 do not contain upper deviation limits for every possible sample size. Rounding the sample size up to the next number in the evaluation table is conservative. An alternative approach would be to audit a sample of 77 items and calculate the achieved upper deviation limit using interpolation.

Step 9: Evaluate the sample results.

Evaluating the results of an attribute sampling application involves:

- Formulating a statistical conclusion.
- Making an audit decision based on the quantitative sample results.
- Considering qualitative aspects of the sample results.

Formulating a statistical conclusion. A key advantage of statistical sampling over nonstatistical sampling is that statistical sampling enables the internal auditor to quantify, measure, and control sampling risk. In attribute sampling, the internal auditor explicitly controls the risk of assessing control risk too low, which is the complement of confidence. In the example, the internal auditor specified a 10% risk of assessing control risk too low, and this value was used to determine the appropriate sample size. When determining the achieved upper deviation limit for the example, refer to the table for a 10% risk of assessing control risk too low.

The internal auditor's best estimate of the deviation rate in the population for the first hypothetical outcome of 1 sample deviation is $1/80 = 1.25\%$. The internal auditor's best estimate of population deviation rate for the second hypothetical outcome of 2 sample deviations is $2/80 = 2.5\%$. However, there is uncertainty in these estimates due to the fact that the internal auditor performed the audit procedure on a sample basis as opposed to testing 100%. In other words, the internal auditor cannot conclude with certainty that the population deviation rate is 1.25% or 2.5%.

For hypothetical outcome number 1 (one sample deviation), the internal auditor can express the statistical conclusion:

I am 90% confident that the true, but unknown, population deviation rate is less than or equal to 4.8%.

For hypothetical outcome number 2 (two sample deviations) the internal auditor can express the statistical conclusion:

I am 90% confident that the true, but unknown, population deviation rate is less than or equal to 6.6%.

Note that the difference between the best estimate of the population

EXHIBIT 9-9

ATTRIBUTE SAMPLING EVALUATION TABLES
(Upper Deviation Limits)
5% Risk of Assessing Control Risk Too Low

Sample Size	Actual Number of Deviations Found								
	0	1	2	3	4	5	6	7	8
25	11.3	17.6	——	——	——	——	——	——	——
30	9.5	14.9	19.6	——	——	——	——	——	——
35	8.3	12.9	17.0	——	——	——	——	——	——
40	7.3	11.4	15.0	18.3	——	——	——	——	——
45	6.5	10.2	13.4	16.4	19.2	——	——	——	——
50	5.9	9.2	12.1	14.8	17.4	19.9	——	——	——
55	5.4	8.4	11.1	13.5	15.9	18.2	——	——	——
60	4.9	7.7	10.2	12.5	14.7	16.8	18.8	——	——
65	4.6	7.1	9.4	11.5	13.6	15.5	17.4	19.3	——
70	4.2	6.6	8.8	10.8	12.6	14.5	16.3	18.0	19.7
75	4.0	6.2	8.2	10.1	11.8	13.6	15.2	16.9	18.5
80	3.7	5.8	7.7	9.5	11.1	12.7	14.3	15.9	17.4
90	3.3	5.2	6.9	8.4	9.9	11.4	12.8	14.2	15.5
100	3.0	4.7	6.2	7.6	9.0	10.3	11.5	12.8	14.0
125	2.4	3.8	5.0	5.1	7.2	8.3	9.3	10.3	11.3
150	2.0	3.2	4.2	5.1	6.0	6.9	7.8	8.6	9.5
200	1.5	2.4	3.2	3.9	4.6	5.2	5.9	6.5	7.2

10% Risk of Assessing Control Risk Too Low

Sample Size	Actual Number of Deviations Found								
	0	1	2	3	4	5	6	7	8
20	10.9	18.1	——	——	——	——	——	——	——
25	8.8	14.7	19.9	——	——	——	——	——	——
30	7.4	12.4	16.8	——	——	——	——	——	——
35	6.4	10.7	14.5	18.1	——	——	——	——	——
40	5.6	9.4	12.8	16.0	19.0	——	——	——	——
45	5.0	8.4	11.4	14.3	17.0	19.7	——	——	——
50	4.6	7.6	10.3	12.9	15.4	17.8	——	——	——
55	4.1	6.9	9.4	11.8	14.1	16.3	18.4	——	——
60	3.8	6.4	8.7	10.8	12.9	15.0	16.4	18.9	——
70	3.3	5.5	7.5	9.3	11.1	12.9	14.6	16.3	17.9
80	2.9	4.8	6.6	8.2	9.8	11.3	12.8	14.3	15.8
90	2.6	4.3	5.9	7.3	8.7	10.1	11.5	12.8	14.1
100	2.3	3.9	5.3	6.6	7.9	9.1	10.3	11.5	15.5
120	2.0	3.3	4.4	5.5	6.6	7.6	8.7	9.7	12.7
160	1..5	2.5	3.3	4.2	5.0	5.8	6.5	7.3	8.0
200	1.2	2.0	2.7	3.4	4.0	4.6	5.3	5.9	6.5

—— More than 20%.

deviation rate (the sample deviation rate) and the achieved upper deviation limit is referred to as the *achieved allowance for sampling risk or achieved precision*.

Making an audit decision based on the quantitative sample results.
The attribute sampling application was designed so that the internal auditor would conclude that the control activity was effective, based on the sample results, if 90% confidence could be achieved that the true, but unknown, population rate was less than or equal to 5% (the internal auditor's specified tolerable deviation rate). The first hypothetical outcome meets this test because the achieved upper deviation limit (4.8%) is less than 5%. The second hypothetical case does not meet this test because the achieved upper deviation limit (6.6%) is greater than 5%.

If the achieved upper deviation limit is less than or equal to the tolerable deviation rate, the quantitative attribute sampling results indicate that the tested control activity is effective (that is, that it can be relied upon to reduce residual risk to an acceptably low level). Conversely, if the achieved upper deviation limit is greater than the tolerable deviation rate, the quantitative results indicate that the tested control activity is not effective (in other words, that it cannot be relied upon to reduce residual risk to an acceptably low level).

At this point, the internal auditor is ready to interpret the quantitative sample results. Recall that the audit objective expressed in our illustrative situation is to determine whether all purchases of materials have been authorized properly. The internal auditor predetermined that the goal was to be 90% confident that the true, but unknown, deviation rate is less than 5%. As indicated above, the first hypothetical case meets this test, but the second does not. Accordingly, the internal auditor should conclude for the first case that the level of control effectiveness over the validity of merchandise shipments is acceptable—that is, the sample results indicate that the control activity can be relied on to reduce residual risk to an acceptably low level. For the second case, however, the internal auditor should conclude that the level of control effectiveness is not acceptable—that is, the sample results indicate that the control activity cannot be relied upon to reduce residual risk to an acceptably low level. The second case constitutes an audit observation that the internal auditor should document and include in the engagement communication.

It is important to note that the internal auditor's interpretation of the quantitative sample results pertain to the effectiveness of the control activity over the past 12 months (the last three months of the preceding fiscal year and the first nine months of the current fiscal year). It would be inappropriate for the internal auditor to draw a conclusion based on the sampling results regarding the effectiveness of the control activity over the last three months of the current fiscal year because the sample did not include purchase orders from these three months.

Considering qualitative aspects of the sample results. In addition to evaluating the quantitative attribute sampling results, the internal auditor should consider the qualitative aspects of any deviations from prescribed controls uncovered. Of particular importance is the possibility that the deviations might be the result of fraud. Assume, for example, that the quantitative sample results support the conclusion that the control activity is operating effectively. Evidence that deviations from the control activity found in the sample were caused by fraud might very well offset the quantitative results and prompt the internal auditor to conclude that the control activity is not effective (that is, that it cannot be relied upon to reduce residual risk to an acceptably low level). The internal auditor must also consider what, if any, impact the discovery of fraud might have on other aspects of the audit.

Cases of missing or voided documents. What should an internal auditor do if documents pertinent to tests of control activities are missing or have been voided? Consider the following cases:

> **Case 1.** As in the illustrative example above, the internal auditor vouches a sample of purchase orders to corresponding purchase requisitions, and two purchase requisitions cannot be found. The two missing purchase requisitions are clearly control deviations; there is no documentary evidence of authorization to prepare the two purchase orders.

> **Case 2.** The internal auditor has randomly selected purchase orders by number to be tested and finds that one of the purchase orders selected was voided. It is determined, after follow-up on the voided purchase order is done, that nothing is amiss. It would be appropriate in this case to select another purchase order for testing purposes. A significant number of voided purchases orders could be indicative of a separate problem warranting further audit attention.

> **Case 3.** The internal auditor has randomly selected purchase orders by number to be tested and finds that one of the purchase orders is missing. The internal auditor follows up on the missing purchase order and is unable to obtain a reasonable explanation for why it is missing. The internal auditor obviously cannot apply audit procedures to a selected item that cannot be found. Should this be considered a deviation from the prescribed control activity? The American Institute of Certified Public Accountants (AICPA) says yes—"If the auditor is not able to apply the planned audit procedure or appropriate alternative procedures to selected items, he should consider the reasons for this limitation, and he should ordinarily consider these selected items to be deviations from the prescribed policy or procedure for the purpose of evaluating the sample."[3] Some internal auditors disagree with this view because it is impossible to perform the prescribed test of controls to a missing document. They further argue that the missing document represents a different problem that warrants separate consideration. They would select another purchase order for testing purposes. Regardless of whether the missing purchase order is considered a deviation from the prescribed control activity or a different problem that warrants separate consideration, the internal auditor should document the missing purchase order in the working papers and decide whether it is significant enough to be written up as an audit observation.

NONSTATISTICAL AUDIT SAMPLING IN TESTS OF CONTROL ACTIVITIES

Selecting and Evaluating a Nonstatistical Sample

Statistical sampling requires two fundamental things: the sample must be selected randomly, and the sample results must be evaluated mathematically based on probability theory. Nonstatistical sampling allows the internal auditor more latitude regarding sample selection and evaluation.

However the internal auditor must still select a sample that is thought to be representative of the population, taking into consideration the factors that affect sample size. *Haphazard sampling* is a nonrandom selection technique that is used by internal auditors to select a sample that is expected to be representative of the population. Haphazard, in this context, does not mean careless or reckless. It means that the internal auditor selects the sample without deliberately deciding to include or exclude certain items.

An internal auditor using nonstatistical sampling must also project the sample results to the population. Moreover, the internal auditor must still gather sufficient competent evidence to support a valid conclusion. It is not appropriate, for example, to use nonstatistical sampling to avoid having to justify the size of the sample chosen. In fact, it can be argued that internal auditors applying nonstatistical sampling should err on the side of selecting larger samples to compensate for the less rigorous selection method and the inability to quantitatively control sampling risk.

The inability to quantify sampling risk statistically is the key feature of nonstatistical sampling that differentiates it from statistical sampling. The internal auditor's conclusion about the population from which the sample is drawn is strictly judgmental instead of being based on probability theory.

If this is true, why would internal auditors ever choose not to use statistical sampling? The answer is twofold: (1) it is not always practical in audit sampling applications to meet the stricter conditions of statistical sampling, and (2) nonstatistical sampling is generally thought to be less costly and time consuming to apply than statistical sampling.

Commonly Used Nonstatistical Sampling Approaches

One common approach to nonstatistical sampling is to select a relatively small sample haphazardly, such as 25 items for all sampling applications based on a presumption of no control deviations in the population, and to conclude that the control activity is not acceptably effective if one or more deviations are found. This approach is convenient, but also has a significant shortcoming—it does not take into consideration two of the fundamental factors internal auditors should consider when determining appropriate sample sizes: risk of assessing control risk too low and tolerable deviation rate.

To reinforce this point, take a closer look at Exhibit 9-8 (page 9-34).

Haphazard Sampling

A nonrandom selection technique that is used by internal auditors to select a sample that is expected to be representative of the population.

Where in Exhibit 9-8 is there a sample size of 25 items or fewer? The answer is only in the first row of the lower table in the last two columns. What does this mean? It means that if the internal auditor had used statistical sampling to determine the sample size, the following parameters were used: 10% risk of assessing control risk too low, 9–10% tolerable deviation rate, and 0% expected deviation rate. These are very liberal parameters that may not be appropriate across all audit sampling applications used to test the operating effectiveness of control activities.

Exhibit 9-10 illustrates a slightly more conservative approach used by some internal auditors to determine nonstatistical sample sizes. This is one firm's view of the sample sizes required to support conclusions that control activities are operating effectively if no deviations are found for samples taken from populations of varying sizes. The internal auditor adjusts the sample size within each range, taking into consideration the factors that affect sample size. If, for example, the control activity being tested is deemed to be critical and the internal auditor wants to assume less sampling risk, sample size at the high end of the relevant range will be used.

A Nonstatistical Sampling Example

Consider the following hypothetical situation:

An internal auditor has been instructed to test, on a nonstatistical sample basis, whether the bank reconciliations prepared over the past 10 months were completed correctly. The company has 10 bank accounts, all of which were reconciled over the past 10 months by the same person using a prescribed template and method. The internal auditor's expectation is that no incorrectly completed reconciliations will be found. If one or more reconciliations are found that were not completed accurately, the internal auditor will conclude that the operating effectiveness of the bank reconciliation control activity was not acceptable over the past 10 months.

Using Exhibit 9-10 as a guide, how many bank reconciliations should

ILLUSTRATIVE NONSTATISTICAL SAMPLE SIZES	
Frequency of Control Application	**Appropriate Sample Size**
Annually	1
Quarterly	2
Monthly	2 to 5
Weekly	5 to 15
Daily	20 to 40
Multiple times per day	25 to 60

Source: Adapted from Sarbanes-Oxley Act: Section 404 – Practical Guidance for Management, PricewaterhouseCoopers, July 2004, p. 61.

EXHIBIT 9-10

the internal auditor test? The internal auditor could reasonably decide to test two to five reconciliations for each bank account since the accounts are reconciled monthly. This approach would require the internal auditor to reach a separate conclusion for each account. Another reasonable approach would be to consider the 100 bank reconciliations as one population, because the reconciliations for the 10 accounts are subject to the same control activities. In this case, the proper sample size range per Exhibit 9-10 falls between the ranges prescribed for control activities applied weekly and control activities applied daily. They might logically decide, in this case, to test 20 to 25 of the 100 bank reconciliations. This approach allows the internal auditor to reach one overall conclusion. Care must be taken, however, to select a sample that can be expected to be representative of the population. Consequently, haphazardly selecting sample items across the entire population of 100 bank reconciliations would be appropriate.

Assume the internal auditor haphazardly selects 25 bank reconciliations. After properly testing the 25 reconciliations, it is determined that each reconciliation was performed correctly. What can the internal auditor conclude? A statistical conclusion about the population of 100 bank reconciliations cannot be expressed, but it would be appropriate to say that the sample result supports the conclusion that bank reconciliations were performed correctly (that is, that the bank reconciliation control was acceptably effective) over the past 10 months.

Assume instead that the internal auditor finds that one of the 25 reconciliations was not performed correctly, which is inconsistent with the expectation that none would be found. Now what should be concluded? Because a control deviation was found, the internal auditor should conclude that the bank reconciliation control activity was not acceptably effective over the past 10 months. This constitutes an observation that the internal auditor should document and include in the engagement communication.

STATISTICAL SAMPLING IN TESTS OF MONETARY VALUES

In addition to using sampling within the context of testing control activities, internal auditors also apply sampling when performing tests designed to obtain direct evidence about the correctness of monetary values—for example, the recorded value of an account balance such as inventory. When performing tests of monetary values, the internal auditor is concerned with two aspects of sampling risk:

The risk of incorrect acceptance (Type II risk, beta risk). This is the risk that the sample supports the conclusion that a recorded value (for example, an account balance) is not materially misstated when it is.

The risk of incorrect rejection (Type I risk, alpha risk). This is the risk that the sample supports the conclusion that a recorded amount (for example, an account balance) is materially misstated when it is not.

Probability-proportional-to-size Sampling

Probability-proportional-to-size (PPS) sampling, also called monetary-unit sampling or dollar-unit sampling, is a modified form of attribute sampling that is used to reach a conclusion in dollar amounts rather than rates of occurrence. PPS sampling is primarily applicable for testing recorded dollar amounts for overstatement, especially when the expected number of individual overstatements in the population is small. It is not likely to be a cost-effective sampling approach if these conditions are not met.

Selecting the sample. As with attribute sampling, it is very important in PPS sampling that the sample be randomly selected—that is, each item in the defined population should have an equal opportunity of being selected. The population in a PPS sampling application is the population of individual dollars contained in the particular account being tested. The sampling unit is the individual dollar. The internal auditor uses a systematic sampling approach to select every nth dollar in the population after a random start. However, the individual dollars selected are not the items of audit interest. The items of interest are the "logical units" containing the individual dollars. A logical unit might be, for example, a specific item of inventory recorded in the inventory records. Larger logical units are more apt to be selected for testing than smaller logical units. In fact, the likelihood of a logical unit being selected is proportional to its size—thus the name probability-proportional-to-size sampling.

The following factors affect PPS sample sizes:

- **Monetary book value of the population.** The book value of the population (for example, the recorded total value of year-end inventory) has a direct effect on sample size.

- **Risk of incorrect acceptance.** The risk of incorrect acceptance was defined above as the risk that the sample supports the conclusion that a recorded value (for example, the recorded inventory balance) is not materially misstated when it is materially misstated. The risk of incorrect acceptance is a component of sampling risk and has an inverse effect on sample size.

- **Tolerable misstatement.** Tolerable misstatement is the maximum misstatement than can exist in the recorded value before the internal auditor considers it materially misstated. It has an inverse effect on sample size.

- **Anticipated misstatement.** Anticipated or expected misstatement is the amount of misstatement the internal auditor expects there to be in the recorded value. It has a direct effect on sample size.

Evaluating the sample results. After selecting and auditing the sample, an internal auditor, using PPS sampling, extrapolates the sample results to the population, formulates a statistical conclusion, and determines whether the quantitative and qualitative sample evidence indicates that the recorded monetary value is fairly stated or materially misstated. A description of how an internal auditor performs these steps is beyond the scope of this textbook.

Probability-Proportional-to-Size (PPS) Sampling

A modified form of attribute sampling that is used by internal auditors to reach a conclusion in dollar amounts rather than rates of occurrence.

Classical Variables Sampling

Classical variables sampling is based on normal distribution theory. It generally is considered more difficult to apply than PPS sampling, largely because it involves much more complex calculations in determining appropriate sample sizes and evaluating sample results.

Selecting the sample. Again, it is very important in classical variables sampling that the sample be randomly selected. The two approaches used to select random classical variable samples are simple random sampling and systematic sampling with a random start.

The following factors affect classical variable sample sizes:

- **Population size.** The population size is the number of items in the population (for example, the number of different inventory items recorded in the accounting records). It has a direct effect on sample size.

- **Estimated population standard deviation.** The estimated population standard deviation, a measure of population variability, has a direct effect on sample size.

- **Risk of incorrect acceptance.** The risk of incorrect acceptance was defined above as the risk that the sample supports the conclusion that a recorded value (for example, the recorded inventory balance) is not materially misstated when it is materially misstated. The risk of incorrect acceptance is a component of sampling risk and has an inverse effect on sample size.

- **Risk of incorrect rejection.** The risk of incorrect rejection was defined above as the risk that the sample supports the conclusion that a recorded value (for example, the recorded inventory balance) is materially misstated when it is not materially misstated. The risk of incorrect rejection, the second component of sampling risk, has an inverse effect on sample size.

- **Tolerable misstatement.** Tolerable misstatement is the maximum misstatement than can exist in the recorded value before the internal auditor considers it materially misstated. It has an inverse effect on sample size.

Evaluating the sample results. As with PPS sampling, after selecting and auditing the sample, an internal auditor using classical variables sampling extrapolates the sample results to the population, formulates a statistical conclusion, and determines whether the quantitative and qualitative sample evidence indicates that the recorded monetary value is fairly stated or materially misstated. The sample evaluation process is more complex for classical variables sampling than for PPS sampling. A description of how an internal auditor performs the evaluation process is beyond the scope of this textbook.

Probability-proportional-to-size Sampling Versus Classical Variables Sampling

Both PPS sampling and classical variables sampling have significant advantages and disadvantages that internal auditors must consider when choosing which approach is best for a particular sampling appli-

EXHIBIT 9-11

PROBABILITY-PROPORTIONAL-TO-SIZE SAMPLING VS. CLASSICAL VARIABLES SAMPLING

Probability-proportional-to-size Sampling

Key advantages:
- Simpler calculations make PPS sampling easier to use.
- The sample size calculation does not involve any measure of estimated population variation.
- PPS sampling automatically results in a stratified sample because sample items are selected in proportion to their size.
- PPS sample selection automatically identifies any individually significant population items—that is, population items exceeding a predetermined cutoff dollar amount.
- PPS sampling generally is more efficient (that is, requires a smaller sample size) when the population contains zero or very few misstatements.

Key disadvantages:
- Special design considerations are required when understatements or audit values less than zero are expected.
- Identification of understatements in the sample requires special evaluation considerations.
- PPS sampling produces overly conservative results when errors are detected. This increases the risk of incorrect rejection.
- The appropriate sample size increases quickly as the number of expected misstatements increases. When more than a few misstatements are expected, PPS sampling may be less efficient.

Classical Variables Sampling

Key advantages:
- Samples are generally easier to expand if the internal auditor should find it necessary.
- Zero balances and negative balances do not require special sample design considerations.
- The internal auditor's objective may be met with a smaller sample size if there is a large number of misstatements—that is, differences between audit values and recorded values.

Key disadvantages:
- Classical variables sampling is more complex. The internal auditor may need to use a computer program to cost-effectively design and evaluate a sample.
- Calculation of the proper sample size requires that the internal auditor first estimate the population standard deviation.

cation. Exhibit 9-11 presents the key advantages and disadvantages of each approach.

SUMMARY

This is the first of four chapters referred to as Internal Audit Processes chapters (page 9-1). This chapter focused on gathering and documenting audit evidence. It began with a high-level introduction to the activities involved in planning and performing an internal assurance engagement and reporting engagement outcomes. The second section covered audit evidence and the procedures, both manual procedures and computer-assisted audit techniques, that internal auditors use to gather sufficient competent evidence. The third section addressed working papers, which serve as the principal record of the procedures completed, evidence obtained, conclusions reached, and recommendations formulated by the internal audit team during the engagement. The chapter concluded with a relatively in-depth discussion of how to apply both statistical and nonstatistical audit sampling in tests of controls and a brief overview of two statistical sampling approaches internal auditors use when testing monetary values.

1. Explain why it is critically important to obtain a thorough understanding of the auditee.

2. Define *inherent risk*.

3. Explain why it is useful for an internal auditor to express risks in terms of causes and effects.

4. Why must an internal auditor consider both the "design adequacy" and "operating effectiveness" of key control activities?

5. What purposes does a well-written work program serve?

6. Briefly describe the key elements of an audit observation.

7. What are the key quality characteristics of internal audit engagement communications?

8. Explain the difference between "negative assurance" and "positive assurance."

9. Define *professional skepticism*.

10. What are the defining characteristics of persuasive audit evidence?

11. Explain the relationship between audit objectives and audit procedures.

12. Explain the difference between vouching and tracing.

13. Identify the different types of analytical procedures used by internal auditors.

14. What are some examples of the things that internal auditors can do with generalized audit software?

15. Explain the purposes of internal audit working papers.

16. Describe the key characteristics of well-prepared working papers.

17. Define "audit sampling."

18. List the steps involved in attribute sampling.

19. Identify and define the factors that affect the size of an attribute sample.

20. Explain the steps involved in evaluating the results of an attribute sampling application.

21. Explain what an internal auditor should do if documents pertinent to tests of control activities are missing.

22. What is the key advantage of statistical sampling over nonstatistical sampling?

23. Explain how the purpose of statistical sampling in tests of monetary values differs from the purpose of statistical sampling in tests of control activities.

Select the best answer for each of the following questions.

1. The tasks performed during an internal audit of a business process should address the following questions:

   1. What are the reasons for the results?
   2. How can performance be improved?
   3. What results are being achieved?

   The chronological order in which these questions should be addressed is:

   a. 3, 1, 2.
   b. 1, 3, 2.
   c. 3, 2, 1.
   d. 2, 3, 1.

2. Reported internal audit observations emerge by a process of comparing "what should be" with "what is." In determining "what should be" during an audit of a company's treasury function, which of the following would be the least desirable criterion against which to judge current operations?

   a. Best practices of the treasury function in relevant industries.
   b. Company policies and procedures delegating authority and assigning responsibilities.
   c. Performance standards established by senior management.
   d. The operations of the treasury function as documented during the last audit.

3. Audit evidence is generally considered sufficient when:

   a. It is competent.
   b. There is enough of it to support well-founded conclusions.
   c. It is relevant, reliable, and free from bias.
   d. It has been obtained via random sampling.

4. Documentary evidence is one of the principal types of corroborating information used by an internal auditor. Which one of the following examples of documentary evidence generally is considered the most reliable?

   a. A vendor's invoice obtained from the accounts payable department.
   b. A credit memorandum prepared by the credit manager.
   c. A receiving report obtained from the receiving department.
   d. A copy of a sales invoice prepared by the sales department.

5. The internal auditor compares the inventory turnover rate of a company subsidiary with established industry standards during the planning stage of an assurance engagement focused on operational objectives to:

   a. Evaluate the accuracy of the subsidiary's internal financial reports.
   b. Test the subsidiary's control activities designed to safeguard assets.
   c. Determine if the subsidiary is complying with organizational procedures regarding inventory levels.
   d. Assess the performance of the subsidiary and indicate where additional engagement work may be needed.

6. An internal auditor must weigh the cost of an audit procedure against the persuasiveness of the evidence to be gathered. Observation is one audit procedure that involves cost-benefit trade-offs. Which of the following statements regarding observation as an audit procedure is (are) correct?

    1. Observation is limited because individuals may react differently when being watched.

    2. Observation is more effective for testing completeness than it is for testing existence.

    3. Observation provides evidence about whether operating activities are aligned with prescribed policies.

    a. 1 only.

    b. 2 only.

    c. 1 and 3.

    d. 1, 2, and 3.

7. An internal auditor is concerned that fraud, in the form of payments to fictitious vendors, may exist. Company purchasers, responsible for purchases of specific product lines, have been granted the authority to approve expenditures up to $10,000. Which of the following applications of generalized audit software would be most effective in addressing the auditor's concern?

    a. List all purchases over $10,000 to determine whether they were properly approved.

    b. Take a random sample of all expenditures under $10,000 to determine whether they were properly approved.

    c. List all major vendors by product line. Select a sample of major vendors and examine supporting documentation for goods or services received.

    d. List all major vendors by product line. Select a sample of major vendors and confirm with them that they actually provided goods or services.

8. Which of the following most completely describes the appropriate content of internal audit engagement working papers:

    a. Objectives, procedures, and conclusions.

    b. Purpose, criteria, techniques, and conclusions.

    c. Objectives, procedures, facts, conclusions, and recommendations.

    d. Subject, purpose, sampling information, and analysis.

9. The primary reason for an internal auditor to use statistical sampling rather than nonstatistical sampling is to:

    a. Allow the auditor to quantify, and therefore control, the risk of making an incorrect decision based on sample evidence.

    b. Obtain a smaller sample than would be required if nonstatistical sampling were used.

    c. Reduce the problems associated with the auditor's judgment concerning the competency of the evidence gathered when nonstatistical sampling is used.

    d. Obtain a sample more representative of the population than would be obtained if nonstatistical sampling techniques were used.

10. An internal auditor selects a sample of sales invoices and matches them with shipping documents. This procedure most directly addresses which of the following assertions?

    a. All shipments to customers are recorded as receivables.

    b. All billed sales are for goods shipped to customers.

    c. All debits to the accounts receivable subsidiary ledger are for goods shipped to customers.

    d. All shipments to customers are billed.

11. If all other factors specified in an attribute sampling plan remain constant, changing the expected population deviation rate from 1% to 2% and changing the tolerable deviation rate from 7% to 6% would cause the required sample size to:

    a. Increase.

    b. Decrease.

    c. Remain the same.

    d. Change by 2%.

DISCUSSION QUESTIONS

1. In anticipation of an upcoming engagement, an internal audit team of CEF Co. recently toured the company's receiving, warehousing, and production facilities to obtain a better understanding of day-to-day operations. Listed below are selected items noted by the audit team during the tour:

- A large quantity of materials was sitting in a corner near the unloading docks. The receiving manager informed the audit team that the delivery trucks had already left. The materials had not yet been counted or inspected.

- One section of the warehouse contained large quantities of items with inventory tags from several physical inventory counts. The warehouse manager told the audit team that this was the company's inventory of spare parts that it was required by law to keep on hand for specified time periods.

- Hazardous chemicals are used in the inventory finishing process. Waste chemicals are stored in large plastic barrels in a designated area of the factory before being shipped for disposal.

Required: For each item noted by the audit team:

    a. Describe the potential business risk(s) associated with the item.

    b. Discuss how the auditors' knowledge of the risks identified might affect a subsequent audit of the materials acquisition and production processes.

2. AVF Inc. manufactures several lines of packaging equipment. The company considers product reliability and outstanding customer service to be critical to its success. The customer service department is responsible for:

- Providing prospective customers with product information.

- Monitoring spare parts availability.

- Providing equipment operating and maintenance information to customers.

- Developing and delivering customer training courses.

- Responding to customer complaints and making service calls.
- Handling customer warranty claims.
- Maintaining good customer relations.

The company recently made a sizeable investment to upgrade its customer service department computer system. The upgrade is expected to improve operational efficiency and customer satisfaction. The outputs of the new system include management reports used to monitor performance in the areas listed above. The audit committee has asked the internal audit function to audit the operational effectiveness and efficiency of the customer service department that covers the following areas:

- Security of assets, including information.
- Compliance with applicable laws and company policies.
- Reliability of financial records.
- Effectiveness of performing assigned responsibilities.
- Valuation of the spare parts inventory.

Required:

a. Discuss why each of the five areas specified by the audit committee may or may not be appropriate for this assurance engagement.

b. Identify three other areas of the customer service department that may warrant the internal auditor's attention.

c. What are the primary audit tasks the internal auditors should perform to evaluate the operational effectiveness and efficiency of the customer service department in meeting the following responsibilities?

- Developing and delivering customer training courses.
- Responding to customer complaints and making service calls.
- Handling customer warranty claims.

3. The following information is available for MVF Co. (dollar amounts are in millions):

	2007	2006	2005	2004
Net sales	$23.2	$21.7	$19.6	$17.4
Cost of goods sold	17.1	16.8	15.2	13.5
Beginning finished goods inventory	2.3	2.1	1.9	1.5
Ending finished goods inventory	2.9	2.3	2.1	1.9
Materials purchased	10.6	8.8	7.5	7.1

Required:

a. Calculate the following ratios for each year:

- Gross profit percentage.
- Inventory turnover.
- Cost of materials purchased to cost of finished goods produced.

b. Analyze the results obtained in a above.

- Describe the change in each ratio you observe in 2007.
- Discuss at least two possible causes of each change observed.

4. All of Kola Co. sales are credit sales shipped Free on Board (FOB) shipping point. Kola typically records sales transactions (that is, sales and cost of sales) throughout the year on the billing date. The internal auditor gathered the following information and documented it in his working papers.

Invoice Number	Date Shipped	Date Billed
8351	12/28/2006	12/29/2006
8352	12/29/2006	1/2/2007
8353	1/2/2007	12/31/2006
8354	1/2/2007	1/3/2007

Required:

a. Describe the specific audit procedures that should be performed to determine whether sales transactions occurring immediately before and after year-end are recorded in the proper period.

b. Record the adjusting journal entries (ignore dollar amounts) the internal auditor should propose based on the cutoff information documented above. Include a clear and concise explanation for each proposed entry.

5. A staff internal auditor found the following possible deviations from prescribed control activities and documented them in her working papers.

Invoice Number	Prescribed Control Activity	Possible Deviation
248	Written authorizations of sales by sales order department.	Verbal authorization by phone by sales order department.
333	Verification of sales order quantities and prices.	No evidence of verification; quantities and prices are incorrect.
377	Verification of sales order quantities and prices.	No evidence of verification, but quantities and prices are correct.
617	Billing department verification of unit prices.	Price verification indicated on invoice; by reperformance, you ascertain that the prices do not agree with the price list in effect at the time of sale.

Required: For each of the items listed above, indicate whether there is or is not a deviation from a prescribed control activity. Briefly explain each answer.

6. AVF Company processes an average of 400 vouchers payable every month. Each voucher package contains a copy of the check disbursed and supporting documents such as vendor invoices, receiving reports, and purchase orders. The internal auditor plans to examine a sample of vouchers listed in the voucher register using attribute sampling to evaluate the effectiveness of several control activities. The attributes of interest include the following:

● Agreement of voucher amounts with invoice amounts.

- Voucher canceled after payment.

Based on past experience, the auditor expects a deviation rate of 2% for the first attribute and 1% for the second. He decides on a tolerable deviation rate of 7% for the first attribute and 6% for the second. He sets the risk of assessing control risk too low at 5%.

Assume that the auditor's tests uncovered two occurrences of voucher amounts not agreeing with invoice amounts and two occurrences of vouchers not being canceled after payment.

Required:

a. Complete the following schedule. (Note: Round sample size per table up to next number ending in zero for sample size used.)

	Attribute 1	Attribute 2
Risk of assessing control risk too low		
Tolerable deviation rate		
Expected population deviation rate		
Sample size per table		
Sample size used		
Number of deviations uncovered		
Sample deviation rate		
Achieved upper deviation limit		

b. Evaluate the sample results for the two attributes. Your answer should include:

- A statistical conclusion for each attribute.
- The audit decision you would make based on the quantitative sample results for each attribute. [9]

REFERENCES

[1] Information Systems Audit Control Association, Guideline-Use of Computer Assisted Audit Techniques (CAATs) (Document G3), (Rolling Meadows, IL: Information Systems Audit Control Association). Available at: http://www.isaca.org/AMTemplate.cfm?Section=Standards_Guidelines,_Procedures_for_IS_Auditing&Template=/ContentManagement/ContentDisplay.cfm&ContentID=18546 (as of February 19, 2007).

[2] American Institute of Certified Public Accountants, Audit and Accounting Guide: Audit Sampling (New York, NY: American Institute of Certified Public Accountants, 1992), p. 24.

[3] American Institute of Certified Public Accountants, AU Section 350, Audit Sampling, paragraph 40, (New York, NY: American Institute of Certified Public Accountants). Available at: http://www.aicpa.org/download/members/div/auditstd/AU-00350.PDF. (as of February 19, 2007).

[4] Adapted from: Ratliff, Richard L. and Kurt F. Reding, Introduction to Auditing: Logic, Principles, and Techniques, (Altamonte Springs, FL: The Institute of Internal Auditors, 2002).

[5] Adapted from: Protiviti, Senior Audit School Participant Guide, (Protiviti, Inc., 2006).

[6] Adapted from: Protiviti, Senior Audit School Participant Guide, (Protiviti, Inc., 2006).

[7] Adapted from: Ratliff, Richard L. and Kurt F. Reding, Introduction to Auditing: Logic, Principles, and Techniques, (Altamonte Springs, FL: The Institute of Internal Auditors, 2002).

[8] Adapted from: Ratliff, Richard L. and Kurt F. Reding, Introduction to Auditing: Logic, Principles, and Techniques, (Altamonte Springs, FL: The Institute of Internal Auditors, 2002).

[9] Adapted from: Ratliff, Richard L. and Kurt F. Reding, Introduction to Auditing: Logic, Principles, and Techniques, (Altamonte Springs, FL: The Institute of Internal Auditors, 2002).

[10] Adapted from: Ratliff, Richard L. and Kurt F. Reding, Introduction to Auditing: Logic, Principles, and Techniques, (Altamonte Springs, FL: The Institute of Internal Auditors, 2002).

CASE

1. Ira Icandoit is a staff auditor in the internal audit function of a small manufacturing company located in western Kansas. Ira recently completed a professional development course on statistical sampling and is very excited about the new knowledge he has gained. He decided to apply his newly gained knowledge during the audit to which he had just been assigned. He used attribute sampling when he performed his tests of control activities over the company's purchase transactions.

   Ira figured that a tolerable deviation rate of 10% and a 5% risk of assessing control risk too low were appropriate for the tests he planned to perform. He had no idea of how many deviations actually might exist in the population, so he set the expected deviation rate at 2% to be conservative. Ira selected a sample of 100 items.

   Because Ira believed larger items deserved more attention than smaller items, he selected 75 items with values greater than or equal to $2,500 and 25 items with values less than $2,500. He thought it would be most appropriate to select transactions near the end of the fiscal year, so he randomly selected items for testing from the last two months.

   Ira was relieved when he found only six deviations from prescribed control activities. One deviation was a missing vendor's invoice, so Ira called the vendor to make sure the transaction was valid. The phone conversation convinced him that the transaction, was in fact, valid. Three deviations were missing signatures by an authorized manager. The manager explained that he had not approved the invoices because he had been out of the office on the date the invoices were prepared. He reviewed the invoices and told Ira there were no problems with them. The other two deviations involved dollar errors. One was an error in the extension of an invoice, and the other was a misclassification error between expenses, which did not affect net income. Ira considered these two dollar errors to be the only two actual control deviations. He determined that the achieved upper deviation limit was 7% at a 5% risk of assessing control risk too low.

   Based on these results, Ira concluded that purchase transactions for the year were unlikely to contain more deviations than the allowable rate. Accordingly, he concluded that control activities over purchase transactions were effective and could be relied on by management.

Required: Identify and explain any deficiencies you note in Ira's attribute sampling application.

2. The purpose of this case is to familiarize you with the ACL Software and to give you an opportunity to practice applying it.

Required:

a. Install the software on your computer.
b. Print and read the *Getting Started manual.*
c. Print the *ACL in Practice manual.* Work through the tutorial contained in the manual. Beginning in Chapter 2, Examine Employee Data, print the outcomes of the tasks you are asked to complete.

3. The purpose of this case is to familiarize you with the IDEA Software and to give you an opportunity to practice applying it.

Required:

a. Install the software on your computer.
b. Print the *IDEA Version Seven User Guide.* Read:

- The Forward and Preface.
- Section One, IDEA Overview.
- Section Two, What's on the IDEA Screen.
- Section Three, IDEA Windows and Toolbars.

c. Work through Section Four, Getting Started Tutorial. Print selected task outcomes as you go. The outcomes you print should clearly show that you completed the entire tutorial.

CHAPTER 10
CONDUCTING THE
ASSURANCE ENGAGEMENT

Learning Objectives

- Describe how the purpose of an assurance engagement impacts the audit objectives.

- Determine engagement objectives and scope statements.

- Describe different types and sources of information that will help the auditor understand the process of conducting an assurance engagement.

- Document simple process flows, showing key process steps, interfaces, and departments involved.

- Perform a process-level risk assessment.

- Distinguish key control activities from non-key control activities.

- Describe how to evaluate the design adequacy of process-level control activities.

- Design different types of testing approaches, depending on the design of the process and engagement objectives.

- Develop a general work program to guide the engagement process.

- Describe the resource considerations that must be evaluated when determining how to staff and schedule an engagement.

- Conduct and document certain types of audit tests to gather evidence.

- Evaluate evidence from assurance procedures to reach conclusions based on the results of testing.

- Develop audit observations and formulate recommendations.

EXHIBIT 10-1

PROFESSIONAL STANDARDS AND PRACTICE ADVISORIES RELEVANT TO CHAPTER 10

2200 – Engagement Planning
2201 – Planning Considerations
2210 – Engagement Objectives
2220 – Engagement Scope
2230 – Engagement Resource Allocation
2240 – Engagement Work Program
2300 – Performing the Engagement
2310 – Identifying Information
2320 – Analysis and Evaluation
2330 – Recording Information
2340 – Engagement Supervision

Practice Advisory 2200-1: Engagement Planning
Practice Advisory 2210-1: Engagement Objectives
Practice Advisory 2210.A1-1: Risk Assessment in Engagement Planning
Practice Advisory 2230-1: Engagement Resource Allocation
Practice Advisory 2240-1: Engagement Work Program
Practice Advisory 2240.A1-1: Approval of Work Programs
Practice Advisory 2300-1: The Internal Auditor's Use of Personal Information in Conducting Audits
Practice Advisory 2310-1: Identifying Information
Practice Advisory 2320-1: Analysis and Evaluation
Practice Advisory 2330-1: Recording Information
Practice Advisory 2330.A1-1: Control of Engagement Records
Practice Advisory 2330.A1-2: Legal Considerations in Granting Access to Engagement Records
Practice Advisory 2330.A2-1: Retention of Records
Practice Advisory 2340-1: Engagement Supervision

This chapter describes the various steps necessary to conduct an assurance engagement. Specifically, as depicted in Exhibit 10-2, which was introduced as Exhibit 9-2 in the previous chapter, you will learn the key steps necessary to plan and perform the assurance engagement.

The first section of this chapter focuses on the planning steps. This will be covered in considerable depth as effective planning is integral to conducting a successful engagement. Executing these steps will give you confidence that the engagement will (1) be comprehensive, (2) align with the organization's objectives, and (3) support the internal audit function charter. After reviewing this section, you should fully appreciate the expression, "failing to plan means you're planning to fail."

The second section of the chapter will focus on executing the test program designed during the planning stage. While performing audit tests typically will take more time than planning an engagement, this section is shorter than the planning section as there are relatively few key steps; these steps are simply performed over and over again to test different control activities. The assurance engagement performance activities are discussed in Chapter 9, "Gathering and Documenting Audit Evidence." Additionally, techniques to evaluate and report on audit observations are covered in Chapter 11, "Communicating Assurance Engagement Outcomes and Performing Follow-Up Procedures." Therefore, the performance section of this chapter will focus on applying those concepts, rather than restating them. The information contained in this chapter will provide a solid understanding of how to plan and

EXHIBIT 10-2

THE ASSURANCE ENGAGEMENT PROCESS

Plan

- Determine engagement objectives and scope.
- Understand the auditee, including auditee objectives.
- Identify and assess risks.
- Identify key control activities.
- Evaluate adequacy of control design.
- Create a test plan.
- Develop a work program.
- Allocate resources to the engagement.

Perform

- Conduct tests to gather evidence.
- Evaluate evidence gathered and reach conclusions.
- Develop observations and formulate recommendations.

Communicate

- Perform observation evaluation & escalation process.
- Conduct interim and preliminary engagement communications.
- Develop final engagement communications.
- Distribute formal and informal final communications.
- Perform monitoring and follow-up procedures.

perform almost any assurance engagement.

To help facilitate learning in this chapter, examples are provided for certain of the key steps to illustrate how the step can be conducted and documented. These examples are for a fictitious company, Books R Us, and focus on the accounts payable and disbursements process (referred to as the *cash disbursements* process throughout the chapter). This particular process is being illustrated as it is common to most organizations, regardless of size or industry. Key facts regarding Books R Us can be found in Exhibit 10-3; these facts will help make the examples more realistic.

TYPES OF ENGAGEMENTS

Before discussing planning steps, it's important first to understand the different types of engagements that may be performed. This chapter focuses on planning assurance engagements, which typically are one of the following types:

- **Financial Assurance.** Providing assurance related to the achievement of one or more financial assertions (existence or occurrence, completeness, valuation and allocation, rights and obligations, presentation, and disclosure).

- **Controls Assurance.** Providing assurance related to the design and operation of key control activities; the controls may be operational, financial, or compliance related.

- **Information Technology (IT).** Providing assurance related to the design and operation of general IT control activities or specific application control activities.

- **Compliance.** Providing assurance related to the design and operation of control activities and procedures in place to assure compliance with laws, regulations, policies, etc.

Assurance Services

An objective examination of evidence for the purpose of providing an independent assessment on risk management, control, or governance processes for the organization.

EXHIBIT 10-3

FACTS SUPPORTING BOOKS R US EXAMPLES IN CHAPTER 10

- Books R Us is a textbook publisher, providing educational tools for the K-8, high school, and post-secondary education markets.
- The company is publicly traded, is based in Dallas, Texas, and has customers in the United States, Canada, England, South Africa, Japan, Australia, and New Zealand.
- Books R Us employs a professional editorial team and contracts with noted academics and other professionals to write the textbooks.
- All printing and binding activities are outsourced, which represents one of the most significant costs to the company.
- The company leases space for its distribution centers, which are located in all of the countries in which it does business.
- Annual revenues for Books R Us total $550 million, cash expenditures approximate $480 million, non-cash expenditures (for example, depreciation and amortization) approximate $25 million, and long-term capital expenditures approximate $40 million.
- On average, the $480 million in annual cash expenditures are disbursed as follows:

	% of Disbursements	% of Dollars
Electronic or wire transfers	10%	60%
Computer generated checks	88%	38%
Manual checks	2%	2%

- While disbursements may be made in different currencies, all are processed out of a centralized disbursements function located in Dallas, Texas.

- **Operations.** Providing assurance related to the effectiveness and efficiency of an organization's operations, including performance and profitability goals and safeguarding resources against loss.

- **Integrated.** Providing assurance related to any combination of the above, for example, a full-scope audit may include assurances on all of the above types of engagements.

In addition to assurance engagements, internal auditors may perform consulting engagements that typically focus on providing advice to improve control activities and/or performance. Conducting consulting engagements is covered in more detail in Chapter 12, "The Consulting Engagement."

Finally, internal auditors may be asked to perform or assist in investigations. These activities may include the following:

- Conducting an investigation to determine whether a fraud has been committed and, if so, to gather evidence that can be used to support disciplinary actions and, potentially, filing criminal or civil charges.

- Investigating allegations from a third party to determine whether there is any basis for such allegations, and to gather evidence that will support management's response and actions to the allegations.

- Serving in a supporting role to internal or outside counsel. Some investigations must be conducted under the leadership of counsel, but the skills and discipline that internal auditors provide can provide valuable support to such counsel.

The approach to conducting investigations is considered outside the scope of this textbook. However, it's important for individuals to understand that such activities may be included within the charter of the internal audit function.

Note that while engagements may be any of the types described above, the most common internal audit engagements focus on assurances relating to internal controls. As a result, the examples and illustrations used in the rest of this chapter focus on these types of engagements.

The first step when beginning an assurance engagement is planning. Planning involves several tasks. Refer to Exhibit 10-4 for a list of these specific tasks, each of which will be discussed in more detail later in the chapter.

DETERMINE ENGAGEMENT OBJECTIVES AND SCOPE

Purpose of the Engagement

As indicated above, there are different types of assurance engagements. Additionally, there may be different reasons for conducting any of those types of engagements. The type of engagement and purpose for performing it may have a significant influence on how the engagement is performed. Therefore, it is important to understand the purpose of the engagement before beginning the planning.

There are a number of reasons for performing assurance engagements, including, but not limited to, the following:

- The engagement was identified in the annual audit plan because of inherent risks identified during the business risk assessment process, risks detected the last time the area was audited, and other relevant factors. For these engagements, the auditor must ensure they understand what underlying business

THE ASSURANCE ENGAGEMENT PROCESS

Plan

- Determine engagement objectives and scope.
- Understand the auditee, including auditee objectives.
- Identify and assess risks.
- Identify key control activities.
- Evaluate adequacy of control design.
- Create a test plan.
- Develop a work program.
- Allocate resources to the engagement.

Perform

- Conduct tests to gather evidence.
- Evaluate evidence gathered and reach conclusions.
- Develop observations and formulate recommendations.

Communicate

- Perform observation evaluation & escalation process.
- Conduct interim and preliminary engagement communications.
- Develop final engagement communications.
- Distribute formal and informal final communications.
- Perform monitoring and follow-up procedures.

EXHIBIT 10-4

risks caused the engagement to be included in the plan, and then design the engagement plan to provide the appropriate assurances relating to those risks.

Purpose of Engagements

· **Part of annual audit plan.**

· **Compliance requirement.**

· **Post mortem.**

· **Significant changes.**

- The engagement is part of an annual requirement to evaluate the organization's system of internal controls for external reporting purposes, such as the Sarbanes-Oxley, Section 404 requirements in the United States and similar financial reporting laws in other countries. For these engagements, the internal auditor must ensure that the engagement is designed to test the areas covered by the underlying regulations; for example, provide assurances regarding the design adequacy and operating effectiveness of internal controls over financial reporting.

- A recent event (for example, natural disaster, fraud, customer bankruptcy, etc.) has tested the process under unusual circumstances and management desires a "post mortem" to determine where the process was effective and where it was not. For these engagements, the internal auditor must tailor the testing and evaluation around the specific event that occurred.

- Changes in the business or industry require immediate modifications to the process and management desires a quick validation that these modifications appear to be designed appropriately to address the changes. For these engagements, the internal auditor may perform a full control activities-focused audit or they may scope it to focus only on the control activities that changed.

Although there may be other factors in addition to those listed above, it is important for the internal audit team to be aware of the reasons or drivers that caused the engagement to be performed. This will help ensure that the overall objectives, scope, and focus of the engagement address those drivers and time is not devoted to other, less important drivers.

> **Books R Us Example:** The purpose of the cash disbursements process engagement is to conduct an audit that was included in the annual audit plan because of inherent risks identified during the business risk assessment process (refer to Chapter 4, "Business Processes and Business Risks," for discussion of the business risk assessment process).

Establishing Engagement Objectives

Once the purpose of the assurance engagement is understood, formal engagement objectives should be established. These objectives, which typically will be stated in the final assurance engagement communication, articulate specifically what the engagement is trying to accomplish. While objectives may be stated in a variety of ways, it should be clear what assurances the engagement will provide. For example, objectives could start with the following phrases (obviously different verbs can be substituted for those used in these examples):

- Evaluate the design adequacy of …
- Determine the operating effectiveness of …
- Assess compliance with …
- Determine the effectiveness and efficiency of …
- Evaluate the accuracy of …
- Assess the achievement of …

Establishing engagement objectives at the beginning of an engagement is a critical step. Without establishment of formal engagement objectives, the internal audit team may not be aligned with the purpose of the engagement and, as such, conduct inadequate or unnecessary steps.

> **Books R Us Example:** The engagement objective is to *evaluate the design adequacy and operating effectiveness of control activities within the cash disbursements process.*

Scope of the Engagement

Once the engagement objectives have been established, the scope of the engagement must be determined. Since an engagement may not cover everything that can be audited related to the engagement objectives, scope statements must specifically state what is or is not included within an engagement. Such scope statements may include the following:

- **Boundaries of the process.** While some processes are small and self-contained, many processes are very broad and overlap with other processes. Therefore, it's important to define at what point in the process the engagement will begin (for example, the initial inputs from transactions or other processes) and where it will end (for example, reports, financial statements, or outputs to other processes).

- **In-scope versus out-of-scope locations.** For processes that cover multiple locations, only some of those locations may be included in the engagement.

- **Sub-processes.** Larger processes may be composed of a series of sub-processes (for example, the cash disbursements process may include the invoice matching/validation, disbursements input, and payment processing sub-processes).

- **Components.** Certain portions, or components, of a process may be omitted. For example, the manual procedures may be included in the scope, while the automated procedures are omitted.

- **Time frame limitations.** An engagement may cover a calendar year, the previous 12 months, or some other time frame.

Decisions regarding these scope statements require a great deal of judgment. However, the internal auditor must ensure that the scope is sufficient to meet the engagement objectives. By articulating the specific scope statements, the internal audit team will better be able to focus the specific test steps and the recipients of the communication will be able to interpret the findings within the context of the engagement objectives.

Books R Us Example: The following will be included within the scope of this engagement:

- Procedures that are executed beginning with the receipt of an invoice or a similar document evidencing the creation of a liability to pay.

- Procedures that are executed through the disbursement of funds and recording of such disbursement in the general ledger.

- All three types of disbursements (electronic wires, computer generated checks, and manual checks).

- Disbursements in U.S. dollars and other currencies.

- Disbursements that were processed during the last 12 months.

Expected Outcomes and Deliverables

Before moving on to the next step in the planning process, one final task should be performed. While the objectives and scope have been determined, it's helpful to apply one of the *Seven Habits of Highly Effective People*: "Begin with the end in mind."[1] There are two important "ends" to consider that will help validate the objectives and scope that have been determined: (1) the potential outcomes that may arise from the tests to be performed during the engagement and (2) the expectations for deliverables to communicate the outcomes and assurances. Each are described more fully as follows:

- Potential outcomes that may arise from the tests to be performed during the engagement—being able to anticipate the different types of testing exceptions that may be identified in a given engagement will help the internal auditor plan their tests to provide reasonable assurance that such discrepancies will be detected. Typical exceptions include the following:

    - **Financial misstatements.** Errors or misclassifications within financial accounts, balances, or disclosures.

    - **Control weaknesses.** Specific control activities are not achieving the desired effect, that is, mitigating the corresponding risks to the desired level.

    - **Shortfalls in objective achievement.** The related objectives, currently or in the future, may not be achieved.

    - **Inefficiencies.** Resources are not being deployed in an optimal manner.

    - **Out-of-compliance situations.** Laws, regulations, or policies are not being complied with on a consistent basis.

- The expectations for deliverables to communicate the outcomes and assurances—understanding the final communication format will help the internal auditor ensure that all necessary information is gathered during the engagement.

- Full-scope, internal reports typically have a wide internal distribution and, thus, will require sufficient evidence to support conclusions and recommendations for improvements.

- Internal memoranda may be for more limited distribution, stating the work performed and support for the conclusions and recommendation only to the extent necessary for the intended audience to understand the underlying weaknesses.

- Reports for third-party use should assume such parties are less familiar with policies and procedures unique to the organization and, therefore, may require greater levels of detail to ensure the readers understand the nature and context of the observations and recommendations.

- Sometimes, a higher level of confidentiality may be necessary for certain engagements. Such instances should be fully discussed up-front with process management to ensure the deliverables support the necessary level of confidentiality.

Books R Us Example: All of the potential testing exceptions could occur during this engagement and, as such, the internal audit team will need to design tests accordingly. The deliverable will be a standard, full-scope internal audit communication. (Examples of possible deliverables will be discussed in Chapter 11, "Communicating Assurance Engagement Outcomes and Performing Follow-Up Procedures.")

UNDERSTAND THE AUDITEE

When planning an engagement, one must first understand the relevant process or processes. Failure to gain a comprehensive understanding of the area under review may result in an incomplete testing plan or a misallocation of internal audit resources deployed in the engagement. Therefore, gaining an understanding of the process is the next key step in planning.

Determining Process Objectives

The first step in understanding the process is to determine the key process objectives. This helps the internal auditor understand why the process exists, which will be important when identifying and assessing process level risks and control activities. It should be noted that this engagement step aligns with the objective setting component of the COSO *Enterprise Risk Management (ERM)—Integrated Framework,*[2] which is discussed in more detail in Chapter 3, "Governance and Risk Management" as well as elsewhere in this textbook.

There may be different types of objectives for a given process. These types of objectives can be described to align with the four objective types in the COSO ERM framework. Specifically, process-level objectives may be described as follows (as well as in examples for the Books R Us cash disbursements process):

Objectives

What an entity desires to achieve. When referring to what an organization wants to achieve, these are called business objectives, and may be classified as strategic, operational, reporting, and compliance.

- *Operational objectives* are the most common type of objectives at the process level and usually define the reason the process exists. These objectives typically are governance or task-oriented, and, as a result, frequently focus on accuracy, timeliness, completeness, or control attributes. Additionally, some operational objectives may focus on ensuring the effectiveness and efficiency of operations, and safeguarding of assets.

  Books R Us Example: A cash disbursements process may have objectives that include the following:

  - Pay bills accurately to avoid adjustments to future bills or penalties due to underpayment of current liabilities.
  - Pay bills timely to take advantage of discounts (if available and appropriate) or avoid late-payment penalties.
  - Record all disbursements accurately in the accounting records and in the appropriate accounting period.
  - Process disbursements within the cost-per-transaction metrics established to ensure cost-effective use of resources.

- *Reporting objectives* at the process level are those designed to meet the organization's reporting needs, whether internal or external.

  Books R Us Example: Information from the cash disbursements process may be used for:

  - Internal reporting of cash flow information that helps the Treasurer in preparing weekly cash flow forecasts.
  - Supporting the liquidity disclosures in the organization's regulatory filings.

- *Compliance objectives* at the process level may relate to compliance with external laws and regulations (COSO's definition) or internal policies (included in The IIA's definition along with external laws and regulations).

  Books R Us Example: Cash disbursements compliance objectives may include the following:

  - Ensure disbursements comply with applicable banking regulations.
  - Ensure disbursements are approved in accordance with the organization's delegation of authority policy.

- *Strategic objectives* at the process level are those created to specifically align with the organization's strategic objectives. While not always evident to individuals performing the specific process tasks, these objectives are important to create a link between the day-to-day activities and the strategies that drive an organization's success. Note that this discussion of strategic objectives differs from the definition of strategic objectives in COSO's *Internal Control—Integrated Framework* discussed in Chapter 5, "Internal Control." Strategic objectives per COSO exist only at the entity level. However, when conducting an assurance engagement, the internal auditor needs to approach the process as a component of the organization as a whole and, thus, certain process-level objectives can be considered strategic in nature.

Books R Us Example: A cash disbursements function my have the following objective in an organization with a specific cash flow or liquidity strategy:

- Pay bills in accordance with the cash flow directives provided by the Treasury department to support the ongoing liquidity of the organization.

● *Other objectives* may also be created for a specific process related to individual department initiatives.

Books R Us Example: If the cash disbursements function wanted to develop bench strength among the staff, the following objective may be applicable:

- Cross-train individuals in all department jobs to ensure at least two people are capable of performing all key departmental tasks.

The process owner or staff involved in the process may be able to provide a list of process objectives. However, in many cases such objectives may not have been articulated formally. In such situations, the internal auditor may need to facilitate discussions with process individuals to determine the key process objectives. The following questions may prove helpful when facilitating such discussions, or when brainstorming among the internal audit team if process individuals are not available:

● Why does this process exist; that is, what is its primary purpose?

● Which of the organization's strategic objectives does it affect or influence and how?

● What initiatives does/should the process undertake to help the organization achieve its strategic objectives?

● What does this process provide the organization, without which the organization would have a difficult time being successful?

● At the end of the day/week/month/year, what gives employees a sense of accomplishment with their job?

● What accomplishments tend to get employees recognized by management or internal customers?

Once the process objectives are understood, the internal auditor is ready to gather information about how the process operates.

Gathering Information

There are a variety of ways to gather information about a process. The internal auditor should consider different types and sources of relevant information to leverage readily available information. Additionally, analysis of data and entity-wide controls can help provide additional insights into a process.

Types and Sources of Relevant Information

The starting point for understanding a process is reviewing documentation that already exists. For example, the following may be available from process owners or others familiar with the process that may provide useful information regarding how the process works:

- Policies relating to the process.
- Procedures manuals.
- Organizational charts or similar information outlining the number of employees and key reporting relationships.
- Job descriptions for people involved in the process.
- Process maps depicting the overall flow of the process.
- Narrative descriptions of key tasks or portions of the process.
- Copies of key contracts with customers, vendors, outsourcing partners, etc.
- Relevant information regarding laws and regulations affecting the process.
- Other documentation that may have been developed to support required reporting on the effectiveness of the system of internal controls.

This information may provide the auditor with much of what is needed to understand the process. However, it still may be necessary to discuss certain aspects of the process with key individuals involved in performing the process. If the available documentation is not sufficiently comprehensive, questions may need to be asked of individuals involved in the process, such as the following:

- What key tasks are you responsible for performing?
- What inputs (information, documentation, etc.) do you need to perform these tasks?
- What, specifically, do you do with these inputs?
- What are the outputs that you produce from each task?
- Which other people or areas do you depend on in order to perform these tasks?
- Which other people or areas depend on you performing these tasks effectively and timely?
- What systems do you utilize when performing these tasks?
- How long does each task take to complete?
- What types of exceptions or errors do you typically encounter?
- How do you handle these exceptions or errors?
- What other barriers or challenges do you typically encounter when performing these tasks?
- What do you do to remove the barriers or meet the challenges?
- In the end, how do you ensure that you perform the task correctly?

These and other questions can help provide the auditor with the information needed to fully understand the process. It can be gained through individual interviews, or through performing a walkthrough, which involves following a transaction through each step of a process. Regardless of the approach, it is important to understand the key tasks in sufficient detail to provide the foundation for the subsequent steps in the planning process.

Analytical Procedures

Understanding the tasks in a process, as described above, is an important step in planning an engagement. However, these tasks describe the way a process is designed to perform, but provide little indication regarding how effectively these tasks are carried out. Performing analytical procedures is one means by which internal auditors conduct high-level assessments that may reveal process activities that warrant closer attention and, accordingly, more detailed testing.

Analytical procedures involve reviewing and evaluating existing information, which may be financial or non-financial, to determine whether it is consistent with expectations.

> **Books R Us Example:** For the cash disbursements audit, this analysis may include any or all of the following:
>
> - Comparisons of financial information to prior periods, for example, trends in accounts payable balances from one quarter to the next.
> - Ratio analyses, for example, current ratio (that is, current assets divided by current liabilities); and accounts payable turnover (cost of goods sold divided by accounts payable).
> - Comparisons of financial or non-financial information against budgeted information, for example, actual cash balances versus forecasted cash amounts.

Data Analysis Using Computer-assisted Audit Techniques (CAATs)

Data analysis involves compiling and analyzing large amounts of data, typically through the use of technology. This technique is described in greater detail in Chapter 9, "Gathering and Documenting Audit Evidence." While most data analysis is conducted to test the effectiveness of a process, some data analysis tests may provide useful information during the planning process. These data analysis steps may provide information about the population of transactions that could prove useful when determining the audit approach.

> **Books R Us Example:** When conducting an audit of the cash disbursements process, the internal audit team may perform the following data analysis tests during the planning phase:
>
> - Number or percent of payments that are made well before or after the due date – this may provide insights into how closely cash flows are managed.
> - Number of manual checks – this may indicate process design weaknesses or potential circumvention of established control activities.

Computer-assisted Audit Techniques (CAATs)

Automated audit techniques, such as generalized audit software, utility software, test data, application software tracing and mapping, and audit expert systems, that help the internal auditor directly test control activities built into computerized information systems and data contained in computer files.

- Stratification of payment amounts – this may provide information about the level of small payments made, indicating the potential for procurement cards.

- Distribution of the first digits of payment amounts (Benford's Law analysis) – a distribution that does not follow Benford's Law may be an indication of unusual disbursement practices (for example, split invoicing), which may, in turn, influence the audit approach. Benford's Law estimates the number of times each of the ten digits (zero through nine) will typically occur at the beginning of each member in a population with certain characteristics.

- Duplicate payment amounts to the same vendor – this may indicate potentially duplicate payments, or provide insights about vendors for which recurring payments are made for like amounts.

Obtaining information about a population during the planning phase can help the auditor design audit tests that most effectively address the inherent risks in the process.

Entitywide Controls Analysis

While it is important to understand the process-level tasks and controls, it is also important to understand how the entity-wide controls may influence the performance of a process. Weaknesses in entity-wide controls can circumvent well-designed controls within a process. For example, if organizationwide policies tend to be informal and inconsistently enforced, then policies specific to the process being audited may not be as important to understanding the process. Similarly, if there is little commitment to attracting, training, and developing competent employees in key areas requiring decision-making abilities and complex judgments, the testing approach may need to be altered as less reliance can be placed on individuals being able to perform complex or highly judgmental tasks.

Entitywide controls are commonly evaluated on a companywide basis at periodic intervals (for example, annually). Therefore, it typically will not be necessary to perform an assessment of the effectiveness of entitywide control on each engagement. However, as described in the previous paragraph, the auditor should consider the results of the entitywide control assessment when planning individual engagements to ensure the approach to testing is relevant and efficient.

Documenting the Process Flow

As discussed above, there may be many types of information that can be gathered about a process from a variety of sources. To demonstrate that the internal auditor understands how the process actually operates, the key steps must be documented. This process flow documentation will facilitate a review of the workpapers by the internal auditor's supervisor or others. The most common ways of documenting process flows are process maps (high-level or detailed maps) and narrative memoranda. Following is a brief description of each.

Entitywide Control

A control that operates across an entire entity and, as such, is not bound by, or associated with, individual processes.

High-level Process Maps

The purpose of a high-level process map is to depict broad inputs, tasks, workflows, and outputs. A high-level process map helps reviewers understand the overall activities, systems, reports, and interfaces with other processes or sub-processes. This understanding will provide a frame of reference for identifying key sub-processes and systems that may be considered for the scope of the engagement. Process maps typically are drawn like a flowchart, with additional information added as necessary to support the understanding of the process flow.

For those not familiar with flowcharts, these charts utilize a collection of symbols, arrows, and words to provide a visual depiction of a process or system. Many people find this visual depiction helps them gain a quick understanding about the inputs, processing, and outputs that are embedded in a process or system. The common flowcharting symbols were discussed in Chapter 4, "Business Processes and Business Risks," and are repeated in Exhibit 10-5.

Books R Us Example: A high-level process map depicting the cash disbursements process is shown in Exhibit 10-6.

A simple, high-level process map can be used to confirm the internal auditor's overall understanding of the process with the process owner, help in determining which areas or sub-processes are within scope for

COMMON FLOWCHARTING SYMBOLS

Symbol	Description
▭	**Process or operation** – A process, sub-process, or activity.
◇	**Decision** – Indicates alternative choices (for example, yes/no or accept/reject), each of which results in different flows of activities and/or documents.
⬒	**Document** – A hard copy input source document or output report.
→	**Flow line** – The direction of activities, workflow, information flow, documents, and handoffs.
⛁	**Computer System or Application** – Information technology that is used to store data, run an application, or perform other computer-based functions.
◯	**On-page connector** – Used to connect different parts of a flowchart on the same page without the use of flow lines.
⬠	**Off-page connector** – Used to connect parts of a flowchart documented on different pages.
⬭	**Terminator** – The start or end of a flow.
⌐	**Annotation** – An explanatory note attached to a specific point in a flowchart.

EXHIBIT 10-5

EXHIBIT 10-6

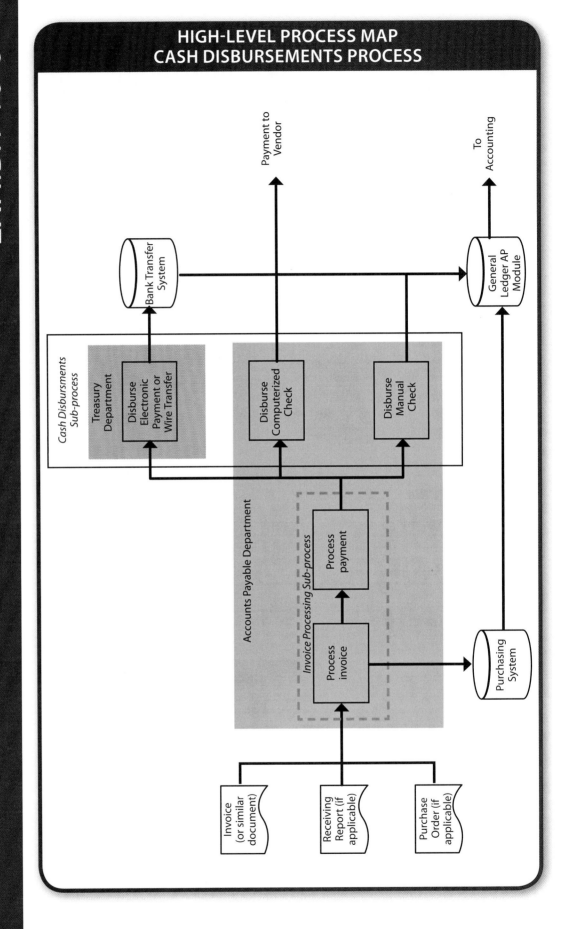

HIGH-LEVEL PROCESS MAP
CASH DISBURSEMENTS PROCESS

the engagement, and serve as a summary view of the detailed process maps.

Detailed Process Maps

While the high-level process map is an important starting point, it doesn't provide the depth and level of detail needed to support the internal auditor's judgments regarding the design of the process. A detailed process map documents the more specific inputs, tasks, actions, systems, decisions, and outputs. In addition to providing a more detailed depiction of the process flow, detailed process maps provide additional information that enhances the understanding of the process. For example, detailed process maps may include some or all of the following:

- Key risks, which may also be denoted by a symbol identifying the points in the process where something could go wrong and cause the process to not operate as designed.

- Key control activities, which may be denoted by a symbol identifying the tasks, actions, or decisions that are considered critical to the design of the process.

- Individuals or positions performing the key tasks or making decisions.

- The timing of when key tasks, actions, or decisions occur.

- The elapsed time it takes to perform a task or make a decision (this may be included if the process map is used to evaluate the efficiency of the process).

  Books R Us Example: An example of a detailed process map is shown in Exhibit 10-7. This example depicts the invoice processing sub-process in the cash disbursements process for Books R Us. The invoice processing sub-process is shown in the high-level process map in Exhibit 10-6.

Because many people are visual learners and thinkers, detailed process maps are an effective way of presenting a great deal of information in an intuitive and understandable format. The level of information in detailed process maps should be sufficient to support the internal auditor's judgments regarding the identification of key control activities, the adequacy of the overall process design, and the gaps between the current and desired level of specific control activities.

Narrative Memoranda

There may be situations in which the internal auditor believes it is more appropriate to document the understanding of the process in narrative write-ups instead of on process maps. These situations typically exhibit one or more of the following characteristics:

- The process is simple and, thus, the visual depiction created in process mapping is not of great value.

- The steps are complicated, making it difficult to describe them effectively in the limited space provided in a process map icon.

- The process owner would like the output to support other

Business Process
The set of connected activities linked with each other for the purpose of achieving a business objective.

EXHIBIT 10-7

10-18

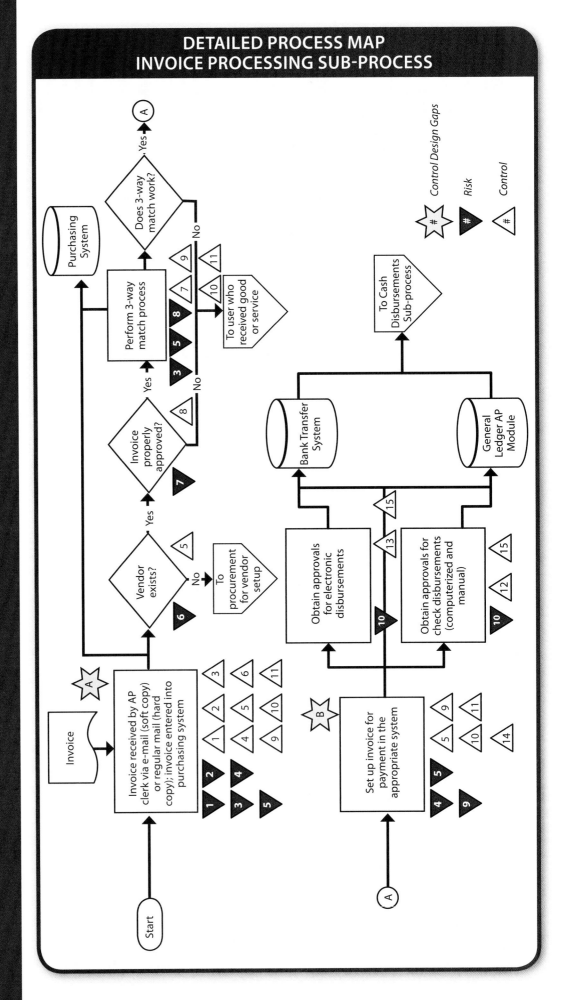

DETAILED PROCESS MAP
INVOICE PROCESSING SUB-PROCESS

Control Design Gaps

Risk

Control

EXHIBIT 10-7 (continued)

Detailed Process Map
Invoice Processing Risks

1 Invoice is not received timely by accounts payable, resulting in liability not being properly reflected in the financial statements.

2 Invoice is not processed timely by accounts payable, resulting in lost opportunities to take discounts or incurring late-payment fees.

3 Invoice information is entered inaccurately into the purchasing system, resulting in inaccurate or inappropriate payments.

4 Duplicate invoices are entered and processed for payment, resulting in payment for the same invoice twice.

5 Accounts payable personnel have inappropriate access to the the various systems, allowing them to establish ficticious vendors, purchase orders, or other payments.

6 Payments are processed to the wrong or non-existent vendor, resulting in late payments to the correct vendor, the need to collect refunds from the incorrect vendor, or a fraudulent payment.

7 Payments are processed for invoices that have not been approved yet, resulting in payment before the good or service is received.

8 Invoices are processed that do not match purchase orders, receiving reports or other relevant documentation, resulting in establishing a liability and paying an incorrect amount.

9 Payments are made before the due date, resulting in lost time value of money.

10 Payments are made without approval, resulting in payments being made by a costly or inefficient means, or in a manner inconsistent to meet the cash flow requirements.

---

process documentation and prefers narrative write-ups over visual process maps.

- The process mapping skills of the auditor are not well developed, thus narrative write-ups are a more efficient means of documenting the process.

Narrative memoranda should include the same type of information as is contained in process maps. While the specific sections of such a memorandum may vary between processes, a memorandum generally should include the elements from the following outline:

1. Overall description of the process.

2. Key inputs

   a. Documents or communications from outside sources (for example, invoices, checks, etc.).

EXHIBIT 10-7 (continued)

DETAILED PROCESS MAP — INVOICE PROCESSING CONTROL ACTIVITIES AND DESIGN GAPS

 As part of the month end close process, the AP Manager will solicit information on unprocessed invoices and will prepare an accrual accordingly.

 Once an approved invoice is entered, the system will automatically book the credit to AP and debit to the appropriate expense or balance sheet account.

 Open purchase orders are reviewed once per month by the Purchasing Manager to determine their status.

 The AP clerk runs a report at the end of each week showing invoices entered but not approved. For invoices outstanding more than a week, a reminder is sent to the user.

 The purchasing system requires that all invoice fields are completed before processing is allowed. An invoice cannot be entered without a match to an approved vendor.

 The Purchasing System alerts the AP clerk if the vendor number, invoice number, and invoice amount match an invoice previously entered.

 The Purchasing System confirms a match between quantities and prices on an invoice, purchase order, and receiving documents. If they do not match, the invoice is placed on hold.

 Invoice approval limits are confirmed with department heads annually and updated if necessary.

 A user name and password is required to access all of the systems. Passwords are subject to naming parameters, and must be changed every 90 days.

 System access rights are reviewed semi-annually with department heads to ensure access capabilities align with job responsibilities.

 AP personnel cannot access the vendor masterfile, nor can they make changes to previously entered purchase order and receiving information.

 Only the AP Manager can initiate the processing of a computerized check batch.

 Only treasury department personnel are entitled to process bank transfers.

 The purchasing system interfaces with the general ledger AP module and the bank transfer system.

 Computerized checks over $50,000 require a manual signature of the Treasurer. Computerized checks over $100,000 requires a manual signature of the CFO. Manual checks require dual signatures; the Treasurer's and CFO's signatures are required consistent with those for large computerized checks. The Treasurer must authorize individual bank transfers in excess of $100,000.

 There is no check with users to determine whether any goods or services have been received but not invoiced yet (engagement observation written up on working paper Z-1).

 While the system does alert the AP clerk to potential duplicate invoices, it does not prevent the AP clerk from continuing to process such an invoice (engagement observation written up on working paper Z-2).

b. Outputs from other processes or sub-processes.

c. Information from outside sources.

d. Data from internal systems.

3. Key steps in the process

a. Tasks that handle, check, change, or monitor the inputs.

b. Analysis that is completed.

c. Decisions or judgments that are made.

d. Systems that are updated.

e. New documents or information that is created.

f. Key individuals performing the tasks.

g. Elapsed time for tasks or groups of tasks.

4. Key outputs.

a. Documents to be sent to outside parties (for example, bills, checks, statements, etc.).

b. Reports for internal use.

c. Inputs into other processes or sub-processes.

d. Data to be stored in systems.

e. Hard copy of documentation to be stored internally.

5. Risk that are managed.

6. Key control activities (refer to section later in this chapter on Identifying Key Control Activities).

Regardless of whether process maps, narrative memoranda, or a combination of the two are used, documenting the process flows helps provide an understanding that is critical to the next steps in engagement planning. Therefore, care should be taken to invest enough time in understanding the process to ensure the foundation for assessing process design is effective.

It is important to remember that in an assurance engagement, process maps and narrative memoranda are used to depict the current or "as is" state, not the desired or "should be" state. A common audit objective is to evaluate the design and operation of a process. The current state is documented to help the internal auditor assess the current design adequacy. The auditee obtains the desired state only after addressing any design weaknesses identified by the internal auditor.

Identifying Key Performance Indicators

After gaining an understanding of the process flow, it is helpful for the internal auditor to also understand how process-level management monitors performance. Frequently, there will be process-level key performance indicators (KPIs) which are monitored on a periodic basis to provide process owners with information about how well the process is performing. Some of these KPIs may be similar to the analytical procedures the auditor performed, as described in the previous section, and some may be quite different. There are certain characteristics of good key performance indicators. They should be:

- Relevant, that is, they measure what is important (for example, disbursement accuracy) as opposed to what is quantifiable (for example, dollar value of disbursements processed).

- Measurable, that is, there is quantifiable information to determine successful performance (for example, inaccurate disbursement information is tracked and compiled to monitor accuracy of disbursements).

- Available, that is, the information needed is available at the right time and to the right people, allowing for timely measurement of process performance (for example, disbursements statistics are available to the Accounts Payable Manager at the close of each pay cycle).

- Aligned with key objectives of the process (for example, duplicate payment information is captured because there is an objective to have none).

- Articulated to the people involved in the process so that they understand what is being measured and the importance of executing within those performance levels (for example, Accounts Payable employees can see the statistics timely and adjust their performance accordingly).

Key performance indicators, whether formal or informal, can define the process owner's tolerance to performance deviations. Management determines what level of errors they are willing to accept when the process does not perform as expected. Knowing these tolerance levels will help the auditor evaluate the results of audit testing. For example, if the auditor finds a two percent error rate in a test, knowing whether this frequency of errors is acceptable will help the auditor determine the significance of these errors.

Books R Us Example: Examples of key performance indicators for the cash disbursements process are as follows:

- 100% of the disbursements are accurate; for example, for the amount on the invoice.

- 98% of disbursements are paid by the due date; under no circumstances should the company ever have to pay interest or penalties on late payments.

- There are no duplicate payments.

- 90% of payables with early pay discounts exceeding 2% are paid in time to take the discount.

Evaluating Process-level Fraud Risks

The final step in understanding the process is to identify and evaluate the potential process-level fraud risks. As discussed in the next section in this chapter, most risks are based on the uncertainty of events that may occur due to the inherent nature of the process. However, the likelihood of certain risks occurring increases if there is intent to commit fraud and/or collusion among multiple individuals involved in the process. Therefore, before commencing the formal risk assessment process in an engagement, it is important to identify potential fraud scenarios in the process. This involves the following steps:

- **Identifying potential fraud scenarios.** Brainstorming with individuals involved in the process the possible means by which individuals, working alone or in collusion with others, could circumvent the process.

  Books R Us Example: Examples of potential cash disbursements fraud:

  - An employee creates a fictitious vendor with his/her own address, submits an invoice for processing to that vendor, and deposits the payment into his/her own account.

  - An accounts payable employee processes a duplicate payment and, through collusion with the vendor, agrees to split the proceeds of the additional payment with an individual at that vendor.

  - A Treasury employee arranges to have funds wire transferred to an offshore account he/she set up by a company in which they have a significant interest.

- **Understanding potential fraud impacts.** Determining what the potential impacts of such fraud scenarios might be. For example, an organization could:
  - Suffer direct financial loss (through misappropriation of assets).
  - Misrepresent financial results (through financial reporting fraud).
  - Suffer reputational damage if the fraud reflects very negatively on the governance or oversight of the organization.

- **Determining whether to test for specific fraud risks.** Assessing whether, based on the inherent risk of fraud within the process, the auditor should design specific tests for fraud.

The intent of this step is not to identify the occurrence of fraud, but rather to evaluate the likelihood of fraud scenarios occurring. If such likelihood is more than remote, the internal auditor should consider designing specific tests to identify the occurrence of or potential for the fraud scenarios.

IDENTIFY AND ASSESS RISKS

Identifying Process-level Risk Scenarios

An organization establishes processes to execute its business plan and achieve its objectives. These processes may be discrete and focused, or they may be cross-functional. Regardless of the breadth, location, or focus of a process, there are risks embedded in all processes. Therefore, the first step in assessing process-level risks is to identify the risk

Fraud
Any illegal acts characterized by deceit, concealment, or violation of trust. These acts are not dependent upon the application of threat of violence or of physical force. Frauds are perpetrated by parties and organizations to obtain money, property, or services; to avoid payment or loss of services; or to secure personal or business advantage.

scenarios that are inherent in the process. Risk scenarios are potential real-life events that may adversely impact the achievement of objectives.

While the detailed process map shown in Exhibit 10-7 includes risks, it is possible that those risks won't be identified until the internal auditor has completed this step in the planning process. It is common for these two phases: Understand the Auditee and Identify and Assess Risks, to be conducted iteratively.

The focus on this step is to answer the question: What can happen that would prevent the achievement of each of the process-level objectives? To answer this question, internal auditors should brainstorm the possible risk scenarios. The following provides an outline of how this can be done.

1. Choose a single process-level objective. This exercise works best if done one objective at a time.

2. Brainstorm barriers (events, scenarios, issues, or circumstances) that might cause the objective to fail. Examples include the following:

    a. External events for which the organization was not prepared or did not react to in a timely or appropriate manner.

    b. Inadequately designed or poorly documented procedures or tasks.

    c. Breakdowns in existing procedures or tasks.

    d. Lack of the right people, with the right skills, deployed in the right manner.

    e. Inadequate supervision or monitoring of activities.

    f. Inadequate communication between interfacing areas.

    g. Employees who intentionally violate policies or act in an unethical manner.

    h. Inadequately designed or underperforming systems.

    i. Untimely, inaccurate, or lack of information for decision-making.

    j. Lack of or inadequate performance measurements.

3. Continue the exercise for the remaining process-level objectives.

4. Since some of the risk scenarios will be similar across process-level objectives, categorize and combine similar risk scenarios. The reason for combining similar risk scenarios will become more evident in the next step where risks are defined.

This brainstorming exercise would be optimized if individuals involved in the process participate. They may be able to identify risk scenarios based on first-hand experience. However, experienced internal auditors should be able to conduct this exercise without assistance from process-level individuals.

An effective way for auditors to perform such a brainstorming session is to write the different scenarios on self-sticking notes and put them

Risk

The possibility that an event will occur and adversely affect the achievement of objectives.

up on a wall or large board. Once the brainstorming is completed, the notes can be (1) arranged by objective to ensure comprehensive coverage of each objective and (2) categorized by similar scenario type to support risk definition.

Books R Us Example: The following are a few of the many risk scenario examples for the cash disbursements process:

- Invoices are not approved timely to permit processing by the due date.

- A duplicate payment is made due to an invoice being input twice, once from an approved invoice and a second time off of a statement sent by the vendor.

- An accounts payable clerk accidentally enters the wrong amount into the system, resulting in payment for the wrong amount.

- Due to employee turnover in accounts payable, input delays are experienced resulting in late payments.

- Unauthorized individuals change payment terms within the system resulting in late or incorrect payments.

Defining Process-level Risks

As indicated above, similar risk scenarios provide the foundation for identifying process-level risks. The risk scenarios represent the specific real-life events that could affect the achievement of objectives. Risks are broader descriptions of the causes and effects of such events. The next step in assessing process-level risks is to define the relevant risks.

There are a variety of ways to define risks. The optimal approach to defining risks will depend on the culture and "risk language" of the organization. However, regardless of the unique approaches that may exist from one organization to the next, it is important to be consistent in the approach to defining risks. Lack of consistency may make it more difficult for risks to be broadly understood throughout the organization.

One common and effective approach for defining risks is to use a "cause and effect" protocol. Under this approach, risks begin with a "cause" (for example, failure to …, lack of …, inability to …) and continue with the effect (for example, financial loss, personal injury, data corruption, reputational damage).

Books R Us Example: A sample of possible cash disbursements risks:

- Expectations Risk. Lack of well-developed and well-articulated policies, procedures, and other forms of communications from management may result in employees carrying out their responsibilities in a manner that is inconsistent with management's expectations and desires.

- Duplicate Payments Risk. Failure to identify multiple inputs of invoices may result in duplicate payments to vendors that could go undetected or prove difficult to collect.

- Timeliness Risk. Inability to process payments on a timely basis may result in fines or penalties (for late payments) or missed discounts.

- Systems Security Risk. Lack of effective logical security controls may create opportunities for unauthorized individuals to manipulate or delete key disbursements data.

- Human Resources Risk. Inability to attract, develop, deploy, and retain competent individuals may result in the cash disbursements process performing at a sub-optimal level, which could cause inaccurate or untimely payments.

Once the risks are defined, they should be linked to the process-level objectives to ensure there is correlation between the risk effects and the success factors for each objective. As will be discussed below, risk assessment involves consideration of the impact on the ability to achieve objectives. Therefore, ensuring linkage to the objectives is a necessary task during this step.

One final task is to validate that the definitions "speak the language" of the process-level employees. Since these employees are responsible for managing the process-level risks, it is important that they have a uniform and consistent understanding of those risks. Therefore, internal auditors should make efforts to share and discuss the risk definitions with process-level management and employees to validate that the risk listing is complete and that the definitions make sense. Success with this task will help facilitate success in the risk evaluation step that follows.

Evaluating the Impact and Likelihood of Risks

Now that the risks have been identified and defined, the internal auditor is ready to perform a risk assessment. In this step, the focus is on determining the potential impact and likelihood of each risk. The purpose of this evaluation is to help identify the risks (and corresponding controls) that will have the greatest adverse effect on the achievement of process-level objectives. Such risks are the ones that deserve most of the attention during an assurance engagement.

The process for conducting a process-level risk assessment generally involves the following steps:

- For each risk, determine the impact of various outcomes associated with the risk. The following tips may prove helpful when performing this step:

  - Recall that, by definition, risk represents uncertainty; therefore, there may be several possible risk outcomes. The internal auditor must be cautious to avoid focusing only on one possible risk outcome, and ignoring more impactful or likely outcomes.

  - Risk is typically measured in terms of the financial impact, which is the most common and easily measured impact. However, there may be other risk outcomes that either cannot be measured in financial terms, or such outcomes may be considered more severe than the financial impact.

Effect

The risk or exposure the organization and/or others encounter because the condition is not consistent with the criteria (the consequence of the difference).

For example, harm to an employee's health and safety, or impairment of an organization's reputation due to negative publicity, may be considered a more severe outcome than the direct financial impact of such risks.

- Impact should focus on the potential exposure over a specific period of time, typically one year. Because risks may occur more than once during the period, it is important to avoid concentrating on a single-event impact. Estimating the impact over a period of time ensures that the potential worst-case exposure is considered.

- It is not necessary to obtain a high degree of precision when estimating the impact of a risk. Using a generic scale (for example, high/medium/low) will typically suffice. However, it is still important to have some definitions around the scale. For example, high impact may be defined as a financial impact greater than $1 million, medium impact may be between $250,000 and $1 million, and low impact less than $250,000.

- The next step is to estimate the likelihood of each of those risk impacts occurring. The following tips may be helpful when performing this step:

  - As discussed above, risks have a range of possible outcomes which will have different likelihoods of occurring. It is important to focus on a single risk outcome—that is, the same outcomes as determined in the previous step.

  - Since there are a variety of risk outcomes, there may also be a variety of root causes for why a risk occurs. Each root cause may have a different likelihood. Therefore, it is important to consider the underlying root cause of the chosen outcome when evaluating the likelihood of a risk occurrence.

  - As is the case when determining risk impact, it is not necessary to obtain a high degree of precision when estimating the likelihood of a risk. Using a generic scale (for example, high/medium/low) will typically suffice. For example, high likelihood may indicate that the risk impact is more likely than not to occur (for example, greater than 50%), medium likelihood may indicate that the risk impact is possible (for example, between 10% and 50%), and low likelihood may indicate that the risk impact is remote (for example, less than 10%).

  - When evaluating likelihood, it is important to focus on the inherent likelihood—that is, considering likelihood without consideration for the control activities management may have put into place. Since the internal auditor already has some understanding of the process, it is common to estimate likelihood based on the effect of these control activities. However, internal auditors should not assume that those controls operate effectively when planning the audit, otherwise, they may under-assess the

Risk Assessment

A process whereby the potential impact and likelihood of one or more risks are estimated.

related risks and fail to test such control activities.

- The final step is to combine the assessment of impact and likelihood into a single risk assessment. The best way to accomplish this is to create a risk matrix that shows the interrelationship between the impact and likelihood of each risk. Assuming a high/medium/low scale is used for the impact and likelihood assessments, the risk matrix can be shown in Exhibit 10-8:

  - A number is assigned to each box to signify the overall level of risk. Once each risk is placed in one of the boxes, they can be classified as follows:

  - Risks in boxes 8 or 9 (red shading) are considered high risk.

  - Risks in boxes 5, 6, or 7 (yellow shading) are considered medium risk.

  - Risks in boxes 1, 2, 3, or 4 (no shading) are considered low risk.

High and medium risks should be included in every audit engagement. Low risks may or may not be included, depending on the internal audit function's charter, objectives of the engagement, and resource considerations. Refer to Exhibit 10-9 for an example of a cash disbursements risk matrix.

Using a matrix or some other means to visually depict the results of the risk assessment will facilitate an overall review of the judgments made in the risk assessment process by internal audit management and the process owners. Such reviews, particularly by the process owner, will help validate the judgments made by the auditor.

Understanding Management's Risk Tolerance

Traditionally, judgments of the internal audit team are the sole source for evaluating risks. This reflects the internal auditor's overall governance role in the organization. However, an underlying premise in enterprise risk management is that management must establish tolerances to business risks, consistent with the organization's overall risk appetite. This premise applies at the process level as well.

EXHIBIT 10-8

EXAMPLE OF A RISK MATRIX

IMPACT		Low	Medium	High
	High	7	8	9
	Medium	4	5	6
	Low	1	2	3
		Low	Medium	High

LIKELIHOOD

Therefore, it is important for the internal auditor to validate the reasonableness of the high, medium, and low impact thresholds that were employed. It is possible that management may have a different level of risk tolerance for the process. To gain an understanding of management's risk tolerance levels, the following steps should be conducted:

- **Identify Possible Risk Outcomes.** As previously discussed, by definition, risks represent a range of possible outcomes. While such outcomes typically are measured in financial terms, there may be other risk outcomes that either do not lend themselves to financial measurement or may have other outcomes that are more severe than the financial impact. For example, the safety of employees may be more severe than potential fines or penalties due to safety violations. Similarly, protecting the privacy of customer data may be more severe than the cost to

EXHIBIT 10-9

EXAMPLE OF A CASH DISBURSEMENTS RISK MATRIX

IMPACT		Low	Medium	High
	High	7 Expectations Risk	8 Duplicate Payments Risk Systems Security Risk	9
	Medium	4	5 Human Resources Risk	6 Timeliness Risk
	Low	1	2	3
		Low	**Medium**	**High**
			LIKELIHOOD	

Expectations Risk is considered *high impact* as lack of sufficient direction and oversight from senior management could result in material disbursements being made in an inappropriate or fraudulent manner. This risk is considered *low likelihood* as there are many examples of good policies and procedures governing disbursements activities, and management is not likely to ignore such an important area.

Duplicate Payments Risk is considered *high impact* as a single duplicate disbursement could be material and would represent lost funds if undetected. This risk is considered *medium likelihood* as it is fairly common for duplicate invoices to be presented to a company, however, most vendors are generally honest so it is less likely that a material duplicate payment would go undetected over time.

Systems Security Risk is considered *high impact* as unauthorized access could result in changes that might conceal material misdirected disbursements. This risk is considered *medium likelihood* as such misdirected disbursements may be detected through other means.

Human Resources Risk is considered *medium impact* as failure to recruit, develop, and maintain competent people in the Accounts Payable department could result in a higher-than-desirable number of inaccurate or late payments. This risk is considered *medium likelihood* as the necessary skill sets are not that difficult to find in the market.

Timeliness Risk is considered *medium impact* as the penalties and interest for being late would not be material, although bad vendor relations would still be of concern. This risk is considered *high likelihood* as there is heavy reliance on others to begin the cash disbursements process and, with generally tight payment terms, there are a variety of delays that could occur in the process, causing a payment to be late.

recover or protect such data.

- **Understand Established Tolerance Levels.** Once the different risk outcomes are determined, discussions can be held with process management to identify tolerance levels that they have already established. Such levels may be documented in key performance measures, individual performance goals, or other departmental communications.

- **Assess Tolerance Levels for Outcomes that Haven't Been Established.** To the extent that established tolerance levels have not comprehensively addressed all possible risk outcomes, discussions should be held with process management to determine other tolerance levels. Questions to facilitate this discussion include:

  - How much variability can you or senior management tolerate relative to achievement of process objectives?

  - What types of outcomes would you consider to be unacceptable?

  - What examples or risk scenarios would you be uncomfortable dealing with?

Understanding management's tolerance levels is important, but does not necessarily supersede the internal auditor's judgment. Remember, the internal audit function has many stakeholders; its fiduciary responsibility to other stakeholders should not be subordinated if process-level management appears to have a higher level of risk tolerance than the auditor perceives other stakeholders may have. However, having a good understanding of process management's tolerance levels will help the internal auditor finalize the risk assessment judgments, as well as gain an understanding that may prove helpful when evaluating the significance of audit findings later in the engagement.

IDENTIFY KEY CONTROL ACTIVITIES

Identifying Process-Level Control Activities

A variety of actions make up a process. All may have a role in achieving the final result, but only a few are truly critical to the outcome; that is, their absence would make it difficult to achieve the desired result. These critical actions are referred to as key control activities. Chapter 5, "Internal Control," provides a definition of internal control and a detailed discussion of the system of internal controls. Recall also, from earlier in this chapter, that entity-wide controls may have an impact on the operation of control activities at the process level. Therefore, the internal auditor must consider the impact of entity-wide controls on the process under review before proceeding with the identification of key process-level control activities.

To execute this step in engagement planning, it is important to understand the different types of control activities that may be considered key control activities at the process level. Although not an exhaustive list, the following represent examples of common control activity types:

- **Approving.** Authorization to execute a transaction by someone

Risk Appetite

The amount of risk, on a broad level, an organization is willing to accept in pursuit of its business objectives.

empowered to do so (for example, approval of a write-off).

- **Calculating.** Computing or re-computing an amount that results from other data obtained in the process (for example, using historical write-off data to compute a bad debt reserve, or checking a depreciation calculation to ensure the systematically computed amount is reasonable).

- **Documenting.** Preserving source information or documenting the rationale behind judgments made for future reference (for example, scanning receiving documentation, invoices, and checks to support a payment, or writing a memorandum to the files that outlines the judgments used in determining an accrual).

- **Examining.** Verification that an attribute exists or occurred (for example, goods being paid for were in fact received).

- **Matching.** Comparisons between two different attributes to verify that they agree (for example, a payment amount agrees with the invoice amount).

- **Monitoring.** Checking to ensure an action is occurring (for example, monitoring that an invoice approver does not exceed his or her limits).

- **Restricting.** Not allowing an unacceptable action (for example, prohibiting speculation on interest rate fluctuations, or not allowing unauthorized individuals to access certain data within key systems).

- **Segregating.** Separating incompatible duties that would create the potential for an undesirable action (for example, separating check signing and invoice approval authority).

- **Supervising.** Providing direction and oversight to ensure actions and tasks are carried out as designed (for example, supervisor approving a batch before computer processing).

Key Control Activity
An activity designed to reduce risk associated with a critical business objective.

Similar to the previous comments regarding risk in the detailed process map shown in Exhibit 10-7, it is possible that control activities won't be completely identified until the internal auditor has completed this step in the planning process. As previously stated, it is common for these two phases: Understand the Auditee and Identify and Assess Risks, to be conducted iteratively.

The process of determining which control activities are key control activities is highly subjective. There are no checklists or formulas that provide the internal auditor with absolute information on which control activities are key and which are not. Rather, determining key control activities is a judgmental process that can be accomplished best by the internal auditor answering the following question: Which of these control activities, if not performed as designed, would likely result in the inability to achieve the process-level objectives? Those control activities that would significantly impair the achievement of process-level objectives are probably key control activities. The following are important when determining which control activities are key control activities:

- The internal auditor must have a clear understanding of the process-level objectives.

- The consequences of inadequate control execution must also be evaluated to determine whether a control activity would significantly impair achievement of the objectives.

- Other compensating control activities should be considered as they may indicate that the operation of a given key control activity is not as critical as first presumed.

- The effect of one control activity on other control activities must also be considered. For example, the execution of a control activity may not appear to significantly impair the achievement of an objective, but it could impact the execution of other control activities which could impair an objective.

- The impact of entity-wide controls should also be considered. That is, weaknesses in entity-wide controls may diminish the effectiveness of process-level control activities. By understanding the effectiveness of entity-wide controls, the internal auditor can better assess the impact key control activities at the process level will have on the achievement of objectives.

- Redundant control activities, or those that are not cost effective, may need to be changed or eliminated. This should be a consideration of the internal auditor since such control activities are probably not key control activities.

Linking Control Activities to the Underlying Risks

The final step in this stage of engagement planning is to link the process-level control activities to the process-level risks. The achievement of objectives is subject to different risk scenarios, and certain control activities may only mitigate certain risks. Ultimately, if a control activity is determined to be ineffective, it may impact a single risk or multiple risks. The documentation of this linkage can be accomplished in a simple matrix, referred to as a Risk and Control Matrix, an example of which is shown in Exhibit 10-10.

Later in this chapter, you will see how this matrix can be used as the beginning for an audit program.

EVALUATE THE ADEQUACY OF CONTROL DESIGN

The next phase in the engagement planning process is to evaluate the adequacy of process design. The key to this phase is determining whether the key control activities reduce or manage the individual process risks to an acceptable level. The following questions should be considered when evaluating the adequacy of process design:

- Do the key control activities, taken individually or in the aggregate, reduce or manage the corresponding process risks to an acceptable level?

- Does the internal auditor understand what an "acceptable level" is, based on management's tolerance levels for the process?

- Are there additional compensating control activities from other

EXHIBIT 10-10

EXAMPLE RISK AND CONTROL MATRIX

Process-level Risk	Key Control Activity	Design Adequacy
Risk A – Definition (associated process-level objectives)	• Control Activity A • Control Activity B • Control Activity C	The indicated key control activities are adequate to manage this risk to an acceptable level.
Risk B – Definition (associated process-level objectives)	• Control Activity A • Control Activity D	The indicated key control activities are not adequate to manage this risk to an acceptable level (describe design gap).
Rick C – Definition (associated process-level objectives)	• Control Activity C • Control Activity E • Control Activity F	The indicated key control activities are adequate to manage this risk to an acceptable level.

processes that may further reduce the level of residual risk related to this process?

- Does it appear that the key control activities, if operating effectively, will support the achievement of process-level objectives?

- To the extent appropriate, does the process design address effectiveness and efficiency of operations, reliability of financial reporting, and compliance with applicable laws and regulations?

- What gaps, if any, exist that impede the effectiveness and efficiency of the process?

  - What specific gaps exist in the design of the process?

  - What are the possible outcomes or impacts of those gaps?

  - Why do these gaps exist—that is, what are the root causes (for example, inadequate procedures, unclear policies, non-interfacing systems, lack of segregation of duties)?

Once the internal auditor has completed the evaluations of design adequacy, any gaps that were identified should be discussed with management and documented as preliminary audit observations. Note that the matrix in Exhibit 10-10 contains a column titled "Design Adequacy" where the internal auditor's judgments can be documented. As indicated in that exhibit, the internal auditor's judgment typically is one of the following:

- The indicated key control activities are adequate to manage this risk to an acceptable level.

- The indicated key control activities are not adequate to manage this risk to an acceptable level (describe design gap).

Once the internal auditor has formed judgments on design adequacy for each individual risk, an evaluation can be made regarding the design of the process taken as a whole. Examples of conclusions for that column include the following:

- Design is adequate; no significant gaps – Overall, the process and systems appear to be designed adequately to manage the risks to an acceptable level.

- Design is adequate; however, gaps exist – Overall, the process and systems appear to be designed adequately to manage the risks to an acceptable level. However, the existence of one or more gaps may result in some exposure that the process owner may find unacceptable.

- Design is inadequate; significant gaps exist – Overall, the process design does not appear to be adequate to manage the risks to an acceptable level. Significant gaps create an intolerable level of exposure that process-level objectives will not be achieved.

These individual observations and overall evaluation will influence the nature, extent, and timing of tests to be performed.

CREATE A TEST PLAN

Now that the internal auditor fully understands how the process operates and has evaluated the adequacy of process design, the next phase is to develop a test plan. A test plan should be designed to gather evidence sufficient to support an evaluation as to how effectively the key control activities are operating. This evaluation, taken together with the evaluation of the process design adequacy, provides the internal auditor with enough information to evaluate whether the process-level risks are being managed to a level that supports achievement of process-level objectives.

Based on the understanding gained from the previous engagement planning phases, the internal auditor is now prepared to: (1) determine which control activities are important enough to test, (2) develop an approach for testing those control activities, and (3) document judgments supporting the chosen audit tests. Each of these steps is discussed in more detail in the following sections.

Determining Which Controls to Test

As indicated above, the primary focus of testing is to determine whether the key control activities are operating effectively enough to ensure process-level risks are managed sufficiently. While this may be accomplished by simply testing all of the identified key control activities, there are other factors the internal auditor must consider when determining which control activities to test.

- Are there higher level control activities that might, by themselves, provide reasonable assurance that the relevant risks are managed sufficiently? Higher level control activities may be reconciliation, monitoring, or supervisory controls performed by individuals independent of the detailed control owners, for example, their supervisors or managers. As part of a top-down risk assessment, the internal auditor should give consideration to these higher level control activities, just as the impact of entity-wide controls should be considered (as discussed earlier in this chapter).

Controls are Adequately Designed

if management has planned and organized (designed) the control activities or the system of internal controls in a manner that provides reasonable assurance that the organization's entitywide and process-level risks can be managed to an acceptable level.

- Are there other mitigating or compensating control activities that address multiple risks? If so, it may be more efficient to test these control activities rather than focusing on testing of each of the detailed key control activities.

- Was the design of control activities assessed as being adequate? If not, it may not be necessary to test the control activities as, even with effective operation, the risks may not be mitigated due to the inadequate design.

  - However, the internal auditor may decide to perform tests to determine the extent of error resulting from inadequate control design. The types of tests to quantify the errors (for example, data extraction and analysis) will likely be different than those performed to test control activities.

- When do the key control activities operate and, based on the period within scope for the engagement, is it practical to test certain key control activities? For example, certain control activities may operate only at year-end. If the engagement is being conducted during the year it may not be practical to test some of those control activities.

- Have there been changes in the process during the period that result in certain key control activities operating for only a portion of the period within scope? If so, consideration must be given to how these changes might impact the testing of key control activities.

Once these factors have been considered, the internal auditor is ready to develop a specific testing approach. As indicated above, the testing approach typically will focus on evaluating the effectiveness of control activities that are adequately designed, but some testing may be appropriate to quantify the impact of control activities that are not adequately designed.

Developing a Testing Approach

A testing approach involves determining the nature, extent and timing of tests to perform. The primary objective of testing is to determine whether the control activities are operating as designed to manage the corresponding risks to an acceptable level. The different types of audit tests are described in greater detail in Chapter 9, "Gathering and Documenting Audit Evidence." However, the following outlines the decisions that must be made when developing a testing approach.

- **Nature of Tests.** Different types of tests provide different levels of assurance and will take different amounts of time to conduct.

- **Extent of Tests.** Control activities can be tested on a partial or complete basis, that is, a sample of transactions or 100% of the transactions. Obviously, larger samples provide greater, assurance, but require more time to conduct the tests. Sampling techniques are discussed in much greater detail in Chapter 9, "Gathering and Documenting Audit Evidence."

- **Timing of Tests.** Tests can be performed at different frequencies or intervals, depending on the period covered in the engagement's scope, the nature of the control activity, and the type of test being performed.

There may be other factors influencing the nature, extent, and timing of tests. The key is to ensure that the testing approach provide sufficient evidence regarding the management of all key process-level risks.

Documenting the Testing Approach

The example Risk and Control Matrix shown in Exhibit 10-10 can be expanded by adding a column to include the Testing Approach for each risk. Exhibit 10-11 provides an example of what this matrix might look like (note that the Design Adequacy column from Exhibit 10-10 has been removed to illustrate the thought linkage between the Key Control Activity and Testing Approach columns).

Note that some of the individual tests may apply to multiple control activities, that is, they are multi-purpose tests.

> **Books R Us Example:** Exhibit 10-12 shows a partially completed Risk and Control Matrix for the cash disbursements function.

DEVELOP A WORK PROGRAM

The next step in engagement planning is to document all of the judgments and conclusions made during the planning phase. As can be seen by the breadth of activities covered in this chapter, there are many different but important tasks that were completed, as well as many more yet to be performed (for example, testing and reporting). In order to ensure all engagement team members understand what has been completed and what remains to be performed, it is common to prepare an engagement work program. This work program may take different forms, such as:

- A standard template or checklist that the lead internal auditor prepares to document the completion of the planning steps. Standard templates are frequently used to ensure each engagement covers all of the necessary tasks.

EXHIBIT 10-11

EXAMPLE RISK AND CONTROL MATRIX WITH TESTING APPROACH

Process-level Risk	Key Control Activity	Testing Approach
Risk A – Definition (associated process-level objectives)	• Control Activity A • Control Activity B • Control Activity C	• Test A • Test B • Test C
Risk B – Definition (associated process-level objectives)	• Control Activity A • Control Activity D • Control Activity E	• Test A • Test D • Test E

- A memorandum summarizing the steps completed. In situations where the planning is dynamic and not consistent from engagement to engagement, this free-form approach may be more appropriate.

- Additional columns in the Risk and Control Matrix if the internal auditor desires to have everything captured in one document.

- A combination of the three.

The format will vary from internal audit function to internal audit function. The key point is that there must be some means of:

- Ensuring all engagement team members understand what has been done and what still needs to be done.

- Communicating who is responsible for performing each engagement task.

- Providing a record of which steps are completed.

- Facilitating review by an engagement manager or director, who provides oversight and direction during the engagement planning process.

Regardless of the format, the following are covered in a typical work program:

- Key administrative steps, such as preparation of a planning memorandum, scheduling resources, establishing milestone dates, etc.

- Conducting a kick-off meeting with process-level management to discuss the objectives and scope of the engagement, process-level risks, timing of the engagement, information needs from process-level employees, reports or other deliverables, and any expectations management has of the engagement.

- Planning steps, which list each of the steps discussed in this chapter (for example, understanding the process, assessing process-level risks, identifying key control activities.).

- Fieldwork steps, which lists the specific tests that will be conducted (this may be documented in the Risk and Control Matrix discussed previously).

- Wrap-up steps, such as clearing open review notes, conducting a closing meeting with process-level management, finalizing the workpapers, etc.

- Reporting steps, such as preparing a draft engagement communication, soliciting feedback from process-level management, and issuing a final engagement communication (covered more fully in Chapter 11, "Communicating Assurance Engagement Outcomes and Performing Follow-up Procedures").

Even though the discussion of developing a work program is covered at the end of this chapter, its preparation typically will be done throughout the engagement planning process. As indicated, the format of the work program is not what's important. The key is to communicate the primary steps, judgments, and conclusions that were made during this process, and to facilitate the execution of the rest of the engagement.

Engagement Work Program

A document that lists the procedures to be followed during an engagement, designed to achieve the engagement plan.

EXHIBIT 10-12

EXAMPLE RISK AND CONTROL MATRIX FOR CASH DISBURSEMENTS

Process-level Risk	Key Control Activity	Testing Approach
Expectations Risk – Lack of well-developed and well-articulated policies, procedures, and other forms of communications from management may result in employees carrying out their responsibilities in a manner that is inconsistent with management's expectations and desires (accuracy, timeliness, recording, compliance, and approval objectives).	• Delegation of authority policy establishes approval levels for procurement and disbursement decisions. • Accounts Payable has developed detailed procedures covering all key disbursements tasks.	1. Review delegation of authority policy and evaluate whether it appears to be current and appropriate given the present responsibilities of individuals. 2. Select a sample of 80 disbursements (10% risk, 5% tolerable deviation rate, and 1% expected deviation rate) and test for approvals in accordance with the policy. 3. Review and discuss procedures with Accounts Payable personnel to determine whether the procedures accurately reflect the required tasks and could be followed by others.
Duplicate Payments Risk – Failure to identify multiple inputs of invoices may result in duplicate payments to vendors that could go undetected or prove difficult to collect (accuracy and recording objectives).	• The purchasing system alerts the AP clerk if the vendor number, invoice number, and invoice amount match an invoice previously entered. • The cash disbursements run will flag any payments of identical amounts to the same vendor for review prior to disbursement.	1. Test the system's duplicate invoice functionality by attempting to enter duplicate invoice numbers. Also, test what happens if a digit or symbol is added to the end of a duplicate invoice number. 2. Since the system only alerts the user to the possibility of a duplicate payment, extract 100% of the payments for the last year and test for possible duplicate payments. 3. Test to ensure the cash disbursements flag operates as designed.
Timeliness Risk – Inability to process payments on a timely basis may result in fines or penalties (for late payments) or missed discounts (timeliness and cash flow objectives).	• The system requires that a payment date be input during invoice data entry. • An edit report is generated whenever a payment date is more than 30 days after the invoice date. • The invoice input screen has a field that can be checked if the invoice is eligible for an early-pay discount.	1. Test the system functionality for the three key control activities. 2. Using data analysis software, compute the difference between the payment date and invoice date for 100% of payments made during the last year. Follow up on any late payments or missed discounts.
Systems Security Risk – Lack of effective logical security control activities may create opportunities for unauthorized individuals to manipulate or delete key disbursements data (accuracy, recording, and cash flow objectives).	• Logical security is administered by IT in the same manner as for all applications. • The Accounts Payable Manager must review and confirm access rights to the cash disbursements system twice per year.	1. IT logical security is tested in a separate audit by the IT audit specialists. Check the results of that audit to ensure there were no design weaknesses relating to the cash disbursements security. 2. Discuss with the Accounts Payable Manager the process for confirming access rights. Examine documentation supporting this procedure.

ALLOCATE RESOURCES TO THE ENGAGEMENT

The final step in planning the engagement is to determine the necessary resources that will be required to carry out the planned steps. This step involves: (1) estimating, or budgeting, the resources that will be needed, (2) allocating the appropriate resources to the engagement, and (3) scheduling those resources to ensure the engagement can be completed on a timely basis.

Budgeting

The first task is to estimate the resources that will be needed to conduct the engagement. A budget should be prepared that considers both the number of hours needed to complete the engagement, as well as other costs that may be required.

- **Hours needed to complete the engagement**. An experienced internal auditor is in a position to develop a reasonable estimate of the number of hours it will take to complete the planning, execution, and reporting tasks on an engagement. The estimate should be realistic, but it cannot always be precise as there may be unexpected events that can delay an engagement (for example, unavailability of key process-level employees, delays in obtaining requested information, illness of internal auditors.). A reasonable estimate should be determined, but it may be appropriate to allow for a variance from that estimate (for example, +/- 10%).

- **Other costs.** In addition to the human resource costs, some engagements may require additional expenditures. Common examples include:

    - Travel and related costs, when the engagement must be performed, all or in part, away from the location of the internal auditors.

    - Technology costs, when access to unique or non-routine technology is needed to complete the engagement (for example, data analysis software licenses, network security analysis software licenses.).

    - Supplies, when non-routine supplies are needed (for example, steel-toed shoes or hard hats for inventory count observations, special paper or ink for deliverables that are heavy in pictures or colored charts and graphs.).

The internal auditor supervising the engagement typically will prepare these budgets as they have the experience to do so and will be held accountable for managing the engagement in a manner that will be within the budget parameters that were established. The chief audit executive (CAE) relies on the effectiveness of engagement budgeting when determining the overall department budget. Refer to Chapter 8, "Managing the Internal Audit Function," for more details.

Allocating Resources

Once the engagement budget has been determined, it is time to identify and allocate the resources needed to complete the engagement. The allocation of human resources is the most important and challenging task. This involves answering the following questions:

- What types of skills are needed on this engagement (for example, financial reporting, IT)?

- What previous experience will be required on the engagement (for example, knowledge about the area, previous experience with similar audits)?

- Who in the department has the skills and experience to meet these needs?

- Is there a need for any specialty skills that do not exist within the internal audit function (for example, derivatives expertise, environmental expertise)? If so, where can these skills be obtained at a reasonable cost?

- Are there professional development considerations that might impact the allocation of resources to this engagement, for example, do certain internal auditors need a particular type of experience to help them learn and grow professionally?

- Are there any other unique departmental considerations that may impact which resources should be allocated to the engagement?

After determining the appropriate human resources for an engagement, the next task is to formally schedule those resources to the engagement. Resource scheduling can be a very dynamic process. For example, the following need to be considered when establishing a schedule:

- **Availability of Key Process Personnel.** Just because it's convenient for the internal audit function to start an engagement on a certain date, that doesn't mean the timing works for process personnel. There may be certain times of the month or quarter that are inconvenient (for example, the period when accounting personnel are focused on closing the books), absences of key personnel (due to travel, vacation, training, etc.), or other department initiatives that will divert the attention of key personnel to other matters.

- **Availability of Engagement Resources.** Similar to key process personnel, internal audit employees may have other commitments (for example, vacations, training, department initiatives, etc.) that could impact the scheduling of an engagement.

- **Availability of Outside Resources.** If specialty skills or additional manpower are needed to complete an engagement, the availability of those resources must also be considered. Sometimes, the service firms providing such resources have different schedules than the organization (for example, different holidays, block training weeks, internal initiatives, etc.).

- **Availability of Key Reviewers.** Even if the key engagement resources are available to complete the field work, unavailability of the internal audit manager or director to perform the level of review required on an engagement may delay the completion of the engagement. This should also be considered to ensure that

EXHIBIT 10-13

THE ASSURANCE ENGAGEMENT PROCESS

Plan

- Determine engagement objectives and scope.
- Understand the auditee, including auditee objectives.
- Identify and assess risks.
- Identify key control activities.
- Evaluate adequacy of control design.
- Create a test plan.
- Develop a work program.
- Allocate resources to the engagement.

Perform

- Conduct tests to gather evidence.
- Evaluate evidence gathered and reach conclusions.
- Develop observations and formulate recommendations.

Communicate

- Perform observation evaluation & escalation process.
- Conduct interim and preliminary engagement communications.
- Develop final engagement communications.
- Distribute formal and informal final communications.
- Perform monitoring and follow-up procedures.

the engagement can be completed in an appropriate time frame.

Once the allocation and scheduling of resources is completed, the engagement is ready to commence. Exhibit 10-13 highlights the next fundamental phase in the assurance engagement process: performing the engagement. The essential tasks involved in the performance phase are also listed in this exhibit.

CONDUCT TESTS TO GATHER EVIDENCE

At this point, the assurance engagement transitions from the plan phase to the perform phase. The testing approach developed in the plan phase and outlined in the Risk and Control Matrix (refer to Exhibit 10-11) must now be executed to determine whether the controls are operating as designed. As each test is conducted, evidence will be gathered to support the internal auditor's conclusions regarding how effectively the control activities are operating.

The results of testing can be documented in the Risk and Control Matrix. The example Risk and Control Matrix shown in Exhibit 10-11 can be expanded by adding a column to include the Results of Testing. Exhibit 10-14 provides an example of what this matrix might look like. Note that the Key Control Activity column from Exhibit 10-11 has been removed for this illustration. This was done to simplify this example as the Key Control Activity column is not critical to the thought process at this point. However, when conducting an assurance engagement, all of the columns are necessary to evaluate the design adequacy and operating effectiveness of key control activities. A complete Risk and Control Matrix can be found in Exhibit 10-21 at the end of this chapter.

Books R Us Example: Exhibit 10-15 shows a partially com-

EXHIBIT 10-14

EXAMPLE RISK AND CONTROL MATRIX WITH RESULTS OF TESTING

Process-level Risk	Testing Approach	Results of Testing
Risk A – Definition (associated process-level objectives)	• Test A • Test B • Test C	• Result A • Result B • Result C
Risk B – Definition (associated process-level objectives)	• Test A • Test D • Test E	• Result A • Result D • Result E

pleted Risk and Control Matrix for the cash disbursements function. At the end of each Results of Testing entry is a cross reference to the audit working papers where the test was documented (X-#). Examples of two tests are included in Exhibits 10-16 and 10-17. If an exception or weakness was found during testing, reference is also made to the working paper documenting the engagement observation (Z-#).

Examples of select working papers supporting this testing are shown in Exhibits 10-16 and 10-17.

EVALUATE EVIDENCE GATHERED AND REACH CONCLUSIONS

Conducting audit tests allows the internal auditor to gather the evidence needed to evaluate the design adequacy and operating effectiveness of key control activities, and reach conclusions about the effectiveness of the process or area under review. The following are questions that the internal auditor may need to answer, depending on the charter of the internal audit function, the objectives of the engagement, and the expectations of the auditee and other internal audit stakeholders:

● Are the key control activities designed adequately?

● Are the key control activities operating effectively, that is, as they are designed?

● Are the underlying risks being mitigated or managed to a tolerable level?

● Overall, is the process or area under review achieving its objectives?

The answers to these questions require the internal auditor to make judgments based on the information gathered during the planning phase for the audit and the execution of audit tests. While the conclusions typically require a great deal of judgment, there is a logical thought process that flows from the steps described throughout this chapter. These conclusions can be documented in the Risk and Control Matrix. Similar to past steps, the example Risk and Control Matrix shown in Exhibit 10-14 can be expanded by adding a column to include the Testing Conclusions. Exhibit 10-18 provides an example of what this matrix might look like. Note that the Testing Approach

EXHIBIT 10-15

EXAMPLE RISK AND CONTROL MATRIX FOR CASH DISBURSEMENTS

Process-level Risk	Testing Approach	Results of Testing
Expectations Risk — Lack of well-developed and well-articulated policies, procedures, and other forms of communications from management may result in employees carrying out their responsibilities in a manner that is inconsistent with management's expectations and desires (accuracy, timeliness, recording, compliance, and approval objectives).	1. Review delegation-of-authority policy and evaluate whether it appears to be current and appropriate given the present responsibilities of individuals. 2. Select a sample of 80 disbursements (10% risk, 5% tolerable deviation rate, and 1% expected deviation rate) and test for approvals in accordance with the policy. 3. Review and discuss procedures with Accounts Payable personnel to determine whether the procedures accurately reflect the required tasks and could be followed by others.	1. The delegation of authority policy lists seven individuals who are no longer with the company. Additionally, nine individuals who are new in their positions or new to the company should be on the listing but are not (Z-3). All other responsibilities appeared to be appropriate (WP X-1). 2. No observations were identified in this test; all approvals were in accordance with the delegation of authority policy, after taking into consideration necessary changes to the policy as described on working paper X-1 (WP X-2). 3. Based on discussions and observations, it appears that the documented procedures continue to be appropriate, current, and well-understood (WP X-3).
Duplicate Payments Risk — Failure to identify multiple inputs of invoices may result in duplicate payments to vendors that could go undetected or prove difficult to collect (accuracy and recording objectives).	1. Test the system's duplicate invoice functionality by attempting to enter duplicate invoice numbers. Also, test what happens if a digit or symbol is added to the end of a duplicate invoice number. 2. Since the system only alerts the user to the possibility of a duplicate payment, extract 100% of the payments for the last year and test for possible duplicate payments. 3. Test to ensure the cash disbursements flag operates as designed.	1. The system rejected all duplicate invoice entries. However, it accepted invoices where a digit or symbol was added to the end of the invoice number, creating the opportunity for a duplicate payment (Z-4) (WP X-4). 2. Fourteen (14) potentially duplicate payments were identified, totaling $357,782. A/P management is following up on all items, which appear to be due to the weakness noted on working paper X-4 (X-5). 3. The test transactions for this control were all flagged in the cash disbursements run. The 14 transactions identified in the duplicate payments test were from different disbursement batches and, thus, were not flagged by this control (WP X-6).
Timeliness Risk – Inability to process payments on a timely basis may result in fines or penalties (for late payments) or missed discounts (timeliness and cash flow objectives).	1. Test the system functionality for the three key controls. 2. Using data analysis software, compute the difference between the payment date and invoice date for 100% of payments made during the last year. Follow up on any late payments or missed discounts.	1. The benchmark testing of all three control activities indicated that they operated as designed (WPs X-7, X-8, and X-9). 2. There were 172 payments (1.1% of total disbursements) made late. Late payment fees were charged on 21 of the payments. Follow-up by A/P management resulted in such fees being waived for nine of the 21 late payments, Fees paid totaled $24,489 (Z-5). There were no missed discounts identified (WPs X-10 and X-11).
Systems Security Risk — Lack of effective logical security control activities may create opportunities for unauthorized individuals to manipulate or delete key disbursements data (accuracy, recording, and cash flow objectives).	1. IT logical security is tested in a separate audit by the IT audit specialists. Check the results of that audit to ensure there were no design weaknesses relating to the cash disbursements security. 2. Discuss with the Accounts Payable Manager the process for confirming access rights. Examine documentation supporting this procedure.	1. No design weaknesses were noted in the IT logical security testing. 2. Based on the discussion and observations of appropriate documentation, access rights appear to be reviewed appropriately and timely.

EXHIBIT 10-16

EXAMPLE OF EXPECTATIONS RISK TEST #1

X-1
Prepared by: Steve Braveheart
Reviewed by: David Richardson

Purpose of Test: To test whether the delegation of authority policy is complete, appropriate, and current relative to establishing the authority for approving procurement and disbursement transactions.

Testing Approach: Review delegation of authority policy and evaluate whether it appears to be current and appropriate given the present responsibilities of individuals.

Sampling Considerations: There are 147 individuals included in this policy. Given the small population and the nature of the assertion (that all and only appropriate individuals are delegated authority to approve procurement and disbursement transactions), a non-statistical sample was chosen. Beginning with the first person on the list, every third person was evaluated as to the appropriateness of their inclusion on the delegation of authority policy.

Results of Testing: Following are the results of the test:

- After completing the initial sample, three individuals were identified who were no longer employees of the company.

- Because of this observation, the test was extended to include all 147 individuals, which indicated that seven individuals on the list were no longer employees, one of whom had left the company 15 months ago.

- Recognizing that the list was not being updated timely, the auditor also tested new employees and promotions during the preceding 18 months and found that five of the new employees and four promoted employees should have been on the list based on their assigned responsibilities.

Conclusion: Based on the results of testing, the control activity relating to reliance on the delegation of authority policy is **not** operating consistently effectively due to failure to update the listing timely for changes in employee status (see engagement observation on working paper Z-3).

column from Exhibit 10-14 has been removed for this illustration. This was done to simplify this example as the Testing Approach column is not critical to the thought process in this example. However, as previously stated, all of the columns are necessary to evaluate the design adequacy and operating effectiveness of key control activities when conducting an assurance engagement. A complete Risk and Control Matrix can be found in Exhibit 10-21 at the end of this chapter.

Books R Us Example: Exhibit 10-19 shows a partially completed risk and control matrix for the cash disbursements function.

DEVELOP OBSERVATIONS AND FORMULATE RECOMMENDATIONS

After completing the testing, gathering the evidence needed, evaluating the evidence, and reaching conclusions, the final step for the internal auditor to complete is to develop the observations and formulate the recommendations that should be communicated to the auditee and other internal audit stakeholders. The key elements of a well-written observation are discussed briefly in Chapter 9, "Gathering and Documenting Audit Evidence." Further elaboration of these elements can be

X-5
Prepared by: Jerry Coxswain
Reviewed by: David Richardson

Purpose of Test: To test whether any duplicate payments were made during the last year.

Testing Approach: Since the system only alerts the user to the possibility of a duplicate payment, extract 100% of the payments for the last year and test for possible duplicate payments.

Sampling Considerations: It is possible to extract all of the disbursements made during the last 12 months. Therefore, all disbursements made during that timeframe were extracted from the cash disbursements system. Using the generalized audit software licensed by the department, we selected all payments of equal amounts for a given vendor, regardless of invoice number or payment date. We also reviewed payments of the same amount regardless of vendor to determine if there were payments to a vendor that may have been using different names.

Results of Testing: After analyzing all of the disbursements that met one of our criteria, we determined that the following represent potential duplicate payments:

Vendor	Invoice #	Payment Date	Amount
ABC Office Supplies	8641032	February 21, 200x	$2,316.50
ABC Office Supplies	8641032A	February 28, 200x	$2,316.50
Alpha Printing and Binding	48637899	March 15, 200x	$125,414.22
Alpha Printing and Binding	48637899-1	March 15, 200x	$125,414.22
Alpha Printing and Binding	48637977	May 15, 200x	$86,213.47
Alpha Printing and Binding	48637977-1	May 31, 200x	$86,213.47
Alpha Printing and Binding	48638102	August 15, 200x	$91,236.17
Alpha Printing and Binding	48638102*	August 31, 200x	$91,236.17
Daily Shipping Services	12587	April 22, 200x	$487.95
Daily Shipping Services	12587X	April 22, 200x	$487.95
Dewey Cheatem Tax Services	489752	April 30, 200x	$19,495.00
Dewey Cheatem Tax Services	489753	April 30, 200x	$19,495.00
Dewey Cheatem Tax Services	489960	September 30, 200x	$21,250.00
Dewey Cheatem Tax Services	489961	September 30, 200x	$21,250.00
Newtown Catering	NC1568	February 14, 200x	$685.73
Newtown Catering	NC1568A	February 28, 200x	$685.73
Newtown Catering	NC1598	March 17, 200x	$443.65
Newtown Catering	NC1598A	March 31, 200x	$443.65
Newtown Catering	NC1677	July 4, 200x	$772.43
Newtown Catering	NC1677A	July 31, 200x	$772.43
Newtown Catering	NC1751	October 31, 200x	$875.00
Newtown Catering	NC1751-1	November 30, 200x	$875.00
Newtown Catering	NC1803	December 12, 200x	$966.47
Newtown Catering	NC1804	December 31, 200x	$966.47
Spellmen Training	667305832	June 18, 200x	$7,500.00
Spellmen Training	667305833	June 18, 200x	$7,500.00
Thompson Florists	1567	August 22, 200x	$125.82
Thompson Florists	156X	August 31, 200x	$125.82

$357,782.41

Conclusion: It appears that duplicate payments are being made in instances when invoices are presented twice, either with slightly different invoice numbers or with the same invoice number, and the individual entering the invoice has added a digit to the end to prevent the system from rejecting the transaction. Therefore, the control activities are **not** operating effectively on a consistent basis (see engagement observation on working paper Z-4).

EXHIBIT 10-18

EXAMPLE RISK AND CONTROL MATRIX WITH TESTING CONCLUSIONS		
Process-Level Risk	**Results of Testing**	**Testing Conclusions**
Risk A – Definition (associated process-level objectives)	• Result A • Result B • Result C	Conclusion covering Risk A
Risk B – Definition (associated process-level objectives)	• Result A • Result D • Result E	Conclusion covering Risk B

found in Chapter 11, "Reporting on Assurance Engagement Outcomes and Performing Follow-up Procedures."

> **Books R Us Example:** Five potential audit observations were identified. These key elements of audit observations are documented in Exhibit 10-20 for each of these five audit observations.

The examples above reflect the documentation that the internal auditor can complete while conducting the fieldwork. However, there is additional information that may be necessary before including such observations in an engagement communication. Refer to Chapter 11, "Communicating Assurance Engagement Outcomes and Performing Follow-Up Procedures," where the resolution and reporting of observations are discussed in further detail.

SUMMARY

Chapter 9, "Gathering and Documenting Audit Evidence," introduced an expression known as the six Ps: Proper Prior Planning Prevents Poor Performance. This expression means that it is critical to effectively plan engagements to ensure success. Time spent up-front in the planning phase of an engagement will likely pay great dividends later, helping to ensure the overall audit will be conducted in an efficient, effective, and comprehensive manner.

The first phase of an assurance engagement is the planning phase. The key steps in planning an engagement are as follows:

- **Determine Engagement Objectives and Scope.** Each assurance engagement will be a little different, depending on the reason for performing the engagement and the desired end results. The first step is to establish the objectives of the engagement and outline the scope to articulate the time, geographical, and procedural boundaries.

- **Understand the Auditee** (including auditee objectives). In order to conduct an engagement, the auditor must first understand the auditee's objectives, the tasks undertaken within the area under review to achieve those objectives, and the ways in which

---

Observation

A finding, determination, or judgment derived from the internal auditor's test results from an assurance or consulting engagement.

EXAMPLE RISK AND CONTROL MATRIX FOR CASH DISBURSEMENTS

Process-Level Risk	Results of Testing	Testing Conclusions
Expectations Risk – Lack of well-developed and well-articulated policies, procedures, and other forms of communications from management may result in employees carrying out their responsibilities in a manner that is inconsistent with management's expectations and desires (accuracy, timeliness, recording, compliance, and approval objectives).	1. The delegation of authority policy lists seven individuals who are no longer with the company. Additionally, nine individuals who are new in their positions or new to the company that should be on the listing are not (Z-3). All other responsibilities appeared to be appropriate (WP X-1). 2. No observations were identified in this test; all approvals were in accordance with the delegation of authority policy, after taking into consideration necessary changes to the policy as described on working paper X-1 (WP X-2). 3. Based on discussions and observations, it appears that the documented procedures continue to be appropriate, current, and well-understood (WP X-3).	Based on the results of the sample chosen, we can conclude with 90% confidence that all disbursements are approved in accordance with management's expectations. However, expectations regarding approval authority are not being met due to the fact that the delegation of authority list is not updated consistently to reflect changes in employment status (see working paper Z-3). Therefore, this risk is only partially mitigated.
Duplicate Payments Risk – Failure to identify multiple inputs of invoices may result in duplicate payments to vendors that could go undetected or prove difficult to collect (accuracy and recording objectives).	1. The system rejected all duplicate invoice entries. However, it accepted invoices in which a digit or symbol was added to the end of the invoice number, creating the opportunity for a duplicate payment (Z-4) (WP X-4). 2. Fourteen (14) potentially duplicate payments were identified, totaling $357,782. A/P management is following up on all items, which appear to be due to the weakness noted on working paper X-4 (X-5). 3. The test transactions for this control were all flagged in the cash disbursements run. The 14 transactions identified in the duplicate payments test were from different disbursement batches and, thus, were not flagged by this control (WP X-6).	While the systematic controls appear to be operating effectively, it is possible to circumvent these controls through submission and input of a different invoice number or adding a digit on the end of the existing invoice number (see working paper Z-4). This represents a weakness in the design of control activities relating to this risk, which, along with the design weakness noted on working paper Z-2 indicates that this risk is not adequately mitigated.
Timeliness Risk – Inability to process payments on a timely basis may result in fines or penalties (for late payments) or missed discounts (timeliness and cash flow objectives).	1. The benchmark testing of all three controls indicated that they operated as designed (WPs X-7, X-8, and X-9). 2. There were 172 payments (1.1% of total disbursements) made late and late-payment fees were charged on 21 of the payments. Follow-up by A/P management resulted in such fees being waived for nine of the 21 late payments. Fees paid totaled $24,489 (Z-5). There were no missed discounts identified (WPs X-10 and X-11).	All of the systematic control activities are operating effectively. However, delays earlier in the process (for example, getting invoices approved and processed by initiators of the purchase) result in a relatively small number of payments being delayed. These delays have resulted in an insignificant financial impact (late-payment fees). Therefore, this risk appears to be only partially mitigated.
Systems Security Risk – Lack of effective logical security control activities may create opportunities for unauthorized individuals to manipulate or delete key disbursements data (accuracy, recording, and cash flow objectives).	1. No design weaknesses were noted in the IT logical security testing. 2. Based on the discussion and observations of appropriate documentation, access rights appear to be reviewed appropriately and timely.	The controls appear to be designed adequately and are operating effectively to mitigate this risk.

EXHIBIT 10-19

EXHIBIT 10-20

BOOKS R US AUDIT OBSERVATIONS FOR CASH DISBURSEMENTS

Z-1

Condition: There is no check with users to determine whether any goods or services have been received but not invoiced yet.

Criteria: All goods received for which title has passed to the company, or services that have been rendered, should be recorded in the financial statements.

Cause: Accounts Payable management had not previously considered or recognized the value of performing such a check.

Effect: Unrecorded liabilities, along with the corresponding unrecorded assets or expenses, may result when the books are closed at month-end, quarter-end, or year-end.

Z-2

Condition: While the system does alert the AP clerk to potential duplicate invoices, it does not prevent the AP clerk from continuing to process such an invoice.

Criteria: The receipt of goods or services should be recorded and processed only once.

Cause: The system was coded to remind the user, but not to prohibit the user from entering an invoice again if circumstances warranted.

Effect: Liabilities, and the corresponding assets or expenses, may be overstated and funds disbursed inappropriately.

Z-3

Condition: The delegation of authority policy lists seven individuals who are no longer with the company. Additionally, nine individuals, who are new in their positions or new to the company, who should be on the listing are not.

Criteria: Authority over the disbursing of funds should only be delegated to individuals whose responsibilities justify such authority.

Cause: The delegation of authority policy is updated semi-annually, rather than each time there is a change in personnel or responsibilities of authorized individuals.

Effect: Disbursements may be made that are not in accordance with management's direction.

Z-4

Condition: The system rejected all duplicate invoice entries. However, it accepted invoices in which a digit or symbol was added to the end of the invoice number, creating the opportunity for a duplicate payment.

Criteria: The receipt of goods or services should be recorded and processed only once.

Cause: In some instances, the AP clerks appear to be entering certain invoices a second time when sent by the vendor. The clerks are not recognizing that these invoices may have been received before, and, given the control design weakness as described in Z-3, are adding a digit to the end to facilitate processing. In other instances, the vendor is issuing a duplicate invoice with a different invoice number (typically one higher than the last one) and the AP clerks did not detect the potential that these were duplicate invoices.

Effect: Liabilities, and the corresponding assets or expenses, were overstated by $357,782.41 and the same amount of funds were disbursed inappropriately.

Z-5

Condition: There were 172 payments (1.1% of total disbursements) made late resulting in late-payment fees being charged on 21 of the payments. Follow-up by A/P management resulted in such fees being waived for nine of the 21 late payments. Fees paid totaled $24,489.

Criteria: Payments should be made in a timely manner, consistent with management's expectations regarding avoidance of late payment fees.

Cause: For a variety of reasons, invoice approvals were not timely in 19 of the 21 instances; thus, the payments missed the company's disbursement processing deadlines. In the remaining two instances, the delays were a result of management's decisions to withhold payment until a disagreement with the vendor could be resolved.

Effect: The company incurred late payment fees totaling $24,489.

performance is monitored and success is measured.

- **Identify and Assess Risks.** The specific events or scenarios that could prevent the achievement of the auditee's objectives must be identified and assessed. This assessment typically involves an evaluation of the impact and likelihood of the risk scenarios.

- **Identify Key Control Activities.** Key control activities are those that, individually or when aggregated with other control activities, will mitigate the auditee's risk to an acceptable level. While the auditee may have implemented many different control activities to achieve a variety of purposes, the key control activities are the ones that are truly integral to achievement of objectives.

- **Evaluate Adequacy of Control Design.** The first key evaluation is the adequacy of control design. This step requires the internal auditor to evaluate whether the collection of controls mitigate the totality of the risks that could prevent the achievement of objectives.

- **Create a Test Plan.** The test plan outlines how each of the key control activities will be tested to help the internal auditor evaluate how effectively those control activities are operating. The tests also must be linked to the underlying risks so that any weaknesses identified during testing can be evaluated relative to the impact on risk mitigation.

- **Develop a Work Program.** A formal work program outlines the key steps in the engagement process and any judgments made regarding the objectives and scope of the engagement.

- **Allocate Resources to the Engagement.** Based on the steps to be performed during an engagement, resources with the appropriate level of experience and skills must be identified and assigned to ensure the engagement can be completed in a timely and effective manner.

Planning an engagement requires more than just carrying out the steps above. It also requires effective documentation of the information gained and judgments made. While the format of such documentation created during the planning phase may take various forms, typically it will include the following:

- Planning memorandum or checklist to document the audit approach and judgments made.

- Process maps or narrative write-ups describing key process flows.

- Risk maps, depicting the judgments made regarding process-level risks.

- A Risk and Control Matrix that documents the linkage between risks, controls, testing approach, results of testing, and testing conclusions.

The second phase of an assurance engagement involves performing the tests that were outlined in the planning phase and evaluating the results. Specifically, the internal auditor conducts the following steps:

- **Conduct tests to gather evidence**. This involves completing each of the tests identified during the planning stage. During this step the internal auditor gathers and documents sufficient evidence to support the conclusions regarding how effectively the control activities are operating.

- **Evaluate evidence gathered and reach conclusions.** This step requires the internal auditor to consider the initial evaluation of control design as well as the results of testing, and to form a conclusion as to whether the underlying risks are being mitigated to an acceptable level.

- **Develop Observations and Formulate Recommendations.** Finally, any control weaknesses identified during the engagement should be written up to facilitate discussion with appropriate management and, ultimately, communication to appropriate stakeholders.

A Risk and Control Matrix is an effective way of documenting the many judgments made and results of testing during the assurance engagement. An example of the full matrix is shown in Exhibit 10-21.

EXHIBIT 10-21

RISK AND CONTROL MATRIX

Process-level Risk	Key Control Activity	Design Adequacy	Testing Approach	Results of Testing	Testing Conclusions
Risk A – Definition (associated process-level objectives)	• Control A • Control B • Control C	The indicated key control activities are adequate to manage this risk to an acceptable level.	• Test A • Test B • Test C	• Result A • Result B • Result C	Conclusion covering Risk A
Risk B – Definition (associated process-level objectives)	• Control A • Control D	The indicated key control activities are **not** adequate to manage this risk to an acceptable level (describe design gap).	• Test A • Test D • Test E	• Result A • Result D • Result E	Conclusion covering Risk B
Risk C – Definition (associated process-level objectives)	• Control C • Control E • Control F	The indicated key control activities are adequate to manage this risk to an acceptable level.	• Test F • Test G • Test H	• Result F • Result G • Result H	Conclusion covering Risk C

NOTES

1. Describe the four different reasons why an assurance engagement might be conducted.

2. List five types of scope limitations.

3. Which is the most common type of process objective and why?

4. Explain why the internal auditor must understand how entity-wide controls may influence the performance of a process.

5. Why is it important for internal auditors to identify and understand key performance indicators for a process?

6. Describe the difference between a process-level risk scenario and a process-level risk.

7. Besides financial reporting impact, list five different types of risk outcomes that could be considered when assessing the impact of risks.

8. What are the key questions that must be answered when evaluating the design adequacy of control activities?

9. What are the key steps covered in the typical work program?

10. What four questions must be answered to evaluate the evidence gathered from audit testing?

Select the best answer for each of the following questions.

1. Which of the following is *not* likely to be an assurance engagement objective?

    a. Evaluate the design adequacy of the payroll input process.

    b. Guarantee the accuracy of recorded inventory balances.

    c. Assess compliance with health and safety laws and regulations.

    d. Determine the operating effectiveness of fixed asset control activities.

2. Analytical procedures can be applied both in planning and performing an assurance engagement.

    a. True

    b. False

3. Which of the following auditee-prepared documents will likely be of greatest assistance to the internal auditor in their assessment of design adequacy?

    a. Policies and procedures manual.

    b. Organization charts and job descriptions.

    c. Process maps depicting the flow of the process.

    d. Narrative memoranda listing key tasks for portions of the process.

4. Which of the following is *not* typically a key element of process maps or narrative memoranda?

    a. Overall process objectives.

    b. Key inputs to the process.

c. Key processing steps involved in the process.

d. Key outputs from the process.

e. Key risks and control activities.

5. Which of the following external risks is *least* likely to impact the accuracy of financial reporting?

    a. The standard setting body in the organization's country issues a new financial accounting standard.

    b. A recent judicial court case increases the likelihood that pending litigation will result in an unfavorable outcome.

    c. Changes in standard industry contracts now allow for netting of payables and receivables.

    d. Competitor pressures cause the organization to pursue new sales channels.

6. Which of the following groups' risk tolerance levels are least important when conducting an assurance engagement?

    a. The audit committee or other board governance committees.

    b. Senior management.

    c. Process-level management.

    d. The internal audit function.

    e. Vendors and customers.

7. Which of the following types of control activities is likely to be least important when evaluating the design adequacy of a cash collections process?

    a. *Approving* the deposit of cash receipts into the company's bank account.

    b. *Calculating* the amount of cash received.

    c. *Documenting* the rationale behind the bank account in which the deposit will be made.

    d. *Matching* the total deposits to the amounts credited to customers' accounts receivable balances.

    e. *Segregating* the preparation of deposit slips from the adjustment of customer account balances.

8. An internal auditor determines that the process is *not* designed adequately to reduce the underlying risks to an acceptable level. Which of the following should the internal auditor do next?

    a. Write the audit report, there's no reason to test the operating effectiveness of control activities that are not designed adequately.

    b. Test compensating control activities in other processes to see if the impact of inadequate design is mitigated to an acceptable level.

    c. Test the existing key control activities anyway to prove that, despite the design inadequacy, the process is still meeting the process objectives.

d. Postpone the engagement until the design inadequacy has been rectified.

9. All testing exceptions are indications of control deficiencies and, thus, represent reportable observations.

a. True

b. False

10. Which of the following is an appropriate conclusion that can be drawn when the internal auditor identifies an observation from testing control activities?

a. The process objectives cannot be achieved.

b. The area may be vulnerable to fraud.

c. Overall, the process is not operating effectively.

d. Certain risks are not effectively mitigated.

11. Once an observation is identified by the internal auditor, it should be:

a. Documented in the working papers.

b. Discussed with the audit committee.

c. Included in the final audit report.

d. Scheduled for follow-up.

DISCUSSION QUESTIONS

1. Why is it so important to "begin with the end in mind" when planning an assurance engagement?

2. COSO defines an organization's strategic objectives as being "high-level goals, aligned with and supporting its mission" that exist at the entity level. With this definition in mind, how can an administrative, task-oriented process have strategic objectives?

3. Why do internal auditors focus on inherent risk while management tends to focus on residual risk?

4. If the internal auditor identifies too many or too few key process-level risks, what impact might that have on the overall assurance engagement?

CASE

You are the audit senior responsible for conducting an assurance engagement of the Books R Us payroll process. This process has not been audited for three years and, as such, is due in the normal audit cycle. There have been no significant changes since the previous audit; that is, there were no system changes, no reorganization of personnel, and no substantive procedural changes. However, during the last assurance engagement, the internal audit function identified several observations, some of which were considered significant. The significant observations related to the following:

- Information pertaining to employees leaving the company was not communicated to the IT department, resulting in extended delays before those employee's systems rights were terminated.

- Hours paid to non-exempt employees were not supported by approved time sheets.

- Amounts withheld for employees were not consistent with elections made by employees.

- The possibility existed that phantom (ghost) employees could be included in the payroll without detection.

Payroll management implemented actions to address all significant observations, and the internal audit function conducted limited follow-up procedures to validate that the planned actions were completed. This is the first audit since the follow-up procedures were completed.

The following is pertinent information to the payroll assurance engagement:

- Books R Us employs approximately 4,400 employees. Approximately 2,700 of those employees are salaried, the rest are hourly.

- Employees are paid bi-weekly.

- Hourly employees earn pay at straight-time for the first 10 hours in bi-weekly pay period, time-and-a-half for the next 10 hours in a pay period and double time for any hours exceeding 20 hours in a pay period.

- The company utilizes a widely-used and market tested payroll package (PayPal) for processing of all payroll transactions.

- The payroll system interfaces with the general ledger system.

- Books R Us has established a separate payroll imprest account for the processing of payroll checks. Amounts are deposited in this account from the company's general account to cover any checks presented against the imprest account each day.

- Certain non-payroll items are deducted from the payroll checks, including the following:
  - Employee loans to cover the cost of extra benefits or computer purchases.
  - Contributions to long-term retirement plans.
  - Contributions to charitable organizations, such as the United Way.
  - Contributions to Political Action Committees (PACs).

- Payroll expenses, and the related payroll accruals, are considered material to the company.

Based on the above information, perform the following steps to conduct a payroll assurance engagement.

1. Determine at least four payroll department objectives that would be relevant to this engagement.

2. Create a list of potential risk scenarios for each objective.

3. Based on the identified risk scenarios, define the key payroll risks and assess the risks.

   a. You will need to make assumptions regarding impact and likelihood for this assessment. Document the assumptions made.

   b. Also, make assumptions about and document process-level management's risk tolerance levels.

4. Document a potential process flow in a detailed process map. Make sure that this flow identifies key risks and control activities, and has at least one potential design inadequacy.

5. Develop potential key performance indicators for the process you documented in step 4.

6. Identify which control activities are considered key control activities. As part of this analysis, document your assumptions regarding the effectiveness of entity-wide controls, and how such controls affect the payroll process-level control activities, if at all.

7. Link the key control activities to the identified risks.

8. Prepare a Risk and Control Matrix to cover the appropriate information from steps 3 through 7. Conclude on the overall design adequacy of the payroll process.

9. Create a test plan for gathering evidence regarding the operating effectiveness of all key control activities.

10. Develop potential test results of testing for all tests conducted. Make sure to identify at least two observations related to the operating effectiveness of key control activities.

11. Add the results of steps 9 and 10 above to the Risk and Control Matrix. Document your conclusions on the effectiveness of control activity operation.

12. Develop observations based on the engagement results that outline the condition, criteria, cause, and effect for each observation.

REFERENCES

[1] Covey, Steven, *Seven Habits of Highly Effective People*, New York, NY: Free Press, 1989.

[2] The Committee of Sponsoring Organizations of the Treadway Commission, *Enterprise Risk Management — Integrated Framework*. Jersey City, NJ: The Committee of Sponsoring Organizations of the Treadway Commission, September 2004.

puter tech
ch allow p
ia applica
oth definit
into the tra
a authoring
trainers,
ly 83% plan
, more train
eware for at
y Boston-ba
n various au
a developme
rainers in m
e near ubiq
ber of off
ional de
to ex

CHAPTER 11
COMMUNICATING ASSURANCE ENGAGEMENT OUTCOMES AND PERFORMING FOLLOW-UP PROCEDURES

Learning Objectives

- Understand why it is appropriate and necessary to communicate assurance engagement outcomes.

- Identify the different forms of assurance engagement communications.

- Identify the steps involved in creating an effective assurance engagement communication.

- Understand the distribution process for effectively communicating assurance engagement outcomes.

- Understand what is involved in effective monitoring of and follow-up on assurance engagement outcomes.

- Understand what it means to report on an assurance engagement versus a consulting engagement.

Chapter 9, "Gathering and Documenting Audit Evidence," provided an overview of the assurance engagement process that depicted three fundamental phases: planning, performing, and communicating. Chapter 10, "Conducting the Assurance Engagement," discussed the first two phases (planning and performing) in detail. Exhibit 11-2 reviews the components of each of these phases. In this chapter, we will focus on the communicating phase.

We will begin by outlining why it is appropriate and necessary to communicate engagement outcomes. We will identify and explain the different forms of communications used to disseminate assurance engagement results and delineate the appropriate usage for each one. We will also outline the steps involved in creating the appropriate communication for the engagement performed and the distribution process to communicate assurance engagement outcomes effectively. We will then identify the necessary steps to monitor and perform follow-up on engagement outcomes that have been communicated. Finally, we will also clarify what it means to report on an assurance engagement as opposed to a consulting engagement.

EXHIBIT 11-1

2330—Recording Information

2400—Communicating Results

2410—Criteria for Communicating

2410.A1—Criteria for Communicating (Assurance Services)

2410.A2—Criteria for Communicating (Assurances Services)

2410.A3—Criteria for Communicating (Assurance Services)
2420—Quality of Communications
2421—Errors and Omissions
2430—Engagement Disclosure of Noncompliance with the *Standards*
2440—Disseminating Results
2440.A1—Disseminating Results (Assurance Services)
2440.A2—Disseminating Results (Assurance Services)
2230 —Engagement Resource Allocation

2500—Monitoring Progress

2600—Management's Acceptance of Risks

Practice Advisory 2330-1: Recording Information
Practice Advisory 2400-1: Legal Considerations in Communicating Results
Practice Advisory 2410-1: Communication Criteria
Practice Advisory 2420-1: Quality of Communications
Practice Advisory 2440-1: Recipients of Engagement Results
Practice Advisory 2440-2: Communications Outside the Organization
Practice Advisory 2500.A1-1: Follow-up Process

Because so many engagement communications involve reporting on the adequate design and operating effectiveness of internal control activities, here, as in Chapter 5, "Internal Control," the COSO Internal Control Framework will be used to study the engagement communication process. See Chapter 5 for an exploration of the Committee of Sponsoring Organizations of the Treadway Commission (COSO) as compared to other internal control frameworks. It is important to note, however, that many assurance engagements are performed with a scope intended to assess or evaluate internal control activities related to matters more narrowly focused than an overall assessment of internal control activities of a business process or area, such as accuracy of account balances, compliance with certain regulations or operating policies and procedures, or the achievement of specific business objectives. In those cases, the corresponding engagement communications will focus on, and provide management with, independent feedback on the internal audit function's results of assessing other such matters. The content of such communications will vary somewhat from the internal control activity illustrations provided throughout this chapter, but the concepts, methodologies, and approaches described are still applicable.

ENGAGEMENT COMMUNICATION OBLIGATIONS

As discussed in detail in Chapter 8, "Managing the Internal Audit Function," the chief audit executive (CAE) has the responsibility to "report periodically to the board and senior management on the internal audit activity's purpose, authority, responsibility, and performance relative to its plan. Reporting should also include significant risk exposures and control issues, corporate governance issues, and other matters needed or requested by the board and senior management" (Standard 2060). The CAE evidences the completion of these professional responsibilities by periodically reporting, among other things, the results of assurance engagements to senior management and the audit committee during routinely scheduled meetings throughout the year.

Assurance engagements, in part, evidence the internal audit function's independent evaluation of senior management's assertion that the organization's system of internal controls is adequately designed and operating effectively. That independent evaluation is typically submitted to the board audit committee and outlines management's conclusions regarding the proper design and efficacy of the organization's system of internal controls. This assessment must consider the impact, if any, of the results of individual assurance engagements performed by the internal audit function throughout the year. The internal audit function independently assesses the process that management undergoes to come to their conclusion and communicates the results of this assessment to senior management and the board audit committee.

Communication is an integral part of any assurance engagement and occurs on an ongoing basis as the engagement progresses. Results are communicated throughout the span of the engagement using various forms of communication, including memoranda, outlines, discussions, and draft working papers. In conjunction with concluding an engagement, final results are communicated to affected parties. This final engagement communication is often referred to as an "audit report" and is the formal way an internal audit function communicates the results of an engagement to management and other appropriate parties relying on the engagement outcomes.

As explained in Chapter 10, "Conducting the Assurance Engagement," individual assurance engagements are designed to meet specific audit

Assurance Services
An objective examination of evidence for the purpose of providing an independent assessment on risk management, control, or governance processes for the organization. Examples may include financial, performance, compliance, system security, and due diligence engagements.

THE ASSURANCE ENGAGEMENT PROCESS

Plan

- Determine engagement objectives and scope.
- Understand the auditee, including auditee objectives).
- Identify and assess risks.
- Identify key control activities.
- Evaluate adequacy of control design.
- Create a test plan.
- Develop a work program.
- Allocate resources to the engagement.

Perform

- Conduct tests to gather evidence.
- Evaluate evidence gathered and reach conclusions.
- Develop observations and formulate recommendations.

Communicate

- Perform observation, evaluation, and escalation process.
- Conduct interim and preliminary engagement communications.
- Develop final engagement communications.
- Distribute formal and informal final communications.
- Perform monitoring and follow-up procedures.

EXHIBIT 11-2

objectives. These audit objectives are directly tied to the annual audit risk assessment and audit plan. This chapter will focus on reporting on assurance engagements and the follow-up procedures related to observations identified during individual assurance engagements.

Chapter 10 also outlined the steps of conducting an assurance engagement. During the engagement, the internal audit function tested control activities to ensure that they had been adequately designed and are operating effectively to meet specific internal control assertions (objectives). Exhibit 11-3 describes some of these fundamental control assertions. An observation is indicated if, during testing, the internal audit function concludes that any of the control activities identified in the engagement are not properly designed or operating as intended. Of course, an engagement will occasionally result in no observations. Once an observation has been identified, however, there are several steps the internal audit function must go through to determine what impact, if any, the observation has on the internal audit function's ability to concur with management's assertion that the system of internal controls is adequately designed and operating effectively. Additionally, the internal audit function must consider the impact indicated observations have on communication obligations under the *Standards*, as described later in this chapter. Even if no observations are identified in an engagement, a formal, final communication is still necessary to indicate this fact and to fully discharge the internal audit function's obligations under the *Standards*.

The internal audit function is able to make this determination by progressing through a series of steps that allow them to evaluate factors affecting the observation relative to its impact, its likelihood, its

EXHIBIT 11-3

CRITERIA FOR ASSESSING MANAGEMENT'S ASSERTIONS

Criteria for Assessing Management's Financial Statement Assertions

Existence or occurrence	Is everything that is there supposed to be there?
Completeness	Is everything that is supposed to be there really there?
Rights and obligations	Are the items real, and are they authorized and approved?
Valuation or obligation	Are they accurately calculated and recorded?
Presentation and disclosure	Are they properly classified?

Criteria for Assessing Management's Internal Control Assertions

Authorization	Did an approved party authorize the transaction?
Validity	Were the transactions approved?
Accuracy	Were the terms, amounts, etc. correct?
Timeliness	Was everything recorded in the proper period?
Confidentiality	Was the information kept private?
Integrity	Was the information free from corruption and alteration?
Availability	Was the information stored and readily retrievable?

classification, and the way in which it affects the mitigation of risk. The internal audit function must also determine the cause of the observation, specifically whether the control activity in question is inadequately designed or operating ineffectively. After those factors have been identified for each observation detected during an engagement, the internal audit function must use judgment in determining the impact of all of the observations when taken together (aggregated). For example, an engagement might result in three observations with none of the three individually constituting a "significant" observation; however, the internal audit function might determine that the three observations, when taken together, do constitute a "significant" observation. While the process of evaluating observations applies to all control activities whether they are related to operations, compliance, or financial reporting, as discussed in Chapter 5, "Internal Control," the assessment of internal controls over financial reporting requires additional consideration of specific communication obligations dictated by the specific financial reporting regulations of the countries in which a given organization operates. Consequently, when communicating an observation regarding a control activity that pertains to financial reporting, the internal audit function has less discretionary power when deciding how and to whom that communication should be made.

Exhibit 11-4 gives a visual representation of this complex process and shows the various combinations that the internal audit function will encounter when determining the appropriate escalation and form of assurance engagement communication. This final engagement communication has particular significance because it includes the internal audit function's independent assessment on the adequate design and operating effectiveness of the control environment covered within the scope of the assurance engagement in question, as well as an independent assessment of management's opinion relative to the control environment covered by the assurance engagement. Taken collectively, the final communications from all of the engagements included in the annual audit plan form the basis on which the internal audit function is able to independently assess the validity of management's opinion on the organization's system of internal controls.

Although determining how and to whom to communicate observations requires the internal audit function to make judgment calls throughout the process, Exhibit 11-4 breaks the process down into manageable steps. The process begins with determining if any observations were identified during execution of the assurance engagement and concludes with direction on how and to whom to communicate observations identified during the assurance engagement.

PERFORM OBSERVATION EVALUATION AND ESCALATION PROCESS

As indicated earlier, an observation is usually indicated when testing identifies evidence that a control activity is not operating effectively. However, an observation can also result from improper design when evaluating the control activity against the fundamental control assertions described in Exhibit 11-3. Regardless of how an observation is identified, once one or more observations are identified, the internal auditors must assess each observation using an evaluation and escalation process, similar to the one depicted in Exhibit 11-4, and determine the implication those observations have on the resulting

Observation

A finding, determination, or judgment derived from the internal auditor's test results from an assurance or consulting engagement.

EXHIBIT 11-4

OBSERVATION EVALUATION AND ESCALATION PROCESS

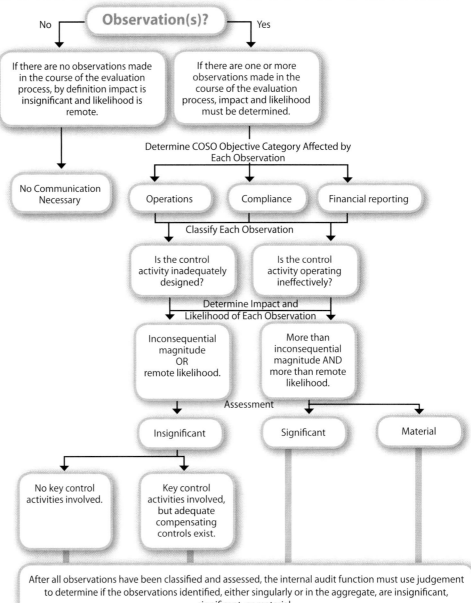

Observation(s)?

No → If there are no observations made in the course of the evaluation process, by definition impact is insignificant and likelihood is remote.

Yes → If there are one or more observations made in the course of the evaluation process, impact and likelihood must be determined.

No Communication Necessary

Determine COSO Objective Category Affected by Each Observation

- Operations
- Compliance
- Financial reporting

Classify Each Observation

- Is the control activity inadequately designed?
- Is the control activity operating ineffectively?

Determine Impact and Likelihood of Each Observation

- Inconsequential magnitude OR remote likelihood.
- More than inconsequential magnitude AND more than remote likelihood.

Assessment

- Insignificant
- Significant
- Material

- No key control activities involved.
- Key control activities involved, but adequate compensating controls exist.

After all observations have been classified and assessed, the internal audit function must use judgement to determine if the observations identified, either singularly or in the aggregate, are insignificant, significant, or material.

Form of Communication Required

If observations, either singularly or in the aggregate, are assessed insignificant with no key control activities compromised, communication of any observations relating to secondary control activities will be informal and does not need to include senior management. However, a formal communication to senior management is still necessary to indicate that no observations relating to primary control activities were identified.

If observations, either singularly or in the aggregate, are assessed insignificant with key control activities compromised but adequate compensating controls exist, communication will be formal and must be made to senior management and the organization's outside independent auditor.

If observations, either singularly or in the aggregate, are assessed significant communication will be formal and needs to include senior management, the organization's outside independent auditor, and the audit committee.

If observations, either singularly or in the aggregate, are assessed material, communication will be formal and needs to include management, the audit committee, the organization's outside independent auditor, and, if the observations relate to internal control over financial reporting, the communication must be provided to other interested parties, as defined by reporting requirements dictated by financial reporting laws in the countries in which the organization operates.

communications for the area (process) under review. They are able to make this determination by progressing through a series of steps that allow them to evaluate factors affecting the observation relative to its impact, its likelihood, its classification, and the way in which it affects the mitigation of risk. The internal audit function staff must also determine the cause of the observation, specifically, whether the control activity in question is inadequately designed or operating ineffectively. As indicated in Exhibit 11-4, each time a decision is made in each step of the process, it is carried through to the next step.

COSO Category

The first step, once one or more observations have been identified, is to determine which COSO category the compromised control activity affects. Control activities mitigate risks that threaten the achievement of objectives in three COSO-defined categories:

- Effectiveness and efficiency of operations.
- Reliability of financial reporting.
- Compliance with applicable laws and regulations.[1]

Classification

After the COSO category has been determined for the observation, the next step is to classify the observation in terms of how the control activity is compromised. The shortcoming will be in one of two areas. Either the control activity is inadequately designed or operating ineffectively.

Impact and Likelihood of the Observation

The next step in the process involves determining the impact and likelihood of the specific observation in question. This requires a judgment to be made regarding whether the observation represents an insignificant, a significant, or a material breach in the ability of the control activity to mitigate a specific risk or group of risks. Like all of the other

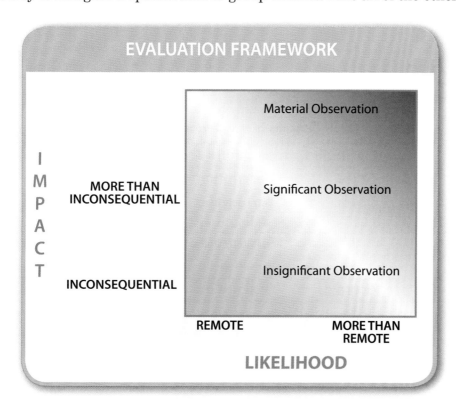

EVALUATION FRAMEWORK

EXHIBIT 11-5

steps, this one will be done for each observation identified during the engagement. After each observation has gone all the way through the process and is through this step, however, it will be performed again for all of the observations taken in aggregate. Refer to Exhibit 11-5 for a visual depiction of the relationship and interdependency of impact and likelihood.

There are three different degrees of importance: insignificant, significant, and material. Although the specific terms *significant* and *material* come from the financial reporting regulations that have been instituted in many countries and have particular relevance to internal control over financial reporting, they are used here to apply to internal control activities in the areas of operations and compliance as well as financial reporting. The definitions for each of the three terms will be given shortly, but it is important to keep in mind that they are primarily conceptual. When applying them practically, internal audit functions do well to leverage the organization's existing risk appetite parameters that are developed and maintained by its risk management function(s). In many organizations, the risk appetite parameters take into consideration planning materiality of the independent outside auditor, which simplifies the observation assessment process and

EXHIBIT 11-6

RISK PRIORITIZATION METRICS
IMPACT (SEVERITY)

Metric	Score	Description	Example (Pre-tax Income Basis)	EPS
Impact	1	**Small Loss** (De Minimus)	< $ Million	< $.$$$
	2	**Medium Loss** (Inconsequential)	≥ $$ Million < $$Million	< $.$$$
	3	**Large Loss** (Significant)	≥ $$ Million < $$$ Million	≥ $.$$$ < $.$$$
	4	**Major Impact on Operations** (Material)	≥ $$$ Million < $$$$ Million	≥ $.$$$ < $.$$$
	5	**Impact Requiring Board Action**	≥ $$$$ Million < $$$$$ Million	≥ $.$$$ < $.$$$
	6	**Potential of Imperil to Survival**	≥ $$$$$ Million	≥ $.$$$

Likelihood (Probability) = Frequency + Warning

Metric	Score	Description	Range
Frequency	1	**Extremely Rare**	Once every 5 years or greater
	2	**Seldom Occurs**	Once every 1-4 years
	3	**Periodically Occurs**	Once to 11 times a year
	4	**Occurs Often**	12 or more times a year

Metric	Score	Description	Example
Warning	1	**Months or years of warning**	Legislative or regulatory change
	2	**Hours or days of warning**	Windstorm or flood
	3	**No warning**	Fire or hacker attack

OBSERVATION EVALUATION CRITERIA IMPACT (SEVERITY)	
Examples of Planning Materiality and Tolerable Error	
DESCRIPTION	RANGE
Planning Materiality	5% of Pre-Tax Income
Tolerable Error	50% of Planning Materiality
Observation Evaluation Criteria	
OBSERVATION CLASSIFICATION	RANGE
Inconsequential	<20% of Planning Materiality
Significant	20%–50% of Planning Materiality
Material	>50% of Planning Materiality

EXHIBIT 11-7

allows the relevant terms and definitions to be consistently applied to control activities related to operations and compliance in addition to internal control over financial reporting. Exhibit 11-6 provides an example of typical enterprise risk management risk prioritization financial metrics, while Exhibit 11-7 illustrates the observation evaluation criteria, including an example of tolerable error and independent outside auditor planning materiality calculation.

Insignificant

An individual observation, or a group of observations, is considered insignificant if the control activity in question has a remote likelihood (slight chance)[2] of failing or the impact of its failure is inconsequential (trivial). If the observation, or a group of observations, is assessed to be insignificant, the internal audit function must further evaluate whether key control activities are involved. This is an important consideration when determining how and to whom the observation will ultimately be reported. If the observation(s) is insignificant with no key control activities involved, communication will typically be informal and will not need to include management outside of the area(s) subject to the audit. However, a formal communication to senior management is still necessary to indicate that no observations relating to key control activities were identified. Remember that Chapter 5, "Internal Control," defined key (primary) control activities as those that are designed to mitigate significant risks associated with an organization's critical business objectives. If key control activities were involved and adequate compensating controls exist to mitigate the negative impact of the compromised key control activity, the observation is still considered insignificant. However, communication will be formal and will be escalated to management external to the area subjected to the audit (that is, those management representatives with oversight responsibility of the area audited), as well as to the organization's independent outside auditor.

Significant

Again, the term *significant deficiency* is taken from the financial reporting regulations that exist in many countries and refers specifically

Insignificant

An individual observation, or a group of observations, is considered insignificant if the control activity in question has a remote likelihood (slight chance) of failing or the impact of its failure is inconsequential (trivial).

Significat
Observation

An individual
observation,
or a group of
observations,
is considered
"significant" if the
control activity
in question has
a reasonable
possibility of failing
and the impact of its
failure is significant.

to observations related to internal control over financial reporting. However, as indicated earlier, many organizations choose, for the sake of continuity, to apply the same definitional criteria to observations related to operations and compliance. The term *significant observation* is applied in this way here. An individual observation, or a group of observations, is considered significant if the control activity in question has a more than remote likelihood of failing and the impact of its failure is more than inconsequential. If the observation, or a group of observations, is assessed to be significant, communication must be formal and include senior management, the organization's independent outside auditor, and the audit committee.

Material

Like significant deficiency the term *material weakness* is taken from financial reporting legislation and specifically applies to observations related to internal control over financial reporting. Again, many organizations apply the same definitional criteria of a material weakness to observations related to compliance and operations. The term *material observation* is applied in that manner here. An individual observation, or a group of observations, is considered material if the control activity in question has a more than remote likelihood of failing and the impact of its failure is not only more than inconsequential, but also exceeds the financial statement materiality threshold. Refer to Exhibit 11-7 for example observation evaluation criteria. If the observation, or a group of observations, is assessed to be material, communication must be formal and include senior management, the organization's independent outside auditor, and the audit committee. Additionally, if the observation concerns internal control over financial reporting, the U.S. Sarbanes-Oxley Act of 2002 and financial reporting regulations in other countries require management to qualify their opinion on internal control over financial reporting and formulate a remediation plan to correct the weakness identified in the control activities in question. Management must continue to qualify its opinion on internal control over financial reporting until the material weakness (observation) is remediated and management has verified such through control retesting that indicates the control activity in question is adequately designed and operating effectively. If management determines it is necessary to qualify their opinion on internal control over financial reporting, this fact must be reported to its stakeholders according to the laws of the country in which it operates.

Material
Observation

An individual
observation,
or a group of
observations, is
considered "material"
if the control
activity in question
has a reasonable
possibility of failing
and the impact of its
failure is not only
significant, but also
exceeds the financial
statement materiality
threshold.

Documentation of the conclusions reached as a result of performing the observation evaluation and escalation process is essential to evidencing that the internal audit function has appropriately determined how and to whom to communicate observations indicated by the test results of the assurance engagement. As previously discussed, the process begins with determining if any observations were identified during execution of the assurance engagement and concludes with direction on how and to whom to communicate observations identified during the assurance engagement. Many internal audit functions will use working paper templates or checklists to assist in documenting these results. Exhibit 11-8 is an example of such a template. Additionally, this template helps fulfill the documentation obligations as indicated in the *Standards* and discussed in Chapter 10, "Conducting the Assurance Engagement." Specifically, the *Standards* state, "Internal

EXHIBIT 11-8

OBSERVATION ASSESSMENT TEMPLATE

Assurance Engagement and Audit Observation Description
Engagement Performed: as of DATE

1.	**Observation Summary:**	
2.	**Condition (Facts)** – Factual evidence and description of control activities as they exist (what is). What was found through testing, examination, questioning, and analysis?	
3.	**Criteria** – Standards, measures, expectations, policy, or procedures used in making the evaluation (what should exist).	
4.	**Cause** – What allowed or caused the condition to exist (the why).	
5.	**Effect** – Risk or exposure encountered because the condition is not consistent with the criteria (what could go wrong, both past and possible future—impact). What is the impact (financial, reputational, in terms of associate safety, etc.)? What is the likelihood?	
6.	**Compensating Control Activities** – What other control activities, including monitoring activities, are in place to mitigate the observation?	
7.	**Conclusion** – Detailed analysis, assessment, and justification for evaluation classifications and final conclusions.	
8.	**Detailed Recommendation** – What does the internal audit function recommend? This recommendation must reconcile with management's solution as discussed during the preliminary communication process.	
9.	**Management Solution** – What will management do to fix the existing condition or prevent the problem from happening again?	

10.	**Observation Evaluation:** • COSO Category • Classification • Assessment **Evaluation performed by:** • Internal Audit Function • Business Unit Management • Outside Independent Auditor	Financial Reporting ____ Material (Weakness) ____ Operations ____ Significant (Deficiency) ____ Compliance ____ Insignificant ____ Inadequate Design ____ Key (primary) Control ____ Ineffective Operations ____ Secondary Control ____ Name Date
11.	**Working Paper Reference**	

auditors should record relevant information to support the conclusions and engagement results" (Standard 2330). Practice Advisory 2330-1 goes on to indicate, "Engagement working papers should be complete and include support for engagement conclusions reached. Among other things, engagement working papers may include: ... results of control evaluations, [and] ... results of analytical procedures."

Chapter 10 includes examples of the various steps involved in per-

EXHIBIT 11-9

OBSERVATION ASSESSMENT TEMPLATE
OUTDATED DELEGATION OF DISBURSEMENTS AUTHORITY

Books R Us Holding Corp. Cash Disbursements Process
Engagement Performed: as of Feb. 10, 200X

1.	**Observation Summary:**	Outdated Delegation of Disbursements Authority Policy
2.	**Condition (Facts)** – Factual evidence and description of control activities as they exist (what is). What was found through testing, examination, questioning, and analysis?	The delegation of authority policy lists seven individuals who are no longer with the company. Additionally, nine individuals were identified who are new in their positions or new to the company that should have disbursement authority, but are not listed in the policy.
3.	**Criteria** – Standards, measures, expectations, policies, or procedures used in making the evaluation (what should exist).	Authority over the disbursing of funds should only be delegated to individuals whose responsibilities justify such authority.
4.	**Cause** – What allowed or caused the condition to exist (the why).	The delegation of disbursements authority policy is updated semi-annually and not as changes in personnel or responsibilities of authorized individuals occur.
5.	**Effect** – Risk or exposure encountered because the condition is not consistent with the criteria (what could go wrong, both past and possible future—impact). What is the impact (financial, reputational, in terms of associate safety, etc.)? What is the likelihood?	Disbursements may be made that are not in accordance with management's or the board's direction.
6.	**Compensating Control Activities** – What other control activities, including monitoring activities, are in place to mitigate the observation?	• Once an employee leaves the company, all access rights to the system are eliminated. Therefore, even though seven individuals who have left the company remain in the policy as authorized signers, they could not get online to approve transactions. • A budget-to-actual analysis is performed monthly by all department heads and cost center owners.
7.	**Conclusion** – Detailed analysis, assessment, and justification for evaluation classifications and final conclusions.	Based on the compensating control activities, the risk of an inappropriately authorized disbursement is minimal. While management may make efforts to update the policy more frequently, they are relying on other key control activities to mitigate the risk and are willing to live with the current level of risk. Therefore, this audit observation will *not* be included in the final report.
8.	**Detailed Recommendation** – What does the internal audit function recommend? This recommendation must reconcile with management's solution as discussed during the preliminary communication process.	Management should implement procedures to update named individuals and corresponding disbursement limits listed in the delegation policy.
9.	**Management Solution** – What will management do to fix the existing condition or prevent the problem from happening again?	Management believes the risk is minimal relative to this observation and, therefore, is willing to live with the weakness as identified between policy updates. **Responsibility:** N/A **Target Date:** N/A
10.	**Observation Evaluation:** • COSO Category • Classification • Assessment **Evaluation performed by:** • Internal Audit Function • Business Unit Management • Outside Independent Auditor	Financial Reporting _X_ Material (Weakness) ____ Operations _X_ Significant (Deficiency) ____ Compliance ____ Insignificant _X_ Inadequate Design _X_ Key (primary) Control ____ Ineffective Operations ____ Secondary Control _X_ Name Date Robert Cratchert mm/dd/yy
11.	**Working Paper Reference**	Z-3, X-1

forming assurance engagements using the fictitious organization "Books R Us." Exhibits 11-9 and 11-10 are observation assessment templates that have been completed using the information obtained during the assurance engagement process for Books R Us in Chapter 10. Exhibit 11-9 documents an observation regarding delegation of disbursement authority which is determined to be insignificant with no key control activities affected. Consequently, it will be communicated informally only to management of the cash disbursements process. Exhibit 11-10 documents an observation regarding the potential for duplicate payments. Because this observation is determined to be insignificant and key control activities are affected, this observation must be communicated formally to senior management, the audit committee, and the independent outside auditor in addition to management of the cash disbursements process.

CONDUCT INTERIM AND PRELIMINARY ENGAGEMENT COMMUNICATIONS

As previously discussed, communication is an integral part of any assurance engagement and occurs on an ongoing basis as the engagement progresses. During the course of performing an assurance engagement, the internal audit function communicates routinely and regularly with the key individuals in the area subject to audit. Much of this communication will be done via e-mail and in face-to-face meetings or on conference calls. The purpose of these communications is to discuss observations as they are identified during the engagement. This allows the internal audit function to make sure the facts are accurate and also initiates dialogue regarding the best method of remediation for identified observations. When an observation calls for immediate attention, interim communication allows it to be brought to the attention of the appropriate individuals in a timely manner and increases the likelihood of prompt resolution. The internal audit function will use the information gathered during these interim communications to finalize the observations that will ultimately go into the final communication and to formalize management's action plan for inclusion in the final communication.

Although the observation evaluation and escalation process took the engagement observations through a step-by-step process to determine what will be required for final communication, the internal audit function must confirm these preliminary facts and conclusions with appropriate management representatives of the area that was subject to the audit before it is distributed in its final form. This can be accomplished in many ways, but most commonly is done through a formal meeting with management, typically referred to as an exit interview or closing conference, followed by a draft of the final communication in whatever form it will take. As part of this process, the internal audit function meets with individuals from the functional area(s) subject to the audit and confirms agreement with preliminary findings and conclusions discussed throughout the engagement. This allows all parties to review what is anticipated to be contained in the formal audit engagement communication and provides a final opportunity for any misunderstandings to be resolved. Additionally, it provides the management of the functional area(s) that was the target of the assurance engagement a way to present their thoughts and planned actions regarding the items to be covered in the final engagement communication and to

Audit Observation
Any identified and validated gap between the current and desired state arising from an assurance engagement.

EXHIBIT 11-10

OBSERVATION ASSESSMENT TEMPLATE
POTENTIAL DUPLICATE PAYMENTS

Books R Us Holding Corporation
Cash Disbursements Process
Engagement Performed as of Feb.10, 200X

1.	**Observation Summary:**	Potential Duplicate Payments
2.	**Condition (Facts)** – Factual evidence and description of control activities as they exist (what is). What was found through testing, examination, questioning, and analysis?	The system rejected all duplicate invoice entries. However, it accepted invoices where a digit or symbol was added to the end of the invoice number, creating the opportunity for a duplicate payment.
3.	**Criteria** – Standards, measures, expectations, policy, or procedures used in making the evaluation (what should exist).	The receipt of goods or services should be recorded and processed only once.
4.	**Cause** – What allowed or caused the condition to exist (the why).	In some instances, the AP clerks could be entering invoices a second time when a duplicate invoice is submitted by the vendor. The clerks are not recognizing that these invoices may have been received before, and, given the control design weakness as described in Z-4 (WP X-5), are adding a digit to the end to facilitate processing. In other instances, the vendor is issuing a duplicate invoice with a different invoice number (typically one higher than the last one) and the AP clerks did not detect the potential that these were duplicate invoices.
5.	**Effect** – Risk or exposure encountered because the condition is not consistent with the criteria (what could go wrong, both past and possible future -- impact). What is the impact (financial, reputational, in terms of associate safety, etc.)? What is the likelihood?	Liabilities, and the corresponding assets or expenses, were overstated by $357,782.41 and the same amount of funds were disbursed inappropriately.
6.	**Compensating Control Activities** – What other control activities, including monitoring activities, are in place to mitigate the observation?	A budget-to-actual analysis is performed monthly by all department heads and cost center owners.
7.	**Conclusion** – Detailed analysis, assessment, and justification for evaluation classifications and final conclusions.	While the compensating control activities may detect very large duplicate payments, the duplicate payments still must be collected from the vendor. Also, smaller, inconsequential payments may not be detected (as proven in the audit test). Management agrees with the observation and has proposed a plan to address the weakness. Therefore, this audit observation will be included in the final report.
8.	**Detailed Recommendation** – What does the internal audit function recommend? This recommendation must reconcile with management's solution as discussed during the preliminary communication process.	It is recommended that AP create a query routine that mirrors the tests run by the internal audit function and perform it prior to processing each batch. The results of this query then need to be reviewed by the AP supervisor and if any payments are identified as potentially duplicative, those transactions should be removed from the batch and researched before payment.
9.	**Management Solution** – What will management do to fix the existing condition or prevent the problem from happening again?	A query routine will be written that operates similarly to the test performed by the internal audit function. This routine will be run before a batch is processed and reviewed by the AP Supervisor. If there are any potentially duplicate payments identified, these transactions will be removed from the batch and researched before payment. **Responsibility:** AP Supervisor **Target Date:** mm/dd/yy
10.	**Observation Evaluation:** • COSO Category • Classification • Assessment **Evaluation performed by:** • Internal Audit Function • Business Unit Management • Outside Independent Auditor	Financial Reporting _X_ Material (Weakness) ____ Operations ____ Significant (Deficiency) ____ Compliance ____ Insignificant _X_ Inadequate Design _X_ Key (primary) Control _X_ Ineffective Operations ____ Secondary Control ____ Name Date Elliott Nest mm/dd/yy
11.	**Working Paper Reference**	Z-4, X-5

give feedback regarding how well the engagement team executed the assurance engagement. Management's action plan to address and resolve control weaknesses identified during the assurance engagement is commonly referred to as *management's response*. These corrective actions are formulated with input from the internal audit function, but are ultimately the responsibility of management to implement. Many internal audit functions include management's response in the final engagement communication.

> "As part of the internal auditor's discussions with the engagement client, the internal auditor should try to obtain agreement on the results of the engagement and on a plan of action to improve operations, as needed. If the internal auditor and engagement client disagree about the engagement results, the engagement communications may state both positions and the reasons for the disagreement. The engagement client's written comments may be included as an appendix to the engagement report. Alternatively, the engagement client's views may be presented in the body of the report or in a cover letter.[3]

> "The use of interim reports does not diminish or eliminate the need for a final [communication]." [4]

In conjunction with concluding an engagement, final results must be communicated to the appropriate and affected parties. This final engagement communication can take on different forms, as discussed in detail later in the chapter, and is the formal way an internal audit function discharges its professional communication obligation under the *Standards*, also discussed in detail later in the chapter.

DEVELOP FINAL ENGAGEMENT COMMUNICATIONS

The final assurance engagement communication is important for a number of reasons. As discussed in both Chapter 1, "Introduction to Internal Auditing," and Chapter 2, "The Professional Practices Framework: Ethics and Standards of Practice," a primary difference between an assurance engagement and a consulting engagement is that in an assurance engagement there are three parties involved: (1) the person or group directly involved with the process, system, or other subject matter—the auditee, (2) the person or group making the independent assessment—the internal audit function, and (3) the person or group relying on the independent assessment—the user. A consulting engagement, on the other hand, typically involves only two parties: (1) the person or group offering the advice—the internal audit function, and (2) the person or group seeking and receiving the advice—the customer. Because the results contained in the final assurance engagement communication will be used by someone other than the internal audit function and auditee (for example, the audit committee), it is imperative that the communication be concise, comprehensive, and accurate. In addition, the final communication evidences the internal audit function's independent assessment of the organization's or area's system of internal controls and serves as the permanent record of the work performed on the assurance engagement and its results.

Final assurance engagement communications ensure the internal audit function fulfills the following obligations:

Auditee

The subsidiary, business unit, department, group, or other established subdivision of an organization that is the subject of an assurance engagement.

Customer

The subsidiary, business unit, department, group, individual, or other established subdivision of an organization that is the subject of a consulting engagement.

- Communicate timely, pertinent information to management concerning weaknesses in internal control activities (lack of adequate design or operating effectiveness), strengths in internal control activities, opportunities to maximize resource utilization or cost reduction, and areas for increased productivity or efficiency.

- Document the scope, conclusion, observations, and resulting management action plans of an engagement.

- Become a part of the permanent record of the work performed during an engagement and the results of that engagement.

Like all engagement communications, the final communication should be professional, accurate, comprehensive, and distributed in a timely manner. Accomplishing all of these objectives is often a balancing act since a quality engagement communication must offer the assurance that an appropriate amount of time has been allocated to complete the work accurately and thoroughly and still be disseminated timely in order to meet management's need for current information. The time required to send out an engagement communication will vary depending on the amount of time spent on the engagement and the number and complexity of any observations contained in the communication. However, a leading practice is to provide final engagement communications to management within ten business days after completing the preliminary engagement communication (exit conference or closing conference).

A well designed final communication should include the following elements:

- **Scope and purpose of engagement.** The area or process subject to the engagement and its corresponding business objectives, related risks, and control activities (the control environment) as indicated by the annual audit risk assessment and audit universe. Practice Advisory 2410-1 specifies that "scope statements should identify the audited activities ... [Additionally,] related activities not reviewed should be identified if necessary to delineate the boundaries of the engagement. The nature and extent of engagement work performed also should be described."

- **Time frame covered by the engagement.** The period of operations covered by the engagement scope typically either as of a point in time or a period of operations that is in the past.

- **Observations as required by the evaluation and escalation process (see Exhibit 11-4) and recommendations.** Details regarding the communication of observations and recommendations will be discussed later in the chapter.

- **Engagement conclusions and rating (if applicable).** The internal audit function's opinion as to the adequacy of the area's system of internal controls for the control environment subject to audit, in addition to the internal audit function's rating of the area if a rating system is used. Ratings will be discussed in more detail later in the chapter. In order to comply with the

Standards, Practice Advisory 2410-1 provides the following information regarding conclusions: "Conclusions and opinions are the internal auditor's evaluations of the effects of the observations and recommendations on the activities reviewed. They usually put the observations and recommendations in perspective based upon their overall implications. Engagement conclusions, if included in the engagement report, should be clearly identified as such. Conclusions may encompass the entire scope of an engagement or specific aspects. They may cover, but are not limited to, whether operating or program objectives and goals conform with those of the organization, whether the organization's objectives and goals are being met, and whether the activity under review is functioning as intended."

- **Management's action plan to appropriately address reported observations (if applicable).** Summarized response of management to the audit observations contained in the final communication including the agreed upon action plan for remediation with a projected time line for completion that will be used as a basis for the internal audit function's follow-up work. The action plan should include the name(s) of the specific individual(s) that are accountable and/or responsible for carrying it out.

In addition, Practice Advisory 2410-1 states that, "engagement final communications may include background information and summaries. Background information may identify the organizational units and activities reviewed and provide relevant explanatory information. It may also include the status of observations, conclusions, and recommendations from prior reports and an indication of whether the report covers a scheduled engagement or is responding to a request. Summaries, if included, should be balanced representations of the engagement communication's content." Practice Advisory 2410-1 also recommends that "engagement client accomplishments, in terms of improvements since the last engagement or the establishment of a well-controlled operation, may be included in the engagement final communications. This information may be necessary to fairly present the existing conditions and to provide a proper perspective and appropriate balance to the engagement final communications."

Rating Systems

There is no single prescribed way for expressing engagement conclusions (observations, recommendations, and effects these observations and recommendations have on management's assessment of the activities reviewed). Options range from listing and prioritizing observations indicated from the assurance engagement to expressing an overall conclusion on the effectiveness and efficiency of control activities reviewed. As indicated in Chapter 9, "Gathering and Documenting Audit Evidence," the internal audit function's assessment of control activities that is included in the final engagement communications can be stated either positively or negatively. If an internal audit function chooses to state that the system of internal controls is adequately designed and operating effectively, it has given positive assurance. If, on the other hand, the internal audit function chooses to communicate that nothing has come to their attention that leads them to believe

Negative Assurance

A communication indicating that nothing negative has come to the internal auditor's attention.

that the system of internal controls is not adequately designed and operating effectively, it has given negative assurance. Either expression of assurance is acceptable and constitutes compliance with the *Standards*. However, many CAEs consider positive assurance to be a best practice. Guidance from The IIA supports this position, stating that "… positive assurance is one of the strongest types of audit opinions. In providing positive assurance, the auditor is taking a position on the strength of the internal controls." This translates into providing "the reader a high level of information, which generally brings a higher level of confidence or comfort in the accuracy of the opinion."[5] Conversely, when the internal audit function provides negative assurance, they take "no responsibility for the sufficiency of the audit scope and procedures to find all concerns or issues. Such an opinion is less valuable than a positive assurance opinion as it provides limited assurance that sufficient evidence was gathered to determine whether internal controls were inadequate [in design or ineffective in their operation]."[6]

Many internal audit functions and board audit committees have chosen to use a formal rating system in conjunction with their conclusions. Such a system provides a way for management and the audit committee to compare the results of assurance engagements across functional areas within an organization, as well as provides a means to trend audit results for a given functional area over time. Many rating systems exist from numerical based systems to systems more descriptive in nature (for example, a descriptive rating system may include ratings such as satisfactory versus unsatisfactory). If an internal audit function chooses to employ a rating system, there must be congruence between the rating assigned and the internal audit function's conclusion regarding management's assertion that the system of internal controls subject to the assurance engagement are adequately designed and operating effectively. In a case when the internal audit function's conclusion and/or rating is inconsistent with management's initial assertion, management would be compelled to re-evaluate that assertion in order to reconcile it with the internal audit function's conclusion (rating). For example, an unsatisfactory rating would indicate that the internal audit function has discovered a material control concern and either management's initial self-assessment would have also identified such or management would need to consider this fact and re-assess the system of internal controls for their control environment in light of this additional information. No matter how the internal audit function chooses to provide its engagement conclusions, ultimately the intent is to provide the auditee and users of the communication with the internal audit function's evaluation of the effects of the observations and recommendations on the activities reviewed and included in the scope of the assurance engagement.

Some internal audit functions make a conscious choice not to rate audit reports because of the perception that if they distribute a communication that received a rating denoting the area or process audited as less than satisfactory, it will result in an antagonistic relationship between the internal audit function and the rest of the organization. Moody's Investor Services disagrees with this perspective, however, and argues that rating audit reports is a best practice. " … audit professionals [should] adopt a simple, yet sensible, grading or rating of their reports, to help users distinguish problematic reports from other audit reports. The audit committee should be able to distinguish the various kinds of reports generated from the audit team:

- Highly critical reports where significant remedial actions are recommended.

- Reports that cite deficiencies that need to be corrected, but where the lapses are not significant.

- Reports that are, effectively, a clean bill of health, even though some improvement opportunities are identified."[7]

Engagement Observations and Recommendations

As discussed earlier in the chapter, engagement observations are items that have come to the attention of the internal audit function that can affect management's opinion on the adequate design and/or effective operations of the control environment. Engagement observations must be handled in a way consistent with and as indicated by the evaluation and escalation process previously discussed. In those cases where formal communication is indicated, the internal audit function makes recommendations to provide the auditee with guidance on appropriate ways to resolve the observation and enhance either the design or operation of the control environment. "Engagement observations and recommendations emerge by a process of comparing what should be with what is. Whether or not there is a difference, the internal auditor has a foundation on which to build the report [communication].... Observations and recommendations should be based on the following attributes:

- Criteria—The standards, measures, or expectations used in making an evaluation and/or verification (what should exist).

- Condition—The factual evidence that the internal auditor found in the course of the examination (what does exist).

- Cause—The reason for the difference between the expected and actual conditions (why the difference exists).

- Effect—The risk or exposure the organization and/or others encounter because the condition is not consistent with the criteria (the impact of the difference). In determining the degree of risk or exposure, internal auditors should consider the effect their engagement observations and recommendations may have on the organization's operations and financial statements."[8]

Criteria

The criteria states what should be. This component of an observation identifies the standard of performance that should be accomplished. The criteria may already be outlined in a policy, procedure, law, regulation, etc., or, it may need to be determined by the auditor based on reasonable standards for achievement of the organization's objectives.

Condition (Facts)

The condition describes control activities as they exist and are functioning at the time of the audit or evaluation. It states what was found through testing, examination, questioning, analysis, etc. This is the heart of the audit observation and must be supported by sufficient, competent, and relevant investigative information and audit evidence.

Cause

The cause explains what allowed the condition to exist. The cause describes the elements of management's processes that either did not exist or that failed, thus allowing the condition to occur. This is an essential component because unless it is known, recommendations or corrective action may not be possible, thus allowing recurrence of the condition.

Effect

The effect outlines the consequence (both past and possible future) of the observation. It describes what did or could happen as a result of conditions not meeting the criteria (in other words, adverse consequences). This component is necessary to convince management that corrective action is necessary. Whenever possible, this component should be quantified by indicating the dollar amount of exposure, number of occurrences, etc.

Detailed Recommendation

The recommendation offers suggestions regarding how to correct the condition. It describes the course of action management should consider to correct the condition and eliminate its adverse effect. The recommended action should address the condition's cause and should include measures to prevent its recurrence.

As indicated in the *Standards*, "Engagement communications should include recommendations for potential improvements, acknowledgements of satisfactory performance, and corrective actions. Recommendations are based on the internal auditor's observations and conclusions. They call for action to correct existing conditions or improve operations" (Practice Advisory 2410-1).

DISTRIBUTE FORMAL AND INFORMAL FINAL COMMUNICATIONS

Practice Advisory 2410-1 reiterates that "observations are pertinent statements of fact. Those observations necessary to support or prevent misunderstanding of the internal auditor's conclusions and recommendations should be included in the final engagement communications. Less significant observations or recommendations may be communicated informally."

Practice Advisory 2440-1 indicates that "the chief audit executive or designee should review and approve the final engagement communication before issuance and should decide to whom the report will be distributed." In general, "final engagement communications should be distributed to those members of the organization who are able to ensure that engagement results are given due consideration. This means that the report should go to those who are able to take corrective action or ensure that corrective action is taken. The final engagement communication should be distributed to management of the activity under review. Higher-level members in the organization may receive only a summary communication. Communications may also be distributed to other interested or affected parties such as external auditors and the board."[9]

Additionally, Practice Advisory 2410-1 states that "certain information may not be appropriate for disclosure to all report recipients because it is privileged, proprietary, or related to improper or illegal acts. Such information, however, may be disclosed in a separate report. If the conditions being reported involve senior management, report distribution should be to the board of the organization."

Final assurance engagement communications are formal or informal depending on the outcome as determined by the observation evaluation and escalation process. For every assurance engagement, however, there will always be a final, formal communication, even if there are no observations to report to management.

Formal

Formal communications are assurance engagement communications for which the intended recipient is senior management, the audit committee, the organization's independent outside auditor, and/or management to whom the key auditee individuals report. Formal communications are indicated when the control activities within the control environment evaluated during an assurance engagement are assessed to be:

- Insignificantly compromised with key control activities affected.
- Significantly compromised.
- Materially compromised.

Historically, formal audit communications have been in hard copy (written reports), or, if distributed electronically, in a Word document. As technology has become more pervasive, however, internal audit functions are beginning to migrate to other formats such as Power-Point presentations. The format used to communicate is less important (as long as it is appropriate to the information presented and the audience receiving it) than covering all of the elements of a formal communication.

As indicated earlier in the chapter, formal communications are the final, permanent record of the results of an assurance engagement. As such, they need to contain the information necessary to reflect accurately the work performed and conclusions drawn. Remember, as stated earlier, all formal communications should include the following information:

- The purpose and scope of the audit.
- The timeframe of the audit.
- The observations and recommendations (results) of the audit, if any.
- The conclusion (opinion and/or rating) of the internal audit function.
- Management's response (action plan) to the recommendations.

The information listed above should be organized clearly and incorporated into the communication using concise, specific language that leaves no room for ambiguity. An example of a final, formal communication is included as Exhibit 11-11.

Informal

When observations are determined to be insignificant as a result of the application of the evaluation and escalation process, the internal audit function will usually opt to communicate these observations to management informally via memoranda, e-mail, in face-to-face meetings, or on conference calls. No matter the form or format chosen, informal assurance engagement communications of insignificant observations are still considered final communications and serve to fulfill the internal audit function's reporting obligations under the *Standards*. The audience for informal, final communications is limited to management of the area that was the target of the audit. Informal communication is considered appropriate only when, during the observation evaluation and escalation process, all observations were assessed to be insignificant with no key control activities compromised. The informal communication will cover insignificant observations related to secondary control activities that might be compromised and, again, will only be distributed to management of the area that was the target of the audit. Even when an informal communication is indicated, in order to fully discharge the obligations outlined in the Standards relative to communicating assurance engagement outcomes, it is still necessary to issue a formal communication to senior management, the audit committee, and the independent outside auditor indicating that no observations were identified related to key control activities. An example of a final, informal communication is included as Exhibit 11-12.

Additional Assurance Engagement Communication Standards

The *Standards* offer guidance regarding the quality of assurance engagement communications as well as what is required in the event of an error or omission. The relevant standards and practice advisories are included here.

Quality of Communications

Standard 2420 of the *Standards* states that "communications should be accurate, objective, clear, concise, constructive, complete, and timely." Practice Advisory 2420-1 goes into greater detail:

- Accurate communications are free from errors and distortions and are faithful to the underlying facts. The manner in which the data and evidence is gathered, evaluated, and summarized for presentation should be done with care and precision.

- Objective communications are fair, impartial, and unbiased and are the result of a fair-minded and balanced assessment of all relevant facts and circumstances. Observations, conclusions, and recommendations should be derived and expressed without prejudice, partisanship, personal interests, and the undue influence of others.

- Clear communications are easily understood and logical. Clarity can be improved by avoiding unnecessary technical language and providing all significant and relevant information.

- Concise communications are to the point and avoid unnecessary elaboration, superfluous detail, redundancy, and wordiness. They are created by a persistent practice of revising and editing a

EXHIBIT 11-11

FINAL, FORMAL COMMUNICATION EXAMPLE
(Audit Report)

TO: Chief Accounting Officer
               Books R Us Holding Corp.

FROM: Audit Director/Manager
               Books R Us Holding Corp.

SUBJECT: Books R Us Holding Corp.
               Cash Disbursements Audit Report

               SATISFACTORY RATING

DATE: April 27, 200X

The Books R Us internal audit function completed an internal control review of the Cash Disbursements function on March 24, 200X. The scope of the review, performed as of Feb. 10, 200X, was to evaluate the design adequacy and operating effectiveness of the system of internal controls within the cash disbursements process. The review included verification procedures to ensure proper authorization, validity, accuracy, timeliness, completeness, existence, classification, confidentiality, integrity, and availability of books, records, and other relevant documentation supporting cash disbursements processed during the fiscal year ended Dec. 31, 200X

The scope of the review included, but was not limited to, documenting, evaluating, and testing the following:
- Procedures for receiving and validating requests for disbursements,.
- Procedures for approving and processing disbursements (wires or checks).
- Procedures for validating disbursements for distribution.
- Procedures for recording and balancing cash disbursements.
- Procedures for reconciling detailed records to general ledger control accounts for cash disbursements.

CONCLUSION

In our opinion, the cash disbursements process is reasonable and the system of internal controls is acceptable, resulting in a SATISFACTORY audit rating. This rating indicates that overall internal controls are acceptable to safeguard assets and minimize exposure to loss. This rating also indicates that there are relatively few deficiencies and that an appropriate level of management attention exists. The internal control environment rating definitions are included as Attachment A.

MANAGEMENT'S ACTION PLAN

Management has established a satisfactory action plan to resolve the observation presented in this report. A detailed explanation of our findings and recommendations, together with management's response, is provided in the attached report.

Copies to:

Chairman of the Board	Board Audit Committee
CEO	Independent Outside Auditor
CFO	Controller
General Counsel	Chief Compliance Officer
Chief Administrative Officer	

CONFIDENTIAL
CONTROLLED

Final, Formal Communication Example
Page 2

1. Enhance cash disbursement review and approval procedures.

Our testing of the cash disbursements system confirmed that the system appropriately rejects all duplicate invoice entries based on invoice number. However, the system edit is not comparing other invoice information for potential duplicates. Our testing indicated the system accepts invoices where a digit or symbol is added to the end of the invoice number, creating the opportunity for a duplicate payment. The receipt of goods or services should be recorded and processed only once. *(continued on next page)*

EXHIBIT 11-11 (continued)

As a result, we expanded our testing to include all invoices processed for payment from Jan. 1, 200X through Dec. 31, 200X for possible duplicate payments. Using generalized audit software, we selected all cash disbursement payments of equal amounts for a given vendor, regardless of the invoice number or payment date. Our query revealed several instances (14 invoices totaling $357,782) where the Accounts Payable clerks possibly entered certain invoices a second time when a duplicate invoice was submitted by the vendor. Follow-up with the clerks indicated they are not recognizing that these invoices may have been received before and were adding a digit to the end to facilitate processing. In other instances, the vendor issued a duplicate invoice with a different invoice number (typically one higher than the last one) and the Accounts Payable clerks did not detect that these were potentially duplicate invoices. As a result, liabilities, and the corresponding assets or expenses, were overstated by $357,782 and the same amount of funds were disbursed inappropriately. A budget-to-actual analysis is performed monthly by all department heads and cost center owners, but is not designed to detect inconsequential errors such as these.

We recommend that a query routine be developed that compares the vendor name, invoice amount, invoice date, and any other key invoice characteristics considered appropriate by Accounts Payable and compares these characteristics to previously processed invoices prior to processing each cash disbursements batch. The results of this query should be reviewed by the Accounts Payable Supervisor for potentially duplicative invoices. Any suspect transactions should be removed from the batch and investigated before processed for payment.

Management Response:

A query routine will be written that compares "key" invoice characteristics (invoice dollar amount, vendor description, invoice number, and invoice date) to previously processed invoices flagging the invoice as a potential duplicate if any characteristics are a match. This routine will be run before a batch is processed and reviewed by the Accounts Payable Supervisor. If there are any potentially duplicate invoices identified, these transactions will be removed from the batch and researched before processed for payment.

Accountability: Chief Accounting Officer
Responsibility: Accounts Payable Supervisor
Implementation Date: June 30, 200X

CONFIDENTIAL
CONTROLLED

Example Final, Formal Communication Example
Attachment A

Books R Us audit reports include an overall rating of the control environment based on the objectives, scope, and conclusions of detailed work performed. The control environment ratings are defined as follows:

SATISFACTORY
Overall internal controls are acceptable to safeguard assets and minimize exposure to loss. This rating indicates that there are relatively few minor deficiencies and that an appropriate level of management attention exists.

NEEDS IMPROVEMENT
Overall internal controls need improvement to safeguard assets and minimize exposure to loss. This rating indicates that the number and nature of deficiencies requires prompt management attention to reduce exposure to a more acceptable level.

UNSATISFACTORY
Overall internal controls are not acceptable to safeguard assets and minimize exposure to loss. This rating indicates that the number and nature of deficiencies are of a critical importance and require substantial management attention. Immediate corrective action is essential to prevent further deterioration.

*Communications
Should Be:*

• **Accurate**
• **Objective**
• **Clear**
• **Concise**
• **Constructive**
• **Complete**
• **Timely**

presentation. The goal is that each thought will be meaningful and succinct.

- Constructive communications are helpful to the engagement client and the organization and lead to improvements where needed. The contents and tone of the presentation should be useful, positive, and well-meaning and contribute to the objectives of the organization.

- Complete communications are lacking nothing that is essential to the target audience and include all significant and relevant information and observations to support recommendations and conclusions.

- Timely communications are well-timed, opportune, and expedient for careful consideration by those who may act on the recommendations. The timing of the presentation of engagement results should be set without undue delay and with a degree of urgency to enable prompt, effective action.

Errors and Omissions

Although a lot of attention is spent on accuracy and completeness in an engagement communication, there will be times when an error or omission will occur. The *Standards* have accounted for that with Practice Advisory 2421-1:

> If it is determined that a final engagement communication contains an error, the chief audit executive should consider the need to issue an amended report that identifies the information being corrected. The amended engagement communications should be distributed to all individuals who received the engagement communication being corrected.

An error is defined as an unintentional misstatement or omission of significant information in the final engagement communication.

PERFORM MONITORING AND FOLLOW-UP

The internal audit function's responsibilities do not end when engagement results are distributed. Remember that during the course of the engagement, as observations were identified, management of the area that was the target of the assurance engagement either committed to take corrective action to remediate the observations or they chose not to take action. The collaborative process that took place during the engagement ensured the internal audit function was in agreement with the proposed action plan as documented in the final engagement communication. As a result, monitoring and follow-up procedures are designed to ensure observations have been addressed and resolved in a manner consistent with management's response included in the final engagement communication. The CAE is instructed by the *Standards* to "establish a follow-up process to monitor and ensure that management actions have been effectively implemented or that senior management has accepted the risk of not taking action" (Standard 2500-A1). In other words, management must make one of two choices: either implement changes to remediate the observation or accept the risk associated with making no changes to the control activity. In either situation, the internal audit function must have a process in place to

Monitoring
A process that assesses the presence and functioning of governance, risk management, and control components over time.

EXHIBIT 11-12

FINAL, INFORMAL COMMUNICATIONS EXAMPLE
(MANAGEMENT DISCUSSION MEMORANDUM)

TO: Chief Accounting Officer
        Books R Us Holding Corporation

FROM: Audit Director/Manager
        Books R Us Holding Corporation

SUBJECT: Management Discussion Findings – Cash Disbursements Process

DATE: April 27, 200X

The internal audit function performed a review of the cash disbursements process to evaluate the design adequacy and operating effectiveness of the system of internal controls within the cash disbursements process. During the course of the review, the following observation came to our attention that affects the operational efficiency of your area. In our opinion, this observation does not constitute a reportable control deficiency and, as a result, is not included in the formal audit report.

We recommend Management evaluate the impact the observation has on operational efficiency and the cost/benefit of implementing corrective action, if any.

1. Enhance the process for updating and maintaining the delegation of disbursements authority policy.
Our review of the delegation of disbursements authority policy indicated there were seven individuals listed with disbursements authority in the policy who are no longer employed by the company and nine individuals acting with disbursements authority that are not identified in the policy as having such disbursements authority. Authority over the disbursing of funds should be limited to individuals currently employed by the company, individuals authorized to perform cash disbursements under the policy, and individuals whose job responsibilities justify such authority. The absence of such limits creates the risk disbursements might be made by individuals not authorized by the policy.

Upon further investigation, we determined the delegation of disbursements authority policy is only updated semi-annually. Currently, no updates are made when there is a change in personnel or a change in responsibilities affected by the policy. For individuals acting with disbursements authority, but not listed in the policy, all were appropriately approved to perform disbursements and required such to perform assigned job responsibilities. Additionally, our testing revealed that access rights to the cash disbursements system are eliminated upon an individual leaving the company. Therefore, even though individuals who have left the company remain in the policy as authorized signers, they could not access the system to approve disbursement transactions. In all seven cases noted during our review, system access had been disabled at termination of the individuals. Finally, we noted that a budget-to-actual analysis is performed monthly by all department heads and cost center owners. Any unauthorized disbursements of consequence would be identified and investigated immediately.

We recommend management consider enhancing procedures for updating the delegation of disbursements policy. Individuals named with disbursement authority should be incorporated into the policy via an exhibit that would list individuals with disbursement authority. The exhibit could be updated and maintained as part of the new employee on-boarding and terminated employee exit processes in a similar manner as system access rights are added or deleted allowing for the policy to be updated as changes occur.

Management's Response:

Management believes the risk of an inappropriately authorized disbursement is minimal and, therefore, is willing to live with the current level of risk as identified between policy updates. However, management does see value in separating the listing of individuals with disbursement authority from the policy itself, as well as incorporating the maintenance of this listing as part of the processing of new and terminated employees. Management will evaluate the cost/benefit of making these changes to the process for updating and maintaining the delegation of disbursements authority policy.

Accountability: Chief Financial Officer
Responsibility: Chief Accounting Officer
Implementation Date: Not Applicable

CONFIDENTIAL
CONTROLLED

monitor and follow up on agreed upon actions to ensure management has done what they intended.

If management chooses to accept the risk, the *Standards* indicate that the CAE must make a judgment regarding the prudence of that decision. Furthermore, "when the chief audit executive believes that senior management has accepted a level of risk that may be unacceptable to the organization, the chief audit executive should discuss the matter with senior management. If the decision regarding residual risk is not resolved, the chief audit executive and senior management should report the matter to the board for resolution" (Standard 2600).

If, on the other hand, management accepts responsibility for implementing changes to remediate the observations, the internal audit function must monitor the progress management makes relative to the remediation of the observations. Regular follow-up procedures should ensure that enhancements are made on schedule with the time frame outlined in the final engagement communication. Ultimately, it is the CAE's responsibility to establish and maintain a system to monitor the disposition of results communicated to management (Standard 2500). This system should be delineated in the internal audit function's audit manual. At minimum, follow-up actions should be documented and retained in the internal audit function's working papers of the next assurance engagement relating to the area that was subject to audit originally. Additionally, in the case where engagement observations were evaluated as significant or material, another audit, commonly referred to as a *follow-up* engagement, is typically scheduled with a targeted scope to evaluate and test whether the control environment of the area has been brought up to an acceptable level. This engagement should be planned, executed, and reported on in a manner consistent with any other assurance engagement.

In terms of communication, the internal audit function has the responsibility to communicate the outcome of the targeted review of the enhanced control environment to the same audience that received the communication from the original assurance engagement that resulted in the significant or material observations. Additionally, when the control activities that were assessed to be significantly or materially compromised in the original assurance engagement communication represent internal control over financial reporting, the financial reporting regulations relative to the countries in which the organization operates must be followed in terms of communication requirements. In addition, the remediation of the significant deficiency or material weakness, as well as the outcome of the targeted review, must be reported to senior management, the audit committee, and the independent outside auditor. In the case of a material weakness, the remediation and corresponding control enhancements must also be disclosed to the organization's stakeholders according to the laws of the country in which it operates.

OTHER TYPES OF ENGAGEMENTS

This chapter addresses reporting on assurance engagement outcomes only. Consulting engagements, including investigations, projects, due diligence efforts, etc., have different communication requirements. Refer to Chapter 12, "The Consulting Engagement" for details on the requirements pertinent to consulting engagement communication.

SUMMARY

In this chapter, the factors that must be addressed when disseminating the results of an assurance engagement were discussed in detail. Specifically, this chapter outlined why it is appropriate and necessary to communicate the outcomes of performed engagements to the interested parties. Next, the different types of communications internal audit functions use to disseminate engagement results were identified and explained and the appropriate usage for each one was delineated. From there, the steps involved in creating the appropriate communication for the engagement performed and the distribution process to communicate engagement outcomes effectively was outlined. Finally, the necessary steps to monitor and perform follow-up on engagement outcomes that have been communicated were identified. This chapter has provided a comprehensive understanding of all of the factors that come into play when reporting and following up on assurance engagement outcomes.

1. What is the purpose of a closing conference (exit interview)?

2. What elements need to be present for each observation when communicated in the final assurance engagement communication?

3. What is the internal audit function's responsibility after the assurance engagement communication is disseminated?

4. What is the difference between final formal communications and final informal communications and when is each one indicated?

5. What information should be included in a well-designed final assurance engagement communication?

Select the best answer for each of the following questions.

1. Recommendations should be included in final audit communications to:

   a. Provide management with options for addressing audit observations.

   b. Ensure that problems are resolved in the manner suggested by the auditor.

   c. Minimize the amount of time required to correct audit observations.

   d. Guarantee that audit observations are addressed, regardless of cost.

2. According to the Professional Practices Framework, which of the following is part of the minimum requirements for an engagement final communication?

   I.   Background information

   II. Purpose of the engagement

   III. Engagement scope

   IV. Results of the engagement

   V.   Summaries

       a. I, II, and III only.

       b. I, III, and V only.

       c. II, III, and IV only.

       d. II, IV, and V only.

3. Which of the following would not be considered a primary objective of a closing or exit conference?

   a. To resolve conflicts.

   b. To discuss the engagement observations and recommendations.

   c. To identify concerns for future audit engagements.

   d. To identify management's actions and responses to the engagement observations and recommendations.

4. During a review of purchasing operations, an internal auditor found that procedures in use did not agree with stated company procedures. However, audit tests revealed that the procedures used represented an increase in efficiency and a decrease in processing time, without a discernible decrease in control. The internal auditor should:

a. Report the lack of adherence to documented procedures as an operational deficiency.

b. Develop a flowchart of the new procedures and include it in the report to management.

c. Report the change and suggest that the change in procedures be documented.

d. Suspend the completion of the engagement until the engagement client documents the new procedures.

5. The primary reason for having formal audit engagement communications is to:

a. Provide an opportunity for the engagement client to respond.

b. Document the corrective actions required of senior management.

c. Provide a formal means by which the independent outside auditor assesses potential reliance on the internal audit function.

d. Record observations and recommended courses of action.

1. Review the engagement observation that follows and record the specific information that represents the recommendation and each of the following observation attributes: criteria, condition, cause, and effect. Does the observation as presented adequately address all of the suggested observation attributes? If not, explain why.

Audit Observation and Recommendation:

Corporation X associates are required to abide by the organization's formal Code of Business Conduct & Ethics (the Code). To ensure all associates are aware of the Code and their obligations under it, Corporation X requires all associates to acknowledge receipt of the Code. A global e-mail was sent to all associates on July 1st informing them of their obligation to read and acknowledge the Code. Associates were instructed to complete and return acknowledgements by December 1st. Our audit testing indicated the following relative to the acknowledgement process:

● As of March 1st, fewer than 50% of associates had completed and returned acknowledgements,

● Follow-up procedures have not been performed by HR or department management to date,

● There is not a formal policy indicating actions to be taken if and when associates do not return acknowledgements, and

● No disciplinary actions have been taken regarding associates who have not completed acknowledgements of the Code to date.

Improving the acknowledgement process will help Corporation X demonstrate compliance with NASD and SEC regulations requiring a Code of Ethics. It will also help to ensure all associates are aware of their responsibilities and obligations to the organization under the Code.

We recommend management enhance the acknowledgement tracking process to ensure all associates acknowledge receipt of, compliance with, and understanding of the Code. Policy and procedures need to be developed and implemented to take appropriate action when associates do not respond. Disciplinary action should be taken if associates refuse to complete and return acknowledgements, as required by policy.

Management Response:

Associates who have not acknowledged the Code as of March 24 will be sent a reminder notification the week of April 3 informing them of the requirement to acknowledge the Code. A report of all associates who continue to be delinquent in acknowledging the code will be provided to the applicable HR liaison for review and follow-up the week of April 17. The HR function will partner with the department business heads of delinquent associates to obtain the necessary acknowledgements. A final report will be generated the week of April 24 to determine the remaining associates who have not acknowledged the Code. A verbal warning will be issued to all associates who have not acknowledged the Code by April 24 and a written warning will be provided to associates who have not acknowledged the Code by April 30th.

Accountability: Jane Doe

Responsibility: John Smith

Implementation Date: May 1

2. Consider the facts presented below. Utilizing the Observation Evaluation and Escalation Process (see Exhibit 11-4) assess the facts presented and determine the following: What observation(s) is (are) indicated? What COSO objective categories are affected? Classify the observation(s) as inadequately designed, ineffectively operating, or both. Determine the impact and likelihood of the observation(s).
Assess whether the observation(s) is (are) insignificant, significant, or material. Based on your answers, how and to whom would you communicate the observation(s)?

Facts:

1. ABC Company is a major wholesaler of electrical lighting fixtures and ceiling fans.

2. The company opened a large store in a growing metropolitan area near the beginning of the company's fiscal year.

3. The following facts surfaced during post-year-end audit procedures performed by the company's financial statement auditor (independent outside auditor):

- The manager of the new store had booked a large year-end adjustment—a debit to sales and a credit to accounts receivable. The journal entry explanation indicated that the entry was made to adjust the general ledger accounts receivable account to the accounts receivable subsidiary ledger.

- The year-end gross margin percentage at the new store was significantly lower than the average gross margin percentage of the company's other stores.

- The manager of the new store was stealing payments customers made on account. That's why the general ledger was out of balance with the subsidiary ledger. The store manager made the large year-end adjusting entry to cover up the theft, which is why the store's gross margin was lower than the average of other stores.

- The year-end adjustment was material to the store but not to the company as a whole.

CASE

Facts:

1. During its assessment of the accounts payable department, the internal audit function identified the following observations:

   - Inadequate segregation of duties over certain information system access controls. Potential loss exposure of $45 million.

   - Several instances of transactions that were not properly recorded in subsidiary ledgers. Transactions were not material, either individually or in the aggregate. Potential loss exposure of $60 million.

   - A lack of timely reconciliations of the account balances affected by the improperly recorded transactions. Potential loss exposure of $25 million.

2. Based on the context in which the observations occur, management and the internal audit function agree on the potential loss exposure represented by these observations individually.

3. The organization has a risk management function that, together with the independent outside auditor, has determined that an amount less than $20 million is inconsequential in impact and that an amount greater than $80 million is material in impact.

Question:

Based only on these facts, determine the COSO objective category affected by each observation, classify each observation in terms of its design adequacy and operating effectiveness, determine the impact and likelihood for each observation, and assess whether each observation is insignificant, significant, or material. After that has been done, outline the next steps an internal audit function should take and the ramifications of the overall conclusion including how and to whom communication should be made.

REFERENCES

[1] Committee of Sponsoring Organizations of the Treadway Commission. Internal Control—Integrated Framework. (Jersey City, NJ: The Com mittee of Sponsoring Organizations of the Treadway Commission, 1994, p. 13).

[2] Financial Accounting Standards Board of the Financial Accounting Foundation. Statement of Financial Accounting Standards No. 5: Ac counting for Contingencies. (Norwalk, CT: Financial Accounting Stan dards Board of the Financial Accounting Foundation, 1975, p. 4).

[3] The Institute of Internal Auditors. The Professional Practices Frame work. (Altamonte Springs, FL: The Institute of Internal Auditors, Practice Advisory 2410-1).

[4] The Institute of Internal Auditors. The Professional Practices Frame work. (Altamonte Springs, FL: The Institute of Internal Auditors, Practice Advisory 2410-1).

[5] The Institute of Internal Auditors. Practical Considerations Regarding Internal Auditing Expressing an Opinion on Internal Control. (Altamonte Springs, FL: The Institute of Internal Auditors, p. 6-7).

[6] The Institute of Internal Auditors. Practical Considerations Regarding Internal Auditing Expressing an Opinion on Internal Control. (Altamonte Springs, FL: The Institute of Internal Auditors, p. 8).

[7] Watson, Mark, Moody's Special Comment Report Number 99909. (New York, NY: Moody's Investor Services, Inc., p. 3).

[8] The Institute of Internal Auditors. The Professional Practices Frame work. (Altamonte Springs, FL: The Institute of Internal Auditors, Practice Advisory 2410-1).

[9] The Institute of Internal Auditors. The Professional Practices Frame work. (Altamonte Springs, FL: The Institute of Internal Auditors, Practice Advisory 2440-1).

CHAPTER 12
THE CONSULTING ENGAGEMENT

> **Learning Objectives**
>
> - Understand the various types of internal audit consulting activities and services provided by internal auditors.
>
> - Understand how to conduct a consulting engagement.
>
> - Understand the benefits to an organization when the internal audit function acts as an agent of change for risk management.
>
> - Be able to identify situations when it is more appropriate to perform consulting services than assurance services.
>
> - Understand the need for the internal audit function to set boundaries for consulting activities.
>
> - Be able to effectively set customer expectations for consulting activities.

Many internal auditors love the excitement of getting a call from the chief executive officer (CEO) who needs someone to go to India next week to look at a problem with the customer service call center. The call center has had a significant increase in complaints and the CEO wants the internal audit function to report back by the end of the week with recommendations for both short-term and long-term corrective actions. A team of internal auditors will fly out over the weekend to interview key personnel and report back on the state of call center operations in India.

Another call is from the manager who oversees an outsourced payroll operation that has been having difficulty getting employee paychecks out on time. Complaints have come from the president's office that his paycheck, among others, was posted at least a day late and that some employee checks bounced. They would like someone from the internal audit function to review these issues and facilitate the implementation of appropriate corrective actions immediately. An audit team needs to be on site with the vendor in the morning in Dallas, Texas, to help management resolve the issue.

Another team is assembled to review the control activities of an organization that is a potential acquisition target in China. This due diligence assignment involves looking at what it will take to implement

EXHIBIT 12-1

PROFESSIONAL STANDARDS
RELEVANT TO CHAPTER 12

1000.C1—Purpose, Authority, and Responsibility (Consulting Engagements)
1130.C1—Impairments to Independence or Objectivity (Consulting Engagements)
1130.C2—Impairments to Independence or Objectivity (Consulting Engagements)
1210.C1—Proficiency (Consulting Engagements)
1220.C1—Due Professional Care (Consulting Engagements)
2010.C1—Planning (Consulting Engagements)
2030—Resource Management
2040—Policies and Procedures
2050—Coordination
2060—Reporting to the Board and Senior Management
2100—Nature of Work
2110—Risk Management
2110.C1—Risk Management (Consulting Engagements)
2110.C2—Risk Management (Consulting Engagements)
2120—Control
2130—Governance
2130.C1—Governance (Consulting Engagements)
2200—Engagement Planning
2201—Planning Considerations
2201.C1—Planning Considerations (Consulting Engagements)
2210—Engagement Objectives
2210.C1—Engagement Objectives (Consulting Engagements)
2220—Engagement Scope
2220.C1—Engagement Scope (Consulting Engagements)
2230—Engagement Resource Allocation
2240—Engagement Work Program
2240.C1—Engagement Work Program (Consulting Engagements)
2300—Performing the Engagement
2310—Identifying Information
2330.C1—Recording Information (Consulting Engagements)
2440.C1—Disseminating Results (Consulting Engagements)
2440.C2—Disseminating Results (Consulting Engagements)
2500.C1—Monitoring Progress (Consulting Engagements)

Add Value

Value is provided by improving opportunities to achieve organizational objectives, identifying operational improvement, and/ or reducing risk exposure through both assurance and consulting services.

the same level of control activities at the newly acquired company as the control activities of the existing organization. The chief operations officer (COO) wants a report back at the end of the month.

These are just a few examples of the challenging and rewarding consulting engagements an internal auditor may be called upon to perform.

Internal audit functions that perform consulting services have great opportunities to add value to their organizations. With the current increased focus on systems of internal controls by regulators, independent outside auditors, and management, internal auditors are being asked more frequently to train managers on the effective design, implementation, and operation of risk management methodologies and internal control activities. These requests are often special requests for which no provision has been made in the annual internal audit plan. At times, this may result in a need to increase staff or reduce some of the planned assurance work. In many cases, the chief audit executive (CAE) is able to justify the expansion of internal audit staff based on the need to help the organization improve its risk management, control, and governance processes while still keeping pace with required assurance engagements.

A very exciting part of internal auditing is coming to work on Monday and not knowing exactly what you may be working on that week. Consulting services, such as fraud investigations, special task force assignments, merger and acquisition studies, due diligence reviews, third-party vendor or service provider reviews, executive management special requests, and requests to identify root causes of operational performance problems can hit the internal auditor's desk on any given day. These projects can cause an unexpected diversion from day-to-day internal audit assurance activities and tax available resources. Many of these projects require a very timely response to management and may have stricter deadlines than already scheduled assurance projects.

David Richards, current president of The IIA has long been an advocate of internal audit consulting services. In his former role as CAE at First Energy, he noted:

> For some internal auditors, the concepts of consulting and auditing are at odds with one another because they see consulting as putting the auditor too close to the customer and potentially compromising the auditor's independence. Actually, consulting has been part of internal auditing for years ... The current definition of internal auditing recognizes that the focus of internal auditing should include both assurance and consulting services. It is clear that internal auditors can add value to consulting assignments by providing the methodologies, facilitation, focus, knowledge, technology, best practices, and independence that help solve customers' problems.[1]

INTERNAL AUDIT CONSULTING STANDARDS

If the internal audit function's charter includes such a provision, a portion of its audit plan should be allocated to providing consulting services to the organization. The internal audit function is well-positioned to perform consulting services, and the payback to the organization often is more significant than when it performs only assurance services. To ensure that it has sufficient resources to address management's concerns, the internal audit function needs to plan for and allocate a portion of available resources to consulting projects, even though such projects may not be known when preparing the annual audit plan and budget. As illustrated in the previous scenarios, many consulting projects cannot be foreseen when the annual audit plan is developed.

As noted in Exhibit 12-2, consulting services are advisory in nature and many times are conducted at the request of management. Consequently, the nature and scope of the consulting engagement are subject to agreement with the engagement customer. Consulting services generally involve two parties:

1. The person or group offering the advice—the internal audit function.
2. The person or group seeking and receiving the advice—the engagement customer.

In contrast, assurance services are performed for the purpose of independently assessing a risk management, control, or governance process and typically involve three parties:

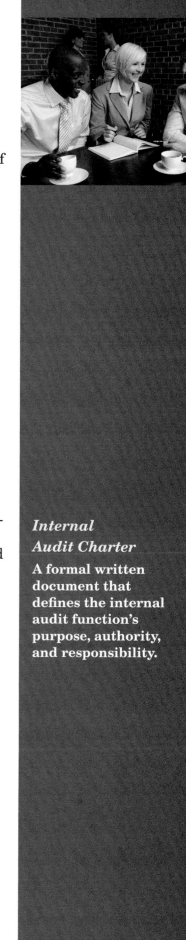

Internal Audit Charter

A formal written document that defines the internal audit function's purpose, authority, and responsibility.

EXHIBIT 12-2

DEFINING AND COMPARING CONSULTING AND ASSURANCE SERVICES

Consulting Services – Advisory and related client service activities, the nature and scope of which are agreed with the client and which are intended to add value and improve an organization's governance, risk management, and control processes without the internal auditor assuming management responsibility. Examples include counsel, advice, facilitation, and training.[1]

Assurance Services – An objective examination of evidence for the purpose of providing an independent assessment on risk management, control, or governance processes for the organization. Examples may include financial, performance, compliance, system security, and due diligence engagements.[1]

The Institute of Internal Auditors, The Professional Practices Framework, (Altamonte Springs, FL: The Institute of Internal Auditors,

1. The person or group directly involved with the process, system, or other subject matter—the auditee.

2. The person or group making the independent assessment—the internal audit function.

3. The person or group relying on the independent assessment—the user.

The internal auditor must be diligent about maintaining objectivity and the internal audit function must maintain independence when performing consulting engagements. It must also be cognizant of its objectivity and independence responsibilities when providing assurance services to recent consulting customers. Standard 1130.C2 states, "If internal auditors have potential impairments to independence or objectivity relating to proposed consulting services, disclosure should be made to the engagement client prior to accepting the engagement."[2]

TYPES OF CONSULTING SERVICES

Internal audit services range from conducting traditional financial statement reviews to operational, performance, and compliance reviews, and frequently include a combination of assurance and consulting services. Examples of internal audit services that internal auditors provide is presented in Exhibit 12-3. Although not all inclusive, this list represents a wide spectrum of consulting and assurance services an internal audit function can provide to an organization. Those that typically fall into the consulting category include: F2, F4, O1, O2, O3, O4, O5, O6, CR1, and CR4. Depending on the nature of due diligence work (F6), it could be considered consulting or assurance. If the internal audit function is asked to provide an independent assessment on risk management, control, or governance processes as part of the due diligence work, the services would be considered assurance in nature. Otherwise, due diligence support work is considered a consulting service.

As organizations go through changes such as reduction of staff or redesign of business processes, the internal audit function can be called on to assist. For example, the internal audit function may be asked by senior management to assist in reviewing and recommending improve-

EXHIBIT 12-3

EXAMPLES OF INTERNAL AUDIT SERVICES
(ASSURANCE AND CONSULTING)

Financial (F)

1. Verify the accuracy of records.
2. Cost analysis of historical data.
3. Evaluation of internal controls.
4. Facilitating the identification of risks and performing risk assessments.
5. Supporting external auditors.
6. Due diligence of pending acquisitions, divestitures, and restructuring.

Operational (O)

1. Facilitation of groups for process improvements.
2. Documenting and analyzing processes and related costs and volumes.
3. Performing functional analysis of functions performed.
4. Performing customer satisfaction surveys.
5. Evaluating the products and services offered.
6. Benchmarking with others to identify best practices.
7. Confirmation of internal employees' compliance with laws, regulations, policies, and procedures.
8. Confirmation of external parties' compliance with laws, regulations, policies, and procedures.

Safeguarding of Assets (SA)

1. Comparison of records to physical assets.
2. Reconciliation of independent records to corporate records.

Computer Related (CR)

1. Participation/review of systems development projects.
2. Review of general computer control activities.
3. Evaluation of application control activities.
4. Conducting investigations into alleged fraud situations.

From First Energy Internal Audit Group

ments in the effectiveness and efficiency of process internal control activities or to participate in quality initiatives, such as improving processes through the use of a maturity model, similar to the control maturity model introduced in Chapter 5, "Internal Control." As described at the beginning of this chapter, consulting can accommodate a wide range of services that are often based on senior management's needs and tailored to resolve specific issues that senior management has identified as requiring attention.

Many organizations have migrated to calling the internal audit function "Internal Audit and Consulting Services" in recognition of the fact that these internal audit functions go beyond the typical assurance work performed in the past. No matter what the internal audit function is called, it is important to recognize the amount of consulting and nonassurance services it provides to the organization. Many organizations feel this is where the "real" value of internal auditing to the organization can be gained. The CAE should review and approve the mix of consulting and assurance audit services with senior management and the audit committee.

The skill set necessary to perform consulting services effectively typically includes a healthy dose of business acumen in addition to customary internal audit knowledge. In many organizations, internal auditors have become known as the experts on risk management processes and techniques, as well as the go-to experts when senior management seeks assistance with the design and implementation of efficient and effective internal control activities. Exhibit 12-3 illustrates the broad range of service that many internal audit functions now provide their organizations.

THE INTERNAL AUDITOR AS CONSULTANT

Internal auditors have all the skills necessary to serve as consultants to senior management. Consequently, some internal audit functions have started adding positions titled "internal audit consultant" or "senior internal audit consultant" as a way to place emphasis on the consulting services their audit group offers. Doing a search on the internet of "internal auditing and consulting services" will produce a number of internal audit functions now using "consulting services" as part of the departmental title. Internal audit functions that provide consulting services are generally viewed as being more progressive than their counterparts who continue to offer only assurance services.

The internal audit consultant needs to be very versatile and have the ability to learn new things quickly. To be effective as a consultant, an internal auditor needs to have significant experience and expertise in process design and engineering, facilitation skills, strategic thinking, consensus building, and creative problem-solving. Those auditors who operate with a "checklist" mentality and are more comfortable using common standardized audit techniques are significantly challenged when asked to provide consulting services due to the diversity and unpredictability of the work that is required.

Christian Desjardins, Director of Audit and Consulting Services for Essilor of America, adds that:

> Consulting has been around for a while, but has not been commonplace. With an emphasis on added value, executives are more likely to turn to internal audit to leverage their knowledge for consulting engagements. Veteran internal auditors have been clamoring to do this work for years, and welcome their new role. Establishing with management a clearly-defined benefit to the company as a whole is an important criterion for accepting a consulting engagement.

> Many times, the lines between assurance and consulting engagements get blurred. Our experience at Essilor is that managers and executives will accept competent help in many forms. Internal auditing is part of the overall resource pool of the organization, so both assurance and consulting engagements are received as adding value. For some throughout the organization, there is no difference.[3]

THE INTERNAL AUDIT FUNCTION AS AN AGENT OF CHANGE

The internal audit function has the opportunity to be a positive change agent and assist in balancing control activity effectiveness and process efficiencies. As a business partner and consultant, the internal audit function can help ensure that implementing strong controls does not translate into over-control and harm the operational efficiency of business processes. As noted in Chapter 5, "Internal Control," excessive control activities can negatively impact the agility and timeliness of a process. Internal auditors who review the effectiveness and efficiency of business processes can help owners optimize those processes to improve cycle times, productivity, quality, employee turnover, customer satisfaction, and financial results. Internal auditors can help the organization by serving as catalysts for change. For internal auditors to be successful change agents, they must be forward looking, strategic thinkers and know where the organization is going. Exhibit 12-4 outlines what to expect when auditors become agents of change.

The Internal Auditor and Process Improvement

Internal auditors should take financial, physical, and human resource constraints into consideration when assisting management by aligning consulting project plans with the organization's mission and strategy. A six-step approach, as described in "Change Champions," published in *Internal Auditor* magazine and outlined in Exhibit 12-5, can assist the internal auditor in moving the organization forward with positive change and process improvement.

Control self-assessment (CSA) is one method that can be used to facilitate discussions regarding business processes and control activities. The internal auditor can focus a CSA discussion on the goals of the organization. The first step is to look at the organization's goals the business processes needed to support them. Analysis of the gaps between where the processes currently are and where they need to be provide the basis for planning how to best move the organization in the right direction.

EXHIBIT 12-4

LEADING THE WAY

For change to take hold in an organization, it must be linked explicitly to real performance goals, and it has to be in the hands of people who understand the business first and change second. Change agents ask what the goals of the organization are, and they focus on how reaching their own objectives affects the organization's operation.

The key to making change happen is to create an environment where people gravitate in the direction you want them to go. The best way to accomplish this is to make people aware of best practices. They'll naturally use a better way if you make one available. Change agents enable change.

If you're going to get something done, you're going to discomfit people around you. Change agents often interrupt routines, reveal problems, and make more work on the way to making less work.

A change agent must always be in two places at once: where the organization is and where it's going. They must also be equally comfortable dealing with senior management and frontline workers because change agents need the support of both groups.

Once you begin to work as a change agent, you're automatically subject to a higher level of scrutiny and a tougher standard of judgment — from those both above and below you. People watch change agents even more closely than others to make sure that they measure up.

Jacqueline K. Wagner, "Leading the Way," The Institute of Internal Auditors, www.theiia.org.

EXHIBIT 12-5

SIX STEPS FOR PROCESS IMPROVEMENTS

1. DEFINE THE PROBLEM AND DETERMINE NEEDS.
   Basic diagnostic tools, such as questionnaires and checklists, can help auditors determine where redundancies, bottlenecks, manual tasks, and risk points exist within the organization.

2. DOCUMENT THE "AS IS" PROCESS.
   A detailed understanding of the inputs, activities, and outputs of the existing processes can enable auditors to identify ineffective or inefficient processes, areas for automation, and unmitigated risks.

3. DETERMINE THE "SHOULD BE" PROCESS.
   Auditors can benchmark and identify best practices within and outside the organization by conducting primary research, such as interviews with customers, partners, and suppliers, or by participating in an industry best practice initiative.

4. IDENTIFY AND PRIORITIZE GAPS.
   Auditors should review the "as is" process versus the "should be" process to locate deficiencies in the current process. Once they understand the financial, physical, and human resource constraints to changing an existing process, auditors should prioritize their recommended improvements.

5. DEVELOP ACTION PLANS AND COMMUNICATE RESULTS.
   An action plan gives auditors a formal approach to convert ideas into organized game plans for implementation. Auditors should use an action plan template to convey prioritized ideas that they recommend putting into action.

6. MEASURE AND MONITOR.
   After recommended changes are put in place, auditors should check periodically to determine whether processes are functioning as designed and work with process owners to deploy a performance measurement system that can monitor and control problems.

Jeff Berk, "Change Champions," Internal Auditor, *April 2006.*

Control Self-assessment (CSA)

A methodology encompassing facilitated meetings and surveys that enables internal auditors and managers to collaborate in assessing business risks and evaluating internal control activities.

Internal auditors have the opportunity to work in an expanded role as internal control consultants and assist in the expansion of major control projects of the organization. Examples of projects where internal auditors have an opportunity to expand their role can include risk assessment of information security and contingency planning, assistance with the development and deployment of regulatory compliance processes addressing new requirements, or assistance with the resolution of known compliance-related issues through internal control activity remediation. These, along with other areas that involve the evaluation of risk and the system of internal controls, are areas in which internal auditors can provide immediate value to the organization in the review of processes and enhancement of control activities. By linking the future goals of the organization to the present conditions, the organization can look closely at its current strengths as well as obstacles that will likely affect the business process on its path to success and the future end state.

Assurance/Consulting Continuum—
Providing a Full-service Internal Audit Function

Internal auditing covers a spectrum of types of work that may be performed. Many times, the line is blurred as to whether the work is an assurance or a consulting type of engagement. In some cases, the engagement is a blended and requires assurance as part of the consulting services (for example, due diligence activities). Exhibit 12-6 shows a continuum of six basic types of internal audit services: financial auditing, performance auditing, quick response auditing, assessment services, facilitation services, and remediation services. The continuum depicted in Exhibit 12-6 underscores the importance of, and the need for, both assurance and consulting implementation standards.

The extreme left of the continuum represents traditional financial attestation audit work and, as one moves to the right, goes from traditional attestation (pure assurance) to operational auditing to fraud investigation—then into consulting with activities such as control self-assessment, and finally, to remediation services in which the internal audit function is assisting senior management with the performance of its duties rather than providing assurance.

Exhibit 12-7 depicts the assurance versus consulting services as a scale, balancing the amount of assurance and consulting services offered by the internal audit function. Both assurance and consulting services are necessary for the internal audit function to optimize its value to the organization. The depiction of the continuum illustrated in Exhibit 12-6 represents the potential for value-added services as the internal audit function moves more toward the consulting services realm and there is increased opportunity to assist management with implementing best practices in control design and risk management practices.

THE CONSULTING ENGAGEMENT

Clearly, the range of consulting services that an internal audit function can undertake is vast and varied in nature and scope. One of the issues in performing consulting engagements is how far a internal auditors should go when providing consulting services. Will they stop with advising management or will they actually perform management

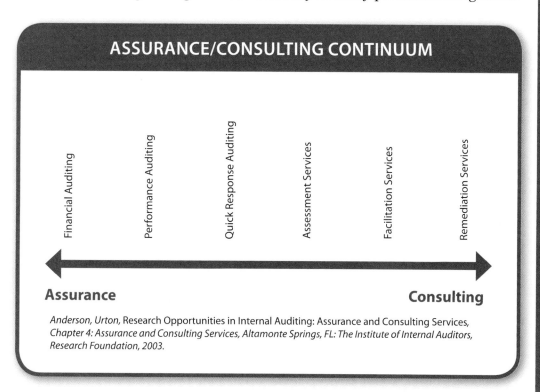

ASSURANCE/CONSULTING CONTINUUM

Financial Auditing

Performance Auditing

Quick Response Auditing

Assessment Services

Facilitation Services

Remediation Services

Assurance   **Consulting**

Anderson, Urton, Research Opportunities in Internal Auditing: Assurance and Consulting Services, Chapter 4: Assurance and Consulting Services, Altamonte Springs, FL: The Institute of Internal Auditors, Research Foundation, 2003.

EXHIBIT 12-6

duties? The U.S. Government Accountability Office (GAO) has put forth a set of basic principles and seven safeguards that significantly restrict consulting activities for governmental internal auditors, and subsequent interpretations have set some further specific limits on what governmental internal auditors are allowed to do without assuming management's role and responsibilities. For more details on auditor independence and the GAO standards, refer to www.gao.gov. Two overriding principles of these new internal audit rules include: (1) Audit groups should not provide nonaudit services that involve performing management functions or making management decisions, and (2) Audit groups should neither audit their own work nor provide nonaudit services that are significant or material to the subject matter of audits.[4] While the GAO standards apply only to governmental internal auditors, the concepts are consistent with The IIA's *Standards* and are relevant for auditors in any industry.

These types of restrictions create challenges and issues for traditional governmental internal audit functions that want to provide value-

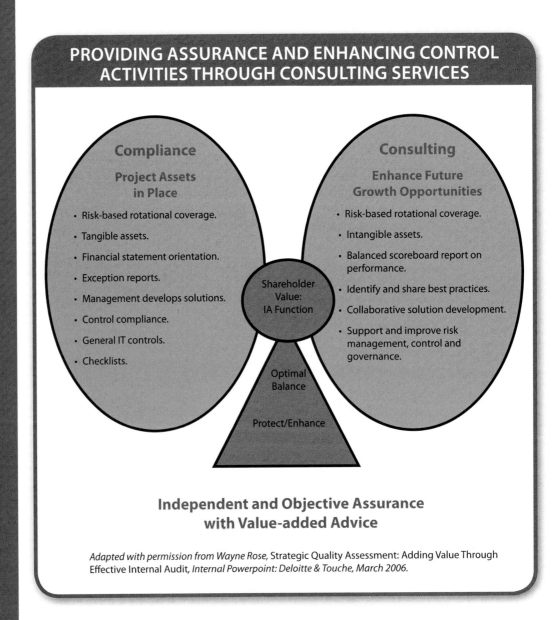

EXHIBIT 12-7

PROVIDING ASSURANCE AND ENHANCING CONTROL ACTIVITIES THROUGH CONSULTING SERVICES

Compliance

Project Assets in Place

- Risk-based rotational coverage.
- Tangible assets.
- Financial statement orientation.
- Exception reports.
- Management develops solutions.
- Control compliance.
- General IT controls.
- Checklists.

Consulting

Enhance Future Growth Opportunities

- Risk-based rotational coverage.
- Intangible assets.
- Balanced scoreboard report on performance.
- Identify and share best practices.
- Collaborative solution development.
- Support and improve risk management, control and governance.

Shareholder Value: IA Function

Optimal Balance

Protect/Enhance

Independent and Objective Assurance with Value-added Advice

Adapted with permission from Wayne Rose, Strategic Quality Assessment: Adding Value Through Effective Internal Audit, Internal Powerpoint: Deloitte & Touche, March 2006.

added consulting services to their organizations. As of late, and on the heels of the many financial reporting laws adopted by countries worldwide, audit committees in the private sector are also more sensitive to the nature and scope of consulting services that the internal audit function is providing to their organizations.

To understand the difference between assurance services and consulting services, and to apply appropriately the attribute and performance standards, internal auditors must keep in mind two key phrases found in the definitions of consulting services and assurance services: (1) "the nature and scope of which are agreed with the client" (consulting) and (2) "independent assessment" (assurance). These phrases reflect a fundamental difference in the structure and relationships involved in the delivery of the two types of services (see Exhibit 12-2).

The structural difference in consulting engagements compared with assurance engagements is an important factor to consider when planning and executing the engagement or project. In consulting, the internal audit function typically has direct contact with an identifiable customer from the start to the end of the engagement or project who will be the ultimate user of the end product. Thus, the two parties are able to work closely together to assess and tailor the work to the customer's needs. The work product is advice and recommendations, which ultimately may or may not be followed by the customer.

However, as was made apparent in Chapter 10, "Conducting the Assurance Engagement," the relationships involved in assurance services are different and more complex. First, the assurance engagement results in an independent assessment, not just advice. Users are expecting an objective assessment, which meets a higher standard than consulting advice. Second, the key parties using the internal audit function's assessment, such as the audit committee, are often remote from any direct involvement with the internal audit engagement and are placing reliance on the internal auditor's work without any direct involvement. It is critical that the internal audit function ensure that the nature and scope of the engagement are well defined and understood by both the auditee and the user of the results. For the results to have meaning and value to the user, the internal audit function must maintain independence and the internal auditor must maintain objectivity in both appearance and fact. Reporting of the results must be objective, accurate, and complete for the independent assessment to have value to the user of the results. Many of the attributes and practices required by the *Standards* are particularly concerned with keeping the interests of the internal audit function and the third-party users aligned. Because of this issue, there are considerably more stringent requirements and higher numbers of implementation standards for the delivery of assurance services than there are for consulting services.

Business process outsourcing (BPO) has become common, as evidenced by the outsourcing of various critical functions such as information technology and other critical business processes by many organizations. This allows organizations to focus on their core business areas. As third parties are asked to perform certain activities as an exten-

Engagement

An internal audit assignment, task, or review activity, such as an internal audit assurance service, consulting service, control self-assessment review, fraud examination, or compliance examination.

Customer

The subsidiary, business unit, department, group, individual or other established subdivision of an organization that is the subject of a consulting engagement.

sion of the organization, the internal audit function may be requested by management to provide pertinent services such as reviewing the transition to the BPO vendor, monitoring the vendor, and consulting on implementation of control activity recommendations.

MAINTAINING INDEPENDENCE

One of the issues in performing consulting engagements is how far an internal audit function can go when providing services on the consulting end of the spectrum without sacrificing independence for future assurance engagements. As previously indicated, the GAO has set out a set of basic principles and safeguards that significantly restrict consulting activities that governmental internal auditors can provide to their organizations. While these types of restrictions create significant limitations for traditional governmental internal audit functions, they help ensure independence at the internal audit function level and objectivity at the individual internal auditor level are maintained when providing assurance services.

In some organizations, concerns of external regulators or of the organization's board about maintaining independence and objectivity have resulted in strictly limiting the level of consulting services that the internal audit function and its internal auditors may perform.

Two key requirements essential to ensuring that the consulting services the internal audit function provides do not impair its ability to perform future assurance activities effectively are:

- Ensuring the internal audit function does not assume management responsibilities. Internal auditors should not make ultimate decisions or execute transactions as if they were part of management. The *International Standards for the Practice of Internal Auditing* highlights this requirement in the glossary definition of consulting services, which states that consulting services "are intended to add value and improve an organization's governance, risk management, and control processes without the internal auditor assuming management responsibility."

- Ensuring that internal auditors do not audit their own work. This one requires some judgment, as the prohibition is not a lifelong prohibition. The restriction is not intended to prevent the internal audit function from providing consulting services, but rather to limit internal auditors' participation in assurance engagements that evaluate control activities on which they may have consulted. While there is no explicit rule in the *Standards*, an individual internal auditor's objectivity is "presumed to be impaired if an auditor provides assurance services for an activity for which the auditor had responsibility within the previous year" (Standard 1130.A1). While providing advice does not have the same impact on objectivity as having management responsibility, it is still an important consideration. By contrast, internal auditors are allowed to provide assurance services for an activity even if they previously have provided assurance services over the same activity.

Independence

The freedom from conditions that threaten objectivity or the appearance of objectivity.

Clearly, judgment is required to ensure that objectivity is maintained. Standard 1130 ensures complete transparency of the internal audit function's past roles in serving the organization by requiring that "if independence or objectivity is impaired in fact or appearance, the details of the impairment should be disclosed to appropriate parties."

Practice Advisory 1000.C1-3, Additional Considerations for Consulting Engagements in Government Organizational Settings, provides further guidance on ensuring the internal audit function remains independent and objective. It states that internal "auditors should be independent [and] avoid relationships and situations that compromise auditors' objectivity." In addition, the practice advisory notes other threats to internal auditor objectivity that have been identified, "including the conduct of non-audit (consulting) work that:

- Creates a mutuality of interest.
- Places auditors in the role of advocate for the company."

Practice Advisory 1000.C1-3 provides examples: "providing advice on appropriate controls during system design with the clear understanding that management has responsibility for accepting or rejecting the advice would have a limited impact on the auditor's objectivity toward that system in the future. By contrast, if the auditor led the system design team, decided which controls to select, or oversaw the implementation of the recommended controls, the auditor's future ability to objectively evaluate that system would be significantly impaired. However, other nonaudit assignments may not be as clear-cut."

Practice Advisory 1000.C1-3 further suggests that the internal audit function "should implement controls that assist in reducing the potential for consulting projects to compromise objectivity of individual auditors, or the independence of the audit function as a whole," and provides the following example of techniques:

a. Defining consulting service parameters in the charter.
b. Limiting type, nature, and/or level of participation in consulting projects in policies and procedures. (Exhibit 12-3 provides examples of such services.)
c. Using of a screening process for consulting projects, with limits on accepting engagements that might threaten objectivity.
d. Segregating consulting units from units conducting assurance engagements within the same audit function.
e. Rotating auditors on engagements.
f. Employing outside providers for carrying out consulting engagements, or for conducting assurance engagements in activities where the audit function's prior involvement in consulting work has been determined to impair objectivity/independence.
g. Disclosing in audit reports where objectivity may be impaired by participation in a prior consulting project.

Maintaining balance between consulting and assurance services and the internal audit function's independence is the responsibility of the

Individual Objectivity

An impartial, unbiased mental attitude and avoidance of conflicts of interest, allowing internal auditors to perform engagements in such a manner that they have an honest belief in their work product and that no significant quality compromises are made.

Impairments to Independence or Objectivity

The introduction of threats that may result in a substantial limitation, or the appearance of a substantial limitation, to the internal auditor's ability to perform an engagement without bias or interference.

CAE. The CAE should periodically review the nature and scope of the internal audit function's services and the level of resources allocated to consulting services with senior management and the audit committee to ensure that there is continued agreement on the focus and balance of these activities. To this end, the expectations of the organization and the audit committee as to the internal audit function's role in consulting should be clearly defined. Standard 1000.C1 asserts that "the nature of consulting services should be defined in the internal audit charter."

UTILIZING THE SPECIALIST

The internal audit function may not always have the specialized skill sets required to perform certain consulting engagements. Specialized technical skills such as technology, financial reporting, treasury/cash management, forensic accounting, environmental compliance, engineering, and regulatory compliance, may need to be obtained from internal or external subject matter experts. "If the internal audit staff lacks the knowledge, skills, or other competencies needed to perform all or part of [an assurance] engagement," then the CAE is responsible for obtaining "competent advice and assistance" (Standard 1210. A1). For consulting engagements, Standard 1210.C1 similarly states that "the [CAE] should decline the consulting engagement or obtain competent advice and assistance if the internal audit staff lacks the knowledge, skills, or other competencies needed to perform all or part of the engagement."

Supplementary advice and assistance may be acquired from internal audit service providers, actuaries, accountants, appraisers, environmental specialists, fraud investigators, lawyers, engineers, geologists, security specialists, statisticians, information technology specialists, the organization's independent outside auditors, and other consulting organizations. The level of outside help varies from total outsourcing of the internal audit function to partial outsourcing or "cosourcing" of selected pieces of audit work. However, certain audit management activities, such as responsibility for the internal audit plan, cannot be outsourced. Whenever the CAE is considering the use of outside assistance, care must be taken to retain ultimate ownership over those elements that the *Standards* describe as the CAE's responsibility.

The *Standards* clearly recognize that the key point is quality and adding value, not who does the internal audit work. There is an emerging view by many CAEs that seeking stronger overall resources and knowledge through sourcing providers is a sign of strength, not a sign of weakness.

CONSULTING ENGAGEMENT PROCESS

The consulting engagement process is similar to the assurance engagement process. As noted in Exhibit 12-8, the process begins with the selection of which consulting engagements to undertake. In many cases, consulting engagements may be at the request of senior management and may not be specifically planned at the beginning of the year. Unforeseen events such as fraud investigations, special projects, committee meetings, review of new procedures, and providing advice to management all require resources out of the planned budget. Many of these projects are time sensitive and may require other assurance projects to be interrupted. At the same time, consulting engagements may not require a full-time effort during the engagement. The five stages of the typical consulting engagement are shown in Exhibit 12-8 and described below.

Selection

Some internal audit functions have an elaborate risk assessment process to determine which engagements to undertake. During the annual planning phase, the internal audit function should determine how much of the annual budget will be dedicated to consulting engagements. Some larger projects such as systems development, due diligence, and large change initiatives, can be planned during the annual planning process. These projects should be risk evaluated and included in the annual planning process. Some consulting engagements can be anticipated and, like assurance engagements, may be required and are therefore automatically included in the annual audit plan.

Engagement Preparation

Since consulting engagements typically are time sensitive, it is critical for internal auditors to be responsive to management when a request for consulting services arises. Timely selection of the internal audi-

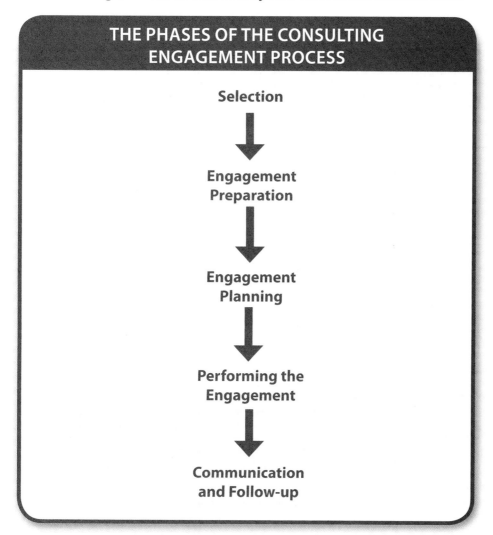

THE PHASES OF THE CONSULTING ENGAGEMENT PROCESS

Selection

Engagement Preparation

Engagement Planning

Performing the Engagement

Communication and Follow-up

Third-party Service Provider

A person or firm, outside of the organization, who provides assurance and/or consulting services to an organization.

EXHIBIT 12-8

tors assigned to the consulting engagement is critical. Typically, more experienced internal auditors are assigned to the consulting engagements, with assistance coming from more junior internal auditors. The assigned internal auditors typically will have the most functional business experience relative to the area that has requested the consulting services. Initial scope discussions with management to determine the appropriate level of services, along with consulting engagement expectations, should be performed by the CAE.

As noted in Exhibit 12-3, there are many types of consulting engagements and the type of engagement will determine the expertise and skills needed by the internal auditors that will be assigned to the consulting engagement. As discussed in Chapter 10, "Conducting the Assurance Engagement," the first phase of the audit project is to determine the purpose of the engagement. With consulting engagements, determining and documenting the purpose of the engagement is even more critical than in assurance engagements because the purpose is typically more ambiguous and more diverse as to the needs of management that the consulting engagement is requested to address.

Similar to the assurance engagement, formalizing objectives at the beginning of the consulting engagement is important. However, in the consulting engagement, the objectives may be more vague and are apt to change during the engagement as more information becomes known. Objectives of the consulting engagement are more likely to pertain to the following:

- Reviewing the design of the controls and providing suggestions.
- Providing input on a new process.
- Reviewing a new system prior to implementation.
- Providing suggestions during a merger due diligence review.
- Providing forensic accounting expertise as part of a fraud investigation.

Similar to the assurance engagement, after the objectives of the consulting engagement are determined, the scope should be determined. During the consulting engagement, the scope can change based on the information that is gathered along with additional input from management. Since audit resources are limited, it is even more important that the consulting engagement have boundaries set related to scope and timeframe. Since these engagements are often at the request of management, and the internal audit function is focused on being responsive to the auditee, it is imperative that the scope and timeframe be established.

Engagement Planning

As is the case when beginning an assurance engagement, it is important for the internal auditors assigned to the consulting engagement to gather information about the functional area in which consulting services are being performed. The internal audit function brings value to each consulting engagement it undertakes by leveraging the broad perspective it has of the organization as a whole. As stated in Standard 2201.C1 "Internal auditors should establish an understanding with consulting engagement clients about objectives, scope, respective responsibilities, and other client expectations." For significant engagements, this understanding should be documented. In most consulting engagements internal auditors will choose to document the engagement scope and responsibilities and review it with the engagement customer prior to performing the work. This helps avoid misunderstandings as the consulting engagement progresses.

Also important to the consulting engagement is discussion with the customer to determine the deliverable and outcomes. The expectation of what will be delivered at the end of the engagement should be established with management. This could vary based on the type of consulting engagement and may be handled formally or informally.

The steps in planning the consulting engagement are similar to those presented in Chapter 10, "Conducting the Assurance Engagement." However, engagement planning is typically more time sensitive for consulting engagements and will need to be completed on a stricter timeline. The timeframe and the deliverables should be agreed upon early in the engagement process so they can be modified based on feedback from management.

Performing the Engagement

Execution of the consulting engagement can take on many forms. Standard 2300 provides the overriding guidance regarding the execution of consulting engagements, stating that "Internal auditors should identify, analyze, evaluate, and record sufficient information to achieve the engagement's objectives." In consulting engagements, those objectives would be determined in the first three phases of the audit.

As described in Chapter 10, "Conducting the Assurance Engagement," some of the same steps involved in performing the assurance engagement are similar to those performed during the consulting engagement. However, much of the work done to create documentation and perform testing of the control activities may not be performed and there may be a greater reliance on user department documentation. Although each consulting engagement may involve different steps and phases, some areas that may be covered by the consulting engagement include:

- Gathering information.
- Various analytical procedures.
- Reviewing various department documentation, including organization charts, process flows, and departmental procedures.
- Potentially using computer-assisted audit techniques.
- Identifying and evaluating key control activities and determining what control activities need to be enhanced.
- Identifying and assessing key risks.
- Understanding the management issues related to the consulting engagement.
- Evaluating the adequacy of control activity design and operating effectiveness.
- Developing observations and formulating recommendations

Some engagements, such as fraud investigations, may involve only the gathering of information, forensic evaluation of the information, and development of the observations and recommendations.

The documentation required for consulting engagements will vary by internal audit function. However, in most cases, the amount of documentation and time spent documenting will be significantly less than for an assurance engagement. The focus typically will be on the final product and providing observations and recommendations to management. Sufficient documentation should be maintained to support those overall internal audit recommendations.

Communication and Follow-up

Communication for a consulting engagement can take many forms. Because timeliness is of the utmost importance for these engagements, it is important to provide oral feedback and dialogue during the project to ensure that there are no surprises and that corrective actions are taken during the engagement. Specific time frames for communication to take place can be outlined at the beginning of the consulting engagement and may correspond with significant dates of particular projects. As more details of the project are known, or as factors change, the consulting requirements may change and consequently must be communicated. As noted in Chapter 11, "Communicating Assurance Engagement Outcomes and Performing Follow-up Procedures," communication of the final audit results can take on many forms. This is true of consulting engagements as well.

Typically, consulting communications will be less formal than in an assurance engagement and are often documented in a memorandum, or the observations may be integrated into a much bigger project. The internal audit function may be part of a committee or project team that is evaluating a process or product and controls may be part of that document. The deliverable from these engagements may be integrated with observations from other areas within the bigger project. In other situations, management may ask the internal audit function to express an oral opinion, which could be requested on the spot with limited information available.

Monitoring and follow-up procedures related to consulting engagements may not be necessary due to the fact that management is asking for an assessment during a major initiative of the project. Part of the normal assurance process will address the ongoing risks and potential future audit engagements. As part of the conclusion of the consulting engagement, the internal audit function should communicate with management any ongoing monitoring or follow-up that will be performed related to the engagement area.

SUMMARY

The expansion of services provided by internal audit functions to the organization will only continue to grow. This area continues to evolve and change based on many factors. Internal auditors must have an understanding of where the organization is in this pendulum of assurance versus consulting work. Additional training and resources may be required to enhance the internal audit function's ability to provide these additional services. The internal auditor must maintain objectivity, just as the internal audit function must maintain independence while taking on these additional services and responsibilities. Clarification of individual consulting engagement responsibilities, as well as clarification of the responsibility the internal audit function has to deliver consulting services to the organization as a whole, must be specifically delineated to avoid misunderstandings at every level.

1. Identify five types of consulting engagements the internal audit function can perform.

2. Describe the different skills required of an internal auditor performing consulting engagements as compared with an internal auditor performing assurance engagements.

3. Who is considered the ultimate customer of internal auditing when it comes to consulting engagements?

4. What would be the appropriate way to address consulting services within the internal audit function's charter?

1. Which of the following would be a typical consulting engagement activity performed by the internal audit function?

    a. Compliance testing of accounts payable procedures.

    b. Determining the scope of an audit to test application controls.

    c. Review and comment on a draft of a new ethics policy created by the company.

    d. Performing testing on the adequacy of control activities over terminated employees.

2. Which of the following is not a required consideration regarding due professional care when choosing to perform an internal audit consulting engagement?

    a. Adequate skills and resources to complete the engagement.

    b. Possible motivations for performing the consulting service.

    c. Potential impact on the financial statement attestation work.

    d. Potential impact on the audit plan to complete the other engagements for the year.

3. When the internal audit function performs advisory and customer service activities, the nature of which are agreed upon by the audit customer, this type of work is considered:

    a. External audit services.

    b. Third party audit services.

    c. Internal audit assurance services.

    d. Consulting services.

4. Senior management of an organization has requested that the internal audit function provide ongoing internal control training for all managerial personnel. This is best addressed by:

    a. A formal consulting engagement.

b. An information consulting engagement.

c. A special consulting engagement agreement.

d. An emergency consulting engagement.

5. A consulting activity appropriately performed by the internal audit function is:

a. Designing systems of internal control.

b. Drafting procedures for systems of internal control.

c. Reviewing systems of internal control before implementation.

d. Installing systems of internal control.

6. Sales representatives for a manufacturing company are reimbursed for 100 percent of their cellular telephone bills. Cellular telephone costs vary significantly from representative to representative and from month to month, complicating the budget forecasting processes. Management has requested that the internal audit function develop a method for controlling these costs. Which of the following would most appropriately be included in the scope of the consulting project?

a. Control self-assessment involving sales representatives.

b. Benchmarking with other cellular telephone users.

c. Business process review of procurement and payable routines.

d. Performance measurement and design of budgeting and forecasting processes.

7. Who has primary responsibility for providing information to the audit committee on the professional and organizational benefits of coordinating internal audit assurance and consulting activities with other assurance and consulting activities?

a. The independent outside auditor.

b. The chief audit executive.

c. The chief executive officer.

d. Each assurance and consulting function.

8. The internal audit function has recently experienced the departure of two internal auditors who cannot immediately be replaced due to budget constraints. Which of the following is the least desirable option for efficiently completing future engagements given this reduction in resources?

a. Using self-assessment questionnaires to address audit objectives.

b. Employing information technology in audit planning, sampling, and documentation.

c. Eliminating consulting engagements from the engagement work schedule.

d. Filling vacancies with personnel from operating departments that are not being audited.

9. The definition of internal auditing states that internal auditing is an independent, objective assurance and consulting activity. Which of the following is not a consulting activity?

a. An internal auditor is assigned to reconcile the monthly corporate bank accounts.

b. At the request of management, an internal auditor writes procedures for outsourcing work to independent contractors.

c. At the request of the audit committee chair, the internal audit function reviews the content of the organization's code of conduct and the effectiveness of the organization's ethics training.

d. At the request of senior management, two internal auditors participate on a team to re-engineer the information technology group's system development process.

1. Explain how the internal audit function can maintain its independence while working with management to deploy improved risk management practices and improve the system of internal controls throughout the organization.

2. How should internal audit consulting engagements be communicated to management?

3. Describe a situation in which the internal auditor could be accused of stepping over the independence line while providing consulting services.

4. How do characteristics of the organization such as industry, size, regulatory environment, and organizational structure change the type and degree of consulting services provided by the internal audit function?

5. How do internal audit functions determine the degree of consulting services to perform and which consulting engagements to accept?

6. Can consulting engagements be structured to provide assurance? Why or why not?

7. Are there consulting services that the internal audit function should not provide? Explain your answer.

8. What are the benefits to the organization when the internal audit function provides consulting services and how can the benefits be measured?

9. Can an internal audit function provide consulting services exclusively? Why or why not?

CASES

CASE 1   Privacy

You are working for a new company that is primarily an Internet-based seller of goods whose business model is similar to eBay. The company was founded on similar principles as eBay and is an on-line auction, but has the added benefit of having one common site that deals with customers worldwide. The CEO knows that privacy is very important in the online business and has requested that the internal audit function draft a best practices privacy policy for customers since the motto for the new company is "Your Privacy is Our Policy." The company neither has, nor plans to hire, a privacy or compliance officer. The CEO expects the CAE to lead this effort and to ensure the campaign meets the company's motto.

With the advertising campaign slated to launch in a month, the CEO wants the privacy documentation finalized as soon as possible.

Identify:

- The key sources on privacy that are available for you to reference as you define best practices.

- The consulting engagement steps you would take and the areas of the company you would ask to participate in the project.

- The consulting engagement documentation you would prepare and the information you would present to the CEO.

CASE 2   Outsourcing

A large, international bank is considering outsourcing all facets of the human resources function including recruiting, benefits, payroll, employee training and development, compensation, and information systems. Three potentially viable vendors have been identified. The internal audit function has been asked to review the vendor selection process and to evaluate each vendor's system of internal controls. Senior management has decided they want a 10% equity stake in the company that performs the outsourcing function.

The original terms of the agreement call for 1,000 employees to be moved from the previously mentioned functions to the company who ultimately receives the contract. The vendor will then be responsible for evaluating the employees' performance and determining which employees will be terminated after a six-month period.

CASES

The vendor has the option to determine which computer systems are used. The length of the contract will be either five or ten years, depending on its pricing structure.

The international bank expects to achieve significant financial gains from this outsourcing arrangement, including significant cost reductions associated with the conversion to standard applications provided by the vendor. The vendor will be expected to leverage existing systems, processes, and personnel and be able to make a profit based on the economies of scale, particularly in the systems areas.

Required:

- Describe the characteristics the internal audit function should look for in the potential vendors.

- What role should the internal audit function play in the bank's plan to take an equity position in the vendor?

- What specific areas should the internal audit function review during the transition phase?

- What are the biggest areas of risk to the bank during the transition phase? After the transition?

- What types of internal audit consulting activities could be performed of the outsourced functions?

REFERENCES

[1]Richards, Dave, "Consulting Auditing—Charting a Course," *Internal Auditor,* December 2001, pp 30-35.

[2]The Institute of Internal Auditors. *International Standards for the Professional Practice of Internal Auditing.* (Altamonte Springs, FL: 2006).

[3]Desjardins, Chris, Audit Director, Essilor, Personal interview. February, 2007.

[4]Comptroller General's introduction to the Government Accountability Office's, Government Auditing Standards. Amendment No. 3 Independence (GAO-02-388G, January 2002).

[5]The Institute of Internal Auditors. *International Standards for the Professional Practice of Internal Auditing.* (Altamonte Springs, FL: 2006, Standard 1130.A1).

GLOSSARY

NOTE: Many of the definitions in this glossary are taken from the glossary in The IIA's Professional Practices Framework, or have been modified as appropriate to conform to the discussions in this textbook.

Add Value – Value is provided by improving opportunities to achieve organizational objectives, identifying operational improvement, and/or reducing risk exposure through both assurance and consulting services.

Adequately Designed – See Control Activities are Adequately Designed.

Application Systems – Sets of programs that are designed for end users such as payroll, accounts payable, and in some cases, large applications such as enterprise resource planning (ERP) systems that provide many business functions.

Asset Misappropriation – Acts involving the theft or misuse of an organization's assets (for example, skimming revenues, stealing inventory, payroll fraud).

Assurance Services – An objective examination of evidence for the purpose of providing an independent assessment on risk management, control, or governance processes for the organization. Examples may include financial, performance, compliance, system security, and due diligence engagements.

Audit Engagement – See Assurance Services.

Audit Observation – Any identified and validated gap between the current and desired state arising from an assurance engagement.

Audit Risk – The risk of reaching invalid audit conclusions and/or providing faulty advice based on the audit work conducted.

Audit Sampling – The application of an audit procedure to less than 100% of the items in a population for the purpose of drawing an inference about the entire population.

Auditee – The subsidiary, business unit, department, group, or other established subdivision of an organization that is the subject of an assurance engagement.

Board – An organization's governing body, such as a board of directors, supervisory board, head of an agency or legislative body, board of governors or trustees of a nonprofit organization, or any other designated body of the organization, including the audit committee, to whom the chief audit executive may functionally report.

Business Process – The set of connected activities linked with each other for the purpose of achieving a business objective.

Business Process Outsourcing (BPO) – The act of transferring some of an organization's business processes to an outside provider to achieve cost reductions, operating effectiveness, or operating efficiency while improving service quality.

Cause – The reason for the difference between the expected and actual conditions (why the difference exists).

Chief Audit Executive – The top position within the organization responsible for internal audit activities. In the case where internal audit activities are obtained from outside service providers, the chief audit executive is the person responsible for overseeing the service contract and the overall quality assurance of these activities. The chief audit executive typically reports to the board and executive management. The term includes such titles as general auditor, chief internal auditor, internal audit director, and inspector general.

Code of Ethics – The Code of Ethics of The Institute of Internal Auditors contains principles relevant to the profession and practice of internal auditing and Rules of Conduct that describe behavior expected of internal auditors. The Code of Ethics applies to both parties and entities that provide internal audit services. The purpose of the Code of Ethics is to promote an ethical culture in the global profession of internal auditing.

Compensating Control Activity – An activity designed to supplement key control activities that may be either ineffective or do not fully mitigate a risk or group of risks by themselves to an acceptable level.

Competent Evidence – Any piece or collection of evidence gained during an engagement that provides relevant and reliable support for the judgments and conclusions reached during the engagement.

Complementary Control Activity – A control activity that is not directly related to the risk it mitigates, and is not enough to fully mitigate the risk by itself, but when taken together with other control activities that are in place, does contribute to the overall effective mitigation of risk. Frequently, complementary control activities operate across multiple processes and risks.

Compliance – Conformity and adherence to applicable laws and regulations (COSO definition). May also include conformity and adherence to policies, plans, procedures, contracts, or other requirements.

Computer-assisted Audit Techniques (CAATs) – Automated audit techniques, such as generalized audit software, utility software, test data, application software tracing and mapping, and audit expert systems, that help the internal auditor directly test control activities built into computerized information systems and data contained in computer files.

Condition – The factual evidence that the internal auditor found in the course of the examination (what does exist).

Conflict of Interest – Any relationship that is, or appears to be, not in the best interest of the organization. A conflict of interest would prejudice an individual's ability to perform his or her duties and responsibilities objectively.

Consulting Services – Advisory and related services, the nature and scope of which are agreed to with the customer and which are intended to improve an

GLOSSARY

organization's governance, risk management, and control processes without the internal auditor assuming management responsibility. Examples include counsel, advice, facilitation, and training.

Control – See Control Activities, Internal Control, or System of Internal Controls.

Control Activities – Any action taken by management, the board, and other parties to manage risk and increase the likelihood that established objectives and goals will be achieved. Management plans, organizes, and directs the performance of sufficient actions to provide reasonable assurance that objectives and goals will be achieved.

Control Activities are Adequately Designed – Present if management has planned and organized (designed) the control activities or the system of internal controls in a manner that provides reasonable assurance that the organization's entity-wide and process-level risks can be managed to an acceptable level.

Control Activities are Operating Effectively – Present if management has executed (operated) the control activities or the system of internal controls in a manner that provides reasonable assurance that the organization's entity-wide and process-level risks have been managed effectively and that the organization's goals and objectives will be achieved efficiently and economically.

Control Environment – The attitude and actions of the board and management regarding the significance of control within the organization. The control environment provides the discipline and structure for the achievement of the primary objectives of the system of internal control. The control environment includes the following elements:

- Integrity and ethical values.
- Management's philosophy and operating style.
- Organizational structure.
- Assignment of authority and responsibility.
- Human resource policies and practices.
- Competence of personnel.

Control Maturity Model – A tool that an organization may use to assess the sophistication and sustainability of its system of internal controls.

Control Risk – The potential that control activities will fail to reduce controllable risk to an acceptable level.

Controllable Risk – The portion of inherent risk that management can reduce through day-to-day operations and management activities.

Corrective Control – A control activity in which detected omissions and errors are corrected.

Corruption – Acts in which individuals wrongfully use their influence in a business transaction in order to procure some benefit for themselves or another person, contrary to their duty to their employer or the rights of another (for example, kickbacks, self-dealing, conflicts of interest).

Criteria – The standards, measures, or expectations used in making an evaluation and/or verification of an observation (what should exist).

Customer – The subsidiary, business unit, department, group, individual or other established subdivision of an organization that is the subject of a consulting engagement.

Database Systems – A system of programs that enable the storage, modification, and extraction of data.

Detective Control – A control activity that is designed to discover undesirable events that have already occurred. A detective control must occur on a timely basis (before the undesirable event has had a negative impact on the organization) to be considered effective.

Directive Control – A control activity that gives explicit direction regarding what actions need to take place to cause or encourage a desirable event to occur.

Effect – The risk or exposure the organization and/or others encounter because the condition is not consistent with the criteria (the consequence of the difference).

Engagement – An internal audit assignment, task, or review activity, such as an internal audit assurance service, consulting service, control self-assessment review, fraud examination, or compliance examination. An engagement may include multiple tasks or activities designed to accomplish a specific set of related objectives.

Engagement Work Program – A document that lists the procedures to be followed during an engagement, designed to achieve the engagement plan.

Entity-Wide Control – A control that operates across an entire entity and, as such, is not bound by, or associated with, individual processes.

External Auditor – See Independent Outside Auditor.

Framework – A body of guiding principles that form a template against which organizations can evaluate a multitude of business practices. These principles are comprised of various concepts, values, assumptions, and practices intended to provide a yard stick against which an organization can assess or evaluate a particular structure, process, or environment or a group of practices or procedures.

Fraud – Any illegal acts characterized by deceit, concealment, or violation of trust. These acts are not dependent upon the application of threat of violence or of physical force. Frauds are perpetrated by parties and organizations to obtain money, property, or services; to avoid payment or loss of services; or to secure personal or business advantage.

Fraudulent Financial Reporting – Acts that involve falsification of an organization's financial statements (for example, overstating revenues, understating liabilities and expenses).

GLOSSARY

General Information Technology Control Activities – Control activities that operate across all IT systems and are in place to ensure the integrity, reliability, and accuracy of the application systems. Also represents a specific example of an "entity-wide control."

Governance – The process conducted by the board of directors to authorize, direct, and oversee management toward the achievement of the organization's objectives.

Impairments to Independence or Objectivity – The introduction of threats that may result in a substantial limitation, or the appearance of a substantial limitation, to the internal auditor's ability to perform an engagement without bias or interference.

Independence – The freedom from conditions that threaten objectivity or the appearance of objectivity. Such threats to objectivity must be managed at the individual auditor, engagement, functional, and organizational levels (also see Organizational Independence).

Independent Outside Auditor – A registered public accounting firm, hired by the organization's board or executive management, to perform a financial statement audit providing assurance for which the firm issues a written attestation report that expresses an opinion about whether the financial statements are fairly presented in accordance with applicable generally accepted accounting principles.

Individual Objectivity – An impartial, unbiased mental attitude and avoidance of conflicts of interest, allowing internal auditors to perform engagements in such a manner that they have an honest belief in their work product and that no significant quality compromises are made. Objectivity requires internal auditors not to subordinate their judgment on audit matters to that of others.

Information Technology Operations – The department or area in an organization (people, processes, and equipment) that performs the function of running the computer systems and various devices that support the business objectives and activities.

Inherent Limitations of Internal Control – The confines that relate to the limits of human judgment, resource constraints and the need to consider the cost of controls in relation to expected benefits, the reality that breakdowns can occur, and the possibility of collusion or management override.

Inherent Risk – The combination of internal and external risk factors in their pure, uncontrolled state, or, the gross risk that exists assuming there are no internal control activities in place.

Internal Audit Charter – A formal written document that defines the internal audit function's purpose, authority, and responsibility. The charter should (a) establish the internal audit function's position within the organization, (b) authorize access to records, personnel, and physical properties relevant to the performance of engagements, and (c) define the scope of the internal audit function.

Internal Audit Function – A department, division, team of consultants, or other practitioner(s) that provides independent, objective assurance and consulting services designed to add value and improve an organization's operations.

Internal Control – A process, effected by an entity's board of directors, management, and other personnel, designed to provide reasonable assurance regarding the achievement of objectives in the following categories:

- Effectiveness and efficiency of operations.
- Reliability of financial reporting.
- Compliance with applicable laws and regulations.

Key Control Activity – An activity designed to reduce risk associated with a critical business objective.

Key Performance Indicators – A metric or other form of measuring whether a process or individual tasks are operating within prescribed tolerances.

Material Observation – An individual observation, or a group of observations, is considered "material" if the control activity in question has a reasonable possibility of failing and the impact of its failure is not only significant, but also exceeds the financial statement materiality threshold.

Monitoring – A process that assesses the presence and functioning of governance, risk management, and control components over time.

Networks – A configuration that enables computers and devices to communicate and be linked together to provide transfer of data and operations.

Objectives – What an entity desires to achieve. When referring to what an organization wants to achieve, these are called business objectives, and may be classified as strategic, operational, reporting, and compliance. When referring to what an audit wants to achieve, these are called audit objectives or engagement objectives.

Objectivity – See Individual Objectivity.

Observation – A finding, determination, or judgment derived from the internal auditor's test results from an assurance or consulting engagement.

Operating Effectively – See Control Activities are Operating Effectively.

Operating Systems – Software programs that run the computer and perform basic tasks, such as recognizing input from the keyboard, sending output to the printer, keeping track of files and directories on the hard drive, and controlling various computer peripheral devices.

Opportunity – The possibility that an event will occur and positively affect the achievement of objectives.

Organizational Independence – The chief audit executive's line of reporting within the organization that allows the internal audit function to fulfill its responsibilities free from interference (also see Independence).

GLOSSARY

Preventive Control – A control activity that is designed to deter unintended events from occurring.

Process-Level Control Activity – A control activity that operates within a specific process for the purpose of achieving process-level objectives.

Professional Skepticism – The state of mind in which internal auditors take nothing for granted; they continuously question what they hear and see and critically assess audit evidence.

Reasonable Assurance – A level of assurance that is supported by generally accepted auditing procedures and judgments. Reasonable assurance can apply to judgments surrounding the effectiveness of internal controls, the mitigation of risks, the achievement of objectives, or other engagement-related conclusions.

Residual Risk – The portion of inherent risk that remains after management executes its risk responses (sometimes referred to as net risk).

Risk – The possibility that an event will occur and adversely affect the achievement of objectives.

Risk Appetite – The amount of risk, on a broad level, an organization is willing to accept in pursuit of its business objectives. Risk appetite takes into consideration the amount of risk that management consciously accepts after balancing the cost and benefits of implementing control activities.

Risk Management – The process conducted by management to understand and deal with uncertainties (that is, risks and opportunities) that could affect the organization's ability to achieve its objectives.

Risk Response (Mitigation) – An action or set of actions taken by management to achieve a desired risk management strategy. Risk responses can be categorized as risk avoidance, reduction, sharing, or acceptance.

Secondary Control Activity – An activity designed to either reduce risk associated with business objectives that are not critical to the organization's survival or success or serve as a backup to a key control.

Significant Observation – An individual observation, or a group of observations, is considered "significant" if the control activity in question has a reasonable possibility of failing and the impact of its failure is significant.

Standard – A professional pronouncement promulgated by the International Internal Auditing Standards Board that delineates the requirements for performing a broad range of internal audit activities, and for evaluating internal audit performance.

Strategic Objectives – What an entity desires to achieve through the value creation choices management makes on behalf of the organization's stakeholders.

Strategy – Refers to how management plans to achieve the organization's objectives.

System of Internal Controls –Comprises the five components of internal control: the control environment, risk assessment, control activities, information and communication, and monitoring that are in place to manage risks related to the financial reporting, compliance, and operational objectives of an organization. See also Internal Control.

Third Party Service Provider – A person or firm, outside of the organization, who provides assurance and/or consulting services to an organization.

Tone at the Top – The entity-wide attitude of integrity and control consciousness, as exhibited by the most senior executives of an organization. See also Control Environment.

Work Program – See Engagement Work Program.

APPENDICES

Appendix A
The IIA Code of Ethics

Introduction

The purpose of The Institute's Code of Ethics is to promote an ethical culture in the profession of internal auditing.

> *Internal auditing is an independent, objective assurance and consulting activity designed to add value and improve an organization's operations. It helps an organization accomplish its objectives by bringing a systematic, disciplined approach to evaluate and improve the effectiveness of risk management, control, and governance processes.*

A code of ethics is necessary and appropriate for the profession of internal auditing, founded as it is on the trust placed in its objective assurance about risk management, control, and governance. The Institute's Code of Ethics extends beyond the definition of internal auditing to include two essential components:

1. Principles that are relevant to the profession and practice of internal auditing;

2. Rules of Conduct that describe behavior norms expected of internal auditors. These rules are an aid to interpreting the Principles into practical applications and are intended to guide the ethical conduct of internal auditors.

The Code of Ethics together with The Institute's Professional Practices Framework and other relevant Institute pronouncements provide guidance to internal auditors serving others. "Internal auditors" refers to Institute members, recipients of or candidates for IIA professional certifications, and those who provide internal auditing services within the definition of internal auditing.

Applicability and Enforcement

This Code of Ethics applies to both individuals and entities that provide internal auditing services.

For Institute members and recipients of or candidates for IIA professional certifications, breaches of the Code of Ethics will be evaluated and administered according to The Institute's Bylaws and Administrative Guidelines. The fact that a particular conduct is not mentioned in the Rules of Conduct does not prevent it from being unacceptable or discreditable, and therefore, the member, certification holder, or candidate can be liable for disciplinary action.

Principles

Internal auditors are expected to apply and uphold the following principles:

Integrity

The integrity of internal auditors establishes trust and thus provides the basis for reliance on their judgment.

Objectivity

Internal auditors exhibit the highest level of professional objectivity in gathering, evaluating, and communicating information about the activity or process being examined. Internal auditors make a balanced assessment of all the relevant circumstances and are not unduly influenced by their own interests or by others in forming judgments.

Confidentiality

Internal auditors respect the value and ownership of information they receive and do not disclose information without appropriate authority unless there is a legal or professional obligation to do so.

Competency

Internal auditors apply the knowledge, skills, and experience needed in the performance of internal auditing services.

Rules of Conduct

1. Integrity

Internal auditors:

1.1. Shall perform their work with honesty, diligence, and responsibility.

1.2. Shall observe the law and make disclosures expected by the law and the profession.

1.3. Shall not knowingly be a party to any illegal activity, or engage in acts that are discreditable to the profession of internal auditing or to the organization.

1.4. Shall respect and contribute to the legitimate and ethical objectives of the organization.

2. Objectivity

Internal auditors:

2.1. Shall not participate in any activity or relationship that may impair or be presumed to impair their unbiased assessment. This participation includes those activities or relationships that may be in conflict with the interests of the organization.

2.2 Shall not accept anything that may impair or be presumed to impair their professional judgment.

APPENDICES

2.3 Shall disclose all material facts known to them that, if not disclosed, may distort the reporting of activities under review.

3. Confidentiality

Internal auditors:

3.1 Shall be prudent in the use and protection of information acquired in the course of their duties.

3.2 Shall not use information for any personal gain or in any manner that would be contrary to the law or detrimental to the legitimate and ethical objectives of the organization.

4. Competency

Internal auditors:

4.1. Shall engage only in those services for which they have the necessary knowledge, skills, and experience.

4.2 Shall perform internal auditing services in accordance with the International Standards for the Professional Practice of Internal Auditing.

4.3 Shall continually improve their proficiency and the effectiveness and quality of their services.

Adopted by The IIA Board of Directors, June 17, 2000.

Appendix B
The International Standards for the Professional Practice of Internal Auditing

Attribute Standards

1000 – Purpose, Authority, and Responsibility

The purpose, authority, and responsibility of the internal audit activity should be formally defined in a charter, consistent with the Standards, and approved by the board.

> **1000.A1 -** The nature of assurance services provided to the organization should be defined in the audit charter. If assurances are to be provided to parties outside the organization, the nature of these assurances should also be defined in the charter.

> **1000.C1 -** The nature of consulting services should be defined in the audit charter.

1100 – Independence and Objectivity

The internal audit activity should be independent, and internal auditors should be objective in performing their work.

1110 – Organizational Independence

The chief audit executive should report to a level within the organization that allows the internal audit activity to fulfill its responsibilities.

> **1110.A1 -** The internal audit activity should be free from interference in determining the scope of internal auditing, performing work, and communicating results.

1120 – Individual Objectivity

Internal auditors should have an impartial, unbiased attitude and avoid conflicts of interest.

1130 – Impairments to Independence or Objectivity

If independence or objectivity is impaired in fact or appearance, the details of the impairment should be disclosed to appropriate parties. The nature of the disclosure will depend upon the impairment.

> **1130.A1 –** Internal auditors should refrain from assessing specific operations for which they were previously responsible. Objectivity is presumed to be impaired if an internal auditor provides assurance services for an activity for which the internal auditor had responsibility within the previous year.

> **1130.A2 –** Assurance engagements for functions over which the chief audit executive has responsibility should be overseen by a party outside the internal audit activity.

APPENDICES

1130.C1 - Internal auditors may provide consulting services relating to operations for which they had previous responsibilities.

1130.C2 - If internal auditors have potential impairments to independence or objectivity relating to proposed consulting services, disclosure should be made to the engagement client prior to accepting the engagement.

1200 – Proficiency and Due Professional Care

Engagements should be performed with proficiency and due professional care.

1210 – Proficiency

Internal auditors should possess the knowledge, skills, and other competencies needed to perform their individual responsibilities. The internal audit activity collectively should possess or obtain the knowledge, skills, and other competencies needed to perform its responsibilities.

1210.A1 - The chief audit executive should obtain competent advice and assistance if the internal audit staff lacks the knowledge, skills, or other competencies needed to perform all or part of the engagement.

1210.A2 – The internal auditor should have sufficient knowledge to identify the indicators of fraud but is not expected to have the expertise of a person whose primary responsibility is detecting and investigating fraud.

1210.A3 – Internal auditors should have knowledge of key information technology risks and controls and available technology-based audit techniques to perform their assigned work. However, not all internal auditors are expected to have the expertise of an internal auditor whose primary responsibility is information technology auditing.

1210.C1 - The chief audit executive should decline the consulting engagement or obtain competent advice and assistance if the internal audit staff lacks the knowledge, skills, or other competencies needed to perform all or part of the engagement.

1220 - Due Professional Care

Internal auditors should apply the care and skill expected of a reasonably prudent and competent internal auditor. Due professional care does not imply infallibility.

1220.A1 - The internal auditor should exercise due professional care by considering the:

- Extent of work needed to achieve the engagement's objectives.
- Relative complexity, materiality, or significance of matters to which assurance procedures are applied.
- Adequacy and effectiveness of risk management, control, and governance processes.
- Probability of significant errors, irregularities, or noncompliance.
- Cost of assurance in relation to potential benefits.

1220.A2 - In exercising due professional care the internal auditor should consider the use of computer-assisted audit tools and other data analysis techniques.

1220.A3 – The internal auditor should be alert to the significant risks that might affect objectives, operations, or resources. However, assurance procedures alone, even when performed with due professional care, do not guarantee that all significant risks will be identified.

1220.C1 - The internal auditor should exercise due professional care during a consulting engagement by considering the:

- Needs and expectations of clients, including the nature, timing, and communication of engagement results. Relative complexity and extent of work needed to achieve the engagement's objectives.
- Cost of the consulting engagement in relation to potential benefits.

1230 – Continuing Professional Development

Internal auditors should enhance their knowledge, skills, and other competencies through continuing professional development.

1300 – Quality Assurance and Improvement Program

The chief audit executive should develop and maintain a quality assurance and improvement program that covers all aspects of the internal audit activity and continuously monitors its effectiveness. This program includes periodic internal and external quality assessments and ongoing internal monitoring. Each part of the program should be designed to help the internal audit activity add value and improve the organization's operations and to provide assurance that the internal audit activity is in conformity with the Standards and the Code of Ethics.

1310 – Quality Program Assessments

The internal audit activity should adopt a process to monitor and assess the overall effectiveness of the quality program. The process should include both internal and external assessments.

1311 – Internal Assessments

Internal assessments should include:

- Ongoing reviews of the performance of the internal audit activity; and
- Periodic reviews performed through self-assessment or by other persons within the organization, with knowledge of internal audit practices and the Standards.

1312 – External Assessments

External assessments should be conducted at least once every five years by a qualified, independent reviewer or review team from outside the organization.

APPENDICES

The potential need for more frequent external assessments as well as the qualifications and independence of the external reviewer or review team, including any potential conflict of interest, should be discussed by the CAE with the Board. Such discussions should also consider the size, complexity and industry of the organization in relation to the experience of the reviewer or review team.

1320 – Reporting on the Quality Program

The chief audit executive should communicate the results of external assessments to the board.

1330 – Use of "Conducted in Accordance with the Standards"

Internal auditors are encouraged to report that their activities are "conducted in accordance with the International Standards for the Professional Practice of Internal Auditing." However, internal auditors may use the statement only if assessments of the quality improvement program demonstrate that the internal audit activity is in compliance with the Standards.

1340 – Disclosure of Noncompliance

Although the internal audit activity should achieve full compliance with the Standards and internal auditors with the Code of Ethics, there may be instances in which full compliance is not achieved. When noncompliance impacts the overall scope or operation of the internal audit activity, disclosure should be made to senior management and the board.

Performance Standards

2000 – Managing the Internal Audit Activity

The chief audit executive should effectively manage the internal audit activity to ensure it adds value to the organization.

2010 – Planning

The chief audit executive should establish risk-based plans to determine the priorities of the internal audit activity, consistent with the organization's goals.

2010.A1 - The internal audit activity's plan of engagements should be based on a risk assessment, undertaken at least annually. The input of senior management and the board should be considered in this process.

2010.C1 - The chief audit executive should consider accepting proposed consulting engagements based on the engagement's potential to improve management of risks, add value, and improve the organization's operations. Those engagements that have been accepted should be included in the plan.

2020 – Communication and Approval

The chief audit executive should communicate the internal audit activity's plans and resource requirements, including significant interim changes, to senior management and to the board for review and approval. The chief audit executive should also communicate the impact of resource limitations.

2030 – Resource Management

The chief audit executive should ensure that internal audit resources are appropriate, sufficient, and effectively deployed to achieve the approved plan.

2040 – Policies and Procedures

The chief audit executive should establish policies and procedures to guide the internal audit activity.

2050 – Coordination

The chief audit executive should share information and coordinate activities with other internal and external providers of relevant assurance and consulting services to ensure proper coverage and minimize duplication of efforts.

2060 – Reporting to the Board and Senior Management

The chief audit executive should report periodically to the board and senior management on the internal audit activity's purpose, authority, responsibility, and performance relative to its plan. Reporting should also include significant risk exposures and control issues, corporate governance issues, and other matters needed or requested by the board and senior management.

2100 – Nature of Work

The internal audit activity should evaluate and contribute to the improvement of risk management, control, and governance processes using a systematic and disciplined approach.

2110 – Risk Management

The internal audit activity should assist the organization by identifying and evaluating significant exposures to risk and contributing to the improvement of risk management and control systems.

> **2110.A1 -** The internal audit activity should monitor and evaluate the effectiveness of the organization's risk management system.
>
> **2110.A2 -** The internal audit activity should evaluate risk exposures relating to the organization's governance, operations, and information systems regarding the
>
> - Reliability and integrity of financial and operational information.
> - Effectiveness and efficiency of operations.
> - Safeguarding of assets.
> - Compliance with laws, regulations, and contracts.
>
> **2110.C1 -** During consulting engagements, internal auditors should address risk consistent with the engagement's objectives and be alert to the existence of other significant risks.

APPENDICES

2110.C2 – Internal auditors should incorporate knowledge of risks gained from consulting engagements into the process of identifying and evaluating significant risk exposures of the organization.

2120 – Control

The internal audit activity should assist the organization in maintaining effective controls by evaluating their effectiveness and efficiency and by promoting continuous improvement.

2120.A1 - Based on the results of the risk assessment, the internal audit activity should evaluate the adequacy and effectiveness of controls encompassing the organization's governance, operations, and information systems. This should include:

- Reliability and integrity of financial and operational information.
- Effectiveness and efficiency of operations.
- Safeguarding of assets.
- Compliance with laws, regulations, and contracts.

2120.A2 - Internal auditors should ascertain the extent to which operating and program goals and objectives have been established and conform to those of the organization.

2120.A3 - Internal auditors should review operations and programs to ascertain the extent to which results are consistent with established goals and objectives to determine whether operations and programs are being implemented or performed as intended.

2120.A4 - Adequate criteria are needed to evaluate controls. Internal auditors should ascertain the extent to which management has established adequate criteria to determine whether objectives and goals have been accomplished. If adequate, internal auditors should use such criteria in their evaluation. If inadequate, internal auditors should work with management to develop appropriate evaluation criteria.

2120.C1 - During consulting engagements, internal auditors should address controls consistent with the engagement's objectives and be alert to the existence of any significant control weaknesses.

2120.C2 – Internal auditors should incorporate knowledge of controls gained from consulting engagements into the process of identifying and evaluating significant risk exposures of the organization.

2130 – Governance

The internal audit activity should assess and make appropriate recommendations for improving the governance process in its accomplishment of the following objectives:

- Promoting appropriate ethics and values within the organization.
- Ensuring effective organizational performance management and accountability.

- Effectively communicating risk and control information to appropriate areas of the organization.
- Effectively coordinating the activities of and communicating information among the board, external and internal auditors, and management.

2130.A1 – The internal audit activity should evaluate the design, implementation, and effectiveness of the organization's ethics-related objectives, programs, and activities.

2130.C1 – Consulting engagement objectives should be consistent with the overall values and goals of the organization.

2200 – Engagement Planning

Internal auditors should develop and record a plan for each engagement, including the scope, objectives, timing, and resource allocations.

2201 - Planning Considerations

In planning the engagement, internal auditors should consider:

- The objectives of the activity being reviewed and the means by which the activity controls its performance.
- The significant risks to the activity, its objectives, resources, and operations and the means by which the potential impact of risk is kept to an acceptable level.
- The adequacy and effectiveness of the activity's risk management and control systems compared to a relevant control framework or model.
- The opportunities for making significant improvements to the activity's risk management and control systems.

2201.A1 – When planning an engagement for parties outside the organization, internal auditors should establish a written understanding with them about objectives, scope, respective responsibilities, and other expectations, including restrictions on distribution of the results of the engagement and access to engagement records.

2201.C1 - Internal auditors should establish an understanding with consulting engagement clients about objectives, scope, respective responsibilities, and other client expectations. For significant engagements, this understanding should be documented.

2210 – Engagement Objectives

Objectives should be established for each engagement.

2210.A1 – Internal auditors should conduct a preliminary assessment of the risks relevant to the activity under review. Engagement objectives should reflect the results of this assessment.

2210.A2 - The internal auditor should consider the probability of significant errors, irregularities, noncompliance, and other exposures when developing

APPENDICES

the engagement objectives.

2210.C1 – Consulting engagement objectives should address risks, controls, and governance processes to the extent agreed upon with the client.

2220 – Engagement Scope

The established scope should be sufficient to satisfy the objectives of the engagement.

2220.A1 - The scope of the engagement should include consideration of relevant systems, records, personnel, and physical properties, including those under the control of third parties.

2220.A2 - If significant consulting opportunities arise during an assurance engagement, a specific written understanding as to the objectives, scope, respective responsibilities, and other expectations should be reached and the results of the consulting engagement communicated in accordance with consulting standards.

2220.C1 – In performing consulting engagements, internal auditors should ensure that the scope of the engagement is sufficient to address the agreed-upon objectives. If internal auditors develop reservations about the scope during the engagement, these reservations should be discussed with the client to determine whether to continue with the engagement.

2230 – Engagement Resource Allocation

Internal auditors should determine appropriate resources to achieve engagement objectives. Staffing should be based on an evaluation of the nature and complexity of each engagement, time constraints, and available resources.

2240 – Engagement Work Program

Internal auditors should develop work programs that achieve the engagement objectives. These work programs should be recorded.

2240.A1 - Work programs should establish the procedures for identifying, analyzing, evaluating, and recording information during the engagement. The work program should be approved prior to its implementation, and any adjustments approved promptly.

2240.C1 - Work programs for consulting engagements may vary in form and content depending upon the nature of the engagement.

2300 – Performing the Engagement

Internal auditors should identify, analyze, evaluate, and record sufficient information to achieve the engagement's objectives.

2310 – Identifying Information

Internal auditors should identify sufficient, reliable, relevant, and useful information to achieve the engagement's objectives.

2320 – Analysis and Evaluation

Internal auditors should base conclusions and engagement results on appropriate analyses and evaluations.

2330 – Recording Information

Internal auditors should record relevant information to support the conclusions and engagement results.

2330.A1 - The chief audit executive should control access to engagement records. The chief audit executive should obtain the approval of senior management and/or legal counsel prior to releasing such records to external parties, as appropriate.

2330.A2 - The chief audit executive should develop retention requirements for engagement records. These retention requirements should be consistent with the organization's guidelines and any pertinent regulatory or other requirements.

2330.C1 - The chief audit executive should develop policies governing the custody and retention of engagement records, as well as their release to internal and external parties. These policies should be consistent with the organization's guidelines and any pertinent regulatory or other requirements.

2340 – Engagement Supervision

Engagements should be properly supervised to ensure objectives are achieved, quality is assured, and staff is developed.

2400 – Communicating Results

Internal auditors should communicate the engagement results.

2410 – Criteria for Communicating

Communications should include the engagement's objectives and scope as well as applicable conclusions, recommendations, and action plans.

2410.A1 – Final communication of engagement results should, where appropriate, contain the internal auditor's overall opinion and or conclusions.

2410.A2 – Internal auditors are encouraged to acknowledge satisfactory performance in engagement communications.

2410.A3 – When releasing engagement results to parties outside the organization, the communication should include limitations on distribution and use of the results.

2410.C1 – Communication of the progress and results of consulting engagements will vary in form and content depending upon the nature of the engagement and the needs of the client.

2420 – Quality of Communications

Communications should be accurate, objective, clear, concise, constructive, complete, and timely.

APPENDICES

2421 – Errors and Omissions

If a final communication contains a significant error or omission, the chief audit executive should communicate corrected information to all parties who received the original communication.

2430 – Engagement Disclosure of Noncompliance with the Standards

When noncompliance with the Standards impacts a specific engagement, communication of the results should disclose the:

- Standard(s) with which full compliance was not achieved,
- Reason(s) for noncompliance, and
- Impact of noncompliance on the engagement.

2440 – Disseminating Results

The chief audit executive should communicate results to the appropriate parties.

2440.A1 - The chief audit executive is responsible for communicating the final results to parties who can ensure that the results are given due consideration.

2440.A2 - If not otherwise mandated by legal, statutory, or regulatory requirements, prior to releasing results to parties outside the organization, the chief audit executive should:

- Assess the potential risk to the organization.
- Consult with senior management and/or legal counsel as appropriate.
- Control dissemination by restricting the use of the results.

2440.C1 - The chief audit executive is responsible for communicating the final results of consulting engagements to clients.

2440.C2 – During consulting engagements, risk management, control, and governance issues may be identified. Whenever these issues are significant to the organization, they should be communicated to senior management and the board.

2500 – Monitoring Progress

The chief audit executive should establish and maintain a system to monitor the disposition of results communicated to management.

2500.A1 - The chief audit executive should establish a follow-up process to monitor and ensure that management actions have been effectively implemented or that senior management has accepted the risk of not taking action.

2500.C1 – The internal audit activity should monitor the disposition of results of consulting engagements to the extent agreed upon with the client.

2600 – Resolution of Management's Acceptance of Risks

When the chief audit executive believes that senior management has accepted a level of residual risk that may be unacceptable to the organization, the chief audit executive should discuss the matter with senior management. If the decision regarding residual risk is not resolved, the chief audit executive and senior management should report the matter to the board for resolution.

GLOSSARY

Add Value – Value is provided by improving opportunities to achieve organizational objectives, identifying operational improvement, and/or reducing risk exposure through both assurance and consulting services.

Adequate Control – Present if management has planned and organized (designed) in a manner that provides reasonable assurance that the organization's risks have been managed effectively and that the organization's goals and objectives will be achieved efficiently and economically.

Assurance Services – An objective examination of evidence for the purpose of providing an independent assessment on risk management, control, or governance processes for the organization. Examples may include financial, performance, compliance, system security, and due diligence engagements.

Board – A board is an organization's governing body, such as a board of directors, supervisory board, head of an agency or legislative body, board of governors or trustees of a non profit organization, or any other designated body of the organization, including the audit committee, to whom the chief audit executive may functionally report.

Charter – The charter of the internal audit activity is a formal written document that defines the activity's purpose, authority, and responsibility. The charter should (a) establish the internal audit activity's position within the organization; (b) authorize access to records, personnel, and physical properties relevant to the performance of engagements; and (c) define the scope of internal audit activities.

Chief Audit Executive – Top position within the organization responsible for internal audit activities. Normally, this would be the internal audit director. In the case where internal audit activities are obtained from outside service providers, the chief audit executive is the person responsible for overseeing the service contract and the overall quality assurance of these activities, reporting to senior management and the board regarding internal audit activities, and follow–up of engagement results. The term also includes such titles as general auditor, chief internal auditor, and inspector general.

Code of Ethics – The Code of Ethics of The Institute of Internal Auditors (IIA) are principles relevant to the profession and practice of internal auditing, and Rules of Conduct that describe behavior expected of internal auditors. The Code of Ethics applies to both parties and entities that provide internal audit services. The purpose of the Code of Ethics is to promote an ethical culture in the global profession of internal auditing.

APPENDICES

Compliance – Conformity and adherence to policies, plans, procedures, laws, regulations, contracts, or other requirements.

Conflict of Interest – Any relationship that is or appears to be not in the best interest of the organization. A conflict of interest would prejudice an individual's ability to perform his or her duties and responsibilities objectively.

Consulting Services – Advisory and related client service activities, the nature and scope of which are agreed with the client and which are intended to add value and improve an organization's governance, risk management, and control processes without the internal auditor assuming management responsibility. Examples include counsel, advice, facilitation, and training.

Control – Any action taken by management, the board, and other parties to manage risk and increase the likelihood that established objectives and goals will be achieved. Management plans, organizes, and directs the performance of sufficient actions to provide reasonable assurance that objectives and goals will be achieved.

Control Environment – The attitude and actions of the board and management regarding the significance of control within the organization. The control environment provides the discipline and structure for the achievement of the primary objectives of the system of internal control. The control environment includes the following elements:

- Integrity and ethical values.
- Management's philosophy and operating style.
- Organizational structure.
- Assignment of authority and responsibility.
- Human resource policies and practices.
- Competence of personnel.

Control Processes – The policies, procedures, and activities that are part of a control framework, designed to ensure that risks are contained within the risk tolerances established by the risk management process.

Engagement – A specific internal audit assignment, task, or review activity, such as an internal audit, Control Self-Assessment review, fraud examination, or consultancy. An engagement may include multiple tasks or activities designed to accomplish a specific set of related objectives.

Engagement Objectives – Broad statements developed by internal auditors that define intended engagement accomplishments.

Engagement Work Program – A document that lists the procedures to be followed during an engagement, designed to achieve the engagement plan.

External Service Provider – A person or firm, outside of the organization, who has special knowledge, skill, and experience in a particular discipline.

Fraud – Any illegal acts characterized by deceit, concealment or violation of trust. These acts are not dependent upon the application of threat of violence or of physical force. Frauds are perpetrated by parties and organizations to obtain money, property, or services; to avoid payment or loss of services; or to secure personal or business advantage.

Governance – The combination of processes and structures implemented by the board in order to inform, direct, manage, and monitor the activities of the organization toward the achievement of its objectives.

Impairments – Impairments to individual objectivity and organizational independence may include personal conflicts of interest, scope limitations, restrictions on access to records, personnel, and properties, and resource limitations (funding).

Independence – The freedom from conditions that threaten objectivity or the appearance of objectivity. Such threats to objectivity must be managed at the individual auditor, engagement, functional, and organizational levels.

Internal Audit Activity – A department, division, team of consultants, or other practitioner(s) that provides independent, objective assurance and consulting services designed to add value and improve an organization's operations. The internal audit activity helps an organization accomplish its objectives by bringing a systematic, disciplined approach to evaluate and improve the effectiveness of risk management, control, and governance processes.

Objectivity – An unbiased mental attitude that allows internal auditors to perform engagements in such a manner that they have an honest belief in their work product and that no significant quality compromises are made. Objectivity requires internal auditors not to subordinate their judgment on audit matters to that of others.

Residual Risks – The risk remaining after management takes action to reduce the impact and likelihood of an adverse event, including control activities in responding to a risk.

Risk – The possibility of an event occurring that will have an impact on the achievement of objectives. Risk is measured in terms of impact and likelihood.

Risk Management – A process to identify, assess, manage, and control potential events or situations, to provide reasonable assurance regarding the achievement of the organization's objectives.

Should – The use of the word "should" in the Standards represents a mandatory obligation.

Standard – A professional pronouncement promulgated by the Internal Auditing Standards Board that delineates the requirements for performing a broad range of internal audit activities, and for evaluating internal audit performance.

INDEX

INDEX

INDEX

INDEX